The Players League

The Players League

History, Clubs, Ballplayers and Statistics

ED KOSZAREK

McFarland & Company, Inc., Publishers
Jefferson, North Carolina, and London

Ed Koszarek died in March 2005
after delivering the completed
manuscript for this book.
The publishers are grateful to
Eugene Koszarek, his brother,
for his generous assistance thereafter.

LIBRARY OF CONGRESS CATALOGUING-IN-PUBLICATION DATA

Koszarek, Ed, 1942–2005.
The Players League : history, clubs, ballplayers and statistics / Ed Koszarek.
  p.   cm.
Includes bibliographical references and index.

ISBN 0-7864-2079-0 (softcover : 50# alkaline paper)

 1. Players League (Baseball league) — History.
 2. Baseball players — United States — Biography.
 3. Baseball — United States — History — 19th century.
  I. Title.
GV875.P55K67 2006   796.357'640973 — dc22   2005035058

British Library cataloguing data are available

©2006 The Estate of Ed Koszarek. All rights reserved

*No part of this book may be reproduced or transmitted in any form
or by any means, electronic or mechanical, including photocopying
or recording, or by any information storage and retrieval system,
without permission in writing from the publisher.*

On the cover: Game in progress at
Brotherhood Park (Polo Grounds), 1890

Manufactured in the United States of America

*McFarland & Company, Inc., Publishers
Box 611, Jefferson, North Carolina 28640
www.mcfarlandpub.com*

Contents

Preface 1
Prelude in Quotations 3
Introduction 5

1. Origins of the Players League 9
2. Franchises and Clubs 48
3. Base Ball in the Days of the Players League 58
4. Player Biographies 65
5. The Competition 304
6. The Demise of the League 350
7. Closure 358

Bibliography 371
Index 373

To everybody who has made
base ball and baseball great
and in turn provided a source
of enjoyment for a lifetime

Preface

In 1890, some 400 American men played professional major league baseball. All were subject to the rigors and stress which came with their status and occupation. Among these, 140 players also had to endure the unique dilemma of being ostracized and reviled by the baseball establishment as it was then.

Herein is told the tale of this singular situation, with primary focus given to the baseball biographies of the 140 who dared to defy the status quo for a cause they believed in. Among them, by consensus, were most of the best players of their exciting era.

Many historian experts affirm that these players, as a league, may have produced the finest baseball season of all time on the playing fields. They had no such success in the front office, or behind the scenes. It is left for each reader to judge the Players League, and foremost, its players.

For all that they have contributed to this book, my thanks to that most reliable of all premises for baseball endeavors, the National Baseball Hall of Fame and Museum, Inc., at Cooperstown, New York. From within their files and archives have come literally a plethora of relevant and worthy documents.

Mike Wyne, of Seattle, is at Cooperstown temporarily; to have corresponded with him in the quest for data and information has proven as much friendly conversation as taking care of business.

In addition to his many professional credits and years of personal service, Mike is at the Hall of Fame as its first volunteer in history. His diligence and enthusiasm are evidenced by the many prized documents he's discovered which are essential to my text.

He suggested as a possible source of more valuable information a certain book not known to exist by this author; Mike at the Trawood Branch of the El Paso Public Library found it in the interlibrary loan system and made possible the obtaining and use of it, a credit to his skills and to the others involved.

Mike and Mike have helped to make running the gauntlet of compiling and scribbling a manuscript somewhat like doing that in cruise control. Their assistance is much appreciated.

There isn't any book about baseball, whether one word or two or hyphenated, worth its weight in paper which in some way doesn't owe credit to SABR.

John Zajc, the society's executive director, offered his time and guidance; Frederick Ivor-Campbell, David Pietrusza, Bill Ryczek and David Nemec — each among SABR's most respected authorities on early baseball — lent their expertise; Joe Overfield, long a denizen expert on baseball of Buffalo and western New York, pitched in; and Pete Palmer helped solve a statistical dilemma, an enormous contribution that affected the format of the entries.

Thanks to these and many others of the Society for American Baseball Research, SABR.

My thanks also to my parents, Edward Joseph Koszarek (1916–1993) and Jane Genevieve Koszarek, nee Stefanski (born 1917), and family, immediate and extended, of whom there were and still are a great many, each and all appreciated and well remembered.

My thanks go out as well to friends and teachers at SUNY–Buffalo; Buffalo State Teachers College; Erie Community College; Seneca Vocational High School and Assumption School, both in Buffalo; and the Buffalo Public Library.

Finally, thanks to the United States Marine Corps and the soldiers of Parris Island.

Prelude in Quotations

"Since 1871 there have been seven major leagues: the National Association, the National League, the American Association, the Union Association, the Players National League, the American League, and the Federal League.... What led John Ward to his position of leadership in the Brotherhood of Professional Base Ball Players and to his founding of the Players National League was, in part, his lifelong awareness that professional baseball was not just a sport. As he reminded players and fans alike in a reflective article in the *New York Clipper* newspaper in 1896, '(Baseball) is not a summer snap, but a business in which capital is invested. A player is not a sporting man. He is hired to do it as well as he possibly can.'"

— *Bryan DiSalvatore*

"1889 November 4 — Members of Monte Ward's Brotherhood of Professional Base Ball Players sever all ties with the NL and form the Players League, a rebel loop that at first is endorsed by several AA moguls but will eventually help sink the AA."

— *David Nemec*

"The establishment of the Players League (P.L.) was announced on November 6, 1889. The league was to be operated on a cooperative basis with both backers and players on the boards of directors. To lend some stability to the clubs, in lieu of a reserve clause players were signed to three-year contracts. Gate receipts were split evenly among clubs, so that there was no financial disadvantage for clubs from smaller cities. The backers were to keep the first $10,000 in profits per club, the rest going back to the league and eventually to be shared with the players...."

— *Andrew Zimbalist*

"King Kelly, Boston's most popular player in the nineteenth century, was the heart and soul of the Players League Reds ... more generally, Kelly's initial willingness to join the P.L. gave the new league credibility, and his subsequent unwillingness to accept an unprecedented $10,000 advance to return to the National League bolstered the circuit's sagging spirits."

— *Dewey and Acocella*

"The one-year stand of the Players League (1890) was actually a movement motivated by players who were members of the National Brotherhood of Professional Players. This was a benevolent organization which used dues of five dollars a month from its members to aid its sick and needy. Players in the new circuit signed three-year contracts at their 1889 figure, which could be raised at the discretion of the club, but not slashed. More interesting, the players abandoned the reserve rule by allowing players to switch clubs at the close of the season. However, the latter plan never got a trial, since the new league lived only one year. The secessionist movement was popular. Four out of five NL regulars jumped to the P.L. Though forced to operate with makeshift lineups the NL magnates boldly took on the insurgents...."

— *Turkin and Thompson*

"The Players League of 1890 arose out of the long smoldering hostilities between major league players and owners, dating back to the NL seizure of power in 1876. Under NL control, players lost money and freedom of movement, and were subjected to harsh disciplinary codes backed by threats of expulsion and blacklisting. To the list of players' grievances was added the reserve clause in players contracts, which players viewed as a device for lowering salaries and a denial of one's right to sell his services to the highest bidder. For their part, owners credited the clause for stabilizing teams and increasing profits. Although legal challenges sustained the players' position, such victories were too limited (in legal magnitude and scope) to overturn the reserve clause. Frustrated on these fronts, in 1885 the players resorted to collective action by forming the Brotherhood of Professional Base Ball Players."

— *David Q. Voight, in Thorn et al.*

"'There was a time when the League [the original National League] stood for integrity and fair dealing; today it stands for dollars and cents,' said John Montgomery Ward, the star player and union president. 'Players have been bought and sold as though they were sheep instead of American citizens.' Noble words, but the Players League lasted just one season."

— *John Helyar*

Introduction

This book is not specifically about rounders or town ball, or the game of baseball, but the ideas and principles that shaped the game for the late 1800s and well into the next century.

The place was the United States of America, at the close of a horrific war. With the formalities done and conclusions officially written, the men of blue and gray returned as best they could to their families and their homes, or what was left of them. Then came a great rebuilding and restructuring — "Reconstruction," it was called — the redefining of a nation torn asunder.

For many there was nothing with which to begin to rebuild. Some were left neither spiritual nor material wherewithal. For other American men, however, the prevailing condition represented a grand opportunity. For them, the question became how to best avail themselves of chances for wealth.

Some win in war; some lose. Even on the winning side there have always been losers, most often those who can least afford to lose. In the Civil War, they were farmers and tradesmen, craftsmen and apprentices. Many who had gone away to fight returned to find their farms and shops had been subject to foreclosure. "Not to despair," said the new men of wealth; "we shall provide. It is now our duty to guide and drive the engine of the new American economy." This they did, with unprecedented vigor and industry — and the blood and sweat of the workers who migrated from their rural homes to the cities in search of a new, "modern" life.

Scottish-born Andrew Carnegie, man of steel; John Pierpont Morgan, man of finance; scion and legend John D. Rockefeller, man of oil; these were America's new captains of industry. Mr. Carnegie used the Pennsylvania State Police to suppress those in service to him when they protested working conditions. Mr. Morgan became America's richest man yet never knew labor or toil. Mr. Rockefeller devised a staggering business trust that would extend past his lifetime into generations beyond. Others would learn from their example and emulate them within a vast variety of domains, including the emerging industry of baseball.

Social classes and economic classes have existed since man first discovered the advantages of advancing to positions of dominance. Such classes have existed on American shores since before the Boston Tea Party. Never before, however, had they been so structured and so widely separated as they became after the Civil War, when the Industrial Revolution was in progress, evolving as the dominant socioeconomic force.

Readily and abundantly, it became evident which men were which. An obvious clue was time and money and energy for leisure activities. Energetic and wealthy young men took to the game of base ball. The friendly club games they played evolved to competitive sport, then to business enterprise.

The lesser classes could still be amused by the game; if all was well, the father of a household might find a quarter that would allow his family to witness an afternoon of the new game. The investment was probably worthwhile; the family might see Al Reach at the bat (among the first to take money and gratuities for playing the game), or Candy Cummings tossing his mysterious curves toward home plate.

In many cities and large towns were entrepreneurs, adventurers willing to sponsor and finance the operations of for-profit teams. Through their efforts, Father and his family might see the traveling roadshows with the likes of Davy Force or Dickey Pierce, John Chapman or Bob Ferguson. Each team had its stars and its particular rivals.

Much has been made of the evolution of the "great American game" from amateur amusement to moneymaking enterprise. In fact, perhaps too much has been made of it. The professional baseball team was a natural phenomenon, grown and tailored to satisfy the culture. Social, economic, and political forces had joined to produce baseball as business. And, as part of the natural order, some men would pursue baseball for economic reasons—not always propitiously so.

Quite simply, a game was devised that became popular with the masses; the game found owners; the owners devised means to reap profits, then bigger profits; and by the unspoken, unwritten code of the new American business environment, they would resist all demands to release more of the profits than absolutely necessary.

At the same time, along came a cadre of lessers, blessed by nature to play the game folks of the United States had embraced. They could play the game well enough to demand salaries for the work they did. All of this is part of the natural order of economic enterprise. At this point, however, the laws of human mechanics came into play.

By these laws of human mechanics, established power would be confronted by a counterforce. There was justified will to change; there was justified will to resist.

So it was that baseball's men of money began to devise mechanisms of authority to assure their position would prevail. Agreements and clauses, codes and rules were created and implemented.

After a decade of such innovations, the owners of the game had only one thing to fear. It was not a protest by the players in their service, whom they believed they could easily control. Nor was it fan reaction; fans would always come, they thought, if fed the right blend of rhetoric and condescension.

What the baseball owners feared was politicians. Even a man as powerful as John D. Rockefeller was brought to heel by the United States Congress, his domain split and broken by antitrust legislation. Baseball's men of money, too, were beginning to hear noises from the political realm. Despite the laws of ten states and one territory already hot in pursuit of the power and realm of Rockefeller, baseball owners hewed to the line of one senior Rockefeller executive who wrote, in 1888, "I think this anti-trust fever is a craze to be dealt with by judicious avoidance." This avoidance did not alter the path toward bigger, better, and more.

No man of the baseball enterprise had power or wealth remotely comparable to Rockefeller's, but all were of the same will: to have and to hold their establishment and its gains. They had won their victory over the amateur game, turning it into a professional business enterprise. They did not see their position in that enterprise as a matter of monopoly. Players who had the skills necessary to play at a professional level disagreed; they had no alternate venue for play. When aggrieved beyond their line of reason, the players organized as a collective.

The word *collective* itself was anathema to business leaders, politicians, and the judiciary of the United States. Collectivism, as they saw it, was infesting the very substance and foundation of the Industrial Revolution, representing a real and severe threat that had to be eradicated by any means. The grand innovations reaped as a harvest of a bloody war were at risk; the new realm of free enterprise was at risk; the gains of the wealthiest men, and the means to hold them, were at risk. The enterprise of baseball had evolved into a microcosm of clashing forces in the larger society: the oligarchy of ownership versus the workers' collective, in this case the Brotherhood of Players, which evolved into the Players League of 1890.

The rise and fall of that league have been expounded upon in the literature. The events have been compared to the Revolutionary War, the Civil War, and by one fine author with the War of 1812. Never before, however, has the phenomenon of the Players League been examined as a whole, or its elements—the men who formed it, and the events of its brief lifetime—been rigorously scrutinized. Nor has the league been studied against the environment that created and, eventually, destroyed it. In all these tasks, this book hopes to excel, and to provide the reader with the complete story of the Players League and the men who made it.

1

Origins of the Players League

During the 1889 season, a small cadre of aggrieved major league baseball players incited insurrection. With the support of their fellow League and Association players, these men demanded a meeting with N.L. owners to discuss the player classification system adopted in 1888. Devised by John Brush, owner of the Indianapolis club, the system called for players to be grouped according to their performance and conduct both on and off the field. A salary cap was to be imposed on each class. For the players who had long resented the owners' reserve system, which bound an athlete to a team and left them powerless to negotiate salary, Brush's plan was the final straw. The Players League was the outcome.

When the owners failed to address their grievances, the players threatened to strike and secretly met with potential financial backers for a new league.

By the offseason, most of the best players abandoned the established major leagues to move toward a league of their own; they would do well enough on the playing fields to win the competition for popular attendance in 1890, but they were out of their element in the back rooms and business offices.

Although more adept at playing the game on the field than their rebuilt rivals, and even with commitments of help from monied men to support their cause, lack of business acumen would prove to be the evident primary cause of the business difficulties of the Players League of 1890.

While the question whether the daring hundred were right or wrong is still arguable more than a century later, there can be no realistic doubt that money and power prevailed. Baseball on the playing fields would change in many ways through the years, but for players bound by contracts, which all have had to be to wear a major league uniform, the status quo of the late 1800s would prevail until the early 1970s.

According to some authorities, the Players League of 1890 was not a legitimate entity, therefore the records they established during that singular season should not be included in the history of baseball. Herein the reader is given the data and facts to establish an informed and independent opinion.

The terms "franchise," "club," and "team" have been used interchangeably by many; herein the baseball terms are used in accord with what they were in fact.

Though not written in stone, these are firm definitions: The *franchise* is the owner(s), granted authorization by a higher power (the league) to operate as a business enterprise; the *club* is the administrative element of the franchise, which extends through the plethora of office duties and tasks onto the playing fields in the position commonly called the manager; the *team* is the players, that element of the franchise and club working in unison on the playing fields to achieve success, measured by baseball in terms of games won and lost.

The Players League did exist, for one year, in the tangible form of eight franchises, clubs, and teams; herein the term "Players" is indicative of the individual core of these elements ideally striving in unison to achieve the baseball goal.

The "league" was their league, a league of, by, and for players, in principle if not in principal; the players had power and the authority to control league policies, operations, rules, even the philosophy underlying the league, and foremost over the P.L. (Players League) constitution, their charter of existence.

What the players of the P.L. did not have, enough of at least, was money to establish and sustain the existence of the league, which made it necessary for them to share their power and their authority (control) with monied men, financiers, commonly in P.L. vernacular referred to as "backers," who in reality became the owners of the franchises and their subordinate elements.

To state this situation minimally, this made for an odd business relationship, for in concept and principle the men of money would be sharing the franchise executive suites with the labor force; it was not the way U.S.A. business was done then, the decisions and deals done by the whole of the franchise entity.

Adding to the complexity, given the proper name in legal form of "Player's [sic] National League of Base Ball Clubs," the Players League in its inception was the product of a rebellion. As with most such events involving confrontation throughout history, this rebellion had causes; it did not happen as any whim, nor in one moment of radical excess.

Foremost among the causes were documents, the historic essence of legitimacy, written and decreed by the monied men who owned and thus were the National League, and to lesser extent the American Association; these were the two professional major leagues of baseball at the time.

Players and franchises had come and gone since 1876 (when the National League was established) and 1882 (when the American Association was established), but one rule of the Base Ball Code of Law enacted in 1879 proved to be so valuable to the established owners that it survived and was sustained for a century. This was despite its arguable unfairness from the beginning. Its legitimacy was argued in venues varying from stadium grounds and beer halls to the highest U.S. state and federal courts.

To make complexity more confounding, a small percentage of the players circa 1890 supported this rule, while contrarily a small proportion of owners despised it. This rule, the catalyst which gave cause for the founding of the P.L., was with minor variations over the years called the reserve rule; its purpose, the players pleaded, was to take away their basic rights to offer their services in return for the greatest gain.

If a parallel might be found in the American Revolution of 1776, Albert Goodwill Spalding of the National League and baseball, circa 1876–1890, would be cast in the role of King George III of an unjust and oppressive England, while other established owners (Soden, Robison, Day and Brush, among others to come) might represent the power and law of the British Parliament.

If the Players League represented a confrontation of enemies, then the consensus choice for the role of George Washington must be John Montgomery Ward; other such roles would equate via the accepted version of American history with Madison, Hamilton, John Jay, Robert Morris, and Benedict Arnold. Each side had its own Prussian elite.

A significant moment in the course of Players League and baseball events was 1876, but to find all the facts it's necessary to search further back in time, beyond that awful American Civil War, for a concrete date — September 24, 1845.

The stage was New York City, at a social club populated by a group of youngish, upscale professional gentlemen; they had given themselves and their club the identity of the Knickerbocker Club.

Their precise numbers are not known, nor the number who chose to participate in their own game of baseball for exercise, for recreation, for fellowship and camaraderie. Their game was purely amateur, played with propriety.

The name Knickerbocker Club merits mention, as they are generally recognized as the first formally organized club in the game which evolved to what it was in 1890, and further to what major league, minor league, and most amateur baseball is today in the U.S.A., Japan, mainland Asia, the Caribe and Central America, Australia, Europe, Canada, and the rest of the world.

Among the Knickerbocker founders were Dr. Daniel L. Adams and Alexander Joy Cartwright. Louis F. Wadsworth was one of the earliest members, and Charles S. DeBost may have been their best baseball player.

Dr. Adams was their first president, serving in that capacity for a dozen years. Mr. Cartwright, the club umpire rather than a player, relocated to Hawaii a decade later, taking the New York game with him.

Baseball as they played it was called the Knickerbocker Game, primarily because their club established a code of rules, and in the early 1850s published the code as a booklet explaining how the game should be played. It was readily adopted by other clubs locally and regionally.

Theirs became the "how to" manual for other clubs of gentlemen who found pleasure in playing baseball. The Knickerbockers held formal practice sessions twice weekly, weather permitting, on the Elysian Fields at Hoboken, New Jersey, "a beautiful spot at the time."

As the first president and team captain, it fell to Dr. Adams to "employ all my rhetoric to induce attendance." He was a medical doctor, with offices in New York City, a graduate of Yale College (1835) and the Harvard Medical School (1838).

There had previously been a club called the New York Base Ball Club, but it had no definite organization. There were no rivalries then, as no other club formed until 1850. The first was the Gotham Club, and its members became the Knickerbockers' special rivals.

The membership of the Knickerbocker Club included merchants, lawyers, bank and insurance clerks, and others with free time after 3 P.M. As the club leader, Dr.

Adams was meticulous in determining the rules and in finding tradesmen to manufacture bats and balls for his club.

It's been proposed that Dr. Adams should have had the title of "father of baseball" rather than Henry Chadwick, as he was directly involved with the early game, while Mr. Chadwick merely wrote of the Knickerbockers, and later other baseball events.

Mr. Chadwick was still writing, and the editor of the *Spalding Baseball Guide* in 1906; he died of pneumonia on April 20, 1908, after attending the Brooklyn Dodgers' home opening game.

A bit more on the Knickerbocker game to amplify how it was and how it changed. While other clubs were forming, the Knickerbockers stayed to themselves, playing intramural contests. When other clubs became competitive and games began to be played between clubs, it was for the victors to provide a banquet dinner for the vanquished.

The city of Brooklyn became the baseball hot bed during the 1850s and into the 1860s, with the Eckford, Exelsior, and Atlantic clubs dominating the competition.

In 1858, the National Association of Base Ball Players was formally established, intended by its charter to be a permanent organization. The original count showed 25 member clubs; by 1860, when the Brooklyn Exelsiors made the first Eastern tour, the N.A.B.B.P. count was then 60. By 1862 the formality of opening day had become an annual event, with May 1 serving unofficially as the date, though some clubs played games as much as a month earlier.

All-black baseball clubs are known to have been organized by then in Brooklyn and in Harlem, in New Jersey, and at Jamaica, Long Island. Black clubs were reported playing in July, and as late as November 15, 1859; some members of the N.A.B.C. played a game occasionally against black clubs which nevertheless were banished in unison from the organization in 1867.

What was to become of the game can be surmised from within two historical anecdotes; one involves two leagues, or three, the other is of a very confused oligarchy.

After the 1890 playing season, the National League franchise of Cincinnati (the Reds) was left hanging in the financial winds. The franchise was purchased by a syndicate of soon-to-be dispossessed Players League owners and executives. Some players (contracts) were included as part of the package. When added to in numbers the club was able to put a team on the field. They didn't have a ballpark, but did play some exhibition games late in October. When the dust of business disorder settled, a National League man owned the franchise, while the primary P.L. buyer maneuvered his way into the soon-to-fail American Association.

Like any business organization, a major league of baseball would be expected to have one presiding officer (president) at a time; not always quite so apparently, as by reports of two usually very reliable sources, the National League of 1890, the year the P.L. played, Mr. Abraham (A.G.) Mills and Mr. Nicholas (N.E.) Young both held that office throughout the whole P.L. year. Both these men are known to have been, before and after, prominent in the baseball establishment.

While the senior major league may or may not have had two presidents—most sources cite only Young—its established lesser almost didn't have a league. During the meeting of the American Association on November 12 and 13, 1889, the discontented owners of the Brooklyn and the Cincinnati franchises quit that league to accept N.L. membership.

The Kansas City owner quit to join the minor Western League; the representative of Baltimore quit his Eastern League franchise in the hope of playing a coup and landing the Washington franchise of the National League.

Apparently quite early in these proceedings the American Association's attorney, also involved in ownership of the Louisville franchise, was by default elected the A.A. president for 1890. This had to have happened early, as otherwise their charter and rules indicate that there would not have been a quorum present to do any business at all.

The issue had been the presidency. Two factions of four clubs each proposed a candidate. A witty trick took two of one side out of the meeting room, whence the election was done, which led to the first two resignations. The losing man was of Kansas City; he relocated his status and players contracts to a minor league. A Columbus man was elected vice president of the A.A. for 1890; the former president has been inadvertently lost in the executive and franchise shuffle.

All ended well that went well for the American Association to be extant through the P.L. year, almost. The little cities of Toledo and Rochester were granted franchises, as was Syracuse. The man of Syracuse reneged or was removed and was replaced in January.

The lesser-established league was still lacking a team to make an eight-team league. In mid–January a young adventurer from Brooklyn took up the void, aided by the owner of the local Sunday stadium. Entering the 1890 playing season only one remained of the original A.A. 1882 entourage. He was the man of St. Louis, Chris Von der Ahe.

As will be seen, these are only a few among the many facts and events which would shape the chaotic 1890 season.

By the mid–1860s there were rumors and reports that amateur players with the most active successful clubs were being paid salaries or stipends, or given jobs which took little time from their game practice and schedules. Two of the most notable were Al Reach of the Philadelphia Athletics and Dickey Pearce of the Brooklyn Atlantics, both prized middle infielders. After the 1868 playing season was done the N.A.B.B.P. Committee of Rules established a qualification system which distinctly separated the professional from the amateur players, the basis of which was compensation for their services as players. No longer was baseball thought to be seedy as work. Many of the best players promptly declared as professional. An issue of 1890 within the greater issue would involve qualification of the players, though the players had no role in making the decisions.

The fading sham of collegial amateurism was dealt a severe blow of reality early in 1869 when the sponsor of the Cincinnati Red Stockings Club, Aaron Champion, as club president declared that all his players were professionals, playing for pay. The list of salaries ranged from $800 to $1,400; the total payroll for his team was $9,500. These Cincinnati Reds made a national tour in 1869, traveled some 12,000 miles, played before some 200,000 fans, and won 64 or 65 games without being defeated. Only a disputed tie game at home late in August against the Haymakers of Troy, New York, spoiled their unprecedented almost-perfect record.

The Red Stockings resumed in 1870, extended their unbeaten streak to 92 games (the number differs in various sources between 84 and 100+) before losing to the Brooklyn Atlantics in 11 innings by a score of 6 to 5. The game is recorded as a baseball classic. Henry Chadwick was the umpire that day. The game was played at Capitoline Grounds on June 14. The victorious home team had chosen to bat last, contrary to the custom of the time.

By the end of calendar year 1869 the professionals had seized control of the N.A.B.B.P. and promptly eliminated the classification rule despite being a small numerical minority of the 1,000 organized baseball clubs. In turn this small group of professionals was condemned by men of the media for their self-serving actions; their conduct was deemed reprehensible and injurious to the all–American game of baseball. Hypocrisy is an element of human mechanics, historically proven an essential element of the human condition.

The date March 17, 1871, is unknown to history despite its being as significant to baseball as April 12, 1861, to the greater record of history, when a Union army captain with the name of Abner Doubleday fired the first shot to defend Fort Sumter at Charlestown, South Carolina. The place was Collier's Rooms, Broadway and 13th Street, New York City, reserved for the evening by the Mutual Club, which was originally composed of city firemen till the local political machine took control, giving priority to those interests. The time was 7:30 P.M. when an idea of Nicholas E. Young took material form: to have the secretaries or other representatives of all the professional baseball clubs meet to discuss their schedules for the 1871 playing season.

The idea was recent. Henry Chadwick had taken to it and gave his approval, the same man who a few months prior had written vile commentary and reviled against professionalism in the *New York Clipper*.

Most recently he'd published notice of the meeting, advising the clubs intending to attend to grant their representatives the full authority to act as they would at a convention; the scenario was not at all unlike the unwritten Annapolis and famous Philadelphia conventions which created the extant American Constitution.

Men of 10 professional clubs came. Eight had been given broad authorization to act; those of Chicago and New York Mutual were not. There are analogies to be found between this scenario for an evening and that of Philadelphia, which may have set a record for the longest convention, and that at Annapolis, which failed in intent and purpose miserably.

Mr. J. W. Schofield of the Troy Union Club by some authority called the Collier's Rooms convention to order. James N. Kerns of the Philadelphia Athletics was promptly elected chairman; Mr. Nick Young of the Washington, D.C., Olympics was chosen to be secretary.

Mr. J. M. Thatcher of the Chicago club made a motion to expand the planned agenda to include selection of umpires, and further to establish rules and protocol to decide the annual championship among these best of professional baseball clubs. All his motions were agreed upon, approved, and done for history.

The presiding officer kept matters well in hand, the first and quite likely the last time among these men and clubs. The agenda was further advanced when the men present were advised of another meeting held the previous evening, by the amateur clubs; the context was presumed hostile to professionalism. He moved to establish the body present as a permanent professional organization.

Then were done matters of business common to any such orderly convention. Meanwhile a chosen committee of three discussed both the merits and the contrary of such an organization. Their consultation was quick; they reported to the body unanimously in favor. They were Mr. Schofield, A.V. Davidson of the Mutual, and Harry Wright representing Boston. This Mr. Wright had been occupied in 1869 and 1870 with the duties of manager and captain of the near-perfect Red Stockings, soon to be announced ex-of-Cincinnati; he was also the center field player, fair at it but considered a great manager. George Wright, his 12-year-younger brother, was and would be a star player for the Boston Red Stockings.

By the end of this momentous evening of baseball business, as it was done, a constitution and by-laws had been adopted by the men present, based on and reflecting those of the N.A.B.B.P. in their convention the prior November, to the extent they would not interfere with the operations of the new professional organization.

The evening of that St. Patrick's Day in New York City has been reported rainy and stormy. That was the day major league baseball was born in the U.S.A. A title was needed, and was given, the National Association of Professional Base Ball Players.

More rules were adopted, none of which stipulated the common name of their organization would be National Association, which it became. There were also resolutions, duly prefaced by "whereas" as business was and is done, and concluded "resolved" which in baseball's future would seldom be done. As an aside, the other clubs present that seminal evening and their representatives were W.H. Ray, Brooklyn Eckford; J.S. Evans, Cleveland Forest City; H.H. Waldo, Rockford (Illinois) Forest City; and O.R. Hough, National of Washington, D.C.

Recall that Mr. Davidson of the Mutual, host for the evening, and Mr. Thatcher of Chicago, the chairman, were not authorized to vote during what became this most momentous event of baseball business. The men present knew the hostility to be expected from their lesser professionals and the amateur contingent of the N.A.B.B.P,. but none among them except perhaps Nick Young and Henry Chadwick (never involved but never distant) could have envisioned what would evolve from the specific entity which was created on that evening in New York City.

It took five playing seasons for what goes around to come around to the N.A. as they had done to their amateur brethren, when precedent was set for what would become how to do the business of the major league game. Before the proverbial ink was dry on their founding documents, the concept and fact of a league of, by, and for the players was on its way to the dustbin of history. By the time the National Association began to play its schedule, individualized in accord with the powers and preferences of the member clubs, the game had already undertaken many changes, and there would be many more of the most basic sort during the brief term of its existence. The teams of the N.A. all began equal in one respect, as the won and lost records of all were 0 and 0. This was despite the fact that nearly the whole of the Cincinnati team switched their services to Boston, even taking the name Red Stockings with them.

A total of nine clubs played that first N.A. season. The Kekiongas of Fort Wayne, Indiana, failed financially in August and were replaced by the Brooklyn Eckfords; after the season, an Association committee ruled that neither team's record would be recorded in the official standings.

Many a lesson was available to be learned from the N.A. The Knickerbockers had written the book on how to play the game. The men who were the N.A. could have written theirs on the theme of how not to run a baseball business major league.

These were the eight clubs that began and survived the seminal 1871 playing season, the records of which are not to be found among those which have been decreed official.

Rank	City Team	Won	Lost	Win %
1st	Philadelphia Athletics	22	7	.759
2nd	Chicago White Stockings	20	9	.690
3rd	Boston Red Stockings	22	10	.688
4th	Washington Olympics	16	15	.516
5th	Troy Haymakers	15	15	.500
6th	New York Mutuals	16	18	.471
7th	Cleveland Forest Cities	10	19	.345
8th	Rockford Forest Cities	6	20	.231

The Kekiongas before they left made a record of seven won and 21 lost (.250 win percent), which if they are included places them eighth with Rockford below, as the N.A. ruled that win percent had precedence over any set of raw data of games won and lost.

The rank status of the Brooklyn Eckfords for 1871 is uncertain. In fact, their records are arcana, and incredibly are not to be found in any of the most comprehensive works of modern baseball literature. Some among readers with historic insight might suggest that such would be found in the musty archives of media which existed then. The historic tie game between the 1869 Cincinnati and Haymakers became the object of such pursuit. This fan and author contacted in writing six newspapers known to exist after the year 2000 that were in business then (New York City three, Cincinnati two, and Troy one). None could provide the missing information.

In the N.A. of 1871 the Red Stockings of Boston achieved the surprise of the season. They'd been expected to virtually stroll away with the gonfalon. Less than equal on paper, the Athletics proved their team the best of two better competitors, as Chicago was also able to produce a record better than Boston.

Standards had been established before the season, many of which were simply ignored or arbitrarily revised by individual clubs in the interim. A post-season meeting of club representatives was deemed necessary to determine which really won the right to display the first N.A. pennant.

Admission fees to games were set at 50¢ but when and where better teams and the best players weren't scheduled tickets might be discounted to a quarter, and profits at the gate could be enormously variant. Some games attracted a few hundred. The Mutuals at home against Chicago were reported to have drawn 6,000 within their fences, with another estimated 3,000 watching the action from beyond.

Gate receipts were to be shared by a set formula. Some of the clubs did and others wouldn't. The Mutuals of New York City gained repute as the most prolific offenders. After October 8 the White Stockings of Chicago didn't have a gate; that was when the Great Chicago Fire devastated their ballpark.

As the season evolved the Eastern clubs became more and more reluctant to make the expensive road trips to the distant locale of Illinois, for example. How the Athletics became the first major league baseball champions became a matter of backroom political business.

During the season Philadelphia had lost two apparently inconsequential games to lowly Rockford, which required much administrative correction for them to win after the fact; the rationale and justification involved Rockford's Scott Hastings. He'd been in the Rockford lineup during those two games. That he played in 23 other regular season games didn't seem to matter, nor did his 30 hits, 27 runs scored, 11 stolen bases, and later calculated 20 runs batted in. Nor that he was the field manager of that Forest Cities team for the entire season. The hierarchy of the N.A. ruled that Rockford had been out of order during those two meaningless games—that Scott Hastings then and there only had not been eligible to play.

For 1872 the N.A. leaders chose a player as league president—Bob Ferguson, who'd been with the Mutuals in 1871 as manager and catcher. That had also been his status in the 1870 game when the Brooklyn Atlantics defeated the unbeatable Cincinnati.

He'd be with the Brooklyn Atlantics again in 1872. They were one of four new franchises created by the N.A. The others were the Lord Baltimores of Baltimore, the Mansfields (so called in honor of Union General Joseph Manfield*) of Middletown, Connecticut, and the Nationals of Washington, D.C. The White Stockings still had no ballpark to call their own and missed the whole second season.

Adrian Constantine "Cap" Anson relocated to the Philadelphia Athletics after his original team, Rockford, left the N.A. His record is still among the most impressive and his tenure among the longest; he continued with the Athletics through 1875, the last season of the National Association. Another star who exited Rockford demands note; he left them to join Boston when the N.A. began. A rule change, one of hundreds, permitted "snap and jerk" deliveries by pitchers. Though pitching by mandate was still underhanded, this enabled Albert G. Spalding to improve from merely outstanding to one of the greatest ever.

Both Spalding and Anson would return to Illinois, to the White Stockings of Chicago, where both became very prominent parts of history for both baseball and baseball reasons. Significantly both would have an enormous impact on the Players League of 1890, with two decades each of skills and wisdom then at their disposal. Neither would be a friend to the P.L.

That Boston had finished third in 1871 soon ceased to matter. With Spalding at the fore and Harry Wright as manager, their team won every other National Association championship handsomely, improving as they went till the N.A. was put to an end. With their lineup filled with stars of Hall of Fame quality, the Red Stockings became most popular with the growing American baseball public. They also became

---

*A fact David Nemec relates in his book *The Great Encyclopedia of 19th Century Major League Baseball* (Donald I. Fine, 1997).

the prohibitive favorites to win every game they played with bookmakers and professional gamblers who'd infested the game since the '60s and now were of numbers and influence far beyond proportions of tolerance.

It seems almost frivolous to say that corruption corrupts, which given time and opportunity will become absolute, but that was the greatest threat to the game then, and in the minds of more than a few men had become the sum condition of the professional game. As prudent men of business, the higher class of gamblers tried to obtain every advantage for their particular enterprise; many risked tens of thousands of dollars on the result of one game, making their stake much greater than that of the club owners.

To the contrary of immorality and illegality, religion posed a threat, especially on Sundays, especially in Pennsylvania and New York. Commonly called Sabbatarians, zealots of various Christian persuasions banded together to assure by whatever means their day would be given its purpose, which surely was not playing games for pay, or paying to witness them. Contrary to gamblers, they had with them the force of law and created problems regularly.

Strange bedfellows perhaps, but both gambling and religiosity were as problematic in the 1920s as in 1890, as in the 1870s. Some owners and clubs found remedy for the holy difficulty by relocating Sunday games to towns or counties where puritan law had evolved along the lines of the greater whole. There never was found remedy for the unholy except to banish players who were judged culpable, but nary a gambler was ever prosecuted.

These virtues and vices were not the only problems. Drunkenness and the demeanor which typically accompanies it had become a general nuisance at major league games, if not a hazard to a majority of more mature and rational folks in attendance. By the 1890s, acts of stupidity and violence were commonplace.

Further harm was done to the N.A. by some of its own. Players jumped from team to team and club to club at the least hint of monetary incentive. This practice, called revolving, had been a prominent problem for the amateur game while that illusion still existed. Common knowledge suggests that a prudent, clever, or cunning businessman can and will avail the greatest problem to great advantage.

The Red Stockings of Boston had taken home the championships of the original professional players league each year after the first—four consecutive, a record rarely matched in the annals of the game. They began with Spalding and the Wright brothers of baseball. With the additions of Ross Barnes, Deacon White, and Jim O'Rourke, they became nearly invincible as a team. These were some of their achievements as a team of that first players' league.

Year	Won	Lost	Win %	Rank	By
1871	20	10	.667	2nd	2.0 games
1872	39	8	.830	1st	7.5 games
1873	43	16	.729	1st	4.0 games
1874	52	18	.743	1st	7.5 games
1875	71	8	.899	1st	18.5 games
Sums	225	60	.789		

As Boston became stronger its league became disordered. The end became inevitable when a man of business decided he'd intervene. His intent and purpose were to reorganize and then restructure a baseball organization, enable it to do business, and sell the public the product they more and more wanted.

William Hulbert deplored gambling as commerce, consumption of alcohol in public, and believed players should stay with the clubs to which they'd committed. These were the core principles of his vision of baseball as business.

And business he did, cautious but unrelenting. He also kept faith with the premise that capital as profits should flow to only capitalists of the first class, as the more of the gross going their way would assure better business. In turn both the business and product would improve, for the good of all, of course.

Early in the N.A. season of 1875, the financially struggling Chicago club invited him to take charge as their president. He paused long enough to survey the possibilities and to consult with Al Spalding when Boston came to his city. He convinced Spalding to come home for the next playing season.

He accepted the offer to become the presiding Chicago officer, with higher office already in mind. He would make Spalding the star pitcher of his White Stockings team in 1876. In his turn Spalding helped Hulbert steal from the Boston club Barnes and White, and Cal McVey, a star in his own right. Spalding also convinced Adrian Anson to come to Chicago.

There would be difficulties he knew, Hulbert did, with Boston's fans. When they were informed of the desertion of their best players those men became seceders, as vile an epithet as any New Englander could summon.

Nor were the Philadelphians to be ignored, surely aggrieved over the loss of their Anson. Still further the National Association as a body would have to be dealt with. This wise man of business, Hulbert, devised one simple solution for many difficult problems. He disposed of the N.A. and created his own league.

This was a burdensome task made simple by chaos, the whole of which can be depicted by the final standings of the N.A. Four teams didn't finish the 1875 season, while a second and a third franchise had been placed in Philadelphia, a true stroke of executive mismanagement if ever there was one in baseball.

There had been other failures and replacements between 1871 and the end. It's worth taking note of the geographical placement of the N.A. at its end; herein the acronym "DNF" indicates that the franchise did not finish the final N.A. season.

Rank	City Team	Rank	City Team
1st	Boston Red Stockings	8th	New Haven Elm Citys
2nd	Hartford Dark Blues	DNF	Washington Nationals
3rd	Philadelphia Athletics	DNF	St. Louis Red Stockings
4th	St. Louis Brown Stockings	DNF	Philadelphia Centennials
5th	Philadelphia (Uncertain)	12th	Brooklyn Atlantics
6th	New York Mutuals	DNF	Keokuk Westerns
7th	Chicago White Stockings		

Along the road to oblivion the National Association of Base Ball Players passed through 17 cities and towns, including Fort Wayne, Indiana; Elizabeth, New Jersey and Middletown, Connecticut. This first players league never had a set of eight teams stay in place through an entire calendar year and wasn't much interested in keeping records, or about business.

Having all his moral bases well covered, the premise used by Hulbert to sell his idea of a new league to potential owners was incredibly elementary. They would take absolute control. They would take the entirety of the gate receipts; after the coffers were full and secure, they could pay the players what they thought was right and proper.

For all its executive and administrative deficiencies, the N.A. could be judged a success based on the five years it existed. Very badly managed businesses seldom survive that long. To their credit they did nothing directly to diminish the quality of the product they put on the playing fields.

Their last mortal mistake as a body was to not see the coming of William A. Hulbert, who himself never realized or plainly ignored the fact of baseball business that the players are essential to the game; with them there could not be a major league of baseball. But then Mr. Hulbert wasn't quite at the business wizardry level of Andrew Carnegie or the other contemporary masters, he was merely very near to it.

William A. Hulbert was a man of Chicago, mind, heart, and soul. He was a man of strong will, sound of mind, determined that his city would be the hub of major league baseball and that he would be the presence at the center of that. His concept was still in force a half century later when Judge K.M. Landis of the (Chicago) U.S. District Court of the Northern District of Illinois was chosen to be the first commissioner of baseball.

Hulbert was also as strict and rigid as Judge Landis, who was the consensus choice of the owners cabal of 1920 due to his dour disposition, able to precipitate fear in any person who might imagine to have offended him. For K.M. Landis and such men it isn't necessary to render a word to gain reverence or fear.

For Mr. Hulbert in his chosen capacity there would not be any nonsense; questions about his judgments were not permitted. There was a code, there were rules to be complied with and to be obeyed to the letter, if not with subservient willingness, then with tolerant obedience. Contrary to the business misconception that autocracy can be democracy, Mr. Hulbert held fast and firm to the principle that when you first begin to rule over an empire, you must be an autocrat, but as you discover loyal subordinates you may begin to become a bit of a democrat. How this article of ancient philosophy might fit a collective such as the Players League of 1890 shall be left for scholars among readers to ponder. Suffice it to say here that Hulbert found only one such subordinate, whom he crafted into a master greater than himself.

The P.L. leaders could have learned much by observing and analyzing the wisdom and work of William A. Hulbert but they did not, as the record will show. Albert Goodwill Spalding certainly did.

It came to pass that a new major league of baseball was founded on February 2, 1876. It granted franchises. Protocol required a president. A charter was needed, of organization, a constitution and bylaws, rules and regulations, a code of conduct for players. All were duly and properly done. It was decreed that a minimum metropolitan population standard should be set at 75,000 for a city or town to have a chance at a franchise. Judge Orrick C. Bishop of St. Louis wrote the new constitution, and a standard player's contract, as a goodwill gesture to Hulbert, at the behest of Spalding.

Had any among the men of the Players League to come been present at the creation, he might have conveyed his knowledge to his brethren — in which case the P.L. might have had a chance to survive. As it would come to pass, the P.L. would stand no chance at all. Experientially, logistically, strategically, the P.L. men were beaten long before the idea was conceived of a second league of, by, and for the players.

The whole of this impossibility would lie in the person of one man of business, who also had been a great player. He was not Solomon, nor Abner Doubleday, not a ruler nor a soldier, merely a man who'd learned very well how to do business the U.S.A. way. When 1890 would arrive he'd have witnessed and taken part in the annihilation of two enemy leagues.

Ptolemy I learned from Alexander of Macedonia; Cleopatra VII in turn learned from the heritage of Ptolemy how to be a ruler and a leader: play to your strengths, concurrent with the weaknesses of your enemy. Any capable baseball field manager knows that. Albert G. Spalding learned from William A. Hulbert; no ruler and leader ever learned better. William Hulbert had bought the core of a terrific baseball team, his moral bases were all well covered, and the premise used to sell his idea of a new league was incredibly successful. Eight franchises were granted for his new league; it existed officially the instant its constitution was approved, by acclamation. ("It" was the National League of Professional Clubs. If Father Chadwick wrote accurately in the *New York Clipper* of February 12, 1876, the term baseball was not part of the official title, an error of omission corrected in record time.)

The original Midwest alliance of Chicago, St. Louis, Cincinnati, and Louisville seemed certain; earlier in the year Hulbert had gone East to secure the support of men in Boston, Hartford, New York City, and Philadelphia. In a gesture of propitious condescension, Hulbert gave the men of the East Morgan S. Bulkeley as the first president of his National League; Mr. Bulkeley was a Connecticut politician and governor, who knew little about baseball and cared less.

He presided officially through the first National League (N.L.) season but was prominently absent when the final 1876 meeting of the National League took place. He'd well served the purpose of alleviating (actually) Northeast concerns about relocation of major league baseball authority to the Midwest.

With a bit of trickery, William A. Hulbert had himself elected N.L. president for 1877. He continued in office till his death on April 10, 1882, of heart disease. He'd begun by operating a combined enterprise of groceries and coal, and was fairly granted the title of "Founder of the National League."

His first act as the N.L. founder had been to put in place a 13-point plan of organization. In the N.L. there would be no place for gambling or drinking and there would be no baseball played on Sundays. He became the enforcer.

Upon taking the office of N.L. president, Hulbert ruled the New York City and Philadelphia franchises out of order for failing then refusing to complete the last parts of their assigned 1876 game schedules; these involved lengthy and costly Midwest road trips. He summarily revoked the franchises of these two biggest major league commercial markets; his decision was sustained until after his death. By the code of baseball, constitutionally grievous offenses had been committed. The offenders were relegated to the status of nonentities. It was a judgment and judgment call by William A. Hulbert. Authority prevailed over commerce, for the moment, in the National League.

The players were made subject to demanding contracts, which were to be rigorously enforced; there would be no jumping allowed. All was fair because there was regional balance in the league at the end of the 1876 calendar year.

Challenge had been made, quickly and firmly undone; there was no doubt about the force of Hulbert. He proved himself again as the absolute authority of baseball before the year of 1877 ended.

As the Louisville team was cruising to the 1877 championship, near the end of the season unexplainable hitches appeared in their drive mechanism. A report had first been made to the club, by the son or nephew of a primary owner of the franchise, who also owned the powerful local newspaper; four players were suspected of contriving to lose games they should have won. They did lose, which made their offenses deeds done, if in fact they were done.

Money was involved, considerable sums of money. Too often plays were made or not made which might come under the term boneheaded by a couple of lesser players. A tough veteran named Bill Craver, who'd been in the game since the Haymakers were amateurs, was also often suspected of at least being connected with New York City gamblers. The fourth suspect player at Louisville was George Hall, a legitimate and proven star. There were inquiries at the club level, but no action done. The son or nephew by some chance happened to be a reporter with the city newspaper and began writing scandal.

The issue was given way to the league level; there was a formal investigation and interrogations were done. The four offenders, lessers, veteran, and star, were judged guilty by Hulbert, and timely baseball justice was done: the four accused were banned from professional baseball for life, in any and all capacity.

Would the Players League executive have banished franchises? Players? Brothers? Brethren? Questions without answers. There were no offenses such as these done which are known. Still the premise of potential and resolution should be considered.

Louisville left the N.L., in part because of this incident, and St. Louis and Hartford for their reasons. The N.L. began 1877 with six pennant aspirants; when the 1878 season began six of the original eight cities were missing. Only Chicago and Boston were still in the league with their founding franchises intact. The balance of the 1878 N.L. roster included Cincinnati, Indianapolis, Milwaukee, and Providence. The National League had taken on a very different and distinctly western look.

Arthur Soden was primary among three Boston owners: Bryan DiSalvatore, in *A Clever Base-Ballist*, calls him "miserly and the most notorious flinty-skinned of the owners." His players were assessed 50¢ per day on road trips for board and meals, had to pay $30 per season for their uniforms, pay for lost and damaged equipment, and submit to random medical examinations. Such salary debits and deeds were common to the baseball condition.

In 1879 the N.L. took to the fields with eight teams. There were no significant challenges to authority, nor corruption, which condition sustained through the balance of the life of William A. Hulbert.

There had been a meeting of the N.L. men in Buffalo in 1879. A primitive reserve clause had been inserted into all players' contracts, about which they had no say at all, for now.

In the beginning Hulbert had made Spalding his team captain and field manager, then awarded the concession for league equipment to the new manufacturing company formed by Spalding and family. Then Spalding was chosen president of the White Stockings club, and in 1880 he became a prominent owner of the Chicago franchise. By the time of the demise of Hulbert, Mr. Spalding was fully prepared for any and all eventualities; he'd become a man of iron will, a leader of leaders. By the mid–1880s Mr. Spalding was the sovereign of baseball.

With eight teams in the N.L. of 1879 it had become a league of little cities, all enthusiastic for major league baseball but few big enough in population to adequately support a franchise; the little cities became subject to a National League policy of membership by revolving door. A monopoly tends to do whatever it wills.

Year	In	Out
1879	Buffalo, Cleveland, Syracuse, Troy	Indianapolis, Milwaukee
1880	Worcester	Syracuse
1881	Detroit	Cincinnati
1882	Stabilized…	But…

The year Hulbert died a most formidable rival was born to the N.L., formally named the American Association of Base Ball Clubs. Its philosophy was grounded in the premise of opposition to monopoly in professional major league baseball. At least this was so expounded in the beginning. The American Association (A.A.) was also originally different from the N.L. in various administrative methodologies.

Oliver Perry (O.P.) Caylor wrote in the *Cincinnati Enquirer* of November 3, 1881, that the A.A. was formed as an independent league; by his account both "base" and "ball" began with lower case b's and their motto was published as "Liberty to All."

Their standard gate admission would be 25¢, not 50¢. Each club was free to decide the issue of beer and liquor to be sold at their ballparks and each could choose in accord with prevailing local opinion whether or not the whole of each Sunday during the season had to be observed as Sabbath.

On the whole it could be said, and has been said, the A.A. intended to cater to the masses, the common folk, offer a product which could be perceived as competitive with that of the N.L., but at lower prices and with options. The further philosophy would go where the N.L. had been and left, or had never gone.

Cincinnati, Philadelphia, and St. Louis were awarded the new A.A. franchises, and Pittsburgh, Louisville and Brooklyn. Beginning with six represented a departure from established precedent. All six teams finished the first A.A. season, and all six A.A. clubs had profits to show for it.

The A.A. hired a corps of its own umpires in July of the first year, previously unheard of as economic absurdity. The N.L. soon emulated this move as wise competitors in any venue of commerce often do. Contrary to N.L. policy, philosophy, whatever, the A.A. players for the season of 1882 had contracts which included no reserve clause; salaries could be expected to be appreciably greater.

Such inducements at both ends of the player's career spectrum assured the immediate survival of the American Association, and future successes could be imagined within the realm of reality. The formula and illusion were fast undone by the men of the N.L.; rather than immediately confront and do battle with their new competitor for the public baseball dollar, they chose to abide the A.A. and ignore the threat it represented, albeit very temporarily, till when N.L. was sure to prevail.

Between the first and second seasons of the A.A. its public face was made over as if decided and done in the N.L. board room. There was communication, there was compromise; the new rival could exist, but only conditionally as the N.L. willed.

The A.A. would be given major league status, verified by an invitation to unofficial team versus team exhibition contests, and perhaps by agreement there could be a post-season series if the parties to be involved were able to contract amenably.

"But" is such a little word, and "if" is even less; but the senior league would do these courtesies and civilities only if the newcomer would be amenable to inserting the sacred reserve clause in the A.A. players' contracts; the players need not know until signing time, if not before the fact, and of course would have no say at all about it.

The deed of mutuality was done, which word "mutuality" soon was to become the essence of battles in legal courts, which in turn would lead to a revolution, a civil war in baseball. There was no formal public notice, but the gauntlet was down. Credit for this act of compromise is due Abraham G. Mills, then the N.L. president, and Denny McKnight, then the A.A. president. McKnight had been a founder of the A.A. and a major owner of the Pittsburgh club. He took a chance not long after and tried to apply reason and common sense to an agitated situation: His credit came in the form of a label, "persona non grata" in his association.

In terms of their players, within a year the A.A. had become a concordant copy of the N.L. The players were again left with no major league where fair play might be found in the offices. As it had been since 1876, more so since 1879 when the reserve clause became an official part of the way of baseball life, their sole alternative was to quit the game and go home.

McKnight would be replaced as the A.A. president and soon after stripped of his partnership in the Pittsburgh franchise by his colleagues, the other lesser league owners. As for A.G. Mills, he'd served as a colonel with the Union blue during the Civil War; there are reports that he played in games on the fields for recreation and amusement, its original intended purposes.

Mr. Mills served as the fourth N.L. president. He was chosen by Al Spalding as one of the seven finest men of the game who could be trusted to perform a historic task which in the baseball realm became tantamount to sacred service.

Esteemed Henry Chadwick had written his opinion that baseball had evolved from English ball games, namely cricket. Spalding saw his duty clear; he formed a blue ribbon committee, which equates with prestige and status second only to a comparable commission. Spalding gave his committee an identity, and Mr. Mills the highest of honors, his Mills Commission by then was given the duty to deny and refute the allegations of Chadwick absolutely.

Spalding appointed to his commission Morgan Bulkeley as one of the most trustworthy, the first N.L. president, a governor, and U.S. senator who'd not been bothered to do due diligence to his president duty that first year the N.L. had played.

There were also on the Mills Commission another U.S. senator, and Al Reach and George Wright, by then both prosperous via their (separate) baseball equipment manufacturing companies; also the president of the U.S. Amateur Athletic Union, and Nicholas E. Young, the fifth N.L. president, who'd held the office from 1884 till 1902, including 1890.

Spalding assigned himself no official status with the committee, though he did lead in seeking input from the public. They were said to have been literally inundated with evidence; documents, artifacts, sworn testimony, affidavits in support of their given cause. Three years later, in 1908, they took their account and rendered a public report.

The Mills Commission decided that above all meritorious evidence stood a letter from a mining engineer in Colorado, who claimed to have been present and witness when Abner Doubleday used a wooden stick to lay out the first baseball diamond as it is now known; the prevailing letter also alleged Doubleday had taken the initiative to decide the proper number of players per side, as they have remained since that historic day in 1839.

All of which claims were later proven to have been done elsewhere first, but Spalding and Mills, and these other finest of baseball men had done their duty far beyond due diligence, and while at it had proven their patriotic virtue to the complete satisfaction of all Americans who were interested and held the same opinion. Truth was what they manufactured, despite proof irrefutable, and the written words of Henry Chadwick.

Spalding knew well the worth of documents toward legitimacy, and the advocacy of other fine men in achieving purposes of will; they'd used the reserve rule and the National Agreement to maintain primacy over the players of baseball despite legitimacy at its core being nothing more than the self-given authority of the National League of Professional Base Ball Clubs. The American Association had chosen to be partner to these and other N.L. capital devices, but the A.A. as a body never proved sufficiently enthusiastic for the N.L. men to sense the confidence in them that the public gave to the truth of Albert Spalding and the Mills Commission.

The A.A. put a pretty good baseball product on the fields, if judged in terms of the postseason championship contests which were initiated after the third season, though not a thought was given to including the Union Association which dared to intrude into the established domain.

Few historians and other experts give credence to these World's Series, as they came to be called, but they serve as evidence that the A.A. did accomplish its purpose of striking down the N.L. monopoly. Fact and history inform that these series of mid– to late–October games were staged for other than the cause alleged by the franchise owners who stood to gain financially from them, to ascertain which major league champion was truly the American national champion.

The public was usually amused while the weather held well, but nearly every account that's been written of any of these is void of praise by the players who had to endure their work year being extended. The owners of the two competing clubs chose the venue, set the schedule, and collected the whole of the gate receipts. There was little if any other income then except a pittance from some concessions sales, and the players were rewarded in dollars as their owners chose; $100 seems generous, better than nothing.

Still there was the competition, and these games for whatever reasons did serve as precedent for the real World Series which began in 1903, and true-to-the-game competition is cause for a brief review of these 1880s annual baseball events.

Year	National League	Games Won	American Association	Games Won
1884	Providence	3	New York	0
1885	Chicago	3	St. Louis	3
1886	Chicago	2	St. Louis	4
1887	Detroit	10	St. Louis	5
1888	New York	6	St. Louis	4
1889	New York	6	Brooklyn	3
1890	Brooklyn	3	Louisville	3

Both the 1885 and 1890 series produced a tie game, and both series ended tied. The officiating norm was one umpire chosen by each owner, nearly all from the appropriate league; the umpires played more of a role in deciding winners than any players. Typical starting times for games was 3:00 P.M., although they usually took little more than an hour to play, squabbling and dawdling could extend them till dusk when the leading side which did the most lagging would complain it was too dark to continue.

The A.A. St. Louis owner, Chris Von der Ahe, once went to excess to support his plea for a call to an end: he placed lit candles along the bench for his side. In a hostile ballpark they were promptly pelted with an assortment of flying objects. He also was one of two who contracted for a 15-game championship contest. As if it were necessary the whole farce was played out, all over the land, no matter that his club was impossibly behind in game count when 11 games had been played.

Whether pure avarice or plain silliness, this 1887 classic went to 10 cities, beginning at St. Louis on October 10 and ending at St. Louis on October 26. Fans at Washington, D.C., almost missed their scheduled showcase by a rainout on October 20; executive innovation prevailed as the game was postponed, then played on the morning of the 21st. The durable players were given a second opportunity to show their skills that day in an afternoon game played at Baltimore.

The American Association as an entity began by agreement on the 10th of October, 1881, at a meeting in Pittsburgh. The formal founding date of the A.A. was November 2, when at Cincinnati the six franchises were officially awarded. The Brooklyn grant was withdrawn by the league in March 1882 and presented to Baltimore.

At that time it was decided the A.A. would not honor the list of players blacklisted for minor offenses by the N.L. It also chose to deviate from the N.L. rules in other ways. An expert on the A.A. has provided insight that its creation was an act antecedent to October, whence at Philadelphia in September an alliance of sorts was formed between scribe and lawyer O.P. "Opie" Caylor on behalf of Cincinnati and Horace Phillips on behalf of Philadelphia who conspired to aver the need for another baseball major league.

With their success manifest the A.A. played out its seminal season with Cincinnati emerging as the champion. Audacity in the name of Caylor and arrogance by the name of Spalding were partners on behalf of their own league in scheduling the first legitimate championship game for October 6; it was played.

Charles "Pop" Smith was the umpire, a reserve player with two A.A. teams during their first season; the place was Cincinnati, the ballpark called "Bank Street Ground." Approximately 2,700 fans could have made valid claims that "I was there!"

If a man would have been willing to wager, the White Stockings of manager Cap Anson would have been the sure favorites to win. If the baseball world was stunned in 1869 and 1870 then that happened again; the Reds (nee Red Stockings) of manager Charles "Pop" Snyder achieved a stunning victory.

A second game was played the next afternoon, which prompted a telegram from A.A. president McKnight to the Cincinnati team which screamed "Stop!" the games, and it was done.*

On February 17, 1883, at New York City, representatives of the American Association, the National League, and the Northwestern (minor) League drafted and agreed to comply with the terms and conditions of the Tripartite Agreement, an early form of the National Agreement, thus properly sealing the bonds of mutual interest.

Eight months later the three leagues would have in place their refined edition of essentially a peace treaty stipulating that each of their franchises and clubs had exclusive rights, safe and secure, to a specified area of territory, and to each hold in reserve a specific number of players under contract.

The terms and conditions would be further revised in the following years, including what had begun in Buffalo in 1879 as the reserve clause agreement, to which the N.L. and A.A. were the primary signatories. Other elements would be added which would remain in place till after the 1890 season. Of course the Players League was not a party to any part or parcel of any such treaties, the worth of which were to be found in treaties of the time agreed between Washington, D.C., and American Indian nations to the west of baseball and the baseball domain.

The 1883 games of the A.A. drew some 300,000 in attendance, an excess beyond their fledgling year of 80,000 when all club ledgers showed financial gains. The combined gate total for the two major leagues of 1883 was estimated at 1 million; the owner of the St. Louis A.A. territory and players bragged of $70,000 in profits for the year.

On October 27, 1883, the same seven men who drafted the winter agreement met at the same place to do the same business; they further reinforced their reserve clause and added 10 amendments as supplements. A parallel can be found in the American Constitution devised at Philadelphia, although it is essential to keep in

---

*David Nemec argues that McKnight probably never issued such an order, as contemporary sources suggest that only two games had been scheduled.

mind that a constitution and any such agreement are completely separate and distinct documents of legitimacy; the parallel here is the Bill of Rights being added to the text for American governance.

That particular American original required from January 1786 till March 4, 1789, for procedure and protocol to be achieved, and a further period until December 1, 1791, for those after-the-fact 10 amendments cited Bill of Rights to be effected and "in force"; some men of business are more efficient in their means and methods than others.

What are decreed as rights for some may also impose restraints upon others. The 10 baseball amendments of 1883, for example, enabled clubs as franchises to transfer from one league to another in their entirety, with the proper approval mechanism in place, and obligated clubs to wait 10 days to sign players who had been properly released by other clubs for reasons of economy.

Thus the leagues granted rights to themselves to relocate, taking with them in theory their ballpark and office furniture, and in fact their players' contracts and players; the players were thus restrained from having any say in their relocation, other than to quit baseball as a source of income or switch to other leagues which were not parties to the agreement(s) and to be restrained for 10 days after one club decided they were of no further use before securing employment with another which was party to the agreement(s).

Complexity aside, this latter restraint ruled away the chance to sign quickly for a bonus when their services were highly in demand, and perhaps for a significant increase in salary, to give all clubs a fair crack at a player, thus protecting the clubs from themselves in the event one might for self-serving reasons assign a peak value to a player in excess of others' opinions.

While A.G. Mills was chairman at these agreement meetings, and O.P. Caylor there for the A.A. interests, also Elias Mather for the party of the third part, until 1890 these men were building a wall of paper and ethos which grew to such proportions that they precluded any possibility of communication and cooperation between themselves and the other party, the players of professional major league baseball.

In addition to the three noted, present and participating for their leagues and their clubs, and their interests, were of the N.L. Arthur Soden of Boston and John B. Day of New York; their A.A. counterparts were Lew Simmons of Philadelphia and Billie Barnie of Baltimore; Caylor was titular chairman of the A.A. contingent, though neither a league official nor primary owner.

There then existed a formal peace agreement between the leagues by virtue of the first constitution that would govern all of baseball, as these men perceived their domain to be.

In November 1883, Henry Van Noye Lucas implanted himself upon the domain; then on December 18 while in Philadelphia he met with men of five other cities — his was St. Louis — to verify the existence of his envisioned Union Association.

Richer than rich, in his mid–20s, he was the son of the owner of a major Midwestern railroad company who was also a banker and a lawyer. The son had made application for a franchise of the major league class and had been rebuffed; he'd created his own club, and semi-pro league and was the third baseman and field manager.

With his credentials in place, and brother in law, Frederick Espenscheid, in tow to serve as point man and operations chief, he established a third baseball major league. His allies in this enterprise were at first Warren White, of Washington, D.C., and Justus Thorner and John McLean of Cincinnati. The former was a former owner of a Cincinnati league club, the latter the owner of the *Cincinnati Enquirer* who had been an employer of O.P. Caylor till disputes on baseball philosophy caused them to part company.

Thomas Pratt of Philadelphia was there, he would be chosen as the vice president of the Union Association (U.A.); Lucas had himself elected president of his league; he embarked upon his grand venture with Mike Scanlon also on his side, a player of major league status who operated a pool hall. He represented Baltimore as the sixth among the new Lucas entourage.

He'd wished for eight, not six, and promised the equipment contract to the sporting goods company of George Wright in exchange for a Boston club. The imagination of Lucas went beyond excess on the playing fields of 1884; by various counts 12 or 13 cities represented his eight franchises.

The men of the U.A. were not party to any agreements, but did make themselves privy to players of the leagues that were; there were player raids back and forth throughout the playing season; for his part in a raid on Providence Henry Lucas was branded a felon in Rhode Island.

The avowed goal of Henry Lucas and his U.A. company writ noble was to establish and operate a league wherein players would have both rights and dignity. These proved a great attraction when came the time to sign contracts. There were promises of bigger pay and better working conditions; players might no longer have to pay to have their team uniforms laundered, for example.

For the St. Louis club the Lucas family and clan built a grand facility on their vast estate, called Normandy. Their ballpark had the stylish name Ball Park of America. As for the others who were the U.A., everything Lucas had to be bigger and better.

The fans of St. Louis were amused with them, but not for long; those of other cities found no enjoyment in the U.A. at all; the president accumulated a team so superior that none of the others were competitive by the end of the first month of play. The U.A. became chaos just trying to keep teams in place. The enterprise went the way of the N.A. after the first and only season. It was swept away from the domain by the prevailing forces like a nest of pesky gnats, after which young Mr. Lucas was permitted to purchase his own real major league franchise.

On April 18, 1885, the St. Louis Maroons were admitted to the National League. Lucas had his wish at last. It's nearly impossible to ascertain with certainty which of the eight U.A. franchises landed where and when during their season of play. This representation is an indicative approximation of those that managed to stay in one place through the whole or much of their season, with further notes to follow; "G.B." herein means "Games Behind" the Union Association champions, of course.

City Team	Won	Lost	G.B.
St. Louis Maroons	94	19	—
Cincinnati Outlaw Reds	69	36	21.0
Baltimore Monumentals	58	47	32.0
Boston Reds	58	51	34.0
Chicago Browns	34	39	40.0
Washington Nationals	47	65	46.5

The men of the U.A. also played games as the Cream Cities of Milwaukee; the Mountain Cities of Altoona, Pennsylvania; the Stogies of Pittsburgh; Keystones of Philadelphia, White Caps of St. Paul, Minnesota; and the Wilmington (Delaware) Quicksteps, which set an official major league record that can be matched but never beaten.

Attendance being a prominent factor in the business of baseball, at one home game during their weeks in the U.A., the Quicksteps of Wilmington counted an attendance of zero (0). During the term the Quicksteps won two games and lost 16, for a .111 win percentage, which arguably constitutes another major league record akin to baseball. The U.A. executive body formally voted to disband as such in January 1885.

By one account, James Jackson had been the catalyst of the U.A. organization in September 1883. Its constitution was almost an imitation of those existing except that the purposes writ included being in direct competition with the establishment, and it "would not honor the reserve clause." Unknown then but after the fact, with stimuli provided by the Monumentals of Washington, D.C., the league established a salary cap for the 1885 season of $2,000 for their players. As a last bit aside, the Maroons won their first 20 games, and at the end of August were 59 and nine.

Harry Wright had played for the Knickerbocker Club. By then the game was no longer as pure as clover honey. By the latter 1880s the business end done in league offices had become as dirty as baseball players would become on their playing fields during the decade after the Players League played.

There was posturing and gesturing, and written words. The players complain about the rating at which they are classified. The brotherhood made no specific statement of grievances against the league; their communication to the president simply indulged in glittering generalities. One of the principal points at issue was the rule.

The Metropolitan Company had sold the New York Metropolitans in 1881 for $25,000 to Erastus Wiman, who owned the Staten Island Amusement Company and the Staten Island Ferry; his plans for relocation of the home park of his team never materialized.

Once in power as N.L. president Col. Abraham G. Mills set about quashing other would-be major leagues. After the 1884 season, Mills was replaced by Nick Young. Though perhaps no less devoted to eliminating the competition, Young's methods were smoother and subtler.

Sporting Life began printing its periodical in 1883. *The Sporting News* was first published in 1886, involving the Spink brothers, Al and Charley. Newburger was an owner of the Indianapolis (N.L.) franchise in 1887; his team won 37 games and lost

89, for a .294 win percentage. It finished eighth and last by 43 games. Such teams do not stimulate many revolutions of the turnstile at the gate.

Caylor was out in Cincinnati by 1887, relocated to Philadelphia to continue working as a newspaper reporter, to publish his own scandal sheet. Perhaps his legal training helped him style his insults with childish word games and cynical poetry and verse.

Nicholas E. Young was N.L. president in 1887. Crassus had been triumvir III in Rome and James B. Billings was triumvir III in the N.L. Boston; on May 22, 1889, the Louisville Colonels embarked on an all-time record 26-game losing streak. Mordecai Davidson was an owner, but in late June turned over the franchise to the association, which sold it to a jumble of new owners.

In *The Beer and Whiskey League*, David Nemec calls Mordecai Davidson "a furniture dealer who ventured into baseball on the assumption that he could run a major league franchise much the same as he did his business."

Davidson, Nemec writes, "was hounded out of baseball in 1889, later did well in business and was feted for being one of Kentucky's last surviving Civil War veterans. His obituary in 1940 mentioned everything but the fact that he had once been a major league owner." And, such was the condition.

In the N.L. in 1886, Detroit jumped several notches to second place due to the acquisition of Dan Brouthers and Hardy Richardson. Late in 1885 Detroit bought the entire Buffalo team for $7,000 specifically to acquire Dan Brouthers, Hardy Richardson, Jack Rowe, and Deacon White.

Regarded as four of the best players in the game, these men turned Detroit into a contender practically over night. In 1886 they were the Detroit Wolverines infield, and in 1887 when that team was the world's champions. They were still together there in 1888.

In 1889 Brouthers and Richardson wore the uniforms of the N.L. Boston Beaneaters the whole season. Rowe was in service to the Pittsburgh Alleghenys which had switched leagues from the A.A. to the N.L.; he played in 75 games after holding out. White, who joined him far into the season, had refused to play there at all.

Chattel are any kind of property except land and buildings. Baseball chattel then could appreciate in appraised value much faster than furniture.

Before the Players League played the owners said for the record that there was no general protest by players. The leaders, they said, were not affected by the reserve clause and classification system. Over 70 were on the list and only five had complained of the rating given them.

"It is not yet perfect, its sponsors did not claim it to be, it is simply an experiment, with a few modifications will be accepted by a large majority of the clubs, there is room for improvement, all the players, stars and otherwise should be classified, and the good men will draw good salaries." Vague generalities, promises, there was more than one issue, about which the players had no say at all, of course.

The Syracuse Stars would play in the American Association during the 1890 season, the first major league season for the fans of that little city since 1879. R.C. Morse was an owner and director. Rich, young, and brash George Frazier put him out on the street while he was reorganizing the business of the franchise.

The Toledo Maumees, also called the Black Pirates, played the 1890 season in the American Association; Valentino H. Ketcham was their owner. The 81,000 fans represented that smallest major league city. After the Players League played the A.A. wasted little time getting rid of Toledo, although it didn't go without a fight.

After a long gestation, this was the environment into which the Players League was born. On June 15, 1889, the Browns were in Louisville to play a series of games. There and then both teams formed chapters of the Brotherhood of Base Ball Players.

Billie Barnie was an Orioles executive on November 1, 1889. He declared that his club quit the A.A. while contriving a deal to join the N.L. as Washington, which deal never came to pass. Chris Von Der Ahe was still A.A. St. Louis and William Whittaker was A.A. Philadelphia. Beyond that the A.A. then became chaos.

Charles Byrne was Brooklyn, which did achieve a switch to the other established league. Wheeler Wyckoff and Zach Phelps were Louisville; the latter was the league attorney and was elected A.A. president for 1890.

Unknown Conrad Burn of Columbus was chosen the vice president of the A.A. for 1890. Aaron Stern as club president and Harry Sterne as club secretary on the 13th of November, 1889, stated their Cincinnati franchise quit, which franchise became a maze. Louis Krauthoff was Kansas City; he quit to join the Western League, whence he took his club, field, furniture, and player contracts.

John T. Brush, of this league and the other, established written standards for the players' salary scale imposed in 1889; the high was set at $2,500 and the low at $1,500. Where each player fit depended on skill, which raises the issue of who would be granted the authority to decide these decisions, which might be as much as 67 percent greater or less than that should be (consider 67 percent more or less of a $40,000 salary income circa the year 2000).

"Shortly after the 1888 World's Series ended, Monte Ward accompanied a raft of other major league stars on a world tour organized by Chicago [N.L.] owner Al Spalding. The tour boat had scarcely left the dock when Indianapolis [N.L.] owner John Brush bolted into action."

"Brush devised a meeting of all the League owners on November 21, 1888, at the Fifth Avenue Hotel in New York [City], where he introduced his 'Salary Limit and Graded Plan' to divide players into five classifications depending on their skill."

"And [such a little word] establish a pay scale that restricted the best players to a salary max of $2,500 while granting those at the bottom of the totem pole $1,500 ... a similar kind of salary limit had been endorsed by League owners three years earlier ... these classifications ranging from 'A' to 'E.'"

The earlier plan was "only to fail because too many teams [sic, clubs] disobeyed it. Now that the Brush plan was about to become law the players hit the roof ... it robbed them of initiative and paid them much less than they could obtain in a free market."

Of course there was no free market. At its core this plan was simply a business device to restrain and protect the owners from themselves, completely at the expense of the players, who could accept, quit major league baseball, or devise a league and rules of their own; these were the only options then.

Another source has added to this, "Players would be placed into classes based upon their ability — and — 'personal behavior.'" The plan was explicit in its financial restrictions, implicit in citing public demeanor as a factor, and insidious in its intent to facilitate the judgment of players by their attitudes toward their status of bound servility.

The Chicago (N.L.) owner had taken a raft of players on a tour of the world. The challenges inherent to the planning and logistics would have been overwhelming to most men then, but not for Albert Goodwill Spalding.

The entirety of the entourage sailed from San Francisco, after playing a series of games for West Coast fans, and against some of the better West Coast teams; they sailed toward the Orient, then wended their way to Egypt, and on toward Paris and London.

They'd been on the road since late October 1888 and wouldn't return to contiguous U.S.A. till early in April 1889. They'd stopped to play a series of baseball games in England. This is an accounting of the first of these games.

London Times, March 13, 1889: a game had been played at Prince's Ground, Manchester, the first display of the American game in England since the Boston Red Stockings and Philadelphia Athletics had visited the land of cricket and rounders in 1874.

Three more games were set to be played in England within a week. For this contest the All America team wore white and Chicago wore gray and black. These were the reported players:

America:	*Chicago:*
Ned Hanlon (OF)	Mark Baldwin (P)
Monte Ward (SS)	Jimmy Ryan (OF)
Tom (OF) or Willard (C) Brown	Marty Sullivan (OF)
Egyptian Healy (P)	Fred Pfeffer (2B)
Fred (C) or Cliff (OF) Carroll	Cap Anson (1B)
George Wood (OF)	John Tener (P)
Jim Fogarty (OF/UT)	Tom Burns (3B)
Jim (OF/UT) or Jack (OF) Manning	Bob Pettit (OF/UT)
Billy Earle (OF/C)	—————

There is no mention of a ninth Chicago player. These surnames are certain; first names are speculative but informed. The positions were their regular major league positions. Many players could and did play a variety of positions, thus are noted as utility (UT). Seven of the America team would play in the Players League. Both named Manning were out of the major leagues in 1890. Three of the Chicago team would be P.L. players. Pettit didn't play in 1890.

It had rained at the site the morning of game day. When the players entered the field conditions were misty, which made it difficult for fans at the distant football (soccer, rugby) end of the field to follow the ball.

Attendance was about 6,000 which only the greatest games played in the U.S.A. could match or better. Spectators were reported as lukewarm to the play of the game generally and puzzled by the frequent changes from batting to fielding. The fielding by both sides was brilliant but their batting form was disappointing.

It had rained that morning, and the turf was slick and wet. Chicago won this first game in England near the end of the world tour. John Monte Ward was not a factor. Extra base hits known were a pair of triples by Anson for Chicago. Fogarty hit a double or triple for the America side; two errors would have been charged, both to America, one to pitcher Healy, one to the America catcher.

Innings	1	2	3	4	5	6	7	8	9	=	
America	0	4	0	0	0	0	0	0	0	=	4
Chicago	2	0	0	0	0	2	0	3	X	=	7

Runs scored by:
America: Carroll, Wood, Fogarty, Manning
Chicago: Ryan, Sullivan, Anson 2, Pfeffer 2, Tener

Fogarty would have had two runs batted in for America while Pfeffer of Chicago would have led all players with four r.b.i.

According to the *New York Clipper* of April 13, 1889, the tour captured the imagination of fans in the United States. At a celebration in New York City, with DeWolf Hopper ("Casey at the Bat" reciter) and Mark Twain in attendance, master of ceremonies Abraham G. Mills told the audience that patriotism and research had established that the game was American in origin then there came from the audience staccato cries of "No rounders!"

The tour converted few foreigners to baseball. The group left San Francisco on Nov. 18 and arrived in New York April 6. The return celebration continued at a game between New York and Brooklyn teams, and culminated at Palmer's Theatre that evening.

The theater was decorated with flags and an emblem of flags of all nations. A sign proclaimed "positively no more money taken tonight." Decor included an emblematic eagle and shield with crossed bats, a pair of baseball gloves, and a catcher's mask.

The pomp and frivolity continued long after 10 P.M. when A.G. Mills called the diners to order, explaining that Governors Hill and Bulkeley had sent notices of regret, unable to attend. Many such dignitaries were in attendance though. To them and the other elite of the baseball world Mr. Mills said, "The boys were not only star baseball players, but they were, in every sense, representatives of American manhood and citizenship."

Truth was spoken and hypocrisy done, for such commendations were not put to paper in the obligatory, forever binding contracts of the players. A.G. Spalding was said to be drunk standing. This was truly one grand scheme; Ward as leader of the Brotherhood was out of the country during what became critical times. Spalding advertised his game and manufacturing business around the world. At home the mechanisms of baseball continued to grind.

The army of malcontent N.L. and A.A. players began to form, to fight the reserve clause, the National Agreement, the rules and the laws to which they'd been made subject with no say of their own. This was not the national slavery issue, this was a baseball issue which required resolution: Were the contracts, by their assumed authority to oblige servitude, perhaps not proper but legal?

Nothing of any law imposed has ever been certain. Since Solomon and Rome laws have been matters of situational convenience, when not arrogant malice or outright whimsy, to dispense with and dispose of demands and dilemmas imposed on the finest men.

According to lawyer and scholar John Phillip Reid, one such law enacted in 1773 was among the finest examples: the imposition by British law of a tea tax on their American colonists. It was done by force of regal authority, with common disposition supportive but at variance. By some on one side this was said then to be sufficiently insidious and nefarious to warrant a writ declaring independence; others claimed it was a trivial cause and reason for war.

To further expound on the validity of law done for cause by U.S. senators Henry Clay and Daniel Webster, between March and the winter of 1850–51, within the highest court of the American parliament, the legal merits of slavery were profoundly and properly debated. Then pen was put to paper which brought forth laws henceforth regarded by the subjects as oppressive to such an extent as to constitute cause and reason for war.

Early in 1885 baseball menial Charlie Bennett brought before the bench of law the covenant issue of involuntary servitude. The judiciary in attendance could have ruled he had no cause and no case, and dismissed the lawsuit for no reason, or for reason of further inquiry accept his case and cause as an issue of indenture by a written contractual agreement, which was no agreement but submission.

To the contrary, the judiciary ruled that the reserve clause was not a contract in and of itself despite its intent. Plaintiff Bennett emerged victorious from the court, wherein had been decided the first significant litigation on the merits of the reserve clause by which the players were bound.

When the baseball season of 1890 would come Charlie Bennett, by choice of free will, would wear the colors of the National League; his win in court in 1885 which legally negated the power of the owners' proprietary right in the player became reservation by the Brotherhood.

No doubt the Tripartite executive was dismayed by the Bennett decision, perhaps said better nom- or nonplused, now their precious reserve clause became priceless, the clause to rule had been ruled illegal and hung on the brink of irrelevance.

The most formidable weapon in the arsenal of the owners versus players written realm seemed to have been rendered worthless and useless; with their birthchild of authority in jeopardy no less than the conglomerate wisdom was needed of Rockefeller and Carnegie and Morgan, perhaps Madison and Hamilton and Jay.

On the 29th of September in 1879, at the Buffalo Pierce Hotel, had joined in conference all the National League franchises in the persons of their owners; self-appointed as the League Board of Directors they devised the first system for reservation of their players, the first reserve clause.

Hulbert was then league president and present. The prototype of 1879 said the members of the National League agreed that in contracting with players for 1880 those named would be assigned as followed.

Each of the six franchises reserved five players, who were to be considered and treated as members of their respected clubs and under contracts to the clubs as assigned. The meaning of being a member of a baseball club had changed significantly since the 1850s, and now again; the rule was inviolate, the reserved players were untouchable.

The players were thus bound by signing contracts for the next season with no say as to their employer for the next year. Five players reserved in 1879 grew to 11 in 1883, to 12 in 1886 after the Bennett decision, to 14 in 1887. Effectively the whole roster of each club was reserved. The one-year rollover became self-renewing; each player reserved belonged to his owner forever if his owner so chose. Clause became rule became law became tyranny.

According to its premier documents written for public consumption in 1876, the National League was founded to "encourage and to foster and to elevate" the game of baseball, to make playing the game "respectable and honorable" and further to "protect and promote the mutual interest of baseball clubs."

The original owners of 1876 also agreed and declared their intent was to "promote harmony and good-fellowship among ourselves ... and to protect the interests of our players." Thus then from 1876 forth the interests of the players as understood by their owners were under the cover of the public preamble clauses; the players were tangible assets with monetary value, like office furniture.

When push came to court early in 1890, Judge O'Brien of the New York State Supreme Court duly adjudicated after due contemplation that he was an ardent fan of the game, and by his readings of it the standard reserve clause was lacking mutuality, after which his judgment and legal wisdom were summarily ignored by those who were better informed, the owners of the game.

As for the part of the American Association in all this business, the most important meeting in association history took place on September 5, 1887, at the Fifth Avenue Hotel in New York City; its purpose was to propose a new National Agreement by making revisions to that to which they'd agreed and existed.

With their vision thus accommodated a system would be established for equalizing the playing strength of teams to end competition for players between teams and leagues, for fairly grading salaries of players thus improving the A.A.'s probability of economic survival by regulating the inflation of salaries.

Further changes would involve creating a self-sustaining reserve corps of players to bring in the new and put out the expensive, for more equitable contracts and dealings between employers and players. The more closely these innovations are read, the more they come to mean double entendre and durable inequity.

If as it's been written it is essential to know your enemy in war then it must be doubly so to know your ally in business; the high National League brass must have been left wondering about their ally, the American Association, and the men who were the A.A.

Lesser matters of their business involved altering the division of gate receipts, creating a Ladies Day at their ballparks once per week but not on any holiday or other day when the gate could be expected to be turning busily. Further and more important, they imposed an automatic fine of $1,500 against any of their teams, meaning the owners, which refused to finish a scheduled game in progress without consent of the umpire(s).

This last alteration would cause more squawking among the A.A. men than a fox in the back yard chicken house. Then of utmost importance, the men who were the A.A. would make revisions which would standardize playing rules and maximum salaries and would obligate renegade players to return to their former teams.

These wishes were all put in print, without the knowledge or consent of the National League. It represented the first instance since the N.L.-A.A. alliance was formed that the A.A. men asserted any explicit share in authority to render and impose decisions that might impinge on the business of major league baseball.

With the sense of a baseball civil war in the winds, these men of the A.A. had asserted for the public to know that they would not accept the role which Hitler would allocate to Mussolini when that war would come, they would not accept the leavings of the elite as Montezuma (sic Moctezuma) and his high priests had rendered their lessers and subordinate classes when the Azteca of Meso-America had ravaged that land and peoples.

If there was to be war then the American Association as an ally but an entity until itself would at least participate in choosing which spoils would be consumed by which of the victors; with victory then presumed nearly assured these were the A.A. clubs and leading men circa 1885–1887:

St. Louis (Browns): Christian Frederick Wilhelm "Chris" Von der Ahe, whom baseball owes for two things: introducing the hot dog to the ballpark and for describing as fanatics those who peopled his park, leading to the term "fan."

New York (Metropolitans): John B. Day, Erasmus (sic, Erastus) Wiman, Frank Rhoner, Walter Watrous.

Brooklyn (Grays, Trolley Dodgers): Charles "Charlie" Byrne, Joseph Doyle.

Philadelphia (Athletics): Lew Simmons, Bill Sharsig, Charlie Mason.

Cincinnati (Reds): Aaron Stern, Oliver Perry "O.P." Caylor, George Herancourt.

Baltimore (Orioles): Henry Von der Horst, John Hauck, William H. "Billie" Barnie.

Pittsburgh (Alleghenys): Denny McKnight, Horace Phillips, William "Bill" Nimick.

Louisville (Colonels): Zach Phelps, J.H. Phelps.

Cleveland (Blues): Frank DeHaas Robison, Davis Hawley, Stanley Robison, Jimmy Williams.

Washington (never played): Mike Scanlon.

The name Wyckoff is linked with Cincinnati in various capacities, most often as a proxy (substitute) representative of that and other A.A. clubs. "Opie" Caylor was a firm man of Cincinnati till he was not permitted to have his way; he remained loyal to the A.A. for a while, then became one of its most vocal and severe critics. He became an antagonist, a reporter renegade.

A historic reference of some legal magnitude informs us that on the 19th of December, 1886, the American Association had no legal existence; it was not an incorporated body. Regardless, a Pennsylvania court at Philadelphia ruled that league was subject to its law.

The A.A. executives in 1887 chose to pay their senior umpire the salary of $1,400 of the season; a junior but better-known umpire was paid $1,200 for officiating A.A. games part of that season. The appraised value of their other two men in blue is not known, but it is known that when one was disabled by a game injury, his income ceased with his utility. Such were the conditions then.

As note aside on Chris Von der Ahe, he was as important to the A.A. as Albert G. Spalding was to the N.L. Von der Ahe has been depicted as boorish and brash and worse, with having a bulbous nose, and a dolt. He was also moon-faced in the mind's eyes of some very recent baseball authors, often depicted with a clownish demeanor, physically big and burly or just rotund.

His physical traits were as they were, enhanced no doubt by his affinity for sausages and beer; he was of Prussian birth, thus usually depicted as kin to Kaiser Wilhelm or the Emperor von Bismarck. Von der Ahe emigrated to the U.S.A. as a youth, with typical wishes and a blank card for a future.

Upon landing at Ellis Island, near New York City, he was given employ by a local street vendor of produce and assigned to work in the Hell's Kitchen section. He saved enough money to enable relocation to St. Louis, where he became proprietor of a small grocery store and a saloon, a beer hall by German custom.

No doubt he was happy in his element, and proud of his tradition. Beyond voluminous quantities of food and drink he was fixed with other fundamental appetites; the Great American Dream became his model of life, and he achieved it in every manner and way.

He wore outrageous clothes, bulky checkered pants and spats. He spoke loudly and could sing louder; he began speculating in real estate and as quick as that made a small fortune. He didn't hoard, and while accumulating more he was free and generous to a fault.

He built a brewery and established a company to administer it. He adopted St. Louis as his hometown and was as proud of it as himself. Intent upon enjoying U.S.A. life to the fullest, and very well able, he purchased an embryonic baseball franchise.

Von der Ahe was there when the American Association began and he'd still be there when it would end. His team was the Browns, and champions like no others of the 1800s except the Red Stockings of Cincinnati and Boston, legend and lore.

He built an estate and within it a ballpark. To assure town folks would come he added carnivals and circuses, restaurants and game parlors, and places to play and to relax; he brought Buffalo Bill Cody and his road show to the people of St. Louis.

No doubt he stuffed considerable sums of money into his no-doubt oversized mattresses, and was eccentric in public; he marched his team to the ballpark, leading them in parade, for which he was criticized by those who did not or would not understand that such frivolity represented a legitimate and proud tradition.

Some among the public did not respect him, the media used him as the image of a buffoon, and his owner peers didn't desire him as one of them. Von der Ahe was a character bigger than life, and in most if not all ways was vastly superior to most if not all of them. Von der Ahe made every day a good day, and fun. He made an awful lot of money while he was at it, his Great American Dream realized and achieved.

He was a big and free spender, peculiar in some ways but clever in business. He was loyal to his men but too quick to react, too often without thinking. He cared for and about people, but in a tirade with his diamond stickpins flashing in the sun would offend men.

Von der Ahe was very naive about the game of baseball; once he was told of the quality of the diamond of another owner, he had to insist on having one bigger and better, till Charlie Comiskey helped him understand that the "diamond" is made of spots on the field all 90 feet apart, everywhere baseball was played.

In a moment of distress one day when his team was in difficulty, he had to inquire why his pitcher was allowing the other fellows to hit the ball. Every baseball day was pomp and circumstance, every game was cause for a holiday for Mr. Chris Von der Ahe, whose emotions would run to an overflow of ecstasy when employees in his service would refer to him as "Der Boss."

He had no qualms about letting umpires, opponents, and fans in the grandstands know his very one-sided opinions, often in language less than decorous; on the spur of the moment he'd fine one of his players for some trivial offense, then just as quickly he'd rescind the unjust debit.

Von der Ahe wasn't a man to be trifled with. His anger came slow but once in place tended to run long and deep. He was neither tyrant nor miser, just the boss.

He wasn't afflicted with a common American cerebral deficiency. Once upon a game of exhibition against a colored team his team refused to play except two. When the Cuban Giants of Philadelphia threatened to sue him for their expected $700 gain, Von der Ahe in his turn fired his team — except two — for an hour.

This braggart of grand proportions, obdurate as a rock, ignorant in the technicalities of the game, who occasioned to be outspoken, had another side; he was a happy man who tried to be fair in all matters, often as not contrary to his business associates.

When came the time the American Association suffered the wrath of Spalding and the National League, he was assigned the position of point man in the surrender negotiations; in the end Von der Ahe was made fodder for slaughter by the men of the A.A.

With his team and club decimated, he pushed for consolidation of the leagues. *The Sporting News* confirmed the official consolidation, which never happened. He also led the corps of owners in efforts to consolidate with the Players League, before and after they played. Chris Von der Ahe was a man of compromise; when all was written and done he was a man nearly destitute by his effort.

Christian Frederick Wilhelm Von der Ahe was born on November 7, 1851; he died June 7, 1913, at St. Louis, Missouri. The cause of death has been written as cirrhosis of the liver.

While his peers in baseball pursued bigger and better and more, Von der Ahe made the Great American Dream his life and for more than a decade he lived his dream. In the end the men and ethos of baseball prevailed. He ran his grocery store and butcher shop, he had his saloon. Chris Von der Ahe in fact had no business being in baseball.

A Look at the Game in the Nineteenth Century: Buffalo

Here follow reports and reminiscences of the game as gathered in the *Sports in Buffalo Scrapbook* housed in the public library of Buffalo and Erie County, N.Y., one exemplary locale during the latter 1800s. Such reports were often included in the sporting sections of the local newspapers, that word "sporting" then having an illicit analogy in "sporting house."

In 1877 "admission to the ball park was 25¢, you paid 10¢ more if you wanted to sit in the covered grandstand." In 1878 "a deal was made with a street car railway company which would enable a fan to buy a ticket for 50¢, entitling him to a round trip to the park and a grandstand seat."

Also in Buffalo in 1878, "a sign board was placed at a major intersection to announce all approaching games." Gimmicks like season tickets were not overlooked, "A ticket for 24 regularly scheduled home games cost ten dollars; the financial report showed that 16 were sold."

Circa 1817–1825, "There were 'Black Laws' of varying degrees of rigor in every Free State, segregating them as an inferior class" which were the written laws, which were continued explicitly with an enthused vigor after the Civil War and into the 20th century in every free state, which were all.

In Buffalo in 1884, "The covered grandstand was in the shape of a half-octagon. An innovation was in the fact that it was completely enclosed in the back and thus offered protection in event of inclement weather; louvers were built to provide ventilation."

"A special section was set apart for ladies, [their seats were] gaily painted arm chairs. Gentlemen if accompanied by ladies could occupy the arm chairs upon payment of an additional dime."

The seating capacity was about 4,000, "with room for about a thousand standees, it [the ball park] cost about $6,000.00."

"The 1884 Bisons opened on the road. Opening Day at the new Olympic Park was scheduled for May 21."

In 1885, "The Buffalo owner [who] sold the team for $7,000 [was named] Jewett, who was anxious to get out of baseball; he and his brother were in the midst of setting up a covered horse-race track."

Venerable Connie Mack didn't mention it in his autobiography, but Frank Grant, who played in Buffalo from 1886 through 1888,

> was a colored second baseman from the disbanded Meriden Connecticut club. During fall and winter there were rumblings of discomfort about the several Negro players in the (International) League. In 1886, Grant joined the Bisons, secured at considerable expense by the team owners.
>
> Grant was likely to prove a favorite among baseball enthusiasts, quick and active as a cat, a ballplayer who aroused enthusiasm of the spectators. He accomplished sterling feats while habitually nursing tender ankles and a sore throwing arm.
>
> Fellow Blacks in the International League had strong campaigns; left-handed pitchers George Stovey (34–15, .694) of Newark and Robert Higgins (19–8, .704) of Syracuse, these men represented cracks in the walls of racial prejudice.
>
> A much-quoted article in *Sporting Life* discussed the state of race relations in professional baseball: "probably in no other business in America is the color line drawn as in baseball. An African who attempts to put on a uniform and go in among a lot of white players is taking his life in his hands."
>
> Frank Grant for the 1887 season showed a .340 batting average, with 28 doubles, 10 triples and 11 home runs; the issue was finally compromised with each club permitted to carry two Negro players. In 1888 Grant hit 14 home runs, an almost unheard of total for those days. Grant became captain of the Cuban Giants [professional Negro touring team] the following year.

> The *Buffalo Express* had referred to them in 1888 as "alleged Cubans." They'd played a game against the I.L. Bisons on September 28th, "they never once drew a razor at a bad decision" wrote the *Courier*; another game was set for the next day but "an unprecedented snow storm, followed by thunder and lightning, put an end to the contest after ten minutes."
>
> From the outset, players resented the reserve-type contract. Their disorganized grumbling failed to arouse much sympathy, especially since the dissidents could offer no workable alternative. In 1885 the National Brotherhood of Professional Baseball Players was formed to give more concerted voice to their grievances.
>
> In 1886 a ceiling of $2,000 was placed on salaries, nothing more than a subterfuge to keep a lid on the pay of mediocre players, for the outstanding ones entered into side agreements which brought them additional remuneration.
>
> The players were further nettled by a plan put into effect in 1888, by which the President of the league rated each player either A, B, C, D, or E, his pay being determined automatically by his classification; this was effected while many star players were on a world tour.
>
> Ned Hanlon, a great player and manager of that era and one of the leaders of the Brotherhood, often said that it was the Buffalo [1879 reserve clause] incident that sparked the players revolt of 1890.

Plans were established; the National League Board of Directors for 1890 consisted of Frank DeHaas Robison of Cleveland and John B. Day of New York, both of whom had been involved in the American Association. Also on the N.L. Board for 1890 were Charles H. Byrne of Brooklyn and M.J. (?) Nimick of Pittsburgh; both had been owners of A.A. clubs and moved them to the N.L. most recently. Secretary to the Board was Nicholas E. Young, the N.L. president.

Others among owners of N.L. franchises and clubs as the year of 1890 approached were Gus Abel of Brooklyn, J.P. O'Neill of Pittsburgh, George Howe and Davis Hawley of Cleveland, John I. Rogers and A.J. Reach of Philadelphia, Arthur Soden and W.H. Conant of Boston, A.G. and Walter Spalding of Chicago, and John T. Brush of Indianapolis. These men as a union had a century of knowledge and experience in baseball on the field and baseball where business was done.

The N.L.-A.A. cooperative Playing Rules Committee members for the P.L. season were Al Spalding, John Day, and John Rogers; there for the A.A. were Billie Barnie, the field manager and part owner of the Baltimore club, and Patrick Powers, field manager at Rochester, possibly a part owner. To say the Committee was stacked toward the N.L.'s favor would represent gross understatement of the fact. Its task was to rule over and regulate the game on the fields of play of the establishment while the Players League played.

Gymnastics of Rationalization in Extremis

On October 22, 1885, nine players from the New York Giants composed and then signed a preamble for the Brotherhood constitution. The preamble, reproduced here from *The Players' National League Base Ball Guide 1890*, spells out both the need for and the aims of baseball's first labor union:

We, the undersigned professional base ball players, recognize the importance of united effort and impressed with its necessity in our behalf, do form ourselves this day into an organization to be known as the Brotherhood of Professional Base Ball Players.

The objects we seek to accomplish are:

> To promote and benefit ourselves collectively and individually
> To foster and encourage the interests of the game of Base Ball
> To promote a high standard of conduct.

The document was signed by John M. Ward, G.G. Gerhardt, William Ewing, Roger Connor, Daniel Richardson, Michael Welch, Michael C. Dorgan, Jas. H. O'Rourke, and T.J. Keefe. John Ward was chosen president, committees were formed, the work of the day was done; the foundation of the Players Brotherhood had been laid. If it was an act done in self-defense fair and just, or if it was an act done to usurp fair and just authority is still more than a century after the fact a matter of judgment.

Protocol and propriety were done then. The written words were no different in substance than any preamble of any American organization being established for reasons and purposes of business. It was not writ public as push was not yet shove.

There had to be fear, the sort of fear known by species when the laws of survival of the fittest come into play; further, these were the men of only one team, owned by one club, by raw numbers a majority among 11 or 13 of the 1885 New York (N.L.) Giants.

In 1886 Ward and his small band of Giants began to organize chapters of the Brotherhood in other cities. The first were of N.L. Detroit (May 11, 1886) with seven members and four more would join later. Next was Chicago (May 15, 1886) with three members and two to come later, including Mike "King" Kelly.

Next came Kansas City (May 19, 1886) with six members and four more soon after. St. Louis was represented by eight then four more. Boston joined with 16 players in June. Philadelphia joined in July with eight originally and eight more later; also in July came three from Washington, D.C. More followed from all the N.L. clubs, including eight of Pittsburgh, and five more joined from the city of Andrew Carnegie.

"Heroic treatment was necessary in order to rid the game of the disagreeable features and fetters that bound it and its exponents ... selling and buying of players, the reserve clause, the classification system, and the clumsy transferring of players. The Brotherhood was forced by the arbitrary actions of the National League to secede from the latter organization."

It was written in the *Spalding Base Ball Guide for 1890*: "The revolt of the players was headed by one man who was the mastermind of the whole revolutionary scheme from its inception to its consummation in the organization of the Players' League."

On November 4, 1889, after a war committee meeting of the Brotherhood, President John Montgomery Ward announced that the Brotherhood had severed all ties with the National League. Play was war, and vice versa; there is no statistical calculus to prove it, but most players in all the major leagues played inspired baseball in 1890 throughout this civilized war.

The status of American Association players was not yet certain as calendar year

1889 was nearing its end. John Reilly later assigned fault to Arlie Latham; after being put in charge of gathering signatures, which he'd allegedly done diligently, he lost the list.

This single miscue could have led to calamity. On the 16th of December, 1889, the Brotherhood had 97 players under contract to play their next seasons in the Players League; six had also signed National League contracts for 1890, each a cause for court action.

The Brotherhood had chosen officers for its union in 1890: John Ward as president, Dan Brouthers as vice president, Tim Keefe as secretary. These were for the Brotherhood, which did not automatically convey to the Players League offices.

The Brotherhood now had a plan for its league, and a strong corps of players to man the playing positions. What it lacked was sufficient money to put its teams on the playing fields. Actually, at that point, the Brotherhood didn't have playing fields.

Nor did it have ballparks, or offices in which to do money business; accommodations would have to be made, the officers decided. For those counting faults and flaws now there were two. At this point the basic premise of a player's league became history.

Variously cited as monied men and backers and contributors does not negate nor minimize the fact that men of money became Players League franchise owners; the accommodation allowed that each club would be operated by an eight-man board, composed of four players and four monied men.

The Players League would have a 16-man senate, two chosen from each club; one would be selected by the players, the other by the monied men. There is some illogic in this part of the plan, in the distribution of power per individual, and further this would invariably result in two cliques when differences arose; consider this then fault and flaw number three.

The senate would elect from among its own the president of the league. As an issue this could be construed as the difference between democracy and republicanism, government by participation or by representation, perhaps fault and flaw number four.

The senate would also elect the vice president, and the same flaw applies. The senate by some rule or protocol was required to select an outsider as the Players League secretary and treasurer; some faults and flaws overwhelm by their weighted deficiency.

The man chosen by some means for this most important position, controller of the records and the money, was Frank Brunell. He like Chadwick and Caylor was a writer for newspapers and various other periodicals and journals. What Frank Brunell was not was a man of business, nor was he experienced as a baseball player.

Never distant but never involved, Frank Brunell had been sports editor for the *Chicago Tribune*, obviously dealing with Spalding frequently if not with regularity; at the time of his selection he'd been a sports writer for the *Cleveland Plain Dealer*. To say it succinctly, this bespectacled man of stooped shoulders, this Casper Milquetoast sort of a fellow, was chosen to be the hub of the Players League. First there was Spalding, then in Cleveland his work must have required close contact with Frank DeHaas Robison, the most hostile, and next to the players and their league. The internal business operations of the Players League, then, involved players, and backers, and Brunell.

Further reason, internal, can be traced through the prior decades to their conflict for power and authority between the leaders of their navy and army; the civilian faction represented the third force in their leadership.

If all three had been willing to cooperate in a unified enterprise, suppressing their own interests, speculation being what it is says Japan might not have suffered the ignominy of unconditional surrender and military occupation.

There are parallels to be found in the Players League structure of players and outsiders as franchise owners. Add the fact of another outsider as chief of operations and reliable hindsight says they had built an organization destined for disaster to provide leadership and authority before their first game was played.

The question has never been answered, perhaps has never been asked, why an outsider was required for the double-duty office of secretary and treasurer. If it was believed necessary that the man chosen be free of influence from within, then why a man of the media, except for his publicity connections?

If ethics and professionalism were issues, a certified public accountant would have sufficed. If knowledge of the game was required, a retired major league player or baseball amateur with enthusiasm for the game and the requisite abilities could have been selected.

The decision was made that Players League clubs would share gate receipts equally; home teams would keep all concessions profits. With these issues resolved, the fiscal order of business for the Players League clubs was presumed done.

Operating expenses would be the problems of each club; players' salaries were to be guaranteed by the backers, as a condition of ownership. A league insurance fund of $40,000 would be put in place before the season began, another condition for ownership by outsiders.

Each club would contribute $2,500 for post-season prizes, to be awarded in accord with ranks in the final standings; these would vary from $7,000 in increments of $1,000 to $0 for the last-place club.

Money left over from all sources would later be distributed by formula to the backers as a unit, and to the players as a unit. The financial operations of the Players League involved a great many presumptions, neither prudent nor how reflective of U.S.A. business was done then.

There would be minimal business difficulties, and all the fiscal contingencies would work themselves out just fine; by this plan there was an inherent sense within the executive body that if it were wished, the sunrise and sunset could meld at midday and at midnight.

Further on the P.L. organization and operations: the charter of organization, the Brotherhood Manifesto, required that each franchise contribute $25,000 to a league fund intended to cover the expenses of clubs which might find themselves with financial difficulties.

All players were guaranteed salaries at least equal to 1889. The Brotherhood would make compulsory assignments of players to teams to equalize the rosters. The standard admission fee would be 50¢. No league games would be played on Sundays. No liquor or other intoxicating beverages would be sold at P.L. ballparks. It was a grand plan the P.L. executives devised, albeit nearly a carbon copy of another which existed.

The original eight P.L. umpires were chosen and would work in teams of two for all games: Ross Barnes, Bob Ferguson, John Gaffney, Tom Gunning, Bill Holbert, Charley Jones, Lon Knight, and Bobby Mathews. Most of these were famous names from the past.

When the season on the field was done 124 players would have been in 10 or more P.L. games: 81 came from the N.L., 28 came from the A.A., and the others came from minor leagues or elsewhere.

Fans who speculated for amusement, or for other reasons, chose the Chicago Pirates by consensus to win the first P.L. pennant; the Buffalo Bisons were picked to finish last.

An early 1890 media report included the statement that Frank Brunell had made a miscalculation by releasing the schedule of P.L. games before the N.L. men had made their schedule known. Another report opined that with both National League and American Association clubs already operating in Philadelphia, the creation of the P.L. Quakers was a strategic error; there just wasn't room for three teams in the city.

The men of the P.L. had done their research less than well with other choices for franchises; they were in place to go head to head in competition for dollars against N.L. clubs in seven cities, while the A.A. men had seven cities to themselves. The Players League of 1890 recorded at least a half dozen errors beyond reconciliation before any players took the field.

This was the major league baseball lineup for 1890, the numbers* in parentheses represent approximate population for each city in hundreds of thousands (561 = 561,000) as potential ballpark customers. These data highlight the most obvious and the least discussed Players League executive strategic error. The actual data were among the census counts for the year 1900.

Players League	National League	American Association
Boston (561)	Boston (561)	
Brooklyn (N/A)	Brooklyn (N/A)	Brooklyn (N/A)
Buffalo (352)		
Chicago (1,699)	Chicago (1,699)	
Cleveland (382)	Cleveland (382)	
New York (3,437)	New York (3,437)	
Philadelphia (1,294)	Philadelphia (1,294)	Philadelphia (1,294)
Pittsburgh (322)	Pittsburgh (322)	
	Cincinnati (326)	
		Baltimore (509)
		Columbus (126)
		Louisville (205)
		Rochester (163)
		St. Louis (575)
		Syracuse (N/A)
		Toledo (132)

Source: *U.S. Department of Commerce, Bureau of the Census for 1896.*

Thus by an approximation of the census count, the Players League had a population of 8,047,000 from which to draw fans to their ballparks. This does not include the city of Brooklyn which was not included in the 1900 census, perhaps due to the fact that the government was in chaos, not able to afford the garbage collection services, and on its way to assimilation by New York City. The potential for the National League was approximately 8,021,000 without Brooklyn, which in 1890 had major league clubs in three Leagues temporarily; their A.A. Gladiators would fail in August. For the American Association the fan potential was 3,004,000 not including Syracuse. The implications are obvious and became reality during the playing season as the A.A. was a distant third at the turnstile gate. To perhaps allow for some adjustment, the population of Syracuse in 1896 was less than 180,000, while the sum for Orange County was about 307,000 in 1990; for Brooklyn as a borough, the datum was about 2,300,000 in 1990.

The whole of which makes the implications more obvious in terms of the American Association. Given its fan base and potential dollar count, it was out of the contest before it began.

There were alternative possibilities for major league franchises in the Players League year, again using 1900 census data these major cities were missing from all the leagues in 1890.

Missing in 1890

Akron 275	Milwaukee (285)
Des Moines (178)	Minneapolis (203
Detroit (286)	Newark (246)
Indianapolis (169)	Richmond (230)
Jersey City (206)	St. Paul (163)
Kansas City (164)	Washington, D.C. (1,279)

There were easily enough major cities to make a league of their own, territorial difficulties notwithstanding, which by National Agreement of those men involved granted exclusivity within the range of 10 then more miles within which to play professional baseball.

Richmond might have presented other difficulties, the Civil War very withstanding. A league of any eight of these markets would have accounted for a potential of 2,500,000 potential customers, not including Washington, D.C., and of course there was always Philadelphia within which to implant another franchise.

Questions thus arise of paramount importance, involving the P.L.'s selection of cities for its franchises, foremost: Why confront the primary hostile force where they were well established? And, why was it necessary to put a franchise in Chicago? Given that a cluster of four league cities was in place between Boston and Philadelphia, and another cluster of three including Cleveland, Pittsburgh, and Buffalo, there were others viable and available.

Who made these all-important decisions? As with these questions and others, the answers can be reduced to business dollars and common sense. The further question is: Who could be expected to dominate and prevail in the Players League business office?

To continue this inquiry in modern terms: How practical were the decisions about "location, location, location" at which to do business, given that interest in baseball historically has spanned all socioeconomic, demographic, and geographic lines? There was neither practical need nor sound reason for the P.L. to challenge the N.L. on its home turf; to do so had nothing in common with the cause for which the P.L. was created. The P.L. could have attracted the players it did, and played an enjoyable and profitable season, for the public would come to see their favorites play, whether the town linked with the team was Philadelphia or Punxatawney, Pennsylvania.

Done sensibly, and not for the cause of self-destructive glory, the major league scenario now could be very different than it is. The point reverts back to the question, Who made the key decisions for the Players League of 1890?

2

Franchises and Clubs

Boston Reds

Owners: Charles A. Prince, Julian B. Hart
Ballpark: Congress Street Grounds
Home Attendance: About 200,000

When this P.L. club took the name "Reds" the N.L. counterpart began to use "Beaneaters" regularly. Presuming the N.L. owner Arthur Soden, to be an unmovable force, Prince went about his private goal of getting a franchise in one of the established leagues by courting the American Association.

To his surprise, Soden agreed to an intrusion into his inviolate territory as a tactic to expedite putting an end to the P.L., but only conditionally; Prince could house an A.A. club in Boston, but couldn't use Boston in its name.

The A.A. Boston club of 1891 would be the same as that of the P.L. of 1890, but only a handful of the P.L. champion players would go along with the move.

The Reds of 1890 had as their field manager and main attraction the star player Mike "King" Kelly, at the time the best-known and most popular player in America. Most every club in every league would have welcomed his presence. He chose for 1890 to play across town from Arthur Soden's N.L. South End Grounds.

His actions and loyalty to the Brotherhood were questioned many times. He was the subject of bribe offers to become a betrayer, but Kelly stayed the course he'd agreed through the P.L. season. What John Monte Ward was as founder and organizer, King Kelly in service to Prince and Hart was to the P.L. at play.

Prince was a lawyer, from a wealthy and prominent family, with firm political ties; he was elected P.L. president early in November 1890, and after the fact planned on a six-team league for the next season.

He was approached by P.L. owner Addison of Chicago, led to believe he'd be taken care of fairly by Spalding if he would surrender. As P.L. president he ordered the P.L. secretary-treasurer, Frank Brunell, to impede Addison from leaving the league, and to advise media that neither King Kelly nor any of his Reds players had abandoned the P.L.

Prince ordered a league conference in Philadelphia in mid-November, based on a report that the New York club leaders had made satisfactory arrangements with the N.L. to leave the P.L., which they denied. Goodwin of Brooklyn was not notified of the meeting, or he ignored the notice. The Buffalo contingent was omitted entirely.

BROOKLYN WONDERS

Owners: Wendell Goodwin, George W. Chauncey, John Wallace, E.F. Linton, John M. Ward
Ballpark: Eastern Park
Home Attendance: Less than 80,000

John Monte Ward was their field manager, a star player, and owned a small interest in the franchise. He was also founder of the players Brotherhood organization, and according to Spalding the prime cause of the existence of the Players League. He'd also authored the manifesto charter for the P.L., and he was an ally to the other Brooklyn Wonders owners. His name and his credentials attracted people to come to the ballpark.

Among the monied men backers of P.L. Brooklyn was E.F. Linton, a banker, and Wendell Goodwin, a streetcar line executive; Goodwin was the figurative leader among this owners cartel. When an urgent league meeting was called for in Philadelphia after the playing season had ended, he chose to not attend, or for reasons unknown he wasn't informed. The P.L. at the time was in a condition of fragmentation toward dissolution.

One of the Wonders backers owned a bread products company, from which came the name, a very useful and gainful public relations tactic.

The owners had to build a ballpark, by public record the cost was in the neighborhood of $100,000. When measured against the ledger of 80,000 at 50¢ per paying unit the basic math becomes indicative of their end result on paper.

Ward was a Wonders owner and he also owned a piece of the P.L. Giants. With his loyalties so split his P.L. mindset had to be constant dilemma. John Day, owner of the Giants, had become a friend to be trusted during his N.L. years.

As attorney for the Wonders club, Ward was challenged in court by John Day for the apparent duplicity in his conflicting roles. As often happens in venues of law, a little issue grew much bigger, leading to a court confrontation involving the cause which had led to the need and existence of the P.L.

In the realm of the New York State Supreme Court, Judge Morgan Joseph O'Brien denied Day's injunction on the grounds that the contract Ward signed in 1889 did not expressly provide the terms of a contract to be made in 1890 and because there was no mutuality in a contract that bound one party for 10 days and the other indefinitely. The ruling was, in effect, a body blow to the reserve clause. All John Day had asked the court was to prohibit Ward from playing in the Players League.

As for the rival Bridegrooms of the N.L., they provided a home attendance figure of 120,000, meaning Ward and the Wonders were beaten at the gate on the home grounds of the P.L. president.

As for their A.A. rival, the Gladiators failed on August 25th, thus becoming the first major league club since 1884 to not complete their season schedule.

On November 10, three of the Wonders owners, major backers, Goodwin, Chauncey, and Wallace reported that they had bought 16 percent of the deceased rival franchise, at a cost of $40,000.

BUFFALO BISONS

Owners: M. Shire, Frank T. Gilbert, Charles B. Fitzgerald, Jack Rowe, James L. White, Connie Mack, William Ellsworth Hoy
Ballpark: Olympic Park
Home Attendance: Approximately 61,000

If this were a situation of local proportions, it would involve the proverbial tangled web without deceit, but such is not the case. Rowe and White were used as pawns in a game of baseball chess circa 1887-1889 which involved a maze of buying and selling clubs and players as much for whimsy as for gains and profits.

The playing board of this chess business extended from Buffalo to Detroit, to Boston, to Pittsburgh, and back to Buffalo. One major league (N.L.) franchise with players was bought for $7,000. Two of the bought players were later transacted elsewhere but refused to go, because they'd bought a minor league franchise and the territory which came with it by National Agreement. It was all done legal and proper, and the men would continue in the game after long and superb careers as players. Nicholas E. Young as N.L. president, by that authority the situation adjudicator, negated their purchase of the minor league franchise, but only to the extent it obstructed the dealings of the maze of established owners who were involved.

Rowe and White were not characters of baseball fiction, though their rights were proven to be. Connie Mack was a virtual novice to ownership, but he would amass a fortune from a career in baseball for 66 years. William Ellsworth "Dummy" Hoy would live for 99 years, in a condition of unjust anonymity.

Not much is known about owner Shire. He was a lawyer and became involved in baseball litigation, which was his only link to the game before the Bisons of 1890 played; his was the only franchise to actually go out of business among the eight of the P.L. The owner-backers of all seven others were able to make deals to be bought out or consolidated with their in-city rivals, of which Buffalo had none at the major league level. There was a minor league club, which was forced by economic pressures to relocate to a neighboring Canadian city midway through the playing season.

Buffalo was unique among cities chosen to host a P.L. franchise. The plan was to challenge the N.L. in each of their eight cities, Buffalo became the only exception when the National League dropped D.C. and Indianapolis to make room for Brooklyn and Cincinnati, both which had quit the American Association to join the more prestigious league.

There is another interesting fact about Buffalo as a baseball town: The infamous reserve clause originated there as the 1879 playing season faded into September.

Having been represented in the N.L. as early as 1879, Buffalo continued as a viable club member into 1885, then relocated to the International (minor) league in 1888. Their ownership group included Charles W. Cushman and Cassius Candee, who sold their I.L. franchise and their stadium, Olympic Base Ball Park, to Jack Rowe and Deacon White.

The new owners—also at the time N.L. players under contract—bought a plot of land for a new ball park, then had the fences and grandstands dismantled and hauled to the new location by horse-drawn wagons.

In the interim the N.L. contracts of Rowe and White were sold to Al Nimick of Pittsburgh by Frederick Stearns of Detroit. Rowe and White, imagining themselves fellow franchise owners, initially refused to report to their new owner, though both recanted and submitted well into the playing season.

The *Cleveland Plain Dealer* observed, "This could mean a baseball war!" the Buffalo-ex-Detroit-Pittsburgh players-now-owners engaged Buffalo lawyer Moses Shire to represent their cause in the public legal courts—of which the *Boston Globe* commented, "It is generally accepted that baseball law is not legal law and could never be upheld in the courts."

The Buffalo P.L. franchise was capitalized at $20,000, most by Moses Shire, ex-sheriff Frank T. Gilbert, and Charles B. Fitzgerald. Rowe and White each put up $1,000. The venture attracted 60,138 to the Buffalo ball park, but in the end the Buffalo backers lost all after the N.L./A.A./P.L. mergers and consolidations were done.

CHICAGO PIRATES

Owner: John Addison
Ballpark: South Side Park
Home Attendance: Almost 149,000

When the Players League ship was declared to be sinking, the great majority of the captains of commerce rushed to be first to abandon it. Owner Addison could have had a significant head start on all of the others.

John Addison was a wealthy Chicago contractor and sole proprietor of the Chicago P.L. franchise. He built a new ballpark for the team, then had them play several games at Westside Park, home of the White Stockings, of which A.G. Spalding was president.

Addison's Pirates did well at the gate, out-drew most other P.L. clubs, and beat Spalding at the gate by almost 50 percent. Still he criticized his players as having lazy methods on the field, of just going through the forms rather than playing with intensity to win.

At an executive meeting of the three major leagues on October 9, Addison proposed that three players be allowed to participate in post-season business; the other owners of his league refused, insisting that negotiations for surrender be brought to an end without them.

Shrewd and cunning, a man of business not averse to employing disingenuous words as a tactic or stratagem, Addison then advised his colleagues that he would not continue his P.L. club in Chicago the next season. He said that his fan base had been lost by his players and could not be recovered. He then alleged inside knowledge that owner Prince of P.L. Boston would be bought out or given an A.A. franchise by Spalding of the N.L.

The name of the man who was in control of Chicago baseball is self-evident. Further along, Addison announced his intention to quit the Players League early in November, that he'd been almost guaranteed a place in the A.A., along with P.L. Boston and a syndicate representing Washington, D.C.

Soon after, Addison announced his intention to sell out to Spalding for $25,000, part cash, part Spalding's team stock. When this deal was done he did get $18,000 in cash, which he distributed among minority owners, player-owners, and his other players.

When his players learned of his pending deal with Spalding they threatened him with lawsuits. Two players, by contract owned by Spalding according to the National Agreement, wrote letters to Spalding pleading they be allowed to return to his fold for the next baseball season.

Threat of legal action became court action. It was not until the 29th of December that John Addison was free to conclude his transaction with Spalding, to be bought out of the P.L. On that date Chicago P.L. formally merged with N.L. Chicago, comparable to the modern business innovation called the hostile takeover.

Which club was phased out of existence is obvious; in the deal John Addison also gained $18,000 worth of N.L. New York Giants stock, and was given a free pass to all the White Stockings home games next season.

John Addison of the P.L. Chicago Pirates had run three ways and got entangled in litigation. Most of the other owner-backers made it to the lifeboats of business; dollar for dollar, the salvation of John Addison became a luxury cruise.

CLEVELAND INFANTS

Owner: Albert L. Johnson
Ballpark: Brotherhood Park

Infants attendance combined with the N.L. Spiders was about 106,000. Albert L. Johnson made the ludicrous declaration that he lost $340,000 in his Players League business adventure. His normal business was managing the affairs of the streetcar lines company he owned and his fortune was made as a coal magnate.

His brother was the mayor of Cleveland, Tom J. Johnson. His streetcar lines were in competition with those owned by the Robison family, one of which, Frank DeHaas, was the primary owner of the N.L. Cleveland Spiders.

Albert L. Johnson seemed genuinely loyal to the P.L. and its cause, but by mid-November of 1890 he was of a mixed mood, not certain whether he should stay with the P.L. through its obvious course, or to make a deal to switch loyalty and club to the A.A. as many of his fellow owner-backers appeared to be doing.

Johnson made a compromise like no other P.L. man, which became a financial disaster. He assembled a syndicate and led the purchase of a mixed Cincinnati franchise, possibly if written accounts are accurate to maintain it as a legacy to the P.L.

He would rebuild Cincinnati in the mold of the P.L., foremost in terms of players rights. By then the financial and emotional conditions of the P.L. backers had become known to Robison and Spalding, and other leading N.L. men. They were losing and they were anxious to change that.

Johnson made an offer to sell his P.L. interests and his new Cincinnati enterprise. The men of the N.L. rejected his offer; his asking price was $40,000 to make the deal done. He was left swinging in the wind, allegedly further from financial success in his P.L. adventure than all his P.L. peer owners combined. His team also had a rather bad season on the field.

When it became evident the end was coming, he released all his players to allow them to be absorbed by other clubs of both surviving leagues as best they could; he did so with little if any financial consideration coming his way.

Late in 1890, Albert L. Johnson was reported by the *Cleveland Leader* as "the man who, more than any other one individual, was responsible for the rise of the Players League." This was a quote from Frank DeHaas Robison.

Johnson was in New York City when the N.L. men met on November 14, 1890; he discussed business with arch-enemy Frank DeHaas Robison, from which came an ultimatum for the surrender of Albert Johnson.

Specifically, his P.L. franchise and his quest in Cincinnati were to be surrendered in return for N.L. men forgiving a $4,000 debt and payment of $25,000, some in fast cash and some by increments through August 1891.

Johnson refused the N.L. cash and consideration. Then with the best of intent John T. Brush, epic N.L. villain and manipulator of the New York Giants and Cincinnati chaos, and J. Palmer O'Neill, the ubiquitous right hand man of the Pennsylvania clubs, urged Johnson to agree, to accept the terms, then to persuade other P.L. owner brethren to do likewise and surrender.

Quoting Robison, this advice and counsel "was given honorably, and with the best of intent." Further, Johnson was to pacify the P.L. players. In the best dramatic fashion, a deadline for unconditional acceptance was set at midnight.

All involved were in attendance as the hands of the clock moved toward closing at the midnight hour, and together they saw the hour pass. After that a second meeting was set for Albert Spalding's office in the middle of next week.

F.B. Robinson of the P.L. New York Giants accompanied Albert Johnson. Upon learning of the prior offer, his comment to Johnson in the presence of Robison and other N.L. men was, "You were foolish that you did not accept. That is more than we will get." 1890 cutthroat baseball was a really tough game, not being able to guess who's on your side and who is against.

The New York Giants contingent of the Players League had done a deal with the men of the N.L. By the end of November the game had become every P.L. man for himself; the P.L. players and player-owners were nowhere in sight.

Albert Johnson then made his own proposal to the N.L., point for point and dollar for dollar exactly the same as the N.L. offer he'd refused. It may be that unconditional surrender somehow is more palatable economically and personally if the surrenderer states the terms and conditions.

A note within a sentence informs that Charlie Byrne of the N.L. Brooklyn Bridegrooms was a participant in the conference and a member of the committee which devised the surrender contract for Albert Johnson.

Recall that he was a first-year member of the N.L. fraternity of elite, as he and Aaron Stern of Cincinnati had quit the American Association in a huff whereupon Albert Johnson somehow took up the Cincinnati vacancy. It was a very tangled web indeed.

New York Giants

Owners: Edwin A. McAlpin, Edward Talcott, Cornelius Van Cott, F.B. Robinson, John M. Ward
Ballpark: Brotherhood Park
Home Attendance: More than 140,000

Excepting Ward from the above, and presuming William "Buck" Ewing as a player-owner, all these were real men of money. McAlpin was in the tobacco business and real estate, Talcott was a broker in stocks, and Van Cott was most notably a former state senator.

As well connected as the P.L. Giants were, they were able to score a preseason win in court over John B. Day, their neighbor N.L. Giants owner and the National League. By some coincidence Mr. Day was also in the tobacco business.

The object of the court case was William "Buck" Ewing, the former captain and catcher of the N.L. Giants, who chose the P.L. as the league to be in for 1890. Mr. Day sought a federal injunction to keep Ewing where he'd been at home since 1884. Day claimed his annual salary was $5,000 and said that was highest in the N.L.

The point at issue relevant to the cause may have been lost. It became the reserve clause of the N.L.-A.A. National Agreement, which of course the P.L. Giants club men were not party to. The presiding judge was William P. Wallace, and after due reading and pondering he articulated, to wit:

"The reserve clause is nothing more than 'a contract to make a contract' for the next season if the parties could reach an agreement." Further, that "The reserve clause only gave Day [by extension the N.L. and A.A. men] 'prior and exclusive' right to negotiate with Ewing [by extension other players]."

Further, ruled the judge, "As a binding agreement it [the reserve clause] was 'wholly nugatory' because no salary was specified and the terms were decidedly one sided." Nugatory normally is said or written within a range of meanings from insignificant to useless.

Buck Ewing proved to be something other than that for his P.L. club, as captain and field manager of the P.L. Giants. His team attracted more than double the numbers of fans to their gate than did their neighbor, the rival N.L. Giants.

The N.L. Giants number of paid at the gate in 1890 was 60,667, an average of less than 1,000 per game; they'd drawn around 200,000 the previous year to approximately half of 131 games. By an estimate in *Sporting Life* the average break-even point in all leagues for all clubs was 1,800 paid per game in 1890.

The P.L. Giants played in a new ballpark, were successful in the final league standings, and would appear to have done well in the business offices. But by the ledgers of their club accountants, when the season on the field was done the owners and backers had lost $8,000.

Owner McAlpin was chosen and served through the playing season as the Players League president. When the after-the-fact conferences were being held he withdrew. When the key conference in November was held, neither he nor his P.L. Giants associates were invited.

Owner Talcott made a deal for himself and McAlpin soon after the playing season was done, to be recipients of N.L. Giants stock in exchange for allowing their P.L. players to be involuntarily absorbed by their rivals.

The owners of other P.L. clubs howled in protest for naught, then they too scurried away to make the best deals they could, after the P.L. New York Giants' monied men had been the first to break ranks and run to surrender.

PHILADELPHIA QUAKERS

Owners: J.M. Vanderslice, George Wagner, J. Earle Wagner, H.M. Love
Ballpark: Forepaugh Park

In this city of three major league teams, J.M. Vanderslice was the chief investor in the Players League franchise, mainly in the company of the Wagner brothers. Their bigger business was wholesale meats. They had been and would continue to be linked to many major league franchises for speculation in Philadelphia and points then far beyond.

The P.L.'ers also called their home Brotherhood Park while the rival N.L. Phillies counted 186,000 cash customers; the Athletics of the A.A. somehow managed to manipulate $42,000 income and $24,000 in players' salaries into a loss of either $18,000 or $26,000.

The Philadelphia A.A. club disbanded on September 17. Owner H.C. Pennypacker said the club was $17,000 in debt and had gone broke on the last road trip. The root of the problem was in the salaries Pennypacker had paid to himself and William Whittaker, the club treasurer.

On November 18, the Philadelphia A.A. franchise was awarded to the Wagner brothers; technically then the A.A. expelled the prior owners as not viable and the P.L. club of the Wagners replaced them.

If the Philadelphia P.L. owners had no problems with their A.A. counterparts, they surely did with the N.L. Phillies executives. In March 1890 Phillies owner and president John Rogers sued to prevent utility man Bill Hallman from joining the P.L. team. He was rebuffed by Judge M. Russell Thayer. The issue became the reserve clause.

Judge Thayer said he took exception to the lack of mutuality in a contract that essentially tied a player to a club for as long as the club desired, but that once a player's services were no longer desired, his employer could dismiss him on 10 days' notice.

The Quakers shortstop during this singular season committed more fielding errors than any other player at any position in any major league on record. The further pursuits of Mr. Vanderslice are unknown.

As for the Wagners, when plans of the P.L.'s monied men were in the process of becoming unraveled, they were planning to jump ship to the American Association. In mid-November one of these brothers mediated a meeting of other P.L. hierarchy.

After which Albert Johnson of Cleveland, Wallace and Linton of Brooklyn, and Talcott and Robison of New York appeared convinced the Players League was sufficiently stable to continue into another season. At least the Wagners believed they were convinced.

Mr. H.M. Love was the titular president of the Philadelphia Quakers club. His regard for the players and player-owners in his charge was simple: he had no respect for the players, and his language toward them was enough to warrant a demand for a formal apology.

Pittsburgh Burghers

Owners: John M. Beemer, M.B. Lennon, C.F. Buiner
Ballpark: Exposition Park
Home Attendance: 117,000

They rebuilt a ballpark and called it home. They beat the local N.L. opposition in attendance by more than 100,000. The N.L. Alleghenys' record on the playing fields was horrendous. The P.L. Burghers were the winners in the contest for Pittsburgh; they were also the second Players League club to have their leadership structure collapse.

William A. Nimick was the National League in Pittsburgh in 1890; his right hand man was J. Palmer O'Neill. Their team set records as one of the worst ever on the playing field, and at one home game a total of 17 fans was counted inside the ballpark.

Nimick had come to the N.L. from the A.A. in 1887, with his club intact, and would leave the club in shambles, with the new earned nickname of "Pirates" after the 1891 season was played.

Meanwhile, Nimick induced the local P.L. men of money to create the Pittsburgh Athletic Company, which in turn at his behest assumed ownership of the N.L. Alleghenys on November 10, 1890, with Nimick as the company boss.

Not only were the Pittsburgh P.L. backers irrelevant, they and their Burghers were not even mentioned in the record of the key Philadelphia Conference of mid-November 1890.

John Monte Ward was present there, representing himself. Who was in control of the Players League then? For that question no viable answer is available to this day.

While the Brotherhood of Players were planning a revolution, the urban U.S.A. was in the midst of the Industrial Revolution. The American elite and leisure classes were buzzing with wonderment about happenings at home and in a variety of strange and distant lands.

A chosen group of major league baseball players was permitted the distinction of visiting some of these lands, allegedly for the cause of promoting the Great American Game. They visited New Zealand and Australia, Ceylon and Egypt, and various others, before reaching the relative security of Europe: Italy, France, and at last England.

Al Spalding planned this grand World Tour and declared what its purpose would be — among more subtle subordinate purposes, of course. A brief study of the names of players who joined the Players League revolution a year later reveals that being sequestered with Spalding for six months didn't result in many converts to the philosophy of the major league owners.

Among bits of baseball news at home after the calendar turned to 1890, on June 16 the Phillies/Quakers beat the Bisons of Buffalo by a record score of 30 to 12, with the victors scoring 14 runs in the sixth inning.

Philadelphia made 28 hits off Lady Baldwin, who pitched the whole scorefest for the Bisons that day, adding three walks and 10 Bisons errors served to increase the record numbers of tallies being posted on the score board.

Each Philadelphia player made at least one hit; Pickett and Milligan, as well as Griffin, each batted their way on base four times; Pickett and Shindle hit home runs; Pickett and Milligan each scored four runs.

Other news bits of the 1890 season: At the admission gate the National League attendance was announced as 813,678; the Players League payee count was about 165,000 more.

Owner Addison of the Chicago P.L. club made news, alleging his financial losses resulted in demoralized players, which in turn resulted in friction between his players and club ownership.

Addison was asked, "Will you pay the players what you owe them?" He replied, "I'll see them hanged first, they've got enough, I'm sick and tired of the whole business."

No doubt his attitude and disclosure were affected by being in direct competition with Al Spalding for the role of favorites of the Chicago baseball fan. Spalding by then was not only the baseball scion of Chicago, but also the recognized leader of the National League owners cartel.

3

Base Ball in the Days of the Players League

To understand and evaluate the statistics of Players League members, it is important to understand the style of the game in and about 1890. For the most part it was station-to-station baseball, playing to score one run. Scores as they were in the amateur club era, 38-25 or 60-12, were history.

One ball might be used throughout an entire game. The home run was a rare commodity. Strategies and tactics common now had not yet been devised. The few following examples are provided to depict what might be expected during a major league game.

First, the ultimate act of batting futility, the strikeout. In the Players League were recorded 2,986 K's, among a total of 38,425 at bats, or 7.77 percent, which indicates that one of every 12.9 (13) at bats would result in a strikeout.

By comparison, in both major leagues in 1988 there were 23,356 K's among 142,568 at bats, or 16.4 percent, meaning one of every 6.09 at bats would end with a K, which implies that many more 1890 P.L. batters became baserunners than 1988 N.L. or A.L. batters.

The pitching counterpart of the batting strikeout would be the walk, but the home runs given up better depicts total futility. Consider both: the entirety of plate appearance data are not available, but the sum of at bats and walks is equitable.

Thus with the sum of 38,425 and 4,182 being 42,607, divided into the 4,182 walks shows that P.L. batters who took their proper place in the batters box to confront the pitcher in his box (there was no mound till 1903) were walked at a 9.82 percent rate.

Meaning in turn that one of every 10.2 P.L. plate appearances resulted in a free pass to first base. In the major leagues of 1988, during which 12,984 walks were allowed, 8.35 percent of plate appearances were walks, evidence the P.L. had a bit more action.

But the spectacle of the home run indicates to the contrary. P.L. batters hit a total of 311 HRs among their 38,425 at bats, 0.81 percent, less than 1 percent, while the major league batters of 1988 produced 3,180 HRs, or 2.2 percent out-of-the park spectacles.

Quite likely, a few of the 1988 version were inside-the-park home runs, perhaps the ultimate in action, while in the P.L. of 1890 such feats were not unusual among the rare few HRs which were hit. In terms of action, the 1890 game appears to have had more, and futility for batters and pitchers was less.

One more factor will be given consideration here, efficiency in the field, transposed as the comparison of runs and r.b.i. By published counts, the P.L. players scored 7,278 runs, but only 5,764 r.b.i. were credited, or 79 percent of the runs scored.

This of course impinges on fielding efficiency, which was at least 10 percent below modern levels, which may also be assessed in an unorthodox manner by divided 7,278 runs scored by 529 games played giving a total of 13.76 runs scored per P.L. game.

It is also known that the composite P.L. earned runs were 4.23 and no matter by which method, doubling or dividing, allowing considerable leeway for exigencies, that 5.30 variation clearly shows that play in the field allowed a lot of runs to be scored.

With the quality of the P.L. game thus fundamentally established, it is possible by a SABR-stat to address park factor, calculated separately for batters and pitchers; above 100 signifies a park favorable to hitters, below 100 a park favorable to pitchers.

Keeping in mind that teams typically play half their games at the home park, the creator(s) of this datum park factor go further by admitting the computation is daunting. Which it no doubt certainly is, involving use of 17 formulas.

When the counting was done, these were the park factors derived for the Players League ballparks.

Players League Park Factors

Team Name: Ballpark	Batting Factor	Pitching Factor	Favorable To
Boston Reds: Congress Street Grounds	107	104	Batters
Brooklyn Wonders: Eastern Park	106	105	Batters
Buffalo Bisons: Olympic Park	92	97	Pitchers
Chicago Pirates: South Side Park	104	103	Batters
Cleveland Infants: Brotherhood Park	92	94	Pitchers
New York Giants: Brotherhood Park	109	107	Batters
Philadelphia Quakers: Forepaugh Park	102	101	Batters
Pittsburgh Burghers: Exposition Park	92	92	Pitchers

The New York (P.L.) park was also called Polo Grounds (IV). "Pittsburg" was the accepted spelling for Pittsburgh when the Players League played. None of these quaint names was a match for that of the Washington (N.L.) Senators 1886–1889 ballpark, Swampoodle Grounds, where the team were also the Statesmen.

All the ballparks of the late 1800s were somewhat different, which surely made a difference in the performances of batters and pitchers. This is a worthwhile factor to consider when assessing the teams and players of the Players League.

This phenomenon continued well into the next century, until the evolution of computer-designed standardized conformity. As for the P.L. players, the sum of park factors appears to favor the batters over pitchers, with three significant exceptions.

To amplify briefly on park factor for purposes of clarification, there is the example of the Phillies home park, Baker Bowl, 1895 through 1938. It was often called a bandbox because the whole of the playing field was inordinately small.

The park factor for their best batter, Chuck Klein, 1928 through 1938, was between 98 and 118 in various years; it was the same for all Phillies batters in a given year. Phil Collins, arguably their best pitcher then, was assigned between 109 and 117.

Baker Bowl was definitely a batter's ballpark. An example of the opposite extreme was Griffith Stadium, home park of the Washington Senators 1911 through 1960, which was often described as cavernous, meaning the playing field was relatively huge.

Joe Kuhel hit the only home park home run for the Senators in 1945, and that was an inside-the-park home run; for him and the other Senators batters in 1945, the park factor was 93. The park factor for their pitchers was 92, a pitcher's park.

The League and Team Stats

Final Standings

Team	Won	Lost	Win%	Games Behind
Boston	81	48	.628	— —
Brooklyn	76	56	.576	6.5
New York	74	57	.565	8.0
Chicago	75	62	.547	10.0
Philadelphia	68	63	.519	14.0
Pittsburgh	60	68	.469	20.5
Cleveland	55	75	.423	26.5
Buffalo	36	96	.273	46.5

The most important fact about the final standings was that the Boston Reds won the right to fly the league pennant. The greater competition was for second place, which never in the history of the game was a great stimulus for attendance.

It's important to note that every team franchise which began the playing season was there at the end. To be said of Buffalo, their record was so bad it shifted the games behind median one place, and the runs per game mean count to lower than seventh.

Average Runs Per Game

Team	Scored	Opponents	+/-
Boston	7.63	5.90	+0.92
Brooklyn	7.25	6.71	+0.54
New York	7.71	6.63	+1.08
Chicago	6.42	5.58	+0.84
Philadelphia	7.13	6.48	+0.65
Pittsburgh	6.52	6.97	-0.45
Cleveland	6.48	7.84	-1.36
Buffalo	5.92	8.95	-3.03

A quick scan of these mean averages and park factors make it abundantly clear there's much more involved in winning than the playing field. Scoring runs wins games and preventing opponents from scoring runs wins games, which are proven statistical facts.

Most historians and informed fans already suspected that, but the premise does not produce a perfect correlation, as shown above; and again but, an unpublished study of these two and 36 other factors prove these are the most reliable predictors.

As all fans know, and historically so, baseball has since its inception been a team game. Valid theories of probability say that the team which leads its league in the most stats, which ideally should be weighted, will win more and the most games.

First glance at the P.L. leading teams may suggest that New York almost owned the batting column, but closer scrutiny will reveal that Boston led in a fair share of these stats, and in stolen bases (station-to-station) and batting runs by vast margins.

The P.L. Team Leaders

Batting:	Pitching:
Games: Chicago 138	Won: Boston 81
At Bats: Chicago 4,968	Lost: Buffalo 96
Hits: New York 1.393	Win %: Boston .628
2B: Boston 223	Games: Pittsburgh 128
3B: Philadelphia 113 / Pittsburgh 113	Starts: Chicago N/A
HRs: New York 64	C.G: Buffalo 125
Runs: New York 1,018	I.P: Pittsburgh 1,117
R.B.I: New York 793	Sh.O: Pittsburgh 7
Walks: Boston 652	K's: Chicago 460
K's: Philadelphia 321	Walks: Pittsburgh 334
B.Avg: Cleveland .286	Hits: New York 1,219
O.B.A: Boston .376	O.B.%: Chicago .321
SL.%: New York .404	E.R.A: Chicago 3.39 (Next 3.80)
S.B: Boston 412 (Next 276)	Saves: Brooklyn 7
B.R: Boston 103 (Next 54)	P.R: Chicago 114 (Next 54)
F.R: N/A	W.A.T: N/A

N/A is intended to indicate not available or not applicable. Add to the above, New York led in fielding percent with .921; made the fewest errors, 450 (in 132 games = 3.41 per game); and Philadelphia, with 118, made the most double plays.

In addition to leading in key batting statistics, New York also led in defense. In pitching Boston has the obvious advantage, otherwise Chicago led in the critical stats. This may prompt the question, "Why did these teams finish in the P.L. standings as they did?"

Individual Stats Leaders

Batting Leaders

Stats	Name (Position)	###	Team
Games:	Hugh Duffy (OF)	138	Chicago Pirates
At Bats:	Hugh Duffy (OF)	596	Chicago Pirates
Hits:	Hugh Duffy (OF)	191	Chicago Pirates
2B:	Pete Browning (OF)	40	Cleveland Infants
3B:	Jake Beckley (1B)	22	Pittsburgh Burghers
	Joe Visner (OF)	22	Pittsburgh Burghers
HRs:	Roger Connor (1B)	13	New York Giants
Runs:	Hugh Duffy (OF)	161	Chicago Pirates
R.B.I:	Hardy Richardson (OF)	143	Boston Reds
Walks:	Bill Joyce (3B)	123	Brooklyn Wonders
K's:	N/A	N/A	
B.Avg:	Pete Browning (OF)	.373	Cleveland Infants
	Dave Orr (1B)	.373	Brooklyn Wonders
O.B.A:	Dan Brouthers (1B)	.466	Boston Reds
SL.%:	Jake Beckley (1B)	.541	Pittsburgh Burghers
	Roger Connor (1B)	.541	New York Giants
S.B:	Harry Stovey (OF)	97	Boston Reds
B.R:	Roger Connor (1B)	+48	New York Giants
F.R:	Fred Pfeffer (2B)	+22	Chicago Pirates

Pitching Leaders

Stats	Name	###	Team
Won:	Mark Baldwin	34	Chicago Pirates
Lost:	N/A	N/A	
Win %:	Bill Daley	.720	Boston Reds
Games:	Mark Baldwin	59	Chicago Pirates
Starts:	Mark Baldwin	57	Chicago Pirates
C.G:	Mark Baldwin	54	Chicago Pirates
I.P:	Mark Baldwin	501	Chicago Pirates
Sh.O:	Silver King	4	Chicago Pirates

Stats	Name	###	Team
K's:	Mark Baldwin	211	Chicago Pirates
Walks:	N/A	N/A	
Hits:	N/A	N/A	
O.B.%:	Harry Staley	.285	Pittsburgh Burghers
E.R.A:	Silver King	2.69	Chicago Pirates
Saves:	George Hemming	3	Cleveland & Brooklyn
	Hank O'Day	3	New York Giants
P.R:	Silver King	+79	Chicago Pirates
W.A.T:	Phil Knell	+6.1	Philadelphia Quakers

Via their formidable tandem of two pitching leaders, the Chicago Pirates had a veritable lock on leadership in their stats. The individual competition in virtually all was intense. They had only one among the batting leaders.

The same holds true for batting, intense individual competition with not really even a hint of dominance by a team among them. If the various batting averages are considered foremost, then the advantage goes to the Boston Reds.

If the raw batting stats, the basic data, are considered alone, in isolation so to say, then the Pittsburgh Burghers would be the choice to lead the league, but both the Pirates and Reds lacked a second among the leaders of these classes.

If only runs stats were to be taken into account — runs scored, runs batted in, and earned run average — Chicago again would have to be considered the prohibitive favorite to take home the P.L. gonfalon. In fact, the media of the year chose the Pirates to win.

But the baseball literature is replete with cases in which the favorites failed, often due to an injury or failure of a star player to perform up to expectations, while a team with two or three whose production was superior finished as the winners.

When all the factors were considered, and after all the games were played, the greater team(s) and the greatest player(s) held ranks at or near the top. Every team had a share of stars, and a considerable number of players had their finest seasons.

It's been written that the Players League had amongst their teams most of the best of that era; the individual biographies firmly support this contention, which is reinforced by another form of assessment: membership in the Baseball Hall of Fame.

The fates and various selection committees representing the baseball valhalla at Cooperstown have not been kind to the P.L. or its players over the years. Nonetheless, by this measure the P.L. prevails over the N.L. and overwhelms the A.A.

Player Notes

These seven players were born in foreign countries:

Tom Brown (England), Jocko Fields (Ireland), Art Irwin (Canada), John Irwin (Canada), Tip O'Neill (Canada), Joe Quinn (Australia), John Tener (Ireland), and Bill Kuehne (possibly Germany).

These seven players lived to age 90+:

Tommy Corcoran (91), Alex Ferson (91), Dummy Hoy (99), Arlie Latham (92), Connie Mack (93), Al Maul (92), Deacon White (91). The seven P.L. players who lived beyond 90 years in relation to the number of 140 who played represents an inordinately high proportion for that era.

These 13 players died before 1900:

Willard Brown (1897), Spider Clark (1892), Ed Crane (1896), John Ewing (1895), Jim Fogarty (1891), Bill Gleason (1893), King Kelly (1894), Kid Madden (1896), Darby O'Brien (1892), Hoss Radbourn (1897), Yank Robinson (1894), Sy Sutcliffe (1893), Ned Williamson (1894). The 13 players who died before a decade passed represent an extremely unusual proportion.

These 19 player careers (more than one year duration) ended in 1890 (number of years in parentheses):

Jack Brennan (five), Spider Clark (two), Jay Faatz (four), Sid Farrar (eight), Tim Fogarty (seven), Jackie Hayes (seven), Gus Krock (three), John Morrill (15), Ed Morris (seven), Con Murphy (two), Hank O'Day (seven), Dave Orr (eight), Tom Quinn (three), John Rainey (two), Jack Rowe (12), John Sowders (three), John Tener (three), Deacon White (20), Ned Williamson (13).

These six players were rookies in 1890 (who played after 1890):

Jocko Halligan, George Hemming, Bill Joyce, Willie McGill, Morg Murphy, Frank Shugart.

These six were not yet states when the P.L. played:

Alaska (1958), Arizona (1912), Hawaii (1959), New Mexico (1912), Oklahoma (1907), Utah (1896).

These two became states while the P.L. played:

Idaho (July 3, 1890), Wyoming (July 10, 1890).

These four were almost too close to call:

Montana (1889), North Dakota (1889), South Dakota (1889), and Washington (1889).

4

Player Biographies

Below is a sample model of the information included for each P.L. player of 1890. In actuality a small number of facts are not to be found, evidently do not exist, and therefore obviously cannot be included, in which cases the space is left blank.

COMMON SURNAME (OTHER), FIRST NAME (AND OTHER)   Baseball Name
Born: Month Day, Year, City, State (or Other)
Died: Month Day, Year, City, State (or Other)
Height: Weight: Batted: Threw:
Major League Career: Number of Years, Number of Games
1889: League(s) and Team(s) Played For
1891: League(s) and Team(s) Played For
1890: P.L.:   1st Team; Games at Each Position
              2nd Team; Games at Each Position
              Other League(s) and Team(s) If Any

These are all listed in chronological sequence.

Statistics

The columns below list the statistics (data) which are included in the players' biographies; then are given a basic definition or explanation for each, and further then some examples. Keep in mind that each pitcher was also a batter, but many batters who were position players did not pitch.

Batting Record

Games:	3B:	Walks:	S.B.:
At Bats:	HRs:	B.Avg.:	B.R.:
Hits:	Runs:	O.B.A.:	F.R.:
2B:	R.B.I.:	S.L.%:	

Pitching Record

Won:	Starts:	K's:	Saves:
Lost:	C.G.:	Hits:	P.R.:
Win %:	I.P.:	O.B.%:	W.A.T.:
Games:	Sh.O.:	E.R.A.:	

It's worth noting that there have been changes in the rules over the years affecting nearly all these statistics, foremost during the 1800s when the game was in its formative and developmental stages. Records of a few were not maintained as parts of the official records until well into the next century. Four which are included here were not created till recently, by members of and generally promulgated by the Society for American Baseball Research; these are often referred to herein as "SABR-stats."

Game(s): A competitive contest between two teams which is played to its conclusion in accord with prevailing rules, which may result in a tie or a forfeit.

At Bat(s): An event in which a player takes the proper place to confront the opposing pitcher with intent to reach base safely by means of a pitch hit in fair territory; will not include any walks or hit by pitch.

Hit(s): A batter hits a pitch in fair territory and reaches base safely before being put out by the opponents. This cannot in any way involve an opponents error. All relevant rules must be fully complied with by the batter and his team.

2B: A hit which achieves one base for the batter is a single; a hit which achieves two bases for the batter is a double.

3B: A hit which achieves three bases for the batter is a triple; in each of these cases the batter can be given credit only if no teammate is put out as a result of the at bat.

HR(s): A hit which achieves four bases for the batter, which is the maximum possible in one time at bat; a home run.

Run(s): A batter or runner on base crosses home plate without first being put out by the opponents while the ball is in play.

R.B.I.: A run (or runs) batted in; by the act of a batter one or more runs score which do not involve any errors by the opponents; the batter may be put out and still be given credit, but not if a double play, two outs, results from the time at bat.

Walk(s): A batter is awarded first base at no risk after, by the judgment of the appropriate umpire, four pitches have been made while an at bat was in progress which were not in the strike zone.

K('s): A strikeout; batter is called out after, by judgment of the appropriate umpire, three pitches have passed which were in the strike zone or which the batter swung at and missed regardless of pitch location or which the batter hit foul but was not caught on the fly excepting the third strike cannot be a foul ball, unless a bunt attempt, or foul tip held by the catcher.

B.Avg.: Batting average; a calculation performed by dividing the number of hits by the number of at bats; no other factors are considered.

O.B.A.: On base average, also referred to as on base percent(age); a calculation performed by dividing the sum of hits and walks by the sum of at bats and walks; each hit has a value of one regardless the number of bases which were achieved.

S.L.%: Slugging percentage, could also be referred to as slugging average; a calculation performed by dividing the total number of bases achieved only by hits, by only the number of at bats; the assigned values for hits are a single = 1, a double = 2, triple = 3, and home run = 4; each at bat has a value of one.

In understanding the difference between batting average and on base average, the math for B.Avg. involves only the number of hits and at bats; each hit and each at bat have a value of one. Neither factor includes walks or hit by pitches. Reaching base on a dropped third strike is an at bat, but if an error is involved, reaching base does not count as a hit, but does count as an at bat.

By O.B.A. is meant reaching base by all the above means except by an error, while the at bats factor is supplemented by walks. There is no case in which a batter is given credit for reaching base by means of an error. Other factors such as hit by pitches and etc. have been, and have not been added to at bats as rules have varied and been revised.

The S.L.% stat involves dividing the total number of bases by the number of at bats only. Consider a scenario of a player going to bat (a plate appearance) 25 times, with no errors involved, with five walks among the plate appearances results in 20 at bats.

If the player gets a total of five hits, dividing 5 by 20 gives a .250 batting average. Dividing the total of 10 times the player reached base, via hits and walks, by the 25 plate appearances, results in a .400 on base average. Note that in baseball math most stats are calculated to three decimal places.

Assume the five hits were a home run (value of 4), two doubles (2 x 2), and two singles (2 x 1) which equal 10 total bases via hits. Divide the 10 total bases by the 20 at bats, the result is a .500 slugging percentage.

S.B.: A stolen base; is credited to a base runner when an advance of one base is made, but may be more, which is achieved solely by the efforts of the base runner, involving no other act by a teammate.

B.R.: Batter Run is the original textbook term, herein revised to Batting Run(s). The definition is linear weights measure of runs contributed beyond what a league-average batter might have contributed, defined as zero. Further, an average player will have a zero rating. For every 10 runs above average the team will win about one more game. The underlining has been added to the original definition, and a synthesized definition of the "B.R." stat follows.

B.R.: Batting Runs: The linear weights measure of runs contributed beyond those of a league-average batter or team, such league average defined as zero. An average player will have a rating of zero. For every 10 runs above average the team will win about one more game. Thus a B.R. of zero is neutral, a B.R. of +10 indicates the team will win about one more game than otherwise, while a B.R. of -10 indicates the team will win about one game less than if the B.R. were 0.

F.R.: Fielding Runs: The linear weights measure of runs saved beyond what an average player at that position might have saved, defined as zero. Thus F.R. are specific to positions, with an average (league average) player at each position given a rating of zero. It is presumed that the +/- 10 variations apply to the numbers of games won, more and less.

Won: A pitcher is credited with a game won who was pitching at the point in a game when the team gained the lead in scoring, which was not relinquished, or if so was pitching when the team regained the lead and maintained until the game was completed. This does not necessarily have to be in fact, but in accordance with the official lineup card at this or these points.

Lost: A pitcher is charged with a game lost who was pitching at the point(s) above; or who was responsible for the base runner(s) who scored to put the team at a deficit.

Win %: A calculation performed by dividing the number of games won by the total number of decisions, won and lost; for example, a pitcher won 10 games and lost 10, the number won (10) divided by the number of decisions gives a result of a .500 Win %; if wins were 20 and losses 10, then 20 divided by 30 equals .667.

Game(s): A competitive contest; the identical definition as is included in the batting record.

Start(s): A pitcher who is the first in a game for the team is credited with a start.

C.G.: Complete Game(s); A pitcher to obtain credit must start and continue as the pitcher of record until the game is concluded.

I.P.: Inning(s) Pitched; A pitcher receives credit for one-third of an inning pitched for each opposing batter put out while the pitcher of record; obviously three opponents put out equal one inning pitched.

Sh.O.: Shutout; A game played to completion in which the opponents score no runs; typically is achieved by one pitcher, but there may be more than one involved. The number of opponents who reach base, by whatever means, is irrelevant.

K'(s): A strikeout achieved by the pitcher, the same definition as in the batting record.

Walk(s): A batter is awarded first base via four pitches called balls, the same definition as in the batting record.

Hit(s): A batter reaches base by a pitch hit in fair territory, the same definition as in the batting record. As in an account ledger, hits, walks, and strikeouts are a credit to one side and conversely are debits to the opposing side.

O.B.%: On Base Percent: A calculation performed identically to that of O.B.A. in the batting record.

E.R.A.: Earned Run Average: A calculation for pitchers: Earned runs times nine, divided by the number of innings pitched. It is essential to know that any run scored which in any way involved an opponent's error cannot be an earned run.

As an example, a pitcher over the course of a season allowed 100 earned runs in 200 innings pitched; the 100 earned runs time 9 is 900, divided by the 200 innings pitched equals an E.R.A. of 4.50; this is an exception to the baseball math rule of three decimal places.

An alternative calculation method which might be preferred is to divide earned runs by innings pitched, then multiply by nine; that is, 100 divided by 200 = 0.50 x 9 = 4.50 E.R.A.

It may be useful to note that although a run may be scored when an error is involved, a run batted in may not be awarded; this might benefit the reader who looks for statistical equity in runs scored and R.B.I.'s. In baseball of the 1800s it was not to be found.

As late in the century as 1890, the year of the Players League, the conditions of the playing fields and the quality of equipment were not nearly at modern levels. Errors were much more common, thus many more runs were scored than there were runs batted in.

As evidence, the composite P.L. fielding average was .913, to be compared with the 1983 A.L. and N.L. numbers of .979 and .978. To elaborate, these data transposed tell that in the P.L. there were 91.3 percent of fielding plays made without an error, while 1983 percentages of plays made without an error were 97.9 percent and 97.8 percent.

P.R.: Pitching Runs: Originally Pitcher Runs, this is the other side of batting runs. This is linear weights measure of runs saved beyond what an average pitcher might have saved, defined as zero. As with the B.R. and F.R. stats, the +/- 10 rule as it affects games won should apply.

W.A.T.: Wins Above Team by text definition, as this also may result in a negative stat herein the acronym is explained as Wins Against Team as it is a measure of a pitcher's success compared to the whole team pitching staff. The definition is how many wins a pitcher had beyond expected for an average pitcher on that team, and the formula is weighted.

ANDREWS, GEORGE EDWARD Ed Andrews
Born: April 5, 1859, Painesville, Ohio
Died: August 12, 1934, West Palm Beach, Florida
Height: 5'8". Weight: 160 Lbs. Batted: Right. Threw: Right.
Major League Career: 8 Years, 774 Games
1889: N.L.: Philadelphia and Indianapolis
1891: A.A.: Cincinnati
1890: P.L.: Brooklyn Wonders; OF 94

Batting Record:

Games: 94	3B: 2	Walks: 40	SL.%: 322
At Bats: 395	HRs: 3	K's: 32	S.B: 21
Hits: 100	Runs: 84	B.Avg: .253	B.R: -14
2B: 14	R.B.I: 38	O.B.A: .323	F.R: -2

Beyond age 30 in the P.L. year, the next would be his last. He'd last played 100+ games in 1888. As a P.L. batter his raw numbers suggest that when he got on base a run was almost sure to score. He didn't show much power at home plate; his production numbers are those of a leadoff batter.

Forty in 1890 was his career high in walks. The B.R. stat reveals deficiencies. He could take a base when the pitching battery was lax. His F.R. stat tells his play in the field was well below average this year.

His best year had been 1887, with Philadelphia (N.L.), batting .325 and scoring 110 runs, with 57 stolen bases. It was one of two years he exceeded the .300+ B.Avg. benchmark level, and one of two years with 50+ stolen bases. He led the N.L. in 1886 with 56 S.B., also for the Phillies. Only once was his defense up to par, with a +15 F.R. in his final season.

He'd been a National League umpire in 1889, a position he resumed after his career as a player, in 1893, 1895, and 1898-1899.

Andrews did well enough to make it to Palm Beach at just about the time that John D. Rockefeller's early business partner, Henry Flagler, made the sunny coast of Florida the place to get away to for residents of the northern climes during the wintry months.

Andrews developed real estate in Palm Beach, and owned a water company. He died of a heart attack.

BAKELEY (BAKLEY), EDWARD ENOCH   Jersey Bakeley
Born: April 17, 1864, Blackwood, New Jersey
Died: February 17, 1915, Philadelphia, Pennsylvania
Height: Weight: Batted: Right.   Threw: Right.
Major League Career: 6 Years, 215 Games
1889: N.L.: Cleveland
1891: A.A.: Washington and Baltimore
1890: P.L.: Cleveland Infants; P 43, OF 1

Batting Record:

Games: 43	3B: 0	Walks: 11	S.L.%: .225
At Bats: 138	HRs: 0	K's: 28	S.B.: 0
Hits: 28	Runs: 10	B.Avg.: .203	B.R.:
2B: 3	R.B.I.: 9	O.B.A.:	F.R.:

Pitching Record:

Won: 12	Starts: 38	K's: 67	E.R.A.: 4.47
Lost: 25	C.G.: 32	Walks: 147	Saves: 0
Win %: .324	I.P.: 326	Hits: 412	P.R.: -9
Games: 43	Sh.O.: 0	O.B.%: .391	W.A.T.: -4.7

As a batter he was less than intimidating, no power, otherwise to be expected of a pitcher. As a pitcher he had one winning season, but 1890 wasn't it. If an objective analysis were to be done to learn whether awful pitchers make an awful team, or the other way round, given that the Infants led their league in batting, the P.L. record of this workhorse pitcher would be a point in favor of the adage that pitching is 80 percent of the game.

His W.A.T. is an obvious result. His P.O. makes it clear that he wasn't effective in crucial situations, nor most any other time either. And how could this not be, allowing an average of more than 15 opponents to earn their way on base per game, with gifts by errors not considered.

Somewhat contrary, his E.R.A. was near enough to the P.L. average of 4.47 to offer some cause for salvation. Perhaps more to the contrary, his 25 losses don't even rank among the top 100 records for a season, all time.

Compared to the whole of his record, 77-125, .381 win %, 1890 was not an unusual year for Jersey Bakely. His best included 25 wins but 33 losses, both beyond the pitching benchmarks. This was for Cleveland (A.A.) in 1888, his only 20+ win season. His first had been his only winning year, 1883, at 5 and 3 for Philadelphia (A.A.).

Each of five years Jersey Bakely exceeded 300+ innings pitched, 533 in 1888, when he started and pitched in 61 games, with 60 complete to his credit.

Edward "Jersey" Bakely died suddenly.

BALDWIN, CHARLES BUSTED Lady Baldwin
Born: April 10, 1859, Ormel, New York
Died: March 7, 1937, Hastings, Michigan
Height: 5'11".   Weight: 160 Lbs.   Batted: Left.   Threw: Left.
Major League Career: 6 Years, 118 Games
1889: Did Not Play
1891: Did Not Play
1890: N.L.: Brooklyn Bridegrooms; P.L.: Buffalo Bisons; P 7

Batting Record:

Games: 7	3B: 0	Walks: 2	S.L.%: .321
At Bats: 28	HRs: 0	K's: 1	S.B.: 1
Hits: 8	Runs: 4	B.Avg.: .286	B.R.:
2B: 1	R.B.I.: 2	O.B.A.:	F.R.:

Pitching Record:

Won: 2	Starts: 7	K's: 13	E.R.A.: 4.50
Lost: 5	C.G.: 7	Walks: 24	Saves: 0
Win %: .286	I.P.: 62	Hits: 90	P.R.: -2
Games: 7	Sh.O.: 0	O.B.%: .407	W.A.T.: +0.1

Lady was a gentleman, which gave cause for the quaint nickname, a demeanor purely proper. 1890 was his last year as a pitcher, among six, one of which was genuinely spectacular. He began the P.L. season with the Brooklyn club of the N.L., worked a total of eight innings in two games, with a 7.88 E.R.A., then escaped to the P.L. and Buffalo.

With the Bisons he didn't get much work, and given the condition of that team, it's to wonder why. He wasn't played in the outfield or at first base, as might seem appropriate occasionally, given his batting stats.

Of his pitching record, very typical of his 1890 P.L. club, it would seem not much was expected of him. Otherwise, or more accurately before, his 1886 record must be discussed. It's one of the best ever compiled by any pitcher.

Detroit Wolverines, National League, let a (*) indicate league-leading stats. He won 42 (*), lost 13, .764 win %; 56 games and 56 starts, 55 complete, 487 innings pitched; seven shutouts (*), 371 hits allowed, 323 batters K'd (*), 100 walks; 2.24 E.R.A.; opponents reached base at a .267 O.B.% rate; his P.R. calculates to an awesome +58.

1886 was the only year Lady Baldwin exceeded 211 I.P., and the only year he won more than 13 games among a career total of 73 with 41 losses (.640 win %), but this one year sure was a dandy.

He was age 26 when a rookie in 1885. His family had moved from New York to Michigan when he was 18. After his brief baseball career he ran a farm, then later achieved great success in the real estate enterprise.

Charles "Lady" Baldwin died of a heart attack. His .660 win % ranks sixth during the period 1876-1889.

He had had to give up work on the diamond because his arm was strained.

BALDWIN, MARCUS ELMORE Mark Baldwin (Fido)
Born: October 29, 1865, Pittsburgh, Pennsylvania
Died: November 10, 1929, Pittsburgh, Pennsylvania
Height: 6'0". Weight: 190 Lbs. Batted: Right. Threw: Right.
Major League Career: 7 Years, 347 Games
1889: A.A.: Columbus
1891: N.L.: Pittsburgh
1890: P.L.: Chicago Pirates; P 59

Batting Record:

Games: 59	3B: 6	Walks: 15	S.L.%: .298
At Bats: 215	HRs: 1	K's: 51	S.B.: 4
Hits: 45	Runs: 27	B.Avg.: .209	B.R.:
2B: 4	R.B.I.: 25	O.B.A.:	F.R.:

Pitching Record:

Won: 34	Starts: 57	K's: 211	E.R.A.: 3.31
Lost: 24	C.G.: 54	Walks: 249	Saves: 0
Win %: .586	I.P.: 501	Hits: 498	P.R.: +52
Games: 59	Sh.O.: 1	O.B.%: .358	W.A.T.: +4.1

Intelligent and outspoken, he ideally fit the Players League. He'd been a member of the Chicago side during Al Spalding's world tour. In 1890, he was the leading pitcher on the best staff in the league.

In fact, he was the league leader in many pitching stats, among which were 34 wins, 59 games, 57 starts, 54 C.B., and with 501 was the only "P" to surpass the mark of 500+ I.P. His fielding was an asset to his record and the team; 146 assists ranks 16th all time among single-season records for a pitcher. In the box his fastball was his forte, but his 183 career wild pitches ranks 10th all time among major league records.

The commentary is mixed about his ability as a batter; 51 K's in 215 at bats is most informative. A .209 B.Avg. ranks as normal for a pitcher, but a slugging percentage 50 percent higher would be a credit to any player. With 11 extra base hits among 45, his slot in the batting order couldn't be overlooked by the opposition.

1890 in many ways was the best of his seven seasons, although he once hit for 10 total bases in a game, including a home run and two triples. Twice he pitched and won two complete games in one day's work, but his reputation included a tendency to let down when his team got behind in the score.

His 1890 E.R.A. of 3.31 was third best in the P.L., consistent with a 3.37 career average. Unusually low for a league best, his 211 K's also led the P.L. The year before he'd also led in K's, with 368 for Columbus (A.A.). Among other career marks he twice led his league in games, passing the 50+ level three years other than 1890.

Baldwin had two seasons of 500+ I.P., including in the P.L., and reached 300+ I.P. a total of seven years. His 54 C.G. was not the league high in 1889, but his 501 I.P. were. His two calculated saves would have been a league best in 1893; his yearly total of wins was about 20, with a career total of 156 wins and 165 losses (.486 win %).

His 1890 P.R. mark of +52 was second in the P.L., he's also ranked second in the uncommon total pitcher's index and total baseball ranking stats.

His signing with Pittsburgh (N.L.) for the 1891 season instead of returning to the Columbus (AA.) Club was a prime reason that Pirates has been the label worn by the Pittsburgh team since. His efforts to persuade others to violate the P.L. surrender agreement landed him in jail for a night.

Eccentric Chris Von der Ahe of A.A. St. Louis, among others, filed a legal complaint against Baldwin; he was arrested but the case was never brought to trial. He subsequently sued Von der Ahe and, after a long and lingering court action was awarded the sum of $2,500 in damages, no small sum at the time. Von der Ahe then refused to pay. Legend tells that he was kidnapped in 1898, and was held until he did pay.

As for Baldwin, he had a knack for being involved in unusual situations. He was a National League umpire in 1892, residing in the Pennsylvania town where Andrew Carnegie used the state police to attack malcontent workers and terrorize their families in his quest to destroy efforts to organize workers unions.

The better side of Mark Baldwin appeared after baseball. Years of rigorous studies earned him the title and license of doctor. He did service in New York City and Pittsburgh, and the famous Mayo Research Clinic. With a certain irony, his death came after suffering a long and lingering illness.

Marcus Elmore Baldwin surely earned the status of Players League star player. Among his further achievements as shown in period stats: His 347 games would rank eighth 1876-1889 and seventh 1890-1899; 328 starts would rank ninth 1876-1889 and fifth 1890-1899; 296 C.G. would rank fourth 1890-1899; 2,811 I.P. would rank 10th 1876-1889 and fifth 1890-1899; 1.307 walks would rank first 1876-1889 and second 1890-1899; 1.354 K's would rank ninth 1876-1889 and third 1890-1899; 165 losses would rank eighth 1876-1889 and first 1890-1899.

Despite the coincidence of his 1887-1893 career overlapping the bounds of these periods, Mark Baldwin does rank sixth from 1890-1899 with his 3.37 career E.R.A.

BARTSON, CHARLES FRANKLIN   Charlie Bartson
Born: March 13, 1865, Peoria, Illinois
Died: June 9, 1936, Peoria, Illinois
Height: 6'0".   Weight: 170 Lbs.   Batted: Threw:
Major League Career: 1 Year, 25 Games
1890: Did Not Play
1891: Did Not Play
1890: P.L.: Chicago Pirates; P 25

Batting Record:

Games: 25	3B: 0	Walks: 11	SL.%: .187
At Bats: 75	HRs: 0	K's: 11	S.B: 2
Hits: 13	Runs: 7	B.Avg: .173	B.R:
2B: 1	R.B.I: 6	O.B.A:	F.R:

Pitching Record:

Won: 8	Starts: 19	K's: 47	E.R.A: 4.26
Lost: 10	C.G: 16	Walks: 66	Saves: 1
Win %: .444	I.P: 188	Hits: 222	P.R: -1
Games: 25	Sh.O: 0	O.B.%: .364	W.A.T: -1.8

One of the many tested and retained to fill the void of new major league players positions created in 1890, his batting was below the norm even for a pitcher, and his pitching was far below the level of the P.L. Pirates. Void of power at the bat, he did manage to get on base and occasionally put a score on the board.

One hundred eighty-eight innings pitched in a 25-game season would later become most commendable, but in 1890 for a competitive team his numbers were indicative of a third reserve pitcher on a staff. None of his numbers rate as terrible, in fact most are near the P.L. norms; but his won-lost record of eight and 10 measures the difference between fourth place, where the Chicagos finished, and finishing in third place.

After his quick major league career, Bartson was owner of a minor league team, and was involved in local politics. An employee of a cigar store, Charles Bartson died of heart disease.

BASTIAN, CHARLES J.   Charlie Bastian
Born: July 4, 1860, Philadelphia, Pennsylvania
Died: January 18, 1932, Pennsauken, New Jersey

Height: 5'6.5".　　　Weight: 145 Lbs.　　　Batted: Right.　　　Threw: Right.
Major League Career: 8 Years, 504 Games
1889: N.L.: Chicago
1891: A.A.: Cincinnati and N.L.: Philadelphia
1890: P.L.: Chicago Pirates; SS 64, 2B 12, 3B 4

Batting Record:

Games: 80	3B: 5	Walks: 22	SL.%: .261
At Bats: 283	HRs: 0	K's: 37	S.B: 4
Hits: 54	Runs: 38	B.Avg: .191	B.R: -20
2B: 10	R.B.I: 29	O.B.A: .287	F.R: -11

Prototype substitute middle infielder and utility player. Mediocre in most every way measurable, but an essential element of every successful baseball team since the New York Knickerbockers took to the playing fields.

Charlie Bastian began with the record-setting Wilmington club of the Union Association in 1884. He played only one game after the P.L. Three sources show him as the shortstop for P.L. Chicago; his alternates were as the third baseman and the reserve catcher, and he was a .189 batter.

If seeking reasons for why the P.L. Pirates didn't do better than fourth place, their six position crew has to rate high among them. This is the composite player destiny brings to home plate with two or three base runners in place; he hits an almost home run, foul by inches, then hits an infield dribbler for the third out.

This utility player did plate a good ratio of R.B.I., and scored well enough on average per hit. He did have at least warning track power (although there were no real warning tracks in 1890), but his B.R. and B.Avg. don't nearly satisfy the minimums for a productive everyday player.

The balance of the earlier career stats of Charlie Bastian doesn't indicate any better with a .189 B.Avg and -84 total B.R. for his eight years. His batting high was .217, with yearly K's in the 70s and 80s in fewer than 400 at bats.

In the field, where such players must excel to sustain, a total +16 F.R. is considerably better than the -11 during his P.L. season.

After baseball, Charles Bastian was a carpenter. He died from chronic heart disease.

BECKLEY, JACOB PETER　　　**Jake Beckley**
Born: August 4, 1867, Hannibal, Missouri
Died: June 25, 1918, Kansas City, Missouri
Height: 5'10".　　　Weight: 200 Lbs.　　　Batted: Left.　　　Threw: Left.
Major League Career: 20 Years, 2,386 Games
1889: N.L.: Pittsburgh
1891: N.L.: Pittsburgh
1890: P.L.: Pittsburgh Burghers; 1B 121

Batting Record:

Games: 121	3B: 22	Walks: 42	SL.%: .535
At Bats: 516	HRs: 10	K's: 32	S.B: 18
Hits: 167	Runs: 109	B.Avg: .324	B.R: +31
2B: 38	R.B.I: 120	O.B.A: .381	F.R: -0

For 20 years, he regularly played at a level just below the greatest stars of his time, and 1890 was no exception. When he retired, his 246 career triples were the most by any player. He was a lefty-lefty. More significantly, he hardly ever missed a game.

Durable and reliable, Jake Beckley was one of the most valuable assets of the lowly P.L. Burghers. His fielding mark shows no deficiency. For a first baseman he demonstrated some speed and good mobility. One hundred nine runs scored and 120 R.B.I. are testament to his batting talents.

His 22 triples tied for the P.L. lead, he was second in doubles and tied for first in SL.%. He was third in R.B.I. and in total bases (279).

Except for 1890, he was with the N.L. throughout all the years of his credible career, which extended into the 20th century. He compiled a .308 career batting average, 1,600 runs scored, and 1,575 R.B.I. One school of baseball theory proposes that equal numbers of runs scored and batted in over the course of a long career is the true measure of an outstanding player.

If this is so, Jake Beckley definitely qualifies; also note him as a Players League star player. Major league players from Missouri weren't often found back them. This rare find was uncommonly exceptional in 1890 and all through his career.

He averaged well over 100+ games per year; mark durability an everyday asset beyond playing statistics. Equity demands note of a career low .235 B.Avg. in 1892 in 614 at bats. If point-counterpoint, cite his P.L. .535 SL.% in favor of this P.L. star.

To explain Jake Beckley, and summarize his career, start with virtually unknown, add all the affirmative adjectives, then start the recitation all over again. Then beyond the accolades estimate his loss to the N.L. Pittsburgh club, to what extent was this a factor in their horrid (23-113) 1890 record season.

His fielding skills rather than batting prowess earned him his rise to the major leagues, verified by a +20 F.R. in 1892, after which that stat fell off to average, with a +24 sum total F.R. for his 20 seasons. His career data include positive notes as a fielder. No big leaguer had more career putouts or chances at the 1B position.

His .308 B.Avg. was built on 13 seasons of .300+. His O.B.A. was .412 in 1894, another year in which he passed the .500+ SL.% level with .518. He scored 100+ runs each of five years, with four years of 100+ R.B.I.; seven years he hit 15+ triples, and posted 10 HRs two years, a lengthy list of benchmark stats.

The SABR-stat B.R. perhaps explains his true value, eight years of +20 and more; his being hit by 183 pitches ranks eighth all time for all players; 2,930 hits ranks 26th; 243 triples are fourth; 4,147 extra bases are the most of the 1800s by any player.

His 1,575 R.B.I. still rank 28th in period stats from 1890-1899. Jake Beckley ranks: eighth in at bats; fifth in doubles, each of five years he had 30+; first in triples; 10th in HRs; second in extra base hits; fifth in total bases; third in R.B.I.; And third in hit by pitches.

He served as an N.L. umpire in 1906, and with the Federal League during its embryonic year of 1913. After ending his major league career he had five very good years in the minors as a player, did a bit of minor league managing and was a minor league umpire.

He never left the game entirely; his name sustains in the record books: first all time among 1B in putouts with 23,709 and ninth in assists with 1,315; but 481 errors were third most all time at the 1B position.

In his later years, Beckley earned his living working for a prominent railroad company; he died of heart disease. Jacob Peter Beckley never played on a pennant winner, which might help to explain the long overdue delay for his admission to the Hall of Fame at Cooperstown, which finally arrived in 1971.

BEECHER, EDWARD H.   **Ed Beecher**
Born: July 2, 1859, Guilford Connecticut
Died: September 12, 1935, Hartford, Connecticut
Height: 5'10".   Weight: 185 Lbs.   Batted: Left.   Threw:
Major League Career: 4 Years, 283 Games
1889: N.L.: Washington
1891: A.A.: Washington and Philadelphia
1890: P.L.: Buffalo Bisons; OF 126, P 1

Batting Record:

Games: 126	3B: 10	Walks: 29	SL.%: .392
At Bats: 536	HRs: 3	K's: 23	S.B: 14
Hits: 159	Runs: 69	B.Avg: .297	B.R: -3
2B: 22	R.B.I: 90	O.B.A: .341	F.R: -5

Pitching Record:

Won: 0	Starts: 0	K's: 0	E.R.A: 12.00
Lost: 0	C.G: 0	Walks: 3	Saves: 0
Win %: —	I.P: 6	Hits: 10	P.R: -5
Games: 1	Sh.O: 0	O.B.%: .447	W.A.T: 0.0

1890 was his only full-time season. There are some positives and one notorious negative to be mentioned among his P.L. numbers. First and foremost in the case of this player are fielding data, testimony to the chance of statistical inconsistency. Skills for an outfielder are by any reasonable estimation less demanding than for other positions, although first base might be an exception.

Good hitters deficient on defense have historically been hidden in left field. It isn't likely that his brief P.L. moment in the pitcher's box involved any great contribution. Among the records specific to the outfield, in 1890 Ed Beecher set the all-time record of 55 errors in a season.

His F.R. for 1890 rates only -5, which must raise some questions, although it need be said that stat is specific to runs saved and not to total defense at OF or any other position. At the bat, Beecher achieved respectably, with a B.Avg. near .300; with O.B.A. and SL.% properly greater there's no fault of note.

Given the fact that he played for Buffalo, his run production at both ends of the spectrum rate excellent; power was adequate, walks and K's not exceptional, but a B.R. of -3 again raises statistical questions.

Compared with the balance of his career, which ended when the A.A. did after the 1891 season, his term in the Bisons outfield represents the better part of his career. A +7 F.R. in 1887 for Pittsburgh (N.L.) is the only point by which he exceeded his 1890 performance.

Later a member of the Hartford Police Department, Edward H. Beecher died after a long illness.

BIERBAUER, LOUIS W.   Lou Bierbauer
Born: September 28, 1865, Erie, Pennsylvania
Died: January 31, 1926, Erie, Pennsylvania
Height: 5'8".   Weight: 140 Lbs.   Batted: Left.   Threw: Right.
Major League Career: 13 Years, 1,383 Games
1889: A.A.: Philadelphia
1891: N.L.: Pittsburgh
1890: P.L.: Brooklyn Wonders; 2B 133

Batting Record:

Games: 133	3B: 11	Walks: 40	SL.%: .431
At Bats: 589	HRs: 7	K's: 15	S.B: 16
Hits: 180	Runs: 128	B.Avg: .306	B.R: +6
2B: 31	R.B.I: 99	O.B.A: .350	F.R: +21

A second baseman who bats .300+ and puts runs on the board, added to a +21 F.R. which, although unknown in 1890, has to be based on excellent play in the field, good enough to rank second among all in the P.L., would surely attract some attention from the competition, and he did.

Lou Bierbauer became the focus of one of the most fierce of all post-P.L. battles to recover and gain players, and by one source was the foremost cause for the Pittsburgh (N.L.) club to forever be called the Pirates.

Add to his P.L. credentials and reasons to pursue his services a minuscule 15 K's in 589 at bats, which equates to 2.5%. Joe Sewell (SS/3B, Indians and Yankees, A.L., 1920 through 1933), was struck out 114 times in 7,132 at bats; his 1.6% K's rate is by most regarded as the best such record in history.

Albeit for only one season, a mark of 2.5% must be given its due and consideration. Further to his credit, Bierbauer played in every Brooklyn Wonders game, during which he accumulated the P.L.'s sixth-highest total of hits. Simply said, there were no negatives among his 1890 numbers.

This was the only season he scored 100+ runs, and one of two with 100+ R.B.I. His +6 B.R. in 1890 appears to be an anomaly, as that stat was almost annually negative, with lows of -31 in 1891 and -27 in 1895, both with N.L. Pittsburgh, and a career B.R. total of -130.

His F.R. were quite the opposite. His best of +36 came in 1889; his 13-year F.R. total of +122 rates highly. But his career sum of 574 errors ranks fifth all time among 2B, offset perhaps by a 6.07 range factor, third best at 2B in history. His career assists adjusted to one 162 game season calculate to 540, which ranks fourth all time at his position.

He hit the benchmark 30+ doubles one year, and posted 649 at bats in 1892, which ranks third in period stats for 1890-1899. After baseball, he worked as a brass molder in a hometown factory, and as a night watchman.

Louis Bierbauer died of pneumonia. His achievements in 1890 justify his status as a Players League star player at second base.

BOYLE, JOHN ANTHONY   **Jack Boyle (Honest Jack)**
Born: March 22, 1867, Cincinnati Ohio
Died: January 6, 1913, Cincinnati, Ohio
Height: 6'4".   Weight: 190 Lbs.   Batted: Left.   Threw: Right.
Major League Career: 13 Years, 1,086 games
1889: A.A.: St. Louis
1891: A.A.: St Louis
1890: P.L.: Chicago Pirates; C 50, 3B 30, SS 16, 1B 7, OF 2

Batting Record:

Games: 100	3B: 5	Walks: 44	SL.%: .320
At Bats: 369	HRs: 1	K's: 29	S.B: 11
Hits: 96	Runs: 56	B.Avg: .260	B.R: -9
2B: 9	R.B.I: 49	O.B.A: .347	F.R: -3

Reserve catchers often spend game time observing, learning the skills to aspire to become a manager. This one doubled his 1890 games played behind home plate by taking a turn at a variety of other positions.

Beginning with a game in 1886, and all the years through 1898, he never played full time at the most demanding of all positions. In 1893, while with the Phillies, he switched to first base, and became a .300+ batter the only time in his career.

Overall, including the P.L. season, label Jack Boyle (not "Dirty Jack" Doyle) an adequate journeyman, utility reserve. Forty-four walks stand prominent among his P.L. numbers. His worth to his team was in his versatility.

Among later numbers of note to Boyle are 105 runs scored in 1893; on defense his F.R. were consistent and ordinary. But B.R.s of -33 in 1887, -25 in 1892, and -36 in 1895 serve to advise why his times in his teams' lineups were limited.

One among the cadre of 1800s "Honest Jacks," he was an A.A. umpire in 1888, and a N.L. umpire in 1892 and 1897; he owned and operated a saloon.

John Anthony Boyle died of nephritis, chronic Bright's disease.

BRENNAN (DORN), JOHN GOTTLEIB   Jack Brennan
Born: c. 1862–1865, St. Louis, Missouri
Died: October 18, 1904, Philadelphia, Pennsylvania
Height: Weight: Batted: Threw:
Major League Career: 5 Years, 183 Games
1889: A.A.: Philadelphia
1891: Did Not Play
1890: P.L.: Cleveland Infants; C 42, 3B 14, OF 6

Batting Record:

Games: 59	3B: 7	Walks: 13	SL.%: .326
At Bats: 233	HRs: 0	K's: 29	S.B: 8
Hits: 59	Runs: 32	B.Avg: .253	B.R: -10
2B: 3	R.B.I: 26	O.B.A: .304	F.R: -6

Also referred to in various texts as "Lee" and "Jim," this Jack Brennan, as second catcher for the Cleveland Infants, probably didn't have much to do on game days. At home, perhaps, he might have taken tickets at the turnstile, a customary task for players then; when the team was playing out of town perhaps he might have helped with transporting the team's equipment, as each carried his own baggage.

He did work some behind home plate, filled in a few games in the outfield, took the place occasionally of the third baseman, after he became the field manager. Sharing the number two position with Brennan were an aged veteran backstop, and for a couple of games a novice with dreams, so he had to keep busy or look busy.

While doing so, he put together the best season of his brief and rather unusual career. His P.L. .253 B.Avg. far exceeded his .220 career mark; both his P.L. O.B.A. and SL.% were well beyond his career numbers.

His P.L. hits, runs, and R.B.I. were all about a third of his wholes of five years. Many players have long argued, "The more I play, the better I play." This is a case in point, although not well enough to win a regular place in the lineup.

His -10 B.R. of 1890 could be used as a point in favor of using stats formulae; during his rather brief major league career he never had a positive B.R., his best being -1 for 1885. More on the unusual, this reserve catcher who could also work in the infield and the outfield in five years played for four teams in four major leagues.

The P.L. Infants were his last, the St. Louis Maroons of the Union Association of 1884 his first. Then came 1885 when the Maroons joined the National League; he didn't play in 1886 or 1887. In 1888 he was with the American Association Kansas City Cowboys, and in 1889 with the A.A. Philadelphia Athletics.

And through all that time, in all those places, nobody bothered to make note of his birth date, his height or weight, or from which side he batted and threw. If this bit of a bio-sketch were to be given a title, it might well be "The travels and travails of the almost anonymous utility catcher."

He ran a saloon after baseball; John Gottleib (Dorn) Brennan died of a heart seizure.

BROUTHERS, DENNIS JOSEPH Dan Brouthers (Big Dan)
Born: May 8, 1858, Sylvan Lake, New York
Died: August 2, 1932, East Orange, New Jersey
Height: 6'2".   Weight 207 Lbs.   Batted: Left.   Threw: Left.
Major League Career: 19 Years, 1,673 Games
1889: N.L.: Boston
1891: A.A.: Boston
1890: P.L.: Boston Reds; 1B 123

Batting Record:

Games: 123	3B: 9	Walks: 99	SL.%: .454
At Bats: 460	HRs: 1	K's: 17	S.B: 28
Hits: 152	Runs: 117	B.Avg: .330	B.R: +40
2B: 36	R.B.I: 97	O.B.A: .466	F.R: +2

He was Players League star player right off the bat, and before and after, of the greatest baseball magnitude. He wasn't quite Babe Ruth class, but comparisons with Bill Terry, Stan Musial, or Ted Williams are not at all excessive when measuring his record on the scale of historic excellence. This star was outstanding, for nearly two decades, consistently.

The Boston Reds won the only P.L. pennant; that required a team effort. Among the team, some players made greater contributions than others. That of Dan Brouthers was the most significant. To just say that he had no negatives would do offense to the facts, and to Players League history.

He led the P.L. in O.B.A., ranked third in B.R. and walks, fifth in doubles, fourth in the seldom-noted Total Average stat. He was competitive in every batting stat except HRs and SL.%. When any player called "Big _____" steals 28 bases, that's worth a mention. If fault must be found, Brouthers' 49 errors in 1890 ranks thirteenth all time for his 1B position.

Even as a youngster he was written of as big and burly. By the time he reached the big leagues in 1879 with Troy (N.L.) the notation of somber had been added. This was a result of trauma beyond repair; at age 19 he'd crashed into an opposing catcher in an effort to score; the young man went down instantly, and tragically died soon after from the force of the collision.

Psychology might say his future success was in part due to the ordeal of having to subsequently cope with the reconciliation process to recover his self-esteem, which he accomplished. Brouthers played major league baseball in four decades, but an asterisk is needed to fully explain. His last complete season was 1896, but he played in two games in 1904, at age 46.

Of this the record books show five at bats, and a resultant string of zeros; if this indicates failure, then let it be so. His whole record must be read and considered just to begin to appreciate his achievements.

All of the following include his excellent P.L. season, and it's worth knowing that during 1890 he played while subject to the duress of serving as the vice president of the Players League Brotherhood Association. Also, he'd been a prime force with the Boston N.L. players, and in persuading others to join the P.L.

During his career, in full seasons, that is restricted to 300+ at bats, he batted .300+ 14 years, reached the .400+ O.B.A. plateau 10 years, and the .500+ SL.% level 11 years. He never did reach 200, but did count 197 hits in 1892. He scored 100+ runs in each of eight seasons and posted 100+ R.B.I. five years. Eight times he hit 30+ doubles, including 40+ twice. Seven times he hit 15+ triples, and in each of three season hit 10+ home runs.

Ninety-nine in 1890 was his greatest single-season accumulation of walks, but he took 50+ each of nine years. If he had 17 K's (1890) in 460 at bats (3.7%) then what can be said about 238 K's in 6,711 career at bats (3.5%)? Further (1890) a ratio of 99 walks to 17 K's is technically 5.8:1.0. His strikeout total is incomplete, lacking his last testimonial year, but 840 walks measured against 238 K's (career), a 3.5:1.0 ratio, is respectable.

Add for the record at bats and K's: 1882, 351 and seven; 1887, 500 and nine; 1894, 525 and nine; this star didn't diminish with time and energy spent. Add for luster these facts of led his league in: B.Avg. five years; O.B.A. five years; SL.% six years; hits three years; doubles three years; triples once; HRs once. He never led in walks.

Further league leadership: runs scored twice, and R.B.I. twice. His career totals of runs (1,523) and RB.I. (1,295) may or may not satisfy the test of equity = excellence.

At risk of going to excess, Brouthers ranks eighth all time with 212 career triples, and ninth with a .342 batting average. Remember that there are variations in all these players stats in the various books of records, but usually the differences are minor and have at most minimal effect on ranks and status.

A couple of Brouthers' one-game achievements: July 18, 1883, six hits in six at bats; September 10, 1886, a total of 15 bases, via three HRs, a double, and a single. Among period stats 1876–1889 he ranks: seventh in runs; seventh in hits; fifth in doubles; third in triples; second in HRs; second in extra base hits; fifth in total bases; third in R.B.I.; seventh in walks; first in B.Avg. (tied); first in O.B.A.; first in SL.%; first in the recently devised stat combining O.B.A. and SL.%.

And, Brouthers is one of only three players in history to lead two major leagues in batting average.

He holds 12 records for single-season achievements during the period 1876–1889. In three consecutive seasons he played for the fans and teams of Boston, in three different leagues.

After 1896, Brouthers continued to be active as a minor league player. After 1906 he worked for John McGraw and the New York (N.L.) Giants in various capacities, where and by whom he had been allowed his two game encore. His services varied from night watchman at the Polo Grounds to player scout.

Dennis Joseph "Dan" Brouthers died of a heart attack. In 1945, a year of corrections for many years of past errors of omission, he was duly elected a member of the National Baseball Hall of Fame.

After his superb major league baseball career, he was on easy street, having saved his money for later needs and security. He was the owner and proprietor of a hotel near Poughkeepsie, New York, and a trustee of his township.

BROWN, THOMAS TARLTON   **Tom Brown**
Born: September 21, 1860, Liverpool, England
Died: October 25, 1927, Washington, D.C.
Heights: 5'10".   Weight: 168 Lbs.   Batted: Left.   Threw: Right.
Major League Career: 17 Years, 1,786 Games
1889: N.L.: Boston
1891: A.A.: Boston
1890: P.L.: Boston Reds; OF 128

Batting Record:

Games: 128	3B: 14	Walks: 86	SL.%: .392
At Bats: 543	HRs: 4	K's: 84	S.B: 79
Hits: 150	Runs: 146	B.Avg: .276	B.R: +8
2B: 23	R.B.I: 61	O.B.A: .378	F.R: +2

If following Dan Brouthers in a biographies book is at all akin to a good Brit having bad luck, then Tom Brown of Liverpool City would have batted behind Lou Gehrig in an R.B.I. contest, with the point formed as a question, "How can you beat that?"

With the exception of 84 K's, Tom Brown had a very good year in 1890, and certainly was a prominent factor in the Boston Reds' successful quest for the P.L. pennant. He was among the fastest from the batter's box to first base, if and when he had to run. His 86 walks in 1890 added another key dimension to the Reds potential, and obviously enhanced his somewhat above-average batting average.

Factor in 79 stolen bases, and make a note aside his name as a real threat to score every time he entered the batter's box, verified by his 146 runs scored for the P.L. Reds. Place him first in the batting order, and feel assured he'll be an asset on every game day, verified by his 128 P.L. games played.

He's ranked second in the P.L. in runs scored and stolen bases, and clearly could hit with power on occasion. Both his +8 B.R. and +2 F.R. are adequate, in sum meaning about a game won rather than not.

He seems to have saved much of his best for the year after the P.L. played, for Boston (A.A.). He batted .321, one of only two years of .300+. He led the league in hits (189) and runs (177), not to mention making almost every hit count. He also led in 1891 in triples (21), and he stole 106 bases, making Brown one of the very rare few to ever achieve 100+ S.B. in any league in any season.

He's also been credited as an excellent outfielder, with a great arm. In fact he ranks fourth all time with 348 OF assists, and fourth in double plays with 85. His 491 errors are the most ever by an outfielder, but adjusted to a 162-game season his career assists equate to 31.62, which ranks fifth all time at his position(s).

Embellish his status with six seasons of 100+ runs scored, add nine seasons with 50+ walks, and six seasons with 50+ stolen bases. Then note that his 177 runs scored record in 1891 was exceeded just once (Billy Hamilton, 192 in 1894), and tied once (Babe Ruth, in 1921). His 657 career S.B. ranks among the top 20, despite such records not being kept his first five years.

Further cite Brown for 30+ doubles one year, and ranks in period stats

(1890–1899) first in hits and second in stolen bases. He was manager of the Washington (N.L.) club parts of two years, (62–74, .471), and a N.L. umpire during his career year of 1891; he also wore N.L. blue in 1898–1899 and 1901–1902.

He came to California from England as a young boy, found his way to the U.S. Midwest, and was a member of the All-American team on Al Spalding's 1888–1889 world tour. After the major leagues, he was a minor league umpire, and operated a cigar store in Washington, D.C.

Thomas Tarlton Brown died of tuberculosis, complicated by the effects of emphysema.

BROWN, WILLARD   **William Brown (Big Bill)**
Born: 1866, San Francisco, California
Died: December 20, 1897, San Francisco, California
Height: 6'2".   Weight: 190 Lbs.   Batted: Right.   Threw: Right.
Major League Career: 7 Years, 418 Games
1889: N.L.: New York
1891: N.L.: Philadelphia
1890: P.L.: New York Giants; C 34, OF 13, 1B 9, 3B 3, 2B 2

Batting Record:

Games: 60	3B: 4	Walks: 13	SL.%: .400
At Bats: 230	HRs: 4	K's: 13	S.B: 5
Hits: 64	Runs: 47	B.Avg: .278	B.R: -3
2B: 8	R.B.I: 43	O.B.A: .320	F.R: 0

Beginning in 1887, with the New York (N.L.) Giants, he shared playing time behind home plate with Jim O'Rourke, of all people. The following two years (Giants) he was stuck behind Buck Ewing. Opportunity appeared on the horizon with the Players League, but there again was Buck Ewing, who was also the P.L. Giants field manager.

Willard Brown did well enough in 1890, filling a utility role. Extra base hits accounted for 25 percent of his total hits. He drove in runs with good consistency when opportunity availed, but his -3 B.R. is on the low side of the fence of expectations.

His career B.R. border on the statistically incredible; between -1 (twice) and -11 (twice), with not a one at or above the zero level. Among the more familiar stats, his P.L. B.Avg. was his next to best, .292 in 1893 in seven games with Baltimore and 111 with Louisville, N.L. of course, as there was no other major league.

That was when he made a position switch from mainly 2B to 3B after which all his data except F.R. reflect the diminished physical demands. He scored 85 runs in 1893, and the same year produced 90 R.B.I.

The next year was his last, and true to his alternate nickname of "California," from San Francisco he came, and to San Francisco he returned.

BROWNING, LOUIS ROGERS   Pete Browning (The Gladiator)
Born: July 17, 1861, Louisville, Kentucky
Died: September 10, 1905, Louisville, Kentucky
Height: 6'0".   Weight: 180 Lbs.   Batted: Right.   Threw: Right
Major League Career: 13 Years, 1,183 Games
1889: A.A.: Louisville
1891: N.L.: Pittsburgh and Cincinnati
1890: P.L.: Cleveland Infants; OF 118

Batting Record:

Games: 118	3B: 8	Walks: 75	SL.%: .517
At Bats: 493	HRs: 5	K's: 36	S.B: 35
Hits: 184	Runs: 112	B.Avg: .373	B.R: +47
2B: 40	R.B.I: 93	O.B.A: .459	F.R: +4

Question: How would you deal with the problem if you could read only at the level of someone with a 60 I.Q.? No offense intended, of course, but give the question a moment of consideration.

Pete Browning contracted an ear infirmity at a young age; it became aggravated from swimming in a local river, which in turn rendered him permanently quite deaf and impaired his education.

Despite his handicaps, he played major league baseball, which included 1890 with the Players League, for more than a dozen years, in well over 1,000 games, producing results on a level with the finest stars of any era.

Next question, told before the fact it's a trick question, how was Pete Browning able to do that?

In 1890, playing for the seventh-place Cleveland Infants, in 118 of their 131 games, he led the P.L. in batting average (tied), was second in on base average, and led in doubles. He was second in batting runs, fourth in hits and slugging percentage.

His 112 runs scored and 93 R.B.I. attest to productive ability; 75 walks versus 36 K's surely pass the tests of eyesight, strike zone judgment, and batting discipline.

Continue with 35 stolen bases, mention again judgment, along with stealth and speed, and a +4 for fielding runs. The sum of this explains this Players League star player on the fields of play.

To achieve completion, add commendable extra base power. He did have quirks, for example refusing to slide, and staring into the sun to improve his eye power, neither of which was as debilitating as drinking to excess at times.

He's been written of as a defensive liability, to an extent for a reason needless to say; his career F.R. is -37, with only a +10 one year as a positive note. This came in his first year, 1882 with Louisville (A.A.); he's ranked 12th all time in OF errors with 209.

He stayed with his home town club(s) through their years as the Eclipse (through 1884) and as the Colonels (through 1889) until the call came for volunteers to challenge the power of the ownership clan.

Coincident with his long tenure at Louisville, he was the first pro player to contract with a manufacturer to have a bat made to his specifications. He accumulated a huge collection of bats and gave each of them a name.

Eccentric? Think not. That's been done by many star players, though made common knowledge by only a few. The manufacturer, by the way, was the shop of J. Frederich Hillerich, whose son, John A. "Bud," was the first custom baseball bat creator.

Resolved: Pete Browning was highly skilled in using his bats. In the peculiar year of 1887, he batted .402, which was 33 points below the league leader. Acknowledging legitimate loss of playing time, he exceeded the .300+ B.Avg. level each of 10 years.

Each of four years his O.B.A. was beyond the .400+ level, and four years he went beyond the .500+ SL.% level. Mark his commensurate career data at .341, .403, and .467.

Two hundred twenty (questionable) hits in 1887 were his most, and his only year of 200+. The next nearest were 184 hits in his P.L. year, during which, by the way, he earned second rank in the unusual Total Average stat, and first in Total Player Rating.

In doubles, Pete Browning once reached 40+, with four years at 30+; once he surpassed the 15+ level in triples. For all his other strengths, his career home run total was only 45. By the unique rules of 1887, he stole 103 bases, more down to earth were 36 in 1888 and 35 in 1890.

With the exception of 1890 his ratios of walks to K's were for the most part ordinary. Three times he exceeded 100+ runs scored. He never got past the 100+ R.B.I. mark, and the A.A. didn't retain counts of R.B.I. during his first six years.

Once he led his league in doubles, and once in hits, four times in B.Avg., twice in O.B.A., and once in SL.%, where hitting HRs counts most. Twice he led in batting runs, but his +47 in 1890 were not among the league highs.

He's one of only three players to have won batting average titles in two leagues. His career B.Avg. of .341 ranks 13th highest in history. Among period stats from 1876–1889 he ranks: first in B.Avg. (tied); third in O.B.A.; fourth in SL.%; fourth in O.B.A./SL.% combination.

He enjoyed a peaceful retirement till, in 1905, a maltreated mastoid infection, combined with longterm drinking, ended in brain damage, and a diagnosis of insanity. He was confined in Lakeland Insane Asylum, near Louisville.

As a youth, Browning is said to have enjoyed competitive kids games. It must be reported, it's been told, that he was not fond of school or studies. Still, as an adult, as a major league baseball player, he was able to produce results at the level of the greatest stars.

How did Browning achieve this? The answer is he did, and he didn't. At least not sufficiently to satisfy all of the criteria required for admission to membership in the hallowed hall at Cooperstown.

His baseball numbers and records speak for themselves. After baseball he owned a saloon, and was a cigar drummer. Browning was a Player League star player, and to that add a note that he was special.

Louis Roger "Pete" Browning, afflicted for most of his mortal existence, died from mastoiditis, following ear surgery.

BUCKLEY, JOHN EDWARD   John Buckley
Born: March 20, 1870, Marlboro, Massachusetts
Died: May 4, 1942, Westborough, Massachusetts
Height: 6'1".   Weight: 200 Lbs.   Batted: Threw: Right.
Major League Career: 1 Year, 4 Games
1889: Did Not Play
1891: Did Not Play
1890: P.L.: Buffalo Bisons; P 4 (Debut Date: July 15)

Batting Record:

Games: 4	3B: 0	Walks: 2	SL.%: .000
At Bats: 15	HRs: 0	K's: 10	S.B: 0
Hits: 0	Runs: 1	B.Avg: .000	B.R:
2B: 0	R.B.I: 0	O.B.A:	F.R:

Pitching Record:

Won: 1	Starts: 4	K's: 4	E.R.A: 7.68
Lost: 3	C.G: 4	Walks: 16	Saves: 0
Win %: .250	I.P: 34	Hits: 49	P.R: -13
Games: 4	Sh.O: 0	O.B.%: .417	W.A.T: -0.1

    He was young and came to Buffalo with expectations. The Bisons needed pitchers and players of most any sort who could play the major league game.

    From which side of home plate he batted isn't known and doesn't matter much. Zero for 15 with 10 K's among his at bats, except as a historical note, it doesn't really matter at all from which side he swung his bat, when he did.

    Pitchers of major league quality were scarce in the Players League year. John Buckley came to Buffalo as a pitcher. To his credit, he completed every game he started. History shows that he did win one more game than millions of aspirants, despite giving up nearly an earned run per inning in the pitcher's box.

    He did collect two walks, and did score a run. Despite a -13 P.R., and a (-) W.A.T. for the Buffalo Bisons of 1890, maybe the club paid his train fare back to Boston.

BUDD, (UNKNOWN)   (Unknown) Budd
Born:
Died:
Height: Weight: Batted: Threw:
Major League Career: 1 Year, 1 Game
1889: Did Not Play
1891: Did Not Play
1890: P.L.: Cleveland Infants; OF 1 (Debut Date: September 10)

Batting Record:

Games: 1	3B: 0	Walks: 0	SL.%: .000
At Bats: 4	HRs: 0	K's: 3	S.B: 0
Hits: 0	Runs: 0	B.Avg: .000	B.R: -1
2B: 0	R.B.I: 0	O.B.A: .000	F.R: 0

"Budd" could have been a misspelled nickname, or a first name. Clifford S. Kachline wrote on phantom ballplayers. Here they're called fantasy players, but they're the same thing. The phenomenon might have been known before 1989, or before 1890, which may have then been written off as arcana. Regardless of the term used, inherent meaning is obvious, such player(s) didn't really exist.

Kachline suggests, "The maxim [axiom] existed almost since the game's earliest days, largely as a consequence of record keepers who sometimes unwittingly entered erroneous data into the record books."

(Unknown) Budd is identified in three reliable sources of data and information only as "Budd." Whether a fellow of this surname or otherwise, someone played in one P.L. game for the Infants of Cleveland.

He was allowed in the batter's box four times, with three K's to show for it, and otherwise a long string of "0's." Which is very possible. His playing position by the books was "OF." further information is unknown.

BUFFINGTON, CHARLES G.   **Charlie Buffington**
Born: June 14, 1861, Fall River, Massachusetts
Died: September 23, 1907, Fall River, Massachusetts
Height: 6'1".   Weight: 180 Lbs.   Batted: Right.   Threw: Right.
Major League Career: 11 Years, 586 Games (Pitched in 414)
1889: N.L.: Philadelphia
1891: A.A.: Boston
1890: P.L.: Philadelphia Quakers; P 36, OF 5, 3B 1

Batting Record:

Games: 42	3B: 2	Walks: 9	SL.%: .340
At Bats: 150	HRs: 1	K's: 3	S.B: 1
Hits: 41	Runs: 24	B.Avg: .273	B.R: -5
2B: 3	R.B.I: 24	O.B.A: .319	F.R: +2

Pitching Record:

Won: 19	Starts: 33	K's: 89	E.R.A: 3.81
Lost: 15	C.G: 28	Walks: 126	Saves: 1
Win %: .559	I.P: 283	Hits: 312	P.R: +13
Games: 36	Sh.O: 0	O.B.%: .366	W.A.T: +1.8

Charlie Buffington was the second of two field managers of the Quakers for 116 games; his won-lost record stands at 61–54, a .530 win percent.

1884 was his biggest if not best year, in 1891 he was great, and 1890 was an off year, despite his impressive winning record. In sum, he ranks among the greatest 1800s pitchers. He took over as the Quakers field manager after 16 games, which might have been a factor in his pitching record.

For Boston (N.L.) in 1884, another year of three major leagues, he won 48 games and lost 16 (.750 win %). His games and starts were 67 and 67; he completed 63, pitching 587 innings. His E.R.A. was a superb 2.15, but not a match for his K's to walks ratio, 5.5:1.0, 417 and 76 respectively. If the term shutting down the opposition applies, he also recorded eight shutouts that season.

His pitching equals that year at most numbered five, Pud Galvin and Charley "Hoss" Radbourn among them. Buffington and Radbourn met in a classic duel on August 4; after 10 innings had been played the score stood at 0 to 0; in the 11th, a light hitting infielder drove a Buffington pitch through a hole in the right field fence; he circled the bases to score the only run of the day.

Charlie Buffington lost 17 games each of three straight seasons, 1887–1889, while winning 21–28–27; he pitched consecutive one hitters on the 6th and 9th of August 1887. The accolade "great" was used in reference to 1891; he won 28 and lost nine (.763) for the Boston club, of the A.A. His 2.55 E.R.A. that year was not near his best, 1.91 for Philadelphia (N.L.) in 1888.

He quit the game after 11 decisions in 1892 (3 and 8), when the Baltimore Orioles management tried to cut his salary, a bit of testimony on the audacity of the owners after the N.L. achieved its major league monopoly. By 1892 the hegemony of the Albert Goodwill Spalding cartel was absolute.

In the interim, having begun (2 and 3) with Boston (N.L.) in 1882, Charlie Buffington led his league only once in win %, and once in the later calculated saves stat. He did achieve beyond +10.0 W.A.T. one year, and among period stats 1876–1889 ranks: eighth in shutouts; ninth in walks; eighth in K's; tenth in wild pitches; second in balks (tied).

His 154 career wild pitches ranks 24th in history; he also set two single-season records in 1876–1889, and one in 1890–1899.

In 1890 he won better than his pitching staff as a whole, and his term as manager produced a better record than the Quakers season as a whole. His E.R.A. was somewhat better than the P.L. average; his on base percent allowed was about equal to the norm.

Buffington was an N.L. umpire in 1883, 1888–1889, and in 1892, the year he quit as a player. After baseball he did well as a broker in cotton and coal, and as the owner-operator of a coal company.

Charles G. Buffington died while being prepared for surgery; he suffered a condition of fatty degeneration of the heart.

CARNEY, JOHN JOSEPH   **John Carney (Handsome Jack)**
Born: November 10, 1867, Salem, Massachusetts
Died: October 19, 1925; Litchfield, New Hampshire
Height: 5'10.5".   Weight: 175 Lbs.   Batted: Right.   Threw: Right.

Major League Career: 3 Years, 252 Games
1889: N.L.: Washington
1891: A.A.: Cincinnati
1890: P.L.: Buffalo Bisons; 1B 24, OF 4; Cleveland Infants; OF 19, 1B 6

Batting Record:

	Buffalo	Cleveland	Totals
Games:	28	25	53
At Bats:	107	89	196
Hits:	29	31	60
2B:	3	5	8
3B;	0	3	3
HRs:	0	0	0
Runs:	11	15	26
R.B.I:	13	21	34
Walks:	7	14	21
K's:	14	5	19
B.Avg:	.271	.348	.306
O.B.A.:	.333	.442	.385
SL.%:	.299	.472	.378
S.B.:	2	6	8
B.R:	-4	+6	+2
F.R:	0	0	0

Handsome Jack had the worst of luck, playing the P.L. season for the last-place and next-to-last-place clubs. None of his numbers nearly correspond with either of their records. Call his a split season.

He played a little more the previous year, his first at the major league level, for Washington (N.L.) and achieved much less than in 1890: .231 B.Avg., .267 SL.%. The year after the P.L. by stats was about half his career.

This involved 130 games for the A.A. Cincinnati and Milwaukee franchise(s) combine; a .283 B.Avg., .394 SL.%; his B.R. sum stands at -5, his F.R. at -2. If there was nothing more to his record, he played in three different leagues during his three seasons, for five teams.

But there is more to tell of John Carney. Compare his calculated batting stats to those of his 1890 teams:

	B.Avg.	O.B.A.	SL.%
Carney	.306	.385	.378
Bisons	.260	.347	.337
Infants	.288	.360	.386

John Carney was clearly superior to his teams, in each of these modes except one; why he left the Bisons, why he didn't play more for either club, must be subject matter left for speculation.

After this three-year career, he was a college baseball coach; and raised a rare breed of rabbits.

John Joseph Carney died of heart failure.

CARROLL, FREDERICK HERBERT   Fred Carroll
Born: July 2, 1864, Sacramento, California
Died: November 7, 1904, San Rafael, California
Height: 5'11". Weight: 185 Lbs. Batted: Right. Threw: Right.
Major League Career: 8 Years, 754 Games
1889: N.L.: Pittsburgh
1891: N.L.: Pittsburgh
1890: P.L.: Pittsburgh Burghers; C 56, OF 49, 1B 7

Batting Record:

Games: 111	3B: 7	Walks: 75	SL.%: .395
At Bats: 416	HRs: 2	K's: 22	S.B: 35
Hits: 124	Runs: 95	B.Avg: .298	B.R: +16
2B: 20	R.B.I: 71	O.B.A: .418	F.R: -13

He made the ranks of period stats 1876–1889 as 10th in hit by pitches. He was not yet of voting age when his major league career began at Columbus (A.A.) in 1884; the remainder of his eight seasons he was a Pittsburgh player, in three leagues.

First at Pittsburgh came the A.A., in 1885 and 1886; then the N.L. 1887 through 1889, then the P.L. and back to the N.L. again for his final season.

He was an N.L. umpire in 1887, and a member of the All-American team during the 1888–1889 world tour. As a player, his batting was considerably better than average, his fielding about as much below; his skills at the bat are evident even when he didn't get a hit.

His speed was better than ordinary. He was typical of catchers then who had versatility in positions. Specific to the Burghers of Pittsburgh, 29 extra base hits among 124, nearly 25 percent, made him a consistent potential run producer; 75 walks and 35 stolen bases made him a legitimate asset to his club.

Just 22 K's measured against 75 walks is worth mention, 22 K's in 416 at bats, 5.2 percent, more so. Include his B.R. SABR-stat as worthy of high note; +16 rates benchmark class for a utility catcher.

Ninety-five funs scored were the most of his career with 71 R.B.I. also. He batted .328 in 1887 and .330 in 1889 was his best; that year he led the N.L. with a .486 O.B.A., 85 walks included.

For these two seasons, 1887 and 1889, his B.R. count +25 and +39, preceded by +27 in 1886. His F.R. the latter two years stand at -12 and -4; why the extreme differences isn't certain. He'd begun as a catcher, which was his primary position until 1891. His first three F.R. marks were +11, 0, +13. Why that decline also is uncertain.

It's been written that Carroll had a constant longing to be in California; there isn't much time to ponder the universe, or California, while working behind home plate, although there have been more than a few outfielders notorious for doing so.

After 1892 he became a batting star in West Coast leagues, and operated a successful freight shipping business, at least for a few years.

Frederick Herbert Carroll died young; the cause has been written as the athletic heart.

CLARK, OWEN F.   Spider Clark
Born: September 16, 1867, Brooklyn, New York
Died: February 8, 1892, Brooklyn, New York
Height: 5'10".   Weight: 150 Lbs.   Batted: Threw:
Major League Career: 2 Years, 107 Games
1889: N.L.: Washington
1891: Did not play
1890: P.L.: Buffalo Bisons; OF 34, C 14, 2B 13, 1B 6, 3B 3, SS 1, P 1

Batting Record:

Games: 69	3B: 1	Walks: 20	SL.%: .327
At Bats: 260	HRs: 1	K's: 16	S.B: 8
Hits: 69	Runs: 45	B.Avg: .265	B.R: -9
2B: 11	R.B.I: 25	O.B.A: .325	F.R: 0

Pitching Record:

Won: 0	Starts: 0	K's: 2	E.R.A: 6.75
Lost: 0	C.G: 0	Walks: 2	Saves: 0
Win %: —	I.P: 4	Hits: 8	P.R: -1
Games: 1	Sh.O: 0	O.B.%: .483	W.A.T: 0.0

From which side of home plate he batted isn't known. During the 1890 P.L. season he played some time at all the nine positions.

His 1890 batting: power minimal, scoring sporadic, not a good situation hitter. On base he was adequate, his fielding neutral. But when having to deal with the different demands at the maximum variety of positions while not playing regularly has to merit at least some consideration. His half-day as a Bisons pitcher produced results quite typical for his team.

Career batting: .262 B.Avg., .311 O.B.A., .351 SL.%, comparable with the most active year (1890) of his abbreviated career. His role with the Statesmen/Senators of (N.L.) Washington, D.C., the previous year: many positions played, at most 14 games, at least two, but none as a pitcher.

His 1889 fielding mark: identical to 1890. At the bat: 35 hits, 12 for extra bases, proportionally near double his Bisons output.

He didn't make any of his hometown teams where he resided all of his short life. Possibly by 1890 he'd already become a victim of the malady which caused his far-too-early demise.

Owen F. Clark: Cause of death, unknown.

COMISKEY, CHARLES ALBERT   Charlie Comiskey (The Old Roman)
Born: August 15, 1859, Chicago, Illinois
Died: October 26, 1931; Eagle River, Wisconsin
Height: 6'0".   Weight: 180 Lbs.   Batted: Right.   Threw: Right.
Major League Career: 13 Years, 1,390 Games
1889: A.A.: St. Louis
1891: A.A.: St. Louis
1890: Chicago Pirates; 1B 88

Batting Record:

Games: 88	3B: 3	Walks: 14	SL.%: .289
At Bats: 377	HRs: 0	K's: 17	S.B: 34
Hits: 92	Runs: 53	B.Avg: .244	B.R: -26
2B: 11	R.B.I: 59	O.B.A: .277	F.R: -2

Charlie Comiskey was the field manager of the Pirates for their entire season of 138 games; his won-lost record was 75–62 for a .547 win %.

In baseball there have been powerful people, and more powerful people; list his name high among them. It would not be difficult to mix Charles Albert Comiskey and Albert Goodwill Spalding. Both have been called natural leaders. There are not nor ever were such men, but both surely learned the requisite skills much better than most mortal men.

"Aggressive, innovative, imperious, and ruthless" is how SABR has depicted Mr. Comiskey; comparisons with Spalding are easy and self-evident.

His father was a Chicago politician and enough said about that for those who know that history. The son learned to value a dollar dearly, and wanted every dollar that passed his way, to have and to hold till eternity.

As a young man, Comiskey went to Dubuque, Iowa, to learn how to play baseball, which he did, and aside he found his wife. All his records show his philosophy was successful, and his plan of order well in order.

As a major league player, he'd earned promotion from Dubuque, under the tutelage of Ted Sullivan, to St. Louis and the Browns of Chris Von der Ahe, who also employed Sullivan in a variety of capacities.

The year was 1882: the American Association was born and with it arrived Von der Ahe, Sullivan, and Comiskey, who, quite incomprehensibly then, and hardly less so now, would have nearly 50 years in the game, as a player, manager, and franchise owner.

This triad formed the most formidable tandem of the A.A.'s 10-year life. Comiskey's playing position was first base almost exclusively, and through 1894 when demands other than play were given priority.

His numbers weren't dazzling, but a check of his clutch hitting by the SABR-stat Clutch Hitting Index for the years which it includes reveals that he averaged above 130, with a high of 157 in 1890; the base number and average is 100.

Comiskey played his position boldly, comparatively speaking, having no fear of standing away from the base. It's said he was a reckless base runner, using tactics both the most notorious teams of all time, the 1890's Orioles and Spiders, would prominently employ a decade later; he also used his vocal capabilities in a manner such as theirs.

His career averages at the bat: .264 B.Avg., .293 O.B.A., .338 SL.%; he had 100+ runs each of three years, and tallied 100+ R.B.I. once. This is despite the fact that the A.A. didn't keep track of R.B.I. most of its years; the same holds true for batting K's, but what is known can be said of Comiskey, that no pitcher was his master with only 84 K's in some 2,500 at bats.

His walks as a rule were also extremely low, 197 in 13 seasons, and tell that when he came to bat he believed his task to be to put the ball in play, a sound and practical philosophy; when the ball is put in play, anything and sometimes beyond that can happen.

His fielding numbers are as low as K's and walks, with a career F.R. balance near zero; but 403 career errors earned him the fifth rank all time at his 1B position.

Comiskey earned the esteem of Mr. Von der Ahe, not an easy task by any means, who appointed him as the Browns field manager, and retained him in that position, completely contrary to his legendary whimsy concerning personnel.

Comiskey duly repaid; in eight years as bench boss, six of which were full time, the Browns twice finished second, the other four years they won pennants, consecutively, 1885 through 1888.

When organizing the Players League, all that was necessary for the Chicago Pirates hierarchy was to ask "Who could do better?" If one year is evidence, then 1890 proved Comiskey was not the best-ever manager of a major league team.

His total numbers as a field manager were won 839 and lost 540, a .608 win percentage; not the best, but outstanding. But, excepting the above, he never won another championship.

When the P.L. arrived, he came to Chicago with a reputation; his first act of authority with the Browns had been to cleanse the team of lushers and other deadweight. He wanted players hell bent and ready to play each game at their best.

As for himself, he was injured the latter half of the 1890 season but still played some. Lead by example is an effective philosophy; let nothing physical stand in your way.

If his numbers as the field manager aren't stunning, check what his pitching staff accomplished. Motivation is an essential element of management, albeit Mr. Comiskey lost sight of this fact while gaining the appellation of "The Old Roman." Titles like that don't come from coincidence.

He never won a stolen base league title, or any in fact, but when driven Comiskey could steal with the best of them: 117 during the aberrant 1887 season, 72 and 65 the next two years. His greatest feats of theft, allegedly, were yet to come.

It would be remiss to not mention that Comiskey pitched a little, 12 innings in all, in four games, including one start, which he finished, for a total record of 0 and 1, with a superb 0.75 career E.R.A.

It would be further remiss to not mention that he played for the Cincinnati Reds three years, 1892–1894, and was their manager through that term, in the second division. The most and notorious in his own realm were yet to come.

His will to take part in the Brotherhood Players League, for all its intentions, represents idiosyncrasy, totally and completely out of character with the man and the Legend predestined which Charles Albert Comiskey would become.

Playing and managing didn't sate his needs. Ban Johnson began to expand his interests in baseball beyond writing about it for Cincinnati newspapers. Like Spalding and Hulbert, he was a man of ideas, with ambitions; list the name Byron Bancroft Johnson among the greater with power.

National League powers had become comfortable with the monopoly scenario, perhaps complacent, and they didn't see Johnson and company coming. He and they were not perceived as a real threat to the N.L. domain; when he tried to communicate with the N.L. he was simply ignored.

Comiskey had joined the fight long before the fact, fully five years before the American League was declared major. Johnson had set him up as the owner of the St. Paul franchise, in the minor Western League, which he ruled as if it were his own.

While Johnson was restructuring and adding wealth, power, and influence to his Western League, Comiskey was founding another major league franchise in the Spalding territory of Chicago. For 30 subsequent years Comiskey owned and ruled the White Sox, franchise, club, and team.

His game on the field would be base running and defense; beyond the fields of play, he would be making hordes of money. The men who then were the N.L. didn't see the A.L. coming, but they were witness to its coming. When they did realize, a legitimate and powerful, and by their choice hostile major league had been born, organized, and established.

Other P.L. players would come to own major league franchises, or parts thereof; with the exception of Connie Mack, no other would endure and sustain longer than Comiskey.

Niggardly, dastardly; Mr. Comiskey was reviled with words and terms the Orioles and Spiders had never thought of. By some he was regarded and reputed to be tighter with a dollar than any of the Rockefeller-Carnegie genre, or the P.L. player who became Mr. Mack, at his miserliest.

In 1913 and 1914 Mr. Comiskey took his White Sox on a world tour, Spalding deja vu, to play against the Giants of Mr. John McGraw. By SABR, this twosome did the same again some 11 years later. About midway between tours, the White Sox won the 1917 and 1919 American League pennants.

In the 1917 World's Series the White Sox beat the Giants 4 games to 2; the 1919 World's Series was different, in more than one way. Set as best-of-nine (two more games = X more $'s), the White Sox lost to the Reds by 5 games to 3.

The number of games and the result were not all that was found to be different. During and soon after, rumors began to flow of a scandal, of White Sox players playing to lose; it became the most despicable and horrific scandal in all baseball history.

There had been the business of Mutuals players banned during the 1850s; the outrage of Richard Higham, found out and banished forever in 1882, the only major league umpire ever found to be dishonest; and the Louisville Four scandal of 1877, effectively and propitiously resolved by President Hulbert.

This scandal, that of the Comiskey White Sox, which media wrote of as the Black Sox scandal, led to creation of the position of baseball commissioner, without which the game, arguably, would have degenerated to such a level of disrepute that it could not have survived.

The skinflint chicanery of Mr. Comiskey has often and widely been cited as the cause of the Black Sox scandal, but never by the baseball establishment, the government of baseball. Nor did the vast majority of media men at the time make much of it.

Perhaps from "Dear Ol' Dad" Mr. Comiskey had learned the needs and the whims of sportswriters. With regularity he provided them presents of liquor, and well-liquored festivities, and with other personal favors.

He died at his sumptuous country retreat in Wisconsin. In 1939 he was among the chosen to forever reside at the Baseball Hall of Fame; his election was as an executive. In 1890 he'd taken the side of the players.

Charles Albert Comiskey died from nephritis, pneumonia, and heart trouble. As a player, he ranks fourth in stolen bases with 295 during the period 1876–1889.

It's been written of him that he spent 29 years as owner of a baseball club, a world record. Half truth — half not.

CONNOR, ROGER   Roger Connor
Born: July 1, 1857, Waterbury, Connecticut
Died: January 4, 1931, Waterbury, Connecticut
Height: 6'3".   Weight: 220 Lbs.   Batted: Left.   Threw: Left.
Major League Career: 18 Years, 1,997 Games
1889: N.L.: New York
1891: N.L.: New York
1890: P.L.: New York Giants; 1B 123

Batting Record:

Games:123	3B: 15	Walks: 88	SL.%: .548
At Bats: 484	HRs: 14	K's: 32	S.B: 22
Hits: 169	Runs: 133	B.Avg: .349	B.R: +48
2B: 24	R.B.I: 103	O.B.A: .450	F.R: +11

The Players League leader in home runs, batting runs, slugging percentage (tied); third in on base average; fourth in batting average; fifth in runs scored and total bases. Also: third in total average and second in Total Player Rating. Roger Connor had a very good year, chosen by at least one expert as Most Valuable Player.

Period stats 1876–1889, with his ranks: ninth in runs scored; sixth in hits; ninth in doubles; first in triples; sixth in HRs; second in SL.%; fifth in O.B.A.; fifth in B.Avg.; fifth in R.B.I.; fourth in walks; sixth in extra base hits; sixth in total bases; third in the O.B.A./SL.% combo stat. Roger Connor had a very good career.

From Troy (N.L.) 1882 to St. Louis in 1897, and including New York (N.L.) 10 years, he led in single-season stats 10 times, with the last coming in 1892. He wasn't a league leader after that. He never led in F.R. or runs scored.

His career B.Avg. is .317, 11 years he batted .300+; career O.B.A. is .397, with eight seasons of .400+, and a .486 career SL.%, with eight seasons of .500+. Also: eight years 100+ runs scored, and four years 100+ R.B.I. for totals of 1,620 and 1,332. Just to be involved in changing the scoreboard close to 3,000 times boggles the mind.

He held the career home run record from 1895 until it was broken by Babe Ruth in 1921. He was also fearsome as a walk-man, with 12 years of 50+ free passes, including 116 in 1892. His career ratio of walks to K's is 2:1 with 1,002 and 449. Note 51 walks and just eight K's in 1885, 63 walks and 10 K's in 1895.

He hit 10+ HRs each of seven years and ranks fifth all time with 233 triples. His 812 extra base hits is the highest total of the 1800s. The stats have spoken; consider Roger Connor among the highest level stars of the 1800s, and a Players League star player.

He hit 30+ doubles each of three years, ranks 20th among 1B with 17,605 putouts, and stands second among 1800s 1B in fielding percentage with .978. His known stolen bases number 244; stats for his first six years are not included in the records.

Hr hit three HRs in one game in 1888 and made six hits in six at bats in a game in 1895; his excellence extended over a decade. Big and powerful, he hit pitches out of ballparks and into the streets. He was deceptively fast, and knew how to run the bases.

Connor was manager briefly at St. Louis in 1895 with eight and 37 won and lost; a .178 win % is not to his credit. He'd played ball games as young as age eight, and worked in a factory while a teenager after his father died.

As an adult, he was quiet and non-controversial, the creed he had been taught as a youth, which extended to work and religion. After baseball he owned and played for a minor league team, and worked as a city school inspector.

Connor, P.L. star player, among the very best of his time, was justly elected a member of the National Baseball Hall of Fame in 1976.

Connor died of throat cancer.

Charley "Hoss" Radbourn, the legendary 1800s pitcher, may have spoken the highest tribute to Connor, saying there was only one man that he could not fool, and that was Roger Connor.

COOK, PAUL   Paul Cook
Born: May 5, 1863, Caledonia, New York
Died: May 25, 1905, Rochester, New York
Height: Weight: Batted: Right.   Threw: Right.
Major League Career: 7 Years, 378 Games
1889: A.A.: Louisville

1891: A.A.: Louisville and St. Louis
1890: P.L.: Brooklyn Wonders; C 36, 1B 21, OF 1

Batting Record:

Games: 58	3B: 3	Walks: 14	SL.%: .294
At Bats: 218	HRs: 0	K's: 18	S.B: 7
Hits: 55	Runs: 32	B.Avg: .252	B.R: -12
2B: 3	R.B.I: 31	O.B.A: .303	F.R: -1

(Comiskey and Connor, names of fame; how does a common catcher follow that?)

Paul Cook was a member of the P.L.'s runner-up team and played in most of their games. His (-) B.R. does not connect with success. But his runs scored were 32, and R.B.I. 31; recall the excellence theorem, with a catch.

With little power, a bit of speed, adequate defense given the diversity of demands which come with being a catcher and playing a variety of other positions, his 1890 Wonders stats prompt the summary comment of basically adequate.

A check of his career stats suggests that nothing different was to be expected; in fact his .252 and etc. of batting data were his best. With three years of R.B.I. missing to measure against 172 runs scored, the void precludes assessment of the theorem mentioned above.

Career B.R. of -76, and 87 K's with three years missing matched against 67 walks equals a vote of "no" for high honors. An F.R. composite of -40 reinforces. Unusual given baseball flukes, but not unique, Paul Cook never hit a major league home run, not one in 1,364 at bats, which might merit some historic attention.

After baseball, he managed a saloon, then a café.

Paul Cook died of lingering illness.

CORCORAN, THOMAS WILLIAM   Tommy Corcoran (Corky)
Born: January 4, 1869, New Haven, Connecticut
Died: June 25, 1960, Plainfield, Connecticut
Height: 5'9".   Weight: 164 Lbs.   Batted: Right.   Threw: Right.
Major League Career: 18 Years, 2,200 Games
1889: Did not play
1891: A.A.: Philadelphia
1890: Pittsburgh Burghers; SS 123 (Rookie)

Batting Record:

Games: 123	3B: 13	Walks: 38	SL.%: .318
At Bats: 503	HRs: 1	K's: 45	S.B: 43
Hits: 117	Runs: 80	B.Avg: .233	B.R: -27
2B: 14	R.B.I: 61	O.B.A: .289	F.R: -3

A major league novice in 1890, his extra bases to hits ratio is as impressive as his batting average(s). Forty-three stolen bases reveal speed. His B.R. is deceptive, and his rookie F.R. much more so. The two Quakers field managers must have had confidence in him, playing him at the shortstop position in all but eight of their games.

His proportion of games played didn't diminish throughout his lengthy career; defensive reasons are self-evident. His career F.R. sum is a positive +26. Beyond that as a whole he achieved distinction in a game played on August 7, 1903, when he recorded 14 assists, still the record by a six-position player.

Among other career notes, Tommy Corcoran is fifth all time at shortstop with 4,550 putouts, sixth in assists with 7,106, also fourth with 956 errors, and ninth with a 5.62 range factor. In 1898 he posted the 1800s 15th highest season fielding average with .932 F.%; he's third among 1800s SS with a .917 F.%. His career assists adjusted to a 162-game season calculate to 555.32, which is tenth all time among shortstops.

But Tommy Corcoran wasn't a one-dimensional player; for the period 1890–1899 he ranks fourth in games, fourth in at bats, and eighth in sacrifices; he also hit the mark of 30+ doubles one year, and stole a total of 387 bases.

Without question he's among the better ever at his position, but an incredible -290 composite B.R. asks where he could be hidden in the batting order. This stat implies he couldn't hit a lick, but he did hit the .300+ B.Avg. mark once, exactly .300 for the Brooklyn club of 1894.

His career batting data read .256 B.Avg., .289 O.B.A., .335 SL.%, average for his time, certainly contrary to that -290 stat. His career runs scored count 1,184 and R.B.I. 1,135. No need to expound here about the veracity of "that" theory.

Twenty triples in 1894 and 15 in 1898 for Cincinnati imply he could both hit and run, well enough to play regularly; the whole of his batting data say this was the ideal number two in the batting order.

After 18 solid seasons in the major leagues, Corcoran was a minor league umpire and manager; his avocation was raising hunting dogs. In his latter years, he was a resident in a nursing home. Near the end Thomas William Corcoran, a genuine credit to the P.L., was still active and self sufficient.

COTTER, DANIEL JOSEPH   Dan Cotter
Born: April 14, 1867, Boston, Massachusetts
Died: September 4, 1935, Boston, Massachusetts
Height: Weight: Batted: Threw:
Major League Career: 1 Year, 1 Game
1889: Did Not Play
1891: Did Not Play
1890: P.L.: Buffalo Bisons; P1 (Debut Date: July 16)

Batting Record:

Games: 1	3B: 0	Walks: 0	SL.%: .000
At Bats: 4	HRs: 0	K's: 0	S.B: 0
Hits: 0	Runs: 0	B.Avg: .000	B.R:
2B: 0	R.B.I: 0	O.B.A:	F.R:

Pitching Record:

Won: 0	Starts: 1	K's: 0	E.R.A: 14.00
Lost: 1	C.G: 1	Walks: 7	Saves: 0
Win %: .000	I.P: 9	Hits: 18	P.R: -10
Games: 1	Sh.O: 0	O.B.%: .509	W.A.T: -0.4

There were a few one-year wonders in the Players League. This gentleman whom not much is known about was a one-game wonder. To his credit he finished what he started for the woeful Bisons of Buffalo.

It must have been like a conscious nightmare; he appeared at home plate four times, most likely with bat in hand; when he left the P.L. his batting record was a long string of zeros.

For a pitcher to win at a rate less than that of the Bisons, what could be said of that? Also consider his P.R. number(s). Not one "K" to show for nine innings but 25 earned base runners; when more than half the batters faced reach base by a combination of their skills and the pitcher's, and when the pitcher during that span watches 14 opponents tally runs, it's time to call an end to a career.

CRANE, EDWARD NICHOLAS   Ed Crane (Cannonball)
Born: May 1862, Boston, Massachusetts
Died: September 19, 1896, Rochester, New York
Height: 5'10.5".   Weight: 204 Lbs.   Batted: Right.   Threw: Right.
Major League Career: 9 Years, 391 Games (Pitched in 204)
1889: N.L.: New York
1891: A.A.: Cincinnati and N.L.: Cincinnati
1890: P.L.: New York Giants; P. 43

Batting Record:

Games: 43	3B: 4	Walks: 10	SL.%: .404
At Bats: 146	HRs: 0	K's: 26	S.B: 5
Hits: 46	Runs: 27	B.Avg: .315	B.R: +1
2B: 5	R.B.I: 16	O.B.A: .363	F.R: -1

Pitching Record:

Won: 16	Starts: 35	K's: 117	E.R.A: 4.64
Lost: 19	C.G: 28	Walks: 210	Saves: 0
Win %: .457	I.P: 330	Hits: 323	P.R: -15
Games: 43	Sh.O: 0	O.B.%: .376	W.A.T: -4.2

Thirty-nine of his cannonballs of 1890 have been recorded as wild pitches. This was a pitcher to beware, given both his nickname and style. He wasn't any sort of slouch in the batter's box either, having hit 12 HRs in his first year, 1884, for the Boston Reds of the erstwhile Union Association.

But 18 HRs in nine years, with 84+ R.B.I. and 199 runs scored don't make a terrific batter out of even a pitcher. His calculated bat-in-hand averages stand .238 B.Avg., .283 O.B.A., .329 SL.%, quite respectable for a wild pitcher.

His 1890 batting data are somewhat exceptional, also his overall pitching record for the third-place Giants. He was a workhorse, no doubt about that, with 330 I.P., though his 28 C.G. in 35 starts, 80 percent, rate below commendable for the time.

As they were, Crane was the least successful numerically among the four-man staff of New York, who shared the box quite equally. His won-lost record counts the difference between third place and second at season's end; his benchmark 210 walks in 1890 ranks 13th among all pitchers in all seasons.

His nickname was "Cannonball" and should have been "Grapeshot," which flies wilder: his 39 wild ones in 1890 rank nineteenth all time, and second during the period 1890–1899. His 145 career wild pitches rank 27th all time and 31 in 1892 are ninth for a season. He ranks sixth in wild pitches for the period 1876–1889.

Other than his proclivity toward aeronautical errancy when he projected the spheroid more or less toward home plate, and his losing win percentage, his numbers differ from his team's:

	Crane	Giants
O.B.%:	.376	.336
E.R.A:	4.64	4.17

The Giants were one of the P.L.'s top batting teams. A pitcher who wields an effective bat can make a difference, as to wit:

	Crane	Giants
B.Avg:	.315	.284
O.B.A:	.363	.352
SL.%:	.404	.404

The Giants led the P.L. in SL.%, and in HRs with 64, also with 1,018 runs scored; they were the only team to exceed .400, 50, and 1,000 respectively. They also led with 2.8 fielding wins, and with 450 made the fewest errors.

A pitcher can make a difference, and some teams can be winners without terrific pitching. As for Crane before and after the P.L. season, wildness aside, he matched his wins peak with 16 in 1892 for the Giants, but lost 24.

He pitched six shutouts during his career, won 72 and lost 96 for a .429 win %; with 720 K's and 887 walks; his career E.R.A. is 3.99. He isn't listed among the top career 100 in Hit Batsmen or high in that stat for the periods, so despite his nickname and his obvious lack of precision control, he wasn't too dangerous.

By the books, this Ed Crane not long after the P.L. played got behind in his rent payments and was given notice he was going to be evicted. He had been despondent, reacted by drinking heavily and brought his mortal life to a close by drinking a bottle of chloral.

CROSS, LAFAYETTE NAPOLEON　　　　　Lave Cross
Born: May 12, 1866, Milwaukee, Wisconsin
Died: September 6, 1927, Toledo, Ohio
Height: 5'8.5".　　Weight: 155 Lbs.　　Batted: Right.　　Threw: Right.
Major League Career: 21 Years, 2,274 Games
1889: A.A.: Philadelphia
1891: A.A.: Philadelphia
1890: Philadelphia Quakers; C 49, OF 15

Batting Record:

Games: 63	3B: 8	Walks: 12	SL.%: .429
At Bats: 245	HRs: 3	K's: 6	S.B: 5
Hits: 73	Runs: 42	B.Avg: .298	B.R: 0
2B: 7	R.B.I: 47	O.B.A: .331	F.R: +4

On his merits, he rates a "very good" grade as a P.L. player, with no faults evident, adequate power, and he could score a run. He produced better than ordinary at the bat and proved himself an asset to his team on defense no matter which position he was assigned to, though he played in only about half the Quakers games.

Cross was raised in Cleveland and ventured south to Louisville, where he began his extraordinarily long and very commendable career. His 1887 and 1888 seasons in that bastion of leisurely elegance were less than distinguished.

He moved north, to Philadelphia, where he played consecutively a total of 14 years, in four leagues, with distinction. He wasn't quite a P.L. star player; his prep year of 1889 (A.A.) was nearly lamentable except for a +15 F.R.

The P.L. season of Lave Cross was the first of many varying between good and terrific. Test his basics against league stats:

	Lave Cross	*Players League*
B.Avg:	.298	.274
O.B.A:	.331	.345
SL.%:	.429	.378

None of his led the league, nor were among the high fives, but Cross set more than a few records during his career. He reached the .300+ B.Avg. level five times, including what was likely an anomaly of .386 in 1894 for the Phillies.

His first .300+ season came the year after the P.L., with .301 for (N.L.) Philadelphia; he made 204 hits in 1894, and 191 in 1898. He also reached base via hits 191 times in 1902, but in an A.L. Philadelphia uniform.

His career B.Avg. is .292, with a .327 O.B.A., and .382 SL.%; all in good order; his only .400+ O.B.A. came in 1894, and his only mark above the .500+ SL.% level. He had 30+ doubles one year, scored 100+ runs once, 100+ R.B.I. three times.

Four hundred sixty-four walks in 9,068 at bats (5 percent), including one season of 600+, tell that he came to play rather than wishing for first base via the judgment of the umpire(s). His K's show 90, but are a full dozen years away from a complete count.

Clearly successful as a batter, his defense is on the edge of outstanding. With a +101 career F.R. total, including a year of +30, almost exclusively as a third baseman. His positions varied for two years after the P.L., then he became as much a fixture at the hot corner as he was in Philadelphia.

Beyond playing the game, Cross was an A.A. umpire in 1889, an N.L. umpire in 1892, and a manager for a baseball moment in 1899 for the worst team on record; he contributed eight wins and 30 losses (.211) to the Cleveland Spiders 20 and 134 (.130).

Cross the player was light years better than that. His 15 assists in a game is still a record; he's fourth all time among 3B with 2,304 putouts, 14th in assists with 3,703, 12th in errors with 394, and holds the highest F.% of 1800s 3B with .938.

At third base, Cross is also seventh all time in range factor with 3.49; his career assists adjusted to a 162-game season are 399.17, which ranks 15th all time among 3B.

Henry Chadwick wrote of Cross as having high character and being a professional exemplar. After baseball, through 1907, he worked as a factory machinist.

Lave Cross played in more than 2,000 major league games; he's nearly unique as a Players League player, with more R.B.I. than runs scored.

Lafayette Napoleon "Lave" Cross died of heart seizure.

CUNNINGHAM, ELSWORTH ELMER   Bert Cunningham
Born: November 25, 1866, Wilmington, Delaware
Died: May 14, 1952, Cragmere, Delaware
Height: Weight: 187 Lbs.   Batted: Right.   Threw: Right.
Major League Career: 12 Years, 341 Games
1889: A.A.: Baltimore
1891: A.A.: Baltimore
1890: P.L.: Philadelphia Quakers; P 14, OF1. Buffalo Bisons; P 25, OF 3

Batting Record:

	Phil	*Bflo*	*Totals*
Games:	15	28	43
At Bats:	52	101	153
Hits:	6	23	29
2B:	1	5	6
3B:	1	1	2
HRs:	0	0	0
Runs:	6	11	17
R.B.I:	3	11	14
Walks:	2	6	8
K's:	11	23	34
B.Avg:	.115	.228	.190
O.B.A:			
SL.%:	.203	.297	.242
S.B:	1	0	1
B.R:			
F.R:			

Pitching Record:

	Phil	*Bflo*	*Totals*
Won:	3	9	12
Lost:	9	15	24
Win %:	.250	.375	.333
Games:	14	25	39
Starts:	11	25	36
C.G:	11	24	35
I.P:	109	211	320
Sh.O:	0	2	2
K's:	33	78	111
Walks:	67	134	201
Hits:	133	251	384
O.B.%:	.407	.405	.406
E.R.A:	5.28	5.84	5.65
Saves:	0	0	0
P.R:	-13	-38	-50
W.A.T:	-3.2	+2.0	-1.2

Many a way it's been written and said, "This guy is pretty good." This guy was less than that. Twelve years, 143–167, .461, E.R.A. of 4.23, not the stuff of 1800s winners, or pretty good pitchers. He couldn't hit a lick either; only his P.L. stats need be read.

Bert Cunningham, pitcher in the P.L. for two teams, not nearly good, then a bit better than that for a team which was terrible. As he didn't do credit to them or himself, it might have been, as some players are valued for intangibles, the 1890 case for Cunningham.

Something must have been the case, at least a factor, to play in the bigs for as long as he did. Consider some standards, then measure Cunningham 1890 against the P.L. 1890, and again against his career (1887 through 1901).

	Bert 1890	P.L. 1890	Bert Career
Win %:	.333	.500	.461
O.B.%:	.406	.345	.368
E.R.A:	5.65	4.23	4.23

He won 22 games in 1888 for Baltimore (A.A.) and lost 29 (.431); he won 28 games in 1898 for Louisville (N.L.) and lost 15 (.651); by leaps and bounds this was his best season, but the Colonels finished ninth (of 12).

Cunningham topped 300+ I.P. each of four years, 453 in 1888 were his most. Seven hundred eighteen career K's and 1,064 walks ratio isn't good; nor is two shutouts in 241 starts. His 201 walks in 1890 beat the benchmark for awful measured against 111 K's.

It was said that Cunningham was ineffective for some reason. He displayed a wildness in the first few innings, after which he settled down, albeit too late. It had to be said he was not a winner.

For the period 1890–1899 he's noted as 10th in hit batters, and ranks second in balks (all four in 1899, not a fault commonly called), but there's another side to this not pretty good pitcher. Quite to the contrary, SABR says "A pretty good pitcher, with a fast ball ... erractic ... his personal habits were exemplary."

With his good side found, in his good year he won 11 consecutive decisions, was an N.L. umpire in 1896 and 1897, and 1900–1901. After baseball he worked as a typewriter salesman. By logical science, if not not pretty good then perhaps not bad either.

DAILY, CORNELIUS F.   Con Daily
Born: September 11, 1864, Blackstone, Massachusetts
Died: June 14, 1928, Brooklyn, New York
Height: 6'0".   Weight: 192 Lbs.   Batted: Left.   Threw:
Major League Career: 13 Years, 630 Games
1889: N.L.: Indianapolis
1891: N.L.: Brooklyn
1890: P.L.: Brooklyn Wonders; C 40, 1B 6, OF 1

Batting Record:

Games: 46	3B: 3	Walks: 15	SL.%: .321
At Bats: 168	HRs: 0	K's: 14	S.B: 6
Hits: 42	Runs: 20	B.Avg: .250	B.R: -7
2B: 6	R.B.I: 35	O.B.A: .315	F.R: -10

He shared a proper first name with a gentleman of much fame. There the similarities end except that both toiled as catchers, in the case of Con Daily it was for 13 years, all part time.

Con Daily also did stints as a National League umpire in 1886, 1891, 1894, and 1896; he could have been the umpire who once put Connie Mack the manager out of a game.

The data for reserve catcher Daily include a batting average best of .320 in 1891, in 206 at bats for N.L. Brooklyn; his next best was .265 in 1893. With a .378 O.B.A. in 1891, and an SL.% a point higher, his other calculated stats follow the same pattern.

He wasn't a producer of runs, not in 1890 or 1891 or any other year, not with career totals of 280 scored and 262 R.B.I. via 541 hits in 2,222 at bats. As further evidence attest his .243 career B.Avg., .314 O.B.A and .299 SL.%, and -70 B.R. with not one positive number to be found in a column of 13.

His defense by SABR-stats is somewhat better, a -10 F.R. which, for a reserve catcher and utility player at all the positions except pitcher in his 630 games, is credible although negative.

Having begun with Philadelphia of the Union Association, passing through N.L. Providence, Boston, and Indianapolis, he went to Brooklyn for the Players League season, and stayed for five more in the city then borough, all in service with N.L. clubs.

He switched to Chicago to play in nine games his final year, to produce a .074 B.Avg. etc. Some bad years are worse than others.

His by all means mediocre major league baseball career ended heroically: Cornelius F. Daily fractured his spinal cord while trying to save a drowning child.

DALEY, WILLIAM   Bill Daley

Born: June 27, 1868, Poughkeepsie, New York
Died: May 4, 1922, Poughkeepsie New York
Height: Weight: Batted: Threw: Left.
Major League Career: 3 Years, 62 Games
1889: N.L.: Boston
1891: A.A.: Boston
1890: P.L.: Boston Reds; P 34, OF 3

Batting Record:

Games: 37	3B: 0	Walks: 9	SL.%: .218
At Bats: 110	HRs: 2	K's: 15	S.B: 1
Hits: 17	Runs: 14	B.Avg: .155	B.R:
2B: 1	R.B.I: 7	O.B.A:	F.R:

Pitching Record:

Won: 18	Starts: 25	K's: 110	E.R.A: 3.60
Lost: 7	C.G: 19	Walks: 167	Saves: 2
Win %: .720	I.P: 235	Hits: 246	P.R: +17
Games: 34	Sh.O: 2	O.B.%: .396	W.A.T: +3.8

1890 was the midpoint of his career, and surely the high point. The years before and after show won-lost records of 11–9, better than average but no match for his season with the P.L. Boston Reds.

His team won the pennant, and he was significant; his won-lost of 18 and 7 counts almost exactly the difference between championship and second place, that difference having been 6.5 games.

Pitcher Bill Daley led the P.L. in Win %; in wins (above) against team he ranks fifth. That's quite a pair of achievements, even though 25 starts weren't considered many then, and 68 percent complete not a mark to rate high esteem.

His contribution to the pursuit of the pennant at the bat was (charitably) minimal, and credit surely is due his supporting cast while in the pitcher's box; 400+ opponents getting on base in 235 innings, to achieve a 3.60 E.R.A. must have involved much defensive assistance.

His personal record is lacking physical essentials. His term as a major league pitcher was brief. A data sketch might somewhat amend the void, and quantitatively depict the magnitude of the contribution of Daley to the Boston Reds and P.L. cause.

	Boston 1889 N.L.	*Boston 1890 P.L.*	*Boston 1891 A.A.*
Won:	3	18	8
Lost:	3	7	6
Win %:	.500	.720	.571
O.B. %:	.379	.396	.374
E.R.A.	4.31	3.60	2.98
W.A.T:	-0.6	+3.8	-1.2

He left the game when the A.A. left the scene, for reasons not known; as for his most exceptional season among three, near as he could be to being a Players League star player, his potential will never be known.

After his somewhat distinguished and very brief career, Daley worked in the rolling mill of a factory, and in an opera house.

William Daley died of heart disease. In one respect he was the most successful pitcher in the Players League.

DARLING, CONRAD   Dell Darling
Born: December 21, 1861, Erie, Pennsylvania
Died: November 20, 1904, Erie, Pennsylvania

Height: 5'8".   Weight: 170 Lbs.   Batted: Right.   Threw: Right.
Major League Career: 6 Years, 175 Games
1889: N.L.: Chicago
1891: A.A.: St. Louis
1890: P.L.: Chicago Pirates; 1B 29, SS 15, C 9, OF 7, 2B 3, 3B 2

Batting Record:

Games: 58	3B: 4	Walks: 29	SL.%: .376
At Bats: 221	HRs: 2	K's: 28	S.B: 5
Hits: 57	Runs: 45	B.Avg: .258	B.R: -1
2B: 12	R.B.I: 39	O.B.A: .352	F.R: 0

How Conrad became Dell is a mystery, perhaps done by a whim of a baseball writer poet laureate. He was a National League umpire in 1887 as "Conrad" and an American Association umpire in 1891 by the name of "Dell C."

As a Players League player he did fairly, certainly kept busy, and less pitching worked part time at all the positions. For the sum of his six-year career 175 games doesn't translate to busy. The year of 1890 was his busiest. The next year would be his last.

His defense reads well enough, no negative F.R. marks, a +2 in 1889; all the others are zero, including the slot for 1890. Other than filling roster spots for the Pirates of Chicago, Darling was almost exclusively a catcher, for which zeroes in F.R. are commendable, even though the stat is adjusted to position.

He wasn't fast or crafty on the base paths, as explained by a career total of 29 stolen bases, including 19 in 1887, when an S.B. often as not was an administrative gift.

His 1890 walks, half as many as hits, say patient at home plate, which can be an asset to players and teams; 18 extra base hits among 57 are impressive, suggesting that when he did swing and connect, he did so with sufficient force to drive the ball some considerable distance.

Ten percent K's among at bats does not impress, not for a utility or any 1800s player, whether or not a powerful batter. Nor do 91 walks versus 96 K's impress, and less so among 628 career at bats. His career .240 B.Avg., .340 O.B.A., and .354 SL.% compared with his P.L. data say Darling was near his batting prime in 1890.

A B.Avg. of .258 grounded in 57 hits is very near the composite historical mean average; when the 57 is isolated and correlated with 45 runs scored, it equates to 79 percent and production success. As runs are the essence of the game, 39 R.B.I. as the result of 57 hits, or 68 percent, also equates with success, well above ordinary.

His .352 O.B.A. being near 100 points higher than his .258 B.Avg. satisfies the standard for span excellence between stats, but .258 and etc. all miss the benchmarks by considerable margins.

For Darling then, only 1887 (Chicago, N.L.) was a better season statistically than 1890; with 45 hits he achieved a .319 B.Avg., .411 O.B.A., and .489 SL.%, stellar numbers. Just a bit of manipulation, a few couched words, and Dell could tilt the scales of excellence in the record books.

After his relatively brief and arguably average major league baseball career, he owned and operated a restaurant and was an employee of a coal company.

The cause of death of Conrad "Dell" Darling is uncertain, but has been written of as related to declining health, and also to an old baseball injury.

DELAHANTY, EDWARD JAMES   Ed Delahanty (Big Ed)
Born: October 30, 1867, Cleveland, Ohio
Died: July 2, 1903, Niagara Falls, New York
Height: 6'1". Weight: 170 Lbs. Batted: Right. Threw: Right.
Major League Career: 16 Years, 1,835 Games
1889: N.L.: Philadelphia
1891: N.L.: Philadelphia
1890: P.L.: Cleveland Infants; SS 76, 2B 20, OF 18, 3B 3, 1B 1

Batting Record:

Games: 115	3B: 13	Walks: 24	SL.%: .416
At Bats: 517	HRs: 3	K's: 30	S.B: 25
Hits: 154	Runs: 107	B.Avg: .298	B.R: 0
2B: 26	R.B.I: 64	O.B.A: .339	F.R: -11

He might have been the greatest player that ever crossed the foul lines, some expert historians have opined affirmatively. What is certain is that his fine career was cut short by his untimely and perhaps mysterious death. It was judiciously ruled accidental, but it could have been suicide, or otherwise.

During the season when the P.L. played, Ed Delahanty played out of position most of the time; the results may be found in his numbers, or perhaps he had not yet reached his prime, which extended through a decade and could have been longer.

Whichever, the clearest evidence is in his numbers; compare P.L. and career, assess the appendages, and consider.

	P.L.	Career	All time	Ranks
B.Avg:	.298	.346	B. Avg.	Fifth
O.B.A.	.339	.412	O.B.A.	27th
SL.%:	.416	.505	SL.%	56th

By the combination of O.B.A. and SL.% Delahanty counts .917 and ranks 37th in baseball history, and further among period stats 1899–1899 ranks: sixth in games; seventh in at bats; third in runs; first in hits; first in doubles; second in triples; second in HRs; second in R.B.I.; first in extra base hits; first in total bases.

These stats don't tell all, though, not by a Canadian mile. He led his league in B.Avg. twice, batted .300+ 12 times, which includes two seasons of .400+; he led twice in O.B.A., among nine seasons of .400+, and is one of the very rare few with an O.B.A. of .500+. He led in SL.% five times, reached .500+ eight times; twice he exceeded .600+ in SL.%, in the 1800s.

Delahanty scored 100+ runs 10 years. He reached 100+ R.B.I. seven years and led three years. He once led in hits and three times had 200+. He also led in triples once, with seven years of 15+, including 21.

Sufficient? Continue. The great ones can do everything with the bat when the ball is put in play. But, was he the greatest?

Nineteen, 13, 11 and 10 HRs in 1800s seasons, his most led a league. Half his K's data are missing; 741 walks don't count at all among 7,505 at bats. As for the B.R. SABR-stat, this might have been devised for Delahanty; he would have led in that if it had been part of the official records then: five times, once with +70, six times above +50. His career B.R. total: +562.

Add 30+ doubles each of 11 years; the Infants managers didn't see this star among the masses and misplayed him to the level of an ordinary star, not even a Players League star. How they missed is some kind of question. Continue the facts of Delahanty.

He regularly recorded 500+ at bats, commensurate with number of games played; add 455 stolen bases to the record, and +54 F.R., best +27, seldom negative. There's more.

He ranks 15th all time with 182 triples (tied). His career assists per 162-game season equate to 29.29, 10th best all time among outfielders. Another source shows 13th in triples with 185; spectacular stars can cause statistical chaos. And more.

Ed Delahanty ranks second among 1800s players in extra base hits with 808, and third in total bases. And more. He had six hits in a game twice, once on June 2, 1890; he hit four HRs in one game in 1896, perhaps this was the game he produced 17 total bases.

He once broke a pitched ball in two pieces. That Ed Delahanty was not a one- or two- or three-dimensional player is fact of evidence. His throwing arm was strong and accurate, his quick release a distinct advantage. He remains one of few to lead both the N.L. and A.L. in batting stats, but his name is not be found among the Players League batting leaders, or any other category.

SABR texts include a comprehensive biography, alleging that he was a big spender, a big eater and a big drinker. Many an author has written the same of George Herman "Babe" Ruth. Also said of both was they were big showboaters, which both lived up to in many ways.

SABR tells the facts of the demise of Ed Delahanty as they officially have been written, but do not mention that this would have set off an international incident of fireworks proportions, if any speculations or literary imaginings had been publicized.

A subtle version of the story tells that he left his Senators team in Detroit to head for New York City; he was angry, and intent to argue. A deal, a transaction which involved him had fallen through; he might not have cared who he would confront, though it's been said the man he most wanted was John McGraw.

A few months earlier the two major leagues made a deal to stop raiding for players, and this was somehow related; Mr. McGraw would have been part of any such deal. He was involved in most every deal and issue connected with the game then.

SABR tactfully blames suppressed anger for what ensued, and it's possible that he's the only person in history to die as he did. He boarded a train in Detroit; by many accounts he got roaring drunk and extremely abusive, mostly with the conductors.

The train took a shortcut through Canada, to Buffalo, then crossed back into the U.S. Something happened, then and there; what is not certain. The official cause of death of Ed Delahanty is that he drowned when he went over Niagara Falls, some 30 miles from that scrawny bridge high above the Niagara River.

The span between the town of Fort Erie, Ontario, and Buffalo, New York, is vast, perhaps a mile; its depth is measured in hundreds of feet. The current, perhaps better said torrent, was and is swift, and as insidious as nature has made anything.

He was put off the train, the official version tells, at Fort Erie, and staggered onto that high scrawny bridge. Did he fall? Was he pushed? Was he dead before his body hit the river? Did he die of shock as he fell, suddenly stunned out of his drunken stupor? Was he dead, by accident or intent, before he was put off that train? A maze of possibilities existed and still exists.

Ed Delahanty certainly did not die as he went over the American Niagara Falls; of that there is absolutely no doubt, no matter what was reported in the media, drawn from the official records.

He didn't play up to his potential in 1890, no doubt of that either; probable cause has been presented. Was he great? Was he the greatest player of his time? Of all time? There are many more and very relevant questions.

1890 was the only year he wore a Cleveland uniform. Otherwise from 1888 through 1901 he was in the service of N.L. Philadelphia, then jumped to Washington of the A.L. He set 11 season records and hold four of the top 10 ranks in the O.B.A. stat in all history.

DeWALD, CHARLES H.   Charlie DeWald
Born: 1867, Newark New Jersey
Died: August 22, 1904, Cleveland, Ohio
Height: Weight: Batted: Threw: Left.
Major League Career: 1 Year, 2 Games
1889: Did not play
1891: Did not play
1890: P.L.: Cleveland Infants; P 2 (Debut Date: September 2)

Batting Record:

Games: 2	3B: 0	Walks: 0	SL.%: .375
At Bats: 8	HRs: 0	K's: 2	S.B: 0
Hits: 3	Runs: 1	B.Avg: .375	B.R:
2B: 0	R.B.I: 3	O.B.A:	F.R:

Pitching Record:

Won: 2	Starts: 2	K's: 5	E.R.A: 0.64
Lost: 0	C.G: 2	Walks: 6	Saves: 0
Win %: 1.000	I.P: 14	Hits: 13	P.R: +6
Games: 2	Sh.O: 0	O.B.%: .325	W.A.T: +1.0

This Cleveland Infants pitcher was a one-year wonder who pitched and played in at least parts of two Players League games. His won-lost record says he was rather terrific, and none of his pitching data dispute this.

In fact the data show his two victories as brief but complete games; the time of year or inclement weather might explain why just 14 innings were played. When Ernie Banks said, "Let's play two!" with his usual enthusiasm, he probably didn't mean seven-inning games.

It isn't known from which side DeWald batted, but whichever it was resulted in a terrific .375 batting average. This one-year and two-game wonder doesn't seem to have any deficiencies at all. The question begs, why is there no more to the career record of this young perfect pitcher and terrific batter?

Check out his E.R.A.; nobody's ever done that over the course of any season. Charlie DeWald did it for the Cleveland Infants of the Players League. Other pitchers have gone through a season unbeaten, but when double figures are brought into play, Elroy Face of the 1959 Pittsburgh Pirates was the closest to perfect.

He won 18 and lost one; the nearest to perfect in the other league after 1900 was Tom Zachary of the 1928 Yankees who won 12 without a loss, and had the distinction of serving home run number 60 the year before that to Babe Ruth, while with the Senators.

Less than a decade after 1890 the people of Cleveland would be shouting and screaming for the heads of their baseball club's owners, the notorious Robison brothers, as in "Off with them!" Of Charlie DeWald the chants would have been more on the order of "More of him!" And why not? Everybody loves a winner!

After his singular career, he was superintendent of cemeteries. Charles H. DeWald (or Dewald) died from declining health.

DOE, ALFRED GEORGE   Fred Doe (Count)
Born: April 18, 1864, Rockport, Massachusetts
Died: October 4, 1938, Quincey, Massachusetts
Height: 5'10".   Weight: 165 Lbs.   Batted: Right.   Threw: Right.
Major League Career: 1 Year, 2 Games
1889: Did not play
1891: Did not play
1890: P.L.: Buffalo Bisons; P 1 (Debut Date: August 23). Pittsburgh Burghers; P 1

Batting Record:

	Bflo	Pitt	Totals
Games:	1	1	2
At Bats:	2	2	4
Hits:	0	1	1
2B:	0	0	0
3B:	0	0	0
HRs:	0	0	0
Runs:	0	0	0
R.B.I:	0	0	0
Walks:	0	0	0
K's:			0

Pitching Record:

	Bflo	Pitt	Totals
Won:	0	0	0
Lost:	1	0	1
Win %:	.000	—	.000
Games:	1	1	2
Starts:	1	0	1
C.G:	1	0	1
I.P:	6	4	10
Sh.O:	0	0	0
K's:	2	2	4
Walks:	7	2	9

Batting Record:

	Bflo	Pitt	Totals
B.Avg:	.000	.500	.250
O.B.A:			
SL.%:	.000	.500	.250
S.B:	0	0	0
B.R:			
F.R:			

Pitching Record:

	Bflo	Pitt	Totals
Hits:	10	4	14
O.B.%:	.514	.359	.462
E.R.A:	12.00	4.50	9.00
Saves:	0	0	0
P.R:	-5	-0	-5
W.A.T:	-0.4	0.0	-0.4

Nicknames of the players were terrific in the 1800s; one of the best was "Count Doe" as in Dracula, for what ever reason Alfred Doe was stuck with that appellation. Another quaint distinction: he was a Players League one-game wonder twice.

Buffalo and Pittsburgh are only a few hours apart by road; for Alfred Doe the distance represented a major league baseball career. It was not a distinguished career, and by the evidence neither he nor management lingered in making prudent decisions.

He could hit, and proved it once, which is once more than many dreamers have achieved. But the fact that he saved his hit for Pittsburgh somehow doesn't seem fair; bad as the Burghers were, the Bisons were much more in need, of even a single.

Apparently he also saved his best pitching effort for Pittsburgh, thus the desperate Bisons were doubly denied. As they are, his numbers are revealing; 10 hits and seven walks in six innings should equate to about a 12.00 E.R.A.; although 14 and nine of the same should calculate better, the actual 9.00 calculation means just an earned run per inning.

Count Doe later was a minor league umpire and a polo player.

DUFFY, HUGH　　　　　Hugh Duffy
Born: November 26, 1866, Cranston, Rhode Island
Died: October 19, 1954, Boston, Massachusetts
Height: 5'7".　　Weight: 168 Lbs.　　Batted: Right.　　Threw: Right.
Major League Career: 17 Years, 1,737 Games
1889: N.L.: Chicago
1891: A.A.: Boston
1890: P.L.: Chicago Pirates; OF 138

Batting Record:

Games: 138	3B: 16	Walks: 59	SL.%: .470
At Bats: 596	HRs: 7	K's: 20	S.B: 78
Hits: 191	Runs: 161	B.Avg: .320	B.R: +24
2B: 36	R.B.I: 82	O.B.A: .384	F.R: +12

Somebody really should write a book about this Players League star player, a whole book, and via due diligence ascertain if his place of birth was Cranston or River Point. Beyond that, nearly 90 years of life allow for much extraneous material.

Prominently note that Hugh Duffy played in two centuries, and did so for more than a decade at a spectacular level. Dare not omit the fact that at Fenway Park (opened April 20, 1912) in 1953, then 86 years of age, Hugh Duffy was the batter during Red Sox infield practice.

He had been a sensational outfielder and line drive hitter and also had great speed. The sum of his array of abilities is well documented by a bronze plaque enshrined in that grand edifice at Cooperstown, New York, which has been in place since 1945.

In 1890 Duffy played in all 138 games for the Chicago Pirates, all in the outfield; manager Comiskey had no problem filling in one slot in the game reports.

Duffy led the P.L. in hits and in runs. His B.R. stands high, but wasn't among the high five. His SABR-stat denotes a very positive +12 F.R., attesting to his defensive skills. In fact, his 34 assists in 1890 rank 30th all time for an outfielder.

His batting averages are also all well above the norm, but not among the P.L.'s high fives. He ranks fourth in the P.L. in doubles, third in stolen bases, and second in total bases, with one less base than necessary to tie for the top spot.

Returning to his great speed, in 1890 Duffy stole 78 bases, and a total of 574 during his 17 major league seasons, although by another count he stole 599; baseball greats = calculated chaos. His personal biographer could likely ascertain the correct number.

There is little dispute that his .438 or .440 batting average in 1894 (Boston, N.L.) ranks first all time among all batters, in all seasons; the .438 for many years the prevailing datum, the .440 represents a recent item of information.

His 85 extra base hits in 1894 ties for the 1800s high, but the whole of this season's counts must be included, as this is perhaps the greatest individual season in history. (Let an asterisk signify league leader.)

At Bats: 539	3B: 15	R.B.I: 145 (*)	Walks: 66
Hits: 237 (*)	HRs: 18 (*)	O.B.A: .502	K's: 15
2B: 51 (*)	Runs: 161	SL.%: .690 (*)	S.B: 48

A chapter of typical length might not suffice to enable proper articulation on just these dozen bits of data; the literature notes that he excelled on defense, hit 18 HRs one year, demonstrated speed and defense, and that hit for average and with power. That's the National Baseball Hall of Fame equation.

Hugh Duffy, Players League, 1890: 59 walks, 20 K's, the ratio is obvious; 20 K's, 598 at bats, equally; 59 extra base hits, 191 total hits, ditto. The P.L. bottom line on Duffy: he was, overall, outstanding.

His career was no less than that, to begin: eight straight years of batting .300+, 10 years in all. He played 120+ games each year 1889 through 1899. His O.B.A. was .400+ five years and his S.L.% .500+ just once, but worth repeating that was .600+, in the 1800s, near .700.

Another source shows a .694 SL.% in 1894; that's 32nd highest in history for an 1800s player. Duffy scored 100+ runs each of nine years, his P.L. datum of 161 is 13th highest of all time; add 100+ R.B.I. eight years, 145 ranks 49th all time.

Further: 200+ hits twice and his 237 ranks 17th all time (tied). He hit 30+ doubles each of three years, including (33rd) that 51. Hugh Duffy was great in 1890 and better in 1894; this is the litany of his period stats for 1890–1899. First in games; first in at bats; second in runs; second in hits; second in doubles; first in HRs; first in R.B.I.; seventh in sacrifices; third in extra base hits; second in total bases; third in stolen bases.

He hit 15+ triples twice, 10+ HRs three years, collected 50+ walks each of nine years, and stole 50+ bases four years, with a high of 85 in 1891 for A.A. Boston.

He began in 1888 in N.L. Chicago and continued there in 1889. After 1891 he went with the only Boston team and continued there through 1900. Then came a season in Milwaukee (A.L.), on a clear day a visible neighbor to the "Windy City, the hog butcher to the World."

He played in only 79 games in 1901 in the "City of Braumeisters" (disculpe, St. Louis), producing a .302 B.Avg., .339 O.B.A., and .439 SL.%; his abilities had clearly diminished to excellent.

He didn't play in the major leagues again until 1904, in the "City of Brotherly Love" for the Phillies, where he continued till 1906. The whole of this involved only 34 games, and he could hardly produce a .300 and stole only three bases in the 34 games; not only his formidable batting skills had been lost, but his speed.

This would not be a proper end to a star of the magnitude of Hugh Duffy; his career B.R. count is +286, with four season above +30, including an incredible +77 B.R. in "The Hugh Duffy Year." His career F.R. mark is otherwise with a -28 sum total, mostly single digits, the only positive exception a +12 F.R. in 1890.

He was the field manager for many major league teams, all or parts of eights years; he won 535 and lost 671 for a .444 win %. He continued to be part of the game, some years as a minor league manager through 1922.

He and Tommy McCarthy, "The Heavenly Twins" of Boston, owned a saloon while still players. He was a recruiter for Milwaukee in 1900 after leaving the Boston club, while the A.L. was in the process of evolving to the status of major league.

Later he was a Boston (N.L.) scout for three years, and then a Boston (A.L.) Scout until 1953. During his playing career, he established 11 season records; as an elder for recreation he batted for fielding practice a half century later.

Some stars shine brighter and longer than others. Mark the name of Hugh Duffy as a Players League star player and member of the National Baseball Hall of Fame. Some stars, much brighter, much longer, perhaps properly, Hugh Duffy died at home.

DUNLAP, FREDERICK C.   **Fred Dunlap (Sure Shot)**
Born: May 21, 1859, Philadelphia, Pennsylvania
Died: December 1, 1902, Philadelphia, Pennsylvania
Height: 5'8".   Weight: 165 Lbs.   Batted: Right.   Threw: Right.
Major League Career: 12 Years, 965 Games
1889: N.L.: Pittsburgh
1891: A.A.: Washington

1890: N.L.: Pittsburgh
P.L.: New York Giants; 2B 1

Batting Record:

Games: 1	3B: 0	Walks: 0	SL.%: .500
At Bats: 4	HRs: 0	K's: 0	S.B: 0
Hits: 2	Runs: 1	B.Avg: .500	B.R: 0
2B: 0	R.B.I: 0	O.B.A: .500	F.R: 0

(It's hard to follow Hugh Duffy, very hard.)

Fred Dunlap virtually owned the top rank in the stats of the Union Association of 1884 (let an asterisk signify league leader) while playing for the league champion St. Louis Maroons club:

At Bats: 449	HRs: 13 (*)	.B.Avg: .412 (*)	K's: N/A
Hits:185 (*)	Runs: 160 (*)	O.B.A: .448 (*)	S.B: N/A
2B: 39	R.B.I: N/A	SL.%: .621 (*)	B.R: +72 (*)
3B: 8	F.R: +25 (*)	Walks: 29	

Some stars prevail over a veritable galaxy of data. In 1884 he practically owned the game on the U.A. fields of play. But in 1890 his capabilities had returned from the stratosphere of baseball statistics.

In fact, in 1890 he hardly played in the Players League at all; in New York City all that was required to jump from the N.L. to the P.L. was to walk around the block, or jump over a canvas cloth fence. His journey to join the Brotherhood involved a great deal more, including his making void an existing legal contract.

He played only 17 games for the Pittsburgh (N.L.) Alleghenys, down from 121 the previous year; he'd only play eight more games after the P.L. year. At Pittsburgh, he'd scored nine times, via seven walks and 11 hits, in 64 at bats, a .172 B.Avg. "Sure Shot" had been a star, illustrious; now he had become like a shadow.

He'd been behind home plate in 1879, the seminal year of the reviled reserve clause of obligatory servitude to perpetuity if the owner so chose. This was before he ever took a stance in a major league batter's box as a player. He began as an umpire.

Dunlap had been made an orphan before age 10, then had been taken in by an older couple with little enthusiasm for education or for kids; baseball became his coping mechanism. As his story has been written by SABR, his 1890 N.L. club released him on the 15th of May, perhaps as an early birthday tribute.

He was accepted by the New York (P.L.) Giants club; he played in one game, then sat out through the balance of the playing season. He resumed the next year, with the Washington (D.C.) Statesmen of the A.A., only to suffer a broken leg on April 20.

An erroneous account elsewhere of Fred Dunlap tells that he was the first and fastest in the A.A. to jump to the P.L. His career did include part-time service as a manager, in 1882 with Cleveland (N.L.) and in 1885 with St. Louis (N.L.)

He was also the field manager with St. Louis (U.A.) For 83 games, of which the team won 66 (.805 win %), of their total record (literally) 94 won and 19 lost, .834, perhaps matched or bettered once or twice in the annals of baseball history.

Though 1884 was surely the year for Dunlap, he did achieve one negative note; not his one game played in the outfield that season, but as a pitcher; he took a quick turn in the pitcher's box, one inning in one game, and took a loss, one of the 19.

Another source shows his won-lost as 0–0, worked an inning, and by calculations done a century later, would have earned a save. Disparity continues; his E.R.A. stands at either 13.50 or 18.00; but no matter all that.

Dunlap never used a fielder's glove; he had hands small as a woman's. He's ninth all time among 2B with 498 errors. Al Spink allegedly wrote of "Sure Shot" in 1910, "Far and away the greatest second baseman that ever lived."

He was also a wonderful ground coverer, having it over every other fielder in this respect.

In the Players League, this one-game wonder achieved zero in both B.R. and F.R.; but he did make plate appearances, which calculate to a .500 batting average, and he slugged at the same rate, arbitrarily comparable to his Union Association season.

Frederick C. Dunlap, foremost of the Union Association, died of rectal disorder. As a major league player, he hit 30+ doubles each of two years; he ranks 10th in doubles for the period 1876–1889, and he scored a run for the Giants of the Players League.

DUZEN, WILLIAM GEORGE   Bill Duzen
Born: February 21, 1870, Buffalo, New York
Died: March 11, 1944, Buffalo, New York
Height: 5'11".   Weight: 165 Lbs.   Batted: Right.   Threw: Right.
Major League Career: 1 Year, 2 Games
1889: Did not play
1891: Did not play
1890: P.L.: Buffalo Bisons; P 2

Batting Record:

Games: 2	3B: 0	Walks: 3	SL.%: .500
At Bats: 4	HRs: 0	K's: 0	S.B: 0
Hits: 1	Runs: 2	B.Avg: .250	B.R:
2B: 1	R.B.I: 1	O.B.A:	F.R:

Pitching Record:

Won: 0	Starts: 2	K's: 5	E.R.A: 13.85
Lost: 2	C.G: 2	Walks: 14	Saves: 0
Win %: .000	I.P: 13	Hits: 20	P.R: -14
Games: 2	Sh.O: 0	O.B.%: .494	W.A.T: -0.9

Duzen was born in Buffalo, New York, and was likely a lifelong resident. Buffalo historically has had a prominent Polish population among its whole. What his credentials were to merit a test with the P.L. Bisons of 1890 is not known. Very likely, the fact of his surname isn't known either.

He didn't play much, or achieve much, this two-game wonder Players League player. The peculiar surname strikes close to home for this author; perhaps Duszynski or another variation, but Duzen doesn't historically fit Buffalo, and prejudice by ethnicity was a prominent fact of life in the 1800s U.S.A.

Still is in fact; that hasn't changed, except that condition of the American mind has migrated to at least one sector of the American Southwest and is as pervasive as Hitlerism there, and has evolved as insidious as any such sickness ever has, no matter the culture, economy, polity.

Duzen pitching didn't fit the Buffalo model either; two stars and two games complete, 13 I.P. tell his games were short if not quick. This somewhat impressive part of his record predicts good things to come for this youngster who had just reached age of majority.

But a 13.85 E.R.A. quickly removed an illusions; nearly half the batters he faced getting on base decreed his future. After the fact his -14 P.R. documents his potential, and that he lost both his decisions concludes his career.

Duzen as a batter evidently could judge the strike zone better than Duzen the pitcher. He left the Bisons after his cameo show to find a real job; he was a member of the Buffalo Police Department for 44 years.

William George Duzen died of a heart attack.

DWYER, JOHN FRANCIS   Frank Dwyer
Born: March 25, 1868, Lee, Massachusetts
Died: February 4, 1943, Pittsfield, Massachusetts
Height: 5'8".   Weight: 145 Lbs.   Batted: Right.   Threw: Right.
Major League Career: 12 Years, 365 Games
1889: N.L.: Chicago
1891: A.A.: Cincinnati
1890: P.L.: Chicago Pirates; P 12, OF 4

Batting Record:
Games: 16	3B: 0	Walks: 0	SL.%: .302
At Bats: 53	HRs: 0	K's: 2	S.B: 1
Hits: 14	Runs: 10	B.Avg: .264	B.R:
2B: 2	R.B.I: 11	O.B.A:	F.R:

Pitching Record:
Won: 3	Starts: 6	K's:17	E.R.A: 6.23
Lost: 6	C.G: 6	Walks: 25	Saves: 1
Win %: .333	I.P: 69	Hits: 98	P.R: -16
Games: 12	Sh.O: 0	O.B.%: .400	W.A.T: -1.7

A young college man when he arrived for P.L. play, he'd served as an N.L. umpire the prior year while pitching for the White Stockings of (N.L.) Chicago. He'd resume again as an official in 1893, continue through 1897, then 1899 and 1901, and again in 1904 with the A.L.

Twelve years as a pitcher then was a long career, and he did well enough with it, averaging nearly 15 wins a year, nine years of which he had the best win % on his team. 1890 though, was not a good year for Frank Dwyer as a pitcher, the Pirates of Chicago had a genuinely dynamic duo who did much better.

By his averages, his 1890 batting was also not up to standards, but his ratios of hits to runs and R.B.I. are terrific, given the small numbers to consider. His data fact of zero walks and 53 at bats is very odd, his two K's nearly as unusual.

Some of his points to ponder might be explained by his games played in the outfield, but his power factor asks why not with greater regularity? But he came to P.L. Chicago as a pitcher, and that must be given first consideration.

Finishing all his starts rates well, and he worked often in relief; his walks to innings are typical, but factor in his hits allowed and that rates below the P.L. norm, which was high for the time, if not excessively so.

But oddly his opponents allowed on base total reads quite well, contrary to both his E.R.A. and his P.R. Clearly he wasn't up to the level of his Pirates staff mates.

Given his age in the P.L. year, his best was yet to come, and did; he won 24 in 1896 for Cincinnati, lost 11 (a .686 win %); this was his personal high in wins. He worked for the Reds from the latter part of 1892 (19–10, 21–18 for the year) through 1899.

The career totals of Frank Dwyer, college man, include 176 won and 152 lost, .537, 3.85 E.R.A.; K's count 563 and walks 764, his other data are comparable. Three years he won 19, three others 18, while all along pitching for a middle of the pack team.

He made the rolls of period stats for 1890–1899, positively and otherwise; he ranks eighth in losses, eighth in games, and ninth in innings pitched (tied). He resigned as a major league pitcher after the 1899 season, then was a college coach and scout.

In 1924 Dwyer became one of the first major league staff coaches, for John McGraw, and he was a member of the New York State Boxing Commission.

John Francis Dwyer died of a heart attack.

EWING, WILLIAM**Buck Ewing**
Born: December 25, 1859, Hoaglands, Ohio
Died: October 20, 1906, Cincinnati, Ohio
Height: 5'10".   Weight: 188 Lbs.   Batted: Right.   Threw: Right.
Major League Career: 18 Years, 1,315 Games (Pitched in nine)
1889: N.L.: New York
1891: N.L.: New York
1890: New York Giants; C 81, 2B 1, P 1

Batting Record:

Games: 83	3B: 15	Walks: 39	SL.%: .545
At Bats: 352	HRs: 8	K's: 12	S.B: 36
Hits: 119	Runs: 98	B.Avg: .338	B.R: +26
2B: 19	R.B.I: 72	O.B.A: .406	F.R: +8

Pitching Record:

Won: 0	Starts: 1	K's: 2	E.R.A: 4.0
Lost: 1	C.G: 1	Walks: 3	Saves: 0
Win %: .000	I.P: 9	Hits: 11	P.R: 0
Games: 1	Sh.O: 0	O.B.%: .368	W.A.T: -0.4

Buck Ewing was the field manager of the Giants for their entire season of 132 games; his won-lost record stands at 74–57, for a .565 win %.

William Ewing — "Buck" or "Buckingham" is not really part of the whole — was born rural, but before teething was done his family had moved to the city. As a young player he had no deficiencies, which some historians inform us lasted throughout his long major league playing career.

As a young man he played the game for pleasure; his industry was driving a distillery delivery wagon. When he reached the major leagues of baseball with Troy (N.L.) in 1880, and through 1897 with Cincinnati, his working gear usually included the tools of ignorance, as catcher's gear came to be called, which was not much then.

The records show that he played every position at some time — no better way to learn than by doing — including pitcher, between 1884 and 1890. He pitched in nine games, with four starts and as many complete, 47 innings in all; his E.R.A. stands a very credible 3.45, won two and lost three, one of the latter for the P.L. Giants.

For the P.L. Giants he had considerable say in who would do the pitching, as he was their field manager through the entire season, and obviously did so quite successfully.

He later managed Cincinnati through five full seasons, 1895 through 1899; he won 394 and lost 297, a .570 win %, all winning seasons, finishes between third and eighth, in a cumbersome 12-team N.L. format. He was at the helm the next year for the New York Giants; after winning 21 and losing 41 of his first 63 games, he was dismissed.

His overall record as a manager counts 489 won and 395 lost, a .553 win %, but no team under Buck Ewing finished higher than third place.

He may have been an A.A. umpire in 1882 and 1889; there's some disparities among names. Whether or not, William "Buck" Ewing has been depicted as a modest gentleman, popular with both his players and the people. After 1900 he was an amateur coach, which is not among his primary credentials.

Buck Ewing was the first catcher elected to the Hall of Fame, chosen and inducted in 1939, after being passed over in 1936 voting. Media elite of the early 1900s provided his finest accolades, identifying him as the greatest catcher and as the greatest player of his century.

Others, including players and common folks, said and wrote that he was treacherous and a traitor to the Brotherhood and to the Players League. His plaque at Cooperstown doesn't mention the P.L., nor does his summary as the scribes there have written it.

As a P.L. player, other than pitching, Buck Ewing did do credit to himself, and to his team and club. To begin with defense, his +8 F.R. while playing mainly as a catcher is well above average; his career F.R. of +100, with a high of +22 in 1881, is superb, indicating excellence and consistency.

His B.Avg. in 1890 was .002 away from the P.L. top five; his career mark is .303, one of the highest among catchers all time. His .406 O.B.A. in 1890 also exceeds the excellence benchmark; his .351 career mark is considerably below though.

Slugging .545 would be excellent for any 1800s player in any year; the P.L. high is written as .541 for this stat, and he's not listed among the top five. A second source also shows .545 though. His exclusion might be a function of 352 at bats. His career SL.% is noted as .456.

Among the other career batting data of Buck Ewing: 1,129 runs, 883 R.B.I.; 392 walks and 294 K's with a year missing; he hit only 71 home runs, but 178 triples and 250 doubles among 1,625 hits would account for the B.Avg./SL.% variance.

His B.R. in 1890 was great, his +130 cumulative is indicative of an excellent batter no matter what the positions and situations.

Buck Ewing led his league's catchers in assists three years and in double plays twice; his throws to the bases were quick and sharp. Thirty-six stolen bases in his P.L. year, and 354 during his career merit the same commentary: quick and sharp.

He ranks 12th all time in errors by catchers with 322 and also 12th all time in passed balls with 360; he led his league in HRs once, and in triples once. One hundred seventeen were his most runs scored, in 1893, his only 100+ runs season. He had 122 R.B.I. that year, also his only 100+, and his best B.Avg. was .344.

His B.Avg. each of 10 years was .300+, O.B.A. .400+ once, for the P.L. Giants; 1890 was his only year of .500+ in SL.%. He stole 53 bases in 1888; B.R.'s of +26 twice and +25 were his highs. Not much question, Buck Ewing was a great 1800s player.

Also not much question, Buck Ewing was a Players League star player, with a status of catcher. As a catcher his career does merit status of excellent or superior, but there were at least a dozen players greater than Buck Ewing in the 1800s. As for the greatest catcher of that era he is a contender.

William "Buck" Ewing died of Bright's disease. A reporter later admitted that "Buckingham," which some record books include, was a product of his imagination put in print. He's still a favorite of historians, and was chosen the greatest by one as recently as the mid-1980s, by "Baseball Guide" editors in the late 1930s and in 1919.

More than one of these ridicules the worth of numbers, except of their own creation. Is Buck Ewing worthy of commendation as a catcher? Certainly. As a batter? Certainly. But kept within the bounds of realistic perspective, he's not as alleged.

Why he played in only 14 games the year after the P.L. is an issue worthy of questions. What is known is that many among the P.L. players suspected him of collusion with various executives of at least one hostile league, which he denied, but again didn't.

He admitted to meeting confidentially with enemy leaders, but insisted that he did no wrong, even though he was well tempted. After the P.L. season ended, while the owner-backers were all scheming to salvage something for themselves, Frank Brunell, the league secretary, issued vitriolic reports about him to the media.

Others were similarly accused of being Judas to the Players Brotherhood and

League, but Brunell excused them, made excuses for them, most prominently for Mike "King" Kelly. The truth can be stretched, and twisted; time has a way of doing that. After all, baseball players are not bound for life to a samurai code of ethics and honor, nor are sportswriters.

The first Hall of Fame elections were conducted in 1936, one by 226 sportswriters, assigned the duty to choose, if any, those worthy who played after 1900; 78 old timers were to choose their counterparts who played prior to that year. No standards were established, no guidelines, no criteria.

The sportswriters chose five for the consummate baseball honor, the old timers chose none. By the time the first induction was set, for June 12, 1939, more than two dozen were elected. Then in 1940 and 1941 there were none, in 1942 Rogers Hornsby, then again none in 1943, and Kenesaw Mountain Landis in 1944.

Some were elected with the status of executive, some as field managers; among the aggregate there was one catcher, and four who had played in the Players League; also one who wrote of it, and one who was vehemently opposed to its very existence.

These are the chosen, the first inducted at Cooperstown, U.S.A., chronologically, alphabetically, by surnames:

1936: Cobb, Johnson, Mathewson, Ruth, Wagner;
1937: Bulkeley, Johnson, Lajoie, Mack, McGraw, Speaker, Wright, Young;
1938: Alexander, Cartwright, Chadwick;
1939: Anson, Collins, Comiskey, Cummings, Ewing, Gehrig, Keeler, Radbourn, Sisler, Spalding.

Contrary to the published judgment of one historian expert, the National Baseball Hall of Fame here is considered a good and a worthy entity, which since its inception has served a variety of, and is expanding, good and worthy purposes.

But, all of this, in isolation. Nefarious? Skulldugger? The politics of baseball. The games within the game. Buck Ewing? Go figure. In his later years, he did hold title to a great deal of real estate in Cincinnati.

EWING, JOHN   John Ewing (Long John)
Born: June 1, 1863, Cincinnati, Ohio
Died: April 23, 1895, Denver, Colorado
Height: Weight: Batted: Threw: Right.
Major League Career: 4 Years, 129 Games
1889: A.A.: Louisville
1891: N.L.: New York
1890: P.L.; New York Giants; P 35

Batting Record:

Games: 35	3B: 1	Walks: 5	SL.%: .298
At Bats: 114	HRs: 2	K's: 35	S.B: 2
Hits: 24	Runs: 18	B.Avg: .211	B.R:
2B: 2	R.B.I: 17	O.B.A:	F.R:

Pitching Record:

Won: 18	Starts: 31	K's: 145	E.R.A: 4.25
Lost: 12	C.G: 27	Walks: 104	Saves: 2
Win %: .600	I.P: 267	Hits: 293	P.R: -0
Games: 35	Sh.O: 1	O.B.%: .357	W.A.T: +1.5

Arcana has revealed that John Ewing's treasured scrapbook included an account of one of his two career home runs, which he hit in a Players League game at Cleveland. Also, that he quotes himself as saying, "Base ball is a big lottery, you can't tell anything about it."

"We were ever so much stronger than Philadelphia, but we couldn't win; when Boston came along, we had no trouble at all with them." Boston finished first, the Giants third, Philadelphia in the second division.

Before baseball, and perhaps between playing seasons, Ewing was a speculator in and a vendor of green goods, a grocer. Once he gambled on potatoes; his specialty was watermelons. He gained the appellation of "hustling huckster," and was known by peers as an honest fellow.

In February 1895, he was afflicted with grip of the lungs, but expected to play that season; he'd been paid $300 in advance money, was soon to be sent $200 more. When he realized the potential severity of his medical condition, he wired the payer to not send the $200, and returned the other $300.

A genuine "Honest John." As a pitcher in 1890 his performance was as good as his integrity, the next season even better. These were his only two full seasons; in 1891 he won 21 and lost eight, his .724 win % led his league.

In 1891 he completed 28 of 30 starts and pitched 237 innings. His 2.28 E.R.A. led his league; his P.R. calculates to +32. There's no indication of his malady in 1891, which was the last of his four major league seasons.

At Louisville (A.A.) in 1888 he'd been less than adequate, 8–13; at Louisville (A.A.) in 1889 he'd been less than that, 8 and 30. He got better in 1890, then better than that at New York (N.L.).

In 1890 his performance was better than the P.L. Giants staff, 27 complete games of 31 starts was better than average pitching. With walks numbering less than K's, he was uncommon among P.L. pitchers; a bit more than a hit allowed an inning was better than most, but his 4.25 E.R.A. doesn't quite match the Giants' 4.17, or the 4.23 of the league.

His P.L. batting was lacking, with 35 K's in 114 at bats (31%) especially, but his hits produced runs; five of 24 hits for extra bases reveal a bit of power at the bat.

He was excellent in 1890, better in 1891; at his worst he proved his best, an honest man; he'd been a fine major league pitcher. "Long John" Ewing, proved "Honest John," died of tuberculosis.

FAATZ, JAYSON S.   Jay Faatz
Born: October 24, 1860, Weedsport, New York
Died: April 10, 1923, Syracuse, New York

Height: 6'4".   Weight: Batted: Right.   Threw: Right.
Major League Career: 4 Years, 298 Games
1889: N.L.: Cleveland
1891: Did not play
1890: P.L.: Buffalo Bisons; 1B 32

Batting Record:

Games: 32	3B: 2	Walks: 9	SL.%: .252
At Bats: 111	HRs: 1	K's: 5	S.B: 2
Hits: 21	Runs: 18	B.Avg: .189	B.R: -8
2B: 0	R.B.I: 16	O.B.A: .297	F.R: 0

Jay Faatz was the second field manager of the Bisons, for 33 games; his record was won 9 lost 24, .273 win %. The team was eighth in the standings when his term began and ended. He was replaced by the same man he had replaced.

Unusually tall for his time, his weight isn't known: behemoth, stick, or normal. Sixty-four stolen bases in 1888 rule out the former, sufficient to get hit by 21 pitches in 1888 rules out the stick. That stat ranks fifth for the period 1876–1889.

He played for four years, including 1884 at Pittsburgh (A.A.), 1888 with Cleveland (A.A.), 1889 Cleveland (N.L.), and Buffalo (P.L.) in 1890. He never played a game at any position except first base; perhaps his height was his strength.

By his numbers, P.L. and the others, three home runs in 1,135 at bats reveal he didn't have much of that. His best batting average was .264 in 1888. His other data are equally mediocre, which is average. It's been written that Jay Faatz had a terrible temper.

In 1890 his best number was his win % as a manager. He quit the major leagues after the 1890 season. As a coincidental interim manager, the Bisons were eighth when he came, and eighth when he left that post.

For Faatz can be said, if hits could be runs, all managers so wish. His proportions would be the stuff of dreams. His run production for the Bisons was above average; 18 scored, 16 R.B.I. via 21 hits and nine walks, no excess to be measured.

That's whether Jay Faatz was large, medium, or a stick of an 1800s major league baseball player.

FARRAR, SIDNEY DOUGLAS   **Sid Farrar**
Born: August 10, 1859, Paris Hill, Maine
Died: May 7, 1935, New York, New York
Height: 5'10".   Weight: Batted: Threw: Right.
Major League Career: 8 Years, 943 Games
1889: N.L.: Philadelphia
1891: Did not play
1890: P.L.: Philadelphia Quakers; 1B 127

Batting Record:

Games: 127	3B: 11	Walks: 51	SL.%: .341
At Bats: 481	HRs: 1	K's: 23	S.B: 9
Hits: 122	Runs: 84	B.Avg: .254	B.R: -12
2B: 17	R.B.I: 69	O.B.A: .331	F.R: -2

Journeyman, a first baseman exclusively, he played in 100+ games each of seven years; the first of eight he played in 99. The entirety of his major league career was played in Philadelphia (N.L.) for the Phillies, other than 1890 which was his last year.

His batting side isn't known; his best B.Avg. was .282 in 1887. During his career he accumulated a .253 B.Avg., .305 O.B.A., and a .342 SL.%.

His P.L. power data are deceptive. In his eight years he hit 157 doubles, 53 triples, and 18 HRs; 51 walks in 1890 were next to his best, among 233, 52 was his best in 1889. Two hundred sixty-nine career K's included a high of 47 in 1886; add 497 runs scored, 412 R.B.I., -32 is the sum of his B.R. stats, his career F.R. stands at +4.

A journeyman is a skilled artisan who has completed his apprenticeship. After his major league years, Farrar owned a turkey farm and 30-acre estate in Connecticut. He'd worked in a box factory prior to 1880. While a player he and his teammates saved and sold tin foil to help finance his daughter's studies in Europe.

He'd kept a men's furnishings store in Melrose, Massachusetts, but sold it, again to finance his daughter's studies. She, Geraldine Farrar, gained fame on two continents as an opera singer, a diva soprano.

Sid Farrar took credit for introducing baseball to France. In 1899, he also took credit for acquainting the French cuisine with baked beans.

Sidney Douglas Farrar died as the result of post surgical complications; he'd been ill for three months and died four months after his operation. The last year of his life he was a director of a local bank.

FARRELL, CHARLES ANDREW   Duke Farrell
Born: August 31, 1866, Oakdale Massachusetts
Died: February 15, 1925, Boston, Massachusetts
Height: 6'1".   Weight: 208 Lbs.   Batted: Both.   Threw: Right.
Major League Career: 18 Years, 1,563 Games
1889: N.L.: Chicago
1891: A.A.: Boston
1890: P.L.: Chicago Pirates; C 90, 1B 22, OF 10

Batting Record:

Games: 117	3B: 12	Walks: 42	SL.%: .404
At Bats: 451	HRs: 2	K's: 28	S.B: 8
Hits: 131	Runs: 79	B.Avg: .290	B.R: +2
2B: 21	R.B.I: 84	O.B.A: .352	F.R: +18

If instead of laboring for 18 years as a major league catcher he'd worked in heavy industry, he'd have taken on the toughest jobs to earn a pittance of a pension, which baseball players got none of then.

In the actual case of Duke Farrell, in 1890 he was the first catcher for the P.L. team with the best pitching staff in the league. When not in service behind home plate, he played elsewhere on the field, and played well enough to rank third among all P.L. players in fielding runs.

All of which makes him an unnoticed most valuable player of the Chicago Pirates. He was a player and a catcher, from 1888 through 1905, in four major leagues; his myths are facts, well documented in the record books.

Duke Farrell set an all-time record on May 11, 1897; the bold and brutal Orioles of Baltimore tried to run on him. Nine tried to steal bases; he threw out eight of them. Throwing out base runners was his baseball forte.

He ranks 11th all time in assists by catchers with 1,417, 10th with 365 errors, and 21st with 285 passed balls, the latter two being hazards of his trade. His career assists when adjusted to a 162-game season rank second all time at his position, 228.87 in that imagined season.

He was an N.L. umpire in 1901 and 1902. Also, it's been written, he was a champion eater of clams. Myth being what it is, he was also the recipient of a 4.5 carat diamond ring as an award.

Broken bones and blood poisoning put him out of action, putting on 60 pounds putting him out of shape. After his long term of major league baseball service, Duke Farrell was a U.S. marshal for a while, then a Boston Braves (N.L.) coach till his demise.

As a youth, he'd worked in a shoe store and played ball for the home town club; when his arm was discovered to be like a whip and that he was agile what had been a game became his work.

He made the Chicago (N.L.) team in 1888, and when he returned to his home town all the factories were shut for a great banquet in his honor. He married a local girl, their contentment came from staying at home, in "Ol' New England Town."

When away on baseball business, his batting was consistently above average, a career .275 B.Avg. There was some authority in his bat; twice he reached 10+ HRs in a season, and once he led his league.

He never reached the level of 15+ triples, but 12 or 13 weren't unusual; his annual doubles count was a little more on average. His hits counted 1,563 in 5,679 at bats, 385 for extra bases, resulting in a typical for his time .383 SL.%.

By the best accounts his walks were 477, with only 246 K's to counter; his O.B.A. stands at .335, his -98 B.R. ask technical questions. Not so with 826 runs scored and 912 R.B.I., quite a good career's worth for an 1800s catcher.

Waiving the number of at bats standards, he reached the .300+ mark in batting average three years, with denominators needed to calculate hits being between 261 and 473. He produced 100+ runs and R.B.I. each only once, in his best year, 1891.

This was with Boston (A.A.); the sums were 108 and 110, in part enhanced by his 12 home runs. His O.B.A. never reached .400+, while playing for a total of 10 different teams. One hundred fifty stolen bases were made by this throw-'em-out specialist catcher.

1890 was one of his better seasons, with no notable negative numbers; if any, his 42 walks stand out, not unusual for him, and he drew 59 walks in his best year. B.R. is adequate, -98 for a career is otherwise.

His +87 career F.R. to the contrary, +18 in 1890 was bettered only by +21 in 1893, for Washington. Duke Farrell has to be considered one of the better 1800s catchers, and add to that he was a stalwart backstop.

Charles Andrew "Duke" Farrell had stomach surgery early in 1925; he died 10 days later.

FERSON, ALEXANDER   Alex Ferson (Colonel)
Born: July 14, 1866, Philadelphia, Pennsylvania
Died: December 5, 1957, Boston, Massachusetts
Height: 5'9".   Weight: 165 Lbs.   Batted: Right.   Threw: Right.
Major League Career: 3 Years, 48 Games
1889: N.L.: Washington
1891: Did not play
1890: Buffalo Bisons; P 10, OF 1

Batting Record:

Games: 11	3B: 0	Walks: 6	SL.%: .219
At Bats: 32	HRs: 0	K's: 7	S.B: 1
Hits: 7	Runs: 4	B.Avg: .219	B.R:
2B: 0	R.B.I: 2	O.B.A:	F.R:

Pitching Record:

Won: 1	Starts: 10	K's: 13	E.R.A: 5.45
Lost: 7	C.G: 7	Walks: 40	Saves: 0
Win %: .125	I.P: 71	Hits: 88	P.R: -10
Games: 10	Sh.O: 0	O.B.%: .403	W.A.T: -2.1

Why he was called "Colonel" probably wasn't a function of 1890, but why he didn't pitch in the major leagues in 1891 probably was. He did try again, in 1892 for Baltimore; he won 0 and lost 1, in nine innings, for an 11.00 E.R.A., no permanent damage to the Orioles.

That Orioles team finished 12th and last; Ferson left and they improved to eighth the next season. The Bisons of 1890 had no such opportunity; the .125 win % by Alex Ferson can hardly be seen within their collective .273.

The sum total of Alex Ferson the pitcher is won 18 and lost 25, .419 win %; 368 I.P., 4.38 E.R.A. The first of his seasons was his best, won 17 and lost 17 for Washington (N.L.) in 1889.

As an 1890 pitcher, 128 base runners in 71 innings of toil is close to his team's mean .387 O.B.%. His 5.45 E.R.A. is better than his team's composite 6.12. His -1.2 W.A.T. tells all there is to know of him during his term at P.L. Buffalo.

As a Bisons batter, he didn't know much success either, .219 B.Avg. and zero extra base hits among seven, which match his K's, he walked from the batter's box one time less, with less cause for despair than he made the trip from pitcher's box to bench.

Why "colonel"? After his baseball career, he owned and operated restaurants.

FIELDS, JOHN JOSEPH   Jocko Fields
Born: October 20, 1864, County Cork, Ireland
Died: October 14, 1950, Jersey City, New Jersey
Height: 5'10".   Weight: 160 Lbs.   Batted: Right.   Threw: Right.
Major League Career: 6 Years, 341 Games
1889: N.L.: Pittsburgh
1891: N.L.: Pittsburgh and Philadelphia
1890: P.L.: Pittsburgh Burghers; OF 80, 2B 30, C 15, SS 4

Batting Record:

Games: 126	3B: 20	Walks: 57	SL.%: .445
At Bats: 526	HRs: 9	K's: 52	S.B: 24
Hits: 149	Runs: 101	B.Avg: .283	B.R: +10
2B: 18	R.B.I: 86	O.B.A: .357	F.R: +7

Although the plurality of his P.L. games were played as an outfielder, the variety of positions played requires a designation as utility. During his rather brief career he played all the fielding positions, pitched an inning in 1887 for Pittsburgh (N.L.), and his concluding season he was foremost a catcher.

Bearing one of the more peculiar 1880s nicknames, as a player he had good power, good speed, and played good defense; include his versatility, and Jocko Fields becomes an essential element to any good baseball team.

1890 was by far his busiest year; 1889 was next, when he took part in 75 games. His career extended from 1887 through 1892, all of his 341 games were played in Pittsburgh uniforms with the N.L. except for the P.L. year, and his final year of 29 games with the Phillies and Giants.

1890 was his best year. He ranks fourth in P.L. triples. The only 100+ among his numbers is his 101 runs scored; his 86 R.B.I. for the Burghers doubled his next highest total. Of his basic data, his 20 P.L. triples was exceeded only by 22 doubles for the 1889 Alleghenys.

His .311 in 1889 was his only .300+ B.Avg.; his O.B.A. high was .376 in 1889, and SL.% .445 in 1890. His B.R. are negative except for +11 in 1889 and +10 in the P.L.; +7 F.R. was his best. Half of his stolen bases came in 1890; fairly said, the P.L. Burghers gained half the prime of Jocko Fields the N.L. lost.

After his major league career in baseball in Pittsburgh, he was an employee of a railway express company, and a county employee.

FOGARTY, JAMES G.   Jim Fogarty

Born: February 12, 1864, San Francisco, California
Died: May 20, 1891, Philadelphia, Pennsylvania
Height: 5'10.5".   Weight: 180 Lbs.   Batted: Right.   Threw: Right.
Major League Career: 7 Years, 751 Games
1889: N.L.: Philadelphia
1891: Deceased
1890: P.L.: Philadelphia Quakers; OF 91, 3B 1

Batting Record:

Games: 91	3B: 6	Walks: 59	SL.%: .357
At Bats: 347	HRs: 4	K's: 50	S.B: 36
Hits: 83	Runs: 71	B.Avg: .239	B.R: -1
2B: 17	R.B.I: 58	O.B.A: .364	F.R: +9

Jim Fogarty was the first of two Quakers field managers; his won-lost record was 7–9, .438; the team was in fifth place when his term ended.

He came from the far West, as the U.S. was then, and played baseball in Philadelphia, where he stayed till his end which, unknown, was imminent. He'd been chosen as a member of the All-American team on Al Spalding's world tour; his P.L. record is stereotype.

Jim Fogarty was the first field manager of the Philadelphia team of the Players League. When he left the post after just 16 games (won 7 lost 9) they were in fifth place, where they were when the season ended 116 games later.

Everything about him in the P.L. year was just a bit below first division level. Best said his hits produced runs; specifically, 71 runs scored and 58 R.B.I. resulted from 83 hits and 59 walks. He also counted 50 K's; when he came to bat he stayed awhile.

Though less than spectacular his raw data are credible; add 36 stolen bases. Among calculations for Jim Fogarty of 1890 are a -1 B.R., +9 F.R., worth nearly a game to the Quakers. His extra base hits imply he had some of both speed and power.

From 1884 through 1889 he played only for the Phillies. His high notes include 113 runs scored in 1887 and 107 in 1889; his highs in R.B.I. were 54 and 50. His 82 walks in 1887 were a league high; 65 in 1889 and 50+ twice more identify him as a leadoff batter.

His 327 career K's might make this arguable; in 2,880 at bats (11%) there's not much of an argument, though his +18 career B.R. may cloud the issue. His +95 career F.R. more than hints he could play the outfield; he's nearly unknown, but there's much to know.

Jim Fogarty twice led his league's outfielders in putouts, and twice in double plays and fielding chances; he made 42 assists in 1889, seventh most by an OF in history. In 1887 he became the second player to steal 100+ bases in a season, 102, with aid of some single-season rules, but in 1889 he had and led with 99.

For the period 1876–1889 he ranks sixth in S.B.; his 99 now rank 21st among S.B. highs. He never batted .300+; his best was .293 in 1886. His O.B.A.s were in the mid- to high .300's range but none .400+; despite some evident power at the bat, his SL.% twice barely passed the .400 level.

His record extends beyond the P.L. playing fields. After the 1890 season was done, and then done again in the back rooms, he was assigned to his prior year's team, which was the rule, but he was bought by the Pittsburgh Pirates, nee Alleghenys.

Fogarty never played for the Pirates, not for any of which became common reasons; in 1891 he came in February to learn the city, the field, the team, to practice a little when the behavior of Lake Erie and the Canadian winds permitted.

Thus becoming cold and wet, he became ill, then was diagnosed with tuberculosis. Disgracefully his good intentions and illness were publicly written of as consumption which generally corresponds with a lust for distilled alcohol or a brew of barley and malt consumed to extremes of excess.

Corrective condescension came four decades later: the *Sporting News* in citation wrote: "No outfielder ever outshone this sparkling wonder of other days for grace of movement, speed, accuracy, and throwing power." This was published in 1932.

The *Reach Guide* gave a generous commendation, with down to earth rhetoric, in 1892. SABR has written well of him much more recently, put him to rest in a manner of speaking. He had not played in 1891.

James G. Fogarty died of tuberculosis a few days before the 1891 baseball season began.

GALVIN, JAMES FRANCIS   Pud Galvin (Gentle Jeems)
Born: December 25, 1865, St. Louis, Missouri
Died: March 7, 1902, Pittsburgh, Pennsylvania
Height: 5'8".   Weight: 190 Lbs.   Batted: Right.   Threw: Right.
Major League Career: 14 Years, 697 Games
1889: N.L.: Pittsburgh
1891: N.L.: Pittsburgh
1890: P.L.: Pittsburgh Burghers; P 26

Batting Record:

Games: 26	3B: 1	Walks: 6	SL.%: .247
At Bats: 97	HRs: 0	K's: 20	S.B: 1
Hits: 20	Runs: 8	B.Avg: .206	B.R:
2B: 2	R.B.I: 12	O.B.A:	F.R:

Pitching Record:

Won: 12	Starts: 25	K's: 35	E.R.A: 4.35
Lost: 13	C.G: 23	Walks: 49	Saves: 0
Win %: .480	I.P: 217	Hits: 275	P.R: -3
Games: 26	Sh.O: 1	O.B.%: .358	W.A.T: +0.3

Pud wasn't pudding as has been alleged in many forms of the literature; its pronunciation doesn't even fit such frivolity. But it does fit well with pudge, which James Francis Galvin certainly was.

He was also among the very best pitchers of the 1800s. Many of his achievements still rank high in the historic records. The P.L. record is not Pud Galvin, but objectivity demands it be considered; 1890 was the next to worst of his only two bad years among 14.

His 1890 W.A.T. shows he was just that much better than the Burghers of Pittsburgh, 60 and 68, .469 win %; their E.R.A. was 4.22 to which he contributed an un-Pud-like 4.35. His O.B.% aren't close to a match, .358 and .322 with the Burghers the better, which was next to lowest in the P.L., bettered only by the .321 of the Chicago club.

As a batter, Galvin contributed little to his team's cause, but eight runs and 12 R.B.I. with 20 hits and six walks. In the other box he did complete all but one of his pitching assignments. He'd trained to be a steamfitter, so surely he was accustomed to tough work. Then he went on to pitch in 697 major league baseball games.

He started 682, completed 639, the 682 ranks ninth all time, the 639 C.G. is second in its class. His 5,941 innings pitched also ranks second. Galvin was the Little Steam Engine That Could and he did. He was the first to win 300 games, and with 361 career wins is tied for second in the historic records.

His career .283 O.B.% ranks 26th all time, and his 56 shutouts ranks 12th; not long ago Bob Gibson tied him in that stat. An issue exists as to whether he pitched 67 or 57 games in which opponents didn't score, and there are other numbers that don't agree among the various record books, but these little points become moot issue when the whole of Pud is considered.

As a fielder, he's ninth in career put outs with 324; Greg Maddux may have recently surpassed that. As a batter in the period of 1876–1889 Pud ranks second in K's with 562, a record nobody was pursuing with deliberate vigor.

Further as a fielder, helping his own and his teams' causes, Pud during his career made 1,382 assists, which ranks fourth all time; he's third among all pitchers with 161 fielding errors. While working at his primary task, he released 226 wild pitches, fifth most in history.

The last datum was recently recalculated by another data source, who reached a count for him of 223 wild pitches; also and more significant, that source revised his career wins upward to 364. His pitching agenda included a fastball, change of speed, and excellent control, and further he was an excellent fielder. It's also been mentioned by a few that Pud Galvin was not reluctant to render the batter a spitball when occasion called.

With this arsenal in place, these are the period stats for 1876–1889 achieved by pitcher Jim Galvin, also cited as "Gentle Jeems." He ranks: first in wins, first in losses, first in games, first in starts, first in C.G., first in I.P., first in shutouts, fifth in K's, seventh in walks, third in wild pitches.

If his career starts number 602, and his complete games 573, the 95% rate is as incredible as the raw numbers. He was also an umpire: A.A. in 1885 and 1886, N.L. in 1886 and 1887, 1889, 1893, and 1895. He was also a manager of the Buffalo Bisons for an N.L. moment in 1885, won 7 lost 17, .293 win %. Put all this together, and one might also refer to him as "Busy Jim" Galvin.

To embellish a bit on the above notes, which quantify to 95%, that calculation among the counts of all pitchers of all time ranks second; perhaps "The Busy And Great" Jim Galvin. By whatever name and how it's interpreted, Mr. Galvin won 46 games in 1883, and 46 in 1884, and along with 37 earlier in 1879, he won 20+ games each of 10 years.

Twice he won two games in one day; only about a half dozen major league pitchers have ever done that. His were the 12th of June of 1879, and the 4th of July in 1882.

In 1884 he started 72 games and completed 71; in 636 innings he recorded 369 K's and 63 walks; the ratio is obvious besides being incredible. More to the point and also incredible, his 1884 E.R.A. was 1.99, much in part due to 12 shutouts. During one week that year he pitched four shutouts, in which he allowed no (0) walks.

Once he did walk three batters in the same inning, and picked off each one at first base; sometimes the really great ones can even erase their baseball mistakes.

Some legends are real and prove themselves. This one recorded appearances in 76 games of which 75 were starts, and he completed 72 for the Buffalo Bisons (N.L.) of 1885. Note 66 games in 1879, among a total of eight seasons in which Mr. Galvin pitched in 50+ as a starting pitcher.

As for starts, note 70+ twice, and eight years of 50+ also; in C.G. then note 70+ twice, 65 in 1879, only these three as 50+, but 40+ C.G. nine seasons. His I.P.: 600+ twice, 593 in 1879, nine seasons of 400+ of 10 with 300+ I.P.

Note also 1,799 career K's, which is not many proportionally, unless measured against 744 walks, of which his high was 78 in a season. SABR-stats show a +69 P.R. for 1884, +38 in both 1886 and 1887, both for Pittsburgh, but of the A.A. then the N.L., and +31 in 1883. His career P.R. sum counts to, lacking the word, +157.

Amazingly, none of these would have led his league; his +17.6 W.A.T. would have in 1883, but not +15.1 in 1884; these are his only W.A.T. of +10.0 or more of a career sum of +55.8.

His career E.R.A. has been measured at 2.87, three times of 14 above 4.00, and three below 2.50, including 2.00 by a source which reconsidered his elite-class 1.99.

Mr. Galvin began with four games in the historic 1875 National Association, pitched for Buffalo (N.L.) 1879 into 1885, jumped to Pittsburgh (A.A.) and continued there in 1886. He went to N.L. Pittsburgh in 1887, through 1889, returned in 1891 and began there in 1892, finishing his spectacular career at St. Louis.

His Players League record withstanding, his presence was a credit to the league and to its cause. Could Pud have been better for the Pittsburghers as a pitcher? Pitching arms and pitchers are mostly only human.

During his incomparable career he led his league in: games and complete once each, innings once, shutouts twice, SABR-stats only one and just once. Given his achievements it stands as a high credit to the pitchers of his era.

Later he was a construction foreman and a bartender. He caught pneumonia and suffered inflammation of the mucous membrane. The official cause of death of James Francis Galvin is recorded as catarrh of the stomach.

Last said of James Francis "Pud" Galvin is that he surely could. He was elected a member of the National Baseball Hall of Fame in 1965.

GILLESPIE, JAMES   Jim Gillespie
Born: September 23, 1858, St. Catherines, Ontario, Canada
Died: September 5, 1920, North Tonawanda, New York
Height: Weight: Batted: Threw:
Major League Career: 1 Year, 1 Game
1889: Did not play
1891: Did not play
1890: P.L.: Buffalo Bisons OF 1 (Debut Date: October 1)

Batting Record:

Games: 1	3B: 0	Walks: 0	SL.%: .000
At Bats: 3	HRs: 0	K's: 2	S.B: 0
Hits: 0	Runs: 0	B.Avg: .000	B.R: -1
2B: 0	R.B.I: 0	O.B.A: .000	F.R: 0

(Tough to follow the Little Steam Engine That Could and did.)

His B.R. of -1 reads much better than the -99 which had been written in error. The remainder of his line in the record is 0's except for an interruption by a "2," and on the whole it would look better without that.

His line also informs that he played in one game and went into the batter's box three times, resulting in 2 K's and an exit pass.

Born a short way from the U.S.-Canadian border at Buffalo, he migrated to the little industrial town where he lived and died. He apparently ventured to Buffalo one day where he became a one-game wonder in the Players League of 1890. He was gone before the ink on the official scorecard was dry.

He was a lumber dealer in his area, and commissioner of police in his municipality.

James Gillespie died of complications of a surgery.

GLEASON, WILLIAM   Bill Gleason
Born: 1868, Cleveland, Ohio
Died: December 2, 1893, Cleveland, Ohio
Height: Weight: Batted: Threw:
Major League Career: 1 Year, 1 Game
1889: Did not play
1891: Did not play
1890: P.L.: Cleveland Infants; P 1 (Debut Date: April 24)

Batting Record:

Games: 1	3B: 0	Walks: 0	SL.%: .000
At Bats: 2	HRs: 0	K's: 1	S.B: 0
Hits: 0	Runs: 0	B.Avg: .000	B.R:
2B: 0	R.B.I:0	O.B.A:	F.R:

Pitching Record:

Won: 0	Starts: 1	K's: 0	E.R.A: 27.00
Lost: 1	C.G: 0	Walks: 6	Saves: 0
Win %: .000	I.P: 4	Hits: 14	P.R: -10
Games: 1	Sh.O: 0	O.B.%: .651	W.A.T: -0.4

When a life ends at about age 25, that is too quick. Nothing is known about this major league pitcher except his team affiliation, enough to estimate his age, and that he was born and died in the city where he played his one baseball game in a major league.

He pitched and batted dismally though. His opponents' on base allowed average could have been the number of a rural farm road and his earned run average an astronomical calculation, .651 and 27.00 respectively.

Batting "zero" with a "K" must prompt an awful feeling, and permitting 20 opponents to reach base in four innings would precipitate nightmares for any pitcher.

There have been other Bill Gleasons. This Bill Gleason lost his only decision. Others have done better; no doubt this one did the best his condition would enable at the time.

This Bill Gleason died soon after, of consumption.

GORE, GEORGE F.   George Gore
Born: May 3, 1852, Hartland, Maine
Died: September 16, 1933, Utica, New York
Height: 5'11".   Weight: 195 Lbs.   Batted: Left.   Threw: Right.
Major League Career: 14 Years, 1,310 Games
1889: N.L.: New York
1891: N.L.: New York
1890: P.L.: New York Giants; OF 93

Batting Record:

Games: 93	3B: 8	Walks: 77	SL.%: .499
At Bats: 399	HRs: 10	K's: 23	S.B: 28
Hits: 127	Runs: 132	B.Avg: .318	B.R: +31
2B: 26	R.B.I: 55	O.B.A: .432	F.R: -20

In a game against Providence on June 25, 1881, he made five hits, all singles, scored five runs, and stole seven bases; the hits and runs were records until 1899. He also had six hits in a game in six at bats; he made five assists in one game, from the outfield.

George Gore had joined Chicago (N.L.) in 1879 and quickly became prominent. He was a splendid fielder and a reliable batter. 1890 was among his best seasons. He was a hard hitter, fine thrower and fielder and demonstrated great success on the field.

He was fifth in his league in 1890 in Total Average, and led his league(s) in a variety of stats. As a talented hitter with good speed he scored 100+ runs with regularity; a hit or a walk by George Gore almost assured a run on the score board.

His career assists adjusted to a 162-game season, 30.35, ranks ninth all time among outfielders. His reputation and a -50 career F.R., -20 in 1890, don't equate; he was old by the time the P.L. played.

He ranks fourth all time in OF errors with 368. He was reputed to be vulnerable to liquor and women; he had bad civilian habits and his latter years were lost in dissipation. He was released by the Giants in July 1892; he went to St. Louis and was let go again in August.

Gore lived to age 76, despite all that; near the end he had to work at almost anything just to survive. At that time he was a resident at Nutley, New Jersey, then was relocated to Utica, New York, not far from Cooperstown.

The facts are hard; Gore had no middle ground. At the bat his K's to at bats count 1:16, walks to at bats 1:7.5, and in 1890 he scored more runs than he had hits. This 28 stolen bases at his age are commendable. George Gore was a significant contribution factor to the New York Giants' successful season.

His 77 walks in 1890 count better than 3:1 against his K's, 10 home runs rank fourth in the league, and then represented a milestone. He wasn't a full time P.L. player, but in only 399 at bats made 127 hits, including 44 for extra bases, 35%.

In one of the more unusual stats, Gore ranks fourth in production, behind only the batting average and home runs leaders; in another such stat, Total Average, he's also fourth, in the same sort of company, this part-time player.

The short- and long-term evidence shows he belongs in such fine company; list the benchmark batting average standards and measure Gore against them:

	Std.	1890	Career
B.Avg:	.300	.318	.301
O.B.A:	.400	.432	.386
SL.%:	.500	.499	.411
B.R.:	+100	+31	+297

On balance, note again his (-) F.R., 1890 and career, despite a variety of commendations. Consider the variables of these averages and after-the-fact stats; his name isn't among the venerable at Cooperstown, only due to the faults and the flaws of the variables of his character, which are highly considered at Cooperstown.

Such are explained as intangibles. Among the tangibles done by Gore are the raw numbers and the averages of 1890, done when he was old; he did nearly as well over the span of 14 major league seasons, from 1879 through 1892.

He played in 100+ games in six of these seasons; the most was 130, in 1891, for the New York (N.L.) Giants. He had 400+ at bats each of these seasons; the most being 528 in 1891. Except for 1890, he was a N.L. player from 1879 through 1886 for Chicago, 1887 through 1892 for New York, and St. Louis.

His 5,357 at bats and 1,612 hits produced 1,327 runs and 582 R.B.I.; his hits include 262 doubles, 94 triples, and 46 home runs. At risk of redundancy, his Players League season stands out. He was walked a total of 717 times, struck out only 332; he stole 170 bases during his career.

Gore eight years batted .300+, six years had .400+ O.B.A., and .499 was the closest he came to .500+ SL.%. He scored 100+ runs seven years, led in that stat twice; he also led in walks three years, in all the batting averages once, all in 1880, with .360, .399 and .463.

He hit 30+ doubles one year and 10+ home runs one year, and had 100+ walks one year. His B.R. are incredible; league high +30 in 1880, twice 40+, positive every one of 14 years except one, -1 in 1888. His -50 career F.R. include -10s in 1889 and 1891, and an unexplainable -20 in P.L. 1890; he has five +30+ B.R. years.

He is included in period stats for 1876–1889, with ranks of: fifth in runs, first in walks, 10th in B.Avg., sixth in O.B.A.

George F. Gore isn't a resident at Cooperstown. The standards for admission there are extremely tough, and it is doubtful he ever could be. He died near there, destitute, in the Masonic Home at Utica; the cause isn't official, a lusher after the fact. For some period of time after his baseball career, he'd been a wholesale liquor salesman.

GRAY, JAMES D. Jim Gray (Reddy)
Born: August 7, 1862, Pittsburgh, Pennsylvania
Died: January 31, 1938, Pittsburgh, Pennsylvania
Height: Weight: Batted: Threw: Right.
Major League Career: 2 Years, 5 Games
1889: Did not play
1891: Did not play
1890: P.L.: Pittsburgh Burghers; 2B 2 (Rookie)
N.L.: Pittsburgh

Batting Record:

Games: 2	3B: 0	Walks: 0	SL.%: .556
At Bats: 9	HRs: 1	K's: 2	S.B: 0
Hits: 2	Runs: 3	B.Avg: .222	B.R: -1
2B: 0	R.B.I: 3	O.B.A: .222	F.R: 0

An unusual case, he was a jumper from the P.L. to the N.L. Also he's almost anonymous. He never played in the major leagues before 1890 and didn't play again till 1893. It must have been his home run that induced the Pirates to obtain him from the Burghers.

If Mr. Al Nimick and his right-hand man, J. Palmer O'Neill, paid Gray big money to change Pittsburgh uniforms, it marked one of the rare few times the Pirates got swampoodled by any player or another club.

Gray went to bat three times for the Pirates in 1890, with nothing to show for it except one "K," but he did pay dividends for them in 1893, with capital gains: two games, nine at bats, same as for the Burghers; four hits including a double, and two R.B.I.

That double the hits sum of his P.L. moment, but not nearly a match for three

R.B.I. and three runs scored. Somehow his B.Avg. and O.B.A. both doubled those of the P.L. and his SL.% kept constant at a phenomenal .556.

That might have been the right word for Reddy Grey, not Jim Gray. Where he came from, where he went, where he was in the early 1890s are all questions supposedly without answers, one or two of which might be found in a tale of legend penned by Zane Grey.

The surnames are spelled a bit differently, but no matter really. What does matter is that Zane Grey wrote more than 50 Western novels and was also a college and professional baseball player. He also wrote, as fiction, "The Redheaded Outfield," a grand tale which might not be all fiction.

When baseball gets into the blood, as must have happened with Zane Grey, the corpuscles become white with what to the uninformed would appear to be red stitching. The name that Zane Grey chose for his team with the red-headed outfield was the Rochester Stars.

His picked manager for his Stars was named just Delaney but reputed to be the image of a rather famous real manager. Two of his probably imaginary outfield trio were named Red Gilbat who played left field, and Reddy Clammer, who played right.

Can you imagine? "Reddy Ray" played center field; he "Had been the intercollegiate champion in the sprints and a famous college ballplayer." The Rochester Stars and Providence Grays were tied for first place. "The September day was perfect."

If Mr. Nimick and his right-hand man would have signed these three with red hair among the dozen they pirated likely the Alleghenys of 1890 would have reversed their record year's sums of won 23 and lost 113.

As for the future of Reddy Ray, "Quien Sabe?" For Jim Gray a bit of his is recorded as great, .556 and all. It's told in the books of records that another "Reddy Grey" did play for the Pirates, but only in 1903, in one game, and did rather well.

This particular Reddy Grey was born at Zanesville, Ohio; the Jim Gray of the Burghers and later Pirates remains virtually unknown. Zane Grey, of course, became rather famous. Now, who really played in the red-headed outfield and for the P.L. Burghers in that one game on June 17, 1890?

A prominent baseball source identifies him as "Reddy Gray." If so, pardon the repetition, but "Quien Sabe?" Jim Gray was also a minor league umpire, and a 50-year employee of the City of Pittsburgh.

James D. Gray died of a heart attack.

GRIFFIN, MICHAEL JOSEPH   Mike Griffin
Born: March 20, 1865, Utica, New York
Died: April 10, 1908, Utica, New York
Height: 5'7".   Weight: 160 Lbs.   Batted: Left.   Threw: Right.
Major League Career: 12 Years, 1,511 Games
1889: A.A.: Baltimore
1891: N.L.: Brooklyn
1890: P.L.: Philadelphia Quakers; OF 115

Batting Record:

Games: 115	3B: 6	Walks: 64	SL.%: .407
At Bats: 489	HRs: 6	K's: 19	S.B: 30
Hits: 140	Runs: 127	B.Avg: .286	B.R: +9
2B: 29	R.B.I: 54	O.B.A: .377	F.R: +15

He began in the A.A., with Baltimore in 1887, batted .301 and continued there the next two years. Then he jumped to the P.L., Philadelphia, then went to Brooklyn of the N.L., where he played eight years, till the end of his fine major league career.

He batted .300+ each of his last four years, with a high of .358 in 1894; he led the N.L. in doubles with 36 in 1891, and with 152 runs scored in 1889. In 1887, Billie Barnie, the man for all tasks at Baltimore (A.A.) had gone to Utica, New York, to observe "Sandy" Griffin.

He signed the wrong Griffin, having gotten the two confused. Mike being the other Griffin proved that Barnie didn't make a mistake for a dozen years.

Mike Griffin consistently played 100+ games, usually 130+ during a season. He wasn't void of power, just lacking; six of his 42 HRs were hit in 1890, which at a 12-year rate doesn't compare to six of 108 triples, though 29 of 313 doubles does.

His 1890 tally of 127 runs scored of 1,405 is typical, as is 54 of 625 R.B.I. (a season is missing in the records). His 64 walks of 809 add another dimension to his offense; 19 K's in 489 at bats in 1890 (3.9%) add more. His 206 career K's are lacking four years.

All considered, the P.L. season of Mike Griffin rates typical; typically and consistently Mike Griffin was a very good major league baseball player. His career batting data are .296, .388, .407; the Philadelphia Quakers had a very good baseball player.

He stole 473 bases in his dozen years, with highs of 94 in 1887 and 65 in 1891. It would have been expected of him in 1890 to steal bases and hit singles, and he produced more than expected.

There's not one (-) among his B.R. stats, but his P.L. +9 don't come near compounding to his career +205 B.R. His F.R. career sum of +69 indicates he was a positively complete player; his P.L. +15 F.R. stand near the top five.

Further on his merits, he's ranked seventh all time among OF with taking part in 75 double plays; his career assists adjusted to a 162-game season equate to 26.63, 16th best among all outfielders of the 1800s and the 20th century.

He led his league's outfielders in fielding percent five years and three years in putouts; he led Players League outfielders with participation in 10 double plays. The offensive record side of Mike Griffin includes 30+ doubles three years; his 36 led the N.L. in 1892, and he scored 100+ runs in 10 years, with 152 in 1891.

He's among the ranked in 1890–1899 period stats as seventh in doubles, eighth in walks, and tied for fifth in single-season runs scored during that period.

His father was a cigar maker, as he was later, also an executive with a local beer brewing company, having proven Billie Barnie made no mistake at all, nor did those who chose for the Quakers.

Michael Joseph Griffin died of pneumonia.

GRUBER, HENRY JOHN   Henry Gruber

Born: December 14, 1864, Hamden, Connecticut
Died: September 26, 1932, New Haven, Connecticut
Height: Weight: Batted: Right.   Threw: Left.
Major League Career: 5 Years, 151 Games
1889: N.L.: Cleveland
1891: N.L.: Cleveland
1890: P.L.: Cleveland Infants; P 48, OF 3, 3B 1

Batting Record:

Games: 50	3B: 3	Walks: 26	SL.%: .276
At Bats: 163	HRs: 0	K's: 29	S.B: 0
Hits: 36	Runs: 21	B.Avg: .221	B.R:
2B: 3	R.B.I: 9	O.B.A:	F.R:

Pitching Record:

Won: 22	Starts: 44	K's: 110	E.R.A: 4.27
Lost: 23	C.G: 39	Walks: 204	Saves: 0
Win %: .489	I.P: 383	Hits: 464	P.R: -2
Games: 48	Sh.O: 1	O.B.%: .395	W.A.T: +3.0

    He did very well for the Infants of Cleveland in 1890, all things considered, and judging by 383 innings pitched wasn't reluctant to work. And that he did, to rank fourth in the P.L. in games and complete games, and fifth in innings pitched.

    Only two among this staff had winning records. The W.A.T. of Henry Gruber is better than the whole, to his credit, while doing a third of the work. His sum won and lost of -1 shows much when compared to his team's -20, which asks why the -2 P.R.?

    Perhaps a factor was 47 wild pitches by Gruber, which ranks eighth most of all time, but he did pitch the Infants' only shutout. His 110 K's were more than a third of the team's 325, his O.B.% and E.R.A. though, .395 and 4.27, exceed their .362 and 4.23.

    His only winner among five seasons was his first, 4 and 3 with Detroit (N.L.) in 1887, when he started and completed his only seven games. His record there the next year was 11 and 14, then for Cleveland (N.L.) the year before the P.L. 7 and 15, and the year after 17 and 22.

    Career totals for Gruber include won 60 lost 78, .435 win % with E.R.As of 2.76 and 2.29 his first two years, and 3.67 for five years. Also, 1,239 innings pitched, twice 300+, with 1,328 hits and 479 walks, not offset by 346 K's. Which may suggest that working long and hard doesn't always assure a winner in the end.

    John Henry Gruber died suddenly, of acute myocardial failure.

    He'd first pitched and worked for a rifle manufacturer, After baseball entered the saloon business. When Prohibition put an end to that, he returned to the same rifle factory, then was the janitor of the Winchester club house.

GUMBERT, ADDISON COURTNEY   Addison Gumbert

Born: October 10, 1867, Pittsburgh, Pennsylvania
Died: April 23, 1925, Pittsburgh, Pennsylvania
Height: 5'10".   Weight: 200 Lbs.   Batted: Right.   Threw: Right.
Major League Career: 9 Years, 262 Games
1889: N.L.: Chicago
1891: N.L.: Chicago
1890: P.L.: Boston Reds; P 39, OF 7

Batting Record:

Games: 44	3B: 1	Walks: 18	SL.%: .366
At Bats: 145	HRs: 3	K's: 26	S.B: 5
Hits: 35	Runs: 23	B.Avg: .241	B.R:
2B: 7	R.B.I: 20	O.B.A:	F.R:

Pitching Record:

Won: 23	Starts: 33	K's: 81	E.R.A: 3.96
Lost: 12	C.G: 27	Walks: 86	Saves: 0
Win %: .657	I.P: 277	Hits: 338	P.R: +8
Games: 39	Sh.O: 1	O.B.%: .364	W.A.T: +1.8

He shared a name with the primary owner of one club. Young in the year of the Players League, in his third major league season, having jumped from Al Spalding's N.L. White Stockings, Addison Gumbert emerged as one of the three big winners of the P.L.'s winning team; this was easily his best season.

His hits allowed to innings pitched ratio is low by the P.L.'s standards, his walks and K's very low, but his O.B.% allowed is above the league norm of .345. He won at a rate better than the Boston staff. In the P.L. he ranks fifth in wins and fourth in win %.

He needed relief half a dozen times, and half a dozen times he came to the aid of staff mates; he relied on control rather than speed or tricks. During one stretch he won 10 straight decisions.

On Labor Day of 1890, he came in to relieve in the morning game, which Boston won by his grand slam home run; then he started and completed the afternoon contest, an 11–2 Boston victory.

He'd begun in 1888, with N.L. Chicago. The next season he won 16 and lost 13 (.552 win %); in 1891, again with the White Stockings, his record was 17 and 11 (.607). 1892 was his last year with the club of Al Spalding, 22 and 19 (.537), his second and last 20+.

He'd proven himself a winner, and on June 20, 1892, Addison Gumbert set records, but to no avail; he pitched all 20 innings of a 7–7 tie game. This was also the first of four years he served as a N.L. umpire, 1892 through 1895.

After Chicago he pitched for Pittsburgh for two years, 12–7 and 15–14 (.632 and .517). Then he moved to Brooklyn for his final season. He arrived always a winner, his first year was 3 and 3, to have his fine record blemished by a count of 11 and 16 (.407).

Persuaded to continue, he began 1896 with Brooklyn, 0–4, ended his career at Philadelphia, winning 5 and losing 3. In 1892 he'd pitched 383 innings, by far his most; among 45 starts in 46 games with 39 complete, his K's were 118 and walks 107, comparable with his P.L. year.

In sum, Addison Gumbert won 124 and lost 102 (.549). His career E.R.A. is 4.28, which includes years of 5.08, 5.19, and 6.02. Not always efficient, he pitched 1,985 innings in all, gave up 2,321 hits and 634 walks, with 546 total K's.

By another measure, his .362 career O.B.% doesn't seem lacking, but a -31 total P.R. contradicts. As a batter throughout, Addison Gumbert was adequate, which is the sum of his 1890 batting stats; a bit below mediocre with an occasional show of power.

After closing out his major league baseball career, he was a county commissioner and sheriff; his business aside was politics.

Nearly always a winner, foremost with P.L. Boston, Addison Courtney Gumbert died of a brain tumor.

HADDOCK, GEORGE SILAS George Haddock (Gentleman)
Born: December 25, 1866, Plymouth, New Hampshire
Died: April 18, 1926, Boston, Massachusetts
Height: 5'11".   Weight: 155 Lbs.   Batted: Right.   Threw: Right.
Major League Career: 7 Years, 204 Games
1889: N.L.: Washington
1891: A.A.: Boston
1890: P.L.: Buffalo Bisons; P 35, OF 7

Batting Record:

Games: 42	3B: 0	Walks: 24	SL.%: .322
At Bats: 146	HRs: 0	K's: 32	S.B: 3
Hits: 36	Runs: 21	B.Avg: .247	B.R:
2B: 11	R.B.I: 24	O.B.A:	F.R:

Pitching Record:

Won: 9	Starts: 34	K's: 123	E.R.A: 5.76
Lost: 26	C.G: 31	Walks: 149	Saves: 0
Win %: .257	I.P: 291	Hits: 366	P.R: -50
Games: 35	Sh.O: 0	O.B.%: .398	W.A.T: -1.2

"Gentleman George" was an N.L. umpire in 1889. He had a great year as a pitcher in 1891 for Boston (A.A.), and in 1892 for Brooklyn, but in 1890, for the Buffalo Bisons (P.L.) his pitching was very much otherwise.

This was a case of a pretty good pitcher having a very bad year for a really terrible team. He led the P.L. in losses, though a Pittsburghers pitcher was as close as close could be. Haddock's 26 ranks only 88th in the record books among most losses in a season.

The next two years, Haddock in terms of won and lost was outstanding, if not spectacular. Consider: 34 and 11 (.756) and 29 and 13 (.690), obviously an average of 30+ wins per season and in sum 63 and 24, .724, a third of a hall of fame career.

But the name of Haddock isn't listed in the Cooperstown roster; his career won and lost of 95 and 87 (.522) is 100 wins and .100 percent away from qualifying credentials. As for his P.L. record, suffice it to say he gave up a lot of runs most pitchers would not have.

He won a dozen fewer games than might have helped the Bisons, and lost a dozen more, but he wasn't alone among the multitude of gentlemen who served time in the Buffalo pitcher's box, which in sum rendered the team 20 games out of seventh place.

His K's to walk ratio was above average for the P.L., his hits per inning not good but more than a few did worse, and his O.B.% isn't so far above the P.L. norm of .345 to result in his won-lost record, had all other team factors been major league level.

Further for Haddock and historic equations, 272 earned base runners in 291 innings pitched could be expected to accrue an E.R.A. in the 4.50 to 5.00 range; his 5.76 informs us that he was far less than outstanding in terms of being up to the task in critical pitching situations.

He did finish about 90 percent of the games he started. His win % is in the ballpark with his team's, seemingly not that far below as a -1.2 W.A.T. would calculate to. As a batter, his stats would have made more than a few of his 26+ teammates envious.

After winning 11 and losing 21 combined during his first two years, with Washington (N.L.) in 1888 and 1889, and going from bad to worse, he led his league in 1891 in wins as above, and in shutouts with five; he'd lost 20 straight decisions in 1888.

His excellent +52 P.R. in 1891, in terms of his career, very neatly offsets his -50 P.R. mark of 1890. His career E.R.A. of 4.08 was as much a function of his 2.91 in 1891 as 5.76 in 1890.

His career W.A.T. of +8.2, in part due to his other fine year in 1892, is equitable with his career win %, and indicative of Haddock much more so than only the year of 1890. Though 599 K's versus 714 walks rates negative, 1.650 hit allowed in 1,580 innings pitched, as above, would equate with a 4.75 E.R.A.

By the hard numbers, Haddock wasn't the best pitcher of the 1890 Bisons, but he carried a heavy part of the load and was clearly their most durable.

George Silas Haddock died suddenly.

HALLIGAN, WILLIAM E.   **Jocko Halligan**
Born: December 8, 1867, Avon, New York
Died: February 13, 1945, Buffalo, New York
Height: 5'9".   Weight: 166 Lbs.   Batted: Threw:
Major League Career: 3 Years, 190 Games
1889: Did not play
1891: N.L.: Cincinnati
1890: P.L.: Buffalo Bisons; OF 43, C 16 (Rookie)

Batting Record:

Games: 57	3B: 2	Walks: 20	SL.%: .355
At Bats: 211	HRs: 3	K's: 19	S.B: 7
Hits: 53	Runs: 28	B.Avg: .251	B.R: -6
2B: 9	R.B.I: 33	O.B.A: .319	F.R: +1

He was an outfielder and catcher. The Buffalo Bisons of 1890 had considerable quantities of both, which is not the best way for a rookie to begin a major league baseball career. He was a local youth, did pretty well overall, but didn't last long working at playing the game.

Within the makings of his career batting average stands a high of .312 in 1891, for Cincinnati (N.L.); in accumulating 247 at bats in 61 games he did much better than the previous year; the power data for his three-year career nicely matches the standards for a single season; 10 Hrs, 15 triples, and 30 doubles, all benchmarks.

For the career of Jocko Halligan these calculate to a .402 SL.%; 86 walks and 206 hits count to a .358 O.B.A.; his B.Avg. is .280. 77 K's are among 737 at bats, 123 runs scored and 132 R.B.I.; if in one season not three would gain him a benchmark star.

His +19 career B.R. include a +13 in 1891; a +1 in F.R. in the P.L. is the only positive of a -3 F.R. There were two 0's in 1892, one for Cincinnati in 26 games, and one for Baltimore in 46 games.

Most of his playing time in 190 games was as an outfielder; he was behind home plate all or parts of 21 games, and put at first base 19 times by the Orioles of 1892.

After enduring the dismal Bisons' drive to last place, the next year his team achieved the same season's end; the next they were fifth when he left and seventh at the end. His switch to the Orioles put him again on a last-place team, but among 12.

Jocko Halligan had had enough. He quit. He had some power at the bat, but not the prescience to imagine the Orioles would be the champions in 1894, and 1895, and 1896. Foresight did enable him to steal 23 bases during his very brief career as a player.

After which, Jocko Halligan was a minor league umpire and a major league scout for talented young players with potential.

HALLMAN, WILLIAM WILSON   Bill Hallman
Born: March 30, 1867, Pittsburgh, Pennsylvania
Died: September 11, 1920, Philadelphia, Pennsylvania
Height: 5'8".   Weight: 160 Lbs.   Batted: Right.   Threw: Right.
Major League Career: 14 Years, 1,503 Games
1889: N.L.: Philadelphia
1891: A.A.: Philadelphia
1890: P.L.: Philadelphia Quakers; OF 34, C 26, 2B 14, 3B 10, SS 2

Batting Record:

Games: 84	3B: 7	Walks: 33	SL.%: .360
At Bats: 356	HRs: 1	K's: 24	S.B: 6
Hits: 95	Runs: 59	B.Avg: .267	B.R: -6
2B: 16	R.B.I: 37	O.B.A: .338	F.R: 0

Finally established at the second base position with the third of his three Philadelphia teams (A.A.) in 1891, the next year he found a home with the Phillies where he'd begun in 1888, then stayed at 2B for the Phillies part way through the 1897 season.

The most notable achievements of this Bill Hallman (there's at least one other in the record books) are scoring 100+ runs in the four seasons 1891 through 1894, of his 14, with a high of 119 in 1893, and 200 stolen bases, his most were 36 in 1894. Neither of these assets is to be found in his P.L. 1890 Quakers record.

Hallman also reached the .300+ B.Avg. benchmark each of four straight years, 1893 through 1896; for the P.L. Quakers, label him not a great batter, or a run producer. He could play any fielding position, and did, fairly well, 0 F.R. in 1890.

That stat of Hallman's is elusive, as his -71 F.R. whole shows, including -25 and -22 (1892 and 1894). The number stands modestly next to his -190 B.R. whole, including -28 and -35 (1897 and 1901).

The -35 B.R. requires a bit of explaining; it was done during 123 games with the Phillies, and five games Hallman had played earlier for Cleveland during the A.L. premier season, which makes him one of the rare players to have played in four major leagues.

Hallman also was a field manager in 1897 at St. Louis; his record was either won 12 lost 46 or won 13 lost 36. He was an umpire, N.L. in 1903. He's in the lists and columns of the record books for a pair of reasons beyond the ordinary.

One of these records could be said neutral, the other as bad as history can read for a player. He played more than 1,000 games at second base, actually 1,100, a record of sorts; during the 1901 season, with the Phillies most of the year, he achieved the lowest official batting average of the 20th century, a .184, which was finally exceeded by Rob Deer, who batted .179 for the Detroit Tigers of 1991.

Hallman was also the subject of a court case, as the Philadelphia (N.L.) club of 1890 tried to prevent him from being an active member of the rival Quakers club.

He was also a vaudeville entertainer between baseball seasons, which he continued later full time while playing for minor league teams. He was also a minor league manager, and became involved in the theatrical business.

William Wilson Hallman died of heart disease.

HANLON, EDWARD HUGH   Ned Hanlon
Born: August 22, 1857, Montville, Connecticut
Died: April 14, 1937, Baltimore, Maryland
Height: 5'9.5".   Weight: 170 Lbs.   Batted: Left.   Threw: Right.
Major League Career: 13 Years, 1,267 Games

1889: N.L.: Pittsburgh
1891: N.L.: Pittsburgh
1890: P.L.: Pittsburgh Burghers; OF 118

Batting Record:

Games: 118	3B: 6	Walks: 80	SL.%: .343
At Bats: 472	HRs: 1	K's: 24	S.B: 65
Hits: 131	Runs: 106	B.Avg: .278	B.R: +3
2B: 16	R.B.I: 44	O.B.A: .389	F.R: -5

Ned Hanlon was field manager for the Burghers through all 128 of their games; his won-lost record stands at 60–68, for a .469 win %.

During his time he was also referred to as Ed in speech and print. Ned Hanlon was a chronological elder among the P.L. players; by 1880 he'd been written of as a star of the first magnitude. He was an able major league outfielder, occasionally a shortstop. He became a much greater star later as a field manager.

He began this second career in 1889, as the third of three managers at (N.L.) Pittsburgh, winning 26 and losing 18 (.591); the team was in seventh place when he took charge and fifth at season's end, as fast as that moving to challenge the first division.

Hanlon chose the Players League for 1890, loyal to the P.L. Brotherhood; he persuaded most of his choice Alleghenys to join the Burghers of 1890. The club was left in such decimated field condition that in the year the P.L. played, the N.L. Pittsburgh edition was established by their 23 won 113 lost, .169 win % as one of the worst teams of all time.

While the P.L. Burghers finished only fifth, the expatriates of their N.L. counterpart performed and produced most credibly. Foremost was Jake Beckley, while Hanlon had a very good year at the bat; on the base paths, it was not quite as good in his and the various other pastures called P.L. outfields.

Including 1890, Mr. Hanlon was a major league manager for 19 years, most notably of the Baltimore Orioles from 1892 through 1898, among which he produced three consecutive championship teams, in 1894 through 1896. Then he went to Brooklyn, took many of his best players with him; this tenure ran from 1899 through 1905, with his teams winning pennants in 1899 and 1900.

From 1889 through 1907, his managerial record stands at 1,313 wins and 1,164 losses, a .530 win percentage, diminished by 97, 104, 87 and 87 losses his last four years, the last two at Cincinnati.

Hanlon as a manager was a canny judge of young talent and a trader and buyer of players. He was meticulous in both instruction and attention to detail. He wrote the book on aggressive offense but did not neglect the essentials and importance of defense.

He was involved in a complex web of ownership of the Baltimore and Brooklyn franchises, and minor league clubs; his shrewd mind led to capital gains wherever he worked and played, and a small fortune in real estate spread around the above two towns. He also had considerable holdings in Pittsburgh.

His baseball interests extended to the Federal League of 1914 and 1915. As a citizen he served as president of the Baltimore City Parks Board. He was an N.L. umpire in 1892. Add to his assets he was a stock holder and member of the board of directors of the Pittsburgh Burghers Base Ball Club, which assets became losses.

His leadership abilities had been observed a decade earlier; he was opposed to hard drinking, and was hypocritically removed from his position as manager of the N.L. Pirates of 1891 when he tried to enforce a code of moral discipline with his players.

As a Players League player, he wasn't a star, nor in fact and truth was he during his 13 years as a major league player. He does merit three marks of distinction for his 1890 play: 106 runs scored, 80 walks, and 65 stolen bases; the last ranks fourth in the P.L.

Hanlon the player was reputed to be an aggressive base runner and he had superb defensive abilities. The fact of 339 career stolen bases, with five seasons of 50+ support the statement, but a total F.R. of -9 does not; his F.R. highs were +12 and +11, in 1882 and 1884.

His S.B. highs are 69 in 1887, and 65 in 1890; only once in the six years known was he successful less than 50 times. With his first six years data missing it might be safe to presume his actual total was at least double what is known.

He began with Cleveland (N.L.) in 1880, but Detroit (N.L.) was the place he played most, from 1881 through 1888; among these Wolverines teams was at least one of the greatest in history, that being their 1887 unit.

Then he played for Pittsburgh (N.L.) in 1888 and 1889, after owner Frederick Stearns auctioned or sold off nearly the whole great team; Hanlon was last an active player in 1892 with the fabled Orioles of Baltimore.

The 80 walks and 24 K's by Hanlon in 1890 for the Burghers are an excellent ratio, adding his 65 S.B. has been a formula for scoring runs since before there were leagues; his O.B.A. of .389 and 106 runs scored attest, also his +3 B.R.

1890 was one of his better years as a player. Overall his batting averages are mediocre, .260, .325, .340; speed rather than power was the force of Hanlon. His career extra base hits count 30 home runs, 79 triples, 159 doubles, less than awesome.

He batted .300+ just once, .302 in 1885; .372 the same year was his O.B.A. high excepting the P.L. year; .397 SL.% in 1881 was his best, far below the benchmark. The 80 P.L. walks were by far his high, and 52 K's in 1884.

A mediocre season total of 69 R.B.I. in 1887 was his best in that production stat; he scored 100+ runs twice, in 1886 and in 1890. His SABR-stat sums are near the baseline, with +15 B.R. and -9 F.R. accumulated during his 13 years as a player.

This was not a star player of high profile at the major league level; the nearest he came was with the Pittsburghers of 1890. Fairly assessed, he was a pretty fair journeyman with speed and discipline at the bat and no glaring faults, lacking only power.

But his results as a manager in 1890 were not within light years of Hanlon at his best, in part verified by his proteges who became successful managers having played and learned the Hanlon style: John McGraw, Hugh Jennings, Wilbert Robinson, directly; there were more, then a second wave, and his lineage continues.

List Hanlon as a definite asset to the Players League; he was elected to the National Baseball Hall of Fame as a manager in 1996.

Edward Hugh "Ned" Hanlon died of complications after a heart attack.

Even before becoming the foremost manager in baseball, he was always doing something unexpected. He was a fine fielder and a slashing batter. He excelled as a baserunner and was as good a fielder and base runner as there was.

He was Eddie in his player days. His traits brought him fame and fortune.

HATFIELD, GILBERT   Gil Hatfield (Colonel)
Born: January 27, 1855, Hoboken, New Jersey
Died: May 26, 1921, Hoboken, New Jersey
Height: 5'9.5".   Weight: 168 Lbs.   Batted: Threw: Right.
Major League Career: 8 Years, 317 Games
1889: N.L.: New York
1891: A.A.: Washington
1890: P.L.: New York Giants; 3B 42, SS 27, P 3, OF 1

Batting Record:

Games: 71	3B: 6	Walks: 17	SL.%: .387
At Bats: 287	HRs: 2	K's: 19	S.B: 12
Hits: 80	Runs: 32	B.Avg: .279	B.R: -5
2B: 13	R.B.I: 37	O.B.A: .328	F.R: -4

Pitching Record:

Won: 1	Starts: 0	K's: 3	E.R.A: 3.38
Lost: 1	C.G: 0	Walks: 4	Saves: 1
Win %: .500	I.P: 8	Hits: 8	P.R: +1
Games: 3	Sh.O: 0	O.B.%: .359	W.A.T: 0.0

Gilbert Hatfield must have been a colonel without portfolio. 1890 wasn't his busiest year as a baseball player; that would be his next. But his best was given for the New York Giants of the Players League, when he got to play.

As a pitcher, he was a "reliefer," and by numbers generally he did well at it. The essence of Gil Hatfield was a player particular to the left side of the infield. His career is lacking order after 1890.

He played for Washington (A.A.) in 1891, in 134 games, with 500 at bats, didn't play in the major league at all in 1892 or 1894, and in 1893 he was in 34 games for Brooklyn. In 1895 he played in five games for amazing Louisville; those were his last.

Hatfield was an N.L. umpire in 1889. In 1890, proportional to his 287 at bats, all his numbers are in order, all rather ordinary, plus bits and flashes of power and speed. During the whole of his major league career, he was sufficiently mediocre that nobody bothered to make a note of which side of home plate he batted from.

During his career, "Colonel" Hatfield served at Buffalo (N.L.) in 1885, was out of service in 1886, played in two games for New York (N.L.) in 1887, then intermittently in 1888 and 1889, then as noted above. His merits might be best explained in columns.

	1890	1891	Career
B.Avg:	.279	.256	.248
O.B.A:	.328	.335	.315
SL.%:	.387	.316	.317
B.R:	-5	-6	-31
F.R:	-4	+4	-6

Virtually without distinction, this "Colonel" might be presumed to have been guided into baseball as the duty of a denizen of hometown Hoboken, an early base and bastion of the game, which transcends the concept of time back beyond the U.S. Civil War.

Among baseball citations relative to standards and benchmarks, he had 50 walks in 1891; otherwise the nearest is 13 triples in 1890. In sum, he played in 317 games, recorded 1,190 at bats and 295 hits, including 54 for extra bases; he scored 173 runs and counted 123 R.B.I.

He did play in the Players League, and later was a bank teller.

Gilbert Hatfield died of a heart attack.

HAYES, JOHN J.   Jackie Hayes
Born: June 27, 1861, Brooklyn, New York
Died:
Height: Weight: Batted: Threw: Right.
Major League Career: 7 Years, 300 Games
1889: Did not play
1891: Did not play
1890: P.L.: Brooklyn Wonders; OF 6, SS 3, C 2, 2B 1

Batting Record:

Games: 12	3B: 0	Walks: 2	SL.%: .190
At Bats: 42	HRs: 0	K's: 4	S.B: 0
Hits: 8	Runs: 3	B.Avg: .190	B.R: -5
2B: 0	R.B.I: 5	O.B.A: .227	F.R: 0

Born in Brooklyn, nearing age 30 in the year of the Players League, nothing more is known of his vitals than that he threw with his right hand. At some point during his major league career, he played all the positions except pitcher.

This dearth of information measures well against his P.L. record. Suffice it to say his season was somewhat less than outstanding. Jackie Hayes, of which there's more than one in the record books, is more easily explained by data than by verbs.

After his first two years, with sums of seven HRs and nine triples, he became near zero in power terms and void of extra base ability. But if $H = R + R.B.I.$ then he was very productive when he played, which wasn't often or much.

And if $W + H = R + R.B.I.$ then his 10 times on base by his own merits, resulting in eight runs on the scoreboard, shows his P.L. season calculus is both productive and commendable. This is contrary to his P.L. -5 B.R.

His K's in 1890 count less than 10 percent of his at bats, a credible ratio for most players. His neutral ±0 F.R. is just that. His zero stolen bases are a question, possibly a matter of judgment and discretion, or situations, or he couldn't run at all.

The adage "The more I play, the better I play" excuses his 1890 batting averages. With his P.L. season thus quantitatively explored, focus on his earlier seasons, as 1890 was his last.

Foremost, playing baseball doesn't seem to have been a matter of economic necessity for this Jackie Hayes. He began in 1882 with Worcester (N.L.), played in 78 games, with 326 at bats, accumulated 4 HRs and a .270 B.Avg., +5 B.R., -3 F.R.

Thus respectably established, when the N.L. cynically, for no reasons other than economic, dropped Worcester in favor of the greater market offered by Philadelphia, Hayes jumped to the A.A., where he played for the next five years.

While with that major league organization, he wore the uniforms of the Pittsburgh Alleghenys, the Brooklyn Trolley Dodgers aka Bridegrooms, and the Baltimore Orioles of Billie Barnie's only relatively successful season as a field manager.

The A.A. career of Jackie Hayes can be synthesized in the form of a line-item chronology:

1883 and 1884, Pittsburgh: 85 and 33 games, 351 and 124 at bats, .262 and .226 B.Avg.;
1884 and 1885, Brooklyn: 16 and 42 games, 51 and 137 at bats, .235 and .131 B.Avg.;
1887 Baltimore: 8 games, 28 at bats, .143 B.Avg.

Thus far witness the decline and fall of Jackie Hayes.

In 1886 he'd returned to the N.L., in service of the Washington Senators aka Statesmen, playing perhaps half of his 26 games at the venerable Swampdoodle Grounds; he accumulated 89 at bats, and a .191 B.Avg.

His career total for 300 games, with 1,148 at bats by the record book, calculate to a .233 B.Avg., .260 O.B.A., .331 SL.%; he scored 106 runs and drove home 68. This is paired with a -18 B.R. is -14 F.R., reflecting two seasons when he labored mainly as a catcher.

In 1888 and 1889 Hayes was mainly away from the major leagues. In 1890 when the P.L. called he became a member of the Brooklyn Wonders club. This John J. "Jackie" Hayes came out of retirement; where there was dearth, he was there.

He met with difficulties the last few years and was destitute. He went stone deaf and was stricken with locomotor ataxia; he could not walk or get around without help.

HEMMING, GEORGE EARL   George Hemming
Born: December 15, 1868, Carrollton, Ohio
Died: June 3, 1930, Springfield, Massachusetts
Height: 5'11".   Weight: 170 Lbs.   Batted: Right.   Threw: Right.
Major League Career: 8 Years, 204 Games
1889: Did not play

1891: N.L.: Brooklyn
1890: P.L.: Cleveland Infants; P 3 (Rookie). Brooklyn Wonders; P 19, OF ?

Batting Record:

	Clev	*Bkln*	*Totals*
Games:	3	19	22
At Bats:	11	57	68
Hits:	2	9	11
2B:	0	0	0
3B:	0	1	1
HRs:	0	0	0
Runs:	1	5	6
R.B.I:	1	8	9
Walks:	0	1	1
K's:	3	11	14
B.Avg:	.182	.158	.162
O.B.A:			
SL.%:	.192	.193	.191
S.B:	2	1	3
B.R:			
F.R:			

Pitching Record:

	Clev	*Bkln*	*Totals*
Won:	0	8	8
Lost:	1	4	5
Win %:	.000	.667	.615
Games:	3	19	22
Starts:	1	11	12
C.G:	1	11	12
I.P:	21	123	144
Sh.O:	0	0	0
K's:	3	32	35
Walks:	19	59	78
Hits:	25	117	142
O.B.%:	.439	.348	.363
E.R.A:	6.86	3.80	4.25
Saves:	0	3	3
P.R:	-6	+6	-0
W.A.T:	-0.4	+1.4	+1.0

After testing the P.L. pitching waters of Cleveland, he quickly switched to Brooklyn. By his 1890 record everything there was more and better. It might be that pitching on the staff of a second place team rather than seventh was somehow more amenable for this major league novice.

After his eighth and last season, he'd proven that a .667 win% in his first had been no fluke (won 8 lost 4). He won a total of 91 games during that term, and lost 82 (.526 win%), including a 20-win season (lost 13, .606) for Baltimore in 1895.

By proportion the next year was his best, won 15 and lost 6 (.714), also for the Orioles. They were in their prime then, the notorious Baltimore Orioles of the mid-1890s: few teams have been able to match their record of success. What George Hemming needed to be a winning pitcher was to be on a winning team.

There's not much to discuss about his 1890 batting, except 14 K's in 68 at bats (21 percent), and not much about that. As for his Infants/Wonders pitching, he won at a rate better than both his teams, completed all his starts, and worked a lot in relief.

His E.R.A. is 0.02 away from the league average; his P.R. of -6 and +6 equaling -0 are matters to consider independently. After the fact Hemming is the P.L. leader in the saves stat, which doesn't equate with 142 hits and 78 walks allowed in 144 innings, which in turn doesn't equate with his win %.

His data allow for about seven opponents runs per game, which is contradictory to both his cumulative E.R.A. and .363 O.B.%. Perhaps Hemming as a P.L. pitcher as a whole is cause for wonder, or there's some unknown to be discovered in the fact of switching from seventh to second; his record defies logic.

Thus, as a rookie, having proven himself to be a much better pitcher than he should have been, he was switched to Brooklyn of the N.L. as part of the P.L. surrender agreement, where he won 8 and lost 15 (.348). He lost a game for Cincinnati in 1892, then went to Louisville for the remainder of the 1892 season.

He continued there through all of 1893, most of 1894, then he was off to Baltimore to prove that common logic can't be applied to baseball of the 1890s. He returned to Louisville to do the impossible in 1897. This endeavor ended in a 3 and 4 mark.

Logic and the baseball enterprise had decreed that no mortal entity could change the destiny of the Louisville club. While there Hemming accumulated 36 wins and 42 losses (.462), with an E.R.A. cumulative of about 5.00. At Louisville, as with the Infants of Cleveland, he was not to be a winner.

To the contrary, while with Baltimore he won 39 games and lost 19 (.672), with an E.R.A. whole about a run less than at Louisville. Add further to statistical dismay his career P.R. later calculated to a -4, while his career W.A.T. counted +7.0.

During his eight major league seasons, Hemming pitched 1,587 innings, including 300+ twice (332 in 1893, 339 in 1894); he struck out 362 and allowed 691 walks, and gave up 1,799 hits. In his case this has no correlation to win %, W.A.T., or whatever premises and theories of baseball that may be applied.

In the baseball case of George Hemming, from Cleveland to Louisville, when he was with a winner, he was a winner. In sum, "quien sabe?"

His obituary reported that he married an actress while in Brooklyn but gave no name or date. Much confusion involves the whole of his life. An obituary written a year after his death stated he was with the recreation department of Springfield, and that upon his retirement was a hotel clerk.

HOY, WILLIAM ELLSWORTH   Dummy Hoy
Born: May 23, 1862, Houckstown, Ohio
Died: December 15, 1961, Cincinnati, Ohio
Height: 5'4".   Weight: 148 Lbs.   Batted: Left.   Threw: Right.
Major League Career: 14 Years, 1,796 Games
1889: N.L.: Washington
1891: A.A.: St. Louis
1890: P.L.: Buffalo Bisons; OF 122, 2B 1

Batting Record:

Games: 122	3B: 8	Walks: 94	SL.%: .371
At Bats: 493	HRs: 1	K's: 36	S.B: 39
Hits: 147	Runs: 107	B.Avg: .298	B.R: +16
2B: 17	R.B.I: 53	O.B.A: .418	F.R: +3

Among outfielders, William Ellsworth Hoy ranks 14th all time with 273 assists, eighth in double plays with 72, second in errors with 394, and 19th among all players with 173 hit by pitches. Nowadays, a player such as "Dummy" would be the subject of both public commendations and quiet curiosity.

Nowadays, major league players are attended to as if mortally wounded, and in turn equally commended, for playing with a sprained this or a pulled that. This

"Dummy" of the 1800s had both a handicap and an excuse throughout his career, but he did not let the handicap hinder him nor permit it to be used as an excuse.

Crude as it might seem, the nickname of "Dummy" given to him and others then was due to the fact that they were severely hearing impaired. The ability and determination of Dummy Hoy enabled him to overcome.

If he'd shown any power at the bat in his 1,796 games and 7,112 at bats (only 40 home runs) he'd long ago have been a legitimate contender for a place of honor at Cooperstown. As it is, he's never even been nominated to have his name inscribed on a bronze plaque there.

Try to imagine, if it's possible, batting near .300 and playing the outfield, unable to hear, not able to speak. As they were in 1890, the Buffalo Bisons of the Players League had among them a silent star who survived 99 years waiting to be recognized; it didn't happen.

Dummy lost his hearing at age three as a result of a meningitic inflammation of related membranes. As a baseball player of his time he was written of as smart and swift. Only three outfielders in history have earned three assists in one game for putouts made by their catcher; Dummy Hoy is among them.

He didn't play in the major leagues till age 26. He led the N.L. in stolen bases (82) for Washington in his first year (1888). He's among 29 who played in four major leagues, and at age 42 played in all 211 games for Los Angeles in a Pacific Coast League season (stole 46 bases).

He may have been the primary reason for umpires developing a system of hand signals, to level the playing field just a bit as it might be said. He stole "only" 39 bases for the 1890 P.L. Bisons, but scored 107 runs, via batting .298 and earning 94 walks, fourth most in the league.

Although the records are lacking data for five of his 14 seasons, his 210 known K's and 1,004 walks are sure evidence of a great batting eye, and good judgment of the strike zone, as well as patience and batting discipline. His 86 walks for A.L. Chicago in 1901 were the most in that league that year.

His 1,796 games in 14 years equals durability, well over 100+ per year. He played with injuries, but then that was no uncommon feat. He scored 1,426 runs via 2,004 hits and 1,044 walks (both milestones), and both his runs and walks rank among the top hundred of all time.

He stole 594 bases in all; only 15 players have accumulated more. Measuring his career batting averages of .287, .384, and .373 against his 1890 marks of .298, .418, and .371 demonstrates the consistency of W.E. Hoy.

Each of five seasons he stole 50+ bases, nine times scored 100+ runs; he counted 119 walks in 1891 and recorded 633 at bats in 1899.

Fans in five cities in addition to those of Buffalo had opportunities to watch this special star play in their hometown colors: Washington (N.L.) 1889–1889 and 1892–1893, St. Louis (A.A.) in 1891, Cincinnati 1894 through 1897 and 1902, Louisville 1898–1899, and Chicago (A.L.) In 1901.

His B.R. career sum is +155, his F.R. -21, almost a pure outfielder, the sole exception being one game in 1890. His data speak the story of a fine major league baseball player of the 1800s.

After baseball, he worked as a farmer; when he died there was no older former player alive. William Ellsworth "Dummy" Hoy has never been permitted the honor of being nominated for the honor of membership in baseball valhalla.

In period stats 1890–1899 he ranks: third in games, sixth in at bats, eighth in runs, third in walks, sixth in hit by pitches, fourth in stolen bases, second in sacrifices.

HURLEY, JEREMIAH JOSEPH   Jerry Hurley
Born: June 15, 1863, Boston, Massachusetts
Died: September 17, 1950, Dorchester, Massachusetts
Height: 6'0".   Weight: 190 Lbs.   Batted: Threw: Right.
Major League Career: 3 Years, 33 Games
1889: N.L.: Boston
1891: A.A.: Cincinnati
1890: P.L.: Pittsburgh Burghers; C 7, OF 1

Batting Record:

Games: 8	3B: 0	Walks: 2	SL.%: .318
At Bats: 22	HRs: 0	K's: 5	S.B: 0
Hits: 6	Runs: 5	B.Avg: .273	B.R: -1
2B: 1	R.B.I: 2	O.B.A: .333	F.R: 0

Jerry Hurley of Boston, Massachusetts, played little in 1890 for the Burghers of Pittsburgh after his single-game, four at bats rookie season of 1889 for his hometown N.L. team. He did more and better for the Burghers after accumulating a long line of 0's with not even a "K" for the records his first year.

His most active year, 1891 in 24 games with 66 at bats for Cincinnati of the A.A., gives him the distinction of playing in three different leagues in three consecutive seasons.

For 1890, his five runs scored and two R.B.I. on the sum of six hits and two walks make him distinctly if minimally a productive batter. Five K's among 22 at bats doesn't calculate as well.

There's almost no evidence of power at the bat, as per his .318 SL.%, but his .278 B.Avg. and .333 O.B.A. are credible; which side he batted from remains a mystery more than a century later.

His P.L. season, as it was, was vastly superior to his brief career; .217 B.Avg., .321 O.B.A., .304 SL.%; 20 hits in 92 at bats included four doubles, two triples, zero home runs. He scored 15 runs, drove home eight, walked 14 times, K'd 18, stole two bases.

His 1890 B.R. from whichever side, or both, is -1, career -2; his 1890 F.R. is -0, career -0. Hurley may have played against his hometown P.L. Reds and possibly played very well; his abbreviated data bank indicate that he was capable.

After his brief major league stay, he was an agent for and later a deputy commissioner of the U.S. Immigration Service.

Jeremiah Joseph Hurley died after a long illness.

HUSTED, WILLIAM J. Bill Husted
Born: October 9, 1867, Gloucester, New Jersey
Died: May 17, 1941, Gloucester, New Jersey
Height: Weight: Batted: Threw:
Major League Career: 1 Year, 18 Games
1889: Did not play
1891: Did not play
1890: Philadelphia Quakers; P 18 (Debut Date: April 29)

Batting Record:

Games: 18	3B: 0	Walks: 3	SL.%: .107
At Bats: 56	HRs: 0	K's: 9	S.B: 1
Hits: 6	Runs: 5	B.Avg: .107	B.R:
2B: 0	R.B.I: 5	O.B.A:	F.R:

Pitching Record:

Won: 5	Starts: 17	K's: 33	E.R.A: 4.88
Lost: 10	C.G: 12	Walks: 67	Saves: 0
Win %: .333	I.P: 129	Hits: 148	P.R: -9
Games: 18	Sh.O: 0	O.B.%: .384	W.A.T: -2.8

It might suffice to say that Bill Husted did not fare well in the Players League as either a pitcher or a batter, which would be unfair. Nor did he do well during his major league baseball career, which was 18 games in 1890, which is fairly fact and truth.

As a pitcher, his 12 complete games among 17 starts calculates far below the norm of his time; an average of seven innings per game does not bode well for a pitcher of that time, nor a -9 P.R. and -1.2 W.A.T. for any pitcher of any time.

Counting walks allowed double the number of K's achieved also never bodes well for a pitcher, nor 1.67 earned base runners per inning pitched. With such sums it would take much good luck and great defense to limit opponents to fewer than five earned runs per game.

As a P.L. batter, Husted clearly did not fare well, at all. That aside, losing three games more than the fifth-place Quakers on average, perhaps it's best that not much more is known about this P.L. pitcher. There might be comfort found in virtual anonymity for a one-year wonder who didn't do well at all.

William J. Husted died suddenly. His business after his major league baseball career is cited as an ice merchant. There is still conflict about his birth date, whether as noted above, or October 11, 1866, where noted, or October 19, 1866, at Philadelphia.

IRWIN, ARTHUR ALBERT Art Irwin
Born: February 14, 1858, Toronto, Ontario, Canada
Died: July 16, 1921, Atlantic Ocean

Height: 5'8.5". Weight: 158 Lbs. Batted: Left. Threw: Right.
Major League Career: 13 Years, 1,010 Games
1889: N.L.: Philadelphia and Washington
1891: A.A.: Boston
1890: P.L.: Boston Reds; SS 96

Batting Record:

Games: 96	3B: 1	Walks: 57	SL.%: .314
At Bats: 354	HRs: 0	K's: 29	S.B: 16
Hits: 92	Runs: 60	B.Avg: .260	B.R: -6
2B: 17	R.B.I: 45	O.B.A: .364	F.R: -6

He was born in the Canadian province of Ontario, unusual for a major league baseball player in 1890; the circumstances of his death were much more unusual and, although resolved, officially remain so.

His family moved to Boston when he was young. By age 15 Art Irwin was playing for the better local amateur teams; he would become a daring and reckless base runner and may have been the first to use a padded fielder's glove.

Family and friends would have enjoyed watching their adopted star become a prominent part of the club that brought the Players League gonfalon pennant to Boston-town. By 1890 he'd become an established veteran, having begun with the Worcester (N.L.) Ruby Legs (sic, Brown Stockings) through the whole of their existence, 1880 through 1882.

If there had been fielding runs then, he would have led the N.L. with +31 in his first major league season, the career sum of which became +30. Among his negative notes of distinction, he ranks 15th all time among shortstops with 594 errors.

He was an N.L. umpire in 1881, and again in 1902. He was also a manager in the N.L., and more prominently in the A.A.; his teams won 416 and lost 427, .493 win %. His only pennant as such came in the last, and his only A.A. year, 1891, which brought to Boston the last gonfalon of that league, with a record of 93 and 42, .689.

His career record as a batter is below average, with a .241 B.Avg, .299 O.B.A., .301 SL.%; he didn't walk much, or often hit with power, with five HRs among 934 hits in 3,871 at bats. He was walked 309 times and K'd 378.

His career production is out of balance, with 552 runs scored and 309 R.B.I. Also among his career data are 93 stolen bases and a -68 B.R., though fairly said somewhat offset by his +30 F.R. at a tough fielding position.

His P.L. manager apparently wanted more production from the "6" position, playing 27 games there himself, and testing half a dozen others for a game of two. Irwin sustained, but in doing so, with 89 games played, became the lowest among P.L. regulars except for catchers in that stat.

He's also consistently low in nearly all batting stats for 1890; his only record above the standards of mediocrity was 57 walks. Prior to and after the P.L., the balance of his career was played at Providence (N.L.) 1883 through 1885, and Philadelphia (N.L.) 1886 through 18 games of 1889, then Washington (N.L.) 85 games to end that season.

He played in six games for Boston (A.A.) in 1891, and one last game for the Phillies in 1894. After that he maintained connections with the game as the owner and manager of an AAA champion club, and was a New York Yankees player scout for five years.

Thus established in Boston and New York City, it was learned he had wives and children in both cities, not legally permitted in Massachusetts or New York, nor morally propitious, with the possible exception of in Utah.

He'd traveled much, and met many people; his financial situation would have allowed for maintaining a household and family, but was not sufficient to comfortably accommodate two. When the two families met by coincidence some time later, this was found to be fact, as the Boston Art Irwins lived well, but New York clan poorly.

A myriad of unknowns were involved in his life. Certainly stress related to such deceit could cause difficulties and likely did; early in 1921 he'd been diagnosed with internal problems and was advised to undergo surgery. Friends testified he was despondent.

He'd been treated in a New York City hospital for stomach troubles, and officially he died on July 16, 1921, but did he? Beyond the obvious bigamist, men such as Art Irwin have long been labeled scoundrels and knaves, synonymous with the mode of deceit he was living.

Deceit done successfully once might invariably lead to further temptation, which might in turn transform such a man from smart and rational to devious and cunning. His idea of a fielder's glove had become a modest industry he owned and operated, very indicative of his innovative capabilities.

He was also said to be an amiable fellow, for business if not for personal reasons. He had business associates in two of the most populous and prominent of cities, and was known to have a good number of social acquaintances and a few close friends.

His place of death officially is the Atlantic Ocean. He'd confided to friends that he was going home to die. His age then beyond 60, his physical condition was poor generally, compounded by the stomach troubles. He bought a steamship ticket from New York City to Boston.

He was listed as a passenger and people affirmed he was on board. The ship sailed and arrived just fine; he did not, at all. Suicide is possible, which was the official and media conclusion, that ex-ballplayer Arthur Albert Irwin had committed suicide.

Accident is also a possibility; he would have been carrying hundreds or thousands of dollars, the subject of a robbery who was killed accidentally, or deliberately. The facts of his death are persuasive but circumstantial, and the conclusion is presumed.

His body was not recovered from the Atlantic Ocean; there are a couple of reasons why not. He might not have boarded that steamship, which required an overnight journey to reach Boston. He might have boarded, left inconspicuously, leaving behind traces of himself to be found, and a reasonable conclusion made.

Irwin then might have begun a new life, free of the burdens and travails which ailed him. Free and frisky, smart and cunning, it's altogether possible that among his business and his social circles had been found an attractive and wealthy widow.

Sufficiently vulnerable, she might have been his for the taking, as wife number three. Subsequent to the publication of his death, there had been two reports that he'd been sighted, at two places both more than a thousand miles away from the Northeast.

One investigation concluded the report as a fraud; the other was not brought to a conclusion. Nor was it necessary for Art Irwin to run and hide; as a born Canadian he could easily have found a new American identity. If he'd found wife number three, and she was a lady of high finance, who among Boston or New York's high society would have questioned her finding new happiness?

IRWIN, JOHN   John Irwin
Born: July 21, 1861, Toronto, Ontario, Canada
Died: February 28, 1934; Dorchester, Massachusetts
Height: 5'10".   Weight: 168 Lbs.   Batted: Left.   Threw: Right.
Major League Career: 8 Years, 322 Games
1889: N.L.: Washington
1891: A.A.: Boston and Louisville
1890: P.L.: Buffalo Bisons; 3B 64, 1B 12, 2B 1

Batting Record:

Games: 77	3B: 4	Walks: 43	SL.%: .295
At Bats: 308	HRs: 0	K's: 19	S.B: 18
Hits: 72	Runs: 62	B.Avg: .234	B.R: -11
2B: 11	R.B.I: 34	O.B.A: .335	F.R: +2

For the reader not really familiar with the distant history of baseball in Canada, John Irwin was born in Canada, and there was organized amateur club competition as early as 1838. It had reached the highest levels in Ontario before Irwin was born.

His baseball pedigree thus extends more than two decades beyond his birth in the emerging industrial cities of Hamilton and Toronto, in the towns Beechville and North Oxford along Lake Ontario, and two additional decades beyond that.

His family migrated to the Boston, U.S.A., area while he was a very young child. Baseball was in the family. His first major league action was with Worcester (N.L.) in 1882; it was just one game and four at bats, with results all 0's.

He didn't play in 1883, or in 1885 when he was an A.A. umpire. He is one of the rare few who played in four major leagues. To cite concisely:

National League: 1882 (noted), 1887 through 1889 for Washington;
Union Association: 1884 Boston;
American Association: 1886 Philadelphia, 1891 Boston, Louisville;
Players League: 1890 Buffalo.

During his eight seasons he played most often at third base and at shortstop, 322 games in all, accumulating +3 F.R. and -14 B.R. He stole a total of 56 bases, drove in more than the known 92 runs, and scored 222 runs. He had 312 hits, 102 walks, and struck out more than the 74 times on record.

He had little batting power: Three HRs, 19 triples, 55 doubles; batted .246 with a .308 O.B.A. and .326 SL.%. There are among his data two seasons with 300+ at bats, of 1,269 total.

One of these 300+ seasons was with the Buffalo Bisons of 1890, the other with Boston of the other single-season league. In 1894 he played his most; in 106 games he had 432 at bats and batted .234 with accompanying data of .260 and .319.

For his Union Association club, Irwin played his best; he made 101 hits, scored 81 runs, and walked 15 times. In both his single leagues, when he got to play and got on base, a run was almost sure to score. In both years production was well above the norm.

While with the Bisons of 1890, he had to compete for playing time with Deacon White, a legend in his own time; thus in order to play for one of the worst teams of all time, standing in his way was one of the best players of all time.

Irwin later became a college baseball coach, proprietor of a billiards and bowling facility, and hotel owner and operator.

John Irwin had surgery for an intestinal disorder, and soon after he died of pneumonia.

JOHNSTON, RICHARD FREDERICK   Dick Johnston
Born: April 6, 1863, Kingston, New York
Died: April 3, 1934, Detroit, Michigan
Height: 5'8".   Weight: 155 Lbs.   Batted: Right.   Threw: Right.
Major League Career: 8 Years, 746 Games
1889: N.L.: Boston
1891: A.A.: Cincinnati
1890: P.L.: Boston Reds; OF 2; New York Giants; OF 76, SS 2

Batting Record:

	Bost	N.Y.	Totals
Games:	2	77	79
At Bats:	9	306	315
Hits:	1	74	75
2B:	0	9	9
3B:	0	7	7
HRs:	0	1	1
Runs:	0	37	37
R.B.I:	0	43	43
Walks:	0	18	18
K's:	1	25	26
B.Avg:	.111	.242	.238
O.B.A:	.111	.288	.284
SL.%:	.111	.327	.321
S.B:	0	7	7
B.R:	-2	-16	-17
F.R:	0	-0	-0

The Players League champion Boston Reds roster included as outfielders three players who a century later would have been known as superstars, and nine others who did fill-in work there.

Dick Johnston opted for the chance of more playing time in the New York Giants' P.L. pastures. There he only had to contend with two stars comparable with the Boston three.

Whether Congress Street Grounds or Brotherhood Park, in any ballpark locale, Johnston possessed speed and base-stealing skills, including 52 in 1887 which might be questioned, but not his 30+ the following two years. His speed had diminished by the P.L. year.

He had a career year in 1888, the fourth of five straight seasons with N.L. Boston. His 18 triples led the league, also evidence of speed, along with benchmarks of 12 HRs and 31 doubles. He scored 102 runs that season, with 173 hits in 585 at bats; he recorded only 15 walks and 33 K's, SABR-stats of +30 B.R. and +5 F.R.

The prior season his B.R. had been -10, with a +23 F.R.; when matched against his P.L. data, and of his career, his decline is evident even in a limited survey:

	1887	1888	1890	Career
B.Avg:	.258	.296	.238	.251
O.B.A:	.281	.314	.284	.285
SL.%:	.393	.472	.321	.366
Runs:	87	102	37	453
R.B.I:	77	68	43	386+
S.B:	52	35	7	151+
B.R.:	-10	+30	-17	-44
F.R:	+23	+5	-0	+42

He hit 20 triples in 1887, not an enhanced stat, which ranks eighth among all players and seasons during the period 1876–1889; he was seldom lacking in defense. The beginning and end of his career are somewhat unusual, both played in the A.A.

The whole consists of eight years, 746 games, 2,992 at bats; his last team was Cincinnati, in the last year of the A.A. They played a partial season, consisting of 100 games; they won 43 lost 57, .430 win%. Their home was Pendleton Park, and their given name was the Porkers.

Said of this A.A. entourage, three-fourths owned by Chris Von der Ahe, who also owned the A.A. St. Louis Browns, "For raucous adventure, wild antics, and just plain fun, the Porkers have never been matched in major league baseball." Johnston played in 99 games for the Porkers; his stats are beside the point.

He'd begun in 1884, with the Richmond Virginias (not Virginians), which played 42 games, perhaps half at their home park, which was Allen Pasture. Their field manager was Felix Moses. They won 12 and lost 30 (.286 win%), and Johnston was among them through their entire existence.

As for Johnston, despite the comings and goings of, he was a pretty average major league baseball player for his time. After that he was a supervisor at a printing plant in Kingston; then he relocated to Detroit, where he was a clerk in a state prison.

Richard Frederick Johnston died of throat cancer.

His father had died the year he was born, after nine months as a Confederate prisoner at Andersonville, Georgia.

Years after he'd played, a peer mused about Dick Johnston, "With Boston I think ... there was a building going up, lots of debris (in the outfield), he fell, put his hand up, caught the ball...."

"...All they could see was his hand, the circus catch was a game-winner, and over the years it attained the stature of a mythic feat."

"Fielding was Johnston's forte, generally considered to be the finest flychaser of his era, 'the phenomenal fielder of the league' some of his catches were simply marvelous; covered more ground than any other fielder with the possible exception of Hanlon."

"The perfect defensive outfielder, covered as much ground as (Tris) Speaker, nor was Johnston a slouch at the plate, he was noted for power in a day when the ball was dead; always was a dapper and dashing gentleman, printed quotes attest to his charm; was a generous soul."

His eulogy includes, "A graceful centerfielder who was considered to be one of the finest ballhawks of his day."

After his major league career, he played in the minors until 1894. Then he played and managed at the city amateur level, and coached and instructed many local nines.

JOYCE, WILLIAM MICHAEL   **Bill Joyce (Scrappy Bill)**
Born: September 21, 1865, St. Louis, Missouri
Died: May 8, 1941, St. Louis, Missouri
Height: 5'11".   Weight: 185 Lbs.   Batted: Left.   Threw: Right.
Major League Career: 8 Years, 904 Games
1889: Did not play
1891: A.A.: Boston
1890: P.L.: Brooklyn Wonders; 3B 133 (Rookie)

Batting Record:

Games:133	3B: 18	Walks: 123	SL.%: .368
At Bats: 489	HRs: 1	K's: 77	S.B: 43
Hits: 123	Runs: 121	B.Avg: .252	B.R: +16
2B: 18	R.B.I: 78	O.B.A: .413	F.R: -12

"Rookie makes good!" could have titled an article of the time. Bill Joyce did lead the league in walks, while playing the hot corner through each of his team's games during the P.L. season.

He also led in walks with 96 for Washington in 1895, and led with 14 HRs the following season, split nine and five between the Senators and the Giants. He wasn't but once a producer of a four-base hit for the Wonders of Brooklyn.

In his eight years he hit a total of 71 HRs, including 17 in each of 1894 and 1895, for Washington, and 10 HRs in his last season, 1889, with New York. In sum, "Scrappy

Bill" (reason unknown) in half of his major league seasons achieved the exceptional mark of 10+ HRs in a season.

He was above the mark with 18 triples for the Wonders and added 18 doubles, but his SL.% stands at just .368; his 123 walks made a very ordinary .252 B.Avg. into an exceptional .413 O.B.A. His +16 B.R. agree, his 77 K's didn't help at all.

He wasn't a kid when a major league rookie. His stats lacking in HRs resulted in 121 runs scored; his 43 stolen bases show he was a legitimate Brooklyn asset. A -12 F.R. doesn't fit well with the whole of his profile, though by formulae count to a game not won, he was a five-position player, durable, reliable.

His 18 triples were fifth most in the P.L.; before his career was concluded he achieved these ranks in period stats for 1890–1899: fourth in walks, third in K's, fifth in hit by pitches, seventh in HRs, fourth in O.B.A., ninth in SL.%, seventh in combo O.B.A./Sl.% (tied).

His 1891 playing time was limited for unknown reason, for Boston (A.A.), but it sure didn't do any harm to his batting averages: .309 B.Avg., .460 O.B.A., and .506 SL.%, all beyond the benchmarks. The raw facts include 243 at bats, nine doubles, 15 triples, three HRs, 76 runs, 51 R.B.I., 51 benchmark walks, 63 K's, and 36 stolen bases.

Twice proven he returned to Brooklyn for 1892, 1894 through 1896 at Washington, then New York and the Giants for the remainder of his very successful major league career. Note that the season of 1893 is missing; so was Joyce. He sat out that season in a salary dispute, true to the Players League tradition.

SABR has written of him as a Texas Western and International League power hitter who came to major league fruition. He's also noted as smart and good on defense.

His career F.R. is -45, he's 10th all time among 3B with 438 errors; in 1890 he set the standing record of 107 errors at his position.

The batting side of the Joyce ledger includes two years of 100+ walks; including the P.L. year, his career walks total 718. His career total K's are 280, lacking two years' data. A speculative projection of the whole wouldn't be much higher.

He learned as he worked at the bat and his K's dropped from a high of 77 in the P.L. to 54 in 1895, down to 34 in 1896. As noted, he beat the HRs benchmark four times, hit 15+ triples twice, 106 during his career, and 152 doubles.

His B.R. best was +51 in 1896, 40+ two other years; add a +30 and others count to a career +252 B.R. With his F.R. not far from positive, for the 1800s, this was one exceptional third baseman. In fact there aren't more than two who may have done better.

	1890	1891	1892	1893	1894	1895	1896	1897	1898
B.Avg:	.252	.309	.245	—	.355	.312	.333	.304	.258
O.B.A:	.413	.460	.392	—	.496	.442	.470	.441	.385
SL.%:	.368	.506	.398	—	.648	.527	.524	.433	.392
Walks:	123	63	82	—	87	96	101	78	88
B.R:	+16	+29	+23	—	+48	+40	+51	+25	+21

He hit for average, hit with power, had plate discipline, and won a slew of games beyond the norm with his batting. The point that the numbers of Bill Joyce are

Cooperstown class is made moot by one number, the 10-year hall of fame eligibility rule.

From another view, his numbers show .300+ B.Avg. five of eight years, .400+ O.B.A. six of eight years, .500+ SL.% four years, including .648; these numbers are not only all above average, but all are 100+ points above average for his time. He set eight season records.

Bill Joyce ranks seventh all time in O.B.A., and in the combined O.B.A. +SL.% stat ranks 43rd in history; in period stats 1890–1899 he ranks: fourth in walks, third in K's, fifth in hit by pitches, fourth in O.B.A., ninth in SL.%, eighth in combo (tied), seventh in HRs.

As a note aside, on May 18, 1897, he tied the record of hitting four triples in one game; no player has done it since. He was a manager, and did it as well as he batted; he won 179 and lost 122, .595 win %. If these were the stats of a pitcher they'd equal a ticket on the fast track to Cooperstown.

After quitting as a major league player, Bill Joyce was a scout for the St. Louis Browns for many years; he also owned a minor league team, operated a tavern, and was an employee of the City of St. Louis. He began as the best rookie in the Players League.

William Michael Joyce died after a three-month illness.

KEEFE, GEORGE W.   George Keefe
Born: January 7, 1867, Washington, D.C.
Died: August 24, 1935, Washington, D.C.
Height: 5'9".   Weight: 168 Lbs.   Batted: Left.   Threw: Left.
Major League Career: 6 Years, 78 Games
1889: N.L.: Washington
1891: A.A.: Washington
1890: P.L.: Buffalo Bisons; P 25

Batting Record:

Games: 25	3B: 0	Walks: 13	SL.%: .215
At Bats: 79	HRs: 0	K's: 14	S.B: 0
Hits: 16	Runs: 15	B.Avg: .203	B.R:
2B: 1	R.B.I: 7	O.B.A:	F.R:

Pitching Record:

Won: 6	Starts: 22	K's: 55	E.R.A: 6.52
Lost: 16	C.G: 22	Walks: 138	Saves: 0
Win %: .273	I.P: 196	Hits: 280	P.R: -50
Games: 25	Sh.O: 0	O.B.%: .444	W.A.T: 0.0

Far too many base runners in 1890, far too many earned runs; his W.A.T. is key and he ideally represents the season sum of the pitching staff of the P.L. Buffalo Bisons. In terms of batting, the dismal Bisons were far and away better. Some batters have warning track power, George Keefe didn't.

As a pitcher he completed every start, regardless, and came in a few times in relief; he won six and lost 16. Who ever said that there's no irony in baseball?

George Keefe won six lost 16, .273 win %; the Buffalo Bisons won 36 lost 96, .273 win %. Was Keefe better than the Bisons, was either better than their league, in any which way?

	Keefe	*Bisons*	*League*
O.B.%:	.444	.347	.345
E.R.A:	6.52	6.12	4.23
P.R:	-50	—	—

Other than a season at Buffalo, his career of six years was spent in Washington (N.L.) 1886 through 1889, Washington (A.A.) 1891. In his first two seasons he lost 4 and won 0; in all he lost 48 and won 20 (.294 win %). In 1891 he lost 3 and won 0.

His best year was 1888, winning 6 and losing 7 (.462); his most were in 1889, when he won 8 and lost 18 (.308). Given, Keefe was once almost a winning pitcher; his record shows further 71 starts and 68 C.G. (96 percent!), 616 I.P., 360 walks and 213 K's, and 721 hits.

Also, .398 O.B.% and 5.06 E.R.A. Keefe did pitch in the 1800s major leagues of baseball, sometimes at Boundary Field, at Gentleman's Driving Park on Sundays, and Swampdoodle Grounds, while in Buffalo at Olympic Park. He finished what he started.

Afterward, he worked in the Washington, D.C., navy yard and was a gardener at a high school. He scraped his leg while getting out of a car.

George W. Keefe died from a leg infection, of blood poisoning.

KEEFE, TIMOTHY JOHN   Tim Keefe (Sir Timothy)
Born: January 1, 1857, Cambridge, Massachusetts
Died: April 23, 1933, Cambridge, Massachusetts
Height: 5'10.5".   Weight: 185 Lbs.   Batted: Right.   Threw: Right.
Major League Career: 14 Years, 600 Games
1889: N.L.: New York
1891: N.L.: New York and Philadelphia
1890: P.L.: New York Giants; P 30

Batting Record:

Games: 30	3B: 0	Walks: 13	SL.%: .185
At Bats: 92	HRs: 2	K's: 26	S.B: 0
Hits: 10	Runs: 18	B.Avg: .109	B.R:
2B: 1	R.B.I: 11	O.B.A:	F.R:

Pitching Record:

Won: 17	Starts: 30	K's: 88	E.R.A: 3.38
Lost: 11	C.G: 23	Walks: 85	Saves: 0
Win %: .607	I.P: 229	Hits: 228	P.R: +22
Games: 30	Sh.O: 1	O.B.%: .338	W.A.T: +1.7

He was well known for his behavior, and his repute was that of a gentleman. 1890 was his last good pitching season; before that he'd been spectacular some years, in others incredible. This is one of the very greatest pitchers in major league history.

He was also a leader in the Players League rebellion and the secretary of the Players Brotherhood. Though his 1890 record doesn't read terrific, mark him as a distinct asset to the league and the cause. His and John Ward's wives were sisters.

As an 1890 player, with his .109 batting average recognized, as a pitcher his 17 and 11 record would have been less had he not between May 7 and June 7 won 10 consecutive decisions.

His P.L. season came to an end on August 19 when the index finger on his pitching hand was broken; prior to that he did enough, and well enough, to rank fourth in O.B.% and fifth in E.R.A.

During the greater part of his career, Tim Keefe had great speed, making his change and curve that much more effective. There's a great deal to be told of the P.L. pitcher and leader; his legend is written in data and facts.

He began with Troy (N.L.) in 1880, and though pitching only 105 innings (won 6 lost 6), he set and holds the official record for lowest E.R.A. in a season; 0.86 doesn't require adjectives.

His career extended through 1893, all N.L. except 1890 and 1883–1884 with A.A. New York. He jumped leagues when the National sold out Troy to put a franchise (back) in New York City.

In 1883 his record was won 41 lost 27 (.603), 41 wins didn't lead the league, but his 68 games, starts and completes, did, as did 619 innings pitched, and 361 K's, and .255 O.B.%; his E.R.A. was 2.41, which didn't lead.

His last two years were with Philadelphia, 19–16 (.543) in 1892 and 10–7 (.588) in 1893; he'd revived from 2 and 5 (.286) in New York and 3 and 6 for the Phillies, 5 and 11 (.313) in 1891. There were issues at play; some critics said his finger had not healed properly, but more subtly was mentioned the residual hostility of the franchise and league owners.

He didn't lead in any statistics after 1890, but prior led in: wins two years (1886 and 1888); win % one year (1888); games two years (1883 and 1886); complete games two years (1883 and 1886); innings pitched two years (1883 and 1886); K's two years (1883 and 1888); O.B.% three years (1883, 1888, 1889); E.R.A. three years (1880, 1885, 1888); P.R. one year (1888).

Measured against benchmarks and other standards of excellence: 20+ wins seven years (42 in 1886, 41 in 1883, 37 in 1884, 35 in 1887 and 1888, 32 in 1885), 28 in 1889; 50+ games and starts five years (68 in 1883, 64 in 1886, 58 in 1884, 56 in 1887, 51 in 1888); 50+ complete games five years (62 in 1886, 54 in 1887; and 1883, 1884, and 1888 same as games and starts); 300+ innings pitched 10 years (619 in 1883, 540 in 1886, 492 in 1884, 479 in 1887, 434 in 1888, 402 in 1881, 398 in 1885, 375 in 1882, 364 in 1889, 313 in 1892); 300+ K's three years (361 in 1883, 333 in 1888, 323 in 1884); 2.00- E.R.A. 3 years (0.86 in 1880, 1.58 in 1885, 1.74 in 1888, and four other years between 2.00 and 2.50); also .300- O.B.% six years, +50+ P.R. five years, among the achievements of Tim Keefe.

His career data: won 341 lost 225, .603 win %, 600 games, 593 starts, 553 complete; 5,061 innings pitched, 2,521 K's, 1,224 walks, 4,452 hits allowed, .295 O.B.%, 2.62 E.R.A.

His ranks all time: eighth in wins, 19th in starts, third in complete games, 12th in innings pitched, 19th in K's, 40th in walks, 38th in E.R.A., his O.B.% by one source is .276, which ranks 15th, and his 233 wild pitches rank third.

The P.R. total for Tim Keefe is +402; +53 in 1888 led his league, but +61 in 1883 did not, nor did three other years of +50+ or another of +40+. His total W.A.T. count +23.2, with a high of +9.1 in 1888, and twice +8.8, in 1883 and 1887, the latter a league leader.

His best win % was .745 in 1888, he also topped .700+ with .711 in 1885. He often pitched 20 games in a season and allowed six hits or less. In 1888 he won 19 consecutive decisions, which was and still is the major league record.

Only Nolan Ryan has accumulated more seasons with 300+ K's. Keefe was the first to have 2,000+ K's, the first to have three 300+ K's seasons, and he ranks as one of only 21 pitchers in history with 300+ career wins.

On July 4, 1883, he pitched both games of a double-header, giving up three hits, the best ever such performance in one day. As a fielder among pitchers he ranks 17th all time with 1,062 assists and first in errors with 167.

His season records are numerous. In period stats 1876–1889 he ranks: second in wins, fifth in losses, 10th in win%, fourth in games, third in starts, third in complete games, third in shutouts (tied), fourth in innings pitched, second in walks, first in K's, eighth in E.R.A., fourth in hit batters, fifth in wild pitches, seventh in O.B.%.

He also ranks first in basic batting average allowed with .223, significantly below the all-time pitching mean for B.Avg.; he pitched 39 shutout games during his career and led his league with eight in 1888; for the period above his starts/C.G. is 98 percent.

Timothy John Keefe was elected to the National Baseball Hall of Fame in 1964. Despite a short season, he was definitely a credit to the Players League, and a P.L. feature player. He was involved in real estate after baseball.

The cause of his death is not certain; the most probable cause was a heart attack.

KELLY, MICHAEL JOSEPH   King Kelly
Born: December 31, 1857, Troy, New York
Died: November 8, 1894, Boston, Massachusetts
Height: 5'10".   Weight: 170 Lbs.   Batted: Right.   Threw: Right.
Major League Career: 16 Years, 1,455 Games
1889: N.L.: Boston
1891: A.A.: Cincinnati and Boston; N.L.: Boston
1890: P.L.: Boston Reds; C 56, SS 27, OF 6, 1B 4, P 1

Batting Record:

Games: 89	3B: 6	Walks: 52	SL.%: .450
At Bats: 340	HRs: 4	K's: 22	S.B: 51
Hits: 111	Runs: 83	B.Avg: .326	B.R: +18
2B: 18	R.B.I: 66	O.B.A: .419	F.R: -5

Pitching Record:

Won: 1	Starts: 0	K's: 2	E.R.A: 4.50
Lost: 0	C.G: 0	Walks: 2	Saves: 0
Win %: 1.000	I.P: 2	Hits: 1	P.R: -0
Games: 1	Sh.O: 0	O.B.%: .359	W.A.T: +0.5

King Kelly was the field manager of the league champion Reds throughout their 130-game season; he led his team to an 81–48 won-lost record, a .628 win %, and thus was selected as the All Star manager of the Players League.

The King's career B.R. count is an awesome +321. As a complete player he's ranked 11th all time with 285 assists; primarily a catcher he's 16th with 259 errors, and sixth with 417 passed balls.

King Kelly began modestly with the Cincinnati Red Stockings in 1878. Their records of less than a decade earlier had already become tradition and legend. They had been the first to declare publicly as a professional baseball club.

Kelly played in 60 of 61 of their games in 1878 as a catcher, outfielder, and at third base. His 237 rookie at bats produced batting averages of .283, .303, .321, better than adequate for his time and his team.

He was established in 1879, still with Cincinnati, batting .348, scoring 79 runs in 78 of their 81 games, while playing a variety of positions. The franchise which owned him was in turmoil, had been since it finished 42.5 games behind Chicago in the N.L.'s seminal season of 1876.

The names Keck and Neff were involved. The baseball elite of Cincinnati would muddle their way through three franchises in nearly as many years, and then end up with none. O.P. Caylor, local sportswriter, was the prime facilitator of the disorder.

He had help from the hostile *Worcester Spy* newspaper, and soon would make his opinions known by means of his own baseball journal. He'd been rebuffed in his quest to become the official scorer for the (by now the name was just) Reds and he made known his wrath as a writer and as a participant in Reds ownership.

On the first of October 1879, the Reds management literally fired the whole team; there was change in ownership, which soon would become irrelevant. In the interim, William Hulbert and Al Spalding sat back in Chicago, scheming to maximize their gain from the troubles at Cincinnati.

The state of King Kelly and the other Reds players was dismay and confusion, for which there was no more regard than for any human chattel. Hulbert was the N.L. president and had been officially since 1877, actually since its origin.

Ownership of the Cincinnatis had passed from the above to Justus Thorner, then again to Menderson and then the iron hand of Hulbert conveyed it to W.H. Kennett, then sent Cincinnati to baseball oblivion on the 6th of October, 1880. Kelly had been fired; he was fair game.

Spalding wanted King Kelly for Hulbert's club, and got him; they were given fine service from the start of the 1880 season until the 1886 season was done. On the playing fields he continued as he'd begun; he became the baseball idol of Chicago, rhetoric and fact made him the star of the nation, as well as the main attraction at the N.L. turnstile gates.

His seven seasons in Chicago uniforms would be a great 1800s career; let an asterisk [*] identify him as the N.L. leader: .300+ B.Avg four years (.323 in 1881, .305 in 1882, .354 [*] in 1884, .388 [*] in 1886); .400+ O.B.A. two years (.414 [*] in 1884, .483 [*] in 1886); .500+ SL.% three years (.524 in 1884, .534 in 1886).

He scored 100+ runs for Chicago each of three years, 120 [*] in 1884, 124 [*] in 1885, and 155 [*] in 1886. King Kelly never did reach the 100+ R.B.I. plateau, but during this phase of his phenomenal career he led the N.L. in doubles twice, with 27 in 1881 and 37 in 1882.

His +64 B.R. of 1886 would not have led, but +49 in 1884 would. Among the years the N.L. kept stolen base records is known that Kelly stole 53 in 1886. His F.R. at Cincinnati were +7 and +6; at Chicago this stat varied between +2 and -14. He'd played at every position.

The N.L. triumvirs of Boston craved Kelly. Hulbert had died in 1882, and had bequeathed his realm of authority and capitalist wisdom to Spalding; he availed as never had been done before in the domain of professional major league baseball.

Arthus Soden was Triumvir I, Caesar; "Conant" was II, Pompey; "Billings" was III, Crassus; he did the deal with Spalding that transacted King Kelly from Chicago to Boston. It was the most startling move of the decade.

The exchange of Kelly for dollars became the first major league transaction of players between clubs. Kelly was consulted and refused, but was induced by a Boston salary suggested at $5,000.

With no fanfare, nor consultation with anyone, on September 29, 1879, the N.L. had held a special meeting at which it passed the first effective, if primitive, reserve rule to curb salaries. The vote of the owners had been unanimous; Hulbert had represented Cincinnati. In 1887 the public maximum was $2,500.

The price paid by the triumvirs for Kelly was $10,000, which was a record at the time, no less stunning than the deal done later which involved Babe Ruth, and a century later involving Catfish Hunter, when the reserve rule was finally broken.

By 1887 the infamous reserve rule had evolved beyond primitive and its original premise to become the foundation of baseball law, despite its legal deficiencies—the law which became cause for the Brotherhood of Players, rebellion, and war.

In accord with the reserve rule, of the record price paid for the transaction of his body and skills, King Kelly received not one dollar. Thus rendered less than a serf, tameme, gokenin or slave, he resumed his superb career whence he'd been sold.

With the fundamental dignity of a man put aside, and his vanity suppressed, which King Kelly had much more than an ordinary share of, he did go to Boston, to play for the Beaneaters in the 1887 season, but the $5,000 salary presumed became less.

That would have been another record for King Kelly, of which triumvir Billings and associates had a different understanding, with a rather peculiar twist, of vanity. When Kelly arrived, Billings informed him that his 1887 pay would be $2,000.

Kelly was furious till he was told he'd be paid $3,000 more for having his picture taken with his new owners. Meanwhile, Spalding was counting his profits, the $10,000 he'd received for the sale of King Kelly.

His presence immediately began dividing the team into two factions, with a little help; media men wrote that Kelly was taking over as field manager, from John Morrill, himself an icon in Boston, with ties to its baseball going back to the era of the National Association, and the Boston Red Stockings.

He denied the allegations publicly, but to little avail, as they had been informed, people tend to believe what they read in the newspapers. They had not been told that King Kelly the player had declined somewhat by then. These are the sums of his three seasons with the Boston Reds of the National League: .300+ B.Avg. two years (.322 in 1887, .318 in 1888); .400+ O.B.A. none (his best was .393 in 1887); .500+ SL. % none (his best was .488 in 1887).

He did score 100+ runs two years, 120 in 1887 and 120 in 1889. He did lead the N.L. with 41 doubles in 1889, his most in that stat. His stolen bases these three years numbered 56, 68, 51; his season totals were high, but he never led his league in S.B.

Spalding and the triumvirs had not swindled Kelly, not exactly, they merely refused to share their gains made by and because of him; the only player in America then with a bigger name than King Kelly might have been Adrian "Cap" Anson of Chicago, who loyally served Hulbert and Spalding for a quarter century.

As for Spalding, the Boston cartel, and their brethren, the twin demons of lust and greed were about to call for their due. The skills of King Kelly on the fields of play had diminished, but his memory and recall were excellent.

The rumblings and grumbling of players which had become the Brotherhood by 1886 were about to become manifestly known as the Brotherhood of Professional Base Ball Players which then would be amended to the Players' National League of Base Ball Clubs.

King Kelly became first prize in the three-way contest for the best players and top gate attractions. The N.L. owners tried to cajole, entice, to induce or seduce and by some legal codes even bribe him to play for their side in the coming war for survival of the boldest and the slickest.

He'd been written of as tempted and more than one time. More than one N.L. executive was directly involved, unofficially of course, independently and without the knowledge of their brethren. It's been said that one of the Boston elite, or John B. Day who owned N.L. New York, or Spalding himself made an offer of $5,000 with no tricks after the jump back to the N.L. was made.

Kelly was said to have agonized, having himself established a grand lifestyle, but he refused that and all other such offers. In this case, his prospective benefactor spurned loaned him $500, for no good reason, and no expectation of repayment.

He was not "The King" of lore whence came the Players League, but Michael Joseph "King" Kelly was great in, and for the P.L. In reference to his physical and behavioral profiles, by the judgment of the wife of a cited author, who writes pretty well herself, King Kelly in his prime was the best looking player of his time.

His autobiography was alleged the first by a famous player; he was smart, creative, and innovative, but had little formal education and was barely literate. There is no disingenuity, and facts need not be embellished to state that King Kelly was a genuine American original, very good and very bad, on and off the field, respectively.

Babe Ruth may have learned mode of behavior for a celebrity and star baseball player from the text on King Kelly; he's been cited the most aggressive baserunner of the 1870s. His batting was superior in every way, his stolen base total excellent, and he was also consistent on defense with a terrific throwing arm.

Babe would have grinned with an inscrutable yet profound smile of an enigma if he'd seen "The King" wearing a silk top hat and an ascot, being driven to the ballpark in an open carriage with clusters of flowers and a bevy of the most lovely young ladies.

He was a scamp without parallel in his prime, and a showman in the mode of modern professional wrestlers on parade. He was literally a fashion model, he sang and did recitations, and he was the original king of the beer halls, bars, and saloons.

He played the game to his capacity and lived life to its fullest; let the further facts illustrate King Kelly, baseball player. He pitched in 12 games but never started any, a grand total of 45 innings.

As a pitcher, he lost a decision in 1884, and won a game in 1887; he won another in the Players League, lost another in the A.A. His record is won 2 and lost 2, his E.R.A. is 4.20; he walked 30 and struck out four; he gave up 45 hits. Somehow King Kelly the pitcher won two decisions out of four.

His batting is not at all a matter of "somehow"; few players have had the capacity to energize fans like he did. In the P.L. he had no faults except fielding runs. He was the field manager of the league champions. He played in more than 80 games, at two of the toughest positions: consider his age at the time.

He batted for average, he hit with power, and he scored a run for every game he played. He drove in runs, and proved the wealth of his batting discipline and judgment; one SABR-stat is clearly in his favor. He led in nothing, yet King Kelly was a complete player.

In 1890, he was well along the chronological downside of a great career, of 1,455 games and 5,894 at bats; his position in the field can only be explained as utility. He played all of them, for the most part outfield and catcher.

His three seasons after the P.L. could be the career of an ordinary 1800s player; 1891 with the A.A., 82 games at Cincinnati, which must be judged less than seriously as a baseball franchise, and that year he put in appearances in four games for A.A. Boston. With 295 at bats he produced .295, .402, .413, one a benchmark stat.

In 1892 he was with the only surviving Boston club, 78 games, 281 at bats; .189, .287, .235; 16 games with N.L. Boston in 1891 are hidden in the records, with .231, .322, .250 maybe reasonably so. King Kelly produced no dazzle in 1891, or in 1892, although 51 walks in 1891 might passively count as such.

In 1893 he brought to an end the playing career of one of the greatest; during that career "The King" batted .308, with 1,813 hits, which included 359 doubles, 102 triples, and 69 home runs; his O.B.A. stands at .368, his SL.% at .438; he scored 1,357 runs, .93 run per game.

He drove in 950 runs, had 549 walks and 417 K's, and stole 368 bases. His lifestyle killed him before reaching age 40; the ashes of the Players League had not yet had time to turn to dust. Chosen for membership at the National Baseball Hall of Fame in 1945, he is surely a Players League feature player, and by virtue of one singular achievement, being the Players League star manager.

There's no redundancy about "the one and only King Kelly." As Michael Joseph Kelly, he officially died of pneumonia, which came as a result of a slight cold.

(The "tameme" was the human beast of burden used by the Spaniards after their conquest of Mexico circa 1521–1600; the "gokenin" was the house servant used by Japanese feudal lords circa 1600–1868, he had previously been the lowest rank of Samurai.)

Beyond innumerable single-season records, these are the period stats 1876–1889 on record for the one and only King Kelly: seventh in games, seventh in at bats, first in runs, fourth in hits, third in doubles, eighth in HRs, second in R.B.I., seventh in walks, seventh in stolen bases, sixth in B.Avg., ninth in O.B.A., seventh in SL.%, seventh in O.B.A./SL.% combo, fifth in extra base hits, fourth in total bases, seventh in stolen bases.

On the fields where he played might still be heard the echo of his fans as they called, "Slide, Kelly, slide!"

KILROY, MATTHEW ALOYSIUS   Matt Kilroy
Born: June 21, 1866, Philadelphia, Pennsylvania
Died: March 2, 1940, Philadelphia, Pennsylvania
Height: 5'9".   Weight: 175 Lbs.   Batted: Threw: Left.
Major League Career: 10 Years, 303 Games
1889: A.A.: Baltimore
1891: A.A.: Cincinnati
1890: P.L.: Boston Reds; P 30, OF 2, SS 1, 3B 1

Batting Record:

Games: 31   3B: 1   Walks: 12   SL.%: .247
At Bats: 93   HRs: 0   K's: 9   S.B: 11
Hits: 20   Runs: 11   B.Avg: .215   B.R:
2B: 1   R.B.I: 8   O.B.A: F.R:

Pitching Record:

Won: 9   Starts: 27   K's: 48   E.R.A: 4.29
Lost: 15   C.G: 18   Walks: 87   Saves: 0
Win %: .375   I.P: 218   Hits: 268   P.R: -1
Games: 30   Sh.O: 0   O.B.%: .378   W.A.T: -5.3

(This involves one of the rare few feats which could follow Tim Keefe and King Kelly.)

In the U.S.A. in the 1930s and '40s, perhaps prior, there was a bit of popular graffiti to be found everywhere which said simply "Kilroy was here." Its intrinsic meaning isn't known, but if it existed in 1886, could well have meant another batter struck out.

He set a record then, Matt Kilroy did, which no pitcher since the modern era began in 1901 has come within 130 of; that was Nolan Ryan (Angels, A.L.) who recorded 383 K's in 1973. That stat only ranks eighth on the all time list; oddly, the players ranking third through seventh all did theirs in 1884.

Further coincidence, and most unfortunate for him, the pitcher who ranks second in most K's in a season also did his in 1886; his sum was only 499 K's in one season. It might seem unlikely that Kilroy struck only 48 P.L. batters in 1890, that is if his four previous seasons hadn't burned him out as a pitcher.

Regarding his epic feat of 1886, it might be prudent to consider the rules for calculating batting averages in 1887, and what were the results. It's safe to speculate that baseball preferred to have the impossible happen only once.

Revising that rule wasn't the only change that year; both the batter's box and the pitcher's box dimensions were also changed, and the requirement was established that home plate had to be made from white rubber, to improve its view for all concerned.

Matt Kilroy pitched for the champion Boston Reds in 1890; if all their staff had done as he did, Boston would have finished in the vicinity of Cleveland. As it was, Kilroy was their fourth pitcher when a major league pitching staff was constructed of, at most, three primary parts.

Matt Kilroy began at Baltimore (A.A.) in 1886 and continued with the Orioles through 1889. In 1887 he led the A.A. with 46 wins and had 19 losses, a .708 win %. His games, starts, complete, his innings pitched, shutouts, in fact all his stats except K's are nearly identical to his numbers for 1886; his won and lost also differ.

With his career data included to measure against, let an asterisk (*) depict the league leader:

	1886	*1887*	*Career*
Won:	29	46	141
Lost:	34	19	133
Win %:	.460	.708	.515
Games:	68 (*)	69 (*)	303
Starts:	68	69	292
C.G:	66 (*)	66 (*)	264
I.P:	583	589 (*)	2,435
Sh.O:	5	6 (*)	19
Walks:	182	157	754
K's:	513 (*)	217	1,170

513 K's in 583 innings in 1886 didn't burn him out, and neither did pitching half of his 10-year career in these two years. His workload declined after this, but he still produced benchmark numbers; in 1889 he won 25, lost 29 (.537), pitched 481 innings, and matched his 217 K's of 1887.

His counts after the P.L. are easy. He won 5 and lost 17 (.227), 243 I.P., one shutout, scattered variously among the Cincinnati-Milwaukee (A.A.) split franchise of 1891; then Washington and Louisville, missing three seasons, coming back for a final season with Chicago. He won 6 and lost 7 (.462); he pitched exactly 100 innings, and recorded exactly 18 K's.

He recorded W.A.T. above +10.0 one year and ranked 10th in walks for the period 1876–1889. He was an A.A. umpire in 1887. Pitching to excess and a base-running crash injured his arm before 1890; he pitched in just five games during August and September.

In his last season he pitched in 13 games and played 12 as an outfielder. As a pitcher he ranks 21st all time in errors with 91 (Nolan Ryan is next with 90). He retired to run a restaurant near Ben Shibe and Connie Mack's new baseball emporium.

Matt Kilroy accomplished something no other pitcher has ever done, and it's safe to speculate that when the Players League played, Kilroy was there. It was later written he was a killjoy to speedsters whenever they made it to first base, and such runners as Kelly, Tom Brown, Stovey, and Hanlon made it a point to hug first base whenever Kilroy was in the box.

KING (KOENIG), CHARLES FREDERICK   **Silver King**
Born: January 11, 1868, St. Louis, Missouri
Died: May 19, 1938, St. Louis, Missouri
Height: 6'0".   Weight: 170 Lbs.   Batted: Right.   Threw: Right.
Major League Career: 10 Years, 398 Games
1889: A.A.: St. Louis
1891: N.L.: Pittsburgh
1890: P.L.: Chicago Pirates; P 56, OF 1, 1B 1

Batting Record:

Games: 58	3B: 5	Walks: 13	SL.%: .249
At Bats: 185	HRs: 1	K's: 22	S.B: 3
Hits: 31	Runs: 24	B.Avg: .168	B.R:
2B: 2	R.B.I: 16	O.B.A:	F.R:

Pitching Record:

Won: 30	Starts: 56	K's: 185	E.R.A: 2.69
Lost: 22	C.G: 48	Walks: 163	Saves: 0
Win %: .577	I.P: 461	Hits: 420	P.R: +79
Games: 56	Sh.O: 4	O.B.%: .321	W.A.T: +2.6

    If there were only two great pitchers in the P.L. of 1890, then he was one of them. He pitched for the Pirates of Chicago, and extremely well at that, which no doubt pleased Charlie Comiskey and boiled the blood of Albert G. Spalding.

    The name of "Silver" was given to Charles F. King by himself. A total of five other major league pitchers reached the mark of 30+ wins in 1890, including two in the Players League. Allow for some perspective and a note of significance.

    Since 1901, 13 major league pitchers have won 30+ games in one season, a total of 21 times; only three of these have not been chosen for honors at Cooperstown. One of the eligibles is Silver King. Among his credentials are these period stats: *1876–1889:* fourth in win %, his period win % is .683. *1890–1899:* 10th in O.B.%, his period O.B.% is .324.

    Among the ranks of Silver King in the Players League of 1890: third in wins, second in games, second in C.G., first in shutouts, second in I.P., first in E.R.A., second in K's, second in O.B.%, first in P.R., first in total pitchers index, first in total baseball ranking.

    His 30 wins for second stands as a tie, the other ranks are his alone; he's one of the few P.L. pitchers with more K's than walks to his credit. Add to exceptions his fewer hits than I.P., and he is the only P.L. pitcher with an E.R.A. below 3.00.

Obviously he won at a rate better than the Chicago staff, but only a +2.6 W.A.T. His ranks of first are indicative of his best assets; by one obscure statistic, with an average of 8.20, he allowed the fewest hits per game in the P.L. On June 21 he pitched a no-hitter, but lost 1 to 0 because of an error.

Silver King had great speed and good control, was weak as a batter, and slow as a runner, but could field his position well. In his 1889 prelude to the P.L. he won 35 and lost 16 (.686) for the St. Louis (A.A.) Browns; in 1888 he was greater and won 45 and lost 21 (.682), also for the Browns.

His first season of 1887 for the incredible St. Louis Browns of Von der Ahe was still better in terms of success: 32 wins and 12 losses count a benchmark .727 win % and he pitched in 46, completed 43 games, with a 3.78 E.R.A. and .330 O.B.%.

1888 was the only year other than 1890 he was a league leader, with 45 wins, 66 games, 64 complete, 586 I.P., six shutouts, and 1.64 E.R.A. He'd just turned age 21 then. His SABR-stat of P.R. also led, +92 for one season, a nine-game gain for his team.

His major league career began in 1886 with Kansas City (N.L.); his four decisions included one for and three against, not a hint of what Silver King would achieve in the coming years. His Browns three-year composite of 112 won and 49 lost (.696) has been equaled or bettered by very few in baseball history.

He began losing after the P.L. season. In 1891 with the Pirates (N.L.) his record was 14 won and 29 lost. Thereafter with New York he won 23 and lost 24 in 1892. He pitched partial seasons in 1893 for the Giants (3 and 4) and Cincinnati (5 and 6) then left the major leagues for two years.

Recall fairly he was the pitching mainstay for three years of one of the greatest teams in baseball history, and in 1887 the leader of one of the greatest pitching triads in history in King, Caruthers and Foutz. Charlie Comiskey worked all to their limit, Silver King foremost. When the P.L. arrived he wanted King with him.

His load was relatively light in 1887, just 390 innings; then in 1888 it was 586 innings. When the Browns fell to second in 1889, he pitched 458 innings. His 10-year career total stands at 3,190.

Silver King won 40+ games once, 20+ each of five years, passed the .700+ win % mark once; worked in 60+ games once, 50+ four years; he made 60+ starts one year, 50+ three years; pitched 60+ complete games once; also 500+ I.P. once and 300+ each of six years.

His E.R.A. was below the 2.00 mark once, 1.64 in 1888. His totals won and lost are 204 and 153, a .571 career win %. He wasn't a strikeout pitcher, 1,229, having allowed 970 walks and 3,105 hits. His career O.B. % is .326, W.A.T. +3.5, and total P.R. is +207, beyond the statistical pitching stratosphere.

He was involved in many salary disputes. He quit to work as a bricklayer with his father's company in 1894 and later became very successful on his own as a construction contractor. He came back to work in the pitcher's box for Washington in 1896 and 1897, 10 and 7, and 6 and 9, pitching a total of 299 innings.

His last E.R.A. was 4.79. He'd just turned age 30 and quit the major leagues for good. His wins, complete games, and innings pitched rank among the top 100 of all time despite a brief career.

His 45 wins in 1888 is tied for 12th rank all time, his 64 complete games is 19th, his 585 I.P. in 1888 ranks 22nd. He had some outstanding seasons, and 1890 ranks as one of his best.

Charles Frederick "Silver" King had surgery to remove gallstones and his appendix; he died soon after of complications. He is a Players League star player, no doubt, but Cooperstown class?

KINSLOW, THOMAS F.   **Tom Kinslow**
Born: January 12, 1866, Washington, D.C.
Died: February 22, 1901, Washington, D.C.
Height: 5'10".   Weight: 160 Lbs.   Batted: Right.   Threw: Right.
Major League Career: 10 Years, 380 Games
1889: Did not play
1891: N.L.: Brooklyn
1890: P.L.: Brooklyn Wonders; C 64

Batting Record:

Games: 64	3B: 6	Walks: 10	SL.%: .409
At Bats: 242	HRs: 4	K's: 22	S.B: 2
Hits: 64	Runs: 30	B.Avg: .264	B.R: -5
2B: 11	R.B.I: 46	O.B.A: .299	F.R: +7

The net result of his Players League stats is that of an average part-time catcher, which is also the sum of his career. Preface with the fact that he was an N.L. umpire in 1892, and note that 1890 wasn't his best or busiest major league season.

But he was the most actively involved of the Brooklyn Wonders' three catchers, and the team did finish second. After the P.L. he stayed in Brooklyn to play for the N.L. Bridegrooms through 1894. He played three years after, 1895, '96 and '98, in a total of 44 games.

The entirety of his career includes 380 games and 1,414 at bats, with 186 runs scored and 222+ R.B.I.; his walks total less than 100, his K's not much more. His single season most and best can be displayed by the years:

1890: 2B (11), HRs (four, tied), K's (22, tied), F.R. (+7, tied)
1891: K's (22 tied)
1892: 3B (11), B.Avg. (.305, tied), SL.% (.443), B.R. (+10), F.R. (+7, tied)
1893: Games (78), At Bats (312), Hits (76), HRs (four, tied), S.B. (four, tied)
1894: Runs (39), Walks (20), O.B.A. (.362), S.B. (four, tied)
1895: S.B. (four, tied).

Some of his data are missing in R.B.I. and K's. They do show he had just one (+) year of B.R., total -42, and +2 total F.R.; his very average for his time batting averages are .266 B.Avg., .301 O.B.A., .361 SL.%.

He stole a total of 18 bases in 10 years; hit 12 HRs, 29 triples and 40 doubles. His major league career began with Washington (N.L.) in 1886 where it ended in 1898; he was with the New York (A.A.) Metropolitans in 1887, and elsewhere in 1888 and 1889.

He played at Pittsburgh in 1895, Louisville in 1896, elsewhere in 1897, and in 14 games for St. Louis in 1898. If his best year wasn't 1890, then it definitely was in Brooklyn; the city which became a borough should have at least a park named after him.

Thomas F. Kinslow died of consumption, exhaustion and phthisis pulmonalis. His age was 35; he died in an unnamed institution.

"A fine ball player, good fellow all around, as a catcher hard to beat through first-class playing and gentlemanly demeanor on the field; as a base-runner he was not brilliant, however his hard hitting and general playing more than made up any deficiency in that line."

KNELL, PHILIP LOUIS   Phil Knell
Born: March 12, 1865, San Francisco, California
Died: June 5, 1944, Santa Monica, California
Height: 5'7.5".   Weight: 154 Lbs.   Batted: Right.   Threw: Left
Major League Career: 6 Years, 192 Games
1889: Did not play
1891: A.A.: Columbus
1890: P.L.: Philadelphia Quakers; P 35, OF 2

Batting Record:

Games: 36	3B: 3	Walks: 7	SL.%: .288
At Bats: 132	HRs: 0	K's: 17	S.B: 3
Hits: 29	Runs: 19	B.Avg: .220	B.R:
2B: 3	R.B.I: 18	O.B.A:	F.R:

Pitching Record:

Won: 22	Starts: 31	K's: 99	E.R.A: 3.83
Lost: 11	C.G: 30	Walks: 166	Saves: 0
Win %: .667	I.P: 287	Hits: 287	P.R: +13
Games: 35	Sh.O: 2	O.B.%: .371	W.A.T: +6.1

He was an off-hand pitcher for whom 1890 was a very good year; in fact it was by far his very best major league baseball year. Compare with his career totals, which are won 79 and lost 90 (.467 win %).

1890 was one of his 20+ win seasons; the other was 1891, with 28 wins and 27 losses (.509) for the Columbus (A.A.) Solons/Buckeyes. He was absent from the major leagues for two years, 1889 and 1893. In 1888 for Pittsburgh (N.L.) he won 1 and lost 2; in 1895 for Louisville he won 0 lost 6, and for Cleveland he won 7 lost 5.

The only continuity of locale in his career came at Louisville; he'd finished the season there, not in the finest style, winning 7 and losing 21 (.250), after a 0 and 0 start with Pittsburgh. In 1892, at Washington, he won 9 and lost 13 (.409) and with Philadelphia he won 5 and lost 5.

Leave 1889 and 1893 blank for Phil Knell, but mark him the best of the Philadelphia P.L. Quakers pitching staff in 1890. His place of origin was San Francisco, and perhaps that's where he spent his off years.

After winning 1 and losing 2 his first year, 1888 for Pittsburgh, perhaps he hadn't found the stimulus to come East again. Among the starting staff of three for the Quakers when he did return, he led in wins, win %, complete games, and gave up the most walks.

His hits allowed exactly equals innings pitched; the 166 extra base runners he put on base didn't do any great harm to his E.R.A.; his +14 P.R. is nicely supplemented by +6.1 W.A.T. As a batter his numbers are those of a pitcher who produced runs.

In the P.L. Knell ranks third in win % and first in W.A.T., in sum almost but not quite a Player League star player. His career numbers are inferior: his won 79 and lost 90 (.467) are below the 68 and 63 (.519) of the Quakers, and they were second division.

Also 192 games, with 141 complete of 163 starts (87 percent) is a bit below the mark for his time; his SABR-stats make somewhat of an issue, +13 P.R. and +5.6 W.A.T., that he pitched for some mediocre and other awful teams:

Year	Team	Place	Teams	Year	Team	Place	Teams
1888	Pittsburgh Alleghenys	Sixth	8	1894	Pittsburgh Pirates	Seventh	12
1891	Columbus Solons/Buckeyes	Sixth	(*)9	1894	Louisville Colonels	12th	12
1892	Washington Senators	10th	12	1895	Louisville Colonels	12th	12
1892	Philadelphia Phillies	Fourth	12	1895	Cleveland Spiders	Second	12

The 1891 asterisk denotes there were actually nine teams in the American Association in that, its last year, but one was two, as the Cincinnati Porkers/Kellys and Milwaukee Brewers. As for Knell the whole shows the Philadelphia P.L. was as good as he got.

His career data continued: 1,453 innings pitched, 1,478 hits allowed, 705 walks and 575 K's, .364 O.B.% and 4.06 E.R.A. His record includes 50+ games and starts one year (1891) when he led his league with five of his eight career shutouts; he pitched a total of 462 innings that year.

Knell as a major league pitcher? About 50–50; for the P.L. of 1890 he produced his best for the Philadelphia Quakers. For Knell to play in 1890, the 3,000 miles he had to travel to go to work must have been a record.

He was an A.A. umpire in 1891, and an N.L. umpire in 1895; as a hometown attraction Horace Stoneham might have traded for him if 1895 had been 1958.

Philip Louis Knell died of a heart attack, coronary thrombosis abetted by arterial sclerosis. After baseball his business was professional. Although a resident of California for 79 years, he died in Santa Monica where he'd been for 14 days.

KROCK, AUGUST H.   Gus Krock
Born: May 9, 1866, Milwaukee, Wisconsin
Died: March 22, 1905, Pasadena, California
Height: 6'0".   Weight: 196 Lbs.   Batted: Threw: Left.
Major League Career: 3 Years, 60 Games
1889: N.L.: Chicago, Indianapolis, Washington
1891: Did not play
1890: P.L.: Buffalo Bisons; P 4

Batting Record:

Games: 4	3B: 0	Walks: 1	SL.%: .083
At Bats: 12	HRs: 0	K's: 4	S.B: 0
Hits: 1	Runs: 1	B.Avg: .083	B.R:
2B: 0	R.B.I: 1	O.B.A:	F.R:

Pitching Record:

Won: 0	Starts: 3	K's: 5	E.R.A: 6.12
Lost: 3	C.G: 3	Walks: 15	Saves: 0
Win %: .000	I.P: 25	Hits: 43	P.R: -5
Games: 4	Sh.O: 0	O.B.%: .464	W.A.T: -1.4

His career happened in 1888, he hung around the next year and the next ostensibly to support the Brotherhood cause, then he was gone. It isn't certain how he ended up with the Buffalo Bisons allocation of P.L. players; it was supposedly done by lottery, but however he got there, neither was any help to the other.

His W.A.T. is below the Bisons,' who were below seventh place by 20 games. His P.R. rates poor, his hits permitted were near double innings pitched, add walks to hits and the total is beyond just poor. His handful of K's just don't make the major league grade.

His data could be juggled and massaged any which way, but won 0 lost 3, a .000 win %, .464 O.B.% and 6.12 E.R.A. still form the August Krock = Buffalo Bisons equation. As for batting, a pair of .083s must match a hit and a walk; an R.B.I. and run scored don't salvage 33 percent at bats lost in the wind.

Best said, he completed all three games he started, but the whole of that counted just 25 innings. The year before wasn't as bad but not much better, winning seven and losing nine for three N.L. teams; expectations in the form of contracts were rendered him by Chicago, Indianapolis, and Washington.

He pitched for Chicago (N.L.) when his career began in 1888. He won 25 decisions and lost 14, .641; games, starts, complete were all 39. In 340 innings he recorded 161 K's and 45 walks, with 295 hits allowed. With a .274 O.B.% and 2.44 E.R.A., Krock was presumed a potentially formidable pitcher.

Suffice it to say that potential wasn't realized, but he did have one terrific season, which is one more than many. As for 1890, the Buffalo Bisons weren't quite what was expected either. After the P.L. season, he relocated to Pasadena, California.

He may have participated in creating the annual Rose Bowl fiesta. He was a contractor, but of what sort isn't known. In the P.L. and baseball he won 32 and lost 25 (.552), and was a winning pitcher.

August H. Krock died of consumption. As a player it was said that he did not drink and was saving his money.

KUEHNE (KNELME), WILLIAM J.   Bill Kuehne
Born: October 24, 1858, Chicago, Illinois
Died: October 27, 1921, Sulphur Springs, Ohio
Height: Weight: 185 Lbs.   Batted: Right.   Threw: Right.
Major League Career: 10 Years, 1,087 Games
1889: N.L.: Pittsburgh
1891: A.A.: Columbus and Louisville
1890: P.L.: Pittsburgh Burghers; 3B 126

Batting Record:
Games: 126	3B: 12	Walks: 28	SL.%: .352
At Bats: 528	HRs: 5	K's: 37	S.B: 21
Hits: 126	Runs: 66	B.Avg: .239	B.R: -25
2B: 21	R.B.I: 73	O.B.A: .277	F.R: +5

His fielding runs stat for the Burghers of 1890 is a +5; his 82 errors at 3B in 1890 rank 13th all time for a season at that difficult and demanding position. A -24 F.R. for his 10 years is more consistent with 373 errors, which ranks 14th all time at 3B.

He played in more than 1,000 games (1,087) with more than 4,000 at bats (4,284), and almost made the milestone mark of 1,000 hits (996) for a .232 career batting average.

In each of seven years he played in 100+ games, had 500+ at bats two years, and 300+ every year; Bill Kuehne came to play. Among his hits are 25 HRs, 145 doubles, and 115 triples, including 15+ of the latter each of four years; 28.6 percent of his hits were for extra bases.

This benchmark doubtful was a result of batting power, but his 21 P.L. stolen bases, 151 career, and five of his HRs were hit in 1890. This doesn't equate with speed either, leaving as the conclusion this P.L. 3B came to play, even if not very well at his position.

The five HRs stand as his career high, set in 1884, tied in 1889. His 73 P.L. R.B.I. stand as his high in that stat; his 66 P.L. runs scored were exceeded just twice, with 73 in 1886 and 68 in 1887. He never accumulated more than 126 hits in one season.

He never had more than 28 walks; when he went to bat he did. His 37 P.L. K's on balance stand negatively against him, but were not near his high of 68 K's in 1888. He beat his 21 S.B. in the P.L. three times, with a high of 34 in 1888.

How or why a -121 career B.R. perhaps was in conjunction with his .232 career B.Avg., which is a few hits one side or the other of a legitimate hitting pitcher; combined with his .258 O.B.A. and .313 SL.% they go a long way toward a statistically logical answer.

Five of his major league years were with the A.A., four with the N.L.; the whole reads like a Midwest U.S.A. travelogue: 1883 and 1884 Columbus (A.A.), 1885 and 1886 Pittsburgh (A.A.), 1887 through 1889 Pittsburgh (N.L.), 1891 Columbus and Louisville (A.A.), 1892 Louisville, St. Louis, and Cincinnati.

He played twice for St. Louis in 1892, the last one game, four at bats with a "K" and long string of 0's. For Bill Kuehne (Knelme) it marked the end of a credible major league baseball career. When the P.L. and 1890 became fact on the field, he came to play.

After suffering many years as an invalid, William J. Kuehne died of lumbar pneumonia. Although his birthplace is shown here as Chicago, he may have been born in Leipzig, Germany, and if not, his father was.

Published on "02-19-1890 With Fred Carroll he invented a curious yet simple means for training the eye to judge swiftly pitched and erratically curved balls, not only excellent practice but a great deal of amusement, will probably apply for a patent."

Previously, on 8-3-1887, "Kuehne has sympathy of friends in his wife, the good-natured player made an unfortunate choice; the woman several times invited members of the club during her husband's absence but non accepted...."

"She is very homely, it is reported she left the city, an officer hunted high and low for her but she could not be found to serve a subpoena; no testimony has been taken yet, he will no doubt get his divorce."

LARKIN, HENRY E.   Henry Larkin (Ted)
Born: January 12, 1860, Reading, Pennsylvania
Died: January 31, 1942, Reading, Pennsylvania
Height: 5'10".   Weight: 175 Lbs.   Batted: Right.   Threw: Right.
Major League Career: 10 Years, 1,184 Games
1889: A.A.: Philadelphia
1891: A.A.: Philadelphia
1890: P.L.: Cleveland Infants; 1B 125, OF 1

Batting Record:

Games: 125	3B: 15	Walks: 65	SL.%: .484
At Bats: 506	HRs: 5	K's: 18	S.B: 5
Hits: 168	Runs: 93	B.Avg: .332	B.R: +33
2B: 32	R.B.I: 112	O.B.A: .420	F.R: -8

Henry "Ted" Larkin was the first of two Infants field managers; through 79 games and a 34–45 won-lost record, the team was in seventh place when his term ended.

He didn't accomplished much as field manager—and 1890 was his only attempt at it—but Henry "Ted" Larkin was a very good baseball player who is practically unknown. The diligent scribes of SABR did include an article about him in a journal on the players and other personalities of the 1800s:

"A hard-hitting first-baseman-outfielder ... one of the disgruntled National league and (American) Association players who formed the rebel Players League in 1890 ... finished his career with some impressive statistics."

These include a .303 B.Avg., .380 O.B.A., and .440 SL.%; he led the A.A. in O.B.A. in 1886. He could hit and had extra base power: 1,430 hits in 4,718 at bats include 259 doubles, 114 triples, and 53 HRs; he led his league in doubles twice, hit 30+ each of three years, reached 15+ triples twice, hit 10 HRs in 1891.

His R.B.I. are incomplete, showing 549 in six years; he reached 100+ twice. He scored 925 runs in his 1,184 games, including 100+ each of four years. His stats accumulated at home plate include 484 walks and an incomplete 141 K's in five years; his known K's include 56 in 1891. He took 50+ walks five years, 83 in 1889.

His 129 stolen bases include 32 in 1886 and 37 in 1887; data for the prior two years are missing. His B.R. is far beyond normal, +262 total, with highs twice in the +40s, twice more +30s. His F.R. are quite the opposite, total -27, only three of 10 positive.

Larkin in the Players League ranks fifth in R.B.I. and fifth in B.R.; he's also ranked third in Adjusted Production, and second in Adjusted Batter Runs. Two of his three batting averages beat the benchmarks, .332 B.Avg. and .420 O.B.A.; his .484 SL.% was close, +33 B.R. among the best the league produced.

To his further credit are 112 R.B.I. and 15 triples. His ratio of 65 walks versus 18 K's is outstanding, as is 52 extra base hits among 168 (30%+).

Among his other data and notable notes are five K's in 319 at bats in 1893 (1.5%), 180 hits in 1886 in 139 games, which adjusted to 162 games would beat the 200+ benchmark by 10; there's not one season his at bats weren't 300+. Hit for average, with power, excellent plate discipline, add durable to reliable.

Among his batting averages: .300+ B.Avg. six years, .400 O.B.A. three years, .500+ SL.% one year; Henry Larkin's batting wasn't lacking in any way. He played the outfield his first four years, 1884 through 1887 for (A.A.) Philadelphia; he switched to first base but stayed with the (A.A.) Athletics in 1888 and 1889, and returned after the P.L. year.

His F.R. as an OF had been near the 0 mark; at 1B they became consistently negative, including -8 in 1890. With this fault a given, his only other option was as a manager; yet the Infants were seventh when he left the position, which is where they finished.

He closed out his career with two years at Washington, 1892 and 1893, and did so credibly; perhaps someday he'll be given his due as a very good 1880s major league baseball player. For the period 1876–1889 he ranks fourth in hit by pitches, and eighth in O.B.A.

After his major league career, he continued as a player in the minors for a few years. He worked as a boilermaker — that's as tough as work has ever been — and otherwise was an employee of the City of Reading.

Henry E. "Ted" Larkin died after a serious illness of several days.

There have been a few major league players named Larkin. One named Frank S., not to be at all confused with Ted, was a pretty good player; he would have been a great feature player in a tale of horror written by Edgar Allan Poe.

As Henry became "Ted," Frank S. somehow became "Terry." He was a pitcher who compiled a record of 89 wins and 80 losses during his five-year career, 1876 through 1880. Then Frank S. "Terry" became a front-page feature in newspapers and no doubt *Police Gazette*.

As it's said now, this Larkin lost it one day, in a manner which would have done justice to Alfred Hitchcock's "PSYCHO." He shot his wife, then cut his own throat, then smashed his head against an iron radiator.

There's a lapse of about a year in his tale, after which Frank S. "Terry" confronted his saloon owner-employer, with two pistols; he was summarily hauled off to jail. The end of Frank S. "Terry" Larkin is left for the reader to decide, as it's not known.

LATHAM, WALTER ARLINGTON   Arlie Latham
   (The freshest man on earth)
Born: March 15, 1860, West Lebanon, New Hampshire
Died: November 29, 1952, Garden City, New York
Height: 5'8".   Weight: 150 Lbs.   Batted: Right.   Threw: Right.
Major League Career: 17 Years, 1,627 Games
1889: A.A.: St. Louis
1891: N.L.: Cincinnati
1890: P.L.: Chicago Pirates; 3B 52
N.L.: Cincinnati

Batting Record:

Games: 52	3B: 2	Walks: 22	SL.%: .294
At Bats: 214	HRs: 1	K's: 22	S.B: 32
Hits: 49	Runs: 47	B.Avg: .229	B.R: -11
2B: 7	R.B.I: 20	O.B.A: .310	F.R: +3

He was often in baseball-throwing contests. One such effort put an end to his long and controversial major league career. He also performed acrobatic stunts to entertain spectators at games. He was a merciless heckler and fierce competitor as well as an outstanding runner. At his size "The freshest man on earth" had to be.

By 1890 he'd played 10 major league seasons. In 1890 he played for two teams, in two leagues. Arlie Latham was one of very few players who jumped the wrong way. He played only at third base in the P.L. and the N.L., but which got the best of Arlie Latham?

Let an asterisk (*) indicate that data is missing:

	Chicago Pirates *P.L. 52 Games*	*Cincinnati Reds* *N.L. 41 Games*	*Arlie Latham's* *Career*
At Bats:	214	164	6,822
Hits:	49	41	1,833
Walks:	22	23	589
K's:	22	18	239 (*)

	Chicago Pirates P.L. 52 Games	Cincinnati Reds N.L. 41 Games	Arlie Latham's Career
Runs:	47	35	1,478
R.B.I:	20	15	398 (*)
B.Avg:	.229	.250	.269
O.B.A:	.310	.346	.334
SL.%:	.294	.311	.341
S.B:	32	20	739
B.R:	-11	-0	-5
F.R:	+3	+5	+48

No matter which answer is decided right, it's probably wrong, as Arlie Latham got the best of both his teams and leagues in 1890; he'd earlier given his best and most to Chris Von der Ahe and his St. Louis Browns, and the American Association.

He was with that team and league from 1883 through 1889. To allow for comparison these were his best and most then:

At Bats: 627 in 1887, 622 in 1892;
Hits: 198 in 1887, 174 in 1886;
Walks: 74 in 1891;
K's: 54 in 1892 (*)
Runs: 163 in 1887;
R.B.I: 69 in 1895 (*)
B.Avg: .316 in 1887, .313 in 1894, .311 in 1895;
O.B.A: .393 in 1894;
SL.%: .413 in 1887, .403 in 1894;
S.B.: 129 in 1887, 109 in 1888;
B.R.: +18 in 1891;
F.R: +37 in 1884.

He could produce with the bat, in every which way except hitting HRs and triples, with only about 100 combined among his total hits. He did reach the 30+ benchmark in doubles once, 35 in 1887 among his 245. Speed and stealth were his strengths, this 3B who could play his position as well as any of his time.

He ranks high twice in period stats 1876–1889: ninth in hit by pitches, and first in stolen bases. His 17-year career began with Buffalo (N.L.) in 1880, with only 22 games and 79 at bats. Near the end, 1896, for St. Louis he played in eight games, had 35 at bats.

The end of the major league baseball career of Arlie Latham was extended, and then again. In 1899 he played six games, with six at bats for Washington; in 1909 he appeared in four games and had two at bats for the New York (N.L.) Giants.

He'd not played the two years after Buffalo. Then he signed with the Browns, and while in service to Mr. Von der Ahe set more than a few records. Of the whole he played in 100+ games 11 years and had 300+ at bats each of 13 years; 1890 was a minimal year for him.

After his part-P.L. season, he continued with the Reds through 1895; then came his career closure in three parts. He provided amusement and created antagonism, but was not a part-time player. He was despised for his antics toward opponents everywhere except at Sportsman's Park in St. Louis.

Some evidence suggests he changed his demeanor and playing style during the year the P.L. played. Perhaps he tired of the notion that "The freshest man..." the more intimately hostile the fans became in retaliation.

The sum of Arlie Latham the player: .300+ B.Avg. four years, 100+ runs scored nine years. There are many benchmarks he didn't reach, but he did achieve 50+ walks five times, and stole 50+ bases eight times; his 793 S.B. ranks eighth in history.

He also ranks 12th all time among 3B in putouts with 1,975, and 19th with 3,545 assists. He's also first among 3B with 822 errors while the next made 614. He's fifth at 3B in range factor with 3.51, and if his career were one 162-game season he'd make 365.56 assists. Only two 3B in major league history would have more.

The year he had his last major league at bats, he became the first to be employed as a full-time coach, by John McGraw of the Giants; his duties included coaching at third base during games and teaching the team base running.

He was an N.L. umpire in 1899 and 1900, and 1902; he was manager of the Cardinals for a baseball moment in 1896, and won 0 lost 3. In 1909 "The freshest man" became the oldest major league player to steal a base; his age was 49 at the time.

In 1952, at age 92, Latham was the New York Yankees press box attendant during the season, and despite being that far along into antiquity, he did a stage performance or two.

The interim, age 49 to 92, is unique; after World War II, Latham lived in England for 17 years, where he served as the administrator, equivalent to the commissioner of baseball.

He also became a friend to the Prince of Wales, Prince Edward, whom one might recall or have read of; he declined the position of king of England, and the British Empire, to marry a commoner.

Arlie Latham was nominated for membership in the U.S. Baseball Hall of Fame in 1936; he received one vote, and one in 1938, and one again in 1942. On the whole, as a good Brit might have explained, Latham was rather a fair baseball player, and more.

He was also a player scout, owned a night club, and delicatessen, and was an actor and comedian.

LEWIS (UNKNOWN) (Unknown) Lewis
Born: Brooklyn, New York
Died:
Height: Weight: Batted: Threw:
Major League Career: 1 Year, 1 Game
1889: Did not play
1891: Did not play
1890: P.L.: Buffalo Bisons; P 1, OF 1 (Debut Date: July 12)

Batting Record:

Games: 1	3B: 0	Walks: 0	SL.%: .200
At Bats: 5	HRs: 0	K's: 0	S.B: 0
Hits: 1	Runs: 1	B.Avg: .200	B.R:
2B: 0	R.B.I: 0	O.B.A:	F.R:

Pitching Record:

Won: 0	Starts: 1	K's: 1	E.R.A: 60.00
Lost: 1	C.G: 0	Walks: 7	Saves: 0
Win %: .000	I.P: 3	Hits: 13	P.R: -19
Games: 1	Sh.O: 0	O.B.%: .714	W.A.T: -0.4

He was born in Brooklyn, almost anonymously. He played and pitched for the P.L. Buffalo Bisons in 1890, awfully bad at that. If skill or luck or both, allowing 20 base runners in three innings of work in the pitcher's box, including three who took the home run tour, nothing better could be said of that.

While at home plate batting he did get a hit, during his part of a game, which he lost as a pitcher, and Lewis did score a run for the Buffalo Bisons in the Players League. If he had continued pitching at his rate, watching 60 opponents score would have made for an awfully long afternoon.

Speculating on why he's listed in the record books only by the name Lewis, this could have been his first name, or the scorekeeper omitted his whole name as an act of public courtesy.

He could have been a fantasy player, or this name was written over that of the real Bisons pitcher that day as an act of mercy.

He could have been the nightmare of a pitcher, or scorekeeper, or newspaper writer, brought to life; he could have been almost anybody. Who would have admitted to this by his true name that eventful day? All in all, it's best that this Lewis remains almost anonymous.

There have been more than a few with the surname of Lewis in baseball. Four are listed among pitchers, including one about his time; eight are among batters, including one who played near the time of P.L. Lewis' brief career. This last Lewis was born in Buffalo, but in this case anonymous is best.

MACK (McGILLICUDDY), CORNELIUS ALEXANDER
Connie Mack
Born: December 22, 1862, East Brookfield, Massachusetts
Died: February 8, 1956, Germantown, Pennsylvania
Height: 6'1".   Weight: 150 Lbs.   Batted: Right.   Threw: Right.
Major League Career: 11 Years, 723 Games
1889: N.L.: Washington
1891: N.L.: Pittsburgh
1890: P.L.: Buffalo Bisons; C 112, OF 9, 1B 5

Batting Record:

Games: 123	3B: 12	Walks: 47	SL.%: .344
At Bats: 503	HRs: 0	K's: 13	S.B: 16
Hits: 134	Runs: 95	B.Avg: .266	B.R: -7
2B: 15	R.B.I: 53	O.B.A: .353	F.R: +12

This was the catcher of the P.L. team that spent the 1890 season in the cellar, some considerable distance below the dim light of seventh place. He endured there all or parts of 112 games, played in 123 of their 134 games, including two no decisions.

Baseball would get better for Connie Mack, then worse, perhaps even worse than the 1890 Bisons, then better, and again worse till the end; the currents of the game tend to ebb and rise during more than half a century.

He was elected to the National Baseball Hall of Fame in 1937, soon after his second rise to the top, before his long-lasting final drop to the depths of the second division of the American League. He was elected to Cooperstown by their *Yearbook* as a field manager; as an executive he suffered no falls at all.

For 66 years, Cornelius McGillicuddy, aka Connie Mack, was among the essential elements of major league baseball; he became a legend long before he passed from a mortal life.

He began as a player, mainly a catcher, with the Washington (N.L.) Senators/Statesmen in 1886, and played for 11 years; he played for only three teams, 100 percent N.L. except for the P.L. year.

He continued with Washington through 1889, after the P.L. went to Pittsburgh, evidently without any pirating, and played there through 1896. He began his long and fabled career as a field manager in 1894 with 23 games left to play, winning 12 and losing 10.

He was the Pirates manager the next two seasons and won 137 and lost 124 (.525 win %). These first three of Connie Mack's teams finished seventh, seventh, and sixth, in a 12-team league. He didn't manage again in the major leagues until a new one began play in 1901; by then he'd also become a franchise owner.

The history of Connie Mack is long and can't be told in whole here. Others have authored the whole tale, including himself in his 1950 autobiography.

He began playing a local form of the game as a young adolescent in the New England town of his birth. Along the way he acquired the appellation from his mates of "Slats," in reference to his long and lanky physique. He learned and did well enough to earn a place on his town team.

His version of the Connie Mack story notes proudly that the manager of his town team invited Cap Anson and his Chicago Colts to play an exhibition contest with them; "Pop" Anson accepted, which pleased all four of the Brookfield villages, but says Mack, "they left their glamour at home." The game was played regardless, and a grand time was had by all.

"Slats" was age 16 then and his father had died recently. He went to work in a local shoe factory to help sustain their large family intact. Both his parents were immigrants from Ireland. His father was a mill worker. All seven McGillicuddy children were instilled with the virtues of honesty and hard work.

At least two siblings died young, as was the way among American families then;

he proudly cites his mother as "a woman of great character." He alleges aspiring to be a baseball player at age nine, which was realized in 1884 with a professional Connecticut club.

Mack advanced fast. The next year he was with Hartford in a high minor league, then "went up to the New York Metropolitans in the old American Baseball Association." They in turn sold him and four other players "to the Washington Senators, then a National League team, for $3,500."

With the Senators, aka Statesmen, Mack played in 10 games in 1886; he came to bat 36 times and batted .361 with a .462 SL.%, levels he'd never again come near as a player. In fact his career B.Avg. is .245, O.B.A. .305, and SL.% an even .300.

1890 was the only year he played in 100+ games; most years his at bats numbered in the 280 to 380 range. His best B.Avg. was .293 in 1889, made with almost no power; except for 16 doubles in 1889 and 10 in 1891, and his P.L. data, he didn't reach any double figures in extra base hits.

His 95 P.L. runs scored nearly equal his next two most, 49 and 51 in 1888 and 1889; he reached his peak in R.B.I. with 42 in 1889. Other than his 47 P.L. walks, both these data and K's per year are minuscule; both are at most near 20. He could steal a base on occasion; his total is 129, with highs of 26, 31, 26 in 1887, 1888, and 1889.

Among SABR-stats his B.R. are all negative except +2 in 1886, followed by -30 in 1887; his F.R. are all positive and total +68 with a best +19 in 1892, highly commendable for a major league catcher.

As a catcher, Connie Mack ranks 19th all time with 281 errors, and 17th in passed balls with 210. He could and did play other positions, in proportion about equal to the P.L., about which he wrote, indexed as "Players League, Buffalo" not much at all: "After three good years with the Washington Senators, I went to Buffalo in the Brotherhood or Players League in 1890, then to the Pittsburgh Pirates." He did participate in the P.L., and did support his franchise, his club, and his team.

His six years as a Pirates player are without distinction. There are a few notes to be mentioned, intermixing Connie Mack the catcher and player and Connie Mack the field manager.

He advanced beyond "Slats" to become "The Tall Tactician," the new name given for more than one reason. The code of baseball did allow trickery, if done within the broad parameters of the rules.

He was known to tip a batter's bat, and devised a quaint use for the technology of refrigeration; when the opponents were to be a tough-hitting team, he'd have the game balls put on ice to deaden them and make them heavy and awfully hard for any batter to hit beyond the confines of the infield.

His Puritan temperament rarely showed anger; there are two exceptions. Only once as a manager was he ejected from a game, for an explosion of outrage, behavior beyond that allowed by the code. This occurred while he was manager of the Pirates.

Circa 1930, he'd had many great pitchers among his Philadelphia Athletics (A.L.) Teams, and the greatest was Lefty Grove. He was having an extremely rare bad day on the mound, so Mr. Mack invited him to view the rest of the game from the dugout.

Grove dutifully turned over the ball, and took that long walk all pitchers dread;

when he arrived he found an isolated place to sit and contemplate, after which he was heard to say to nobody in particular, "Aw, nuts!"

Mr. Mack didn't use bad language, nor did he tolerate it from his players; having resumed his position on the bench, and having heard the words which drifted his way on the wind, he replied clearly "And nuts to you too, Mr. Grove!"

He almost always referred to the players on his teams, and to most other men as "mister," and that's about as angry as Mr. Connie Mack was ever known to behave publicly.

He'd told his widowed mother before he left home in pursuit of the glory and wealth a baseball career could offer that he would not smoke or drink, or swear or lie. He did take up the game of golf in his later years, but never used tobacco.

As for the other parts of his oath, he did tipple a dram of fine liquor on occasion; it was rumored but never proven that he kept a bottle of exclusive stock secreted in his office.

A hundred versions of the story have been told of how it came to pass that he was one of the original American League founders and franchise owners. This is an excerpt from his own version:

"My 'Philadelphia Story' begins in 1900 and continues through 1950, a half-century of glorious experiences.... When the American League was being organized we decided upon making it fifty-fifty between the West and the East....

"I was awarded the Philadelphia franchise, my friend Ban Johnson told me to see Benjamin F. Shibe, one of the owners of the A.J. Reach [baseball equipment] company.... I shall always be indebted to Mister Ban Johnson for his good advice.

"Mister Ben Shibe greeted me enthusiastically, we organized a corporation and he made me president. He asked Charles Somers, a friend in Cleveland, to join us.... We had our franchise, but we had no team and no park."

"We finally decided upon a site ... Columbia Park was the name we gave it.... It didn't take us very long to construct a single-decked grandstand.... I looked over our rivals, the Phillies, and began negotiating with four of their players. I signed up Napoleon Lajoie...."

John McGraw had written a somewhat different recollection of the A.L. origins. "Through the summer of 1900 ... Ban Johnson having decided to call his circuit the American League, had been contemplating his plans for a frontal attack on the National League....

"One called for establishment of a club in Baltimore, Charles A. Comiskey held the A.L. franchise in Chicago.... Fans gave an enthusiastic reception to prove Baltimore was big-league territory.... McGraw learned Johnson was going to drop Baltimore as soon as possible ... transfer [the franchise] to New York.

"Undoubtedly the American League was growing stronger, an all-out fight was sure to come." There is talk of bitterness and animosity of McGraw, Johnson, and Andrew Freedman, who owned the (N.L.) Giants. Baltimore signed Bresnahan, McGinnity, and Cronin. There is no mention of Connie Mack.

From an impartial commentator; "The groundwork for formation of the American League actually was started nine years before its official beginning in 1901.... Byron (Ban) Johnson and Charles Albert Comiskey began their dream of a new diamond empire....

"Ban made his initial move in 1896, after Connie Mack had been fired for making caustic comments against a critical front office. Ban snapped up Mack for his own (Western) League ... offering part interest in the Milwaukee club.

"After the 1899 season, Johnson persuaded Charles Somers to take over the vacated Cleveland franchise. Somers 'steered' the league the next two years [with money invested in many of the franchises]....

"Comiskey switched his St. Paul [Western League] team to Chicago.... The circuit was changing its name to American League. He [Johnson] sent Connie Mack to Boston to lease a plot for a ballpark using Somers bankroll....

"He [Somers] had loaned Comiskey money to build a ballpark in Chicago ... also had a finger in Philadelphia.... Johnson's major league began operations on Wednesday, April 24, 1901."

Mr. Mack did embellish just a bit his role in the seminal events, but like John McGraw his view was from the inside of the fishbowl, where it's most difficult to see the whole well. With the passing of time, Ben Shibe, Charles Somers, Johnson and lesser others, he became the Philadelphia Athletics Inc.

As the president, he appointed himself field manager and continued in that role until 1950, half a century. Waving a scorecard to signal his fielders became his trademark. Ironically, in 1950 he and ancient Burt Shotton were declared by baseball to be the last managers allowed to do dugout business during games while wearing civilian business suits (and sometimes hats).

During these 50 years, the teams of Connie Mack won nine A.L. pennants, and five World Series titles; they also finished eighth and last in the American League 17 times. Twice he built dynasties, and twice he sold off most of his star players. Many fans and some among the media castigated him as purely mercenary.

When he left this life for baseball valhalla, his sons took over control of his franchise, and chaos ensued; they had learned from him the value of money, but not their father's other virtues. His franchise was sold in 1955 and became the Kansas City Athletics. In turn, in 1968, they became the Oakland A's.

The composite record of Mr. Mack cannot be told as the owner, president, treasurer, or business manager, only as field manager: his teams won 3,582 games, lost 3,814 (.484 win%). By far both his wins and losses are the historic records.

He won his last pennant in 1931, in 1930 his last World Series; during his last two decades there were no new gonfalons to adorn the walls of Shibe Park. In 1937 the Athletics finished seventh, and he was chosen for Cooperstown; in 1939 the Athletics finished seventh and he was inducted at Cooperstown. By coincidence only to be found in baseball, these were his only two seventh-place finishes.

When asked why he'd dismantled his first champions, prior to the 1915 season, his rationale was "When a team starts to disintegrate, it's like trying to plug up the hole in the dam to stop the flood, in building teams one has to lay strong foundations."

Upon inquiry on the matter of his second selling of the Athletics stars after the 1931 season he mused, "Another era has come and gone ... the law of diminishing returns is unrelenting.... I have been falsely accused of making a fortune by selling players.... Gate receipts were rapidly diminishing."

Besides his other offices, tasks, and duties, he was also the Athletics' resident philosopher. One of the subtitles he chose for a section of his biography was "Happy Days." In 1890 he had worn the same uniform as Dummy Hoy and Deacon White. He spent most of the P.L. season in the best position to learn how to lose with the pride and dignity of a classic gentleman.

Though playing for the P.L. worst, this was his best year as a major league player; he didn't mention in his book that he'd been financially invested in the Buffalo Bisons. An error of omission? Some facts are best tactfully left unsaid. He did support, and Connie Mack did participate.

Cornelius McGillicuddy, best known as Mr. Connie Mack, died of complications of a broken hip suffered four months earlier.

MADDEN, MICHAEL JOSEPH   Kid Madden
Born: October 22, 1866, Portland Maine
Died: March 16, 1896, Portland, Maine
Height: 5'7.5". Weight: 130 Lbs. Batted: Threw: Left.
Major League Career: 5 Years, 122 Games
1889: N.L.: Boston
1891: A.A.: Boston and Baltimore
1890: P.L.: Boston Reds; P 10, OF 2, SS 1

Batting Record:

Games: 13	3B: 0	Walks: 3	SL.%: .237
At Bats: 38	HRs: 0	K's: 3	S.B: 0
Hits: 7	Runs: 5	B.Avg: .184	B.R:
2B: 2	R.B.I: 4	O.B.A:	F.R:

Pitching Record:

Won: 3	Starts: 7	K's: 24	E.R.A: 4.79
Lost: 2	C.G: 5	Walks: 25	Saves: 0
Win %: .600	I.P: 62	Hits: 85	P.R: -4
Games: 10	Sh.O: 1	O.B.%: .399	W.A.T: 0.0

He was good in 1887, insignificant in 1890, mediocre in between and after, then was gone from the major league scene. Nearest to distinction stand his 21 wins in 1887, for the Beaneaters of Boston (N.L.), while losing 14 times, for a .600 win %.

In that, his best season, he pitched 321 innings in 37 games, with 36 complete, while allowing 317 hits and 122 walks, with 81 K's, a .342 O.B.%, and 3.79 E.R.A., good for a +10 P.R.

He also had a .600 win % for the P.L. Boston Reds. The balance of his pitching ledger reads completely different after that. His E.R.A. calculates to exactly 1.00 per game more, his O.B.% of .399 is consistent, but not his record of won 3 lost 2.

Mike Madden went beyond the flash point after his first season. His course continued with Boston in 1888 and 1889; in 1891 he went with Boston (A.A.), for a game

(0 and 1) then changed to the colors of the Baltimore (A.A.) Orioles, where he won 13 and lost 12.

There's nothing of significance between 1887 and 1893 to be found in his record; he won 10 and lost 10 in 1889. The sum of his stats include won and lost of 54 and 50 (.519), 97 of 109 starts completed, 122 games total, 958 I.P., 987 hits allowed, 336 walks and 284 K's, .343 O.B.% and 3.92 E.R.A., -16 P.R. and a -1.1 W.A.T.

He pitched for Boston teams in three different leagues. If any his standout stats are the .343 O.B.% and 89 percent complete games, neither of which is among any all-time or period stats lists.

As a Players League batter, he produced nine runs (scored and R.B.I.) with seven hits and three walks, but it isn't known from which side of home plate he swung his bat. As a P.L. pitcher, he was a member of the league champions staff, and if judged by his 0.0 W.A.T. he was as good as the whole. Written of on 11-15-90, "Brilliant but erratic, gives cunning to the ball; after a good deal of polishing developed into a first-class twirler, has the greatest curves of about any man but is batted hard sometimes; pitched a few good games this year but has not had much to do."

7-24-1897: "Madden's widow in want, in a pitiful condition, has two children, finds it almost impossible to support them and herself; he died at his home March 16, 1896."

MAUL, ALBERT JOSEPH   Al Maul
Born: October 9, 1865, Philadelphia, Pennsylvania
Died: May 3, 1958, Philadelphia, Pennsylvania
Height: 6'0".   Weight: 175 Lbs.   Batted: Right.   Threw: Right.
Major League Career: 15 Years, 410 Games (187 as a pitcher)
1889: N.L.: Pittsburgh
1891: N.L.: Pittsburgh
1890: P.L.: Pittsburgh Burghers; P 30, OF 15, SS 1

Batting Record:

Games: 45	3B: 2	Walks: 22	SL.%: .321
At Bats: 162	HRs: 0	K's: 12	S.B: 5
Hits: 42	Runs: 31	B.Avg: .259	B.R:
2B: 6	R.B.I: 21	O.B.A:	F.R:

Pitching Record:

Won: 16	Starts: 28	K's: 81	E.R.A: 3.79
Lost: 12	C.G: 26	Walks: 104	Saves: 0
Win %: .571	I.P: 247	Hits: 258	P.R: +12
Games: 30	Sh.O: 2	O.B.%: .354	W.A.T: +3.3

A winning pitcher on the P.L.'s sixth-place team, he also played the field and batted like a player. In sum, he was almost up to the standards of a Players League star player — almost, but not quite.

1890 was the next-to-best year of his long, very average career, his fifth year as a major league pitcher. A different kind of statistical calculation reveals that Al Maul gave up 14 HRs in 1890, of the Pittsburghers' 36 total, or 39 percent of the whole.

Even in an era when pitching staffs included two or three key starters, this 39 percent is beyond any standard of adequacy. Further, if 10+ HRs in a season is the standard of excellence for the batting contingent, then he achieved the opposite of excellent.

He was adequate as a P.L. batter; a gathering of his data shows 42 hits + 22 walks = 31 runs + 21 R.B.I. = production. His B.Avg. wasn't much below the P.L. mean of .274 and his O.B.A. .003 above the league norm. His B.R. counts -4 and his F.R. 0.

That explains his 15 games played as an OF and 1 at the six position. His P.L. SABR-stats at bat and in the field don't well equate with his +12 P.R. and +3.3 W.A.T., which in turn don't equate with 104 walks allowed, also beyond a batter's benchmark.

But then again, his E.R.A. is superior to both the league 4.23 and the Burghers' 4.22; his O.B.% though is in excess of the P.L.'s .345 and Pittsburgh's .322. His ratio of complete games in the P.L. of 93 percent is superior to his career 86 percent.

During that career, Maul's total in C.G., starts and games read 143, 167, 187; pitched 1,433 innings, gave up 1,659 hits and 518 walks, had 346 K's. His composite P.R. is -16, O.B.% .369, W.A.T. +13.3, and E.R.A. 4.44.

The major league career of Al Maul extends from 1884 with the Philadelphia Keystones of the Union Association; he was missing in 1885 and 1886, and 1892, and concluded in 1901 with the New York (N.L.) Giants. During the whole he won 84 and lost 80 (.512).

With Philadelphia (N.L.) in 1887 and Pittsburgh (N.L.) in 1888 and 1889 he accumulated 5 wins and 8 losses; his U.A. record is won 0 and lost 1. With Pittsburgh (N.L.) in 1891 he posted a 1 and 2 mark; Washington 1896 5 and 2; D.C. and Baltimore in 1897 0 and 1; Brooklyn 1899, Philadelphia 1900 and New York 1901 he recorded totals of 4 wins and 6 losses.

That doesn't leave many among his 15 seasons to be counted as major, with the exception of 1890 with the Burghers:

1893 Washington: won 12 lost 21 (.364), 33 starts, 29 complete, 297 innings, .390 O.B.%, 5.30 E.R.A.

1894 Washington: won 11 lost 15 (.423), 26 starts, 21 complete, 202 innings, .401 O.B.%, 2.45 E.R.A.

1895 Washington: won 10 lost 5 (.667), 16 starts, 14 complete, 136 innings, .331 O.B.%, 2.45 E.R.A.

1898 Baltimore: won 20 lost 7 (.741), 28 starts, 26 complete, 207 innings, .295 O.B.%, 2.10 E.R.A.

Thus, Maul won 20+ once, lost 20+ once, and reached the .700+ win % mark once; he never did reach 300+ I.P. He allowed 100+ walks twice (in addition to 1890 there were 144 in 1893). His 2.45 E.R.A. led the N.L. in 1895; his other E.R.A. benchmark and best of 2.10 didn't lead.

Maul could get a hit when his team needed it, and there's some evidence which indicates he could pitch when he had to. When all is considered, 1890 with the sixth-place Burghers may have been his best season. It's a close call.

He's also close to the status of a P.L. star player, but not quite. Considerably more walks than K's isn't star material, and although 104 in 247 I.P. calculates to only four free passes per nine-inning game, there's something symbolic about that 100.

Al Maul stayed in the game after his pitching career. He was a scout and an employee of the ticket department for both the Phillies and the Athletics; both clubs were occupants of Shibe Park in 1927, and from 1938 through 1954.

He was rated one of the outstanding hurlers of his era. He came to the attention of major league officials when he was with Nashville. Maul was sold to the N.L. Philadelphia club for $2,500, which was reported to be the highest price paid for a minor leaguer up to that time.

McALEER, JAMES ROBERT   Jimmy McAleer (Loafer)
Born: July 10, 1864, Youngstown, Ohio
Died: April 29, 1931, Youngstown, Ohio
Height: 6'0".   Weight: 175 Lbs.   Batted: Right.   Threw: Right.
Major League Career: 13 Years, 1,021 Games
1889: N.L.: Cleveland
1891: N.L.: Cleveland
1890: P.L.: Cleveland Infants; OF 86

Batting Record:

Games: 86	3B: 7	Walks: 37	SL.%: .340
At Bats: 341	HRs: 1	K's: 33	S.B: 21
Hits: 91	Runs: 58	B.Avg: .267	B.R: -7
2B: 8	R.B.I: 42	O.B.A: .340	F.R: +9

Although "Loafer" (?) is verified among the lesser lights of the Players League, 1890 was nearly his best year. He did play in the major leagues for 13 years; among them are included six with 100+ games played, and eight with 300+ at bats.

The benchmarks can almost be omitted here; there aren't any to be found in his P.L. data, and only this during the rest of his career: 51 stolen bases in 1891, not the stat of a "Loafer." He also stole 40 bases in 1892, has a +11 in F.R. for 1892, and also in 1892 he earned 63 walks and 54 K's.

He played in Cleveland in 1892, and every year of his career except 1902 and 1907, when he was with the St. Louis Browns of the American League. He was an A.L. initiate in 1901 with the Blues of Cleveland.

His F.R. marks indicate he could play the outfield; all are positive except one (-1 in 1895), and his total F.R. stand at +42. But if B.R. are evidence, he couldn't do nearly as well at the bat; his total B.R. of -128 reads very much in the negative.

A Cleveland sportswriter of the time cited him as the best centerfielder ever seen and Hall of Fame umpire Billy Evans was quoted as saying that McAleer "could project where a fly ball would fall and move to that place."

His fielding numbers serve to verify his fielding abilities, but his B.Avg. in 1890 was nearly 20 points below that of his team; the Infants led the P.L. as a team, with a .286 B.Avg.

His other batting averages aren't that distant from his team, and are considerably above those for his career:

	Players League	McAleer 1890	McAleer Career
B.Avg.	.274	.267	.253
O.B.A:	.345	.340	.321
SL.%:	.378	.340	.310

Jimmy McAleer had some speed but no power. He had 262 stolen bases during his career. Among his 1,006 hits in 3,982 at bats are 114 doubles, 39 triples, and 12 HRs; his single-season high in HRs. is four. He hit triples in double figures once.

He scored 619 runs, not the stat of a leadoff batter, and plated 469 R.B.I., not the stuff of fourth in the batting order; he did make the lists of period stats for 1890–1899, ranking eighth in K's.

When the Cleveland Blues began play in 1901, he was their field manager. When he went to St. Louis for 1902 he was their manager. He played in 3 and 2 games these years. He didn't play in 1903 through 1906, but did continue as the Browns manager through 1909.

Then he took charge of the Washington Senators from the dugout for 1910 and 1911; his composites as a bench boss are 736 won and 839 lost, a .453 win %. His best finishes were second in 1902 and fourth in 1908; his teams were eighth once and seventh in four of 11 years.

Somewhat less than distinguished at this point as both a player and as a manager, the logical thing for him to do by one school of thought was to move up, move higher, go for more; a wizard of the Las Vegas school would advise, "When you're losing, double your bets." He'd been a successful recruiter of players for the A.L., which indirectly led him to the office of president of the Red Sox franchise; as such, and now Mr. McAleer, in 1912 he became a co-owner with Robert McRoy, who'd been secretary and confidant to Ban Johnson.

Like many such business tandems, this one had its secrets and conflicts. McAleer sold out after a year; he would not submit to the others, but did not have sufficient power to deny their demands. Johnson pulled the strings behind the scenes.

One citation gives much greater due to McAleer, stating he was the majority stockholder of the Red Sox franchise for a few years and one of the primary movers in the formation of the American League.

James Robert McAleer became a victim of cancer. He would not submit to the power of nature either, or passively wait for his end; he died of a self-inflicted gunshot wound to the head.

When asked the key to his success, the great British prime minister, Winston Churchill, summed it up in seven words: "Never give up. Never, never give up." The career and life of James Robert McAleer was a parallel, almost till the end.

McGEACHEY, JOHN CHARLES   Jack McGeachey
Born: May 23, 1864, Clinton, Massachusetts
Died: April 5, 1930, Cambridge, Massachusetts
Height: 5'8".   Weight: 165 Lbs.   Batted: Right.   Threw:
Major League Career: 6 Years, 608 Games
1889: N.L.: Indianapolis
1891: A.A.: Philadelphia and Boston
1890: P.L.: Brooklyn Wonders; OF 104

Batting Record:

Games: 104	3B: 4	Walks: 19	SL.%: .323
At Bats: 443	HRs: 1	K's: 12	S.B: 21
Hits: 108	Runs: 84	B.Avg: .244	B.R: -25
2B: 24	R.B.I: 65	O.B.A: .278	F.R: 0

His high was 49 for Indianapolis (N.L.) in 1888; if 164 stolen bases in 608 games indicate speed, then he had speed. If nine home runs in 2,464 at bats indicate power, then he had power. And if 604 hits in those at bats (.245 B.Avg.) indicate a hitter...

His 345 runs scored and 276 R.B.I. (one year is missing) combined nearly equal his games played, which is indicative of a productive batter. He ranks second in the P.L. in Clutch Hitting Index with 129 (100 = average) but his -25 B.R. in the P.L. deny that; the same is true for his career 108 CHI and -109 B.R

With a +17 career F.R., 0 in the P.L., and best of +10 in 1889, his place in major league baseball then was in the outfields. He wasn't highly skilled at the bat; his career sums of 57 walks and 148 K's are indicative.

He began with six games for Detroit (N.L.) in 1886 and finished the season with 59 in St. Louis (N.L.). 1887 through 1889 were spent in Indianapolis (N.L.) with 350 games played in those three years; he batted .269 the first and .267 the last. Along with his high in F.R., his best in S.B. came in the midst of this term.

When the P.L. season began, he came to play, and did, though not exceptionally well, except for an unexplainable 12 K's in 443 at bats; exceptional for the best, far beyond for McGeachey. None of his other P.L. stats or calculations stand out so well, perhaps with the exception of 80 runs scored from 127 earned times on base.

Despite low batting averages across the board, he did produce runs for the Brooklyn Wonders, and his 2.7% wasted opportunities rates highly commendable.

He went to the A.A. in 1891, his last year, played in 50 games in Philadelphia, and 41 at Boston. He didn't nearly play up to his Players League level.

With career batting averages of .245, .265, .314, 133 extra base hits among his 604, and the balance of his career and best years data to consider, despite the dimensions of his P.L. stats being ordinary, Jack McGeachey is among those who did his best in the P.L. when it played.

After baseball he was a businessman in Boston.

McGILL, WILLIAM VANESS   Willie McGill (Kid)

Born: November 10, 1873, Atlanta, Georgia
Died: August 24, 1944, Indianapolis, Indiana
Height: 5'6".   Weight: 170 Lbs.   Batted: Threw: Left.
Major League Career: 7 Years, 168 Games
1889: Did not play
1891: A.A.: Cincinnati and St. Louis
1890: P.L.: Cleveland Infants; P 24, OF 1 (Rookie)

Batting Record:

Games: 24	3B: 0	Walks: 21	SL.%: .176
At Bats: 68	HRs: 0	K's: 16	S.B: 0
Hits: 10	Runs: 10	B.Avg: .147	B.R:
2B: 2	R.B.I: 6	O.B.A:	F.R:

Pitching Record:

Won: 11	Starts: 20	K's: 82	E.R.A: 4.12
Lost: 9	C.G:19	Walks: 96	Saves: 0
Win %: .550	I.P: 184	Hits: 222	P.R: +2
Games: 24	Sh.O: 0	O.B.%: .392	W.A.T: +2.5

Pitching for the next-to-last place team in a league of elders and stars, he did well enough to earn his salary. Rookie Willie McGill was the youngest player in the P.L. and hadn't yet turned 18 when he made his first trip to the box.

On May 8, 1890, he set a record as the youngest to pitch a complete game; in 1891 he became the youngest 20+ game winner. Sportswriters labeled him high living and undisciplined; often when he showed up for a game his mind didn't. His behavior led to a case of "malaria," which then meant a hint of venereal disease.

Nearly unique for his time, McGill was one of the very few major league players who came from the Deep South. He shared the third pitcher's slot for the Infants and did his share adequately, a modest accolade for a pitcher with a winning record for a team that lost 20 more games than they won.

His E.R.A. of 4.12 and O.B.% of .392 are consistent with 4.23 and .362 of the Cleveland staff; he finished 95 percent of his starts and pitched in a handful of other games. The sum of his first year doesn't suggest any excesses or behavioral deficiencies.

His second season shows even less any personal faults. He began with the Cincinnati/Milwaukee (A.A.) franchise, won 2 lost 5, then went to St. Louis (A.A.) and became the second pitcher for a very good second-place team.

Winning 19 and losing 10 with St. Louis produced his only 20+ win season; he pitched 314 innings in 1891, with a 3.35 E.R.A., including 2.93 for the Browns, but finished only 22 of his 31 starts for the Browns, and 28 of 39 overall.

He nearly missed 1892, winning 1 and losing 1 for Cincinnati. He was at full strength the next year, but won only 17 of 35 decisions for Chicago. Same place 1894, 7 and 19, then to Philadelphia for his last two seasons, with totals of won 15 and lost 12.

He was 10 and 8 in 1895, and 5 and 4 in 1896 were winners, but combined don't calculate to a successful season for a pitcher of his time. During his brief career, he won 72 and lost 74 (.493). The remainder of his ledger is along the same lines.

McGill chalked up 168 games, 150 starts, 116 complete; 1,252 I.P. and 1,381 hits allowed; 701 walks and 501 K's; .389 O.B.%, 4.61 E.R.A., -21 P.R., -0.8 W.A.T. He ranks third in the P.L. in Clutch Pitching Index with 111; a 100 is average.

He did well enough at Cleveland in 1890; only at St. Louis in 1891 was he better. This scamp of the South was out of the major leagues by age 25. He continued as a minor league player, and completely contradicted his written image by becoming a college coach and trainer.

His work beyond baseball consisted of employment with a power company, then with a steel company. Indianapolis became his adopted hometown.

MILLIGAN, JOHN   Jocko Milligan
Born: August 8, 1861, Philadelphia, Pennsylvania
Died: August 30, 1923, Philadelphia, Pennsylvania
Height: 6'0".   Weight: 192 Lbs.   Batted: Right.   Threw: Right.
Major League Career: 10 Years, 772 Games
1889: A.A.: St. Louis
1891: A.A.: Philadelphia
1890: P.L.: Philadelphia Quakers; C 59, 1B 3

Batting Record:

Games: 62	3B: 3	Walks: 19	SL.%: .397
At Bats: 234	HRs: 3	K's: 19	S.B: 2
Hits: 69	Runs: 38	B.Avg: .295	B.R: +2
2B: 9	R.B.I: 57	O.B.A: .363	F.R: +4

He was first catcher for the P.L. Philadelphia Quakers and for 10 years was nearly a pure major league catcher, 772 games. He batted far above the norm for his position; more than a third of his hits went for extra bases. He handled the second position duties as well as he batted.

His total F.R. is a positive +70, with only one -1 negative, but he ranks 14th all time among catchers with 304 errors, and eighth with 406 passed balls.

He batted as high as .366 in 1889, 100 hits in 273 at bats; allowing some flexibility in numbers given his position, when he accumulated 200+ at bats in a season, he produced batting averages of .300+ three times, including .303 in 455 at bats in 1891.

His P.L. B.Avg. of .295 is closer to the benchmark than to his career mark of .286, in 2,964 at bats; his .363 O.B.A. in 1890 and career .341 reflect batting skill; .397 SL.% for catcher Milligan in 1890 represents an anomaly.

His career SL.% is .433; in 1889 he posted a phenomenal .623, and .505 in 1891. He hit 12 HRs the former year, 11 HRs in the latter; these were among a total of 50 HRs in 10 years. In 1891 he recorded his only 100+ stat, with 106 R.B.I., and led his league with 35 doubles.

Nine doubles in 1890 are also well below the norm for Milligan; he hit a total of 189. Three triples are also far below his mean of 10 per year. The same holds true for 38 runs scored in 1890 among 440; 57 R.B.I. are among 363 with four years missing.

His 210 career walks calculate close to his P.L. 19. His known 133 K's can't be measured against his P.L. 19, as five years of data are missing. True to a catcher, he had good judgment of the strike zone.

His B.R. of +2 in 1890 is way off the mark of +98, with highs of +36 in 1891 and +31 in 1889. Other than for the Quakers, Jocko Milligan played for A.A. Philadelphia in 1884 through 1887, then A.A. St. Louis in 1889.

He returned to the Jefferson Street Grounds in Philadelphia after the year of the P.L., for its last year of A.A. service. He played at D.C. in 1892 and split his last season of 1893 between Baltimore and New York.

Insight will tell a catcher, and Jocko Milligan knew when it was time to withdraw from the major leagues; he later played for and managed minor league teams, and was a court employee at City Hall in Philadelphia.

John "Jocko" Milligan died after a lengthy illness and a surgery involving an unknown infirmity.

MORRILL, JOHN FRANCIS John Morrill (Honest John)
Born: February 19, 1855, Boston, Massachusetts
Died: April 2, 1932, Boston, Massachusetts
Height: 5'10.5". Weight: 155 Lbs. Batted: Right. Threw: Right.
Major League Career: 15 Years, 1,265 Games
1889: N.L.: Washington
1891: Did not play
1890: P.L.: Boston Reds; 1B 1, SS 1

Batting Record:

Games: 2	3B: 0	Walks: 2	SL.%: .143
At Bats: 7	HRs: 0	K's: 1	S.B: 0
Hits: 1	Runs: 1	B.Avg: .143	B.R: -1
2B: 0	R.B.I: 2	O.B.A: .333	F.R: 0

He'd played consistently since the Boston team was called the Red Stockings of 1876, when the National League began. 1890 was a cameo appearance to demonstrate support for the cause of the Brotherhood of Players.

His Boston Reds manager properly allowed him to substitute for a star at first base in one game and replace his regular shortstop in another game. John Morrill was among the eldest to have a Players League record.

While himself a regular at first base, Morrill accumulated 285 errors, to rank 13th all time in that stat at that position. When adjusted by his 1,265 career games, this calculates to 35 errors in a modern season, far below the 58 and 57 made in 1884 and 1885 by two of the greatest stars of the 1800s.

The only venture away from Boston by Morrill as a player was to Washington in 1889. He was consistently loyal to the National League from its origin through 1889, and was as firmly established as a favorite among baseball fans of Beantown.

Twice he marked B.Avg.s of .300+, .302 in 1877 and .319 in 1883; the latter year his SL.% reached a then-monumental mark of .525 on the strength of 33 doubles, 16 triples, and six home runs.

He's almost unknown now, but Morrill came fast and stayed long as a premier major league player. He hit 12 HRs of a career 43 in 1887; his triples count totals 80, and doubles 239. Among his other raw numbers are 821 runs scored, and 643 R.B.I.

His 358 career walks and 656 K's require elaboration; his K's include 87 in 1884, 86 in 1887, and three more years of 50+ K's. His stolen bases are unknown through 1885, only 61 in the next four years; his SABR-stats have both been calculated positive, with career sums of +69 in B.R. and +28 in F.R., both commendable.

His B.R. high is +28, set in 1883. He hit 30+ doubles each of two years, 15+ triples once, and 10+ HRs once. When he began through his prime teams played between 100 and 130 games in a season, so any benchmarks merit extra weight.

Beyond benchmarks, he'd noted among period stats 1876–1889 with ranks of: fourth in games, fourth in at bats, eighth in doubles, eighth in R.B.I., 10th in walks, first in K's, 10th in extra base hits, eighth in total bases.

He was the manager where he played from 1882 through 1889. His name is closely linked with two of the greatest names from the time of baseball antiquity; his predecessor in the managerial post had been William H. "Harry" Wright, and he replaced George Wright as captain of the Boston team.

After experiencing baseball as a player and manager, he worked as a commercial sportswriter, and retailer, then became the general manager for the Wright and Ditson Company, vendor and manufacturer of sporting goods; he was with the firm for nearly 40 years. The senior partner was George Wright.

Morrill in 1890: 1 hit + 2 walks = 1 run + 2 R.B.I. The tribute granted this gentleman of the game in turn is tribute to the Players League and the Brotherhood of Players. Later he served as an N.L. umpire in 1891 and 1896.

John Francis Morrill died of double pneumonia.

MORRIS, EDWARD   Ed Morris (Cannonball)
Born: September 29, 1859, Brooklyn, New York
Died: April 12, 1937, Pittsburgh, Pennsylvania
Height: Weight: 165 Lbs.   Batted: Right.   Threw: Left.
Major League Career: 7 Years, 311 Games
1889: N.L.: Pittsburgh
1891: Did not play
1890: P.L.: Pittsburgh Burghers; P 18

Batting Record:

Games: 18	3B: 0	Walks: 5	SL.%: .143
At Bats: 63	HRs: 0	K's: 13	S.B: 0
Hits: 9	Runs: 7	B.Avg: .143	B.R:
2B: 0	R.B.I: 5	O.B.A:	F.R:

Pitching Record:

Won: 8	Starts: 15	K's: 25	E.R.A: 4.86
Lost: 7	C.G:15	Walks: 35	Saves: 0
Win %: .533	I.P: 144	Hits: 178	P.R: -10
Games: 18	Sh.O: 1	O.B.%: .356	W.A.T: +1.0

His P.R. total is +177, including seasons of +51, +58, +62 in 1884 through 1886; his W.A.T. total is +31.0, with +12.9 which led his league in 1885, and +10.0 in 1886. His nickname of "Cannonball" by all means should begin with a "K."

His father was well known in Brooklyn, where some of the first organized games of baseball were played, but the family moved to San Francisco to find fortune. Ed Morris learned the game well enough there to be invited back East, where he played for two American Association teams.

The first was Columbus in 1884, where he won 34 and marked 302 K's; he pitched for Pittsburgh in 1885 and 1886 and won 39 and 41, K'd 298 and 326. Then he changed leagues and became ordinary. His first three years were sufficiently awesome to require attention.

Let an asterisk (*) denote league leader:

	1884	1885	1886
Won:	34	39	41 (*)
Lost:	13	24	20
Win %:	.723 (*)	.619	.672
I.P:	430	581 (*)	555
Sh.O:	3	6 (*)	12 (*)
K's:	302	298 (*)	326
O.B.%:	.248	.265 (*)	.277 (*)
E.R.A:	2.18	2.35	2.45

Add to his cluster the league lead in games and complete, both 63 in 1885, and the same in 1888 with 55 and 54; he won 20+ games four of his seven major league years, reached .700+ win % once; he pitched 50+ games, starts, and complete four of his seven years.

Continue the calculus with 300+ I.P. five years; 300+ K's twice; E.R.A. below (-) 2.50 four years. His career sums include 171 won and 122 lost, .584 win %; 311, 307, 297 games, starts, complete; note his rate of C.G. to starts is an incredible 97 percent.

He pitched 2,678 innings, his 2,468 hits allowed are less. Note his ratio of 1,217 K's to 498 walks and his .272 O.B.%, and 2.82 career E.R.A. The sum of

Ed "Cannonball" Morris is Cooperstown, but their 10+ years exclusionary rule says not.

His career O.B.% ranks 10th among all pitchers in history. He holds these ranks in period stats 1876–1889: eighth in shutouts, ninth in O.B.%, fourth in hit batters.

He switched to N.L. Pittsburgh in 1887 and had an awful season; he won 14 and lost 22, 4.23 E.R.A. He rebounded in 1888, still with the Alleghenys, won 29 lost 23, and led the league with 54 C.G. and 55 games. He pitched 480 innings, but his cannonball was gone; a mere 135 K's, his O.B.% was .299, and his E.R.A. a fine 2.31.

Working for Pittsburgh again in 1889, he won 6 and lost 13. Ed Morris was well along the downhill side of a stellar major league career. He changed leagues again for 1890, but not cities; one account has him at times in the leadoff slot in his Players League batting order.

A quick glance at his batting stats might prompt the question "Why?" although when he did get on base a Burghers run would usually go up on the scoreboard. To his credit, he completed all his starts, the relatively few there were in 1890.

The same source cited above alleges that Ed Morris had poor off-field habits. He was an N.L. umpire in 1895 and 1897. For the balance of his mortal term he chose Pittsburgh over San Francisco.

Edward Morris died after an eight-week illness caused by an infected toe.

MULVEY, JOSEPH H.   Joe Mulvey
Born: October 27, 1858, Providence, Rhode Island
Died: August 21, 1928, Philadelphia, Pennsylvania
Height: 5'11.5".   Weight: 178 Lbs.   Batted: Right.   Threw: Right.
Major League Career: 12 Years, 987 Games
1889: N.L.: Philadelphia
1891: A.A.: Philadelphia
1890: P.L.: Philadelphia Quakers; 3B 120

Batting Record:

Games: 120	3B: 15	Walks: 27	SL.%: .430
At Bats: 519	HRs: 6	K's: 36	S.B: 20
Hits: 149	Runs: 96	B.Avg: .287	B.R: -1
2B: 26	R.B.I: 87	O.B.A: .326	F.R: -18

His Players League F.R. of -18 is one of four similar parts of his whole -69 F.R.; this hazard at the hot corner ranks seventh all time at that position with 475 career errors. On the other hand, he could hit well enough for a 3B of his time.

He was lacking in long ball power but produced runs, scored and driven; his B.R. career sum of -74 is far afield from the right side of the statistical fence. His 134 career walks don't count in his 4,063 at bats, but 257 K's weren't the essence of his .261 career B.Avg., nearly the historic major league average.

His minuscule count of walks didn't do much to build an O.B.A., and his is just .287. His .355 SL.% is somewhat more in order with the historic norms. Fifteen triples for the P.L. Quakers is his only benchmark stat among 157 doubles, 70 triples, and 29 Hrs.

The value of Joe Mulvey to his teams calculates to about a run per game: 987 games played, 598 runs scored, 532 R.B.I. Each of eight years he played 100+ games; each of seven years he had 400+ at bats, and 398 another year.

He first played in the major leagues for Providence (N.L.) in 1883, and changed to Philadelphia (N.L.) after two hits in 11 at bats; he continued with the Phillies through 1889, during which time his stats were consistently very ordinary.

His high in runs scored is 93 in 1887, in R.B.I. 78 the same year. In 401 at bats in 1884 he was K'd four times, walked 49. His stolen base data are missing four years; for the balance of his career he has 147 S.B. with a high of 43 in 1887.

With career batting averages of .261, .287, .355, his season in the P.L. stands out; 33 percent of his hits were for extra bases, runs scored were near the benchmark, and his hits and walks near exactly match runs and R.B.I. indicating a productive player.

His games played and at bats are second only to his numbers of 1889, with 129 games and 544 at bats. After the P.L. he went to the Philadelphia A.A. club, thus playing in the same city in three different leagues in three years.

He played a full season in the A.A. in 1891: .254, .287, .364. In 1892 he returned to the Phillies for 25 games. In 1893 he was with Washington and played in 55 games. He missed the 1894 season, then concluded his career with Brooklyn in 1895. There's nothing of an unusual or exceptional nature to be noted during this period.

Mulvey was also an N.L. umpire in 1895. On the whole his dozen years as a major league baseball player were ordinary in all ways except one; some days the fair side of third base can be a dangerous place, even if equipped with a fielder's glove. He played near his best in the Players League of 1890.

Joseph H. Mulvey died suddenly. The cause was identified as heart failure. He had been the night watchman at the Phillies park.

There was some controversy on his joining the Players League. He had signed with the N.L. for $2,750 and paid $1,250.

The issue became a civil and criminal legal action. Was the money paid as an advance or a bonus? He was charged with larceny and had to post bail. His P.L. owner, J. Earle Wagner, agreed to pay his N.L. counterparts the whole sum at $300 a month.

Mulvey also alleged he would pay back the money. He said he had always been an honest ballplayer, had always played to win, behaved well, worked hard, and did good work for Philadelphia for years, facts he thought should be remembered by Messrs. Reach and Rogers of the N.L.

MURPHY, CORNELIUS B.   **Con Murphy (Monk)**
Born: October 15, 1863, Worcester, Massachusetts
Died: August 1, 1914, Worcester, Massachusetts
Height: 5'9".   Weight: 130 Lbs.   Batted: Threw:
Major League Career: 2 Years, 35 Games
1889: Did not play.

1891: Did not play
1890: P.L.: Brooklyn Wonders; P 20, OF 3. A.A.: Brooklyn.

Batting Record:

Games: 23	3B: 0	Walks: 5	SL.%: .246
At Bats: 69	HRs: 0	K's: 7	S.B: 1
Hits: 15	Runs: 11	B.Avg: .217	B.R:
2B: 2	R.B.I: 7	O.B.A:	F.R:

Pitching Record:

Won: 4	Starts: 14	K's: 29	E.R.A: 4.79
Lost: 10	C.G:11	Walks: 82	Saves: 2
Win %: .286	I.P: 139	Hits: 168	P.R: -9
Games: 20	Sh.O: 0	O.B.%: .402	W.A.T: -3.6

His batting side is unknown, but in the P.L. of 1890 it was relatively positive: 15 Hits + 5 Walks = 11 Runs + 7 R.B.I. His pitching side is also unknown, but may have cost his team the P.L. pennant: 4 and 10 = -6 and the Brooklyn Wonders were 6.5 games behind the league champions at the end of the season.

Baseball was a team game then as it is now, and it's not been one player was solely responsible for losing a championship. But Con Murphy was the only pitcher on the Brooklyn staff with a losing record, begging the question why was he a loser?

He pitched during only two seasons; his first had been the year of 1884 when three major leagues were in business. He was with the Philadelphia (N.L.) team; his record of won 0 and lost 3 with nothing positive except three complete games in three starts wasn't much of a factor in the Phillies sixth-place 39–73 (.348) season.

When the lottery and the search for pitchers were in progress, the Wonders management chose Con Murphy to be one of theirs; his only major league experience was the above. They lacked in this sort of business and the choices were a matter of best guess.

With all these teams which didn't exist before pursuing players, the situation in sum was one in which demand exceeded supply, which had happened only that once before; the Wonders were able to secure the services of only one established pitcher.

They used only five P's during the season; other than their ace the staff consisted of an outfielder, a part timer, and another comparable to Con Murphy. When the P.L. season was done and the deeds all recorded, all the others had done exceptionally well, pitching over their heads it might be said.

Their ace posted a gap between won and lost of 14 games; the other three were combined 12 games above the .500 mark. Their E.R.A. including Murphy was 3.95, the league average was 4.23; so they achieved beyond expectations, and better than the league.

Why was Con Murphy the losing pitcher for the Brooklyn Wonders? Runs win games, and runs lose games; his E.R.A. cost his team a dozen runs, by his -3.6 W.A.T. stat many more than that. So, where do runs come from? The answers are obvious.

The O.B.% of the league stands at .345, of the Wonders .348, of Con Murphy much more. His 168 hits allowed and 68 free passes in 139 innings of pitching, 1.80 an inning times 9 = 16+ with the potential to score.

This doesn't take into account bases given by errors, which should be consistent no matter who's pitching, but historically isn't, as fielders just don't do as well behind losing pitchers; when all the counting is done his E.R.A. should be higher.

There's no way that John Ward and Company could have predicted, and it wasn't Con Murphy alone who finished second, but when contemplating the facts of the Players League, arguably he was the pitcher who lost the only P.L. pennant.

He changed to the uniform of A.A. Brooklyn during the season, won 3 and lost 9, 5.72 E.R.A.; that stat had been 6.58 in 1884; his composites are won 7 lost 22, .241 win %, 5.31 E.R.A.; as it is, this losing pitcher was at his best for P.L. Brooklyn.

His real occupation was salesman. Cornelius B. Murphy died of heart disease.

In January 1892 he said he was done with the rum business and would pitch the next season for any club wanting a good pitcher. Suffice it to say he didn't pitch in the 12-team N.L. of 1892.

MURPHY, MORGAN E.   Morg Murphy
Born: February 12, 1867, East Providence, Rhode Island
Died: October 3, 1938, Providence, Rhode Island
Height: 5'8".   Weight: 160 Lbs.   Batted: Right.   Threw: Right.
Major League Career: 11 Years, 566 Games
1889: Did not play
1891: A.A.: Boston
1890: P.L.: Boston Reds; C 67, SS 2, 3B 1, OF 1 (Rookie)

Batting Record:

Games: 68	3B: 2	Walks: 24	SL.%: .309
At Bats: 246	HRs: 2	K's: 31	S.B: 16
Hits: 56	Runs: 38	B.Avg: .228	B.R: -12
2B:10	R.B.I: 32	O.B.A: .301	F.R: -6

His first year was the year of the Players League, and his last was the first year of the American League. In the interim he was with the American Association in its last season, and for eight of 11 years he was a National League player.

As a player, Morg Murphy was almost exclusively a catcher. He was also a National League umpire in 1893, 1896, and 1898, suggesting an affinity for working behind home plate, where the baseball view was best.

He didn't play full time; only a very rare few catchers did then. His only 100+ games season was 1891 for the Boston Reds, who were the last champions of their association. He didn't play for any team in 1899, when there was just one major league.

In the P.L., for the Boston champions, he shared the workload behind home plate with another novice and the team's manager; the time cards show Morg Murphy was there the most.

Two hundred forty-six at bats don't equate with a full year for the player at any position facing in his direction. His .228 B.Avg. and his other batting data wouldn't suffice to keep a player at any of the positions in the starting lineup, and surely not for the champions.

When he did get hits and walks they did create runs, of which no team ever scores enough. He contributed a share of extra base hits. His SABR batting stat of -12 B.R. doesn't suggest his work had great value in the cause of winning.

Murphy the catcher stole 16 bases to add to his value for the P.L. Reds; these and 17 the next year are among the 53 he stole during his career. Neither these nor the results of 1,967 at bats produced any benchmarks. His career B.R. is -120.

A P.L. -6 F.R. among his career -14 doesn't really enhance his value, his +11 in the A.A. of 1891 to the contrary. The whole, including six marks of 0 can be construed as expected for a catcher; that -120 B.R. would require complex analysis.

He played for Cincinnati in 1892 through 1895, for St. Louis in 1896 and 1897, and Pittsburgh and Philadelphia in 1898. After his year of sabbatical he was with the Phillies again in 1900, then became a prize catch for the A.L. Philadelphia Athletics.

Specific and significant mention is made of his defection to the A.L. & Co. far beyond justified by his nine games and 28 at bats for a .214 B.Avg.; but his six hits (0 walks) produced five runs and 6 R.B.I., which must be some kind of record.

This was the career moment for Morg Murphy, during which he produced batting averages of .225, .287, and .281; his extra base hits include 56 doubles, 12 triples, and 10 home runs. He scored 247 runs, with 227 R.B.I. His walks number 157; his K's are uncertain.

He was the primary backstop for the Players League champions, and his team the next year closed out the A.A.'s operations in high style. By the rules for ascertaining excellence, it leaves Morgan E. Murphy a pretty fair 1800s catcher.

NASH, WILLIAM MITCHELL Billy Nash

Born: June 24, 1865, Richmond, Virginia
Died: November 15, 1929, East Orange, New Jersey
Height: 5'8.5". Weight: 167 Lbs. Batted: Right. Threw: Right.
Major League Career: 15 Years, 1,549 Games
1889: N.L.: Boston
1891: N.L.: Boston
1890: P.L.: Boston Reds; 3B 129

Batting Record:

Games: 129	3B: 6	Walks: 88	SL.%: .379
At Bats: 488	HRs: 5	K's: 43	S.B: 26
Hits: 130	Runs: 103	B.Avg: .266	B.R: +7
2B: 28	R.B.I: 90	O.B.A: .383	F.R: +16

Pitching Record:

Won: 0	Starts: 0	K's: 0	E.R.A: 0.00
Lost: 0	C.G: 0	Walks: 0	Saves: 0
Win %:	I.P: 0	Hits: 1	P.R: 0
Games: 1	Sh.O: 0	O.B.%: .1.000	W.A.T: 0.0

Less than a month after the last Rebel troops surrendered, William Mitchell Nash was born in the capital city of the ersatz Confederate States of America. Less than 20 years later Billy Nash was the rookie third baseman for the Richmond club of the American Base Ball Association.

By the turn of the century, Billy Nash had been written of as superior at his position with an outstanding arm and smart, which summarize his cerebral and defensive abilities as a major league baseball player; the calculated comment of +67 F.R. came later.

His batting skills are equally impressive; his +100 B.R. makes it as clear as a sunny day in Richmond that he could get the critical hit and score the essential run for his team.

He led the rebels of the Players League in the SABR-stat of Clutch Hitting Index (C.H.I.) with a rating of 130, wherein 100 is average; his P.L. calculations of +7 and +16 in B.R. and F.R. respectively show positive of his play in 1890.

The value of 3B Nash in his prime was assessed so highly that after the 1895 season he was traded even-up for Billy Hamilton who'd just completed a string of three of the most spectacular seasons in all of baseball history.

Although Nash played in 1897 and 1898, his great career effectively came to an end at the same terrible instant his 1896 season did. In his 65th game of 1896 he was hit in the head by a pitch, damaging his skull and resulting in a case of vertigo; he suffered double vision at times.

His career of 1,549 games adjusted to a season of 162 gives him 345.14 assists for a season, which ranks 15th all time among third basemen; his 78 errors in 129 games in 1890 also ranks 15th all time for a season at his position. His total of 2,219 career putouts is sixth all time among 3B.

Also among players at the fifth position, Billy Nash ranks second with 614 errors, fairly offset by his 3.65 range factor which ranks third all time.

He was the field manager of the Phillies in the year he was injured; his record shows he won 62 and lost 68, a .477 win %. His team finished the season eighth of 12 in the National League. He was also an N.L. umpire in 1901. By demand of Andrew Freedman, the owner of the Giants franchise, he could not officiate games in New York City; no public rationale has ever been given.

The further agenda of Nash of the South included owning a hotel in Buffalo, New York, earning a medical degree, serving as a town health officer, lecturing, and working as a building health inspector.

During the better part of his playing career, after Richmond and before the Phillies, he played only in N.L. Boston, except for his P.L. season; this entails 1885 through 1895, almost always at 3B. Twice he did a bit of pitching, once for the P.L. Reds, the prior year a whole inning, during which he allowed a walk.

As a batter, his at bats were consistently in the 400s and 500s but he never had a B.Avg. higher than .295, in 1887; otherwise his high was .293 in 1893; his career B.Avg. is .275, O.B.A. .366 and SL.% .381.

Among the basics from which the three averages are made, he hit 266 doubles (high 27 in 1893), 87 triples (high 15 in 1888), and 60 HRs (high 10 in 1893 and 1895); add to these sums and benchmarks 1,072 runs scored, with four seasons of 100+ including 1890.

The other years of his benchmark runs output were 1887, 1893, and 1894; at the other end of putting a run on the board, are 977 R.B.I. with a year's data missing. These include seasons of 123 in 1893 and 108 in 1895.

He shows 383 career K's with two years missing; 50 is the most, in 1891. His 803 career walks include 10 seasons of 50+, with highs of 91 in 1894 and 88 in his P.L. season. His total of 265 stolen bases includes a peak of 43 in 1887.

Billy Nash of Richmond, Boston, and baseball: consistent and reliable at a demanding and difficult position, much better than most. As a batter there have been both much better and many less. He ranks fifth in the P.L. in F.R. among all, great for a 3B man.

William Mitchell Nash died of a heart attack.

O'BRIEN, JOHN F.   Darby O'Brien
Born: April 15, 1867, Troy, New York
Died: March 11, 1892, West Troy, New York
Height: 5'10".   Weight: 165 Lbs.   Batted: Right.   Threw: Right.
Major League Career: 4 Years, 136 Games
1889: N.L.: Cleveland
1891: A.A.: Boston
1890: P.L.: Cleveland Infants; P 25, OF 1

Batting Record:

Games: 26	3B: 1	Walks: 2	SL.%: .188
At Bats: 96	HRs: 0	K's: 6	S.B: 0
Hits: 15	Runs: 12	B.Avg: .156	B.R:
2B: 1	R.B.I: 6	O.B.A:	F.R:

Pitching Record:

Won: 8	Starts: 25	K's: 54	E.R.A: 3.40
Lost: 16	C.G: 22	Walks: 93	Saves: 0
Win %: .333	I.P: 206	Hits: 229	P.R: +19
Games: 25	Sh.O: 0	O.B.%: .369	W.A.T: -2.9

Three leagues in three years, N.L., P.L., A.A.; it hasn't been possible in major league (U.S.A.) baseball since 1915. A year after the P.L. he pitched for the A.A. league champions. The next year he was dead; he wasn't allowed much time for either a career or a life.

He was a National League umpire in 1889. As a pitcher and player he was consistently erratic. He began in 1888 with the Cleveland Blues of the American Association, won 11 lost 19 (.367 Win %), then went to the Cleveland (N.L.) Spiders, won 22 and lost 17 (.564 win %) when not officiating in 1889.

He pitched for the Boston (A.A.) Reds in 1891, won 18 lost 13 (.581 Win %). There was another Darby O'Brien active at the time, but he only pitched for the New York Metropolitans and only in 1887. These are among the numbers of the P.L. Darby O'Brien:

	1888	*1889*	*1891*
Game:	30	41	40
Starts:	30	41	30
C.G:	30	39	22
I.P:	259	347	269
K's:	135	122	87
Walks:	99	167	127
Hits:	245	345	300
O.B.%:	.333	.360	.375
E.R.A:	3.30	4.15	3.65

He ranks second in the P.L. in Clutch Pitching Index (C.P.I.). His P.L. batting can be dismissed with three notes: he didn't hit with power, his walks to K's ratio is very bad, and his 15 hits and two walks resulted in 12 runs scored and 6 R.B.I., which is extremely productive for any batter.

His P.L. won and lost complete the wave of bad year, good year, then bad and good again. Further as a pitcher, his rate of C.G. declined consistently; his I.P. were down then up then again. His K's to walks and to I.P. read an erratic scramble.

Further considering his O.B.% and E.R.A., the whole indicate a problem. A second scan and bit of thought will show that the pitching problem of the P.L.'s Darby O'Brien was linked to the strike zone and guiding his pitches within or ideally very near it.

His walks per inning times nine doesn't calculate to a rate calling for a train ticket back home, but four walks per game guarantees at least one opponent's score on the board, probably two, which of course have to be compensated for by at least one more of your own, to achieve the fundamental purpose of the game.

Further, note the correspondence between his walks and E.R.A.s, foremost his highest of two negative benchmarks in the walks stat; the 167 isn't near the single-season record of 289 set in 1890 by Amos Rusie of the N.L., but does rank among the 100 worst of all time.

The pitcher's SABR-stats serve to corroborate the inconsistency of Darby O'Brien; while pitching runs are more specific to the individual, wins against (above) team are a balanced function of both pitcher and team. When he was good they were bad, and vice-versa:

	P.R.	W.A.T.
1888	-7	-0.5
1889	-5	+5.0
1890	+19	-2.9
1891	+2	-2.9
Career	+9	-1.3

In the end he appears better than average, but not as good as his teams. In 1890 the Cleveland Infants were a very bad team, and by won and lost he was .090 below the team's .423 win %. While some of his other stats are as good or better than the team, and some worse, the scientific stats show he was great but not nearly as good as his team: consistently inconsistent.

John F. "Darby" O'Brien died of pneumonia.

O'DAY, HENRY FRANCIS   Hank O'Day
Born: July 8, 1863, Chicago, Illinois
Died: July 2, 1935, Chicago, Illinois
Height: Weight: Batted: Threw: Right.
Major League Career: 7 Years, 199 Games
1889: N.L.: Washington and New York
1891: Did not play
1890: P.L.: New York Giants; P 43

Batting Record:

Games: 43	3B: 1	Walks: 10	SL.%: .273
At Bats: 150	HRs: 1	K's: 27	S.B: 1
Hits: 34	Runs: 24	B.Avg: .227	B.R:
2B: 2	R.B.I: 23	O.B.A:	F.R:

Pitching Record:

Won: 22	Starts: 35	K's: 94	E.R.A: 4.21
Lost: 13	C.G: 32	Walks: 163	Saves: 3
Win %: .629	I.P: 329	Hits: 356	P.R: +1
Games: 43	Sh.O: 1	O.B.%: .371	W.A.T: +3.3

Such a pitcher can be a valuable part of a team if for no other reason than to disrupt the batting mindset of the opposition; Hank O'Day was valuable for that and more reasons. His style was crafty and he had stuff, which explains his junkball pitching.

His pitches were slow, they were heavy, tough on catchers, and tougher on batters who'd seen smoke the previous couple of games.

His career as a pitcher was brief, seven years, with less than an ordinary won 70 lost 110 (.389 Win %) record. He pitched in 199 games, 190 starts, 175 complete (92% of starts), 1,634 innings; he struck out 654, walked 579.

The remainder of his pitching career line includes 1,647 hits permitted, -42 P.R. total, -12.2 W.A.T., also an ordinary 3.79 E.R.A. He won 20+ games only once, pitched 300+ innings three years including 403 in 1888.

In 1888 he pitched for Washington (N.L.), where he worked from 1886 through 1888; he'd begun in 1884 with Toledo (A.A.), badly, winning 7 and losing 29. He had three other seasons of 20+ losses. By an odd combination 1889 was his best year; he won 2 and lost 10 for the Senators, then won 9 and lost 1 for New York (N.L.) for 11 and 11.

1890 was his last and only winning season as a pitcher, the year his three saves would have tied for the league high if there had been saves in 1890; his win % and games pitched are near the leaders.

As a P.L. batter his balance of walks and wasted opportunities counts very negative. He delivered almost no extra bases or power but did produce an adequate sum of runs in proportion to hits and walks. His batting averages are those of a pitcher.

During and after his years of pitching and batting, O'Day worked as a National League umpire; by one count he worked at it for 34 years: 1888–1889, 1893, 1895 through 1911, 1913 and 1915 through 1927.

He mixed in two years as an N.L. manager, 1912 with Cincinnati and 1914 with Chicago; his teams combined won 153 and lost 154, a .498 win % for fourth-place finishes both years.

As such, his career in major league baseball extended from 1884 through 1927, a total of 44 years. Only a few have surpassed that sum in any combination of capacities.

The career of O'Day as an umpire is filled with facts from which myths and legends are made; he's not in the Hall of Fame, but did officiate the first World Series in 1903. He was the only umpire to ever eject manager Connie Mack from a game.

He was behind home plate in the Merkle Game of 1908, and in 1920 was officiating when the only unassisted triple play in World Series history was made. He umpired in 10 World Series in all; only revered Bill Klem did more.

In period stats 1876–1889, O'Day ranks third in hit batters. As an umpire by 1895 he had developed a set of signs and signals that were demonstrative, he was one of the first to implement such a style. One might have been used to toss Connie Mack.

Seldom told, umpire O'Day further imposed a $100 fine on Mack, which was later enforced by the National League. By one account, Mack had put on such a display of temper that police had to intervene. The date was September 6, 1895.

On September 24, 1908, O'Day was behind home plate; Bob Emslie was the umpire on the bases. The inning was the last, and the Cubs and Giants had each scored a run. The Giants had a runner in scoring position; Fred Merkle was on first base.

The batter hit a sure single; the lead runner crossed home plate. Merkle, a rookie, presumed the game over and ran off the field instead of touching second base, which was necessary. Stories vary; who had the game ball has never been certain.

Somebody came up with another ball. There was chaos on and off the field, and in the dugouts. Somebody with a ball went and touched second base, claiming a force-out, negating the run which had scored.

Umpire Emslie claimed he didn't see the play, which left the decisions to umpire O'Day; he'd be wrong no matter what was his call. He shouted "The run doesn't count!" and ran off the field. The game had to be replayed, which decided the N.L. pennant. He'd been involved in a similar incident just 19 days before.

This classic O'Day moment caused baseball officialdom to realize more umpires were needed, at least in crucial games. It didn't happen till the fourth game of the next year's World Series, after a bitter dispute about a ball batted fair or foul.

O'Day was a member of the Rules Committee for Organized Baseball in 1920. He hotly criticized a proposal on R.B.I. counts when a home run ends a game; he was opposed and the rule change was passed by a 5 to 1 vote, after which he shouted, "I'm telling you it's illegal!" Umpires have to be decisive.

He was one of the most colorful umpires in baseball annals and is ranked with Bill Klem. A few days after the Merkle boner he found himself involved in another major incident involving fair or foul?

A lady filed a lawsuit claiming injury when she was hit in the face by the ball; the baseball issue was home run or not, to win a game or not. He'd called the ball fair and a home run; this time he had a court, lawyers, and a witness for support.

Some umpires add character to the game. Hank O'Day gave much. When he'd pitched he wasn't much of a pitcher, but had a good year in the Players League of 1890.

O'NEILL, JAMES EDWARD   Tip O'Neill
Born: May 25, 1858, Woodstock, Ontario, Canada
Died: December 31, 1915, Montreal, Quebec, Canada
Height: 6'1.5".   Weight: 167 Lbs.   Batted: Right.   Threw: Right.
Major League Career: 10 Years, 1,054 Games
1889: A.A.: St. Louis
1891: A.A.: St. Louis
1890: P.L.: Chicago Pirates; OF 137

Batting Record:

Games: 137	3B: 16	Walks: 65	SL.%: .407
At Bats: 577	HRs: 3	K's: 36	S.B: 29
Hits: 174	Runs: 112	B.Avg: .302	B.R: +10
2B: 20	R.B.I: 75	O.B.A: .377	F.R: -13

His batting averages read like the trajectory of a home run shot from point of origin to apogee, which at some time and place will return to Earth level. The list of Tip O'Neill isn't very long in points of years; he played in the major leagues for only 10.

Regardless of this limitation, his record represents one of the greatest baseball careers in history. He began in 1883 and ended in 1892; by 1890 he was well into the phase of decline. The sum of his single-season batting averages is .326, 37th best of all time.

His career O.B.A. is .392, which ranks 80th. Very few from the 1800s rank among the top 100 in SL.%, and O'Neill isn't among them. He hit 92 triples in his 10 years, and 52 home runs, along with 222 doubles, to sum up his .458 SL.%.

These are among his 1,386 hits in 4,255 at bats; he scored 880 runs and 435 R.B.I. are known in five years. His +281 B.R. total is near out of sight. He stole 161 bases in the seven years his league counted them.

His league was the American Association. After 23 games and 76 at bats for the New York (N.L.) Giants in 1883, he switched to St. Louis and the Browns, where he stayed through 1889. The team was spectacular, won a slew of pennants, and he was a vital part.

After his terrific P.L. season, he returned to the Browns; his B.Avg. in 1891 was .321, with a .402 O.B.A. His walks in 1891 were 62, of 421 in all; his K's were 33, of 146+. The ratios and proportions are self-evident and testament to a great batter.

In 1891 O'Neill scored 112 runs and drove home 95. These are among his numbers while with the Browns, along with some of the Browns as a team.

	Tip O'Neill (A.A.)				*St. Louis Browns (A.A.)*			
	B.Avg.	O.B.A.	Runs	R.B.I.	Won	Lost	Win%	Place
1884	.276	.309	49	N/A	67	40	.626	3rd
1885	.350	.399	44	N/A	79	33	.705	1st
1886	.328	.385	106	N/A	93	46	.669	1st
1887	.435	.490	167	N/A	95	40	.704	1st
1888	.335	.390	96	98	92	43	.681	1st
1889	.335	.419	123	110	90	45	.667	2nd

It was a fantastic run for O'Neill and for the Browns. From the Red Stockings of the early 1870s to the Yankees of the latter 1990s, very few teams have compiled such records over a period of so many years. Yet both O'Neill and his team are almost unknowns.

There is definitely a correlation, and it is significant; his 1887 batting data may be adjusted for the rule(s) in effect that year. The four years of missing R.B.I. of course have some effect on perception of him as a player, no fault of his own.

He led the A.A. in hits in 1888 with 177 and a .335 B.Avg.; the next year he had 179 hits. 1887 was his year; he led with 225 hits, 167 runs, with 14 HRs, and with 52 doubles, also with the B.Avg. and O.B.A. above, and +88 B.R.

Analysis of his defensive abilities isn't necessary; by the F.R. stat his sum is -55, with not a positive among the nine years for which there are data. He was an outfielder, exclusively in his last eight years, who began as a pitcher.

In 1883, while with the Giants, he won five and lost 12 (.294 Win %), with a 4.07 E.R.A., 148 I.P., 15 complete in 19 games he started. He began as a pitcher with the Browns and turned it around in his second season for his second team.

He didn't pitch at all after 1884, when he won 11 and lost four (.733), with a 2.68 E.R.A., 141 I.P., 14 starts, all complete among 17 games. His composite P.R. is -7, but in the C.P.I. stat his 122 in 1884 led the A.A.

Much more significant over the long term as a batter, O'Neill posted a B.Avg. of .300+ in seven of his 10 years, an O.B.A. of .400+ three years, and a .500+ SL.%

once; that was .691 in 1887, when he posted a .400+ B.Avg. with or without help from the rules committee.

Recall his 225 hits in 1887; that datum ranks 52nd all time, tied with the likes of Ty Cobb, Bill Terry, Paul Molitor and others. Though he played in the 1880s he's a good fit in such class. His 85 extra base hits in 1887 are tied for most by any 1800s player. The 52 doubles he hit in one of his three years of 30+ ranks 24th all time, tied with Tris Speaker and Lou Gehrig and others, again putting O'Neill in some pretty fair company.

He scored 100+ runs each of five years, had 100+ R.B.I. one of the five years known, 15+ triples twice, and 10+ HRs twice. If his P.L. stats were noted by an asterisk aside, there would be one next to nearly all these benchmarks.

In an era when baseball bats were big and long and some had very strange shapes, his was said to be tiny by comparison. He was popular and a gentleman, not necessarily in that order. As a teenage amateur he pitched his hometown Woodstock club to the Canadian national championship.

His first American major league owners had a franchise in each league. A tricky switch by them that failed freed him to sign with the Browns, with the advice and counsel of Charlie Comiskey, whom he followed to the Chicago Pirates of the Players League.

During the 15-game World's Series of 1887, he started three double plays from the outfield, indicating that despite his -55 career F.R. he had good throwing arm (ex-pitcher) and good speed in the field. Despite his 161 career stolen bases, including 29 for the Chicago Pirates, he's been reported as simply inept at sliding into bases.

His period stats 1876–1889 include ranks of: third in B.Avg., second in O.B.A., third in SL.%, second in combo. O.B.A. & SL.%.

O'Neill was, and remains the only player in history to lead his league in doubles, triples, and HRs in the same season (1887).

After his career as a major league player in the U.S.A. he was president of a Montreal minor league club. He lived with his mother and brothers; together they owned and operated a saloon and restaurant.

James Edward "Tip" O'Neill died of a heart attack incurred while he was walking along a Montreal thoroughfare. He's never been nominated for membership in the American National Baseball Hall of Fame, but he definitely rates the call of a Players League star player.

O'ROURKE, JAMES HENRY   Jim O'Rourke (Orator)
Born: August 24, 1852, Bridgeport, Connecticut
Died: January 8, 1919, Bridgeport, Connecticut
Height: 5'8".   Weight: 185 Lbs.   Batted: Right.   Threw: Right.
Major League Career: 23 Years, 1,999 Games
1889: N.L.: New York
1891: N.L.: New York
1890: P.L.: New York Giants; OF 111

Batting Record:

Games: 111	3B: 5	Walks: 33	SL.%: .515
At Bats: 478	HRs: 9	K's: 20	S.B: 23
Hits: 172	Runs: 112	B.Avg: .360	B.R: +31
2B: 37	R.B.I: 115	O.B.A: .410	F.R: +2

Articulate and intelligent far above the norm, Jim O'Rourke was a member of the elderly gentry by 1890. While playing in the P.L. he posted numbers the length of the list consistent with those that earned him high rank among baseball's elite since 1872.

Nearing age 40 when he played the outfield for the P.L. New York Giants, he achieved one of the best of his many fine seasons. There were no deficiencies; he excelled in every respect. He exuded confidence but never flaunted his baseball or other skills.

There was an exception of sorts; when men of the media insisted that he be interviewed whether convenient or not, or when asked questions he deemed not appropriate, he would confound and dazzle them with scholarly language and sophist vocabulary equal to the most brilliant minds of his time.

He became a law school graduate in 1887, after many years of diligent part-time studies. As an elder O'Rourke was a member of both the Minor League Board of Arbitration and the National League Board of Directors.

He was popular with the public and players, a gentleman of high integrity; once he fined himself for swearing during a game. His demeanor was consistent with his family of Connecticut farmers. His father died when he was young.

Later he worked at law, played at politics, and was a success in his real estate ventures. In 1945, O'Rourke was elected to the National Baseball Hall of Fame, one of a select group judged deserving by a special "Old Timers" committee.

In 1872 he began his major league baseball career with the Mansfields of Connecticut. His next three years, till the end of the National Association, he was with the Boston Red/Red Stockings, after which the balance of his career he was with the National League, except the Players League year.

He was also a manager, five years in all, four with Buffalo, 1881 through 1884, with Washington in 1893; his teams won 246 games, lost 258 (.458 Win %). His playing career actually ended in 1893, but by contract he played a complete game in 1904 for the Giants of John McGraw; O'Rourke got a hit and scored a run.

He continued as a minor league player until 1908. Then he organized a minor league, owned and managed a club, and was president of that league. He played two cameo tribute games by invitation, including a nine-inning game in 1917; he was age 67 then.

Between 1872 and 1893 O'Rourke played in 1,999 games; if he ever had a bad year, it doesn't show in the records. He was primarily an outfielder, although he played considerably at 1B and 3B. He was nothing special as an outfielder, but his batting was second to none.

During his 19th season, the Players League season, he ranked third in batting average and doubles, fourth in runs batted in, and fifth in slugging percentage. His runs scored and R.B.I. were both 100+; his 20 K's in 478 at bats equates to 4.2%. His B.R. is a benchmark +31, his F.R. a positive +2, and he stole 23 bases.

Positive in every way, not a fault to be found, this gentleman merits citation as a Players League star player, and as a Players League feature player. On a level playing field of opinion, O'Rourke would be a viable candidate for the title "Greatest Player of His Century."

It's known that twice he batted .330+, but many data are absent. He scored 278 runs in 225 games during his first four years, in the National Association, predecessor to the National League. His 351 hits in 1,109 at bats calculate to a .317 B.Avg.

His age was 19 when he began with the Mansfields. When the N.L. was created he carried three Boston years to the new league; he continued as a Boston player from 1876 through 1878, and returned for another year after a year with Providence.

In 1877 he led the N.L. with 68 runs, 20 walks, and with a .407 SL.%.; his four-year N.L. Boston cumulatives include 277 games, 1,195 at bats, 369 hits, .309 B. Avg. He led with six HRs in 1880. He scored 244 runs during this period; his R.B.I. were 140.

Among his many notable numbers are nine K's in 265 at bats in 1877 (3.4%), and eight K's in 363 at bats in 1880 (2.2%). His interim year B.Avg. at Providence was .348. His .371 O.B.A. led the N.L., as did his .459 SL.%. He scored 69 runs in 81 games.

While with the Buffalo (N.L.) Bisons from 1881 through 1884, the last was his best season: .347 B.Avg., .392 O.B.A., .480 SL.%. 1883 was his first year with 100+ runs scored, 102. He scored 119 times in 1884.

His long tenure with the New York (N.L.) Giants ran from 1885 through 1889, then again in 1891 and 1892. His first of these seasons included 16 triples, his only benchmark in 3B or HRs during his career.

The best and most of O'Rourke for the Giants before the P.L. year include the 16 triples and 119 runs. He scored 106 times in 1886, marked B.Avg.s of .321 in 1889, .309 in 1886, .300 in 1885 and was K'd 11 times in 297 at bats (2.7%) in 1887.

His best after the P.L. was for the Giants, a .304 B.Avg. in 1892. He ended his actual playing career with Washington in 1893, with batting averages of .287, .354, .356, and 15 stolen bases.

A summary of O'Rourke's career includes 13 years with B.Avg. .300+ (high .362 in 1877), two years with O.B.A. .400+ (high .410 in 1890), one year with SL.% .500+ (1890). He scored 100+ runs each of five years (1883 through 1886 and 1890), had 100+ R.B.I. one year (1890).

His highest walks total was 49 in 1893, his most K's were 34 in 1889; O'Rourke did not come to the ballpark to watch the opposing pitchers pitch. His +303 cumulative B.R. ranks high among the best; his high was +39 in 1884. His F.R. composite is -122; his worst was -22 in 1887.

O'Rourke did not descend upon Mansfield from Mount Olympus; he was just a youngster who came off the farm and was able to learn and do extremely well in the major league game of baseball. He did make a couple of special appearances after he became a legend.

The greatest season of this great player merits special note; the sum of his year with the Players League by basic numbers: 172 + 33 = 112 + 115 = Outstanding. O'Rourke is a P.L. star player, and a feature player. All was for the cause of the greater good; his spirit has continued at Cooperstown since 1945.

When James Henry O'Rourke died the cause was pneumonia. His eulogy called him the fairest and squarest of men. SABR adds, "He would have appreciated that."

His walks and home runs were not many, but he did hit 30+ doubles each of three years; he's one of only three players in history to lead two leagues in batting average. In the Players League of 1890 he ranks third in doubles, fourth in R.B.I., third in B.Avg., fifth in SL.%; he's also fifth in the Production stat.

In period stats 1876–1889 O'Rourke ranks: third in games, third in at bats, third in hits, third in runs, fourth in doubles, fifth in triples, seventh in R.B.I., seventh in B.Avg., seventh in extra base hits, third in total bases.

After his stellar major league career he founded a minor league, organized a club in it, and was the manager and the team's catcher. He was also a practicing lawyer and fire commissioner in his town.

ORR, DAVID L.   Dave Orr
Born: September 29, 1859, New York New York
Died: June 23, 1915, Brooklyn, New York
Height: 5'11".   Weight: 250 Lbs.   Batted: Left.   Threw: Right.
Major League Career: 8 Years, 791 Games
1889: A.A.: Columbus
1891: Did not play
1890: P.L. Brooklyn Wonders; 1B 107

Batting Record:

Games: 107	3B: 13	Walks: 30	SL.%: .537
At Bats: 464	HRs: 6	K's: 11	S.B: 10
Hits: 173	Runs: 89	B.Avg: .373	B.R: +34
2B: 32	R.B.I: 124	O.B.A: .416	F.R: -5

The number of players who could follow O'Rourke is minuscule; Dave Orr with only eight years as a major league player by strict rules couldn't be considered.

Orr's batting average in the Players League of 1890 stands at .373, none was higher and only one tied; his batting side is still an issue in baseball literature.

To allege that his major league beginning was disjointed is truth; a game for the Metropolitans, then one for the Giants, then 12 more for the original Mets. The second "one" was in the National League; the balance of his games were played in the American Association, except 107 in 1890.

His total is only 791 games played, his 464 at bats in 1890 are among 3,289. His 173 P.L. hits, which don't rank among the top five, were part of his whole count of 1,126, which calculate to a .342 career batting average, ninth highest in history.

Allowing for a bit of perspective, the .342 puts Dave Orr in the midst of Dan Brouthers, Babe Ruth, and Harry Heilmann, all comfortably ensconced as parts of Cooperstown heritage.

To list the years Orr did not achieve a .300+ B.Avg. is simple: none. His years with a .400+ O.B.A. total are two; those with a .500+ SL.% are an amazing, for the

1800s, six of eight. His career B.R. sum is an equally amazing +223, and his F.R. total is -0.

He could play in the field, but it's doubtful his physique would have enabled him at any position except first base. To vast proportions, his game was imbalanced toward batting and hitting with power; his .502 career SL.% ranks 61st all time, and fourth of four 1800s players who are in the top 100.

If there were five reasons why the Brooklyn Wonders were able to finish second in the P.L. instead of fourth or seventh, then Orr represents at least two of these reasons. This veritable behemoth even stole 10 bases in 1890, though this was his lowest season total of 66 among the five years known.

If Vince Lombardi had seen the likes of Orr he might have salivated; Jerry Kramer or Forrest Gregg might have been an afterthought rather than enshrined at Canton, Ohio. An athlete by nature of such dimensions as Orr will find a realm in which to excel.

Had not the St. Louis Browns the person and persona of Charlie Comiskey as the third position player and team leader, owner Chris Von der Ahe surely would have pursued to sign Orr as his 1B man and dining companion wherever the A.A. would play their games.

Imagination and speculation put aside, Orr did play in the American Base Ball Association, at first base, for the New York Metropolitans, from 1883 through 1887. His first manager, in 1883 and 1884, was Jim Mutrie, himself somewhat of a legend; Mr. Mutrie defected to the National League New York Giants in 1885.

In those two years, both manager and player established themselves as giants among baseball men. 1883 was the first year for Mutrie in his position and the first for Orr at his. The result was an American Association pennant on the strength of 75 games won and 32 lost (.701 Win %).

Mutrie became the 19th century counterpart of Earl Weaver, and a great PR man, while Orr led the A.A. with a .354 B.Avg., 162 hits, and a then still-to-be-counted +43 B.R. Earl Weaver and Boog Powell would have done wisely and well to have used this dynamic Metropolitans duo as role models.

Orr went on to hit 21 triples in 1885, and 31 in 1886; the 31 among 193 hits ranks second now in the all time single-season records. All these stats were league leaders, as were his .543 SL.% in 1885, and .527 in 1886, when he also led with seven Hrs.

His K's were not counted most years. His walks while with the Mets tally 52 in the four years known, 98 during his career. He could judge the strike zone and had the batting discipline of a master; the name Ted Williams comes to mind.

Consider his 210 extra base hits while with the Mets among 1,818 at bats; the calculation is easy and the term "amazing" does not nearly suffice. During this term he made 634 hits, the 6 by 18 assures a batting average far beyond the benchmark; 33 percent of his hits for extra bases has hardly happened in all history.

He left the Metropolitans to play across town for Brooklyn in 1888. He played in only 99 games, his least except for that peculiar rookie year. He batted .305, registered 57 R.B.I. in the first year the A.A. counted them, and scored only 57 runs.

He switched to Columbus (A.A.) for the 1889 season, which was much more amenable to his style and form. He played in 134 games, produced a .327 B.Avg., drove in 87 runs and scored 70; his F.R. of +9 was the best of his career.

1890 came, and with it the Players League. Orr became a singular part of baseball history; this was overall his best year, but by no choice of his own, it was his last year. While playing in a post-season exhibition game in rural Pennsylvania, he suffered a stroke which ended his career after only eight years.

It was a cruel blow to a star just past age 30. His parents had been immigrants and life could not have been easy. His facts of life include saving a little boy trapped in a train wreck. Despite his massive strength, he himself had become injured.

During his career, Orr hit 30+ doubles three years, 15+ triples two years, and a peak nine HRs in 1884; he had 100+ R.B.I. one year known, in 1890, and his high in runs scored was 93 in 1886. His most walks were 30 in 1890, his most K's were 38 in 1889; his B.R. calculate to +30 four years, of which three are 40+.

He led his league in:	*His ranks in the P.L. include:*
B.Avg. one year	First in B.Avg. (tied)
SL.% two years	Third in SL.%
Triples two years	Second in R.B.I.
HRs one year	Fourth in B.R.
Hits two years	Fourth in Production.
B.R. one year.	

He's omitted in the columns of period stats; the criterion for inclusion is a minimum of 3,000 plate appearances, he had 3,289 at bats. The logic and reason for the omission are unknown. If he was included, his ranks for the period 1876–1889 would be: fourth in B.Avg., 10th in O.B.A., second in SL.%.

After the stroke, and despite his crippled condition, he tried work as a stone mason, did work as a Broadway stage hand, and was a caretaker at Ebbets Field. During the Federal League's 1914 season, he was the Brooklyn press box attendant.

He'd been manager of the New York Metropolitans briefly in 1887, won 3 and lost 5; the year before he became the first player to amass 300+ total bases in a season. He certainly was a Players League star player, and if there were a compassion committee at Cooperstown, Orr would be a star there also.

A photo in a SABR journal shows him batting from the right side, but he's noted in prominent literature as batting left handed. Both players and photographers have been known to play tricks, and though such are rare, they're not as rare as a player like Dave Orr.

David L. Orr died of heart disease during the 1915 baseball season. No doubt there was a void in the Brooklyn press box.

PFEFFER, NATHANIEL FREDERICK   Fred Pfeffer (Dandelion)
Born: March 17, 1860, Louisville, Kentucky
Died: April 10, 1932, Chicago, Illinois
Height: 5'10.5".   Weight: 184 Lbs.   Batted: Right.   Threw: Right.
Major League Career: 16 Years, 1,670 Games
1889: N.L.: Chicago

1891: N.L.: Chicago
1890: P.L.: Chicago Pirates; 2B 124

Batting Record:

Games: 124	3B: 8	Walks: 44	SL.%: .361
At Bats: 499	HRs: 5	K's: 23	S.B: 27
Hits: 128	Runs: 86	B.Avg: .257	B.R: -13
2B: 21	R.B.I: 80	O.B.A: .319	F.R: +22

(O'Neill, O'Rourke, and Orr; the "P" is silent in pronouncing the surname "Pfeffer.")

Though his name appears in many places in the books of records, Fred Pfeffer batted .300+ just once. He regularly led his league in defensive stats, and he was a leader in the Brotherhood movement to establish the Players League.

His .300+ came as .308 in 1894, for Louisville. He never reached .400+ in O.B.A., but in 1884 for Chicago (N.L.), some allege by nefarious means, he amassed a .514 SL.%. 1894 was really his last year, though he played some in 1895 and 1896.

His first year was 1882, for Troy (N.L.). In 83 games and 335 at bats he hit one home run, had a B.Avg. of .221, and walked once. In 1883, with Chicago, in 96 games and 371 at bats he hit one HR, had a .235 B.Avg., but his SL.% were on the rise, improved from .273 to .340.

His F.R. had been +7 and +6 but jumped to +40 in 1884; his B.R. had been -16 and -10 and jumped to +30 in 1884. He played in 112 games and had 467 at bats; he hit 25 HRs which helped to nearly double his SL.% as a rookie. He scored 105 runs and had 101 R.B.I., which both were more than double his first two years combined.

In 1885, Pfeffer played in 112 games, had 468 at bats, hit five HRs, posted a .241 B.Avg. and .328 SL.%. In the year of his 25 HRs only one player hit more in a season, and that was also in 1884. He hit 27 for Chicago. Critics complained throughout the season the home park of the Chicago White Stockings had been adjusted.

His term with the Windy City team extended from 1883 through 1889, resumed in 1891, after which he played for Louisville 1892 through 1895, began 1896 with the Giants, and ended his career that year back with the Chicago club.

Pfeffer scored 100+ runs just once and had 100+ R.B.I. just once. With that, let his greater assets come to the fore. His speed was far above normal; on the base paths, lacking four years' data, he stole 382 bases, including 64 in 1888 and 57 in 1887.

His fielding as judged by the F.R. numbers was superb, a career total of +234, with not one negative; his +40 would have been a league leader, also +37 in 1888 and +22 in 1890.

Further, he ranks first all time among second basemen in putouts with 6,545, he led his league eight straight years; he's fourth all time in 2B assist with 6,905, he led four straight years; also he's 12th all time in double plays with 1,186, led six straight years.

He led his league in 2B chances seven years. He's first all time in range factor with 6.39; his range factor of 6.68 in 1890 ranks 13th all time among single-season 2B records. His 1884 range factor of 7.29 ranks first. His career assists adjusted to a 162-game season calculate to 537.96, sixth all time among 2B.

Pfeffer also ranks second all time in errors by a 2B with 791. One source claims that he didn't use a fielder's glove. With both his worst and best told, his P.L. batting was very average; his walks near double his K's, and his run production at both ends of the base paths above average.

His ratio of extra base hits was also better than average. The B.R. stat of -13 does not concur, but his +22 F.R. was highest in the Players League; his F.R. improved a point in 1891, and his B.R. jumped to a +7. In 137 games, 498 at bats, his B.Avg. was .247, with seven HRs and a .349 SL.%.

His O.B.A. in 1891 was four points higher than his SL.%, via 79 walks, one of four years he walked 50+ times. Another was 67 walks for Louisville in 1892, followed by 53 walks in 1893. He changed his game plan, which improved his usual B.Avg. by 10 points.

H.R.s fell to two and three, then five in 1894, when he batted .308, after which Pfeffer was primarily a part-time player. His career sums are almost multiples of his P.L. raw data and his batting averages variances are minuscule; he was average in 1890 as a batter, and base stealer, typically excellent in the field.

Games: 1,670	B.Avg: .255	SL.%: .369	Runs: 1,094	Walks: 527
At Bats: 6,555	O.B.A: .312	HRs: 94	R.B.I: 1,019	K's: 498 + a few

In period stats 1876–1889, he's tied for third in HRs. He was manager at Louisville most of 1892, in that strange split season when he replaced the original during the first half; he won 9 and lost 14 (.391) to finish 10th of 12. In the second half his team won 33 and lost 42 (.440) to finish ninth of 12.

Thus the sum of the managerial record of Fred Pfeffer is 42 won and 56 lost (.429). After the major leagues he was a college coach and a minor league manager. He owned and operated a tavern until Prohibition (January 16, 1919) and then was an attendant and supervisor of a racetrack press box.

Nathaniel Frederick Pfeffer died of heart disease.

PICKETT, JOHN THOMAS   John Pickett
Born: February 20, 1866, Chicago, Illinois
Died: July 4, 1922, Chicago Illinois
Height: Weight: Batted: Right.   Threw: Right.
Major League Career: 3 Years, 189 Games
1889: A.A.: Kansas City
1891: N.L.: Baltimore
1890: P.L.: Philadelphia Quakers; 2B 100

Batting Record:

Games: 100	3B: 9	Walks: 40	SL.%: .371
At Bats: 407	HRs: 4	K's: 17	S.B: 12
Hits: 114	Runs: 82	B.Avg: .280	B.R: -3
2B: 7	R.B.I: 64	O.B.A: .347	F.R: -23

Kansas City, Philadelphia, Baltimore: three leagues in three years. A quick and fast unusual career; 1890 represents more than half of it. There's evidence of good discipline at the bat, but he must have been a sight to see playing in the field.

For 1890 his F.R. calculates to -23; it's his only such stat. The other two are 0. His P.L. -3 B.R. is best among -12 and -6; the sum is -21. His F.R. sum stands at -23. John Pickett probably didn't render fear among opponents or their managers.

His seven P.L. doubles are sandwiched between another seven and two, his nine triples between zero and three, his four HRs between zero and one. He also had 40 walks between 11 and seven; these are the ingredients of a .252 season B.Avg., .311 O.B.A., and .326 SL.%.

His before and after batting averages are displayed along with his career totals:

	1889	1891	Career
B.Avg:	.224	.213	.252
O.B.A:	.271	.260	.311
SL.%:	.259	.291	.326

For Pickett, the Players League season made a greater difference in his career than for any other individual player. His further composites include for his three seasons 189 games and 749 at bats, 189 hits (one per game), 115 runs and 88 R.B.I.

His 17 K's in 1890 and his 12 stolen bases among 21 also show the influence the P.L. had on him. Pickett wasn't a star, but he sure was a player at his best in the P.L. of 1890.

He was an employee of Albert Spalding's sporting good company for 24 years, much better at designing bats than using them.

John Thomas Pickett died of complications after an unknown surgical procedure.

QUINN, JOSEPH J.   Joe Quinn
Born: December 25, 1864, Sydney, Australia
Died: November 12, 1940, St. Louis, Missouri
Height: 5'7".   Weight: 158 Lbs.   Batted: Right.   Threw: Right.
Major League Career: 17 Years, 1,768 Games
1889: N.L.: Boston
1891: N.L.: Boston
1890: P.L.: Boston Reds; 2B 130

Batting Record:

Games: 130	3B: 8	Walks: 44	SL.%: .411
At Bats: 509	HRs: 7	K's: 24	S.B: 29
Hits: 153	Runs: 87	B.Avg: .301	B.R: +4
2B: 19	R.B.I: 82	O.B.A: .359	F.R: +13

There are two Joe Quinns in the record books. The other one began in 1871 and was done a decade later; the P.L. Joe Quinn began in 1884 and played longer, into the first year of the 20th century.

In the process, the P.L. Joe Quinn gained a flawless record of honesty and integrity along with a few statistical records as a clever baserunner and a respected infielder. In sum, he knew how to play the game.

As to his credits, he was among the smartest and speediest second basemen, and further, when the *Sporting News* conducted a survey in 1893 to identify the most popular player in St. Louis, Joe Quinn was the people's choice.

His family moved to Dubuque, Iowa, when he was a young boy. As a naturalized American, he played in four major leagues of baseball; his position was second base, but he played at all of the positions during his long career.

At first base in 1884, he set the all-time single-season record for errors at that position with 62. During the split-season single-league World's Series of 1892 he was in the outfield for Boston. It was the 11th inning, the score was tied at 0 to 0.

Jesse Burkett, one of the fastest ever to run the bases, had an opportunity to challenge Quinn's throwing arm; when the game was called to conclusion, the score was still 0 to 0.

Quinn played second base in 1890; exceptional then and now, he played in all (130) of his team's games. The keystone position player has often been a liability in the batting order, but Quinn made it into an asset for the P.L. champion Reds.

He didn't lead the league in any stats, but among his there are no negatives. Some such as his benchmark batting average, runs scored and R.B.I. are well above the norm and expectations for a full time fourth position player.

His extra base data are also above the norm for his position and for the era; his walks are nearly double his K's. Combined with 153 hits he produced a good many runs for the Boston Reds that ordinarily would not have been posted on the scoreboard.

His P.L. +4 B.R. commend his batting, but his +13 F.R. contradicts the whole of his calculated fielding record; it's one of only two positives among a total of -109 F.R., with contra-benchmark lows of -32 for St. Louis in 1893 and -31 for Boston (N.L.) in 1889.

If his P.L. numbers were consistent through all 17 years he played in the major leagues, and if accolades were all facts, anyone in search of the greatest second baseman of the 1800s would not have to search any further; as it was, Quinn is cited as a Players League star player.

In terms of the best 2B of his century, hard facts must be given their due. He ranks 19th all time among 2B with 418 errors; nearly all that rank higher also played in the 1800s, including one with more than 800 errors, and two with 700+

On the other side of the errors coin, Quinn and two of the aforementioned three also rank among the top 100 2B in career fielding percent; the more equitable measures put Quinn second in F.% and 13th in errors when limited to the 1800s.

Another side of Quinn, as a complete player, reveals career averages of .261, .302, and .327, all far below his 1890 numbers. He played in 100+ games each of 10 years and had 300+ at bats 12 years; he didn't score 100+ runs any year, now did he ever have 100+ R.B.I.

He didn't reach any of the extra base benchmarks, he didn't walk to first base 100+ times in any season, nor did he collect any horrific sums of K's. His best and most show 44 walks in 1890, and 42 K's in 1892, among 364 career walks and 214 K's with five years missing.

The sum of his stolen bases is 268, with 29 in the P.L. his high. B.Avg.s of .300+ were achieved three years, in a career total of 6,879 at bats. There are no .400+ O.B.A. or .500+ SL.% in his columns; one is 98 points and the other is far from the benchmarks.

In these columns, Quinn's highs stand at .359 O.B.A. in 1890, and .468 in SL.%, also in 1890; his high of 87 runs was scored in 1890, and his 82 R.B.I. high also came in the P.L. His B.R. are almost all (-), -208 sum, +7 in 1888 was his best.

The American Association is missing from the list of the four leagues he played in. All were for one year except the N.L., with the Union Association in its year of 1884, the Players League in 1890, and the American League in its premier year of 1901.

In 1884 the St. Louis Maroons were his team, in 1890 the Boston Reds, both champions. In 1901 he was with the Washington Senators who finished sixth on their way to becoming "First in war, first in peace, and last in the American League."

After his family migrated to Dubuque, the baseball training grounds of the Midwest, Quinn found good stock from which to learn the game. He was found in Dubuque by the discoverer of numerous future major league players, foremost for the St. Louis Browns.

After the year of the U.A. Maroons, Quinn switched with the franchise to the N.L. and played both their seasons of 1885 and 1886 before the club folded. He joined N.L. Boston after missing 1887, and was with that club in 1888 and 1889, and after the P.L. year in 1891 and 1892.

The 1890s were the most successful decade in the Boston organization's history. The franchise was in management chaos, and its success is to be found in league championships in 1891, 1892, and 1893, then again in 1897. The franchise continued through 1952, had World's Series champions twice in that span, in 1914 and 1948.

Quinn departed Boston for St. Louis and the Cardinals in 1893 and continued with them through 48 games in 1896. Then he was off to Baltimore for the remainder of that season through 12 games in 1898, then returned again to St. Louis for 103 games.

He was by then firmly locked in to the Robison Brothers' double franchise family of St. Louis and Cleveland. When the decision was made to move their best chattel to St. Louis for the 1899 season, Quinn was one of the unfortunates made Spiders.

Thus relegated to one of the worst teams in history, he'd gone full circle in a manner of speaking, from champions with Charlie Comiskey, and King Kelly, and Frank Selee with Boston in 1891 and 1892, to a woeful and awful team which made a season record of 20 wins and 134 losses; others were bad but none to this level.

He'd been field manager for the Robisons in 1895, at St. Louis. In his part of that season the team won 11 and lost 28; their season culminated in an 11th-place finish of 12. He endured nearly all their outrages in Cleveland as their 1899 manager.

No matter the skills and wisdom he'd learned from his outstanding mentors, no manager could have offset the machinations of the Robisons, passing their players back and forth like toy soldiers. Their first 1899 Spiders manager quit at 8 and 30, a .211 Win %.

Quinn accepted the onerous duty. The team was 12th and last in the National League; he could only endure through 12 wins and 104 losses, an almost major league impossible .103 Win %. As a player, he was witness to the whole 147-game nightmare.

Quinn had a good year as a batter in 1899, with a .286 B.Avg., .312 O.B.A., and

.345 SL.%. He accumulated 615 at bats, and a -16 B.R.; he stole 22 bases and has been given a mark of -3 F.R. His owners were reduced to one franchise after 1899; four of the N.L. 12 were disbanded as the league returned to a format of eight teams.

Quinn played 22 more games for the Robisons in 1900 at St. Louis, then went to Cincinnati for 74 more. The advent of the American League passed and it became fact on the field. Quinn was prize pickins and ended up with the Washington club.

Contrary to some baseball histories and presumptions, Clark Griffith was not the first owner of that franchise. In the first A.L. season, he was manager of the Chicago White Sox, but long before he owned Washington, Griffith had a seminal influence on the franchise.

He, Ban Johnson, and Charlie Comiskey turned the then-minor A.L. into a major league. Griffith, as a representative of the Ball Players Protective Association (circa 1899–1900), got the first word of the N.L.'s refusal to incorporate the A.L. franchises.

Johnson assigned the Senators franchise to Jimmy Manning, owner and manager of the Kansas City team in the minor A.L. Fred Postal was named the club's first president-owner. It was later found that Johnson himself held 51 percent of the Senators stock.

For Quinn, who must have had some inkling, this must have been deja vu from the Union Association, the Players League, and the brothers Robison. Even though he wasn't a privy insider, he must have had some sense of baseball politics after 16 years.

He played in 66 games for the Senators, batted a normal .252 and posted a -3 F.R. at his position; this concluded his career as a player. Add to his credits the duties of N.L. umpire in 1889, 1894, and 1896.

This flawless and honest man of integrity, this Players League star player, returned to St. Louis; he owned and operated a funeral home for 24 years, half a world away from his land of origin, but not very far from Dubuque.

Joseph H. Quinn died of hardening of the arteries. The condition was claimed due to frailty, and he was in hospital eight months.

QUINN, THOMAS OSCAR   Tom Quinn
Born: April 25, 1864, Pittsburgh, Pennsylvania
Died: July 24, 1932, Swissvale, Pennsylvania
Height: 5'8".   Weight: 180 Lbs.   Batted: Right.   Threw: Right.
Major League Career: 3 Years, 113 Games
1889: A.A.: Baltimore
1891: Did not play
1890: P.L.: Pittsburgh Burghers; C 55

Batting Record:

Games: 55	3B: 3	Walks: 17	SL.%: .275
At Bats: 207	HRs: 1	K's: 8	S.B: 1
Hits: 44	Runs: 23	B.Avg: .213	B.R: -14
2B: 4	R.B.I: 15	O.B.A: .282	F.R: -4

In 1886 he played three games for the Pittsburgh (A.A.) Alleghenys, scored a run, and had no hits or batting averages. He might have been hit by a pitch then stole a base to get in scoring position. He was away from the major leagues the next two years.

When he returned it was with the Baltimore (A.A.) Orioles. He played in 55 games, the same as with the P.L. Pittsburghers. His batting averages were .175, .252, .211, he stole six bases and played the field at a +5 F.R. rate. In all he showed he had some abilities.

1890 was the last year of the career of catcher Tom Quinn. When his records of the years are compared, it's clear 1890 was the better; he hit a home run in 1889 and another in 1890, but for Baltimore he produced only one triple and two doubles, 34 hits in all in 194 at bats. His B.R. for Baltimore calculates to -16.

Where numbers count most for catchers, his -4 Burghers F.R. costs his team about a game measured against his Orioles datum; his counts of 17 walks and 8 K's for the Burghers are to their advantage when measured against 19 walks but 22 K's for the Orioles.

The Burghers' first catcher was much better at the bat than Quinn but played only one game more, his -13 F.R. behind home plate tells much about why. In sum, as Casey Stengel once reasoned for all to know, if Tom Quinn hadn't been there a lot of Burghers pitches would have gone all the way to the backstop.

After his brief major league baseball career, he was a factory inspector for the Commonwealth of Pennsylvania.

Thomas Oscar Quinn died of septic poisoning.

RADBOURN, CHARLES GARDNER　　　Charley Radbourn (Ol' Hoss)
Born: December 11, 1854, Rochester New York
Died: February 5, 1897, Bloomington, Illinois
Height: 5'9".　　Weight: 168 Lbs.　　Batted: Right.　　Threw: Right.
Major League Career: 12 Years, 653 Games (528 as a pitcher)
1889: N.L.: Boston
1891: N.L.: Cincinnati
1890: P.L.: Boston Reds; P 41, OF 4, 1B 1

Batting Record:

Games: 45	3B: 0	Walks: 9	SL.%: .292
At Bats: 154	HRs: 0	K's: 20	S.B: 7
Hits: 39	Runs: 20	B.Avg: .253	B.R: -9
2B: 6	R.B.I: 16	O.B.A: .299	F.R: +4

Pitching Record:

Won: 27	Starts: 38	K's: 80	E.R.A: 3.31
Lost: 12	C.G: 36	Walks: 100	Saves: 0
Win %: .692	I.P: 343	Hits: 352	P.R: +35
Games: 41	Sh.O: 1	O.B.%: .330	W.A.T: +4.5

His parents came from England to New York City, soon moved to Rochester, and then to Bloomington. These were the elements of his infancy and youth. As a young man he worked as a railroad brakeman till he was age 23.

When he arrived in the baseball major leagues, it was with a reputation as a pretty good baseball player. His batting and fielding records confirm this: .235, .283, .281 averages at the bat, with 308 runs scored and 259 R.B.I.; he even stole 26 bases.

His B.R. stat has since been calculated at -77, his F.R. a +4. To "Hoss," also Charley Radbourn, these elements of baseball were all secondary. At the ballpark, on the field, he was ornery and cantankerous; in the pitcher's box he was driven to succeed.

He wanted the ball every day his team was scheduled to play a game, no matter whether it was for a championship, a league game, or an exhibition against amateurs.

His fielding and batting were good enough that he was in the starting lineup 125 times during his career other than as a pitcher; his Players League games as such are extremely out of proportion.

His P.L. batting and fielding work rate adequate or better, his pitching, though outstanding, doesn't measure up to his best. Many of his pitching numbers are beyond compare, and some are beyond comprehension.

These are the pitching ranks of Charley "Hoss" Radbourn in the Players League of 1890: fourth in wins, second in Win %, third in W.A.T., fourth in E.R.A., third in O.B.%, fourth in P.R., third in Total Pitcher Index, fourth in Total Baseball Ranking.

Note that his W.A.T. is measured against the league champions; twice during his career in this stat he's calculated above +10.0; it's +21.0 for 1884. His total W.A.T. counts to +51.5. He was no doubt the leading pitcher for the P.L. champions, but as great as he was in 1890, there's much distance between 1890 and his best.

	P.L. 1890	Most/Best	All Time Rank
Wins:	27	60	First
Win %:	.692	.833	41st
O.B.%:	.330	.254	Not in top 100
E.R.A.:	3.31	1.38	22nd
W.A.T.:	+4.5	+21.0	Not listed

Each and every most and best were achieved in one season, 1884, which as a whole has never been equaled; he pitched for the Grays of Providence (N.L.) that season. It need be said that not all historians of the game accept the 60 wins; some claim just 59.

This is an issue of new information versus great tradition. The greatest season of Charley Radbourn, perhaps the greatest in all baseball history, does not end there, or with the above.

Add (with all-time ranks) 73 starts (fourth), 73 complete games (second), 679 innings pitched (second), 441 K's (fifth), and 98 walks, a 4.5:1 ratio (not ranked), plus 11 shutouts (eighth); he allowed 528 hits in those 679 innings in 1884.

When he retired from the major leagues, after the 1891 season, these were some of his career totals (and all-time ranks): 309 wins (17th), .613 Win % (47th), 503 starts (36th), 489 C.G. (seventh), 4,535 I.P. (21st), 2.68 E.R.A. (50th).

To encapsulate his career in brief: he won 40+ games two years, 20+ nine years; had a .700+ Win % one year; 50+ games five years, 50+ starts five years, 50+ C.G. four years, 500+ I.P. three years, 300+ eight years, 300+ K's two years, E.R.A. below 2.00 one year, and below 2.50 five years.

Probably needless to say, Charley "Hoss" Radbourn clearly was a Players League star player, and a Players League feature player, and there's more to come.

Continue his career summary: his league was the National League 10 of 11 years, he led his league in wins two years, Win % one year, games two years and starts one year, innings pitched one year, shutouts one year, K's two years, O.B.% one year, and E.R.A. one year.

After the fact: he would have led, if such existed, in pitching runs three years, and in W.A.T. once. He was with the Providence Grays from 1881 through 1885, the Boston Reds/Beaneaters 1886 through 1889, the P.L. Boston Reds, and the Cincinnati Reds in 1891.

He did have a couple of bad won and lost seasons: 1886 27 and 31 (.466 Win %), 1887 24 and 23 (.511 Win %), 1891 11 and 13 (.458), with the 31 losses representing a negative benchmark. He also had some good seasons other than 1884 and 1890.

These include 1881 with 25 and 11 (.694), 1882 with 33 and 20 (.623), 1885 with 28 and 21 (.571), 1889 with 20 and 11 (.645). 1883 was omitted because that was the first year Hoss Radbourn went beyond the realm of reality; won 48 lost 25 (.658 Win %).

Also in his prelude to 1884, were 66 complete games in 68 starts, and work in eight other games, 632 innings pitched, 315 K's, a .264 O.B.%, and 2.05 E.R.A.

Recalling that there are some differences between the various books of records, and it seems the greater the player the more differences there are, though rarely involving great dimensions, this was the career of Charley "Hoss" Radbourn: won 310, lost 195, .614 Win %; 528 games, 503 starts, 489 C.B.; 4,535 I.P. with 4,335 hits allowed; 1,830 K's and 875 walks; an even .300 opponents on base percent, and 2.68 E.R.A. Nearly all these data can be found in the columns and lists of records.

For example, he ranks sixth in history with 617 wild pitches. Despite trying to conserve his energy until it was needed he won 18 straight decisions in 1884. His 60 win season included three consecutive shutouts in June. Three other games were the longest in the N.L. that year, 14, 15, and 16 innings; He pitched all to completion.

He was also suspended without pay for a while in 1884, the penalty imposed by the Providence management for some careless pitching and an outburst of temper. His pitching partner, whom he resented, was dismissed from the team for drunkenness. Then "Hoss" was reinstated and paid a bonus to pitch more often.

Virtually a one-man staff, in the ensuing three months he pitched 40 complete games. His record during this period was won 35 and lost 4; this included pitching a string of his team's 22 straight games. He often pitched four and five consecutive days. To conclude his greatest season in proper style, he won three straight World's Series games in three consecutive days.

He had to quit after being gunshot in the face and eye in a hunting accident. In the twilight of his life he owned a pool room and saloon, but because of his deformity became a recluse.

Charley "Hoss" (also Old and Ol' Hoss) Radbourn was one of the first group of inductees at the National Baseball Hall of Fame in June 1939. He'd reached and doubled the impossible dreams of dozens of great major league pitchers. He's both a Players League star player, and a Players League feature player.

These are among his ranks in period stats 1876–1889: fourth in wins, sixth in losses, fifth in games, fifth in starts, fifth in complete games, fifth in innings pitched, seventh in shutouts, fourth in walks, fourth in K's, 10th in E.R.A., fourth in wild pitches.

Charles Gardner Radbourn had long been a married man, but he died of convulsions and paralysis brought on by syphilis.

RADFORD, PAUL REVERE   Paul Radford
Born: October 14, 1861, Roxbury, Massachusetts
Died: February 21, 1945, Boston, Massachusetts
Height: 5'6".   Weight: 148 Lbs.   Batted: Right.   Threw: Right.
Major League Career: 12 Years, 1,361 Games
1889: N.L.: Cleveland
1891: A.A.: Boston
1890: P.L.: Cleveland Infants; OF 80, SS 36, 3B 7, 2B 4, P 1

Batting Record:

Games: 122	3B: 12	Walks: 82	SL.%: .408
At Bats: 466	HRs: 2	K's: 28	S.B: 25
Hits: 136	Runs: 98	B.Avg: .292	B.R: +17
2B: 24	R.B.I: 62	O.B.A: .406	F.R: +3

Pitching Record:

Won: 0	Starts: 0	K's: 3	E.R.A: 3.60
Lost: 0	C.G: 0	Walks: 1	Saves: 0
Win %: —	I.P: 5	Hits: 7	P.R: 0
Games: 1	Sh.O: 0	O.B.%: .374	W.A.T: 0.0

(Radbourn: difficult to follow a legend who did the impossible.)

He was an outfielder by trade. If +39 F.R. in 12 years is some indication, he was very good in the field, and could have been a regular at shortstop. It is doubtful he would have done well as a pitcher; beyond his P.L. bit is a record of won 0 lost 4, with 85 hits and 17 walks allowed in 43 innings, and an 8.58 E.R.A.

Most likely with a basis in career -17 B.R., SABR labeled Paul Radford with "the worst hitting of his era," which his P.L. data contradict absolutely. Further though, by SABR, "He did everything else extremely well, [was] smart about base ball, [and] respected."

There are no faults to be found in the P.L. batting of Radford; his B.Avg. is near the benchmark, his O.B.A. is above it, his SL.% causes wonder given 48 extra base hits among 136 (35 percent), 82 walks and 28 K's rate excellent (3:1), and 28 K's in 466 at bats merits ditto. Twenty-five stolen bases serve as supplement; 98 runs scored and 62 R.B.I. are respectable production numbers. The .292 B.Avg. in 1890 was his best, with a career mark of .242. His P.L. .406 O.B.A. was 1 of 2 at .400+, career .351; .408 SL.% his best of a total .308.

He scored 100+ runs two years, 65 was his R.B.I. high; he collected 106 walks in 1887 which led the A.A., and he ranks ninth in walks for the period 1876–1889. His P.L. doubles and triples were both his most, he hit four HRs in 1887. The Infants of Cleveland got Radford at his best.

SABR tells us that he enjoyed the game and would play six days a week, but his Sabbath was reserved. He's unusual as a major league player of his time as he came from wealth; his father owned an iron foundry in the prime of the Industrial Revolution.

After his respectable major league career, Radford worked as a machinist to not flaunt his wealth; he continued playing regularly as an amateur.

His career itinerary includes 1883 at Boston (N.L.), 1884 and 1885 at Providence (N.L.), 1886 at Kansas City (N.L.), 1887 at New York (A.A.), 1888 at Brooklyn (A.A.), 1889 at Cleveland (N.L.), the Players League of course, 1891 at Boston (A.A.), and 1892, 1893, and 1894 with the Washington Senators, of only 12 possibilities.

In his 1,361 games he had 4,979 at bats, 1,206 hits, including 176 doubles, 57 triples, 13 HRs, 791 walks and 373 K's (one year's data missing). He scored 945 runs and had 417 R.B.I. (one year's data missing). He stole 346 bases in all, including benchmarks of 73 in 1887, and 55 in 1891.

Within his -17 B.R. total are +14 in 1887 and +17 in 1890; among his +39 F.R. total is a best of +14 in 1891. In sum he was very good in the field; 346 stolen bases in a dozen years equals very capable on the base paths, and K's and walks and more equal plate discipline.

At some time he played every position except catcher, which means he was versatile; he played in 100+ games each of eight years and 90+ three other years, which means he was durable. His B.Avg. is lacking 20 points, and SL.% somewhat more, but on the whole, Paul Radford sums up as a complete 1800s major league baseball player who was at his best in 1890 in the Players League.

RAINEY, JOHN PAUL   John Rainey
Born: July 26, 1864, Birmingham, Michigan
Died: November 11, 1912, Detroit, Michigan
Height: 6'1.5".   Weight: 164 Lbs.   Batted: Left.   Threw: Right.
Major League Career: 2 Years, 59 Games
1889: Did not play
1891: Did not play
1890: P.L.: Buffalo Bisons; OF 28, SS 7, 3B 6, 2B 2

Batting Record:

Games: 42	3B: 1	Walks: 24	SL.%: .295
At Bats: 166	HRs: 1	K's: 15	S.B: 12
Hits: 39	Runs: 29	B.Avg: .235	B.R: -5
2B: 5	R.B.I: 20	O.B.A: .349	F.R: 0

1890 wasn't a good baseball year for him; by far it wasn't the better of his two. He was a fit for his Players League team, though the Buffalo Bisons started the season with a blank slate while John Rainey was already writ negative.

His. F.R. of 0, made while coping with the diversity of demands at his variety of positions, is better than his season as a whole, but -5 B.R. with only 10 extra bases to show for 39 hits is weak, as his SL.% affirms. His other batting averages, though, are below the norms rate tolerable for a part-time utility player.

His walks to K's ratio is adequate, neither to any proportional excess; his run production is low but not terribly lacking, and with the whole of John Rainey of 1890 in view, his P.L. season sum is slightly below average, with one notable deficiency.

He didn't play in the major leagues in 1889 or 1889. In 1887 he was in 17 games for the New York (N.L.) Giants, coincidentally marking up the same O.B.A. in 1890. His SL.% was nearly as meager, but his batting average of .293 was near the benchmark.

This last item of data represents the sum difference between his -5 B.R. in the Players League and -0 in 1887; his F.R. are the same for both seasons. He recorded only 57 at bats in 1887, with only three doubles and no other extra base hits among them.

As such, his weakness as a major league baseball player of the 1800s is readily evident; he was exclusively a singles hitter, with next to no power at all at the bat. But, as the Bisons of 1890 were a needy team, he filled a good many voids; by all the historical records, he did so just barely adequately.

After and likely during his time in the major leagues he worked in a meatpacking facility.

John Paul Rainey died of phthisis pulmonalis after a lingering illness.

RICHARDSON, DANIEL   Danny Richardson
Born: January 25, 1863, Elmira, New York
Died: September 12, 1926, New York, New York
Height: 5'8".   Weight: 165 Lbs.   Batted: Right.   Threw: Right.
Major League Career: 11 Years, 1,131 Games
1889: N.L.: New York
1891: N.L.: New York
1890: P.L.: New York Giants; SS 68, 2B 56

Batting Record:

Games: 123	3B: 9	Walks: 37	SL.%: .335
At Bats: 528	HRs: 4	K's: 19	S.B: 37
Hits: 135	Runs: 102	B.Avg: .256	B.R: -21
2B: 12	R.B.I: 80	O.B.A: .307	F.R: +16

He became steady and a regular in 1887, his fourth season with the New York (N.L.) Giants, where he continued through 1889. Primarily an outfielder his first few years, a switch to second base made him an excellent middle infielder.

His. F.R. was +12 in 1887 and +10 in 1888; it would improve to +44 in 1891 and +49 in 1892, numbers rarely found for any player at any position. His career compilation is an outstanding +118 F.R.

His batting was average through the early part of his career; the first of his only two 100+ numbers came with 100 R.B.I. in 1889. His power was moderate, compensated for with stealth and speed; he stole 41 bases in 1887 officially, and 30+ the following three years.

His batting highs during this period all came in 1889, with a .280 B.Avg., .342 O.B.A., .398 SL.%, a better than average start, and neatly spaced increments, but each 20 to 50 points less than would be necessary to establish any benchmarks.

His presence was essential to the P.L. New York Giants, despite his not batting on a par with his fielding and base running. He posted quite ordinary stats in 1890, but made good use of his 135 hits and 37 walks; 102 runs scored beats the benchmark, and 80 R.B.I. by a four and six position player is readily acceptable.

His +16 F.R. explains the terms of his greater value, and his 37 S.B. can be counted as a bonus; -21 B.R. technically contradicts his merits at the bat. His walks to K's is excellent, his 25 extra base hits is low as a percentage of 135, and his batting averages would all look better if they were 50 points higher.

Danny Richardson was a superior infielder but a below-the-norm batter. He did get a share of key hits; in 1889 he became the first player to hit three home runs in a World's Series. Nobody matched or beat that till Babe Ruth in 1923.

In the field, playing either side of second base, he did well what there was to be done; his 6.80 range factor in 1894 ranks first for a season all time at the SS position.

He was manager of the Senators for part of 1892 and won 12 and lost 31 (.279 Win %), which is much more complex than just the numbers. His quiet demeanor changed completely after the 1890 P.L. season; he'd been consistent, not flashy, seldom given media attention.

He'd been a workman at the game who became a troublemaker of top level by those who then assigned assignations. He owned stock in his Players League franchise, as many players did; that was part of the Brotherhood arrangement to form their league.

The power elite of the game in 1890–1891, as with any pride or pack of predators, did not try to attack the whole flock that dared to challenge their eminent domain; Richardson was among the chosen to be attacked, for retaliatory discipline.

He was one of the troublemakers chosen to suffer and to pay for the audacity of rebellion done. His owners in 1891 refused to pay recompense for his investment lost in the P.L.; these were the New York Giants club, to which he'd been ordered returned by the settlement agreed to by the owners, in which players had no say.

Others were granted bonuses and privileges as recompense, and to comply and conform. Richardson was too useful as a public attraction to simply be relegated to the blacklist as were a few or more 1890 P.L. players. He did not whimper into submission in the hope he might be allowed to continue.

Renegade, troublemaker, recalcitrant, he was chosen to be whipped into compliance, to learn subservience to his economic betters; he played the 1891 season for the New York (N.L.) Giants, but he did not rescind his claims, nor suborn himself to ultimatums.

After the 1891 season, his name was left off the Giants reserve list. He'd played well; recall his +44 F.R. led his league, all players at all positions, and his batting averages were a dozen or more points above what they'd been the year before the P.L.

A player such as this isn't just left to drift in the wind, but by that time his issue had become much more involved than some reimbursement of dollars. The 1890–1891 winter games behind the closed doors of the owners had produced tumult.

The owners of the deposed Players League franchises scrambled for status among the owners of the A.A., who were themselves in the process of preparing for a fight to the finish with the greater power and stability of the N.L.; somebody had to lose.

Albert Johnson, who'd lost heavily in the Cleveland franchise, teamed with the P.L. secretary, Frank Brunell, to buy the N.L. Cincinnati franchise, which was on the edge of bankruptcy; their plan was to court and hire King Kelly, then build a team around him; there might have been a place for Richardson.

The play was fast and loose in the back rooms and boardrooms in winter 1890–1891. The A.A. dropped the little cities of Rochester, Syracuse, and Toledo to make room for Cincinnati in their restructured eight-team league; Cincinnati failed.

J. Earle and George Wagner of the failed P.L. Philadelphia club entered into the A.A. as the Athletics, which at the time had more an image of circus clowns than a business organization. They'd wanted to pirate Richardson, but he refused to play for them, and signed on with the Giants for 1891.

The next winter, when the A.A. was beaten and done, it was deja vu all over again as another mad rush of disenfranchised owners shut down their business operations and began looking toward the next fiscal season. Franchise enclaves had declined in number from 24 to 12 in a little more than a year.

The Wagner brothers had garnered substantial profits from the surrender settlements of both the P.L. and the A.A. Philadelphia clubs; they'd also owned the Washington N.L. franchise till it was removed from the league at the end of the 1889 season.

These were men of money, not baseball, fast talking, money-hungry, hit-and-run, abusive self- promoters among the most rapacious in baseball history. They wanted Richardson; if he was to continue he'd have to submit to them, and he did.

But in 1892 he played with an attitude as it's now said. His batting numbers dropped 30–40–50 points. He did not go quietly into the Wagner brothers' (now again N.L.) consortium. They'd bought their way back in with the new (1892) Senators franchise.

They assigned Richardson as their third manager despite his obviously inept performance, won 12 lost 31 (.279), and were going to continue with him into 1893. He still had market value though, and when opportunity and money called, they answered.

He was traded to Brooklyn for Bill Joyce and $2,000; the Wagners got a gate attraction and cash in the bank, they thought. Richardson went to Brooklyn, but Joyce refused to sign with the Wagners when they informed him that his salary had been reduced by $1,000 and he sat out the 1893 season in protest.

Richardson was awful in Brooklyn, drinking heavily and out of control. The drinking and distresses caused internal problems, in turn causing him to be absent from the team. He was suspended without pay, then was summarily shipped off to Louisville.

Richardson went to Louisville. 1894 was his last season, and for him it was a typical season; +3 F.R. and played shortstop in 107 of his 117 games. The team played only 13 more games. He batted .253, hit a home run, stole eight bases and set a SS's record.

He quit baseball after that, perhaps having proved something. The executive rationale? There are always victims in wars. He became co-owner of a department store, the biggest in Elmira.

Daniel "Danny" Richardson died of a heart attack while he was in New York City on business. He was having a restaurant lunch.

During his baseball career, he accrued 4,451 at bats, 1,129 hits, among them 149 doubles, 52 triples, 32 home runs. He had minimal power and good speed. He stole 225 bases, scored 676 runs, and batted in 558; he was walked 283 times, K'd 289.

His SABR-stats read: B.R. -107, F.R. +118. Many players left the game after the year of the Players League; hindsight says Daniel Richardson would have done wise if he'd been one of them. List him as a P.L. casualty.

RICHARDSON, ABRAM HARDING   Hardy Richardson (Ol' True Blue)
Born: April 21, 1855, Clarksboro, New York
Died: January 14, 1931, Utica, New York
Height: 5'9.5".   Weight: 170 Lbs.   Batted: Right.   Threw: Right.
Major League Career: 14 Years, 1,331 Games
1889: N.L.: Boston
1891: A.A.: Boston
1890: P.L.: Boston Reds; OF 124, SS 6, 1B 1

Batting Record:

Games: 130	3B: 14	Walks: 52	SL.%: .483
At Bats: 555	HRs: 11	K's: 46	S.B: 42
Hits: 181	Runs: 126	B.Avg: .326	B.R: +24
2B: 26	R.B.I: 143	O.B.A: .384	F.R: -2

He's been identified variously as "Hardy" and "Hardie" and as the Babe Ruth of the 1800s. Hardy Richardson was admired by all, and was a terrific baseball player. In 1878, the *New York Clipper* chose him as the best defensive center fielder. His major league career began in 1879.

He played for 14 years, including a few great years, among which 1890 was his best. His age was 35 then, and he was an established star. The expectations were high and he delivered, perhaps as no other player could have, providing leadership and stability among a team of stars, the Players League champions.

He was also a statistical team and league leader. His mode of leadership was by example, at which he was as good as there was. His R.B.I. in the P.L. topped the next highest total by 19; he led in runs produced by 22. He tied for second in HRs, was fifth in hits, and fourth in total bases with 288.

His B.R. of +24 is indicative of his productivity, 42 stolen bases added impetus,

46 K's are many but less than 10 percent of his 555 at bats; 52 walks added run potential to his 181 P.L. hits, and only a -2 F.R. marred his perfectly positive P.L. record.

The Hardy Richardson of 1890 ranks as a Players League star player, and he was a star nearly every year. Only in 1888 among his years before the P.L. did he have less than 300 at bats; in the two years that followed, his last, he was well into the 200s in official times at the bat.

Each of seven years Richardson batted .300+, with a high of .351 in 1886; his only .400+ O.B.A. came in 1886, also his only .500+ SL.%; .402 and .504 respectively. He hit 11 HRs. twice, leading the N.L. in 1886. In 1887 he hit 18 triples; among doubles counts are 34 in 1883, and 34 in 1889, his only 30+ seasons.

He never had 200 hits in a season, but 189 in 1886 were the N.L. high. Each of four years he scored 100+ runs, including 131 in 1887. The only year he surpassed 100+ R.B.I. was 1890; 52 walks were also a personal high, as were his P.L. 46 K's.

His best B.R. mark was +47 in 1886, his career B.R. total is an outstanding +223, his F.R. total is a fine +83 with a high of +24 in 1881, when he played the outfield and three infield positions.

At some time during his career he played at all the positions. His pitching was minimal, only five games and 16 innings; his 3.94 E.R.A. is a prime factor of his won 3 lost 0 record.

He began in the major leagues with Buffalo (N.L.) in 1879, and was there till he was sold to Detroit (N.L.) after the 1885 season. In this, he was part of the biggest baseball transaction of players in the 1800s.

Owner Frederick Kimball Stearns, a pharmaceuticals magnate, wanted Richardson and three other Buffalo players; to get them, in the end, he bought the whole Buffalo club for $7,000. Richardson continued with Detroit through 1888, then moved to Boston (N.L.).

He was still in Boston the next season, but in the uniform of the P.L. Boston Reds; the year after his team won the P.L. pennant, he played for the Boston A.A. entry. His career concluded after the 1892 season, when he played 10 games for the Giants, and 64 for the Senators.

Hardy Richardson compiled 5,642 at bats during his 14 seasons, and 1,688 hits included 303 doubles, 126 triples, 68 home runs. He stole 205 bases, walked 377 times, and recorded 445 strikeouts. In all, he scored 1,120 runs and had 818 R.B.I.

Outside the ballpark, and after his major league career, SABR informs us that Hardy Richardson "was a crackerjack at target shooting." As a member of a club he once killed 99 birds in a day to win a contest.

He owned and operated a hotel, and worked for a company which manufactured and sold typewriters.

Abram Harding Richardson died after a brief illness.

The ranks of Hardy Richardson in period stats 1876–1889 include: 10th in at bats, eighth in runs, eighth in hits, seventh in doubles, sixth in triples, 10th in R.B.I., eighth in extra base hits, eighth in total bases.

One of the 1800s players most written about, his citations are many, including some from his time and soon after. They include some errors.

"He was invited to be present for the unveiling of the memorial to Cap Anson," in Chicago in 1923; the invitation was made by John Heydler, N.L. president; he was also invited to the 1939 "Cooperstown Baseball Centennial" but has not been elected as a member.

"Second base was his favorite position; his whole heart was in the Brotherhood organization; earned distinction on the diamond for his hitting; natural bent as a batsman was to make line drives; great left-fielder and all-around player."

"July 9, 1888 broke an ankle and was out the rest of the season; in 1890 his batting and fielding were remarkable, he did not muff a fly ball, 16 home runs led the country; one of the greatest all-around players ever seen on the diamond."

"One of the greatest outfielders in the business, one of the most gentlemanly players that ever wore a uniform; became one of the highest priced players in the United States; one of the greatest second basemen and fielders on the diamond."

"With a splendid record at the bat; was offered $3000 to quit the Brotherhood and $5000 a year (salary); he declined, to stick to the Brotherhood sink or swim; fine fielding and accurate throwing, able to play most any position."

"Works earnestly and honestly and is an excellent batsman; clever all-around player; wonderful fielding and timely hitting; one of the leading batsmen; more than an average baserunner; fast enough to hit in the leadoff spot."

"Was invited to throw out the first ball at Christy Mathewson's tribute game."

Hardy Richardson of the Player's League: "Intended to remain until the very last; owned $1000.00 worth of stock in the Boston club; never played a better game than this season; a credit to the profession, a gentleman under all circumstances."

ROBINSON, WILLIAM H.   **Yank Robinson**
Born: September 19, 1859, Philadelphia, Pennsylvania
Died: August 25, 1894, St. Louis, Missouri
Height: 5'6.5".   Weight: 170 Lbs.   Batted: Right.   Threw: Right.
Major League Career: 10 Years, 978 Games
1889: A.A.: St. Louis
1891: A.A.: Cincinnati and St. Louis
1890: P.L.: Pittsburgh Burghers; 2B 98

Batting Record:

Games: 98	3B: 3	Walks: 101	SL.%: .281
At Bats: 306	HRs: 0	K's: 33	S.B: 17
Hits: 70	Runs: 59	B.Avg: .229	B.R: +7
2B: 10	R.B.I: 38	O.B.A: .434	F.R: -22

"101 walks in 98 games!" wouldn't be found among headlines or sports page features, neither would boosting a batting average 200 points to reach the O.B.A. benchmark. Yank Robinson isn't a prominent name in baseball literature, nor was it in 1890.

While the word versatile might best depict him, quirky may be more accurate. Diversity kept him in good stead with management and media for a decade. He wouldn't use a fielder's glove. He played all the positions during his career, but none very well.

He amassed a -115 F.R. record. His power at the bat was nearly negligible, batting below mediocre. What he could do extremely well was walk and steal bases. Each of three seasons he amassed 100+ walks; his totals of 116 and 118 in 1888 and 1889 led the A.A., as did his .400 O.B.A. in 1888, when he batted .231.

He never reach 100+ stolen bases in a season, but had 50+ each of three years: 75 in 1887 by the rules, 56 in 1888, 51 in 1886. He played in the Union Association in 1884, for the Baltimore Monumentals; the league didn't keep S.B. records.

That's when Yank Robinson really began his major league career, in 1884 with that Baltimore club. All the teams in that league were also called "Onions." He'd played in 11 games for Detroit (N.L.) in 1882, notably with one walk and 13 K's, he batted .179.

Conditions were hard and games were tough. When "beer call!" would sound he could be expected to be first to belly up to the bar. His fondness for the brew grew to excess while the seasons passed.

William H. "Yank" Robinson died of consumption. One report states that he died of pulmonary problems.

In the Players League he did well what he did best on the field. He ranks third in walks and fourth in O.B.A.; in period stats 1876–1889 he ranks third in walks, seventh in O.B.A., 10th in stolen bases, and fourth in hit by pitches (tied).

He made himself in 1884, playing six positions in 102 games, at a +14 F.R. rate; his B.R. was +15, on the strength of a .267 B.Avg., .327 O.B.A., .359 SL.%; he got 111 hits and 37 walks, which led the U.A.

His good show in 1884 got him a contract with the St. Louis (A.A.) Browns for 1885, where he stayed till the Players League called; by then he'd found a regular place on the playing field, at second base.

While with the Browns he batted .305 in 1887, not wholly because of the one-year rules revisions. He had 32 doubles among 131 hits that year, one below his career high of 132 in 1886. He drew 92 walks in 1887, marked up a .445 O.B.A., and his SL.% went above .400 for the only time in 10 years, peaking at .405. Robinson didn't hit for many extra bases.

This was also his second year with 100+ runs scored, one more than his U.A. top mark, though less than his last and best 100+ of 111 in 1888; 100+ R.B.I. might have been a vision. Most of his years no A.A. records were kept, and when they were his R.B.I. high was 70 in 1889. He had 50 and 52 K's during two of six years when there were records kept.

Much of his career -115 F.R. were made in 1888 and 1889, -30 and -34, while he was finding himself at second base; while there in 1890 for the Pittsburgh Burghers he improved to -22.

He returned to the A.A. in 1891. With the Cincinnati/Milwaukee combine he played 97 games, then one with the Browns; combined his 1891 B.Avg. was .177, he drew 68 walks and stole 23 bases. The next year, his last, with the Senators, his numbers included 67 games, .179 B.Avg., 38 walks, and 11 stolen bases.

He ranks 11th all time among 2B in errors with 471. Marched to the beat of a different drummer, and played the game his way.

ROWE, JOHN CHARLES Jack Rowe
Born: December 18, 1856, Harrisburg, Pennsylvania
Died: April 25, 1911, St. Louis, Missouri
Height: 5'8". Weight: 170 Lbs. Batted: Left. Threw: Right.
Major League Career: 12 Years, 1,044 Games
1889: N.L.: Pittsburgh
1891: Did not play
1890: P.L.: Buffalo Bisons; SS 125

Batting Record:

Games: 125	3B: 7	Walks: 48	SL.%: .333
At Bats: 504	HRs: 2	K's: 18	S.B: 10
Hits: 126	Runs: 77	B.Avg: .250	B.R: -16
2B: 22	R.B.I: 76	O.B.A: .324	F.R: -8

Jack Rowe was the first, third and last Bisons field manager. His first-term record in 81 games was won 22 and lost 58, .275 win %, and in his second term of 19 games won 5 and lost 14, .263 win %. At the end of his first term they were in eighth place, as when he resumed, and at the end of their season.

As manager of the Buffalo (P.L.) Bisons for 100 games, and a co-owner of the franchise, he has to bear much of the burden for assembling and operating one of the worst teams in the field of baseball history.

He was originally signed by Buffalo (N.L.) for the 1879 season and worked mainly behind home plate through 1884. When the bruises and fatigue reached tolerable limits, he converted to the shortstop position and stayed there through the remainder of his career.

Jack Rowe didn't play in 1886 for any major league team. After the 1885 schedule was done he and three other players were sold to Frederick Stearns, owner of the Detroit (N.L.) Wolverines, who wanted them so badly for his own that he bought the Bisons.

Before the 1889 season, Stearns sold two of his prime four to Boston, and two to Pittsburgh. Meanwhile Rowe and Deacon White had bought a minor league franchise for Buffalo and had no desire or interest in playing for Pittsburgh.

Al Nimick, owner of that franchise, was still entangled in various legal squabbles resulting from his jumping from the A.A. as a retort for that league's dumping of Denny McKnight, who'd been a founder and the originator of the A.A. Alleghenys.

What Rowe did want was to play for his own team, and manage it, all of which was achieved by rights of territory when the Players League took the field. The whole of these shenanigans would become a prominent part of baseball history.

When he refused to go from Detroit to Pittsburgh, one of the Boston (N.L.) owners, director Billings, wrote him a letter advising him to sign with Pittsburgh. He did, and played in (N.L.) Pittsburgh in 1889.

The next year he was in Buffalo, part owner, in and out and in again the manager of the awful P.L. Bisons; as such this is the record of the only major league adventure of Jack Rowe, manager.

	Won	Lost	Win%
First of 3	22	58	.275
Third of 3	5	14	.263
The Bisons	36	96	.273

Some records identify him as the only Bisons manager, which is not so; Jay Faatz made the notable contribution when apparently Rowe could tolerate no more of 9 wins and 24 losses (.273). If nothing else positive can be said, the P.L. Buffalo Bisons were consistent.

The 1890 P.L. stats of Jack Rowe don't stand out, except 18 K's in 504 at bats (3.6%), which of course isn't an official stat. Eighteen K's measured against 48 walks also rates exceptional; he did better in all the other numbers during his career.

1890 was his last major league season. In 1881 he led his league in triples with 11, his high was 14 in 1884; he hit 30+ doubles one year. His career batting rates were credible, and he hit very well for extra bases (25%).

His career 1879–1890 includes 4,386 at bats, 1,256 hits, a .286 B.Avg. Among his hits were 202 doubles, 88 triples, 28 HRs, and his SL.% is .392. He marked very low sums of 177 K's and his 224 walks, resulting in a .323 O.B.A.

His B.R. SABR-stat is a positive +77, his -160 F.R. belies some accolades; he was better in the field in 1890 than most years. His very negative F.R. is mainly a function of his many years at the second position; his worst marks there were -22 in 1880 and -12 twice. While at SS he earned a mark of -33 F.R. in 1887.

Rather to the contrary, SABR cites Jack Rowe as a "top-notch catcher and shortstop, and a feared hitter." The *New York Clipper* in 1881 went to excess: "A sure catch, a swift and accurate thrower and (he) faces pluckily the swiftest and wildest pitcher. He also excels in batting and, being an earnest and hard-working player, a most useful man."

The *MacMillan Encyclopedia* as compliment notes that he "did not strike out a single time in 308 at bats in 1882." To make that compliment last a career, he struck out only the noted 177 times in 4,386 at bats, which calculates to a commendable 4.0 percent.

During his major league career, Rowe batted .300+ four years in 300+ at bats seasons at shortstop and 200+ while at catcher; he never did reach the plateaus of .400+ O.B.A. or .500+ SL.%. He tallied 100+ runs once, 135 in 1887; his R.B.I. high was 96, also in 1887.

His stolen bases total only 59, with a high of 22 in 1887 by the prevailing rules. When the Players League closed up shop, Rowe closed out his career in good style. Somewhat above average, he experienced all the elements of baseball in the 1800s.

His later years were spent as the owner and proprietor of a cigar store in Buffalo. In about 1910, with his health failing, he moved to his daughter's home in St. Louis. The *New York Clipper* cites him as being from Louisiana, Missouri.

He suffered a general degeneration of health lasting about a year with the reason given as nephritis, a noninfective inflammation of the kidney.

John Charles Rowe died of nephritis, Bright's disease.

RYAN, JAMES EDWARD   **Jimmy Ryan**
Born: February 11, 1863, Clinton, Massachusetts
Died: October 26, 1923, Chicago, Illinois
Height: 5'9".   Weight: 162 Lbs.   Batted: Right.   Threw: Left.
Major League Career: 18 Years, 2,012 Games
1889: N.L.: Chicago
1891: N.L.: Chicago
1890: P.L.: Chicago Pirates; OF 118

Batting Record:

Games: 118	3B: 5	Walks: 60	SL.%: .463
At Bats: 486	HRs: 6	K's: 36	S.B: 30
Hits: 165	Runs: 99	B.Avg: .340	B.R: +27
2B: 32	R.B.I: 89	O.B.A: .416	F.R: -1

Batting right and throwing left was unusual for a major league player. Batting .300+ with power and able to field his position, that's Jimmy Ryan. This complete 1800s player was with the White Stockings of Chicago (N.L.) for 15 years, and Pittsburgh (N.L.) for one year.

He also played for the Washington (A.L.) Senators in 1902 and 1903, with impressive numbers, after rethinking retirement all of 1901. His basic Senators batting averages were .320 and .249, in 120 and 114 games, 484 and 437 at bats, with O.B.A.s of .376 and .278 and SL.% of .448 and .373.

Better than most players, much better than one hinging on age 40, 1902 was clearly the better of his two seasons in D.C., near the composite batting averages for his fine career: .306 B.Avg., .373 O.B.A., .444 SL.%. In sum, this was and is an unknown star.

If the N.L. had an M.V.P. award in 1888, the clear choice would have been Jimmy "Pony" Ryan; he produced an extraordinary set of data that season, certainly worth notice. Let an asterisk (*) indicate league leader, and further consider the benchmarks:

Games: 129	SL.%: .515 (*)	3B: 10	K's: 50
At Bats: 549	Runs: 115	HRs: 16	S.B: 60
B.Avg: .332	R.B.I: 64	Hits: 182 (*)	B.R: +51 (*)
O.B.A: .377	2B: 33 (*)	Walks: 35	

He hit for average, and with power, produced runs. There is the negative 50 K's. He stole benchmark bases, rating superior by one SABR-stat; the other calculates to +2 F.R., above average in the field.

Ryan was an uncommon college player who turned professional. According to Cap Anson, his manager at Chicago 15 years, he didn't learn hustle and he lacked speed. Which does nothing to explain 418 career S.B., including 60 above and 50 in 1887.

After the fact, and contrary to Anson, the composite B.R. of Ryan is an outstanding +311, including +50 above and two more years above +30; his F.R. total is a +5, with +13 in 1889. Anson had his prejudices, and Ryan might have the subject of one.

Further in favor of an excellent player are his ranks in period stats 1890–1899: ninth in runs scored, fourth in doubles, fifth in extra base hits; in the Players League records he ranks fifth in batting average.

He began with Chicago (N.L.) in 1885, with three games and 13 at bats including six hits with two runs scored and two R.B.I.; established that fast, he was a seasoned veteran with an excellent record in 1890 when the Chicago Pirates took the field.

With the exception of -1 F.R., all his P.L. numbers range between excellent and outstanding, foremost his .340 B.Avg., 32 doubles, 60 walks, .340 O.B.A., and +27 B.R. There is no indication of a laggard of any sort, which also has been inferred by opinion.

His .463 SL.% is below the benchmark, but 25 percent of his hits were good enough for extra bases; both his runs scored and R.B.I. are near benchmarks, his 60 walks and 30 stolen bases calculate to nearly 100 bases gratis.

There is some difficulty in articulating his essential utility; he was great in 1888, not quite in 1890, and aspersions aside, there are some Ryan issues to consider.

Given his record and historical status, the critique of Anson stands foremost against him in testimony. Also against Ryan though he was neither the first nor last, he's alleged to have once beat up a sportswriter, general repercussions withstand.

True, such demeanor does not constitute propriety either for a baseball player or a stellar gentleman, albeit during the 1890s that was the means by which more than a few issues and disputes were resolved.

His complete record as baseball facts put this unknown among the class of best players of the 1800s; as great as he was in 1888, as good as he was in 1890, he also excelled in other years.

He scored 100+ runs eight years and his R.B.I. in the P.L. were his career high. Many of his records, best and most have been noted. On July 1, 1897, he scored five runs in a game, and hit a grand slam home run. He played in 100+ games every season but two.

Nothing about him by the numbers hints at negative. It's possible there was animosity between Anson and Ryan. Among the Chicago team Anson was *the boss* and no doubt about it, firm and strict beyond Charlie Comiskey, and Ryan represented a challenge to the batting authority of Anson. But malice by media can be damaging.

His. B.Avg. was .300+ each of 11 years, O.B.A. .400+ four years, SL.% .500+ just once; he hit 30+ doubles seven years, 15+ triples twice, and 10+ HRs four years. With personalities and retribution set aside, Ryan produced meritorious numbers nearly every year including 1890.

In 2,012 major league games he compiled 8,164 at bats, 94th on the all time list; Adrian "Cap" Anson ranks 47th with 9,101. Ryan has 2,502 hits, 74th all time; Anson accumulated 2,995 hits, 21st all time. Overall and on the field, Ryan was lesser.

Ryan's 451 career doubles and 157 triples are well within the top 100 of all time. His 118 home runs are near the top of the 1800s list. His typical K's count about 30 per season, his 803 walks include seasons of 73, 70, 61, the P.L. 60, and five more of 50+; in all facets of batting Jimmy "Pony" Ryan was highly consistent.

He's not much less in the other half of the game; he led his league's outfielders in the chances per game stat twice, and in assists and double plays once. He ranks 10th all time in double plays by an OF with 70. His career assists adjusted to a season of 162 games calculates to 31.27, which ranks sixth all time.

If he didn't have hustle or speed, if Jimmy Ryan of the White Stockings and others including the P.L. Pirates, was a laggard, then the accounting of him as a baseball player is in error by its very dimensions which put him on the edge of outstanding and high among his peers of the 1800s.

As a player he lacks nothing. There is no statistical deficiency which could justify his exclusion from the stars of his century. He was overall among the best of the Players League of 1890, and he is definitely and definitively a Players League star player.

He was there for the cause in 1890 and did fine credit to the Brotherhood of Players. He excelled both before and after 1890. He was an N.L. umpire in 1892, briefly during the 1900s was a minor league manager, and managed for semi-pro teams.

He was one of two among many who jumped from N.L. Chicago to P.L. Chicago who, near the end of 1890, wrote to Albert Spalding pleading for reinstatement. Jimmy Ryan is still an unknown in the literature of the game; the brethren of scribes neither forgives nor forgets evidently.

James Edward Ryan for many years was a deputy sheriff.

SANDERS, ALEXANDER BENNETT Ben Sanders (Big Ben)
Born: February 16, 1865, Catharpen, Virginia
Died: August 29, 1930, Memphis, Tennessee
Height: 6'0". Weight: 210 Lbs. Batted: Right. Threw: Right.
Major League Career: 5 Years, 168 Games
1889: N.L.: Philadelphia
1891: A.A.: Philadelphia
1890: P.L.: Philadelphia Quakers; P 43, OF 10

Batting Record:

Games: 52	3B: 6	Walks: 10	SL.%: .407
At Bats: 189	HRs: 0	K's: 10	S.B: 2
Hits: 59	Runs: 31	B.Avg: .312	B.R:
2B: 6	R.B.I: 30	O.B.A:	F.R:

Pitching Record:

Won: 19	Starts: 40	K's: 107	E.R.A: 3.76
Lost: 18	C.G: 37	Walks: 69	Saves: 1
Win %: .514	I.P: 347	Hits: 412	P.R: +18
Games: 43	Sh.O: 2	O.B.%: .341	W.A.T: -0.2

One of the rare 1800s major league players to have roots in the South, he was also one of few P.L. pitchers with a positive (from a pitcher's perspective) strikeouts to walks ratio. 1890 was the last of his three straight 19 wins seasons.

Big and burly, much about him is different from most players of his era. He would not play on Sundays for religious reasons. He earned a college degree while a player, in engineering. It was he who established the terms and conditions of his contracts.

Ben Sanders played for just five years, four in the City of Brotherly Love, the last in Louisville, Kentucky. With the (N.L.) Phillies he won 19 and lost 10 (.655 Win %) in 1888; still with the Phillies in 1889 he declined to 19 and 18 (.514).

He matched his 1889 won and lost record with the P.L. Quakers, then the following year with the A.A. Athletics won 11 and lost 5 (.688); the last was his only losing season, won 12 and lost 19 (.387), but he added to his run of 19's. His composite won and lost are 80 and 70 (.533).

All his E.R.A.s were higher than his total of 3.24 except the first, a benchmark 1.90, when he struck out 121 and walked just 33, with 240 hits in 275 innings. His next year was good, but not near that level: 3.55 E.R.A., benchmark 350 I.P., but 406 hits and 96 walks, and 123 K's.

There are many similarities between the 1889 and 1890 records of Sanders, including .353 and .341 O.B.%, 44 and 43 games, 34 and 30 complete. If he has a P.L. standout stat it's 107 K's and 69 walks in 347 innings.

He was one of three Philadelphia Quakers pitchers who were almost a matched set, but Sanders ranks fifth in O.B.%, and fourth in the stat Total Pitcher Index.

As a P.L. batter, Sanders beat the benchmark in B.Avg. and did well fielding his position despite being an awkward fielder. It's to his credit that he filled in 10 games among a trio of very good outfielders; only one Quakers regular beat his .312 B.Avg., and he played at shortstop.

The next year, with the Athletics, he was relegated to the role of third pitcher, which reduced his workload by about half, which cut .005 off his O.B.%; his E.R.A. hardly changed, 3.79 in 1891, but he reached his low by SABR-stat with -1 P.R., after +29, +19, and +18.

He recovered in 1892 stat to +2 P.R. with Louisville, a function of his 3.22 E.R.A. and .325 O.B.%, much more so than 12 wins and 19 losses. The sums of the successful major league career of Ben Sanders beyond won and lost begin with a 3.24 E.R.A.

He marked a .328 O.B.%, two seasons of 300+ innings pitched, with an I.P. total of 1.385; he allowed 1,496 hits and 297 walks with 468 K's in 168 games, 157 starts, 144 complete (92 percent C.G.).

Sturdy and reliable, he wasn't distracted from his work by the need to report late a few seasons, which his baseball owners permitted, so he could complete his semesters of study, and of unique significance, was paid his full seasons' salaries.

When his degree studies were done and his first career complete, he worked for an engineering firm for a year then founded his own business firm. He'd done well enough at baseball that for a few years there were solicitations from club executives.

High marks to Ben Sanders, and to the P.L. which he chose when that decision had to be made. Besides playing and schoolwork, he'd been a National League umpire in 1889. His future work was as a civil engineer.

Alexander Bennett Sanders died of a gallbladder infection.

SEERY, JOHN EMMETT   **Emmett Seery**
Born: February 13, 1861, Princeville, Illinois
Died: August 7, 1930, Saranac Lake, New York
Height: Weight: Batted: Left.   Threw: Right.
Major League Career: 9 Years, 916 Games
1889: N.L.: Indianapolis
1891: A.A.: Cincinnati
1890: P.L.: Brooklyn Wonders; OF 104

Batting Record:

Games: 104	3B: 7	Walks: 70	SL.%: .297
At Bats: 394	HRs: 1	K's: 36	S.B: 44
Hits: 88	Runs: 78	B.Avg: .223	B.R: -12
2B: 12	R.B.I: 50	O.B.A: .348	F.R: +7

A generous written account cites him as a clever fielder and base-runner, noting his position as left field. He began with the Baltimore Monumentals of the Union Association in 1884; he played brilliantly at left field and led his team in the official batting averages. Then he played a final game at K.C.

There's a bit of a hitch with the Kansas City Unions at the end of that season (unlike the rest, Kansas City used the nickname of "Unions"), among the greatest one-game seasons in history. He had four at bats, got two hits including a double, scored two runs, earned an R.B.I., and was walked once.

While with the Monumentals earlier, 105 games, 463 at bats, he played the field at a +4 F.R. rate and made batting averages of .311, .340, .408; he scored 113 Baltimore runs via 144 hits and 20 walks, before his U.A. farewell, for him a very good year.

There's not much to compare with Emmett Seery of the Players League, as the U.A. didn't maintain records of R.B.I., K's, or stolen bases, and of course there were no B.R. or F.R. in 1884 or in 1890.

Where there are data there is symmetry with each of his B.Avg. and SL.% down about 100 points, while his O.B.A. is comparable, due to 70 P.L. walks versus 21 in the U.A. His numbers of games corresponds, but at bats not nearly, as if he used up most of his brilliance in Baltimore, then what was left at K.C.

Scribes of the time again wrote appreciatively of him while with the Indianapolis Hoosiers (not Blues) during their stay in the N.L. from 1887 through 1889. It was said of Seery that he garnered an extended reputation not only as an expert left fielder, but also as a good batsman and a most daring and clever base runner.

These are the statistical essence of his three years at Indianapolis, during which he did produce one very good year in B.Avg. and at least very good in near every other official stat, including a considerable array of benchmarks; he seems to have done what the writer wrote, and to his credit no less than that.

	1887	*1888*	*1889*	*Career*
B.Avg:	.224	.220	.314	.252
O.B.A:	.331	.316	.401	.345
SL.%:	.353	.330	.454	.356

	1887	1888	1889	Career
Runs:	104	87	123	695
R.B.I:	28	50	59	300+
Walks:	71	64	67	471
S.B.	48	80	19	240
B.R.:	-3	+7	+30	+55
F.R:	+7	+11	+1	+35

Among the lines and columns are very few deficiencies: two years batting average, one low R.B.I. datum, one negative B.R. mark; otherwise during these three years and his nine-year career, this guy really was a terrific baseball player, in each and every way.

He averaged 100+ games per year during his career and hit a benchmark 15 triples in 1887 with no help. If fault is to be found it's in his K's relative to walks, moreso as data are missing.

	Games	At Bats	K's
1887	122	465	68
1888	133	500	73
1889	127	526	59
Career	916	3,547	426+

If the media were able to consolidate the best of Seery, he might be a match for himself at Baltimore, or Kansas City. There's been no mention here of two interim years, 1885 and 1886, with the St. Louis Maroons during the two-year stay of that franchise in the N.L.; cite B.Avg.s of .162 and .238.

Ethos and objectivity require we note Seery incurred an awful fall after his novice U.A. season of achievements. Perhaps a reason is that no two major leagues have been quite the same.

	1885	1886		1885	1886
Games:	59	126	O.B.A:	.220	.324
At Bats:	216	453	SL.%:	.208	.327
Walks:	16	57	B.R:	-14	+1
K's:	37	82	F.R:	+5	-3

He had some very good if not terrific years, and one very bad — actually awful — year. Suffice it to say the Brooklyn Wonders of the Players League of 1890 got the better Seery. He played two more years, for Cincinnati/Milwaukee (A.A.) and Louisville, and his B.Avg.s were .285 and .201, good reason to end his career.

As a retired baseball player Seery married a recently widowed neighbor lady circa 1904; she was of family as one such might say, who were area pioneers, and had accumulated a great amount of real estate, which she'd claimed for herself, and had.

Seery became partner to the wealth; they traveled, spending leisure time at the resorts Saranac Lake and Sewell's Point; their life of leisure was severely impacted when she contracted tuberculosis.

He suffered a stroke soon after. His death preceded hers by a year. His specific cause is unknown but tuberculosis is highly contagious, and stroke can be lethal or cause complications.

His wife had John Emmett Seery interred next to her first husband and soon after she joined them in eternal leisure.

SHANNON, DANIEL WEBSTER   Dan Shannon
Born: March 23, 1865, Bridgeport, Connecticut
Died: October 25, 1913, Bridgeport, Connecticut
Height: Weight: 175 Lbs.   Batted: Threw:
Major League Career: 3 Years, 242 Games
1889: A.A.: Louisville
1891: A.A.: Washington
1890: P.L.: Philadelphia Quakers; 2B 19. New York Giants; 2B 77, SS 6

Batting Record:

	Phil	*N.Y.*	*Totals*
Games:	19	83	103
At Bats:	75	324	399
Hits:	18	70	88
2B:	5	7	12
3B:	1	8	9
HRs:	1	3	4
Runs:	15	59	74
R.B.I:	16	44	60
Walks:	4	25	29
K's:	12	34	46
B.Avg:	.240	.216	.221
O.B.A:	.278	.274	.275
SL.%:	.373	.315	.326
S.B:	4	21	25
B.R:	-3	-20	-23
F.R:	-7	-2	-9

After 19 games with the Quakers of 1890 he moved up a couple of notches in the standings, but nearly everything else went down. Further on his three-year career, in three leagues, with four teams, what started as mediocre in 1889 declined to utterly awful in 1891.

His Players League season came between one with the Louisville (A.A.) Colonels and one with the Washington (A.A.) Statesmen. The former finished eighth in 1889, 27 and 111 (.196 Win %), 66.5 games behind the league leader; the latter won 44 and lost 91 (.329) in 1891, finishing eighth or ninth depending on whether the analyst prefers Cincinnati/Milwaukee as one or two teams.

For Dan Shannon there were no best of times; they were surely the worst, and consistently at that. He wasn't a field manager in the P.L. but was part time in both other major league seasons; 10 and 46 (.179) with Louisville, 15 and 34 with Washington (.306).

Shannon stood well up in batting and fielding and always worked hard for his club. Fairly consider his key stats in the years before and after the P.L. then close out his career.

	1889	1891	Career
B.Avg:	.257	.134	.233
O.B.A:	.315	.205	.291
SL.%:	.373	.164	.339
Runs:	90	7	171
R.B.I:	48	3	111
S.B:	26	3	54
B.R.:	-3	-8	-33
F.R:	+2	0	-7

Though his time with the P.L. Quakers was brief, this seems to have been the best of Shannon; the distance between their Forepaugh Park and the Brotherhood Park of the P.L. Giants is not great. This was where and when he lost his way in terms of potential of having a successful baseball career.

His further career data include 242 games, 964 at bats, 225 hits of which 65 were for extra bases (29 percent!), 77 walks and 107 K's. Ruminating for a moment on 1880s players, some had it and some didn't, and excepting batting power Shannon was among the latter.

Other than his continuing interests in baseball, he operated a café, was an employee of the City of Bridgeport, and was a messenger for a typewriter company.

Daniel Webster Shannon died after a brief illness.

SHINDLE, WILLIAM   Billy Shindle
Born: December 5, 1860, Gloucester, New Jersey
Died: June 3, 1936, Lakeland, New Jersey
Height: 5'8.5".   Weight: 155 Lbs.   Batted: Right.   Threw: Right.
Major League Career: 13 Years, 1,422 Games
1889: A.A.: Baltimore
1891: N.L.: Philadelphia
1890: P.L.: Philadelphia Quakers; SS 130, 3B 2

Batting Record:

Games: 132   3B: 21   Walks: 40   SL.%: .481
At Bats: 584   HRs: 10   K's: 30   S.B: 51
Hits: 188   Runs: 127   B.Avg: .322   B.R: +21
2B: 21   R.B.I: 90   O.B.A: .369   F.R: +2

A middle infielder who could hit with power, run and steal bases, and add good batting discipline. He led the Players League in total bases by one, ranks third in hits and in triples. He played all but two of his 132 P.L. games out of position which somewhat explains his 119 errors in 1890.

Billy Shindle has been written of as a rock-solid third baseman. One hundred nineteen errors are the most in history by a shortstop in a season, which does not at all relate to his +2 fielding runs; nor does the calculus logically connect to a +36 F.R. in 1888.

He played only third base then. In 135 games, his +36 F.R. was a league-leading stat; nor does the F.R. logic link well with his +36 F.R. again in 1892, when he was at 3B in 134 games, and played nine other games at the six position.

His career F.R. by the way, 13 years and 1,422 games, is a great +85, and it should be fairly said that nobody has ever written that baseball logic has to make sense.

Shindle among 3B ranks fourth in career errors all time with 568. He also ranks 18th in putouts with 1,815, and second in range factor with a 3.70 stat for his career. His 1892 fielding range factor of 4.34 ranks first all time at 3B; if his career assists are adjusted to one 162-game season he ranks second all time.

Logic aside, changing positions on the field by 50 feet should not make that great a difference. This author recalls for a fact that when the positions are five and six it surely can, but those 119 errors (one source shows 122) in a season will not go away.

If this is distressing, then his batting averages are dizzying; during the four-year period 1888 through 1891 his basic B.Avg.s were .208, .314, .322, .210. If it's never been written elsewhere, let it be here: baseball, go figure it.

Shindle got a late start as a major league player, 1886; he didn't play full time till 1888. His first two years, at Detroit (N.L.) involve a total of 29 games and 112 at bats, with B.Avg.s adequate at .269 and .286, and F.R.s of 0 and 0.

The whole of his career extended from 1886 through 1898. After his limited Detroit debut with Baltimore (A.A.) in 1888 and 1889, he joined the Phillies (N.L.). After his fine season with the Quakers, fielding not withstanding, he played for the Orioles in 1892 and 1893, and then for Brooklyn for the remainder of his 13 major league years.

He played exclusively at third base from 1893, with -14 F.R. in 1896 and -13 F.R. in 1897. Somehow his two -30s benchmarks do calculate to +85 F.R., which is a fine mark for a 3B to post for an 1800s career.

He stole a total of 318 bases; his P.L. benchmark sum of 51 were the third consecutive year of 50+, with 52 S.B. in 1888 and 56 in 1889. In 1897 he had 105 R.B.I. for the Superbas/Dodgers, with a next best of 96 in 1894, then his 90 for the P.L. Quakers.

He scored exactly 100 runs in 1892 and 1893, 122 in 1889, and 1890 was his best run scoring season. Among his 1,560 hits in 5,807 at bats count 226 doubles, 97 triples, and 30 home runs; his 10 P.L. HRs. equal his next three most productive HR years.

Shindle produced his triples high in the P.L. year, his next best being 18 in 1892, his only triples benchmarks. Thirty-two doubles in his next to last year were his most, his only 30+ doubles season. He achieved the unusual stat of 600+ at bats in a season in 1892, with 619 for the notorious Orioles of Baltimore.

He walked to first base 66 times in 1893, among a career total of 388. His K's data are missing for three years, but he shows 240 in his other 10 years, with a high of 39 in 1891.

Beyond B.Avg.s of .314 in 1889 and .322 in 1890, he didn't reach .300+ any other year; his career B.Avg. is a very average .269. There were no .400+ O.B.A. seasons for Shindle; his high of .369 was first done in 1889 and again in 1890.

As for the .500+ benchmark in SL.% his lacking .019 in 1890 was by far his best, with his next best of .405 in 1894. His career run counts are 992 scored and 758 driven in. His P.L. +21 B.R. and +15 B.R. are his only positives among a career -91 sum in B.R.

Overall, Shindle reads out as a better than average 1800s player. There's no known method of quantitative analysis to check against, but the rigors and demands of third base surely would calculate to greater than nearly all other positions. When this is taken into account, Shindle becomes a very good player.

He was about 50 feet and 119 (or 122) errors away from that when the Players League played; as such even a countermeasure of a positive F.R. can't really offset, but his durability, base running, 27 percent extra base hits, batting generally, and production counting 188 + 40 = 127 + 90 = a Players League star player.

To his detriment, and significantly so despite very good stats throughout the balance of his career after the P.L., twice in those years Shindle was put off teams by Ned Hanlon, who was as astute a judge of players' abilities as ever there was.

One source which goes beyond baseball statistics reveals that, Hanlon had no use for Shindle. Perhaps Mr. Hanlon knew something that the numbers don't tell. After his fine or otherwise career, Billy Shindle worked for a private local company.

William "Billy" Shindle died of chronic nephritis and heart disease.

SHUGART (SHUGARTS), FRANK HARRY   Frank Shugart
Born: December 10, 1866, Luthersburg, Pennsylvania
Died: September 9, 1944, Clearfield, Pennsylvania
Height: 5'8".   Weight: 170 Lbs.   Batted: Right.   Threw: Right.
Major League Career: 8 Years, 745 Games
1889: Did not play
1891: N.L.: Pittsburgh
1890: P.L.: Chicago Pirates; SS 25, OF 5 (Rookie)

Batting Record:

Games: 29	3B: 5	Walks: 5	SL.%: .330
At Bats: 106	HRs: 0	K's: 13	S.B: 5
Hits: 20	Runs: 8	B.Avg: .189	B.R: -8
2B: 5	R.B.I: 15	O.B.A: .232	F.R: 0

To be judged on his merits as a rookie with the Chicago Pirates would have put him in the position of having to seek some other profession; it must have been good luck that someone in authority of the Pittsburgh (N.L.) Pirates saw some potential and signed him for their club for 1891, among a herd of others.

A few positives can be found in Frank Shugart's Players League record, but none are in the official books; half of his hits were for extra bases, 20 hits + five walks resulting in eight runs and 15 R.B.I. = a very good rate of run production.

But, even with the minimal data he accumulated in 1890, 13 K's versus five walks is not a satisfactory ratio; an SL.% of 150 points higher than the basic B.Avg. would look great if the starting point were .289 and not his actual .189.

He batted better the next season, in the Steel City, a .275 B.Avg. with a .324 O.B.A., on 57 hits in 320 at bats, and 20 walks, in 75 games; 26 K's show slight improvement, a .394 SL.% by choice was a decline, but in dire straits adjustments must be made.

The best year for Shugart statistically was 1894, for the St. Louis Cardinals; these are his best year stats, and career:

1894

Games: 133	O.B.A: .348	Runs: 103	K's: 37
At Bats: 527	SL.%: .436	R.B.I: 72	S.B.: 21
B.Avg: .292	B.R: -10	Walks: 38	F.R: -4

Career

Games: 745	O.B.A: .322	Runs: 483	K's: 174+
At Bats: 3,014	SL.%: .376	R.B.I: 384	S.B: 131
B.Avg: .267	B.R: -51	Walks: 218	F.R: -40

In 1893 he played a split season, 52 games for Pittsburgh and 59 for St. Louis. There is no standout stat, there are no benchmarks; in fact, 1894 was the only year he produced any of either. His career K's are missing two years' data.

His last year in continuity was 1895, with Louisville; his name wasn't on any major league roster in 1896, or 1898 through 1900. He played in 40 games for the Phillies in 1897, then 107 in 1901 for the White Sox in the first year of the American League.

One of his best marks was made in 1897, a .417 SL.%. He was listed on the White Sox roster as a shortstop. His 1901 batting averages were .251, .298, and .345. He finished his major league career much better than it began with the Chicago Pirates.

Frank Harry Shugart (Shugarts) died after a long illness.

The cause of his demise on the official certificate is noted as nitral stenosis due to 92b. He'd been a farm manager for others for many years, who died suddenly, stricken by some malady common to advanced age.

Though essentially undistinguished as a major league baseball player, he became the subject of much written commentary, and as elusive as has ever been. In fact for a few years nothing could be found of him, as if he'd just appeared, played, and vanished.

He played in the minors till about 1908 when he had to quit on account of bad eyes. An erroneous account had him participating in the first triple play, with players who were in two different leagues at the time.

The variety of surnames of his family included Shugart, Shugarts Shugert(s) and Shuckers, his first name(s) varied between Frank and Harry to William to George,

Daniel, Joseph, Elmer and more. He was born in at least three towns and lived in Punxatawney, Pennsylvania.

He was the caretaker of a hunting lodge, and an associate of the father of the famous 1940s movie cowboy Tom Mix; he may have been an employee of Tom Mix, in Arizona. The search for him even led to East Chicago, Indiana.

A researcher in the service of the National Baseball Hall of Fame, in the 1950s or '60s or '70s set out to ascertain who he was, his place of birth and death, what there could be learned. His quest attracted much chatty correspondence, near zero useful.

After some number of years, it was established that Frank Harry Shugart probably was his true identity, and the rest is history.

SLATTERY, MICHAEL J.   Mike Slattery
Born: November 28, 1866, Boston, Massachusetts
Died: October 16, 1904, Boston, Massachusetts
Height: 6'2".   Weight: 210 Lbs.   Batted: Left.   Threw: Left.
Major League Career: 5 Years, 374 Games
1889: N.L.: New York
1891: N.L.: Cincinnati
1890: P.L.: New York Giants; OF 97

Batting Record:

Games: 97	3B: 11	Walks: 27	SL.%: .445
At Bats: 411	HRs: 5	K's: 25	S.B: 18
Hits: 126	Runs: 80	B.Avg: .307	B.R: +7
2B: 20	R.B.I: 67	O.B.A: .352	F.R: -9

Playing in the outfield with Jim O'Rourke and George Gore could have gone two ways for him; there would be minimal expectations or he would be expected to perform and produce at their levels, which he did very well indeed in the Players League.

He didn't prove quite equal to O'Rourke or to Gore —few players did— but Mike Slattery gave the New York (P.L.) Giants one of the two finest outfield trios in the league. Their presence prompted Slattery to levels of achievement his record says he wasn't capable of.

His play in the field by a -9 F.R. SABR-stat was negative; he had only one such positive, a +6 F.R. in his first year, 1884, with the Boston Reds of the Union Association. He didn't play in the N.L. or the A.A. at all during the next three years.

In the U.A. he was in 106 games, had 413 at bats, and scored 60 runs via 86 hits and four walks; he compiled batting averages of .208, .216, .232, distinctly inferior. A further overview of his career puts him in a New York (N.L.) Giants uniform in 1888 and 1889.

He played 103 games the first of these years and 12 games the next, achieving nothing of distinction. In 1891 he was with Cincinnati (N.L.) and Washington (A.A.), and accomplished virtually the same as the year before the Players League.

It was written of Slattery during his time that he was one of Boston's idols on the diamond. For several years he was one of the most prominent baseball players in the East and was considered the equal of any of the fielders in the league.

If there is a place in life for destiny, then it was decided he would have one terrific season as a major league player; fate may have caused opposing pitchers to envision another coming of Gore or O'Rourke to make their day.

Slattery didn't lead or rank near the top in any P.L. stat. His near equal walks and K's might make arguable that he wasn't efficient in the one-on-one game. But when he brought his bat to home plate in 1890 he did business at rates comparable with many historic betters.

His 126 hits and 27 walks producing 80 runs scored and 67 batted in calculates to a terrific rate of productivity where it counts the most, on the scoreboard; 36 extra base hits among 126 (29 percent) made his scoring potential that much greater; to enhance he stole 18 bases.

Compare some of Slattery's P.L. stats with the totals of his five-year career, noting the U.A. didn't keep R.B.I. data.

	1890	Career
Games:	97	374
At Bats:	411	1,481
Hits:	126	372
Runs:	80	229
R.B.I:	67	135+

The call is close, but fairly he can't be cited as a P.L. star, although for that singular year the fates enabled Slattery to be a terrific baseball player.

Viewing the season of the Players League Giants from another perspective, perhaps it was the presence and performance of Slattery which caused Gore and O'Rourke to be as great as they were.

When all was said and done, Slattery had done himself proud, he did well beyond his level best in the cause of his Brethren. A leg injury caused his retirement from the game. Afterward he went into the tailoring business in Boston.

Michael J. Slattery's cause of death was hypertropic cirrhosis of liver and chronic gastroenteritis. He died after a brief illness due to stomach trouble.

When Mike Slattery had played for the Boston Reds of the Union Association in 1884, at age 17 he was the youngest regular in major league history.

SNYDER, CHARLES NICHOLAS Pop Snyder
Born: October 6, 1854, Washington, D.C.
Died: October 29, 1924, Washington, D.C.
Height: 5'11.5".   Weight: 184 Lbs.   Batted: Right.   Threw: Right.
Major League Career: 15 Years, 797 Games
1889: N.L.: Cleveland
1891: A.A.: Washington
1890: P.L.: Cleveland Infants; C 13

Batting Record:

Games: 13	3B: 0	Walks: 1	SL.%: .208
At Bats: 48	HRs: 0	K's: 9	S.B: 1
Hits: 9	Runs: 5	B.Avg: .188	B.R: -6
2B: 1	R.B.I: 12	O.B.A: .220	F.R: 0

He began in the historic National Association in 1873, and played for the New York Mutuals, Lord Baltimore, and Philadelphia, in 28, 39, and 66 games respectively. As with these numbers, his third year B.Avg., .301 in 1875, nearly doubles those of .153 in 1873 and .190 in 1874.

He was a catcher who on rare occasion played the outfields. He was also 10 years past his prime in 1890, and an innovator who is credited with developing basic field techniques for catchers and being among the first to give signs to his pitchers and infielders.

Gifted with astute knowledge, having learned a consistent work ethic, SABR advises that Charles "Pop" Snyder while in his prime was probably the best defensive catcher in baseball.

He seldom played in more than 50 games a year. In his early years the schedules consisted of 60 to 80 games a year. By the annals he still was able to collect 1,295 (and more) assists, which now ranks 20th all time for catchers.

He also was charged with 529 errors, which ranks second all time, and 647 passed balls, which ranks first among all major league catchers. He may have been the best of his era defensively, but Pop Snyder has never been quoted as saying that being an 1800s major league catcher was easy.

SABR tells more about Pop Snyder. "He usually caught 90% of his team's games, including all 60 in 1878 ... [and] led in many defensive stats" including fielding average three years, putouts two years, and passed balls two years.

By 1878 he was working behind home plate in Boston. He'd been with Louisville the first two years the National League was in business; he stayed with Boston through 1881. When the American Association began he jumped to Cincinnati, where he continued from 1882 through 1886.

He was with the Cleveland Blues the two years that franchise operated in the A.A., 1887 and 1888, then returned to the N.L. with the Cleveland Spiders in 1889. His last bit of a season was spent with A.A. Washington in 1891.

During the last three of these years he played in only 27, 13, and eight games, with the issue resolved that he'd done outstanding work behind the plate.

His .895 career fielding percentage tells the better side of Pop Snyder, with a .235 batting average being the offensive counterpart. The extra base hits made in his first three years are lost in history; it is known that while in the N.L., A.A., and the P.L. he hit 110 doubles, 39 triples, and seven home runs.

These hits raise his basic B.Avg. to a .303 SL.%, the stat of a less than awesome slugger; 75 walks added to his 849 hits were the primary parts of a .256 O.B.A. for Pop Snyder; by bits and pieces his count of career K's is 118. In sum he was not any sort of phenom at the bat.

The numbers speak much better of him as a field manager than as a catcher at the bat. He was manager of the Cincinnati Reds in 1882, 1883, and 1884. His first team won the first A.A. pennant. He was manager at Washington his last year, the perpetually fallible city of D.C., his hometown.

The complete record of Pop Snyder as a manager is won 163 and lost 122, a .572 win percentage, with first- and third-place finishes the first two years, when he was in charge the whole season; the second Reds manager took his team to fifth place in 1884.

Pop Snyder was the second of four to steer the Statesmen of D.C. in 1891; the team finished eighth and last, giving him the ironic distinction of first place in the A.A.'s first year, and last place in the last year of the A.A. endeavor.

Pop Snyder was also a long-term umpire. He was with the A.A. in 1886 and 1891, with the N.L. in 1892 and 1893, 1895, and 1898 through 1901. By SABR-stats calculated much later, as a major league batter and catcher Pop Snyder accumulated a total of -85 batting runs (B.R.), and an outstanding +136 fielding runs (F.R.).

This veritable unknown among baseball originals, though he didn't play much or bat well, was there when the Players League played.

SOWDERS, JOHN   John Sowders
Born: December 10, 1866, Louisville, Kentucky
Died: September 26, 1909, Indianapolis, Indiana
Height: Weight: Batted: Right.   Threw: Left.
Major League Career: 3 Years, 65 Games
1889: A.A.: Kansas City
1891: Did not play
1890: P.L.: Brooklyn Wonders; P 39, OF 3

Batting Record:

Games: 40	3B: 0	Walks: 10	SL.%: .235
At Bats: 132	HRs: 1	K's: 12	S.B: 0
Hits: 25	Runs: 14	B.Avg: .189	B.R:
2B: 3	R.B.I: 20	O.B.A:	F.R:

Pitching Record:

Won: 19	Starts: 37	K's: 91	E.R.A: 3.82
Lost: 16	C.G: 28	Walks: 161	Saves: 0
Win %: .543	I.P: 309	Hits: 358	P.R: +14
Games: 39	Sh.O: 1	O.B.%: .386	W.A.T: -1.2

Three teams, three leagues, three years; 0 and 0 at Indianapolis (N.L.) in 1887, 6 and 16 at Kansas City (A.A.) in 1889, Brooklyn (P.L.) in 1890 and he called an end to his career as a major league baseball pitcher.

His performance in the years prior to the P.L., and his batting in the P.L., don't require much discussion; he was not very good in the pitcher's box and was worse in the batter's box. To his credit as a batter, he did score some runs and drove in almost 50 percent more; he got a couple dozen hits, and hit a Players League home run.

In his 0 and 0 pitching year the counts are 1 game, 3 innings, a 21.00 E.R.A.; courtesy suggests nothing more should be said about that. His 6 and 16 equates to a .223 Win %, not as good as the K.C. Cowboys' 55 and 82 (.401), nor as good as their third pitcher who won 8 and lost 6 (.571).

With Kansas City, John Sowders did complete 20 of 23 starts, pitched 185 innings, and struck out 104 opposing batters, but he allowed 105 walks and 204 hits; his 1889 O.B.% is .388, and his E.R.A. an appropriate 4.82. His 1889 SABR-stat P.R. is -20.

For his first season his P.R. count is -6, with a -0.3 W.A.T.; his career SABR-data are -11 P.R. and -5.1 W.A.T. Apparent discrepancies are due to his work in 1890. Sowders was good in the Players League, and the P.L. was good for him.

He was the second pitcher with P.L. Brooklyn, a changed pitcher in terms of production and results, even though his -1.2 W.A.T. is below the team's staff as a whole. A bit of speculation says if his P.L. won and lost of 19 and 16 had been 6 and 16, then the Wonders would have finished in the second division.

Pitcher Sowders exceeded the work standard of excellence in 1890, with 309 innings pitched; his E.R.A. is better than the team's staff 3.95. His and the team's O.B.% are exactly the same.

But his K's and walks are way out of balance, to the negative, though his rate of innings pitched and hits allowed is better than the typical P.L. ratio, and overall Sowders of the Brooklyn Wonders was superior to the league.

To sum up his annotated major league career, he improved from nothing to a loser, then got better than average, his team, and his league. John Sowders was by far at his best in the year of the Brotherhood Players League.

STAFFORD, JAMES JOSEPH   General Stafford (Jamesy)
Born: July 9, 1868, Webster, Massachusetts
Died: September 18, 1923, Worcester, Massachusetts
Height: 5'8".   Weight: 165 Lbs.   Batted: Right.   Threw: Right.
Major League Career: 8 Years, 568 Games (12 as a pitcher)
1889: Did not play
1891: Did not play
1890: P.L. Buffalo Bisons; P 12, OF 4 (Rookie)

Batting Record:

Games: 15	3B: 0	Walks: 7	SL.%: .163
At Bats: 49	HRs: 0	K's: 8	S.B: 2
Hits: 7	Runs: 11	B.Avg: .143	B.R: -6
2B: 1	R.B.I: 3	O.B.A: .250	F.R: 0

Pitching Record:

Won: 3	Starts: 12	K's: 21	E.R.A: 5.14
Lost: 9	C.G: 11	Walks: 43	Saves: 0
Win %: .250	I.P: 98	Hits: 123	P.R: -10
Games: 12	Sh.O: 0	O.B.%: .388	W.A.T: -0.4

His baseball bottom lines are the same as the Buffalo Bisons' bottom line; like Gen. Franklin Pierce, who in 1848, was removed from command in Mexico while in battle, and who in 1857 was refused his party's nomination for a second run at the presidency, General Stafford was equally ineffective in the pitcher's box and at home plate while holding a bat.

Below mediocre in all aspects of the batting game, he did cash in some critical hits, accounting for 11 runs scored and 3 R.B.I. with just seven hits and seven walks, and stole a couple of bases, which would justify his use as a substitute outfielder.

As a pitcher he capitalized his opportunities far less efficiently, as the whole of his account shows; a W.A.T. below that of the P.L. Bisons would have to require many great deficiencies, as his P.R. verifies. In his favor he did complete all of his starts except one, like Mr. Pierce aforementioned.

The O.B.% of the P.L. "General" is only .001 away from the Buffalo stat of .387 and his E.R.A. is 0.98 lower than the team's staff; on the other side of General Stafford are walks double K's, commensurate with giving away positions and games.

After the year of the P.L., General Stafford did not pitch an inning during the remaining years of his major league career. He didn't play in 1891 or 1892; perhaps time was required to recover from the trauma of 1890.

From 1893 through seven games of the 1897 season, his function was utility player; for the New York Giants, then for Louisville, Boston, and Washington through 1899.

Free of the distractions of pitching, he improved generally. In 553 games and 2,079 at bats he made 583 hits and 164 walks; his K's are shown as 95 but three years' data are missing. He hit 60 doubles, 19 triples, and 21 home runs.

His batting average became .274, his O.B.A. improved to .331, his SL.% went up to .350; his stolen base count increased to 117, but the SABR-stat sum of his offense was still B.R. -50.

Apparently he never did get the feel for playing the field, not as evidenced by his sum -41 F.R., all counts being either 0's or -'s. By the record, if General Stafford didn't have to pitch or protect his position in the field, he might have been a pretty good baseball player, maybe even for the Bisons.

After the major leagues, he was a minor league manager and umpire, as well as an American League umpire and a college coach. It's been written of him that he was a subdued athlete and was parsimonious with words. An anecdote is offered as explanation.

During the Civil War in Cuba, circa 1896, he was a member of the New York team, and an ardent supporter of Antonio Maceo, the Cuban patriot. Maceo was Stafford's ideal of what a hero should be. Maceo was lured into the woods and slain by traitors in the patriot camp. Stafford eulogized Maceo, saying he was a good man and it was a darn shame to kill him.

The death of James Joseph "General" Stafford has at least two explanations. The first is that he died following a collapse after finishing a speech at a club banquet. The second is that he died a week after undergoing surgery for an unknown infirmity.

Or, there was more than one "General Stafford." The pitcher for the Players League Buffalo Bisons had owned and worked a farm.

STALEY, HARRY E.   Harry Staley

Born: November 3, 1866, Jacksonville, Illinois
Died: January 12, 1910, Battle Creek, Michigan
Height: 5'10".   Weight: 175 Lbs.   Batted: Right.   Threw: Right.
Major League Career: 8 Years, 283 Games
1889: N.L.: Pittsburgh
1891: N.L.: Pittsburgh and Boston
1890: P.L.: Pittsburgh Burghers; P 46, OF 1

Batting Record:

Games: 47	3B: 2	Walks: 13	SL.%: .268
At Bats: 164	HRs: 1	K's: 16	S.B: 0
Hits: 34	Runs: 25	B.Avg: .207	B.R:
2B: 3	R.B.I: 25	O.B.A:	F.R:

Pitching Record:

Won: 21	Starts: 46	K's: 145	E.R.A: 3.23
Lost: 25	C.G: 44	Walks: 74	Saves: 0
Win %: .457	I.P: 388	Hits: 392	P.R: +43
Games: 46	Sh.O: 3	O.B.%: .310	W.A.T: -0.8

    1890 was his second of four 20+ win seasons, by a margin of .010 better than his .447 Win % (won 21, lost 26) for N.L. Pittsburgh the year before. He'd begun his major league career the year before that, for N.L. Pittsburgh, and won 12 and lost 12. When his career ended, Harry Staley was a legitimate major league pitcher.

    In 283 games, with 257 starts and 231 complete, he won 136 and lost 119 decisions, for a .533 Win %; his 1890 record of 21 and 25 is just about that far the wrong side of .500.

    In a total of 2,270 innings he gave up 2,468 hits. His P.L. sums are nicely in harmony at 388 and 392; he recorded 300+ I.P. each of four years, including an extraordinary 420 in 1889.

    His totals of walks and K's are 601 and 746, and his P.L. ratio of 74 free passes to 145 walks back to the bench is outstanding; his high in K's of 159 came in 1889, as did 116 walks, his high in that stat.

    The career opponents on base allowed rate by Staley is a fine .339, slightly more than his 1890 mark of .310, which was the lowest such in the Players League. His career E.R.A. is 3.81, considerably above his 3.23 (or 3.22) in the P.L., the second-lowest such mark in the league of 1890.

    Staley also tied for second rank in P.L. shutouts. Further, his ranks among the P.L.'s high 5's include: fifth in games, third in C.G., fourth in I.P., fourth in K's (tied), fifth in Total Pitcher Index.

    His P.L. SABR-stats stand at a superb +43 P.R. and -0.8 W.A.T. which is the end product of a terrific season for a losing team. His P.R. in the P.L. serve as the greater part of a +50 P.R. sum.

    1891 wasn't a complete season for Staley; he returned to the N.L. Pittsburgh club, won 4 and lost 5, then changed his pitching address to N.L. Boston. There he won 20 and lost 8; this .714 part season win % was the closest he got to benchmark.

He'd been the dominant pitcher with the P.L. Burghers; there was no place for him on the 1891 Pittsburgh staff along with three other skilled veterans. The Pirates finished eighth and last in the N.L.

Later with Boston that year, he was designated third pitcher, behind a veteran star and a virtual novice who each won 30+ games and the N.L. pennant; his contribution of 20 and 8 is the distance between first and third place for the Beaneaters.

Apparently content with his role, he stayed with the reborn Reds of Boston. In the ensuing three seasons his won-lost marks were 22–10, 18–10, 12–10, during which time his team finished first by 8.5 games, first by five games, and third by eight games.

Staley apparently didn't know the sands of time flow very consistently, or he was just persistent; he insisted on one more major league season, and got it, at Louisville: won 6, lost 13.

Even during the years when the name Knickerbocker ruled the game, during the early 1860s when Eckford and Atlantic were called national champions, far back in time when baseball was a game, compassion had no place for a used pitcher.

There was no compassion for Staley in 1895; he had to know that if opponents on a given day could score 19 or 36 runs they would do it. His capacity declined, and the positives of the past turned in the other direction. The game is cruel.

Twice after the terrific (despite) P.L. season, Staley posted E.R.A.s in the excellent range, 2.58 in 1891 and 3.03 in 1892; they grew to 6.85 in 1894 and 5.26 in 1895. His I.P. fell from benchmarks 324 and 309 to 209 and 159.

An astute pitcher, any major league player, can read the signs in the sands. To know when to quit is an essential element of astute for all of them which some choose to ignore. Despite, Harry Staley was a fine 1800s major league pitcher.

He contributed 46 decisions to the Pittsburgh Burghers, and 388 innings of commendable work to the Players League.

Harry E. Staley died following surgery performed a week earlier.

STOVEY (STOWE), HARRY DUFFIELD   Harry Stovey
Born: December 20, 1856, Philadelphia, Pennsylvania
Died: September 20, 1937, New Bedford, Massachusetts
Height: 5'11.5".   Weight: 175 Lbs.   Batted: Right.   Threw: Right.
Major League Career: 14 Years, 1,486 Games
1889: A.A.: Philadelphia
1891: N.L.: Boston
1890: P.L.: Boston Reds; OF 117, 1B 1

Batting Record:

Games: 118	3B: 11	Walks: 81	SL.%: .470
At Bats: 481	HRs: 12	K's: 38	S.B: 97
Hits: 143	Runs: 142	B.Avg: .297	B.R: +25
2B: 25	R.B.I: 85	O.B.A: .404	F.R: −1

He's a Players League star player, and a Players League feature player, both in a manner best on the field. There were issues about his ancestry, specifically the melanin count of his skin; said simply, in the opinions of some forms of Americans, Harry Stovey wasn't quite white enough to play major league baseball in the late 1800s.

Everything about him as a player speaks to the contrary. While a rookie with Worcester in 1880 he led the N.L. in triples, and in home runs which, though sensational, were merely a portend of things to come. The totality of his record of successes during his 14 years as a player stands among the greatest in the history of the game.

He changed his surname so his mother wouldn't know that he was earning his living playing baseball. Try to imagine the joyful dilemma of his managers struggling to decide which place in the batting order Stovey would be the most effective.

His play in the field ranks among the top 10 percent of all the 1800s players. Due recognition has seldom been done because his career was split almost equally between the outfield and first base, technically diminishing his performance at both positions.

Still he ranks 19th all time among first basemen in errors with 241, a clearly negative achievement but also a commendation to the length of his tenure, and to his hustle and mobility.

Twice he tried the position of field manager, with Worcester in 1881; he won 8 and lost 18 (.308 Win %), which is definitely negative but an indication of his ambitions while just a sophomore, and also a credit in terms of the perception of him held by his owners. As a veteran with Philadelphia (A.A.) in 1885 he tried again, won 55 and lost 57 (.491), then knew his limitations to leave managing well enough to others.

To aid his efforts as a base runner, he's said to have been the first major league player to use sliding pads; to what extent they helped isn't certain, but it is known that he stole a total of 509 bases during his career. Further consider his total is lacking six years of data. Still, only 30 players in history have officially accounted for a greater accumulation.

A player named Sam Morton, more likely Charlie Morton, who played in the major leagues for three years during the 1880s, but doesn't have a stolen base record, has also been credited as the first to use sliding pads; he played in a total of 88 games.

The real record of Harry Stovey is further confounded by the fact that his league didn't maintain R.B.I. records for five years, nor strikeouts for six years. He's not shown with 100+ R.B.I. in any year except 1889, while still with Philadelphia (A.A.). He has been assessed with 68 K's in 1889 and 69 K's in 1891 for Boston (N.L.). His known S.B. high stands at 97, in 1890 for Boston.

These 97 stolen bases led the Players League and ranks 23rd all time among all major league players regardless of pigmentation; his 68 S.B. in 1886 were a league high but 87 S.B. in 1888 didn't lead, nor 74 in 1887, or 63 in 1889, all for the Athletics. Nor did he lead the N.L. in 1891 with 57 stolen bases, among years known.

In one 1891 game the scorekeeper properly marked Stovey with 5 K's. During his career he had five hits in a game five times; once he hit two triples in the same inning, and three during a game in 1884. He was the first to record 20+ S.B. in a season, in 1884.

Each of four years Stovey led his league in triples; Willie Wilson and Sam Crawford each did it five times, Ty Cobb four times. Harry Stovey also led his league in HRs six times, was the first to reach the 100+ career mark in HRs, and held the HR record through the span of years 1889 through 1895.

As a point of perspective on the historical standing of Stovey, measure the six times led his league in HRs against the all time National League record of Ralph Kiner who led seven times, and the American League record of Babe Ruth who did it 12 times.

Stovey was the first to lead two leagues in HRs, the N.L. with six in 1880 and 16 in 1891, and the A.A. with 14 in 1883, 13 in 1885, seven in 1886, and 19 in 1889; he almost led a third league in HRs, and he ranks second (tied) in the Players League of 1890.

For the record, the 174 career triples by Stovey ranks 21st all time. He also ranks third in runs scored in the P.L., and he ranks first in the P.L. in Total Average with a count of 1.207 (the statistical methodology is unknown).

A combination of natural speed and learned skills were wisely used on the 1800s playing fields by this major league baseball player who maybe had the blood of mixed races, which might be an admixture with any of dozens of possible variations. His forte on the field though was power; he had the skills and strength to hit (by one account) 121 home runs, a high number for any of the best 1800s players.

His mix of abilities also produced (by one account) 173 triples — only 20 players have hit more in history — and 347 doubles. The total count of his extra base tallies among 1,769 career hits (6,138 at bats in 1,486 games) adds up to 642, or 36 percent of his hits, which is extraordinarily outstanding by any objective measure.

Each of six years he beat the 1800s HR benchmark; his high of 19 was hit in 1889 and he led his league all six of these years. Each of three years his triples count was 15+; his most were 23 in 1884 and 20 twice, and four times he was the league leader. He hit 30+ doubles each of four years, including 38 in 1889; he led with 31 in 1883.

There's no need to discuss his power factor beyond spectacular. Counted as slugging percentage his sum is .461; including three years of .500+, his high SL.% mark was .545 in 1884.

When he took his bat to home plate he also took discretion; 661 times his skill and discipline earned walks to first base, but patience and prudence failed 343 times when he was put out on strikes. His K count is more, and six years' data are missing.

The result of his judgment is written in a .360 on base average. He never led in walks but took as many as 81 in a season; that was in 1890 in the Players League. His K's that year number 38, an excellent ratio.

He was walked 77 times the year before the P.L., and 78 times the year after, with five other years of 50+ free passes to first base.

Historically, 80 percent of major league players couldn't wish a .288 career batting average; for Harry Stovey .288 has to be declared a deficiency, the price which has to be paid for putting too much vigor into his swings. He never led any league in B.Avg., and posted .300+ only four times. His high mark was .326 in 1884.

SABR-stats by B.R. rates him at the extreme of outstanding, with a career sum of +360 batting runs, including a league-leading +46 in 1884, two years at +40, and three other years above +30. His career F.R. mark is +24, saved from mediocrity by +17 the year before the P.L. and +11 F.R. the year after.

Stovey reached the 100+ runs scored benchmark nine consecutive years, and led his league four years with 110 in 1883, 124 in 1884, 130 in 1885, and 152 in 1889; note his 142 runs scored for the P.L. Boston Reds.

His complete itinerary included Worcester (N.L.) 1880 through 1882, Philadelphia (A.A.) 1883 through 1889, the Players League Reds of course, then Boston (N.L.) 1891 and 38 games in 1892, then 74 with Baltimore, eight more with Baltimore in 1893 and the closure of his benchmark career with Brooklyn for 48 games in 1893.

In 13 of his 14 years Stovey counted 300+ at bats, 500+ in three of these years: 1888, 1889, and 1891. His P.L. at bats were near to 500. We need note his -1 F.R. Only in one of his 118 games was he at first base; Dan Brouthers was fixed there, from which the Rock of Ages might not have been able to displace him.

One hundred seventeen games for the champion Reds were the least among their starting outfield trio; unknown as it was happening, and seldom said since, Stovey was in his environ in 1890. He was one star among a team of great players.

Of the P.L. Boston Reds, three regular position players had better B.Avg.s than Stovey, as did the team's field manager, who also had the duty every game day to organize the whole into a batting order.

Winning that league championship was the result of a unified effort. The excellence of Stovey rates accolades equal to a number of great others. All in all his was a fair contribution.

No known source shows him with a 34-percent rate of extra base among his Players League hits, 48 of 143; he is a legitimate candidate for the title of "Greatest Player of the 1800s!"

These are among his ranks in period stats 1876–1889: second in runs, 10th in hits, sixth in doubles, second in triples, first in HRs, sixth in walks, fifth in S.B., fourth in extra base hits, seventh in total bases, 10th in O.B.A., sixth in SL.%, sixth in combo.

If Stovey wasn't good enough to play major league baseball during the 1800s, then no American man was. If his mother knew and understood, she would have had good cause to be proud, and damn justifiably so. Her skin color may have been any of many.

Then certain species were afflicted with insipid prejudices, in Boston and Chicago, St. Louis and Louisville, and in Washington, D.C.; if it ruffles a few feathers of comparably cerebrally deficient Americans now, then let it be so.

The same still exists within all these major American locales, and further and greater now known within a sector of the Great Desert Southwest, wherein multiple counts are judged by government(s) and law)s) to constitute no offense to us!

Stovey was a member of the Philadelphia or New Bedford police force after baseball, and was known to have been disabled for several years. He was nominated for membership in the National Baseball Hall of Fame in 1936; he received six votes.

Then his name was lost in the will of the winds at Cooperstown. He was known to come to games drunk. Despite his inferior batting average, and "only" 85 runs batted in, Harry Stovey is a Players League star player, and a Players League feature player. Harry Stovey (Harry Duffield Stowe): cause of death unknown.

STRICKER (STREAKER), JOHN A.   Cub Stricker
Born: February 15, 1860, Philadelphia, Pennsylvania
Died: November 19, 1937, Philadelphia, Pennsylvania
Height: 5'3".   Weight: 138 Lbs.   Batted: Right.   Threw: Right.
Major League Career: 11 Years, 1,196 Games
1889: N.L.: Cleveland
1891: A.A.: Boston
1890: P.L.: Cleveland Infants; 2B 109, SS 20

Batting Record:
Games: 127	3B: 8	Walks: 54	SL.%: .320
At Bats: 544	HRs: 2	K's: 16	S.B: 24
Hits: 133	Runs: 93	B.Avg: .244	B.R: −21
2B: 19	R.B.I: 65	O.B.A: .318	F.R: −0

"An earnest, effective, and reliable player excelling at second base where he has but few equals and no superior; a sure catch, swift and accurate thrower; his activity enables him to cover a great deal of ground, some of his catches and stops being extraordinary; also ranks as an expert base-runner and good batsman; is a strictly temperate, honest ambitious young player, always works earnestly for the best interests of his club."

This was the prevailing opinion of Cub Stricker early in his career. It changed considerably when difficulties arose in late 1889 and early 1890 as to which was his club. "Stricker signed a contract with the Cleveland (N.L.) club on November 13, 1888, by the terms of which he agreed to play ball from April 1 to October 1, 1889 for the sum of $2000." No problems here at all.

"The contract, it is claimed, also gave an option on his time for the season of 1890. Stricker is charged with failure to fulfill the option clause of his contract. He also signed to play for Mr. Johnson and the Players' League company during the season of 1890." Papers were served; he made jest of the whole matter.

Baseball as played off the field was a very different game than on the fields of play. "A number of clubs want John for next year and the club getting him can be confident of possessing an honest hard-working player, who knows exactly how second base should be played." He did not understand the game off the field at all, nor did he care to.

Stricker had been with the A.A. Cleveland club in 1887 and 1888. He'd jumped to the N.L. Cleveland club for 1889, with all the blessings due such conduct being given by their hierarchy and friends in the media. Chris Von der Ahe, whose A.A. business was in St. Louis, became involved, as a member of the famous Peace Committee which was to oversee the behavior of all clubs in both major leagues, and rule on alleged offenses when complaints came.

When Stricker went from A.A. to N.L. Von der Ahe recalled a rule which required "players must be paid the amounts called for in their contracts.... Stricker has a contract with that [Cleveland] club which states that he was to receive $2000.... Von der Ahe refused to give him more."

Off the record, so it seems, Von der Ahe, speaking for the A.A.: "affirms that Stricker is entitled to $3000, now is not the time to violate even the smallest obligation entered into." There was another side to the Peace Committee, and they were disgusted. Among the they were Frank DeHaas Robison and John T. Brush, who owned the Indianapolis territory regardless of league, and he'd made a claim on Stricker for his services.

When the subterfuge was done Stricker was assigned to the Cleveland company of the N.L.; Von der Ahe was wrong, and the N.L. had done no wrong at all, although each was disgusted with all of the others, which was how the game was played then off the field. A year hence it was deja vu all over again, but the culprit was Stricker. All wrong was his due, and Mr. Johnson of the Players League company. There were contracts and the National Agreement to prove culpability and liability.

Wrote the media friends of the A.A. as the 1891 season was about to begin on the field, "Stricker is undeniably and contestably the best second baseman that has played for Boston for many a year.... Of all the players that come to Boston none will receive a heartier and warmer welcome than 'Cub.'" In the interim the Players League played, he'd been anathema, and the subject of stalking by lawyers not by baseball club executives. How fast and fully an opinion can change, then again, and then again.

The scenario does not mention that the Boston A.A. club of 1891 was owned by the executives who'd owned the Boston P.L. club in 1890, nor that nearly every club which was party to the National Agreement and subject to the judgment of the Peace Committee selected players to pursue to play for them on the field in 1890 in violation of their P.L. contracts, or they would prosecute the player in public courts. In effect those chosen were like prey isolated by a pack of wolves.

Stricker had been given an accurate appellation, but not for these reasons, nor for his tendency to jump contracts. At 5'3" and 138 pounds, he was considerably smaller physically than his major league peers, much as during the past few decades when a player is less than six feet in height he is labeled by media as being diminutive, which in turn somehow equals deficient.

He was a pretty fair major league second baseman, with sufficient versatility and ability to play the six position or any in the outfields when his team was in need.

What stands out as deficient in his record is power at the bat; overall during his career he made 1,107 hits in 4,635 at bats, which included 128 doubles, 47 triples, and 12 home runs. His extra base rate is 17 percent, and his annual rates of extra bases are all low.

His 29 hits for extra bases among 133 for the Infants of Cleveland (22 percent) exceeds his norm. His benchmark 54 P.L. walks and 16 K's (3.4:1.0) among 544 at bats (2.9 percent) definitely rate commendation. He was walked 414 times in all, including 63 times in 1891, and 50+ each of four other years.

It took four years for him to learn the A.A. strike zone, from his rookie year at

Philadelphia in 1882 through 1885. His K's for these years and through 1888 are missing from the record, his walks the first four were 15–19–19–21, and each of his next five years were 50+, including 1887 and 1888 at A.A. Cleveland and the N.L. in 1889.

Stricker didn't play in the major leagues in 1886, which by the terms and conditions of the National Agreement enabled him to choose his league and team for 1887 as a free agent. That's all that was necessary to lose a year out of a career.

For the seven years known Stricker was K'd 105 times in 2,209 at bats (4.8%). To the contrary scoring runs requires hits and walks; he scored 790 runs, with a peak of 112 in 1887, his only 100+ run production stat.

He was at the front end of the batting order. He counted only 259 R.B.I., with a high of 65 in the P.L. of 1890. His fielding was usually in good order; he led his league in F.R. his first year with +20 (and again in 1891 with +27) but has been marked with a -38 F.R. for his third year; his career F.R. sum is -23.

After Boston (A.A.) in 1891, he split the 1892 N.L. split season between St. Louis (28 games) and Baltimore (75 games), and closed out his career in Washington in 1893. He'd been field manager at St. Louis; he won 6, lost 17 (.261 win %). In 1892 he was a National League umpire.

Of the years known, he was a great base stealer: 86 in 1887, the next year 60, and 54 in 1891, probably his best season on the field. As with many diminutive players, this was a strength of Stricker, what he did best as a player.

His Players League batting average is low, five points better than his career .239, but never higher than .273 in 1883. His P.L. O.B.A. also was better than his whole of .306 with a high of .334 in 1887; his P.L. SL.% of .320 is less than his best of .333 in 1884 and much better than his career .294: Cub had no power at all.

He wasn't a star in the Players League, but he did challenge the most powerful baseball powers. He's in the record books, ranking third all time in errors by a second baseman with 701, offset by fifth rank in range factor with a mark of 5.97.

If Cub Stricker had any outstanding moments on the field, they weren't put in print. Among the most notable was his prelude to the Players League.

John A. "Cub" Stricker (Streaker) was assigned the contributing cause of death bronchopneumonia, generalized arteriosclerosis with myocardial degeneration, with his actual cause of death reading "ruptured left byforne (?) with metastes brain and bone structure." Which reads as if a lawyer was near him till his very end.

STYNES, CORNELIUS WILLIAM   Neil Stynes
Born: December 10, 1868, Arlington, Massachusetts
Died: March 26, 1944, Somerville, Massachusetts
Height: 6'0".   Weight: 165 Lbs.   Batted: Threw:
Major League Career: 1 Year, 2 Games
1889: Did not play
1891: Did not play
1890: P.L.: Cleveland Infants; C 2 (Debut Date: September 8)

Batting Record:

Games: 2	3B: 0	Walks: 0	SL.%: .000
At Bats: 8	HRs: 0	K's: 0	S.B: 0
Hits: 0	Runs: 0	B.Avg: .000	B.R: -2
2B: 0	R.B.I: 0	O.B.A: .000	F.R: 0

He played two games at the second position for the P.L. Cleveland Infants of 1890, went to bat eight times, made no hits, got no walks, didn't "K" at all, scored no runs, and drove in none. His batting averages are all .000, less than expectations by his -2 B.R. He made zero stolen bases and his F.R. is "0."

This is not a major league record for brevity of a career, it's not even close.

On September 21, 1922, the Cleveland (A.L.) Indians put a player up to bat for a look-see, his first at bat; his name was Eucal "Uke" Clanton, also given the name "Cat." He went to bat, he struck out, then he went home to Powell, Missouri.

After his major league career, Neil Stynes was a supervisor with a local water company, maybe also during and before.

SUNDAY (WACHER/WACHTER), ARTHUR (AUGUST) Art Sunday

Born: January 21, 1862, Springfield, Ohio
Died: ?
Height: 5'9". Weight: 193 Lbs. Batted: Left. Threw:
Major League Career: 1 Year, 24 Games
1889: Did not play
1891: Did not play
1890: P.L.: Brooklyn Wonders; OF 24 (Debut Date: May 5)

Batting Record:

Games: 24	3B: 1	Walks: 15	SL.%: .349
At Bats: 83	HRs: 0	K's: 9	S.B: 0
Hits: 22	Runs: 26	B.Avg: .265	B.R: +2
2B: 5	R.B.I: 13	O.B.A: .419	F.R: 0

If he'd been Billy Sunday he'd have been a holy terror on the base paths, but actually he wasn't really even Art Sunday. If 0 stolen bases during the whole of his career of 24 games is any indication, the least of his baseball playing assets was speed.

More walks than K's wasn't unusual for a Players League player, but more runs scored than hits made is unusual for any player. By his +2 B.R. it's a safe guess that many of his 26 runs scored and 13 batted in were very helpful to his Brooklyn Wonders team.

If Sunday had any faults or flaws in the field, they don't show by his very average 0 F.R. stat. His .265 batting average is also very average, but not so his benchmark .418 O.B.A., made with his 22 hits and 15 walks.

His 15 walks and nine K's, though a small sample, is a better than average ratio, his .349 SL.% corresponds well with his six extra base hits of the 22.

In sum, although lacking power at the bat, Sunday was better than average during his brief major league tenure, and potentially could have been better than that.

His illogical departure is more odd than his runs to hits ratio, but then again he wasn't Art Sunday. An inquiry made later notes that he may have been "Arthur Hawker" or "August Hawker" of the U.S. Forest Service who worked in Utah, but they and higher government offices have no record of him by any name.

SUTCLIFFE, ELMER ELLSWORTH   Sy Sutcliffe
Born: April 15, 1862, Wheaton, Illinois
Died: February 13, 1893, Wheaton, Illinois
Height: 6'2". Weight: 170 Lbs. Batted: Left. Threw:
Major League Career: 7 Years, 344 Games
1889: N.L.: Cleveland
1891: A.A.: Washington
1890: Cleveland Infants; C 84, OF 15, SS 4, 3B 2

Batting Record:

Games: 99	3B: 8	Walks: 33	SL.%: .422
At Bats: 386	HRs: 2	K's: 16	S.B: 10
Hits: 127	Runs: 62	B.Avg: .329	B.R: +9
2B: 14	R.B.I: 60	O.B.A: .382	F.R: -6

He was Wheaton's first pro and a prominent research reference gives his name as Edward Elmer. During the period when he was born many boys were named after Elmer Ellsworth, who was an early Civil War hero. Five other major league players were also christened with that name.

As a player Sy Sutcliffe was a courageous and hard-working catcher as well as a swift and straight thrower. The nickname "Cy" or the reduced form of Cyrus was common among 1800s players, but not "Sy."

Nor was a catcher by trade common who could play all the other fielding positions, and bat .300+ with power and discretion. This was the playing composition of Sy Sutcliffe, of the Cleveland (P.L.) Infants.

He wasn't their best defensive player, -6 F.R., but consider the stats he produced in 1890 alongside his team and the league:

	Sy	Team	League
B. Avg:	.329	.286	.274
O.B.A:	.382	.360	.345
SL.%:	.422	.386	.378

Before the 1889 season opened, he was acquired by Cleveland, which was in need of a back-up catcher; prior to 1890 he joined several of his teammates who jumped to the Cleveland team in the new league. He finished among the top 10 batters but he also had the lowest fielding average among the league's catchers.

Judging by batting stats, 1890 represents fully a third of his career, excepting at bats and K's. 1,322 and 87 respectively; with K's accounted for in all his years, 1884–1885 and 1888 through 1892, he shows an adequate 6.6% rate.

His count of walks is only 92; when he went up to bat it was with the intention of putting the ball in play, making things happen. Another equation works well for Sutcliffe: 73 of 381 hits went for extra bases, almost 20 percent, which is the baseline of superiority.

1890 was consistent with his career in terms of extra base ratio; 2:1 walks to K's rates better with B.R. +9 of a career sum +10, and 10 stolen bases of a career 41, on the whole in the P.L. he was not far from a star player. But that -6 F.R. and his production is flawed with 127 + 33 = 62 + 60; no doubt his batting averages suffice.

His two years in two leagues in Cleveland were the longest he was in any city. He accumulated quite a travel log (but didn't play much till the P.L.). He started at Chicago (N.L.) in 1884–1885 (4 and 11 games), and finished 1885 at St. Louis (16 games).

He was elsewhere in 1886 and 1887 and resumed in 1888 at Detroit (49 games); then came Cleveland in 1889 (46 games). He'd been exclusively a National League player, but after the P.L. he went to Washington and the A.A., then finished at Baltimore in 1892 (66 games).

Sutcliffe was signed by the Washington Statesmen and batted .353 during the 1891 season. This was the highest average in the league, although he didn't have quite enough at-bats to qualify for the title. He was in 53 games and had 201 at bats.

Sy Sutcliffe didn't accumulate any benchmarks during his career. He did score 177 runs and batted in 174 (recall the theory that equal equals great). His cumulative batting averages are .288, .336, and he had a .371 SL.%.

His record isn't especially long or impressive on the whole, but he produced a season near excellent in 1890. The Infants and the League were better for his having been there, even though he wasn't the Wheaton iceman.

Elmer Ellsworth Sutcliffe died of Bright's disease.

SWETT, WILLIAM E.   Pop Swett
Born: April 16, 1870, San Francisco, California
Died: November 22, 1934, San Francisco, California
Height: Weight: Batted: Threw:
Major League Career: 1 Year, 37 Games
1889: Did not play
1891: Did not play
1890: P.L.: Boston Reds; C 34, OF 3 (Debut Date: May 3)

Batting Record:

Games: 37	3B: 3	Walks: 16	SL.%: .330
At Bats: 94	HRs: 1	K's: 26	S.B: 4
Hits: 18	Runs: 16	B.Avg: .191	B.R: -3
2B: 4	R.B.I: 12	O.B.A: .321	F.R: 0

This "Pop" might have been too young to be away from home in 1890. For a lad his age to travel to the extreme opposite end of the country must have been quite an adventure, and more so to test his future as a player of major league baseball.

"Pop" wasn't a reference to his age or wisdom; by a hometown account he was given the name as a young amateur for the clever way he could trap foul flies. Fact is, someone from the distant East must have seen in young William some potential.

He came to Boston with credentials as a catcher. He must have been discouraged when he learned his status would be at best second behind the batter with the Boston P.L. Reds, maybe third; it was for the manager to decide who'd play on a given day, and he himself often took a turn as catcher.

Young William also had to compete against another novice for playing time. He was from the neighboring town of Providence. When catcher Swett was permitted to play, he didn't do much to show he should be first, or any part of the Boston roster.

His 0 rate of fielding runs doesn't indicate any faults at the backstop position, but his .191 batting average if he was a regular would have to be a record. To his credit he did show some power: eight of his 18 hits were for extra bases. If done over the course of a season full time the results would be Ruthian.

But 1890 wasn't a full season for Pop Swett, for him it was a major league career; with his Players League adventure done when San Francisco called he answered, by then having reached the age of legal majority.

The hometown media made much of his season in the East. One article has him with the Boston American League team, while another reported he showed up well in some of the game but as Chas. A. Swett.

Still others, through and beyond his life, had him starring with the Boston Brotherhood nine, while less disingenuous reports summarized a brief but brilliant professional career, and the *New York Clipper* in his day said Swett "did excellent work behind the plate" ... [and] aided materially that P.L. team in winning the pennant."

Still others wrote that he did excellent work at the bat and made such a splendid impression that he was asked to join the A.A. Boston Reds in 1891. Finally, he was called one of San Francisco's most famous baseball players in the '90s.

He didn't play in the American Association or American League, but San Francisco was much further from Boston than it is now, and if a scribe took a little literary liberty, who would know? He did go back to the city by the bay. He played in the minor leagues and semi-pro, including one year for a team of 'Frisco Boys in a Southern League for a team based in Nashville, which didn't finish its season.

He did play in the Players League, made more than 100 plate appearances, and behind home plate played at a 0 level which isn't negative. Afterwards he was an employee of the City of San Francisco for many years.

The cause of death of William E. "Pop" Swett was carcinoma of liver which was reported as a short illness.

TEBEAU, OLIVER WENDELL   Patsy Tebeau
Born: December 5, 1864, St. Louis, Missouri
Died: May 15, 1918, St. Louis, Missouri

Height: 5'8".   Weight: 163 Lbs.   Batted: Right.   Threw: Right.
Major League Career: 13 Years, 1,167 Games
1889: N.L.: Cleveland
1891: N.L.: Cleveland
1890: P.L.: Cleveland Infants; 3B 110

Batting Record:

Games: 110	3B: 6	Walks: 34	SL.%: .418
At Bats: 450	HRs: 5	K's: 20	S.B: 14
Hits: 135	Runs: 86	B.Avg: .300	B.R: +4
2B: 26	R.B.I: 74	O.B.A: .353	F.R: +13

Patsy Tebeau was the second of two field managers of the Infants; his record of 52 games stands at won 21 lost 30, .412 win %. The team was in seventh place both when he took the position and at the end of their season.

Wild and dangerous was the Ol' West then, and wild and vile was the ballpark at Cleveland where Patsy Tebeau was the field manager of a major league baseball team.

Once he was fined by the National League administration for assaulting an umpire. He took the case to a court of civil law and the charge was dismissed on a technicality; he had been denied legal due process.

It's confusing as could be, but it involved Tebeau, so it was to be expected: with no explanation of facts or circumstances, he once was assaulted, then paid a bribe to avoid being involved in a lawsuit.

The team he managed, perhaps better said the team he controlled on the field, has been called notorious, and much worse than Spiders. Their style was to win by any means including threats, other intimidation, and actual violence; they were led by example, in the person of their manager.

His won and lost record at the helm as a whole is impressive, won 726 and lost 585 (.555 Win %) in 11 seasons if his last of 92 games in 1900 is counted as a whole season (won 42, lost 50).

His career as a manager began in the Players League, in 1890, which was his first of only two losing seasons; in both, his first and last his teams finished in seventh place. Every other year he brought home a winner, but never a league championship.

He came close once, sort of, as the second-half winner in the 1892 National League split season; having destroyed all the competition, the league had to devise this odd scenario to justify a postseason.

When it happened, the Spiders of Patsy Tebeau were soundly beat. The format was best-of-nine; they lost games two through six, with no winner in game one. Cy Young of the Spiders and Jack Stivetts of the Boston Beaneaters, first-half champions, hooked up in one of the classics. After 11 innings the score was still 0 to 0; on the day only 10 hits were made, and one error.

The great majority of these years he was in service to one or both of the Robison brothers, but not in 1890. Then his team owner was Albert L. Johnson. He didn't sustain in the game; Tebeau and the Robisons did. Tebeau was manager of one of their syndicate teams from 1891 through 1900, the last two years in St. Louis.

Mr. Patsy Tebeau was legally the holder of the same two first names as a prominent legal jurist surnamed Holmes, which was where the resemblance ended; the former has been cited as being the most aggressive base runner of the 1800s.

He instilled this trait in his teams. In addition to expanding their unprintable vocabularies and vocal capacities, he's also been cited as an inspirational leader. Base runners crashing into opponents trying to field their positions is one example.

To trip them, restrain them, by all means and method, the object is to win, and if you're not caught it didn't happen, in accord with the Oliver Wendell Tebeau baseball school. Dirty Jack Doyle and Dirty Jack O'Connor best depicted the curriculum; Ed McKean, though, was master in the mode of conduct.

Their winning records were seldom a match for counterparts Ned Hanlon and John McGraw and company, but in terms of ornery and downright vile they were every bit and bite their equals. Also of the Spiders of Patsy Tebeau were the irony of Jake Virtue, Jess "The Crab" Burkett, Nig Cuppy, and Cupid Childs.

Jimmy McAleer was accused by some of being the rowdiest, as were Chippy McGarr and Bobby Wallace. Many of Tebeau's players were as notable for their abilities as they were for their misdemeanors; a considerable number are now denizens of Cooperstown.

Tebeau, though, isn't in the hall of fame and has never been nominated. He was not a passive bench manager. He played in the field and very well. Early in his career he played at third base, but changed to first base in 1893. This was not just managerial prerogative; he was among the best of 1800s players in most every respect.

Don't confuse him with "White Wings," his elder brother, who in his own right was a very able player. The elder had great speed, stole 228 bases in his six seasons. He chose the A.A. for 1890 and both wore Cleveland uniforms part of 1894 and all of 1895.

Patsy was fast on his feet and good with his hands, never reluctant to join in a fistfight on or off the field, including more than a few which he provoked. He put his foot speed to better use by stealing 164 bases during his career, and at 3B in 1890 played well enough to rate a 4.09 range factor, eighth all time at 3B.

This, his first season as a manager, third as a player, didn't begin in the opening day game of the Infants; when he was made manager the team had won 34 and lost 45 (.430 Win %), and were in seventh place. His 21–30 (.412) made them neither better nor worse.

Both Henry Larkin, who'd been there first, and Tebeau had very good seasons as players, as did others. Both were lacking a first-class pitcher to rely on for critical games and serve as the stopper when losing streaks occurred.

When Tebeau was in the lineup to take a regular turn at bat, the Infants were not a seventh-place team. His 1890 data do not contain a hint of a negative; beyond the bat he was their hot corner man, charged with the task of holding an excellent team of individuals together.

His +13 F.R. reflects his fielding skills, a +4 B.R. is to his favor; his .300 B.Avg. is at the edge of excellence, but not so his .353 O.B.A. or .418 SL.%. Still, these are neither inferior or inadequate numbers.

Twenty-seven percent of his Players League hits were good for extra bases. If he'd had real power in his swings there'd be a closer correspondence between doubles and home runs than 26 and 5. If his speed was high octane there'd be a closer connection between doubles and triples than 26 and 6.

His 26 doubles and 14 stolen bases could be construed completely as aggressive base running. His 34 walks and 20 K's say patient at home plate and a good sense of the strike zone. His 86 runs scored and 74 R.B.I. make a good balance in production.

Add his hits and walks and runs and R.B.I., the result is a very good balance, and very good production. Count his 20 K's as part of 450 at bats and this result is an excellent 4.4% of opportunities gone to waste.

Although there's nothing overwhelming about Patsy Tebeau as a P.L. player, neither is there indication that he was in any way lacking. His beginning, though, was less than auspicious; in 68 at bats in 20 games for Chicago (N.L.) in 1887, the whole of his .162 B.Avg. with a -7 B.R., except his +3 F.R. is deficient.

Not in the major leagues in 1888, he resumed with Cleveland (N.L.) in 1889; 136 games and 521 at bats later he'd found his level in a .282 B.Avg. His career calculation is .280; his .332 O.B.A. that year is exactly that of his career. Some power could be found in his .390 SL.%, well above his career mark of .364.

He never got near the batting benchmarks of .400+ O.B.A. or .500+ SL.%, but 1890 was not his only .300+ B.Avg. season; there was his best of .329 in 1893, and .318 in 1895, also .302 in 1894. Nor were his season stolen base stats beyond ordinary; 30 in 1894 were his most.

A +13 F.R. in 1890 was his best in the field, in 110 games at third base, where the going is always tough. His next best is +6 in 1891 and 1893. Some among these are negative, but the first noted is his only F.R. in doubles figures, of a career +15.

No so good in the B.R. category, his career total is -70, including -24 in 1896, and a modest high of +11 in 1893, worth one game. He earned the term playing manager with six seasons of 100+ games and eight seasons of 300+ at bats.

His high in runs scored was 90 in 1893, with 102 R.B.I. the same season, his only 100+ production benchmark. Walks and K's sums are both minimal; 319 walks include a high of 53 in 1898, typically in the 30s. Thirty-five is the high among 198 K's, in 1894, with 1897–1900 missing as the N.L. downsized its data collection.

After leading the Infants of Cleveland until their end on the field, Mr. Johnson's grief and despair lasted well into the Lake Erie winter. Tebeau resumed with the Spiders and was appointed as their field manager.

He played in only 61 games, and 86 the next year, then switched to first base and played in 116 games. Thus eased of some of the load he hit 32 doubles, his only extra base benchmark, and by combination of choice and chance also had 32 walks.

He was in great batting form in 1893 with only 11 K's in 486 at bats. There is no benchmark but 2.2% is outstanding for any major league player in any season, even when they're abbreviated by less than major league difficulties.

In the last of his years, Tebeau played in only one game and did nothing at all with four at bats; there had been many and much more exciting moments during his generally commendable career.

The 1895 National League World's Series was a contest between the minds and men of Ned Hanlon and Patsy Tebeau, featuring the fare and antics of the Orioles and Spiders, if one might imagine; the prize was the Temple Cup, donated to stimulate interest in the less-than-stimulating season after the season.

With such sham foisted upon the baseball public, and forced on the players, as the standard contract required service until the first of October, their recompense was a matter of whimsy of their owners. The series was scheduled as a best-of-seven event.

Cleveland had finished the regular season schedule in second place, behind Baltimore by three games. The Temple Cup series of 1895 is considered by some to be one of the best as it was the only one that saw the losing side win a game, which is less than classic.

There weren't many Temple Cup series. The New York Giants had finished second in 1894, by a coincidental three games. The Giants took the cup to New York after shutting out the regular season champions, the Baltimore Orioles, 4 games to 0.

(As a very relevant question aside, who took home the National League gonfalon these years? Foremost in the year of 1892?)

The 1895 Cleveland Infants of Patsy Tebeau did nearly as well as the 1894 Giants under manager Monte Ward. The format again was best of seven but it required five games for the Infants to shut down but not shut out the Orioles of Ned Hanlon.

Mr. Temple's purpose in sponsoring the championship was to see his Pittsburgh team win it. Pittsburgh finished no higher than sixth in the 12-team N.L. during the four-year reign of the Temple Cup.

This was as close as Tebeau came to knowing baseball glory as a manager. As for his 1890 Infants, when a team of very good players has a very bad season, virtually all the fingers of blame will point straight to the manager. Very much to the contrary, his Players League season as a player was on the edge of star class.

When his major league career was done he retired to St. Louis, where he'd been born, where he was last a manager and played. He then owned and managed a bar and saloon. Though the reason isn't clear, the means to his end was suicide.

A revolver was found at the scene, close at hand. The body of Oliver Wendell "Patsy" Tebeau was put to rest not far from the ballpark at Cleveland, Ohio. He had been diagnosed with heart disease shortly before he died.

The cause of death was a gunshot wound to the right temple.

TENER, JOHN KINLEY   John Tener
Born: July 25, 1863, County Tyrone, Ireland
Died: May 19, 1946, Pittsburgh, Pennsylvania
Height: 6'4".   Weight: 180 Lbs.   Batted: Right.   Threw: Right.
Major League Career: 3 Years, 61 Games
1889: N.L.: Chicago
1891: Did not play
1890: P.L.: Pittsburgh Burghers; P 14, 3B 2, OF 2

Batting Record:

Games: 18	3B: 0	Walks: 7	SL.%: .286
At Bats: 63	HRs: 2	K's: 10	S.B: 1
Hits: 12	Runs: 7	B.Avg: .190	B.R:
2B: 0	R.B.I: 5	O.B.A:	F.R:

Pitching Record:

Won: 2	Starts: 14	K's: 30	E.R.A: 7.31
Lost: 11	C.G: 13	Walks: 70	Saves: 0
Win %: .214	I.P: 117	Hits: 160	P.R: -40
Games: 14	Sh.O: 0	O.B.%: .424	W.A.T: -3.9

He was a member of the team on Al Spalding's Chicago White Stockings versus All-America World tour, which by account of the *New York Clipper* returned the entourage to the U.S. at New York City on April 6, 1890, just days before the baseball season of three major leagues was scheduled to begin. Further, noted the *Clipper*, the tour had left San Francisco the previous 18th of November.

John Tener was a National League umpire in 1889, a member of the U.S. Congress in 1909, governor of the Commonwealth of Pennsylvania 1911–1915, and president of the National League of Baseball Clubs 1912–1917 (some sources list his term as 1913–1918).

He was the tallest pitcher in the Players League in 1890, and tied for the tallest player, which by common American opinion established his natural superiority, such presumption having existed since the species realized there were advantages to be found in standing upright.

This does not correlate with his record as a major league pitcher for three years of won 25 and lost 31 (.446 Win %); the 1890 season was his worst of the lot. This is supported by the fact of his career earned run average of 4.30; his E.R.A. in the P.L. nearly doubled that mediocre mark.

In this worst baseball year of John Tener, while at the bat he struck twice for home runs. His production by the sums of hits and walks balanced against runs scored and R.B.I. is further distant from normal than his below-average-for-a-pitcher .190 basic batting average. When this season was done he knew well enough to quit and move on to other endeavors.

As for the quality of his P.L. pitching, the SABR-stats all are accurate and indicative: 7.31 E.R.A., .424 O.B.%, -40 P.R. and -3.9 W.A.T. for the lowly Pittsburgh Burghers, the staff marks of which further reinforce, 4.22 E.R.A. and .322 O.B.%.

To his credit, Tener in 1890 did complete 13 of 14 starts. In his 117 innings of pitching he allowed places on base to be taken by 230 opposing players, including gifts of first base to more than double the number he struck out. If the Players League had a representative losing pitcher he would be John Tener.

He achieved this nadir of his very brief major league career after two seasons with the White Stockings of Chicago (N.L.); if he was a member of the other team on Mr. Spalding's world tour, the how and why might be found in his Burghers season statistics.

In 1888 he'd won 7 and lost 5; in 102 I.P. he had an excellent 2.74 E.R.A., an outstanding .298 O.B.%, K'd 39, walked 25, and gave up 90 hits, the numbers of a rookie with great potential. That potential was lost in 1889 with a won 15 lost 15 record; in 287 innings he had 105 K's and gave up 105 walks and 302 hits for a .350 O.B.% and 3.64 E.R.A., a very neutral ledger.

There can be found nothing specific in his 1890 numbers which would indicate his political future. He was genuinely awful in every calculated way; beyond the aforementioned are his raw data of 30 K's and 70 walks, nothing positive whatsoever to be found. He did find his place in the greater world beyond major league baseball. He became a bank president and partner in an insurance company, he was a congressman and a governor, and the president of the National League. He definitely was not cut out to be a major league pitcher.

John Kinley Tener died three weeks after he had a heart attack.

TWITCHELL, LAWRENCE GRANT   Larry Twitchell
Born: February 18, 1864, Cleveland, Ohio
Died: April 23, 1930, Cleveland, Ohio
Height: 6'0".   Weight: 185 Lbs.   Batted: Right.   Threw: Right.
Major League Career: 9 Years, 639 Games (42 as a pitcher)
1889: N.L.: Cleveland
1891: A.A.: Columbus
1890: P.L.: Cleveland Infants; OF 56. Buffalo Bisons; OF 32, P 13, 1B 3

Batting Record:

	Clev	Bflo	Totals
Games:	56	44	100
At Bats:	233	172	405
Hits:	52	38	90
2B:	6	3	9
3B:	3	1	4
HRs:	2	2	4
Runs:	33	24	57
R.B.I:	36	17	53
Walks:	17	23	40
K's:	17	12	29
B.Avg:	.223	.221	.222
O.B.A:	.279	.316	.295
SL.%:	.300	.285	.294
S.B:	4	4	8
B.R:	-15	-9	-23
F.R:	-10	-4	-14

Pitching Record:

	Clev	Bflo
Won:	D	5
Lost:	i	7
Win %:	d	.417
Games:		13
Starts:		12
C.G:	N	12
I.P:	o	104
Sh.O:	t	0
K's:		29
Walks:		72
Hits:	P	112
O.B.%:	i	.398
E.R.A:	t	4.57
Saves:	c	0
P.R:	h	-4
W.A.T:		+1.3

It must have been "The Curse of Larry Twitchell" which put Gene Woodling on the rosters of the Washington Senators and New York Mets in the same year (1962);

in his favor Woodling didn't suffer the humility of having to pitch for either of his teams.

Larry Twitchell did pitch in years other than 1890, but in 1890 the lesser of his teams, the seventh-place Cleveland Infants, didn't use him as a pitcher although they were in dire need of a good one throughout the Players League season.

Neither had the Detroit (N.L.) team put him in the pitcher's box, not much at any rate during his 1886 rookie season; he worked 25 innings, collected a bloated 6.48 E.R.A., and has a record of won 0 and lost 2 for that season.

In 1887 his record was great, still with the Wolverines, who that season as a team were one of the great ones; he won 11 and lost 1 (.910 Win%), the team won the N.L. pennant by 3.5 games, in this one of his two notable seasons.

His pitching career extended from 1886 through 1891 consecutively, and 1894; he played in nearly 600 more games than he pitched. While a pitcher, beyond the above, add Detroit in 1888 to his traveling agenda, Cleveland (N.L.) in 1889, Columbus (A.A.) in 1891, and Louisville the other year.

That's most of the pitching career of Larry Twitchell, except for the Buffalo Bisons of 1890; for them he was one of 16. His record in all those other years was 1 win and 1 loss in 10 games. His whole record including Buffalo was 17 won and 11 lost (.607), a fairly good year for a fairly good 1800s pitcher.

It might be interesting to match some of his data from his one great year, the Players League year, and his career:

	1887	*1890*	*Career*
Won:	11	5	17
Lost:	1	7	11
Win %:	.901	.417	.607
O.B.%:	.346	.398	.373
E.R.A:	4.34	4.57	4.63
P.R:	-4	-4	-19
W.A.T:	+4.7	+1.3	+5.2

Except for the numbers of won and lost and the percentage there isn't much difference to be found at his best with the worst and overall. There's some evidence that he was better than the Bisons, that the '87 Wolverines were greater than he was, and that he was a pretty good major league pitcher by his bottom line.

As a batter, his first two years correspond perfectly with his pitching—1886 B.Avg. = .063, 1887 B.Avg. = .333—beyond which he wasn't as good a batter as a pitcher, and was near his nadir in his Infants/Bisons year. This was his career as a batter:

B.Avg: .263	Runs: 362	K's: 231	Extra Base Hits:
O.B.A: .313	R.B.I: 384	B.R: -37	163
SL.%: .357	Walks: 168	At Bats: 2,571	

While in the pitcher's box and the various outfield pastures, he accumulated enough faults to be rated a -49 in fielding runs; in and from the batter's box he accumulated run production sums which by the equal = great school say he was a great batter.

His Walks to K's ratio say he was not a great batter, which his B.R. confirms;

his basic B.Avg. is just average, on base and SL.% are less than adequate, and his extra base rate of 6 percent isn't fit for a pitcher. He produced no benchmarks of any kind.

Twitchell had a great pitching moment, which lasted through a season; he had one great batting moment, which lasted a game. On August 15, 1889, he went to bat six times and set a record that stood for many years when he hit a home run, three triples, a double and a single for a total of 16 bases.

He was a good outfielder and a hard hitter. His arm went out on him but came back with a whip nearly any man would envy. Somewhere along the way he developed a symbiotic sense of being attracted to some really major league losing teams—1888: Detroit fifth, 1889: Cleveland sixth, 1890: Clev/Bflo. seventh & eighth, 1891: Colombus sixth, 1892: Washington 10th, 1893: Louisville 11th, 1894: Louisville 12th.

In 1889/1890 he caught the slow train to ignominy; it was all downhill personally and professionally after that. The facts were never confirmed, but Larry Twitchell was accused of being the first to give out the Brotherhood's plan for the P.L. to a newspaper editor, Frank Brunell.

He quit when the count of his games reached 639, leaving much behind to consider: Is the whole greater than the sum of its parts (Wolverines of 1887)? Do pitchers and players make the team or can the team make the players (Infants/Bisons of 1890)? What was the role in all this of a newspaper sporting editor?

Lawrence Grant Twitchell died of heart disease.

VANHALTREN, GEORGE EDWARD MARTIN   George VanHaltren
Born: March 30, 1866, St. Louis, Missouri
Died: September 29, 1945, Oakland, California
Height: 5'11".   Weight: 170 Lbs.   Batted: Left.   Threw: Right.
Major League Career: 17 Years, 1,984 Games (93 as a pitcher)
1889: N.L.: Chicago
1891: A.A.: Baltimore
1890: P.L.: Brooklyn Wonders; OF 67, P 28, SS 3

Batting Record:

Games: 92	3B: 9	Walks: 41	SL.%: .444
At Bats: 376	HRs: 5	K's: 23	S.B: 35
Hits: 126	Runs: 84	B.Avg: .335	B.R: +16
2B: 8	R.B.I: 54	O.B.A: .405	F.R: +1

Pitching Record:

Won: 15	Starts: 25	K's: 48	E.R.A: 4.28
Lost: 10	C.G: 23	Walks: 89	Saves: 2
Win %: .600	I.P: 223	Hits: 272	P.R: -1
Games: 28	Sh.O: 0	O.B.%: .377	W.A.T: +0.9

Successful as a pitcher and super at the bat, his work for the Brooklyn P.L. Wonders was worth at least two spots on the roster. He's a valid candidate for

M.V.P. of the P.L., and he came with an established reputation as a major league pitcher.

He'd use those skills only twice more during the next decade. His batting was that of an above average journeyman, who in the Players League established himself as a star.

The starting pont was Chicago (N.L.) in 1887. George VanHaltren had just reached the age of majority. He'd traveled from Oakland, where his family relocated when he was young, to try a career as a major league baseball player.

He did succeed, and definitely so, but at first was of mixed mind whether his priority should be pitching or batting. His first pitching record of won 11 lost 7 (.611 Win %) in 1887, working in 20 games, measured against a .203 batting average in 45 games with 172 at bats, would seem to have given the needed guidance.

Still with Chicago in 1888, his average at bat improved to .283 in 81 games with 318 at bats; his hits for extra bases improved from four doubles to nine, from zero triples to 14, three HRs to four, but his fielding fell off from the later calculated 0 F.R. to -3 F.R.

His second pitching season involved more games, 30 as opposed to 20, more decisions, 13 and 13, and more innings, up from 161 to 246; his E.R.A. was reduced to 3.51 from 3.86, O.B.% from .364 to .331, and then he didn't pitch at all in 1889.

That season he played in 134 games, with 543 at bats, and gained his first benchmark stat with a .309 B.Avg; his power data were mixed with 20 doubles, 10 triples, and nine Hrs. His walks grew phenomenally from 22 to 82 and K's minimally from 34 to 41. He scored 126 runs and drove home 82 White Stockings team mates.

Ambivalence prevailed in terms of league preference for 1890. The decision was made to switch from the N.L. to the P.L., and the move proved positive in every way. VanHaltren was again a winner as a pitcher, but only third pitcher on the Brooklyn staff.

Nonetheless, his work as a pitcher was of sufficient quantity and quality to help his team finish second in the P.L. He completed 23 of 25 starts; SABR-stats show him borderline, with a -1 P.R. and +0.9 W.A.T.

His Brooklyn Wonders O.B.% and E.R.A. were too high, walks double K's is looking for more of the same, 272 hits and 89 walks in 223 I.P. is simply too many to get away with over the course of a whole major league season, but a .600 win % has won more than a few championship pennants.

As a Brooklyn Wonders batter VanHaltren left nothing in doubt, enforced by a +16 B.R.; +1 F.R. had been his norm and it would get worse in the future before it got better. Focus on 1890 and his best and most, and the bottom line of an excellent career:

Stat	Best/Most	Career
Hits:	204 (1898), 197 (1896), 186 (1897)	2,532
2B:	30 (1900), 28 (1896), 23 (1901)	285
3B:	21 (1896), 19 (1895), 16 (1898)	161
HRs:	9 (1889 & 1891), 8 (1895)	69
Runs:	136 (1891 & 1896), 129 (1893 & 1898)	1,639

Stat	Best/Most	Career
R.B.I:	104 (1894), 103 (1895)	1,014+
Walks:	82 (1889), 76 (1892), 75 (1893)	868
K's:	46 (1895)	305+
S.B:	75 (1891), 55 (1892), 50 (1897)	583

His R.B.I. data are noted as incomplete. The strikeout column is blank from 1897 through 1903. His B.R. are of +30 three years, high +33, total +268 B.R. His F.R. high is +9 twice, total +4 F.R. Assess the player VanHaltren from another view.

600+ At Bats: three years, 500+ 13 years, 300+ 15 years;
200+ Hits: one year, 175+ 10 years;
  30+ Doubles: one year, 20+ 10 years;
  15+ Triples: four years;
  10+ HRs: zero years;
100+ Runs: 12 years;
100+ R.B.I: two years;
100+ Walks: zero years, 50+ 12 years;
100+ S.B: zero years, 50+ three years.

Each of 12 years his B.Avg. was .300+, high .351 in 1896, career .316; each of six years his O.B.A. was .400+, high .422 in 1893, career .385; just once did VanHaltren have a .500+ SL.%, with .503 in 1895.

Just twice did he lead his league in stats, with 21 triples in 1896 and with 45 stolen bases in 1900. If his total of stolen bases was 574, as one source shows, then he ranks 18th all time in that statistic.

As a batter, his ranks in period stats 1890–1899 are as follows: second in games, second in at bats, fourth in hits, fifth in triples, ninth in walks, fourth in runs, fourth in total bases, fifth in stolen bases.

After 1890, he pitched in six games in 1891, won 1 lost 0, 23 I.P., 5.09 E.R.A.; two games in 1896, won 1 lost 0, 8 I.P., 2.25 E.R.A.; total all other years with no decisions, seven games, 29 innings, his career O.B.% is .366, E.R.A. 4.06.

The beneficiaries of his services after 1890 were Baltimore (A.A.) in 1891, the only Baltimore and Pittsburgh in 1892, again Pittsburgh in 1893, and the New York Giants from 1894 through 1903.

1890 was a very good year for VanHaltren, after which came a baker's dozen more; he didn't lead the P.L. in any stats or rank in the high fives. He missed many more games than usual, and he hadn't yet reached his batting prime.

Still there is no fault to be found in the P.L. record of VanHaltren at the bat; he had two benchmark batting average stats, good number of stolen bases, excellent B.R., above average F.R., and his walks as a batter nearly double K's.

His rate of 17 percent extra base hits could have been higher. He wasn't a power hitter any time in his career; runs and R.B.I. show him at the front end of the batting order. Both are adequate, but by the calculation Runs + R.B.I.= Hits + Walks his production was somewhat out of order for the Brooklyn Wonders.

During his career in the outfield he accumulated 348 assists, to rank fourth all time in that stat; adjusted to a hypothetical 162-game season his 30.86 assists ranks eighth all time. He's 13th in double plays with 64 and sixth with 358 errors. He occasionally took a turn at the four and six fielding positions.

He was the field manager of the Baltimore Orioles for 11 games in 1892, their first of three; he left with the team in 12th place and the team finished in 12th place, neither better nor worse for his having been there. One hundred twenty-three games later he transferred to Pittsburgh.

He went back to Oakland after his major league playing career to work in construction. He did some scouting along the West Coast for the Pittsburgh club. His career was great overall, and with the Brooklyn Wonders in 1890 he was a star in the making.

His work after baseball was as a latherer, a plasterer, not to be found very often nowadays. The same could be said of his P.L. season; it was unusual, very good in both the batter's box and in the pitcher's box.

Although his season was abbreviated he was a positive presence as both batter and pitcher. His numbers weren't outstanding in either category but overall rate the call of a Players League star player, at the unusual combination of change pitcher and reserve outfielder.

George Edward Martin VanHaltren died of a heart attack.

VAUGHN, HARRY FRANCIS Farmer Vaughn
Born: March 4, 1863, Rural Dale, Ohio
Died: February 21, 1914; Cincinnati, Ohio
Height: 6'3".   Weight: 177 Lbs.   Batted: Right.   Threw: Right.
Major League Career: 13 Years, 915 Games
1889: A.A.: Louisville
1891: A.A.: Cincinnati
1890: P.L.: New York Giants; C 30, OF 12, 2B 1, 3B 1

Batting Record:

Games: 44	3B: 0	Walks: 10	SL.%: .325
At Bats: 166	HRs: 1	K's: 9	S.B: 6
Hits: 44	Runs: 27	B.Avg: .265	B.R: -7
2B: 7	R.B.I: 22	O.B.A: .307	F.R: 0

Behind Buck Ewing on the depth chart would be almost every other 1800s catcher. With the P.L. Giants of 1890, Harry Vaughn became one among the many. There wasn't room for him in the Giants' outfield; his situation was like being stuck behind the proverbial rock and between three hard places.

Ewing was their catcher and field manager. Two of the fielders were a star and a classic and the third had a career year, which meant not much playing time for Farmer Vaughn where he might be functional and comfortable.

He'd really not proven himself. 1890 was his fourth season if 1886 was his first. With Cincinnati (A.A.) he appeared in one game, had three at bats, and nothing else, 000s and 0's across the board except for a .250 O.B.A., but with no walks (hit by pitch?).

He was elsewhere in 1887 and with Louisville (A.A.) in 1888 and 1889, the first of which shows a .196 B.Avg. in 189 at bats. 1889 shows 360 at bats and a .239 B.Avg., and a +6 F.R. as a catcher.

He was less active in 1890 and more capable at the bat. With a 0 F.R. his stats are credible for a second catcher, not to excess either positive or negative.

Beyond and through 1899, with the standards for at bats waived, he batted .300+ each of three years, almost reached the .500+ SL.% level once, and made 946 hits in 3,454 at bats in all, for a .274 B.Avg., with accompanying .306 O.B.A. and .365 SL.%.

The low O.B.A. is a function of only 151 walks; 128 K's are known among eight of his 13 seasons. Obviously very active at the bat, not content to watch many pitches pass, this and his work behind home plate led him to the position of an N.L. umpire in 1892 and 1893.

For Farmer Vaughn 1891 was a year of transition, from the P.L. to the A.A., from New York to the mess of the Cincinnati/Milwaukee franchise. The uncertainty about position day to day sustained, with 64 games at the second position, and one or more at every other position except four and six including a day as the pitcher.

His 1891 data file includes 100+ more at bats than in 1890, his B.Avg. .020 better. He doubled his count of doubles. He went home in 1893 to Cincinnati to play baseball. The worst he showed the home folks was his defense in 1892 which rates -11 F.R.

The summary of his defense, all years at all those positions, calculates to an average 0 F.R. His B.R. stat is otherwise, an accumulation of -'s which total -79 B.R., his one positive being a +2 B.R. in 1898; in 275 at bats he produced a .305 batting average.

1893 was his most productive year at Cincinnati, with a benchmark 108 R.B.I., 35 walks, and 16 stolen bases, all career highs. His work at the bat in 1894 produced his best B.Avg. of .310 in 284 at bats; this nearly halved his prior year's at bats, 483, his most.

Vaughn hit his SL.% peak of .482 in 1894 with a count of 15 doubles; his high was 23 in 1895 of a career 147. There were five triples among a total of 53, a high of 12 in 1893. He hit eight home runs, by far his high among 21. He didn't have warning track power; his best was barely beyond the infield's borders.

1895 was another benchmark year for sometimes catcher Vaughn in terms of a .305 B.Avg. in 334 at bats. Among his hits were 29 for extra bases and nearly a benchmark's worth in doubles. Decline set in and his next two years' B.Avg.s were .293 and .291, in 433 than just 199 at bats. Everything else went down proportionally.

Still Vaughn could have gone out in good style, a repeat of .305 as batting average in 1898 in 275 at bats, but he chose to try again. 1899 was not a good year, with only 108 at bats, an awfully low .176 B.Avg. and neither his O.B.A. or SL.% reached .200.

He beat the benchmarks a few times. He played only two 100+ game seasons. His batting was adequate, about average for all players all time. His fielding wasn't deficient. On the whole he rates the ambiguous call of satisfactory and perhaps better if the whole of day-to-day disorder in positions is taken into account; his season in the Players League was service well done for a cause.

He was stuck nearly his whole credible career at the position of second catcher, and whatever else that called for. After he went back home to play, his manager at Cincinnati from 1895 through 1899 was Buck Ewing, whose games at C declined from 105 to 69 to one during the years 1895 through 1897.

He wasn't only second catcher, he was also the subject of anecdotes. There was an alleged record-breaking throw at Buffalo, but it had not been properly authenticated and John Hatfield's throw remained the best on record. Ed Crane also claimed the record.

Vaughn was recognized as one of the hardest throwers in the league, the heavy-hitting backstop. He was hit by a pitch while at bat. He stood around waiting for a doctor, then walked into the clubhouse and fell into a faint. His right arm near the elbow was fractured putting him out of the game for six weeks. Then stood up to the plate and hit a two-batter.

After his major league career he was a minor league player and manager, with controversy; in 1909 the National Commission was involved. The cause for the case happened in 1907; the facts and truth were misrepresented and misstated.

Vaughn was tricked into a situation of indiscretion involving a woman of uncertain repute by two of his players who both wanted to be manager of the team, and the club. Money for buying players got involved, and a signed contract for his services. The issue degenerated to "he dissipated his salary" and after judgment was done Vaughn applied for a rehearing.

Harry Francis "Farmer" Vaughn died of lobar pneumonia.

VISNER (VEZINA), JOSEPH PAUL Joe Visner
Born: September 29, 1859, Minneapolis, Minnesota
Died:
Height: 5'11".   Weight: 180 Lbs.   Batted: Left.   Threw: Right.
Major League Career: 4 Years, 235 Games
1889: A.A.: Brooklyn
1891: A.A.: Washington and St. Louis
1890: P.L.: Pittsburgh Burghers; OF 127

Batting Record:

Games: 127	3B: 22	Walks: 76	SL.%: .395
At Bats: 521	HRs: 3	K's: 44	S.B: 18
Hits: 138	Runs: 110	B.Avg: .265	B.R: +5
2B: 15	R.B.I: 71	O.B.A: .367	F.R: −10

He led the Players League in triples, along with teammate Jake Beckley, inferring "fast as blazes" which is denied by only 18 stolen bases, and "long ball power" which is denied by only three home runs.

The whole of Joe Visner (Vezina) as a major league player is as illogical as allegations compared to his P.L. season with the Burghers of Pittsburgh. Consider technically his benchmark 22 triples, his benchmark 76 walks, and 138 hits; why is his O.B.A. below .400, and his SL.% below .500?

He produced another P.L. benchmark with 110 runs scored; with his 71 R.B.I. that's production, but way out of balance. Why only a very average .265 batting average? Why only 15 doubles if he was capable of 22 triples? And why only a mere three home runs?

Consider culturally that major league players from Minnesota were scarcely to be found in 1890; players of Italian origin no matter birth locale were hardly to be found at all. With all else on the record, why should his time and place of demise be unknown?

What is technically certain about Visner is that his 1890 P.L. season involved more than the greater half of his very brief career, which could lead to further and more culturally complex questions about why a player with many excellent stats was all but ignored both before and after the Players League.

He was given a moment in 1885, with A.A. Baltimore. His four games and 13 at bats were neither tragedy nor comedy, his B.Avg. was a low but not awful .231, his O.B.A. was .333 by virtue of his two walks. He scored two runs then left no record until 1889.

Then he played less than a stunning season with A.A. Brooklyn, 80 games with 295 at bats; B.Avg. .258, O.B.A. .346, SL.% .447, good stats and a proper balance grounded in 36 walks, 12 doubles, 10 triples, eight HRs, 56 runs scored and 36 R.B.I.

Then add to 1889 36 K's, a +10 B.R. and -12 F.R.: not dazzling, but no real faults. On the whole he was an above-average player. He chose to go with the Brotherhood and its league for 1890, and was the subject of negative criticism and vague innuendo.

"Hard-hitting right fielder, ability to place [hit] a ball is more luck than anything else" wrote Ella Black on August 28, 1890. There had been prior commentary relevant to integrity, that of Joe Visner and the Players League.

Published reports said that Visner received $300 advance money. Folks wondered if the Brotherhood was really paying advance money to players, and if so who was providing the financing.

Commentary by Visner on February 13, 1892: "Baseball is still the national sport and probably will continue to be, instead of having the batteries do all the work let the entire teams take an equal part and that will increase the popularity of the sport, which has fallen off."

He'd played his last major league game in 1891; still his concern was about the game not money. The game creates its own integrity.

1891 had not been much of a season for Visner. He played the outfield primarily, in 18 games for A.A. Washington, then six games for the A.A. St. Louis Browns. His total of at bats reads only 95, with batting averages of .242, .301, .379.

Among 23 hits were two doubles, four triples and one HR, less than in 1890 but similarly balanced; he walked eight times, K'd 10, and scored 15 runs. R.B.I. were not kept count of by the A.A. in 1891.

In 1889 he played 53 of his 80 games as a catcher, none at all in his 127 P.L. games, and only one at catcher in 1891; a -22 career F.R. might indicate he was out of position in the outfield. He has only two F.R. marks, -10 for 1890, -12 as a catcher in 1889.

His whole record might be informative; +14 B.R. is in his favor, 29 doubles, 36 triples, 12 HRs among 240 hits calculates to 32 percent extra base hits which is exceptional. His 122 walks and 90 K's with his bit of a first year missing show nothing negative.

His. R.B.I. count is 147 with his first and last year missing, but neither would make a great difference. He scored 183 runs by those 240 hits and 122 walks. His defense was below standard, but there's nothing to indicate less than a major league player.

The compilations result in a career .260 B.Avg., which is at the all-time average line. His .363 O.B.A. over 100 points higher says he knew how to get on base, but 33 stolen bases ask why not more. His .408 SL.% seems like it should be more but isn't low.

The only true test of Joe Visner was 1890, and he did pass if not with flying colors or rave reviews. He achieved benchmarks and he led in one stat. His whole P.L. season reads above average, then he was on his way down and out of the major leagues.

Being from Minnesota might be a factor, though how is not clear; being Italian more likely was a factor, and the how is very clear. The fact of life that his age was 30 when the Players League played was moreso a factor in his untimely exit. The fact is this was a player with ability and potential who just vanished. Why?

WARD, JOHN MONTGOMERY   John (Monte) Ward
Born: March 3, 1860, Bellefonte, Pennsylvania
Died: March 4, 1925, Augusta, Georgia
Height: 5'9".   Weight: 165 Lbs.   Batted: Left.   Threw: Right.
Major League Career: 17 Years, 1,825 Games (291 as a pitcher)
1889: N.L.: New York
1891: N.L.: Brooklyn
1890: P.L.: Brooklyn Wonders; SS 128

Batting Record:

Games: 128	3B: 12	Walks: 51	SL.%: .428
At Bats: 561	HRs: 4	K's: 22	S.B: 63
Hits: 189	Runs: 134	B.Avg: .337	B.R: +18
2B: 15	R.B.I: 60	O.B.A: .394	F.R: +14

John Monte Ward was the only field manager of the Wonders, for all 133 games of their season; his won-lost record of 76 and 56, .576 win %, shows the team in second place at the end of their season.

A thousand have played longer than 17 years, a thousand have batted above .275 during their career, and four have won more than 47 games in a season. John, also known as Monte, Ward did that in 1879 but did not set a record; Al Spalding had won 47 decisions before him in 1876.

Thousands have been officially ejected from major league games; John Monte Ward is the only player to have been formally expelled from law school. He returned later to complete his assignments and win a degree. He's also the only player to lead a revolution.

That was the Brotherhood Rebellion of 1890, of course, the culmination of which was the Players League, precipitated foremost by Albert Goodwill Spalding. Both Ward and Spalding were pitchers and team owners, Spalding much longer and much more prominently.

The career of Spalding as pitcher and manager ended after the 1877 season. The career of John Monte Ward began at the start of the next season; he was a pitcher exclusively his first year, for Providence (N.L.). He won 22 and lost 13 (.629 win %), starting and completing 37 games; he pitched 334 innings and led the league with a 1.51 E.R.A.

The Grays of Providence played 62 games that year, won 33 and lost 27 (.550 win %), finishing third at eight games out of first place. In 1879 the Grays played 85 games, won 59 and lost 25 (.702), and finished first; Ward won 47 of these games, lost 19 (.712), pitched in 70, started 60 and completed 58 games.

He pitched an incomprehensible 587 innings, allowed a .272 O.B.% and benchmark 2.15 E.R.A.; he led the N.L. in wins and win %, and in strikeouts with 239 — not a phenomenal number until compared with the minuscule 36 free passes to first base he gave away.

The Grays were third in 1880, 15 games behind Chicago; Ward won 39 and lost 24 (.619), 595 I.P., .253 O.B.%, 1.74 E.R.A. Great but not good enough. His pitching slipped after that, still with the Grays in 1881, 18 and 18, 330 I.P.; in 1882 19 and 12 (.613), just 278 I.P. His E.R.A.s were 2.13 and 2.59, one not a benchmark. Only two more seasons were left of John Monte Ward as a pitcher.

He was with the New York (N.L.) Giants in 1883 and 1884; the first year resulted in 16 and 13 (.552), the last was 3 and 3, his I.P. were 277 and 61, E.R.A.s 2.70 and 3.39. An arm injury ended his term as a major league pitcher. His period stats ranks 1876–1889 are second in E.R.A. and eighth in wild pitches.

Prior to 1884 he'd not played in more than 88 games, as an outfielder when not pitching, occasionally at shortstop. He left a pitching record of 164 won and 102 lost, .617 win %; 291 games, 261 starts, 244 complete (93%); in history, his 2.10 E.R.A. ranks fourth, his .617 win % is 43rd.

In 2,462 innings he gave up 2,317 hits, allowed 253 walks, and struck out 920 (1.00:3.64). Extremely few have done better. His career O.B.% is .277, outstanding; his opponents' basic B.Avg. allowed is .253 or .254, and has been confused by one source to rank first.

He won 40+ games only once, had 20+ wins three years; one year of .700+ win %; 50+ games, 50+ starts, 50+ complete two years each; 500+ I.P. two years, 300+ four years; these data all derive from six seasons as a full-time pitcher.

Twice Ward posted E.R.A.s below 2.00, and four years below 2.50. He led his league once in wins and win %, and E.R.A. and K's, and also in shutouts once with eight in 1880. His P.R. total is a superb +138, with league highs of +30 in 1878 and +42 in 1880; his career W.A.T. is a modest +9.8.

He'd gained fame as a pitcher, but no longer able in 1885 he played only at shortstop. The recovery program for his injured right arm had been to play the outfield and throw left handed, but he was not at first as a position player nearly equal to his pitching.

In 1885, and through 1889 for the New York (N.L.) Giants he played only shortstop. The first year, in the field he played at a +2 F.R. rate. As a batter he was terrible; with averages of .226, .255, .285, 17 walks and 39 K's, there was nothing positive.

The sum of his extra base hits that worst of all seasons were eight doubles and nine triples; he scored 72 runs and had 37 R.B.I. He also instigated the founding and formation of the Brotherhood of Players union in 1885.

Ward then might have expected all the players of the N.L. and the A.A., and the minor leagues where potential replacements played to join in union; he might not have expected Cap Anson and dozens of other established stars and players to remain loyal to the status quo.

He could not have anticipated the media brutality which the N.L. hierarchy primarily would have done. There would be continuous denunciations done by men no less famous and reputable than Henry Chadwick and O.P. Caylor. The oligarchy controlled the media, and in fact Spalding had his own *Base Ball Guide*.

Members of the Brotherhood would be written of as recalcitrants, sufficiently ignorant to growl at and then bite the hand that fed them; they were called drunken knaves, and men without principles and no sense of shame.

Ward and his equally less-than-skilled brethren, could not comprehend that a favorite tactic of the elite historically has been to use intermediaries to degrade their presumed lessers by deceitful assignations of them using their own most vile and despicable traits of character.

Neither Ward nor the Brotherhood could have been prepared to play the back room and boardroom and media games in their formative stages, nor know how wisely the cartel could and would use the laws of business and the business of law to its advantage, to confuse and confound any and all efforts toward equity.

Ward had been given elementary instruction while at law school, but obviously did not understand that men of money and power do not play games when the facts of life and material wealth as they know them are challenged.

The law of baseball was not the law of nature; rather than to assure the fittest would survive the advantage would be to the richest, the quickest, and the slickest. Ward and the Brotherhood must have believed they could beat the law, or at least secure their existence as if by herding instinct, as if predators would tread lightly upon them if they were unified.

Innocence was lost while Ward the player wavered between superb and mediocre. On the playing fields now he would be one player, no longer the feature attraction. He'd developed some skills at the bat and fielding his position; composure was recovered and confidence restored when he began the 1886 season.

Albeit unknowing, preparations to confront the redolent smell of money the owners were allegedly hoarding at players expense may have been a distraction; his personal situation was at least as much so, whether he was aware or not.

Ward was married to a celebrity actress, but theirs was not a relationship filled with bliss. He was famous as a baseball player in America; she had won fame on both sides of the Atlantic, and was intent to keep it.

If either was to submit and be subordinate it would be him, not her, had decided Mrs. John Monte Ward; which was the greater of his extraordinary difficulties is debatable, but both took a toll.

He must have realized that soon he would have to confront Spalding head to head, and mind against mind, to resolve as it would come to pass the most egregious issues in the history of off-the-field baseball.

Spalding had all the advantages, including vested authority. He only had to keep his mind focused on baseball business, about which at the time he had more skill and knowledge than any other owner or executive, surely more than an upstart player-lawyer.

Ward was still young, mid-20s, lacking experience in business, in law, in leadership, in matrimony, at playing the position of shortstop at the major league level, and batting commensurately.

He'd been kicked out of law school because of a prank involving stealing chickens. In many and various ways he was lacking the maturity to cope appropriately and successfully with the variety of roles and responsibilities he'd assumed.

At the time he might still have entertained the frivolous presumption that ultimately moral right would prevail over material power, that merely organizing the Brotherhood and doing a bit here and there of posturing and gesturing would remedy the most flagrant abuses of the reserve clause.

Nor could Ward been fully aware of the politics of baseball then, as was his primary adversary, Spalding. An established owner and executive and master propagandist, Spalding knew the rules of the boardrooms and the back rooms. He'd been there when the rules were made, and was a force in their making.

Again, all Ward's games were played at shortstop in 1886, he would count -12 F.R. but was better at the bat with averages of .273, .300, .340; 82 runs scored and 81 R.B.I., 19 walks but 46 K's. He could not get together all facets of his game on or off the field. There was still much to be learned, and he did.

Discipline at the bat, mastery in the field, and unprecedented speed were discovered in 1887. The year of the odd batting rules he was credited with 111 stolen bases; his +27 F.R. was outstanding and his B.Avg. was .338.

Extra base counts were still minimal and never would reach epic sums with 16 doubles, five triples, and one home run; he scored 114 runs, had 53 R.B.I. Walks were 29 and K's wee 12, in 545 at bats (2.2%) helping him to a .371 O.B.A.; his .391 SL.% was comparably meager.

Stars bat .300 but don't hit merely one home run in a season, and Ward had to be a star to retain his professional status, as mediocre men don't lead revolutionary movements; his lack of power at the bat might not suffice in the limelight.

He'd become a flash on the base paths, and flashy in the field. Off the field some concessions were either won or assiduously granted. Just better could not have been good enough for a player fixed with great aspirations; he would press and fall again in 1888.

He'd proven his mettle and now he proved himself an enigma: -1 F.R. in the field, 38 stolen bases, nine walks and 13 K's, 510 at bats in 1888; 14, 5, and 2 were his extra base numbers, 70 runs and 49 R.B.I. His batting averages read .251, .265, and .310.

Then again Ward recovered, in 1889: .299, .339, .349, the latter via 13 doubles, four triples, one home run, with 62 S.B. and +3 F.R. He had 27 walks and seven K's in 479 at bats; seven of 114 games were played at second base and all others at shortstop.

When the season was done playing became secondary and longstanding issues reached the tinder box point of incendiary. The clan of club owners at imperium had given no serious thought to the possibility of conciliation; on the other side stood the Brotherhood of 100.

All proposals toward compromise were pushed off the negotiating table, then the symbolic table itself was overturned and cast aside. The doors of reason were shut tight and all light was blocked out as the year 1890 approached.

The sides were set, the men of Spalding against the men of Ward, and the owners' attitude was firm. The Brotherhood would not delay, for to delay would make no sense; there were historical precedents, and when it is time for war blood will run. In this war it ran green.

Two terms of the basic Latin idiom suffice to explain the owners' singular minds: "Ad Valorem" declaring the Brotherhood was not worthy to exist, and "A Priori" declaring the Players League would be doomed in advance.

Ward made known his decision, given with full consent of the Brotherhood. The playing fields would be transformed to battlefields, the box offices to parapets. Where in Providence or in Satan's domain could he have envisioned being away five months?

The two sides were like ships which could no longer pass quietly in the night. The situation had become corollary to the fact of the land. The very foundation of the American social contract was at risk and the players might not lose but could not be allowed to win.

This situation perceived by Ward globally established the National League as the enemy. The American Association took a side but was ambivalent; those owners might mix loyalties and commit to either side, or to both.

Locally Ward and his celebrity wife had circumscribed their marital dilemma clearly; the wife was expensive and the first evidence of trouble had appeared within 15 months of their union.

She returned to the stage that fall of 1889, in spite of Mr. Ward's protests. The whole on-off affair was like a tiresome joke. She left him on April 19, 1890. She made her choice of sides.

Ward was educated but not erudite. He knew law, but he knew nothing at all. His weaponry consisted of wits and will, both of uncertain quantities. The forces of Spalding included surveillance and spies, of vital utility before, during and after the Players League war. Many were accused, none ever convicted.

When the baseball season of 1890 arrived he'd place his stakes both ways; he would play shortstop on the field, as manager of the Brooklyn Wonders at his own discretion. He was a part owner of the franchise and also part owner of the P.L. Giants.

After the season, divorce, demise and all, he bought a $35,000 home in Brooklyn — the sum of three years' salary and income while he made claims of losing money in his Players League bold business ventures.

As P.L. Brooklyn's manager he was a success, if second best among eight was success for him. On the field he was outstanding, with a +14 F.R. as indication. He stole 63 bases during the season and he made the second-highest total of hits in the league.

Only three players scored more runs, his stolen bases rank fifth in the P.L., and he ranks third in Total Player Ranking. His 51 walks and 22 K's show he'd learned something; beyond his play and his various duties, he was the catalyst of the Brooklyn Wonders team.

Ward represents all the answers to all the questions of how and why his team was able to beat out the neighboring Giants in the final standings, and six other Brotherhood teams.

A critic with sympathy would acclaim that Ward gave his heart and his soul to the Brooklyn Wonders and the Players League, and his money and his all; some numbers would provide for a fair analysis.

	Ward 1890	Best / Next
B.Avg:	.337	.338 (1887)
O.B.A:	.394	.379 (1893)
SL.%:	.428	.415 (1893)
Runs:	134	114 (1887)
Hits:	189	193 (1893)
At Bats:	561	614 (1892)

It becomes a moot point to say that Ward merits status as a Players League star player, and a Players League feature player; his 1890 baseball season stats as a batter are at the epicenter of a seven-year span which has no precedent or equal.

He continued as a player through 1894, with N.L. Brooklyn the next two years, with the New York Giants the latter two years. He led the N.L. in stolen bases with 88 in 1892, and played more than 500 games during this phase of his career. Each year he was the field manager of his team.

During his career he established a total of +93 F.R., as great at defense as he was in the pitcher's box, the batter's box, and on the basepaths. He was as durable a player as ever there's been, his ranks in period stats 1876–1889 reveal: sixth in games, fifth in at bats, 10th in runs scored.

Among his career numbers as a batter are 1,825 games, 7,647 at bats, and further of his record: .300+ B.Avg three years; .400+ O.B.A. zero years; .500+ SL.% zero years; 100+ Runs five years; 100+ R.B.I. zero years; 100+ Walks zero years, 50+ two years; 100+ S.B two years, 50+ five years.

Where he was great he was great, where he was lacking he was lacking. To complete his career chart: 231 doubles, 96 triples, 26 HRs. among 2,105 hits, 1,408 runs scored, 867 R.B.I., 420 walks and 326 K's, 540 stolen bases with eight years' data missing. His 540 in nine years known would rank first in 1876–1889 and second in 1890–1899.

After the P.L. his on-the-field emphases were getting hits, drawing walks, and driving in runs. Despite the revised priority and the years missing he ranks 27th all time in stolen bases. His +93 F.R. is high, including +14 in 1890, and his 105 errors made in 1890 rank fifth highest all time at the shortstop position in a season.

Ward was an N.L. umpire in 1888, very odd all things considered. As a manager for seven years he compiled a record of 412 won and 320 lost (.563 Win %); his best finish was second, twice.

He's alleged in many texts to have pitched the second perfect game in history, but Ward was never perfect. After his divorce from his celebrity actress wife, or vice versa, he had more than a few interludes, and once almost got shot when he wasn't involved.

He married again, a plain, homely woman, and they lived comfortably. No lawyer has lacked for money; he indulged a while with a firm, then established his own business practice and did very well indeed. Among his clientele occasionally were baseball players.

At least once he represented a club and a league in court. His agenda was done at leisure in his sumptuous Broadway Avenue offices; the comforts and amenities allowed lawyers in the courts enabled a good deal of regular relaxation.

He also learned to enjoy casual recreation. He took up golf as a game and became very adept, a tournament class player. He and new wife were solicited for membership in the tonier clubs. He and his wife of subordinate propriety enjoyed many pleasant days and evenings.

They toured while he played at the finest clubs in the nation. Lawyer Ward also dabbled in real estate, with greater material consequences than with baseball clubs. He was nominated for the office of National League president after William Pulliam shot himself on July 23, 1909, but wasn't elected.

He was among a group of New York City investors who bought the Boston N.L. franchise in late 1911, and was president of the club till he quit in August 1912, frustrated and disgusted with his partners and with the leagues.

Ward came from proper middle class family in rural Pennsylvania and achieved an adolescent goal of making it in New York City; he did that, and in Brooklyn in 1890 with the Players League he personally inspired.

His life was a mix of failure and success, much more of one that the other. Allegedly late in 1890 or soon after Spalding told him in the back room of a common saloon that without him the P.L. could not have existed.

A plaque bearing his name scribed in bronze has been in place at the National Baseball Hall of Fame since 1964; he would have had it done in gold or gold leaf at the very least. His place has been assigned in center field, not shortstop or pitcher.

He is not cited as executive nor manager. The inscription is a few words longer than most; he's noted as both a star pitcher and star shortstop with acclaim as having pitched a perfect game. Myth continues: a no-hitter is not a perfect game.

The closure of his distinct Cooperstown euology is given verbatim: "A staunch opponent of the reserve clause, Ward organized the Players' Brotherhood and later formed the short-lived Players' League." Edison and Ford and the Wright brothers, endured their failure at about the same time as did Ward.

Righteous innovation and confident endurance were then essential elements of the real American game. With all due modesty he was a Players League star player and a Players League feature player, almost a legitimately complete baseball player.

John Montgomery Ward and his good wife chose to winter at Augusta, Georgia, said to be the finest of all golfing places. He went on a hunting trip and caught a cold which turned into pneumonia; he died in a hospital near where he'd learned he wanted to be.

WEYHING, AUGUST   Gus Weyhing
Born: September 29, 1866, Louisville, Kentucky
Died: September 3, 1955, Louisville, Kentucky
Height: 5'10".   Weight: 145 Lbs.   Batted: Right.   Threw: Right.
Major league Career: 14 Years, 538 Games
1889: A.A.: Philadelphia
1891: A.A.: Philadelphia
1890: P.L.: Brooklyn Wonders; P 49

Batting Record:

Games: 49	3B: 3	Walks: 16	SL.%: .230
At Bats: 165	HRs: 1	K's: 44	S.B: 2
Hits: 27	Runs: 21	B.Avg: .164	B.R:
2B: 2	R.B.I: 15	O.B.A:	F.R:

Pitching Record:

Won: 30	Starts: 46	K's: 177	E.R.A: 3.60
Lost: 16	C.G: 38	Walks: 179	Saves: 0
Win %: .652	I.P: 390	Hits: 419	P.R: +27
Games: 49	Sh.O: 3	O.B.%: .364	W.A.T: +5.8

He might have been great and certainly was exciting. Louisville produced some fine original baseball products during the latter 1800s. This was one of their best, although wildness in the pitcher's box was a constant nemesis to his career.

Between 1887 and 1901 Gus Weyhing had seven 20+ win seasons, and seven 20+ loss seasons; during his career he won 264 games and lost 232 (.532 Win %). Only 32 pitchers in major league history have won more, and only 16 have lost more.

He's tied at 36th for the most starts, 503 of the 538 games he pitched in. His 448 complete games ranks 11th all time. In 4,324 (29th) innings Weyhing struck out 1,665 (94th) opposing batters, and walked 1,566 (ninth). All in all wildness prevailed.

His 4,562 hits permitted ranks 17th in history among all major league pitchers. His 32 wins in 1892 are among the top 100 single season records, as are his 28 losses in 1887; 470 innings pitched in 1892 is 100th.

His 130 wild pitches in 14 years ranks 33rd all time. His 109 hit batters ranks 30th. He has the distinction, as batter, of ranking sixth in K's during the period 1890–1899.

The 179 walks given up by Weyhing in 1890 have been exceeded only 43 times, his 167 walks in 1887 ranks 63rd, and 161 in 1891 also is among the top 100. Two hundred nineteen K's as a pitcher in 1891 were his high but don't make the list of 100, nor does his lowest 2.25 E.R.A. of 1888.

Weyhing began as a major league pitcher with Philadelphia (A.A.) in 1887, where he returned after the P.L. season; he'd continued with the Athletics in 1888 and 1889. After the A.A. went out of business he went to N.L. Philadelphia through 1894 and into 1895.

He was with Louisville all of 1896, didn't pitch in the N.L. in 1897, with Washington in 1898 and 1899, then 1900 and 1901 drifted among four teams to collect 13 decisions, none in two games with the A.L. Cleveland Blues in 1901.

He was a genuine major league workhorse in five of his first six years with 400+ innings in each, missing that mark by 10 in 1890. He was also a big winner and loser; in 1887 he won 26 and lost 28 (.481 Win %), with 53 complete games in 55 starts, a 4.27 E.R.A. and .338 O.B.%, 193 K's and 167 walks.

1888 was a winning season for Weyhing, 28 and 18 (.609) 45 C.G. in 47 starts, a 2.25 E.R.A. was his benchmark best, .283 O.B.%, 204 K's and a commendable 111 walks.

1889 was the first of three consecutive 30+ win seasons, 30 and 21 (.588), 50 complete in 53 starts, 2.95 E.R.A. and .338 O.B.%, 213 K's and 211 walks (212 by one source ranks 12th all time).

In 1890 he was with the Brooklyn Wonders of the Players League, of course. His batting was no help at all, but his pitching was and these are the P.L. ranks of Guy Weyhing: second in wins (tied), fifth in Win %, third in games, fifth in complete games, third in innings pitched, second in shutouts (tied), third in K's, fifth in P.R., second in W.A.T.

He was their only big winner; without his success the Wonders would have been sure second division, unless another pitcher had been secured and come to the fore as Weyhing did. It was in the Players League that he established his real worth. Consider:

	Weyhing	Wonders	League
O.B.%:	.364	.348	.345
E.R.A.	3.60	3.95	4.23

Where he was lacking the lag was negligible. To allow almost 600 base runners during a season and come out of it with numbers like these reveals a pitcher who can, for any lesser this alone would have been a portent of disaster.

Further consider an estimate of his worth to the Wonders by means of his SABR-stats; by one factor he won three games which could have been lost, by another he produced nearly six wins beyond average, with average meaning .500 of course; apply these to the league:

Team	Win%	G.B.
Boston	.628	—
Brooklyn	.576	6.5
New York	.565	8.0
Chicago	.547	10.0
Philadelphia	.519	14.0

His record and contribution to his team are sufficiently meritorious, and good enough to earn for Weyhing the call of a Players League star player.

He won 31 in 1891, and 32 in 1892, concurrent with 20 and 21 losses, win %'s of .608 and .604; his K's and walks the first of these years were 219 and 161, the second 202 and 168. He had 51 and 49 starts, 51 and 46 complete games.

His. I.P. counts these two years were 450 and 470, E.R.A.s of 3.18 and 2.66, and O.B.%'s of .331 and .316. In these two seasons, as well as the Players League year, Weyhing wasn't lacking.

He was a winner again in 1893, but on the inevitable decline; won 23 and lost 16 (.590), 345 I.P., 40 starts with 33 complete, an ominous ratio of 101 K's and 145 walks, and moreso a bloated to exploded 4.75 E.R.A.

He won again in 1894, though minimally, 16 and 14 (.533), 25 C.G. in a modest 34 starts, only 266 innings, 81 K's and 116 walks; bloated exploded to a 5.82 E.R.A., O.B.% went up to .415. There isn't any need to look for omens or portents, he was worn out.

1895 told the tale, split among three teams. He lost two then was cast out by the Phillies after three fine seasons, won one for the Pirates then was dismissed, and completed the sum of his won 8 lost 21 (.276) with Louisville. His O.B.% hovered near .400 and his E.R.A. a losing 5.81.

With the hometown team again the next year he won 2 and lost 3. He missed all of 1897, then went to Washington for two years, 15–26 (.366) and 17–21 (.447), with E.R.A.s of 4.51 and 4.54; his I.P. were still annually well into the 400+ range.

With St. Louis then Brooklyn in 1900 he posted 3 wins and 2 losses. He began the new century in the new league. Two games, 11 innings, and an 8.18 E.R.A. later he was given a free pass back to the N.L.; he concluded 1 and 1 with Cincinnati, and he was done.

The raw count data are substantial, and add to these a career O.B.% of .351, E.R.A. 3.89, +40 P.R., a significant +23.0 W.A.T., 50+ games four years, 50+ starts and complete games three years, and five years of 400+ I.P. among nine years of 300+ I.P.

His career wins and losses count nearly 500 decisions. His 448 C.G. ranks 11th all time. His 130 wild pitches ranks 33rd. By the end of the 1901 season Weyhing had been pitching major league baseball for 14 years in four leagues.

He won more than most, and lost more than most, set a few records and beat a few benchmarks; these are among his period stats for 1890–1899: fifth in wins, second in losses, fourth in games, fourth in starts, fourth in C.G., fourth in I.P., sixth in K's, fifth in walks, fourth in shutouts, seventh in hit batters (tied), eighth in wild pitches.

He alone might have been worth the cost of an admission ticket, for he certainly made things happen on the field. In 1890 he was a big winner and a Players League star player. Put another like him on the Brooklyn staff, and the P.L. gonfalon might have gone to Brooklyn, the greater prize since there was only one.

Not much is known about Gus Weyhing after his baseball career, other than he was a night watchman for a local water company at age 86.

WHITE, JAMES LAURIE   Deacon White
Born: December 7, 1847, Caton, New York
Died: July 7, 1939, Aurora, Illinois
Height: 5'11".   Weight: 175 Lbs.   Batted: Left.   Threw: Right.

Major League Career: 20 Years, 1,558 Games (2 as a pitcher)
1889: N.L.: Pittsburgh
1891: Did not play
1890: P.L.: Buffalo Bisons; 3B 64, 1B 57, SS 1, P 1

Batting Record:

Games: 122	3B: 4	Walks: 67	SL.%: .308
At Bats: 439	HRs: 0	K's: 30	S.B: 3
Hits: 114	Runs: 62	B.Avg: .260	B.R: -4
2B: 13	R.B.I: 47	O.B.A: .381	F.R: +18

Pitching Record:

Won: 0	Starts: 0	K's: 0	E.R.A: 9.00
Lost: 0	C.G: 0	Walks: 2	Saves: 0
Win %: —	I.P: 8	Hits: 18	P.R: -4
Games: 1	Sh.O: 0	O.B.%: .483	W.A.T: 0.0

The most admired star of the 1870s was a Players League feature player in 1890. He was a gentleman always, and in terms of professional and personal integrity he had few peers through the latter third of the 19th century.

He began before there were any professional baseball leagues, then on May 4, 1871, was listed at the position of catcher for the Forest City club of Cleveland. Their opponents were the Kekiongas of Fort Wayne. It was the first game of the first major league season, played in the National Association.

Deacon White was the first batter to face Bobby Mathews. His first pitch was called a ball, then White hit a double, the first hit in major league history. Twenty seasons later he was a utility player in 122 games for the P.L. Bisons, and part owner of their Players League franchise.

In the interim he was assigned the status of a celestial white dwarf, which is a great force but is seldom seen and the entirety of his record radiates excellence. According to Henry Chadwick, writing of him in 1890, "The integrity of his character is preeminent."

James Laurie "Deacon" White died with the distress of not being among the first waves of 1800s greats chosen for perpetual honor at Cooperstown. Shamefully he was not even invited to be a guest at the inaugural induction event on June 12, 1939.

Chadwick also wrote "He had great skills." There have been more than a few blunders of oversight by the various hall of fame committees during the decades, but this stands as one of their very worst. He'd been age 23 when he made that first of all hits; by 1890 he was a senior elder, given by all then his due respect.

This senior elder, Deacon White, played well enough in 1890 at third base and first base to rank fourth in the league in fielding runs. These are among his ranks in period stats for 1876–1889, keeping in mind the lesser numbers of games played during his first decade, and that the records are lacking much lost data: fifth in games, sixth in at bats, fifth in hits, eighth in B.Avg., fourth in R.B.I., ninth in total bases.

The Forest Cities Club of Cleveland began playing baseball in antiquity. Few records were kept then; all they tell of White in his first year is 23 games played and

73 runs scored. That was in 1868; his line for 1869 is blank except that his positions were catcher and pitcher.

In 1870, in 36 games, his position again is shown as catcher; he made 108 hits, which accounted for 184 bases. No more is known.

There's an item of inconsistency in his very limited National Association record. He changed teams for the 1873 season from Cleveland to Boston. His primary position throughout the five years of N.A. play was catcher. There was no inconsistency in his batting, an average of .300+ each and every year.

That was a players league in title, the National Association of Base Ball Players, proven so by their multitude of administrative disorders. White was one of the few to transcend the brief time frame when players first presumed to be league executives.

While playing in the N.A., White often moved to an outfield or infield position. He was field manager of the Cleveland club the last two games of the 1872 season and lost them both. The team fell from fifth to seventh place.

The Forest Cities played 20+ games in all that season, won 6 and lost 15 (or 16), then dropped out of the association. N.A. teams that played through their 1872 schedule totaled games in the 40s and 50s. Boston, for example, played 48, won 39 and lost 8; they were the league champions.

The year before, the first year of N.A. play, the Athletics of Philadelphia were the league champions, winning 21 (or 22) and losing 7; the Bostons were the champions in 1873, 1874, and 1875, playing schedules of 60, then 71, then 82 games.

The first players league illusion was lost when men of money overwhelmed the players and took the game as their own. In 1876 they founded the National League, the same which continues to exist today.

White was there in 1876. He'd jumped to the Chicago club of Hulbert and Spalding and continued as a stellar and superb player. While in the N.A. he played in 259 games, had 1,316 at bats, made 456 hits, scored 287 runs, and his B.Avg. was .347.

His first year in the N.L., the first year of the N.L., the new league kept records of the various extra base hits, of K's and walks, such that O.B.A. and SL.% could be calculated; R.B.I. became part of the record.

White was the first league leader in this stat, R.B.I., with 60 R.B.I. in 66 games. He had 303 at bats in 1876, hit 18 doubles, a triple, and a home run, walked seven times and was K'd three. He scored 66 runs in that equal number of games.

His K's as a percentage of at bats is the easiest not-in-the-record stat to calculate; three of 303 would have been the first such outstanding stat. He also pitched in a game in 1876, two innings, which shows the long line of 0's the opponents achieved.

It's doubtful there was a term "career year" then, but in 1877 White had one; he led the N.L. in B.Avg. with .387, SL.% with .545, in hits with 103, triples with 11, R.B.I. with 49, and would have led in B.R. with +28 if that stat had existed then.

Further on his career year he played in 59 games, had 266 at bats, scored 51 runs, hit 14 doubles and two HRs. His walks were eight and K's three, and his O.B.A. counts another benchmark with .405.

He jumped back to Boston for 1877, then to Cincinnati for 1878 through 1880, was manager for 18 games in 1879, won 9 and lost 9, then turned over the position to former Boston teammate and star Cal McVey; he didn't manage again during his long career, and was moving away from the C position.

White tried his skill as an N.L. umpire in 1880; there was no more of that either. With all decisions left for others his position became "play me where you most need me," which his managers did with confidence and pleasure.

He played every position, less at 2B and SS than others, with efficiency but not always well, as attests his -59 career F.R. As a 3B he ranks ninth all time in errors with 444; his worst in the field now rates -15 F.R. in 1882 and -13 F.R. in 1883.

A couple of cautions for the reader not too familiar with this era; the careers of Deacon White and Cal McVey often crossed and can easily be intermixed. Both were great; also, Will White, brother of James Laurie, was a major league pitcher between 1877 and 1886 and was one of the best (won 229, lost 166, 2.28 E.R.A.).

As a batter while with Cincinnati, Deacon White posted B.Avg.s of .314, .330, .298, and his at bats were 258, 333, 141, in 61, 78, and 35 games. His O.B.A.s are .340, .342, .340, with SL.% marks of .337, .423, and .355. Nearly all these numbers were below his prior levels.

His total extra base hits these three years—24 doubles, nine triples, one home run—represent precipitous drops for White. In the 174 games he played for Cincinnati he scored 117 runs, and in two years of production with Boston or Chicago, his R.B.I. total was just 88.

One percent K's to at bats increased to 3 percent these three years. The raw numbers of 21 K's and 25 walks tell he had no interest in walking to first base. His stolen base counts can't be included for these three years or previously; there are no N.A. records and the N.L. didn't keep stolen base records until 1886.

His best years were past, but his prime had extended through nearly a decade. White went to Buffalo (N.L.) for 1881, was there through 1885 then, depending on perception, became part of the biggest baseball purchase or exodus of the 1800s.

His position while with N.L. Buffalo was mainly third base. His sum fielding rate for the five years is -42 F.R., including his two worst seasons and a +1 F.R. His batting was steady, if no longer spectacular, with B.Avg.s between .282 and .325, O.B.A. within bounds of .313 and .370, and SL.% in the .341 to .442 range.

One hundred ten games were his most played, with 452 at bats in 1884. His best of the five Buffalo N.L. years was 1884, with highs in all the batting averages; in 1884 he scored 82 runs and drove in 74, he walked 32 times and K's 13 (2.9 percent), he hit 16 doubles, 11 triples, and five HRs. He never was a batter with power.

Then he was off to Detroit to work for owner Frederick Stearns, who bought the whole Buffalo club to obtain him and three others; the bottom line cost for the purchase has been reported at $7,000. He didn't get the Deacon White of his early years, but did get his money's worth.

White played for Detroit for three years, 1886 through 1888. The middle year was the best for him and for the team; in 1887 they led the N.L. in all the batting averages, in runs scored, in hits, doubles and triples.

White didn't lead in any stats. He played 3B at a -6 F.R. rate, batted .303 with a .353 O.B.A. and .416 SL.%. He walked 26 times and struck out 15, had 71 runs scored and 75 R.B.I. in 111 games. In 449 at bats he hit 20 doubles, 11 triples, three HRs, and stole 20 bases.

White and the Detroit Wolverines of 1887 won the right to meet the St. Louis Browns in the (by then) annual N.L. vs. A.A. World's Series. There hasn't been any other at all like it; Detroit won eventually, 10 games to 5, during the span from October 10 through October 26, and played in 10 different cities.

During this most protracted of all post-season contests, White played in all the games, 14 at 3B and one at 1B. His work was not distinguished; with a .207 B.Avg., 12 hits and two walks were good for eight runs scored and three driven in.

He labored through 1888, -11 F.R. in the field, stealing 12 bases in 125 games, making 157 hits in 527 at bats, with 22 doubles, five triples, and four HRs; his runs were 75 and R.B.I. 71, and his K's exceeded walks by 24 to 21.

Executive schemes put him on the Pittsburgh N.L. roster for 1889. He and a teammate had bought a minor league club for Buffalo in the off-season; they were intent upon being active within it, as owners, management, and as players.

White surrendered to coercion though, and played 55 games for the Pittsburgh N.L. club; in 252 at bats he made 57 hits, 10 for doubles, one for a triple, gained first base free 16 times, wasted 18 opportunities at the bat, scored 35 runs and drove home 26. His batting averages for 1889 stand at .253, .314, and .307, and he stole two bases.

The career lines in the record books show White played at every position. His games total including the N.A., though still not official, is 1,558; his at bats total 6,651, hits 2,075, runs 1,136, and R.B.I. 756 in 15 seasons. Also in 15 of his 20 seasons are 292 walks and 215 K's, 217 doubles, 73 triples, and 18 home runs.

In five years he had 46 stolen bases, for 15 years a -59 F.R., +147 B.R.; his O.B.A. for 15 years is .344, and SL.% .382. The whole of his batting average is .312 which, when deemed official, will rank 80th among about 16,000.

With appropriate adjustments for limited possibilities in at bats his B.Avg. was .300+ each of 12 years and O.B.A. .400+ one year. His best after the N.A. was 1877. The same holds true for SL.%, .500+ one year. He never scored 100+ runs or tallied 100+ R.B.I.; most were 77 runs in 1875, and 76 R.B.I. in 1886.

His high count of K's was 35 in 1886, his most walks were 67 in 1890; as mentioned, he led his league two years in R.B.I., one year in B.Avg., one year in SL.%, and also one year in hits and triples, and B.R.

1890 was the last among 20 years as a major league player. His season with the P.L. Bisons judged by +18 F.R. was by far his best in any year at any position. SABR-stats show him batting slightly below average.

Deacon White of the Players League was nearly void of base path speed, as nearly every year with minimal batting power; walking became the strong point of his offense. The sum of the P.L. year cited by one statistical measure is 114 + 67 = 62 + 47 is exceptional for an awful baseball team.

He wasn't the field manager, but a part-owner has to be fairly considered accountable for one of the worst records in history: won 36, lost 96, .273 Win %; to finish 46.5 games out of first place, 20 games out of next-to-last place, has been achieved by other teams, but not many nor often.

The sum of Deacon White in 1890 is that he was still adequate to the demands of the game on the field; this gentleman of highest integrity was the paradigm for his nickname of "Deacon." He was an active tribute to the cause of the Brotherhood of Players, and he is a Players League feature player.

SABR has produced the fairest epilogue: "Though overlooked by Cooperstown, he was not forgotten in his adopted home Buffalo. In 1986 he was inducted into the Buffalo Baseball Hall of Fame."

In 1891 White was fired as the manager of a neighboring minor league team and quit completely as a player. He worked for his brother for a while as an optical assistant, a lens grinder, which requires great vision and hands. He opened his own livery stable, then lived with his daughter in Illinois after 1910.

In a tribute game for Christy Mathewson, probably soon after 1920 Deacon White took up the burden in the sixth inning, pitching remarkable ball for two innings and allowing no hits or scores by the sponsors, the Ilion (N.Y.) Sunset League Young Stars. The calculation of his age then is as remarkable.

Deacon White was invited to the unveiling of the memorial to Cap Anson in Chicago in 1923 and apparently was there, all expenses paid by the National League.

He was past time and out of step soon after the Players League played. The livery stable has become an obsolete and forgotten bit of Americana and American history. James Laurie "Deacon" White is a Players League feature player, and he's still fairly well remembered somewhere.

WHITNEY, ARTHUR WILSON   **Art Whitney**
Born: January 16, 1858, Brocton, Massachusetts
Died: August 15, 1943, Lowell, Massachusetts
Height: 5'8".   Weight: 155 Lbs.   Batted: Right.   Threw: Right.
Major League Career: 11 Years, 978 Games
1889: N.L.: New York
1891: A.A.: Cincinnati and St. Louis
1890: P.L.: New York Giants; 3B 88, SS 31

Batting Record:

Games: 119	3B: 3	Walks: 64	SL.%: .260
At Bats: 442	HRs: 0	K's: 19	S.B: 8
Hits: 97	Runs: 71	B.Avg: .219	B.R: -24
2B: 12	R.B.I: 45	O.B.A: .322	F.R: -5

He was an adept fielder who also played shortstop, but he was never particularly strong at bat. Caution is advised in any further inquiry about this Whitney, for there are two others of the 1800s. One was born in Brocton a couple of years earlier than the Players League Whitney; he played only part of one season, 1876, was known as "Jumbo," probably because of his size, 5'7" and 152 pounds.

The other, Jim Whitney, was born just two months before the P.L. Whitney. He was primarily a pitcher, a very good pitcher; he wasn't part of the P.L. contingent, but his career and that of Art Whitney correspond almost exactly.

Art Whitney was a Players League player and on the whole was inferior to his pitching counterpart by all statistical measures. Art Whitney had no power or speed, and was below the norm for fielding his position, which over the course of his career was mainly third base.

Judgment regarding his fielding is due for the most part to a -13 F.R. in 1885. He was then the shortstop for the Pittsburgh (A.A.) Alleghenys, in his second of three years with that club. His position the years before and after was 3B; his F.R. were 0 and +9.

His basic B.Avg.s for the Alleghenys were .298, .233, and .239. He stole 15 bases in 1886, the first year the A.A. kept such counts. He began in the major leagues in 1880 with Worcester (N.L.), was elsewhere all of 1883, ended when the A.A. did, in 1891 with 93 games for the Cincinnati/Milwaukee combine, then three games for the St. Louis Browns.

At bats his last year were 358 of a career total 3,681. His B.Avg. was .193, but he hit a career high of three home runs of his total of six. Among his other career data are 32 triples and 89 doubles; his triples high was five in 1880 and in 1881 for Detroit (N.L.), and he hit 13 doubles in 1880 and again in 1886.

Whitney drew 302 walks in his 978 games, was K'd 173 times, with three years' data missing still indicative of a good batting eye, strike zone judgment, and discipline at the bat; his runs scored number 475 in all, and his R.B.I. were 266 with three years' data missing.

As a batter his composite B.R. count is -40; his only plus was +1 in 1884. As a fielder he ranks 19th all time among 3B with 344 errors. Of a career sum -18 F.R. his best was +9 in 1886.

He played for Providence and Detroit (both N.L.) in 1882, with B.Avg.s of .119 and .190; his marks in all the batting averages are among the lowest to be found for any 1800s player who was at the major league level longer than briefly.

Probably not the most sought after player, he played for the Pittsburgh (N.L.) Alleghenys in 1887 and for the New York (N.L.) Giants in 1888 and 1889. 1887 was his best year at the bat: .260 B.Avg., .346 O.B.A., .304 SL.%, with 57 runs scored, 51 R.B.I., 55 walks and 18 K's in 431 at bats (4.2 percent).

He was on the roster of the New York (P.L.) Giants in 1890 and as such represents one of two holes in their regular lineup and batting order; his O.B.A. of more than .100 above his B.Avg. would be impressive if not based on a .219 B.Avg.

To his favor as a P.L. player are a benchmark 64 walks and 4.3 percent K's to at bats rate. Somebody had to be assigned to the left side positions of the Giants infield, and Whitney was there all except 13 of their games. He might well represent the dearth of top of the line and mediocres available when three major leagues played.

After his major league career at baseball on the field, he was the founder and manager of a company which manufactured and distributed sporting goods. His business was absorbed by A.G. Spalding & Bros. For many years he was a representative of the latter company.

The cause of death of Arthur W. "Art" Whitney was cardiac failure due to arteriosclerotic heart disease, complicated by the effects of chronic nephritis.

WILLIAMSON, EDWARD NAGLE   **Ned Williamson**
Born: October 24, 1857, Philadelphia, Pennsylvania
Died: March 3, 1894, Mountain Valley Springs, Arkansas

Height: 5'11". Weight: 170 Lbs. Batted: Right. Threw: Right.
Major League Career: 13 Years, 1,201 Games
1889: N.L.: Chicago
1891: Did not play
1890: P.L.: Chicago Pirates; 3B 52, SS 21

Batting Record:

Games: 73	3B: 3	Walks: 36	SL.%: .268
At Bats: 261	HRs: 2	K's: 35	S.B: 3
Hits: 51	Runs: 34	B.Avg: .195	B.R: -15
2B: 7	R.B.I: 26	O.B.A: .311	F.R: -13

To tell first that his father was a manufacturer of awnings seems like a safe place to begin, after which sentiment in literature literally overwhelms. Truth be told, there is little as a major league player which compares with his multitude of accolades.

One source tells that Ned Williamson was also a great boxer; to name source names there was Cap Anson, and Charlie Comiskey, and A.G. Spalding. Only one, James Hart, president of the Chicago club in the mid-1890s, mentioned anything questionable of him.

What did he mean by referring to Williamson as a "generous-hearted fellow, everybody's friend but his own." Also is written, "he liked the good things in life and was socially inclined." Anson was his field manager every year of his career except the first and last, and it's well known that he had no tolerance for nonsense or maladaptive behavior by his players.

Clearly in the affirmative for Williamson the person was that he was level-headed, bright, good-hearted, quiet and gentlemanly, as well as reliable, hard-working, honest, square-dealing, good-natured, well read, observant, articulate, kind-hearted, and very popular with both players and fans.

As a player, no less is said of Williamson. He was called the greatest all-around player and the greatest thrower. He was a magnificent ballplayer with an excellent batting and fielding record and a sure catch. He excelled in all-around play.

Many players and writers of his time are said to have regarded him as the best in the game at third base or at shortstop. He was famous for his strong, accurate throws. He was a speedy runner and an excellent slider. There's more.

He was a good batter, waiting for the right balls to hit. His hitting was hard and heavy although he did not hit for high average. Also, he led his league four years in fielding. His career extended from 1878 through 1890, when he established these ranks in period stats 1876–1889: ninth in games, second in walks, fourth in K's, seventh in HRs, eighth in R.B.I. (tied), ninth in extra base hits.

All was not peaches and cream for Williamson, although the choice of words might entail oxymoron. In the last four years of life his formerly well-constructed physique ballooned to enormous proportions. These years were spent as a co-partner saloon operator in Chicago with 1870s star player Jimmy Wood.

Williamson had been a prominent member of the Brotherhood of Players, such that the signing of his 1888 contract drew much attention from the media. As a P.L. player, Williamson played well for the hog butcher to the world in Chicago.

The whole of his Players League record on the fields of play is exceedingly to the contrary. He did not play in 66 games. His SABR-stats of -15 B.R. and -13 F.R. when he did play give hint of the number of games he did not help win. He showed no speed, but 12 of 51 hits were for extra bases (24 percent) stands to his credit.

Still, his SL.% of .268 is half of a benchmark, his walks and K's as gains and waste offset each other, and his production is far below an adequate norm. His basic batting average is horrendous; still, this was his last year, which might tell why.

There's hardly anything at mediocre level, much less to rave on, but he wasn't a youngster when the P.L. played, and if his weight gain was caused by maladies unknown to medical science then, he may already have been afflicted in 1890.

But still, of Williamson there is too much contradiction in print, and too much uncertainty beyond written words. The facts of his life may have been grounded in intelligence, he may have been perceived as a great baseball player, but Anson, Comiskey, Spalding, et al. may have missed the fact that Williamson lived life in the fast lane as it was then, and he crashed.

For example, he met his wife, said to have been a lovely young lady of propriety, in New Orleans, during spring training with the Chicagos of Cap Anson. She was there with her mother and stayed at the same hotel as Williamson by coincidence.

Mother and daughter were vacationing, as ladies of elite families did then. Mother warned daughter to have nothing to do with those baseball players, but nature had other intentions and plans.

A teammate of Williamson's was there with his wife, one among those that chose to be together that time of year in New Orleans. This one befriended the elite young high society lady, which in part precipitated her inquisitive sense about those players.

By chance she had an interest in baseball, or the players, which all in all enabled her to attend a game unknown to prude mother; the pretty young thing saw Williamson hit the game-winning home run and she tossed him a bouquet of flowers, which was customary and proper then.

He didn't know at the moment he'd hit the home run of his life. Their story could have been the basis of a Victorian romance novel, perhaps even a bit risque. The wife of the teammate introduced them during dinner. Mother was plussed but dignity prevailed.

They were married, circa 1882, and lived happily, but happily ever after didn't happen.

As a member of the White Stockings during the world tour of Al Spalding, some of the questions about Williamson begin to find answers. He was injured in Paris, having torn up his knee when he tried to slide on the French sand and gravel playing surface.

A 1912 editorial by Sam Crane in the *New York Journal* praised Williamson as "the best third baseman of the second decade of baseball from 1880 to 1890" with the opinion based on his "all-around ability in fielding, batting, base running, and throwing," which leaves no baseball faults to be found.

To sustain such an opinion for three decades by one writer, and the litany of other accolades, speaks hall of fame for Williamson; one source says he was given serious consideration. Fact is, he was a nominee in 1936, receiving two votes from the Veterans Committee. There hasn't been another since for him.

Was he "Wonder!" or was he "Wonder?" Ed Crane was a major league pitcher and played in the Players League; his career meshes well with Ned Williamson. They never were on the same team, but nevertheless had to know each other at least as baseball players. After confronting Williamson one-on-one in the most basic baseball format, his comments were complimentary but ambivalent.

He led his league once in home runs, and in fact in 1884 established a season record which sustained till Babe Ruth hit 29 HRs in 1919; it continued as the N.L. season record till broken by Rogers Hornsby with 42 HRs in 1922.

In fact, 1884 for Williamson was a season the likes of which only a few players have ever known. In addition to 27 HRs, he led the N.L. shortstops in assists; his defense that season now calculates to a +22 F.R., but he didn't lead in anything else.

He led in doubles with a spectacular 49 in 1883 and in walks with 75 in 1885. He never led in anything else. He never reached the .300+ B.Avg. plateau; his high was .294 in 1879. His high in hits was 117, in runs 87, both in 1885. His R.B.I. high was 84, in 1884; the 117 hits came in 1887. We need say no more about that.

His career line shows a .255 B.Avg., .332 O.B.A., and a .384 SL.%, at best about average. His O.B.A. high was .377 in 1887. In SL.% he had a .554 in 1884, his only .500+ SL.% season; the next was .447 in 1879. The search for answer about Williamson raises more questions.

His high in walks was 80 in 1886, and during his career he made 506 such walks. His K's are comparable, highs of 71 in 1886 and 1888, during his career 532 swishes in futility. His 809 runs scored and 667 R.B.I. just don't correspond with a spectacular player.

He stole a high of 45 bases in 1887, and again no more will be said, save that he had a total of 88 during his major league tenure, with eight seasons of data missing among the 13. His B.R. sum total of +123 is highly commendable, only two -'s and a high by far of +37 in 1884.

Fielding runs are accounted for all his years, of which seven are -'s and as much so as -35 for 1887; contrary are +'s of +22 in 1884 and +20 for 1879. Whether friend or foe on the field, the numbers do not nearly correlate with the critique or the collective of inordinately complimentary commentary.

Sam Crane further wrote of Williamson that he was "a gentleman on the field" and from others came the further statements that he was superb in action and a ball-bearing-smooth athlete and also a perfect physical machine.

His playing weight is typically written as 170 pounds, but that should be appended with 210 in 1890 for whatever reason(s). His "paunch" is comparable to that of Billy Bonny (or Bonney), better known as Billy the Kid of that era. In his only known photo he's paunchy if not slovenly, and he's also been cited as spunky.

A further minor difficulty involves his name. In most modern and recent literature Williamson is noted as "Ned," but in and about his time the scribes identified him as "Ed." There seems no end to the questions.

A source from the distant past tells of injury to Williamson while on the world tour in the fall of 1888, which may well be, but is really doubtful as the most comprehensive reports available about that seminal event include specific dates, from October 20, 1888, to April 20, 1889, with no mention of him.

And further on that bit of a question, why would a New York City sportswriter identify every member of the Chicago touring team, but mention nothing about the other team? Other than by most accounts they were the All America or All American team.

Williamson played some in the Players League; all that can be said in the affirmative is that he was a Pirate who maybe should be given the label of "Wonder." And his 27 of 1884 is still a disputed issue, but not the fact that he hit those HRs.

Edward Nagle "Ned" Williamson died of dropsy of the stomach. He was a Players League player. He was and is an anomaly.

The sport of hockey maintains records for a stat called assists in scoring goals; the baseball analogy of goals is runs scored, of course. There is no datum in baseball which is in any way comparable to such assists, but there could be in the future.

The first to qualify for these assists would be the pitchers, of course, the first of which come to mind are Robin Roberts and Bert Blyleven. And how about ballparks? If the first thought that comes to mind is "ridiculous!" consider Ebbets Field and the Baker Bowl.

The latter though, as amenable as these bandboxes were, would have to be classed as kid stuff as there would be no contest in the category of home run assists by ballparks with Lake Park in Chicago which, according to John Tattersall was built in 1871, burned in 1871, and was as quickly rebuilt.

Lake Park became home park to the Chicago White Stockings in or about 1878 and still was in 1884 when Williamson hit his longstanding season record of 27 home runs. The team high in the N.L. that year was 142, of an aggregate league sum of 322.

The American Association of 1884, its 12 franchises and 13 teams, hit a total of 238 home runs in 1884; the fledgling and soon to depart Union Association of 1884, its eight franchises and 12 or 13 teams hit a total of 126 home runs; Fred Dunlap hit 13 of theirs.

Tattersall alleges no actual measurements of Lake Park are available but there is much evidence of a short right field fence probably no further than 230 feet from the home plate to the right field corner across the field.

Further, Tattersall says, "During the years prior to 1884, the prevailing ground rule [was] batted ball over the wall [gets] two base hit" and reveals that "17 home runs [were] hit in Lake Park in 1883."

He comments further, "Some brilliant strategist in the Chicago camp [devised] legalize ... right field fence ... home run." It may well be that a home baseball park was awarded an assist before Lake Park, Chicago, in 1884, but if so it's unknown.

Chicago's home opening day that momentous season was May 29. Two games were played; in the afternoon Williamson hit three out of the park at right field. The correspondent added that his hits that day were fortunate.

The three home runs earned a total of seven, and Tattersall cites further along in the season, on August 6, Cap Anson "popped three balls over the [same end of the] fence" as Williamson had. *Boston Herald*: "That over the fence rule is a perfect sham."

Also from Tattersall, "John Manning [did the] three-a-game act on October 9th

... batted only 5 homers all season." Manning was with the Philadelphia Phillies in 1884, and Mr. Tattersall finds further fault with the record of Williamson.

For Williamson in 1884: "HRs: Home 25, Elsewhere 2 = 27. Williamson had indeed been practicing the art of arching balls over the rightfield fence, thus was well prepared when the ground rule change took effect.... White Stockings hit 140 HRs in 1884."

His calculations show 130 of the White Stockings 1884 HRs were hit at home and 10 elsewhere, a record which stood until 1947; the New York Giants that season hit a total of 221 HRs. How many assists were given the Polo Grounds that year is unknown.

That year the next-to-high in the N.L. was 115 by the Pirates, in the A.L. the Yankees led with 115, but in 1884 the Chicagos hit an average of 2.32 HRs per game at Lake Park, still a record which the game of wall ball surely will demolish.

Major league ballparks have changed vastly since 1884. Now all are designed and built by a standard. Baseball is what it is, and baseball was what it was; it's been so since players wore pants called knickers, since someone built a fence and charged a fee.

So, according to Tattersall, "That's the story of a phony (home) park arrangement." But what is a baseball anomaly? And why don't the official records include a datum call assists? Ned Williamson was the beneficiary of 25 in 1884, no sham at all.

WISE, SAMUEL WASHINGTON Sam Wise
Born: August 18, 1857, Akron, Ohio
Died: January 22, 1910, Akron, Ohio
Height: 5'10.5".   Weight: 170 Lbs.   Batted: Left.   Threw: Right
Major League Career: 12 Years, 1,175 Games
1889: N.L.: Washington
1890: A.A.: Baltimore
1890: P.L.: Buffalo Bisons; 2B 119

Batting Record:

Games: 119	3B: 11	Walks: 46	SL.%: .430
At Bats: 505	HRs: 6	K's: 45	S.B: 19
Hits: 148	Runs: 95	B.Avg: .293	B.R: +8
2B: 29	R.B.I: 102	O.B.A: .359	F.R: +2

A National League umpire in 1889 and 1893, he was the first major league player to test the hegemony of the National Agreement in the courts. Prior to the 1882 season he signed with N.L. Boston after signing with A.A. Cincinnati; the triumvirs owners cartel won the case and the services of Sam Wise.

His prior experience was one game for N.L. Detroit in 1881; in four at bats he hit two singles and struck out twice. Both 1882 teams and leagues proved wise in their pursuits; perhaps they saw potential in his .500, .500, .500, and 2 K's. How it was that he was free to sign with A.A. Cincinnati is not told in the records.

Wise led his league in K's in 1884 with 104. This worst sort of a benchmark stat isn't yet among official records; by the book the first batter to reach this plateau didn't do so until 1913. He was Danny Moeller of the A.L. Washington Senators.

Wise also led his league in errors at his position in 1883, with 88. He played only at shortstop that year; by the records this was his preferred position. He also led twice in chances for a season. During his major league term he tried all the positions except catcher and pitcher.

As a batter Wise reached the .300+ level in B.Avg. twice and he scored 100+ runs twice; in 1890 he had his only 100+ R.B.I. year. During the Players League year he was the most productive of the Buffalo Bisons. This record includes almost no faults at all.

Forty-five K's in 505 at bats is too close to 10 percent, and too nearly balances 45 walks; his walks and hits equal almost 200 times on base. His 95 runs and 102 R.B.I. equates with outstanding production, and for the lamentable Bisons might rate something greater than that.

He's not among the P.L. leaders in any stat, but his 46 hits for extra bases (31 percent) is highly commendable; all his batting averages stand above the league norms of .274 B.Avg., .345 O.B.A., and .378 SL.%. His 19 stolen bases merit a bit of extra credit; his SABR-stats being all positive merit that much more.

Not amazing, or awesome, nor bedazzling, Wise of the Bisons middle infield, and played well enough in 1890 to merit the status of a Players League star player.

The year after the P.L. he was mainly at 2B for the Baltimore (A.A.) Orioles. He played 103 games and in 388 at bats made a .247 B.Avg.; 62 benchmark walks were essential to his .364 O.B.A., and 20 hits among 96 for extra bases resulted in a .317 SL.%. He K'd 52 times, scored 70 runs, had 48 R.B.I., and was -10 F.R. for the year. In sum he had a significant decline from his P.L. year.

His last year was 1893; he missed 1892, for Washington, where in 122 games and 521 at bats were 25 K's (5 Percent), 49 walks, 27 doubles, a benchmark 17 triples, and 5 HRs among 162 hits. He scored 102 runs and had 77 R.B.I. in his last major league year; he played 93 games at 2B and 31 at 3B, producing a very positive +16 F.R.

Wise ended well a career of 12 years and 1,175 games, which included eight years of 100+ games; he made 1,281 hits in 4,715 at bats, including 221 doubles, 112 triples, and 49 home runs. His 643 K's don't read well next to 389 walks, but 834 runs scored and 672 R.B.I. are certainly credible sums for a middle infielder.

His composite SABR-stats are +81 B.R. and -12 F.R. Beyond the benchmarks previously mentioned are a .522 SL.% in 1887, and 17 triples that same year. 1888 was the last of his seven Boston years, during which his games varied between 78 and 114, and his at bats between 298 and 467.

His range of batting averages during this period is vast, from .214 through .334. His O.B.A. is more disparate, .234 to .390, and SL.% still more, .319 to .522. Wise was once awarded a silver bat for having made the greatest number of hits of any player on the Boston team. He was considered one of the best shortstops in the business.

In 1889 he was with Washington (N.L.) for 121 games and 472 at bats; his batting averages were less than impressive, .250, .341, and .341, with the first below the norm and the last below any expectations. He amended well the next year for the Buffalo Bisons when the Players League played.

He'd done well off and on for the Boston (N.L.) Reds, and in 1890 he was sufficiently commendable at the bat and second base to rate the call of a Players League star player. After major league baseball he was a production foreman for a major rubber company.

Samuel Washington Wise died of appendicitis.

WOOD, GEORGE A.   George Wood (Dandy)
Born: November 9, 1858, Boston, Massachusetts
Died: April 4, 1924, Harrisburg, Pennsylvania
Height: 5'10.5".   Weight: 175 Lbs.   Batted: Left.   Threw: Right.
Major League Career: 13 Years, 1,280 Games
1889: N.L.: Philadelphia and A.A.: Baltimore
1891: A.A.: Philadelphia
1890: P.L.: Philadelphia Quakers; OF 132, 3B 1

Batting Record:

Games: 132	3B: 14	Walks: 51	SL.%: .429
At Bats: 539	HRs: 9	K's: 35	S.B: 20
Hits: 156	Runs: 115	B.Avg: .289	B.R: +8
2B: 20	R.B.I: 102	O.B.A: .360	F.R: +15

His age was 31 when the P.L. played. The nickname "Dandy" gives a hint of character and demeanor, flashy if not outright bold. His years and stats reveal that he had high levels of skills to play major league baseball. As a P.L. batter he was better than average, and in 1890 his fielding was superior.

He displayed some power at the bat and had patience and a good eye for home plate; 100+ runs and 100+ R.B.I. explain his value to the Philadelphia Quakers. He was their most productive player. The sum of these assets earn him status as a Players League star player.

"Dandy" has been cited as having a rifle arm. During his career he led the outfielders of his league twice in putouts, assists, and double plays. His 35 assists in 1890 rank 23rd all time for a season; his career assists adjusted to a 162-game season (26.69) rank 15th all time. His 276 errors rank 11th.

He was an A.A. umpire in 1889 and 1891, an N.L. umpire in 1898 and 1899, and a manager one year, 1891, with the Philadelphia (A.A.) Athletics. His team won 67 lost 55 (.549 win %) and by one account was a member of the entourage that toured the world.

His only league leading stat was seven HRs in 1882, for Detroit (N.L.); he hit 68 HRs during his 13-year career. The most were a benchmark 14 in 1887 for Philadelphia (N.L.). Among benchmark stats are his 15 triples in 1887 and 19 triples in 1888, also for the N.L. Phillies.

George Wood scored 100+ runs each of three years; the most were 118 in 1887. His 102 R.B.I. for the Quakers of 1890 was his only 100+ in that stat. He never had 100+ walks or K's, but did have 50+ walks three years, and 50+ K's four years, with highs of 72 walks in 1891, and 75 K's in both 1884 for Detroit, and 1886 for the Phillies.

His career stolen base total is 113 known, with six years missing; the most were 22 in 1891. His career SABR-stats are a terrific +125 in B.R., with +26 in 1891 his high, and a total +14 F.R.; his P.L. +15 is by far the best.

His career batting averages are all well above average, all below his P.L. numbers. His career B.Avg. is .273, O.B.A. .329, and SL.% .403. Benchmarks included a .302 B.Avg. in 1883 and .309 in 1891; there are no others. He was better than most, but surely not dandy.

By the vast majority of his 1,280 games and 5,371 at bats, Wood was a National League player: Worcester 1880, Detroit 1881 through 1885, Philadelphia 1886 through 1889; in the minority he was with A.A. Baltimore for three games in 1889 and Philadelphia in 1891.

With no options he returned to the N.L. for 1892 with Baltimore for 21 games. After 30 more with Cincinnati in 1892 he ended his major league career. Among players who knew the Players League from within, a dandy would not have been an Englishman eating spaghetti, but Wood played a dandy game in 1890.

He's a choice as a Players League star player. He may have been the player who posed for the symbolic photo image of Ernest Lawrence Thayer's "Casey at the Bat." After baseball he was a clerk employed by the Commonwealth of Pennsylvania, then a Public Service Commission marshal.

As a player he earned ranks in period stats 1876–1889 of: eighth in triples, eighth in K's.

George A. Wood died of a heart attack.

5

The Competition

Estimates have claimed that 90 percent of established major league players were with Players League clubs in 1890. They were definitely a plurality, probably a majority, but the P.L. did not have a monopoly on such players.

Ninety percent would have left the other two major leagues nearly void of excellence, which was not the case. All roads did not lead to the Players League in 1890; many players switched between teams and between leagues, though the drift was in the P.L. direction.

These are the best who chose to not distinguish the Players League with their presence. Herein neither the career chronology nor compilation of data is complete for some of the players.

ANSON, ADRIAN CONSTANTINE "CAP"
1B. Athletics (N.A.) 1872–75; 1B & Mgr., Chicago (N.L.) 1876–97

His 10,323 at bats are the 1800s record and were the major league record until broken by Honus Wagner. He was an iron man of the game, and just as tough with himself as with the players in his charge. He still holds records and ranks high in many categories.

He was the career leader in hits from 1880 till 1923. He held the career R.B.I. record until 1933; he now ranks ninth in R.B.I. and 19th in runs scored. With the glove he's first at first base with 20,794 putouts and first in errors with 583.

His N.L. total 2,995 hits ranks 21st, his 528 doubles 23rd. As a manager his win % is .578, based on 1,296 wins and 947 losses. In the period 1880 through 1886 his teams won five pennants. He holds the record for longevity as manager of one team. He was elected to the National Baseball Hall of Fame in 1939, as a player.

He began with Rockford of the National Association in 1871, the first year of organized professional major league baseball. When his career was done he'd batted .300+ each of 24 years, led his league two of those years, and led in hits one year.

He reached the .400+ O.B.A. benchmark each of 10 years, .500+ SL.% six years; he scored 100+ runs six years, had 100+ R.B.I. seven years, and led his league eight years. He also led in doubles two years and hit 30+ doubles six years. He hit 10+ HRs three years. He had 100+ walks one year, and led in O.B.A. three years.

Cap Anson was off his game in 1890, far below the standards he demanded of himself each and every year. This was his 20th, as opposed to best and most, which show 1886 as his best year.

	Career	1890	Best / Most
At Bats:	10,323	504	559 (1892)
Hits:	3,425	139	187 (1886)
Runs:	1,996	95	117 (1886)
R.B.I:	1,879+	107	147 (1886)
Walks:	952+	113	113 (1890)
B.Avg:	.332	.312	.399 (1881)
O.B.A.	.395	.443	.457 (1894)
SL.%:	.446	.401	.544 (1886)
B.R:	+564	+39	+51 (1888)
F.R:	+54	+2	+12 (1876)

Many of his data are in the range of incredible. His numbers of at bats and hits, the result of the theorem equal = great when applied to his career runs and R.B.I., more than 1,000 walks, and perhaps foremost the +564 batting runs counted for Cap Anson.

If it appears that he had no faults, the call is close but not quite; as firm as he was with himself and his players, he was as firm, perhaps better said as rigid, in making judgments of other people, primarily relative to the hue of their skin.

At least once he refused to let his team play a game because the opponents had a Negro among their starting nine; this was an exhibition game, against amateurs and semi-pros. He was also one of the most vociferous about forbidding Negroes as players in the major leagues.

BARNIE, WILLIAM HARRISON "BILLIE"
C, Hartford (N.A.) 1874; Mgr., Baltimore (A.A.) 1883–91

His stolen base total is equal to his importance to the game as a player, officially unknown, actually next to none; his primary contributions were as a negotiator, player scout, and manager, the former two being impossible to quantify allow for opinions.

His complete record as a manager was won 632 lost 810 (.438), which includes N.L. teams in 1892–94 and 1897–98; with the A.A. Baltimore Orioles from 1883 through 1891 his teams won 470 and lost 548 (.462).

As a player he had 322 at bats and made 57 hits, for a .177 B.Avg., and he scored 30 runs; as a manager his best finishes were third two years, once in the A.A. and once in the N.L. In the N.L. he was with the Louisville/Pittsburgh and Brooklyn/Baltimore syndicates.

On August 17, 1894, he watched one of his many Louisville pitchers, Jack Wadsworth, give up 36 hits in their game against the Phillies. As manager of the 1890 Orioles his team won 15 and lost 19 (.441) to play their way into eighth place. The franchise went out of business, then it was revived through 1890 and played through 1891.

Billie Barnie was there when major league baseball went through its most troubled and tumultuous times; he was a vital figure in gaining equity if not parity for the American Association, in the clash of three leagues in 1890, and when the A.A. was destroyed.

BENNETT, CHARLES WESLEY "CHARLIE"
C, Detroit (N.L.) 1881–88, Boston (N.L.) 1889–93

His win in a court challenge of the reserve clause in 1885 was viewed as a point in favor of establishing the Brotherhood of Players. In the year the Players League played Charlie Bennett stood loyal to the National League.

He posted .300+ batting averages three years and hit 30+ doubles one year. He ranks eighth all time among catchers with 379 errors, and sixth with 417 passed balls. In 1890 rugged and durable Charlie Bennett worked behind home plate for one of the great pitching triads.

These were John Clarkson, Kid Nichols, and Pretzels Getzein, but the Beaneaters finished only fifth, while their Beantown rivals, the P.L. Reds, won their league championship.

In 1894, Charlie Bennett suffered one of the most horrid of all baseball tragedies: his legs were cut off by a railroad train.

BURKETT, JESSE CAIL "JESSE, THE CRAB"
OF, New York (N.L.) 1890; Cleveland (N.L.) 1891–98

A novice the Players League year, and a rare baseball product of West Virginia, "The Crab" went on to a hall of fame career, inducted in 1946.

He set a major league record of 240 hits in a season exactly a half century earlier, in 1896. He developed and mastered the combination at the bat of extreme proficiency and extra base ability; he began very well and reached his peak in 1896.

	Career	1890	Best / Most
At Bats:	8,421	401	624 (1898)
Hits:	2,850	124	240 (1896)
Runs:	1,720	67	160 (1896)
R.B.I:	952	60	94 (1894)

	Career	1890	Best / Most
Walks:	1,029	33	98 (1893)
B.Avg:	.338	.309	.410 (1896)
O.B.A:	.413	.366	.486 (1895)
SL.%:	.446	.461	.541 (1896)
B.R:	+522	+20	+57 (1901)
F.R:	-33	-1	+8 (1902)

By the SABR-stats his fielding was mediocre but his batting runs total among the highest. His calculations show three other years above +50 and nine years above the benchmark +30. Other benchmarks include an incredible 200+ hits each of six years, including 240 in 1896.

He also had a .400+ B.Avg. two years, .300+ 11 years; .400+ O.B.A. nine years and .500+ SL.% five years. He scored 100+ runs nine years, hit 10+ HRs one year and 15+ triples four years. His combination of 320 doubles, 182 triples, and 75 HRs calculate to 20 percent extra base hits.

His K's were at 50+ in two of the five years known; more than offset by 13 years of 50+ walks, with a high of 98 in 1893. He led his league in hits three years, in B.Avg. three years, O.B.A. one year, and in runs scored two years.

These are among current ranks held by Jesse "The Crab" Burkett:

Single Season:

11th: 240 hits in 1896
14th: 160 runs scored in 1896
26th: 153 runs scored in 1895

Career:

20th: .338 B.Avg.
23rd: .415 O.B.A.
18th: 1,720 runs scored
15th: 182 triples.

He belonged to the Cleveland/St. Louis N.L. syndicate from 1891 through 1901, then played in the American League from 1902 through 1905. There was not a year his proficiency was not extraordinary in some baseball respect; Jesse Burkett was simply extraordinary.

BURNS, THOMAS P. "OYSTER"
OF, Brooklyn (N.L.) 1890–95

He was with the Baltimore (A.A.) Orioles the year that four strikes were last required to call a batter out, and parts of 1884 through 1888, after beginning with the Wilmington (Del.) Quicksteps in the Union Association of 1884.

He had a terrific season with the Orioles of 1887 but wasn't at his best for the Bridegrooms in the Players League year. He was chosen by one source as an N.L. all star that year. In the second game on August 1 he achieved the unusual feat of hitting for the cycle: a home run, triple, double, and single in the same game.

His 1890 B.Avg. was a modest .284, but 134 hits and 51 benchmark walks produced 102 runs scored and 128 R.B.I., the league high, as were his 13 HRs. His choice as one of the prime N.L. team, though, clearly was a function of many stars playing elsewhere.

Just as clearly he was an A.A. all star in 1887, and seems to have been at his best when the scenario was other than normal (data for his 11 year career are in parentheses):

B.Avg: .341 (.300)	B.R: +46 (+199)	Runs: 122 (869)
O.B.A: .414 (.368)	F.R: -22 (-58)	R.B.I: Unknown (673+)
SL.%: .519 (.446)	Hits: 188 (1,389)	S.B.: 58 (263+).

Oyster Burns had another very good year in 1894, again when the rules were adjusted: 179 hits, .354 B.Avg., .409 O.B.A., .503 SL.%, +17 B.R., 106 runs scored, 107 R.B.I., 30 stolen bases, 32 doubles, 14 triples, and five home runs.

Overall he achieved benchmarks in B.Avg. with .300+ four years, .400+ O.B.A. two years, .500+ SL.% two years, 100+ runs four years, 100+ R.B.I. three years known, 30+ doubles one year, 15+ triples three years, 10+ HRs one year, 50+ walks five years, and a high of 68 in 1889 of 464 during his career; his high K's were 42 twice known.

Overall a commendable albeit rather brief career. In the year the P.L. played, Oyster Burns was an all star in another league.

CARUTHERS, ROBERT LEE "BOB"
P, St. Louis (A.A.) 1884–87, Brooklyn (A.A.) 1888–89

He'd be quickly now labeled diminutive, this youngster from Tennessee. Confronted with this dual disadvantage during the span 1885 through 1887 he won 99 games and lost 36 (.733 win %); then he followed up in 1888–1889 with 69 wins and 26 losses (.726 win %).

By common standards he had an excellent season in the P.L. year: won 23, lost 11 (.676), pitched 292 innings, 30 complete games, with a .325 O.B.% and 3.09 E.R.A.; SABR-stats reinforce excellent with a +16 P.R. and +0.7 W.A.T.

By Bob Caruthers's standards this was his downside, as attests his .688 career win % which is the fifth best in major league history; his .676 win % of 1890 was merely the fourth best in the N.L.

He'd switched from the A.A. for the 1890 season, as did many, but few if any brought along a record comparable to his. He'd been a mainstay and catalyst of the great St. Louis Browns teams of the mid-1880s, and done no less for the Trolley Dodgers of 1888–1889.

When both Brooklyn teams in both established leagues became the Bridegrooms he opted for the N.L. version, where he stayed through 1891; he won 18 and lost 14 (.563), had a .353 O.B.% and 3.12 E.R.A., +7 P.R. and +3.3 W.A.T.

He went to St. Louis, where he began, for the 1892 season, which proved to be his last. He won 2 and lost 10, with both SABR-stats later counted negative, and 5.91 E.R.A. an 1892 baseball fact. He'd really hit the downside, but in eight of nine years he was terrific.

A brief survey of his career says with certainty Caruthers produced a record of Cooperstown class, but lacking one year:

	Career	Best / Most		Career	Best / Most
Won:	218	40 (1885 & 1889)	Games:	340	56 (1889)
Lost:	99	N/A	C.G:	298	53 (1885)
Win %:	.688	.784 (1889)	I.P:	2,829	482 (1885)
O.B.%:	.303	.272 (1888)	P.R.:	+213	+63 (1885)
E.R.A.:	2.84	2.07 (1885)	W.A.T:	+30.5	+11.2 (1889)

He led his league in wins two years, in win % three years, two years in shutouts, one year in E.R.A., one year in P.R. and one year in W.A.T.; his collection of benchmark stats is something other than diminutive.

He won 40+ games two years, 20+ six of his nine years, had a .700+ win % three years, pitched 50+ games two years, and 50+ complete games one year; add 400+ innings pitched one year, and 300+ six years. His E.R.A. was 2.50- each of three years, four years he beat the +30 P.R. benchmark, and one year the mark in wins against (above) team.

His major league career wasn't long, his workloads weren't huge, and what he mainly did was win and win. His career data composite would have made Bob Caruthers a leading feature player in the Players League of 1890.

CHILDS, CLARENCE ALGERNON "CUPID"
2B, Cleveland (N.L.) 1891–98

His nickname doesn't fit the image of the tough Cleveland Spiders and a further contradiction in expectations was a four position player leading his league in slugging percentage, which with a .481 SL.% Cupid Childs did for the Syracuse (A.A.) Stars in 1890.

His career extended through 13 seasons. His career total of 3,859 putouts ranks 19th all time at his position; his 644 errors is fourth at 2B, the other side of which is his 5.87 range factor, which is seventh best.

He made enough assists to average 521 for a 162-game season, the 10th highest such mark for a second baseman. At bat his career .416 O.B.A. ranks 22nd in history. His career B.Avg. is .306, with a high of .355 in 1896, and the .481 SL.% in 1890 was his best.

He produced 1,720 hits in 5,618 at bats; the most were 177 in 1892 and 1896. His career count of 205 doubles includes 33 in 1890 plus of 100 triples 14 in 1890. Four of his 20 career HRs came in 1895; he was walked a total of 990 times, and 120 in 1893 were his high.

He stole a total of 269 bases, 56 in 1890. His total B.R. tally was +235, by a middle infielder with minimal power, with a high of +47 for both 1890 and 1892. His total F.R. count is +78, with an astounding +42 calculation for 1896.

After a start of two games for N.L. Philadelphia in 1888, he wasn't in the major leagues in 1889. Beginning with a great 1890 season, he led in O.B.A. one year, runs scored one year, doubles one year, and of course in SL.% one year.

Power hitters were at a premium in 1890, especially in the A.A., as was a B.Avg. of .345 which Childs marked in 1890. He hit the .300+ B.Avg. benchmark five other years and .400+ O.B.A. five other years, but never did get to the .500+ level in SL.%.

He did score 100+ runs seven years, including 109 in 1890 and 145 in 1893 of a career total 1,214. He hit the 100+ R.B.I. mark once, with 106 in 1896 among the years known; he hit 30+ doubles one year.

He didn't play in the Players League in actually his rookie year but did produce exceptionally well in 1890 and many years; if it should occur to wonder "hall of fame, why not?" then ponder no further than to imagine a plaque at Cooperstown scribed "Cupid."

CLARKSON, JOHN GIBSON "JOHN"
P, Chicago (N.L.) 1884–87, Boston (N.L.) 1888–92

Formidable John Clarkson was in a slump in 1890 with only 25 wins. The year before he'd won 49 which led his league, as did his .721 win %, 73 games, 68 complete games, eight shutouts (10 in 1885), 284 K's (308 in 1885 and 313 in 1886), 2.73 E.R.A., +89 P.R. and +12.1 W.A.T., and that was one season.

His career, 1890, best and most stats include:

	Career	1890	Best / Most
Won:	327	25	53 (1885)
Lost:	178	18	N/A
Win %:	.648	.581	.768 (1885)
Games:	531	44	73 (1889)
C.G:	485	43	68 (1885 & 1889)
I.P:	4,537	383	623 (1885)
O.B.%:	.313	.337	.262 (1885)
E.R.A:	2.81	3.27	1.85 (1895)
P.R:	+369	+13	+89 (1889)
W.A.T:	+22.9	+0.7	+12.1 (1889)

His P.R. were greater than +50 two other years, and above +30 two years beyond that. He's ranked 10th all time in wins, eighth in complete games, 19th in win %, 20th in innings pitched, and 12th with 182 wild pitches.

Also among all pitchers as fielders Clarkson ranks 11th with 1,143 assists and second with 162 errors. He led his league in wins three years, win % one year, games three years, C.G. three years, I.P. four years, K's three years, E.R.A. one year, W.A.T. one year, shutouts two years.

Among his benchmarks are 50+ wins one year, 30+ six years, 20+ eight years, .700+ % two years, 70+ games two years, 50+ six years, 60+ C.G. two years, 50+ five years, 600+ I.P. two years, 300+ eight years, 300+ K's two years, 2.00- E.R.A. one year, 2.50- three years.

Before Chicago and Boston, Clarkson had pitched in 1882, for N.L. Worcester; he won 1 and lost 2. He didn't pitch in the major leagues in 1883. After Chicago and Boston he pitched for Cleveland most of 1892 through 1894, and there posted won and lost marks of 17 and 10, 16 and 17, 8 and 10, which was the end.

Clarkson may have been the second most awesome pitcher of the 1800s, sufficient to be a feature player in another league in 1890. That may sum up John Clarkson, in another league and sufficient at the game to be elected to the National Baseball Hall of Fame in 1963.

CLEMENTS, JOHN J. "JACK"
C, Philadelphia (N.L.) 1884–97

He ranks sixth among all major league catchers with 417 passed balls. The toughest of all baseball positions takes this toll only on catchers. He endured almost exclusively at the second post through all his 17 seasons, 1884 through 1900.

A pure National League player, his term with the Phillies began a year after the franchise. He stayed with his team through four Philadelphia ballparks: Recreation Park (1883–86), Huntington Grounds (1887–94), University of Pennsylvania Athletic Field (1894), and the legendary Baker Bowl (1895–1938).

By a very reliable source, he also played through three names other than Phillies; the Quakers is common and familiar, but Live Wires and Blue Jays are the stuff of arcana. While there, he established a very credible record, and did fine service.

The year the P.L. played he was good behind home plate, he did better; As a batter he was great. The whole of his record is well above average. In certain statistics he had one year which would rank among the classic of all time.

His sums of runs and R.B.I. are to be expected of a regular at his position: 619 runs scored with 64 in 1890 his high which was equal to 1893 and 1895; 687+ R.B.I. with 74 in 1890 and a high of 80 in 1893. He stole only 55 bases; 10 in 1890 were his most.

In 1895 he had only 322 at bats and 127 hits. Among comparable calculations this was what he did with those, supplemented foremost by 7 K's (2.2 percent futility), 22 walks (not inclined to stand and wait), 27 doubles, 2 triples (likely not a blazer on the base paths), and 13 HRs (he also hit 17 in 1893).

	Career	1890	1895
B.Avg:	.286	.315	.394
O.B.A:	.347	.392	.446 (best .455 in 1894)
SL.%:	.421	.472	.612

Among his career count of +109 B.R. is +34 for 1895. His total F.R. counts to -27. He hit 77 home runs in 4,283 at bats, not Ruthian but then nobody was. Jack

Clements was awesome in 1895 and produced commendably in the P.L. year. He did credit to himself, to his team, and his town of birth throughout his fine career.

COLLINS, HUBERT B. "HUB"
2B/OF, Brooklyn (A.A.) 1889–89, Brooklyn (N.L.) 1890–92

It isn't often that a player scores more runs in a season than he has hits, but this player did it the year the P.L. played. This is the second baseman management has been searching for since the first baseball dollar changed hands, the unknown most valuable.

He changed leagues for the 1890 season, and beyond. His first year with the N.L. Bridegrooms he scored 148 runs and had 69 R.B.I., he made 142 hits and took 85 walks. The correlations say great, his 85 stolen bases say better, with 170 free bases.

Add a +1 F.R. and the composite is a star-class middle infielder. He led the N.L. in runs scored, was third in doubles with 32, fourth in walks, and second in S.B. His team won its league title in 1890, and he was an essential element in bringing that pennant to Brooklyn.

His B.Avg. was a modest .278, O.B.A. .385, and SL.% .001 higher with that benchmark accumulation of doubles, which tells power was not to be expected from Hub Collins at the bat. His career wasn't long, just seven years, but he had a couple of other very good years.

With emphasis on his assets, this is the sum of a textbook second baseman which, with the myriad changes in the game, has been the same since the Eckfords and Atlantics played in Brooklyn during the 1850s and the 1860s.

	1887	*1888*	*1889*	*1890*	*1891*	*Career*
Hits:	162	162	149	142	120	790
Walks:	39	50	80	85	59	332
S.B:	71	71	65	85	32	335
Runs:	122	133	139	148	82	653
B.Avg:	.290	.307	.266	.278	.276	.284
O.B.A:	.338	.373	.365	.385	.265	.365
F.R:	0	+15	0	+1	-21	-4

Collins was productive and mostly consistent. He could play the field, which he did as an outfielder with Louisville in 27 games in 1886 through most of 1888 before going to Brooklyn. He was at his best in the P.L. year, began to fade, and knew when to end a career.

Never spectacular, not awesome, just reliable, he produced some benchmarks: .300+ B.Avg. two years, 100+ runs four years, 30+ doubles two years; he led his league in runs one year, and in doubles one year. He didn't play in the P.L. but was the composite of what the major league 2B should be.

DAVIS, GEORGE STACEY "GEORGE"
SS, New York 1893–1901

He was a rookie with the Cleveland (N.L.) Spiders in 1890 and began most notably with a .264 B.Avg., 53 walks, and +13 fielding runs. When he left the major leagues after 20 years he'd accumulated a .295 B.Avg., 870 walks, and +203 fielding runs.

His positions were mixed the first few years, but when he settled in at the six position he became one of the best ever. He played the field at a first-class level, played the strike zone game the same way, and developed as a batter into a prominent force.

As a rookie his 35 outfield assists now ranks 23rd among OF on the all-time list. As a shortstop he made assists at a rate of 565 in a 162-game season, which ranks seventh all time among SS. As a batter in 1893 he fashioned a then-record consecutive 33-game hitting streak. His 616 career S.B. rank 15th in history.

George Stacey Davis was elected to the National Baseball Hall of Fame as a shortstop in 1998. He's the earliest switch hitter chronologically of all hall of fame position players. There's some evidence of his future all-round success in his 1890 stats.

His 53 walks joined with 139 hits produced 98 runs and 73 R.B.I., and he's now among the top 40 all time in R.B.I.; he stole 22 bases, and his +13 F.R. alone would have been enough to assure his future. He excelled for a decade; these are his best, most and career:

	Career	1890	Best / Most
At Bats:	9,031	526	597 (1892)
Hits:	2,660	139	195 (1893)
Runs:	1,539	98	120 (1894)
R.B.I:	1,435	73	134 (1897)
Walks:	870	53	66 (1894)
B.Avg:	.295	.264	.355 (1893)
O.B.A:	.359	.336	.435 (1894)
SL.%:	.405	.375	.554 (1893)
B.R:	+246	+6	+42 (1893)
F.R:	+208	+13	+43 (1899)
S.B:	616	22	65 (1897)

The list of "led his league" stats isn't as long as might be expected: R.B.I. one year, 134 in 1897, F.R. two years, +33 in 1898 and +43 in 1899. His list of benchmarks includes every facet of the game.

He had a .300+ B.Avg. nine years, .400+ O.B.A. four years, .500+ SL.% four years, 100+ runs five years, 100+ R.B.I. three years, 30+ doubles three years, 15+ triples three years, 10+ HRs two years, 50+ walks eight years, which includes 65 in 1902 and 60 in 1905. Add to that +30 B.R. two years and +30 F.R. two years.

After his P.L. year beginning he continued with Cleveland through 1892. When he went to New York it was for nine years then again in 1903, interrupted by a season with the A.L. White Sox in 1902, where he returned in 1904 and played out the balance of his long and great career through 1909.

FOUTZ, DAVID LUTHER "DAVE"
P. St. Louis (A.A.) 1884–87; 1B. Brooklyn (N.L.) 1890–93

He career separates into two parts: the first was outstanding, the second was great. His transition year was 1886 with 59 games as a pitcher and 45 as a position player; he led pitchers of the A.A. with 57 putouts.

His career began in 1884 with the St. Louis (A.A.) Browns. His record as a pitcher was a limited won 15 lost 6 (.714 Win %). Still pitching for the Browns 1885 through 1887 he won 99 games and lost 42 (.702 Win %), and each year the Browns were league champions.

The last of these years his batting was sufficient to convince himself and those who make such decisions that he'd mean more to his team if he played every game with an occasional turn in the pitcher's box, a decision which turned out just fine.

In the last of these years his B.Avg. was .357, O.B.A. .393, and SL.% .508, data unheard of for a pitcher. He was with Brooklyn (A.A.) in 1888 and 1889; the latter of these years he scored 118 runs and had 113 R.B.I., data unheard of for almost any player.

Switching to the N.L. for 1890 produced a season which combined some of both the above: a .303 B.Avg., .368 O.B.A., .432 SL.%, 106 runs scored and 98 R.B.I. Numbers such as these don't arise in isolation; in 1889 he had 64 walks and in 1890 took 52 more.

As a batter he didn't strike out much, 136 times in the eight years known, nor did he produce vast numbers of extra base hits. In 4,533 at bats he totaled 186 doubles, 91 triples, and 32 home runs. No matter as he was a prize player with two dimensions.

Batting:

	Career	Best / Most
Hits:	1,254	156 (1888)
Runs:	784	118 (1889)
R.B.I:	584+	113 (1889)
Walks:	300+	64 (1889)
B.Avg:	.277	.357 (1887)
O.B.A:	.323	.393 (1887)
SL.%:	.379	.508 (1887)
S.B:	280	48 (1891)
B.R:	+15	+28 (1887)
F.R:	-13	+7 (1885)

Pitching:

	Career	Best / Most
Won:	147	41 (1886)
Lost:	66	N/A
Win %:	.690	.719 (1886)
Games:	251	59 (1886)
C.G:	202	55 (1886)
I.P:	1,998	504 (1886)
O.B.%:	.306	.265 (1884)
E.R.A:	2.84	2.11 (1886)
P.R:	+147	+75 (1886)
W.A.T:	+10.9	+6.6 (1886)

As a batter he led in no stats. His benchmarks include a .300+ B.Avg. two years, .500+ SL.% one year, 100+ runs two years, 100+ R.B.I. and as a pitcher he led his league in wins and win % one year each, in E.R.A. one year, and in P.R. one year.

His pitching benchmarks include 30+ wins two years, .700+ win % three years, 50+ games one year, 50+ C.G. one year, 300+ I.P. three years, and 2.50- E.R.A. two years; as a pitcher his career .690 win % ranks third in major league history.

No matter whether pitcher's box or batter's box, he excelled, nor did the league matter; 1890 was just one excellent year, but in missing Dave Foutz the Players League missed out on a double star attraction.

GASTRIGHT (GASTREICH), HENRY CARL "HANK"
P, Columbus (A.A.) 1889–91

The 1890 major league situation called for 50 percent more pitchers, he was his second year and one of the most fortunate, as the P.L. year was by far his best year; his benchmarks include one year with 30+ wins (1890), 400+ I.P. (1890), and one year league leader in win %.

The latter was achieved in 1893, for Pittsburgh (won 3, lost 1) and Boston (won 12, lost 4), a combination of 15 wins and 5 losses which obviously equate to a .750 win % which league officials ruled their best despite only 226 I.P. by Hank Gastright.

He had two other marginal years, 1889 and 1891, both with Columbus (A.A.); neither was a winner at won 10, lost 16 (.385) and won 12, lost 19 (.387), with 223 and 284 I.P. respectively. These were among his seven year total of 72 won and 63 lost (.533), with 1,302 I.P.

His E.R.A. in his split year was 5.44, nearly double the 2.94 of 1890 when he won 30 and lost 14 (.682), pitching 401 innings in 48 games, with 41 complete of 45 starts, further accruing a +41 P.R. and +6.6 W.A.T.

In the A.A. of 1890 he ranks third in wins, and win %, fifth in both games and I.P., and second in O.B.%; in his 401 I.P. he gave up just 312 hits. His 135 walks measure well against 199 K's. In 1890 Hank Gastright was the factor which enabled Columbus to achieve second place in their association.

GLASSCOCK, JOHN WESLEY "JACK"
SS, Indianapolis (N.L.) 1889, New York (N.L.) 1890

His major league career extended from 1879 through 1895, he peaked in 1889 and despite relocating stayed there through 1890; the whole of his career can be fairly classed as superior, at the bat, in the field, and on the base paths.

A shortstop who could hit for high average (.290 career, best .352 in 1889), field his position with excellence (+200 career F.R., best +35 in 1887), and steal bases at benchmark levels (372+ in his career, most 62 in 1887), he did well enough to be nominated for a bronze plaque at Cooperstown in 1936, but got just two votes.

The concept in that election, by its structure and process, was destined to elect few or none, as the rigorous standard of 75 percent of the voters applied. There were

78 on that special old timers committee, and the field from which to choose was all the 1800s.

Against Jack Glasscock was his rank of sixth among all shortstops with 632 career errors; for him would have been, if the data had been considered, a rank of eighth with 560 hypothetical assists in a season of 162 games. His 205 hits in 1889 ranks fourth in the period 1876–1889, and his 40 doubles that year ranks eighth.

He led his league in hits two years, in B.Avg. one year, and three years in F.R. This six position player was a complete player, as say his 200+ hit season, .300+ B. Avg. four years, one year of 100+ R.B.I., two years with 30+ doubles, two years with better than +30 F.R., and three years with 50+ stolen bases.

If 1889 was his best season among the many, then 1890 wasn't far off the mark. Longevity didn't diminish his ability in any facet of the game sufficiently to allege any deficiency. These are his career, 1889, and 1890 stats; in the P.L. year in his league he tied for the lead in hits, was first in B.Avg., second in doubles and fifth in O.B.A.

	Career	1889	1890
Hits:	2,040	205	172
Runs:	1,163	128	91
R.B.I:	825+	85	66
Walks:	439	31	41
B.Avg:	.290	.352	.336
O.B.A:	.337	.390	.395
SL.%:	.374	.467	.439
S.B:	372+	57	54
B.R:	+103	+30	+29
F.R:	+200	+31	+15

GLEASON, WILLIAM J. "KID"
P/2B, Philadelphia (N.L.) 1890–91, St. Louis 1892–93

He played the major league game for 22 years, was a pitcher for eight years, won 20+ games each of four years, and lost 20+ games each of three years. The bottom line of his batting is average. His pitching won 138 games and lost 131 (.513 win %). His best year was 1890.

His other three prime years and career in a capsule include:

	1891	1892	1893	Career
Won:	24	20	21	138
Lost:	22	24	22	131
Win %:	.522	.455	.488	.513
I.P:	418	400	380	2,389
O.B.%:	.350	.337	.384	.355

	1891	1892	1893	Career
E.R.A:	3.51	3.33	4.62	3.79
P.R:	-8	-2	+3	+10
W.A.T:	+1.7	+3.8	+3.0	+8.7

As a batter his best average was a .319 B.Avg. in 1897, his only benchmark batting average. He had 106 R.B.I. the same year. The same is fact for 100+ seasons. His extra base hits and walks were both annually minimal. He stole 328 bases in his 22 years.

His total B.R. is -203 and total F.R. +10. He played in 1,966 games, put 7,452 at bats in the record books, with career batting marks of a .261 B.Avg., rather low .309 O.B.A., and below the norm .317 SL.%.

His pitching record in the P.L. year was his best, but his batting was very much to the contrary, to wit:

1890 Batting:

Hits: 47	R.B.I: 17	B.Avg: .210	SL.%: .223	B.R: -17
Runs: 22	Walks: 12	O.B.A: .250	S.B: 10	F.R: 0

1890 Pitching:

Won: 38	Win %: .691	C.G: 54	O.B.%: .327	P.R: +52
Lost: 17	Games: 60	I.P: 506	E.R.A: 2.63	W.A.T: +9.8

For 1890 he ranks second in his league in wins and win %, third in games and C.G., third in I.P., fifth in E.R.A., fourth in K's with 222, and second in shutouts with six. For reasons unknown the year of the P.L. was the year of Kid Gleason the pitcher.

Reason aside, after 1894 he left the pitching to others and switched to second base, which made possible a career span for the 1800s of near-record proportions. Kid Gleason was a very average batter and pitcher, except for one year, and not in the Players League.

Not as a batter, not as a pitcher, his modest +10 career F.R. includes a +20 and +24 for the New York Giants in 1899 and 1900; overall he put in enough time at the keystone position to amass 3,883 putouts, 18th most all time at 2B, and commit 572 errors, sixth all time. His career .938 F.% is among the top 100 at 2B.

HAMILTON, WILLIAM ROBERT "BILLY"
OF, Philadelphia (N.L.) 1890–95, Boston 1896–1901

He came to Philadelphia after two years with A.A. Kansas City to replace Jimmy Fogarty, who switched to the P.L. K.C. and the A.A. obviously lost. The P.L. gained a fine player, the N.L. and Phillies gained one of the greatest players in history.

Billy Hamilton was top of the order in more than one way. He's the only major league player in history to have more runs scored than games played, set multiple batting records, and held career and single-season records in stolen bases for almost a century.

He wasn't without fault; in the field his 288 career errors now rank ninth all time among outfielders. By one credible account he was the fastest base runner of the 1890s and had the worst throwing arm.

Despite a +13 F.R. mark for 1892, his career total is -46 F.R. Only 376 of his 2,158 hits were for extra bases; his extra bases were made with his legs rather than at the bat. With regularity his combination of stolen bases and walks would total near 200.

These skills were evident in 1890: 102 S.B. and 83 walks, a .325 B.Avg. and .430 O.B.A., the difference was consistently .100 or more; his career marks in these stats are .344 B.Avg., which is eighth highest on record, and .455 O.B.A., fourth highest all time.

His R.B.I. count was only 49 in the P.L. year, his SL.% a fair .399, his hits counted 161 and runs scored 133. His B.R. count was +33 and F.R. +3; the commentary above on his fielding is fair. With his negatives accounted, the positives might overwhelm.

Hamilton led his league in hits one year, B.Avg. two years, O.B.A. six years, runs four years, and stolen bases five years; others have been statistical leaders, some in more categories, but few with next best near as great, and next to that, and more.

His benchmarks include 200+ hits two years, a .400+ B.Avg. one year, .300+ 11 years, .500+ O.B.A. one year, .400+ 11 years, .500+ SL.% one year (which requires brief discussion), 15+ triples one year, 100+ runs 11 years, 100+ walks five years, and 100+ S.B. three years.

He beat the mark of 50+ walks in a season 13 of his 14 years and the mark of 50+ stolen bases nine of his 14 years; one season he did have a .500+ slugging percentage, .005 higher than his O.B.A., in 1894 when he produced one of the greatest seasons in all of history.

In 129 games he had 544 at bats, with 220 hits, a nearly unique .400+ B.Avg. at .404; he was struck out 17 times, 3 percent of at bats; he drew 126 walks which compounded his B.Avg. to a very rare .500+ O.B.A. at .523. His SL.% was .528, with 25 doubles, 15 triples, and four home runs; SABR rates this season at +61 B.R.

He stole fewer than 100 bases in 1894; his total was 98, and his high was 111 in both 1889 and 1891; add to his 1894 data 192 runs scored, and 87 R.B.I. These are the current ranks achieved by Hamilton during that singular 1894 season — runs: first, B.Avg: 19th, O.B.A: sixth, S.B: 23rd.

Beyond which his hits and walks rank among the top 100 of all time; further his two 111 S.B. rank sixth, his 102 in 1890 rank 18th, and by every reputable count his 912 career stolen bases rank third in history.

His 1,187 career walks now rank 43rd and his 1,690 runs are 22nd. When Billy Hamilton jumped from the American Association to the National League in 1890, the Philadelphia Phillies, and later to lesser extent Boston Beaneaters, were the beneficiaries of one of the greatest major league leaps in all of baseball history.

HECKER, GUY JACKSON "GUY"
P, Louisville (A.A.) 1882–86

He was virtually insignificant in 1890 for the Pittsburgh (N.L.) Alleghenys, where he'd switched after eight A.A. years. His won 2 and lost 9 (.182 win %) were hardly a factor in the Pittsburgh quest for the worst records in history; they won 23 lost 113 (.169).

After a won 6, lost 6 record in his rookie year, Guy Hecker was benchmark class the next four years, and in 1884 he was spectacular; his won-lost the other years: 26–23 in 1883, 30–23 in 1885, 26–23 in 1886. Each is a benchmark in losses, as is 30 in wins.

His losses in the other year, 1884, were also benchmark at 20, but his wins numbered 52 and rank third among most in one season; his 72 complete games also ranks third, and his 671 I.P. of 1884. In fact the whole of his record that year is benchmark class.

Include his .722 win %, 75 games, 385 K's, and 1.80 E.R.A.; each of these stats also was a league leader, as would have been +106 pitching runs. Further that year his W.A.T. calculation is +18.0. He allowed just 56 walks, nearly a 7:1 ratio with K's. His .242 O.B.% also was a league-leading stat.

Before and after the 1884 season, the other benchmarks by Hecker include the obvious 30 wins, and three more season of 20+, 50+ games two years, 50+ C.G. one year, 400+ I.P. three years, a 2.18 E.R.A. in 1885.

After an 18 and 12 season in 1887 he went negative, 8–17 and 5–13, all with Louisville. Then came the year of the P.L. and the last of Hecker as a major league pitcher; his .182 really wasn't far from his team's .169.

During better years he established a .279 career O.B.%., 19th best all time, and was a much better than average player overall. He played the outfield or first base in 703 games, accumulating 2,866 at bats, with these among his results:

Hits: 810	R.B.I: N/A	B.Avg: .283	SL.%: .376
Runs: 501	Walks: 141	O.B.A: .324	B.R: +52

He had one terrific season as a pitcher, a handful of very busy years, as a batter had 183 extra base hits, 123 stolen bases, and an excellent +15 F.R. mark. When all was done after an awful P.L. year, Guy Hecker proved to be a very good baseball player.

HUTCHINSON, WILLIAM FORREST "BILL"
Chicago (N.L.) 1889–95

He began credibly with Chicago (N.L.) in 1889; he won 16, lost 17 (.485 win %), and pitched 318 innings, with a 3.54 E.R.A. In 1890 he was arguably, but not very, the best pitcher in the National League, and he continued at that level the next two years.

Among his data for the P.L. year—let an asterisk (*) indicate the league leader—were 42 (*) wins (lost 25, .530 win %), pitched in 71 games (*), 65 (*) complete games, and 603 (*) innings; his 603 I.P. ranks 13th all time.

His 44 putouts in 1890 ranks ninth all time by a pitcher, his 289 K's were second in the N.L., his .308 O.B.% was third, Win % fifth, E.R.A. was 2.70, P.R. +58, and W.A.T. +2.2 for the second place team; he allowed 505 hits and 199 walks.

His career win % is a deceivingly modest .530, based on totals of 183 wins and 162 losses in eight years, during which he pitched 3,066 innings, and beyond 1890 led in wins one year, games two years, C.G. two years, and I.P. two years.

His best year may have been 1892 — won 37, lost 36 (.507) aside — with 75 games, 67 complete, 627 innings, and 316 K's; his best win % was .698 based on 44 wins and 19 losses, with 561 I.P. in 1891.

His career E.R.A. is an ordinary 3.59, W.A.T. +8.6, but his work by SABR-stats produced +114 pitching runs. His benchmarks include 40+ wins two years, 30+ three years, 70+ games two years, 50+ three years, 60+ C.G. two years, 50+ three years, 600+ I.P. two years, 300+ five years, and 300+ K.s one year.

Hutchinson had three very impressive years among his eight, which includes the year the Players League played; according to one expert critic, in 1890 Bill Hutchinson was the premier pitcher in the National League.

LOVETT, THOMAS JOSEPH "TOM"
P, Brooklyn (A.A.) 1889, Brooklyn (N.L.) 1890–91

He began in a mediocre fashion, won 7, lost 8 (.467 Win %) for Philadelphia (A.A.) in 1885. He left and didn't return till 1889 with Brooklyn (A.A.), won 17, lost 10 (.630). He again was absent in 1892, then with Brooklyn his last two years, 1893 and 1894 won 3 and 8, lost 5 and 6. These were the lesser of his pitching years.

In 1891 with Brooklyn (N.L.) he won 23, lost 19 (.548), and in the year of the P.L. for N.L. Brooklyn was at the top of his game in leading a very good Bridegrooms staff to the N.L. championship with a record of won 30 and lost 11 (.730).

His winning percentage was the best in his league; 327 hits in 372 I.P. read well among his P.L. year data, which includes ranks of third in wins and second in W.A.T. with +5.4. He was in 44 games and completed 39 starts, with a 2.78 E.R.A., 324 O.B.%, and +32 P.R.

A few of his 1891 stats were comparable, 44 games and 39 C.G., but his E.R.A. was 3.69, O.B.% .335, and the SABR-stats say -14 P.R. despite a +5.2 W.A.T.

These two years, along with 1889, essentially were his career, won 88 and lost 59 (.599), 162 games and 132 complete, 1,306 I.P. with a telling 3.93 E.R.A. and .342 O.B.%, -28 P.R. and his +7.6 W.A.T. inform he didn't play on any championship teams but 1890.

LYONS, DENNIS PATRICK ALOYSIUS "DENNY"
3B, Philadelphia (A.A.) 1887–90, St. Louis (A.A.) 1891

His total of 13 years at the hot corner resulted in a career -30 F.R. mark, with his best being a +10 in the P.L. year. His batting stats for the five years cited are those of a star first baseman or an outfielder.

His name appears with regularity among the ranks for the period 1876–1889. His career began with Providence (N.L.) in 1885 and continued through 1897 with Pittsburgh. Among these ranks for the year 1887 his 209 hits are third highest in a season, his 43 doubles in 1887 also rank third, and 63 extra base hits ranks seventh.

In 1890 his 29 doubles tied for second in the A.A., 7 HRs third, he's fourth in B.R. the P.L. year, and second in total player rating in his league; in fact as a batter Denny Lyons may have been the best offensive 3B of the 1800s, as a concise summary shows:

	Career	1890	Best / Most
At Bats:	4,294	339	570 (1887)
Hits:	1,333	120	209 (1887)
Runs:	932	79	135 (1889)
R.B.I:	569+	N/A	105 (1893)
Walks:	621	57	97 (1893)
B.Avg:	.310	.354	.367 (1887)
O.B.A:	.407	.458	.458 (1890)
SL.%:	.443	.531	.531 (1890)
B.R:	+256	+41	+48 (1887)
S.B:	224	21	73 (1887)

He never led a league in any stat, but his benchmarks include his 200+ hits one year, .300+ B.Avg. seven years, .400+ O.B.A. seven years, .500+ SL.% one year, 100+ runs four years, 100+ R.B.I. one year, 30+ doubles two years, 15+ triples one year, and 10+ HRs one year.

His K's data are missing for many years, but he's known to have hit nothing but the wind 58 times in 1891. His 244 career doubles joined with 69 triples and 62 HRs result in a count of 28 percent of his hits for extra bases.

There's a hint of a free swinger in his stats, at least for his time. His data in the field are fairly acceptable for a third baseman. He could hit, and with power, and run some, the makings of an all star player, which Denny Lyons was in 1890, but not in the Players League.

McCARTHY, THOMAS FRANCIS MICHAEL "TOMMY"
OF, St. Louis 1888–91, Boston 1892–95

When he and Hugh Duffy were joined as the "Heavenly Twins" of Boston he was the lesser celestial statistically, as most other stars would have been. When he joined the ranks of major league players in 1884 his data say he was light years away from being a star.

He was first with Boston of the Union Association and batted .215. In 1885 with Boston (N.L.) he batted .182. In 1886 and 1887 with Philadelphia (N.L.) he batted .185 and .186. The sum of his stats these four years are best left at etc. Then came a breakthrough.

Tommy McCarthy switched to the A.A. for 1888; with St. Louis he batted a bit above average .274. On the same team the next year he batted .291, then .350 in the year of the P.L. for St. Louis of the A.A. He diminished somewhat but still was near .300 in 1895.

His last year was 1896, .249 for Brooklyn; he knew when to quit. He'd learned how to use the batter's box to his best advantage, but what he'd learned best was how to run the bases, for a total of 468 S.B. during his 13-year career. He led his league one year.

He also drew 537 walks, took over 1,000 bases without a hit, but after his long and dismal beginning he ran up a sum of 1,496 hits in 5,128 at bats, for a .292 career B.Avg., a .364 O.B.A., and with only 289 extra base hits a .376 career SL.%.

These latter, though, included 10 HRs in 1894, when he had 126 R.B.I. and a .490 SL.%, both very contrary to the major league player he'd become. His style as evidenced by benchmarks was more along the lines of 600+ at bats two years, a .300+ B.Avg. four years, .400+ O.B.A. three years, 100+ runs seven years, and 10+ HRs once.

As the premier batter in the American Association in 1890, his qualifications for such an accolade include 192 hits, 137 runs, .350 B.Avg., and a .430 O.B.A. Among his other 1890 stats were 66 walks, and one of six years with 50+.

Also in 1890 Tommy McCarthy stole 83 bases, which led the A.A., among four years of 50+. He had an outstanding count of +48 B.R. which led the A.A. in 1890, of a career total +87 B.R., and +3 F.R., of +60 total F.R., his best a benchmark +31 in 1888.

Lacking somewhat in power at the bat, this was a complete baseball player who was in St. Louis the year the P.L. played. This lesser "Heavenly Twin" was elected to the National Baseball Hall of Fame in 1946, noting he mastered the trapped fly ball trick.

McMAHON, JOHN JOSEPH "SADIE"
P, Philadelphia (A.A.) 1889–90, Baltimore (A.A.) 1890–91

A compelling case could be made for Sadie McMahon being on the edge of hall of fame potential. His major league career 1889 through 1897 lacks a year for eligibility, which makes this a moot issue, but his 1890 season record would serve as the catalyst.

He led the A.A. in wins in 1890, one of his many good years, also ranks first in games and complete games, I.P. and K's, and W.A.T. His win % in the P.L. year was a modest fifth. Odd but fact, this league leader pitched for two teams in 1890.

He began the season with Philadelphia, where he began in 1889 with a won 14, lost 12 (.538 Win %) record; in 1890 he won 29 and lost 18 (.617) before switching to Baltimore where he won 7 and lost 3.

While his record was in fine order the P.L. year, those of his teams were very much in disorder; his 29 wins (18 losses, .617) for the Athletics of Philadelphia were half the team's 58 wins (78 losses, .409). This team finished sort of next to last.

His 7 and 3 for Baltimore came after Baltimore replaced the new A.A. Brooklyn Gladiators, who went out of business on August 25; they'd replaced the Brooklyn Bridegrooms club, which had jumped to the N.L. for 1890.

There's more to this bit of 1890 baseball absurdity. The new and quickly gone extinct Gladiators played their home games on weekdays in the borough of Queens near Brooklyn, and Sunday games on the far side of Queens; thus the Brooklyn Gladiators weren't really even a Brooklyn team.

Whether Brooklyn or Baltimore, whatever, this team and club finished last in the A.A. of 1890, despite the efforts of Sadie McMahon. He continued with A.A. Baltimore in 1891 and had another very good year, winning 34, losing 24, .586 Win %.

Among the other data of Sadie McMahon these two 30+ win and 20+ loss season, and career compilations are:

	1890	1891	Career
O.B.%:	.332	.326	.347
E.R.A:	3.27	2.81	3.51
P.R:	+34	+51	+173
W.A.T:	+13.6	+5.9	+29.8

His workload these two years consisted of pitching in 60 and 61 games, with 55 and 53 complete, accumulating 509 and 503 innings; during his nine-year career these data counts were 321 games, with 279 complete, and 2,634 innings pitched.

He wasn't done when the A.A. went the way of the Gladiators to oblivion. He pitched for the halcyon Baltimore Orioles from 1892 through 1896. These are some of his N.L. with no options numbers, including the three consecutive years the Orioles were champions.

	1892	1893	1894	1895	1896	Career
Won:	20	23	25	10	11	173
Lost:	25	18	8	4	9	127
Win %:	.444	.561	.758	.714	.550	.577
Games:	48	43	35	15	22	321
C.G:	44	35	26	15	19	279
I.P.:	397	346	276	122	176	2,634
O.B.%	.352	.370	.378	.311	.358	.347
E.R.A:	3.24	4.37	4.21	2.95	3.48	3.51
P.R:	+2	+12	+35	+25	+17	+173
W.A.T:	+5.7	+5.1	+4.2	+1.1	-2.3	+29.8

During his one-year-too-brief career Sadie McMahon went from losing teams to champions. His name is seldom prominent when the world champion Baltimore Orioles are written of, though he was a prime force and a mainstay, foremost in their first year.

He went back to Brooklyn for the 1897 season, as did most of the Orioles stars, and after a 0 and 6 start closed out his edge of fame career, including a great 1890 season.

He led his league two years in wins, one year in games, two years in C.G., two years in I.P., also in K's one year with his high of 291 in 1890, W.A.T. one year which was 1890, and in shutouts two years.

His benchmarks include 30+ wins two years, 20+ five years, .700+ win % one year, 500+ I.P. two years, 300+ four years, P.R. +30 three years, and his career win % of .577 is tied for 100th on the all-time list.

McPHEE, JOHN ALEXANDER "BID"
2B, Cincinnati (A.A.) 1882–89, Cincinnati (N.L.) 1890–99

His career was long. Born at Massena, New York, and retired to San Diego, he stopped in the Midwest city of Cincinnati and stayed 18 years to play major league baseball. Almost the whole of his 2,135 games were played at the keystone position, second base.

He batted .300+ each of three years, had a .400+ O.B.A. three years, scored 100+ runs 10 years, and hit the mark of 15+ triples three years. The calculations of his B.R. total +145 and his F.R. count is +276, with four years of +30 and more.

He led his league in this stat one year, and in HRs one year, a very unusual combination. With 11 years of 50+ walks and four years with 50+ stolen bases, Bid McPhee proved himself excellent in all the facets of the game.

His career began with the first American Association champions. In his long term he didn't rate a negative F.R. till his next to last year, although he ranks second all time among all 2B with 791 errors.

He's also fourth with 6,545 putouts and in 1886 set the single-season 2B record with 529 putouts. He'd also fourth in assists with 6,905, 12th in double plays with 1,186, and his range factor of 6.33 is second all time among all 2B players.

His combination of hits and walks and stolen bases are the basic stuff of a star four position player. Seven HRs isn't many but in 1886 no A.A. player hit more. His 188 career triples now rank 11th among all players, and his 568 S.B. ranks 21st.

He was a prolific run scorer, the premium front end of the batting order player; he had no deficiencies of any sort at the bat, on the bases, or in the field. This was acknowledged by his election to the National Baseball Hall of Fame in the year 2000.

For 1890 N.L. Cincinnati he scored 125 runs via 135 hits, 82 walks, and 55 stolen bases. His B.Avg. was a below the norm .256, with his O.B.A. ideally by the book 100+ points higher at .362; not so with his .386 SL.%. His +15 B.R. and +26 F.R. explain much.

Many of his single-season data counts are missing; four years of stolen bases, six years of R.B.I., and 10 years of K's, as both major leagues were awfully remiss about maintaining consistent records of their players performance and production.

The best and most and career of McPhee among known data include 18 K's in 433 at bats (4.2 percent) in 1896, 303 doubles, 188 triples, and 52 HRs among 2,249 hits (24 percent for extra bases), 139 runs scored in 1886 of 1,678 total, 94 walks in 1893, and 95 S.B. in 1887.

His B.Avg. high was .305 in 1896, his O.B.A. .420 in 1894. His P.L. season at

Cincinnati was adequate in some respects, but on the whole not up to standards of Bid McPhee. He was the last 2B in the major leagues to not use a fielder's glove.

MULLANE, ANTHONY JOHN "TONY"
P, Cincinnati (A.A.) 1886–89, Cincinnati (N.L.) 1890–93

The list of his teams in all is much longer, including (all A.A.) Louisville in 1882, St. Louis in 1883, and Toledo in 1884. In fact he was the star of Toledo in 1884. He didn't pitch at all in 1885 as the result of a full-year suspension imposed by his league for excessive holdouts and intolerable contract jumping.

He actually held out, refusing to play for three years. Though mediocre in the year of the Players League, he was a sensation during the span of five years he did play during 1882–1887, winning 166 games while losing 109 (.604 Win %).

There are reports that he could pitch well from either side, also that he was mean and liked to throw at batters, and further, as *Sporting Life* reported, he was "a man of the most sordid nature," and openly biased against and hostile to Negroes.

Beyond his odious persona, Tony Mullane was a very good major league pitcher. During his 13-year career, 1881 through 1894 he had more than 500 decisions, with 285 wins and 220 losses, a .564 win %. He ranks ninth all time with 468 complete games, and 22nd if his innings pitched total is 4,531 and not 4,540.

His best year by win % was 1883–won 35, lost 15, .700. His best by E.R.A. was 1882, with a mark of 1.88, won 30, lost 24 (.556). Overall though his best was with Toledo in 1884: 37 wins and 26 losses (.587) in 68 games with 65 complete, 576 innings, 329 K's and 90 walks (3.66:1.00), a +14.8 W.A.T. and +49 P.R.

His best by SABR-stats counted was a +57 P.R. in 1883. He was +49 again in 1887; his total P.R. count is +247. A +14.8 W.A.T. in 1884 was his best, of a total +37.3. There's no doubt that he ranks among the top class of the 1800s as a pitcher.

His list of "led his league" includes win %, games, and K's each one year, and shutouts two years. His benchmarks included 30+ wins five years, 20+ eight years, a .700+ win % one year; 50+ games five years, 50+ C.G. three years, 500 I.P. two years, 300+ eight years, 300+ K's once, 2.00- E.R.A. one year, 2.50- two years, and P.R. at or above +30 five years. His only standout stat in the P.L. year is a 2.24 E.R.A. Otherwise Tony Mullane shows -0.7 W.A.T., 91 K's and 96 walks. He pitched in 25 games, 209 innings, 21 C.G., won 12 and lost 10 (.545). His closing years of 1893 and 1894 included pitching for the Cincinnati club (6 and 6) and Baltimore (12 and 16) in 1893, and for Baltimore (6 and 9) and Cleveland (1 and 2) in 1894; his pitching for many years was superior. Fairly said, Tony Mullane on the whole was otherwise.

NICHOLS, CHARLES AUGUSTUS "KID"
P, Boston (N.L.) 1890–1901

This is one of perhaps a dozen legitimate candidates for the title of "the greatest pitcher in history." As evidenced by his career record, best and most, and benchmarks he was outstanding for more than a decade, and thus properly awarded a place in the National Baseball Hall of Fame at Cooperstown in 1949.

He led his league in wins four years, games two years, I.P. one year, and shutouts three years. His benchmarks include 30+ wins seven years, 20+ 12 years, .700+ win % four years, 50+ games five years, 50+ C.G. one year, 400+ I.P. five years, 300+ 12 years, and 2.50- E.R.A. four years.

	Career	1890	Best / Most
Won:	362	27	35 (1892)
Lost:	207	19	N/A
Win %:	.636	.587	.738 (1897)
Games:	631	48	53 (1892)
C.G:	533	47	50 (1892)
I.P:	5,061	427	454 (1892)
K's:	1,868	222	240 (1891)
O.B.%:	.322	.303	.303 (1890 & 1892)
E.R.A:	2.95	2.21	2.02 (1904)
P.R:	+533	+64	+68 (1897)
W.A.T:	+36.0	+1.2	+7.8 (1896)

The span between his career wins and losses is one of the greatest. The counterpart to his 5,061 I.P. is 4,912 hits, barely less than a hit per inning. His 1,868 K's counters 1,268 walks, and for each of seven years his P.R. calculate to beyond +50.

Kid Nichols was a rookie in 1890, brought in to fill the void left by the loss of Hoss Radbourn to the Players League; 1890 was the beginning of a pitching career which some experts propose was the best of the 1800s after Spalding.

If any fault exists in the record of Kid Nichols it's in the fact that starts aren't included in the data set above; he made 562, for an outstanding 95 percent rate of complete games, none better than 47 of 48 (98 percent) for N.L. Boston in the P.L. year.

In his league in the P.L. year he ranks fifth in games and fourth in C.G., also fifth in I.P.; third in K's, and second in both O.B.% and E.R.A.; by one assessment he's also ranked first in the N.L. of 1890 in the category total pitcher index.

He's also ranked fifth all time in I.P., and by the evidence he could field his position in all-star style; he ranks 14th all time among pitchers with 311 putouts, and 18th in assists with 1,031.

Add to the all-time ranks among pitchers by Nichols 19th in win %, 20th in starts, 13th in batters hit with 133, and 15th with 169 wild pitches; he's sixth all time in career wins.

After his long and great stay in Boston, 100 percent N.L. Kid Nichols was out of the major leagues in 1902 and 1903. He returned for an encore with St. Louis in 1904, won 21, lost 13 (.618 win %); in St. Louis in 1905 he won 1 and lost 5 then switched to Philadelphia, where he won 10 and lost 6. He completed his career 0 and 1 with Philadelphia in 1906.

It's nearly impossible to pick one as his greatest year. If by I.P. it would be 1892 when he won 35, lost 16 (.686); if by win % then 1897, 31–11, .738; 1898 31–12, .712; 1893 34–14, .708; if by P.R. 1897 again; if by W.A.T. then 1896 with 30–14, .682.

There's further support for each of these seasons, and further if by E.R.A. then his finest year was 1904 for St. Louis, or if limited to the Boston segment of his 15-year career then 1898 won 31 and lost 12, 2.13, or at 2.21 allowing for his being then a rookie 1890, the P.L. year, excellent but not quite stellar.

The list of Kid Nichols's achievements in period stats 1890–1899: first in Wins, fifth in Losses, second in Win %, first in Games, first in Starts, first in C.G., first in I.P., seventh in Walks, second in K's, second in E.R.A., first in O.B.%, first in Hit batters, first in Wild pitches, first in Shutouts.

And if there were such a stat then Kid Nichols would be first in saves in the period 1890–1899 with 16.

O'CONNOR, JOHN JOSEPH "JACK"
C, Columbus (A.A.) 1889–91, Cleveland 1892–1897

A major league catcher for 21 years, he didn't lead in any stats and his only benchmark note is .300+ B.Avg. two years. He played game number 1,451 on his ledger in 1910 after being out two years. At that his career closure resulted in a long line of 0's.

Otherwise he had some good seasons, in the A.A. where he began with Cincinnati in 1887 and 1888, then switched to Columbus for the term 1889 through 1891. Then went with Cleveland, where he was known as "Rowdy Jack," where he had the best view of the action.

Whereas with the former, his A.A. teams, his duty was primarily catching pitches, while on the field for Cleveland he would have been calling the hit and run shots for his infielders, advising when to trip, grab a belt, when to let go, to warn and distract.

His best year as a player was easily 1890, for Columbus (A.A.), where he contributed a .324 B.Avg. (career .263), .377 O.B.A. (career .306), .411 SL.% (career .336), 89 runs (career 713) and 38 walks (career 301), all Jack O'Connor highs.

His stolen base high also came in 1890, 29 of a career sum of 220; he had 29 again in 1893 for the Spiders. His most R.B.I. among years known, not 1890, were 75 in 1893 of a known 671 total. His B.R. best is +19 in 1890 of -131 total; his best work in the field rates a +3 in 1892, of -74 total, -5 F.R. in 1890.

His 1890 Columbus pitching staff led the A.A. in shutouts and hits allowed, ranking second in O.B.% and E.R.A. The team finished second in the year of the P.L., the other two of the Solons' brief franchise life were sixth in 1889 and fifth in 1891, for which O'Connor is given due credit as catcher and as a batter.

He played for the Spiders through 1898, was one of the players switched to St. Louis by the Robison syndicate for 1899, continued at St. Louis into 1900 then went to Pittsburgh to end that season and continue through 1902, playing few games.

He switched to A.L. New York for 1903, then A.L. St. Louis for 1904, 1906–07, and 1910, usually batting in the very low .200s while fielding 0's and -'s except 1904 when he batted .294; his lengthy career consisted of 5,380 at bats, most 572 in 1892.

PIKE, LIPMAN EMANUEL "LIP"
OF, National Association 1871–75, N.L. 1876–78

His benchmark is a .351 B.Avg. in 1871 for the Trojans of Troy. His most runs were 73 in 56 games in 1873 for the Lord Baltimore club. His most at bats were 313 and most hits 107 both in 70 games for the St. Louis Reds in 1875.

Including here National Association data which are not yet in the official major league records, between the N.A. and N.L., in 1,987 at bats Lipman Pike made 625 hits for a .315 B.Avg., and scored 436 runs in 423 games.

The amount of N.A. data available is minimal. It's known his B.Avg. was .300+ three of the five N.A. years, that in sum he had a .300+ B.Avg. five years including .323 in 1876 for St. Louis (N.L.) and .311 in 1878 in a season split between Cincinnati 31 games and Providence five games (both N.L. clubs, of course).

While he was with the first professional major baseball league the schedules varied in the range of 50 to 80 games per year. It's possible to pro-rate his data but fairness becomes an issue as players historically haven't been consistent through a season.

For example his 73 runs scored in 1873, if adjusted to a season of 162 games, would calculate to 114 runs, and by his at bats about the same; but he could have been injured or gone into a frenzy, thus scoring 73 runs or as happened not long before nearly 200.

The complexity here of Pike goes beyond leagues and any official records. Foremost he didn't play in the year of the Players League and had not played since one game in 1887 with Brooklyn (A.A.) and prior to that five games in 1881 with Worcester (N.L.).

His service to the N.L. in the year of the P.L. was as an umpire, a tribute to him and by his service moreso to the league. He was born in 1845, in New York City where baseball was born, and he'd gained both popularity and fame before any major league creation.

Then and since he's also been the object of insipid discrimination, as his ancestry was Jewish, since the origins of (sic) civilization an excuse and rationale for moronic presumptions. The fact of 1890 was the N.L. recalled a great star to officiate its games, near as much so just calling "safe" or "out" as any of their many fine position players and pitchers.

His fame was grounded in his forte of daring and speed, on the bases and in the outfield. He's been avowed by credible witnesses as the fastest player in the game during his prime; by testimony of two writers, he once beat a racehorse running in a 100-yard dash.

The tattered and lacking statistics and information which have been garnered and ordered by the diligence of SABR serve as testament to the greatness of Lipman Pike. His official weight was 158 pounds, his height 5'8" so he was of course "diminutive."

His official stolen base sum is given as zero (0), an offense to baseball common sense; for critics and experts who can't accept the N.A. as a major league, his data separated by classification into N.A. and N.L. are these.

He was with the N.A. from its origin, played in 260 games, had 1,254 at bats, and scored 303 runs, mainly by 402 hits, for a .321 batting average; while playing in the N.L. he accumulated a .304 B.Avg., in 163 games, 733 at bats, scored 133 runs, and led the N.L. with four HRs in 1877.

Before the N.L. and N.A. he'd learned the skills of an infielder, primarily 2B and 3B, having begun as a player in 1866 with the Philadelphia Athletic Club; he went over to the New York Mutual for two years, then back to the Athletic for 1869 and 1870.

Hits weren't recorded his first two years, nor at bats. In 1866 his known stats stand remarkable, 49 outs (-) and 100 runs (+) in 16 games. 1867 produced a balance of 78 outs and 78 runs in 29 games. In 1868 83 outs and 82 hits, 60 runs, in 25 games.

1869: 325 total bases, on 175 hits, in 48 games; he'd settled in to 2B. 1870: 153 total bases, 84 hits, 21 games; he was playing the outfield by then. A compilation of his fielding averages of the period 1871 through 1878 range between .779 and .905.

At some point in time, Pike was tagged with the name of "The Iron Batter." Including the P.L. he was part of four major leagues; an unusual then lefty-lefty, this first Jewish baseball player of fame accomplished many brilliant feats.

If the appellation "The Iron Batter" rings not familiar, this was as complimentary in media vernacular in his time as would be a few decades later "The Big Train" (Walter Johnson) and "Big Six" (Christy Mathewson), and later "The Iron Horse" (Lou Gehrig).

As a fielder Pike was a sure catch, and a remarkably fast runner, while also singularly graceful in his movements. He played in the great and historic game of June 14, 1870, when after 11 innings the final score was Atlantics 8 and Red Stockings 7; he played for the winning side.

Lipman Pike died young, in 1893 at Brooklyn. Al Spalding and the N.L. company of 1890 knew a good catch when they could get one. Much about his career is reminiscent of Joe DiMaggio's.

PINKNEY (PINCKNEY), GEORGE BURTON "GEORGE"
3B, Brooklyn (A.A.) 1885–89, Brooklyn (N.L.) 1890–91

With 143 games played in 1888, and 141 games in 1886, unknown George Pinkney held the top two marks during the period 1876–1889; these were his most. His best came the year he moved from Brooklyn A.A. to Brooklyn N.L. His work at the bat and third base helped bring the N.L. pennant to Brooklyn in 1890.

On the lists of N.L. statistical leaders in 1890, his name is third in on base average, fourth in batter runs, and third in total average. He was well above average in hits, walks, and stolen bases, an unusual combination for a player at his position.

His work at the bat somewhat offsets a -16 F.R. at his demanding position.

Overall it was sufficient to assign Pinkney an N.L. star for the P.L. year. He reached his peaks in known R.B.I. with 83, in walks with 80, in B.Avg. with .309, O.B.A. .411, and SL.% with a relatively meager .431 mark.

To measure his relative success in 1890 his career data in these stats for a 10-year career are 391+ R.B.I., 525 walks, a very average .263 B.Avg., .345 O.B.A., and .338 SL.%; viewed from another perspective, he was 40, and 60, and 100 points above himself.

His high in hits came in the years he played most: 156 in both 1886 and 1888, and 150 hits in the P.L. year, 1,212 total. His at bats high was 580 in 1887, 485 in 1890, 4,610 in all. His runs were 134 in 1888, 115 in 1890, and 875 during his career.

He led his league one year in runs scored, 1888, in the midst of five consecutive 100+ runs years. He led in walks one year, 1886. All his other batting benchmarks came in 1890. He'd been at his best on the base paths in 1887, with 59 S.B. recorded, and 51 in 1888, of a career total 296 in the eight years known.

His SABR-stats are informative: his B.R. total +39, with a benchmark +32 for 1890, and +23 for 1888; his F.R. total a deficient -102 overall, +10 for 1887 his only positive mark, a -16 for the year the P.L. played.

His whole record says George Pinkney should have played at a position other than 3B, but even in his record years that's where he was every game, but then his name might have really not been Pinkney, so "quien sabe?"

His major league career began in the N.L., with 36 games in 1884. When the 1885 season began he was playing in the A.A. After the P.L. year he continued with N.L. Brooklyn in 1891, went to St. Louis for 1892, then Louisville 1894, and his career was done.

Seemingly out of place for a decade, he set a couple of unusual records, and had a very good year in 1890, good enough to be an all star at 3B in the National League.

RAMSEY, THOMAS A. "TOAD"
P, Louisville (A.A.) 1885–89, St. Louis (A.A.) 1889–90

Only once in major league history has a pitcher struck out 500+ opposing batters in a season. No pitcher has ever come closer to this impossible benchmark than Toad Ramsey. Both these fantastic feats were achieved in the same year, in the same league.

Ramsey recorded 499 official K's in 1886. His other data for that season include his high of 38 wins, a .585 win % which was tied in 1890, 67 games and 66 complete, 589 innings of pitching, a .292 O.B.% and 2.46 E.R.A., +65 P.R. and +10.2 W.A.T.

His count of walks in 1886 is also incredible, 207, which were reduced to 167 in 1887. His K's fell proportionally to 355, which led the A.A. In 1887 he lost 27 as in 1886, won 37, a .578 win % with 65 games on the record and 61 complete.

He had another good year among his six, but not near these levels. In 1890 he won 24 and lost 17, as noted .585, pitched in 44 and completed 34 games, in 349 innings had 257 K's and allowed 102 walks, O.B.A. .318 and E.R.A. 3.69, +7 P.R. and +0.8 W.A.T.

He also had a very bad year, and more; throughout 1888 he won 8 and lost 30, .211, 40 games and 37 complete, 342 innings, .330 O.B.% 3.42 E.R.A., -14 P.R. and -9.2 W.A.T. He began 1889 by winning 1 and losing 16, .059, 5.69 E.R.A. and went to St. Louis (A.A.).

This is nearly the whole record of Toad Ramsey: won 114 and lost 124, .479 win %, 248 games with 225 complete, 2,101 I.P., 1,515 K's and just 671 walks merit attention, .318 O.B.% and 3.30 E.R.A. are credible, and +96 P.R., -2.6 W.A.T. to the contrary.

He had a good year for his A.A. team in 1890, but not near his maximum performances. In the brief span of six years he recorded benchmarks galore and led his league in a few stats. The most notable of his achievements though is 499 K's in a season, and only one major league pitcher has ever exceeded that, once.

RAY, IRVING BURTON "IRV"
SS, Baltimore (A.A.) 1890–91

He's included here to fill a great void, as there was not in the A.A. of 1890 a shortstop who performed at an all-star level, nor any who played full time adequate to fair major league expectations.

Irv Ray played in just 38 of his teams' 134 games in 1890. His teams were actually one franchise composed of a discordant new Brooklyn enterprise which failed in August, then was taken over by Baltimore baseball entrepreneurs who built a last-place team.

With none among six position players who satisfied standard at bats criteria playing even near mediocre, Ray with 139 at bats must be noted as the best shortstop in the A.A. of 1890, literally by default.

Fairly said, these was nothing at all deficient about his work at the bat except an obvious lack of power, with a .360 B.Avg., .433 O.B.A., and .453 SL.%; he helped his cause with 15 walks and 11 S.B., and scoring 28 runs. His K's and R.B.I. are missing.

He played in 88 games in 1888 and 1889 for N.L. Boston and A.A. Baltimore, accumulating about 350 at bats and a composite .300+ B.Avg. He did play a full season in 1891, bating .278. His B.R. total for his brief career is +18, his F.R. total -45.

He played a bit at other positions, 2B and 3B and OF; the wonder is why he didn't play more all things considered. As little as he did in the P.L. year he was the best shortstop the A.A. had.

REILLY, JOHN GOOD "LONG JOHN"
1B, Cincinnati (A.A.) 1883–89, Cincinnati (N.L.) 1890–91

His 26 triples in 1890 rank ninth all time for a season. He hit for the cycle on August 6, 1890, a rare feat of hitting a home run, triple, double, and single in the same game.

In 1888 he led his league with 13 HRs, a .501 SL.%, and 103 R.B.I. It was not his best season; his 316 career errors as a first baseman rank 11th all time for his position. There aren't any positives among his 10 F.R. marks, but -22 total is tolerable.

He also led in SL.% another year, and home runs another year, and triples one year; his B.Avg. was .300+ each of five years, for his career a solid .289. His SL.% was .500+ two years, and for his career an above the 1800s norm .437. His career O.B.A. was .325, with just 157 walks added to his 1,352 hits in 4,684 times at bat.

He scored 898 runs, had 335 R.B.I. and struck out 156 times in the four years known; the image is that of a power hitter, affirmed by 215 doubles, 139 triples, and 67 HRs. Among his hits 31 percent for extra bases, he also stole a total of 245 bases.

Further affirmation of his batting abilities comes in the form of the B.R. SABR-stat, +164 career, best +46 in 1884, next +44 in 1888 which is his league high; in the P.L. year his B.R. was a good +19. He walked 16 times in 1890, and his high was 34 in 1889.

Further in 1890, John Reilly registered 553 at bats, 166 hits, including 25 doubles, the record one more triples, and 6 HRs, 34 percent of hits for extra bases is reaching the peak for the 1800s. His B.Avg. in the P.L. year was an even .300, his O.B.A. .328 for obvious reasons, and his SL.% .472. As per the above, he stole 29 bases.

He began with Cincinnati (N.L.) in 1880 and missed the next two years. The balance of his career itinerary is above, all Cincinnati. Among the best and most of this 1800s variety slugger were 553 at bats in 1890, 170 hits in 1887, and 114 runs in 1884 and 1890.

His high count of R.B.I. known is 103 in 1888; his batting average highs were all in 1884: .339 B.Avg., .366 O.B.A., and .551 SL.%; he hit 35 doubles in 1887 and the 26 triples noted in 1890. In addition to his 13 HRs in 1888 he hit a benchmark 11 HRs in 1884.

During his career of moderate duration, John Reilly had many good years, among which the year of the P.L. was just one.

RHINES, WILLIAM PEARL "BILLY"
P, Cincinnati (N.L.) 1890–92 & 1895–97

He was a rookie in the year the P.L. played. His nine-year career ended in 1899; he won 20+ games two years. 1890 was by far the better, with 28 wins and 17 losses (.622 Win %); 1890 was also his busiest and best year in a variety of baseball ways.

He pitched in 48 games, with 45 complete, 401 innings, with a career high 182 K's and career low 1.95 E.R.A.; his O.B.% in 1890 was an N.L. best .300, and his 1.95 E.R.A. was also the N.L. best. He walked 113 opponents, and pitched them six shutouts.

His 28 wins of 1890 rank fifth in the N.L. for the P.L. year; his six shutouts and 113 clutch pitching index both rank second. He was out of the major leagues in 1894, but when he was in he never did nearly as well as in his rookie year.

He led in E.R.A. another year, 2.45 in 1896, with an N.L. best .326 O.B.%; he won 20+ again, with 21 wins in 1897, against 15 losses (.583). He had 300+ I.P. one other year, 373 in 1891 when he won 17 and lost 24 (.415).

After a great novice season, all-star class, cite Billy Rhines as sporadic; there's no consistency to be found in his record, though the whole of his career is credible, even commendable:

Won: 114   Win %: .525   E.R.A: 3.48   C.G: 189   P.R: +86
Lost: 103   O.B.%: .341   Games: 249   I.P: 1,901   W.A.T: +3.6

The P.R. best by Rhines was +72 in 1890. He also produced a P.R. of +30 in 1896; his W.A.T. high was +5.1 in 1895, with a +3.0 mark for 1890.

Would his P.R. have been a terrific +72 as a P.L. rookie? Would this rookie at his best have won 28 P.L. games? That's a matter for baseball speculation, but he did just fine in the N.L. the year the P.L. played.

ROBINSON, WILBERT
C, Philadelphia (A.A.) 1886–90, Baltimore ex–Brooklyn 1890–1899

In 1890, after 82 games played for the Athletics, he went to Baltimore for 14 more for the franchise that came and went in 1890, between Brooklyn and Baltimore; he batted .241 with 91 hits in 377 at bats during this his itinerant season.

He also put a .283 O.B.A. in the record book, and a .332 SL.%, with 19 walks and unknown K's, 39 runs scored and unknown R.B.I.; add 18 hits for extra bases. The record isn't very impressive. He stole 21 bases, but behind the plate by SABR-stat he was +15 F.R.

In 1894, 146 pitches he hit found daylight in fair territory. This no doubt was his best all-round year as a player; only a .457 SL.% and 33 S.B. in 1896 aren't high marks of 1894 for Wilbert Robinson, then in his prime with the Baltimore Orioles.

That season included 494 at bats, 146 hits, 69 runs and 98 R.B.I., 46 walks and only 18 K's, 12 S.B. and a +7 B.R., .353 B.Avg., .421 O.B.A., and .430 SL.% with 21 doubles, four triples, and an HR.

After his playing career of 17 years, including 1901 and 1902 with A.L. Baltimore, and a falling out with longtime teammate and cohort John McGraw, he took the position of field manager in the borough of Trolley Dodgers.

Robinson became so popular that he was adopted as "Uncle Robbie." His record as manager of the Dodgers, or Robins as the team came to be called, stands at 1,375 won and 1,341 lost (.506 win %).

His team won just two league pennants during his term of 18 years, 1914 through 1931, but his popularity did not ebb; in 1945 Wilbert Robinson was elected to the National Baseball Hall of Fame as a manager.

As a player, a batter, in a game against St. Louis in 1892, he made a record seven hits and had 11 R.B.I.

RUSIE, AMOS WILSON
P, New York (N.L.) 1890–95 & 1897–98

He held out and did not play the entire 1896 season because of a personal and salary issue between himself and his owner, Andrew Freedman. Think of Amos Rusie as gnarly, especially in terms of K's and walks. The whole of his work earned him a place in the National Baseball Hall of Fame in 1977.

Rusie came back in 1897 a winner on every count in his confrontation with Freedman; when he pitched they passed like flashes, as he's reputed to have been one of the fastest pitchers in history, and one of the wildest.

Even with a losing record, 29 and 34 (.460 Win %), 1890 was a good year for him with 56 complete of 67 games and 341 K's in 549 innings of pitching; his K's led the N.L. as did his .232 B.A.%, his 2.56 E.R.A. was near benchmark, a count of +61 P.R. great, and his W.A.T. for the P.L. year is -2.4.

The owner he held out against has been cited as a superlative species of Tammany Hall bagman by trade a real estate lawyer. Amos Rusie collected a list of benchmarks a yard long and just as wide.

He won 30+ games four years, 20+ eight years, had a .700+ win % two years, pitched in 60+ games three years, 50+ five years, had 500+ innings of pitching three years, 300+ eight years, and tallied 300+ K's two years. He led his league in wins one year, games and C.G. one year each, I.P. also one year, K's five years, B.A.% four years, E.R.A. two years, shutouts four years, and would have led if there were such a stat then in P.R. two years, including an incredible +126 P.R. in 1894. He also led in W.A.T. one year. (Note that B.A.% is batting average not O.B.%)

Further on Rusie, his 289 walks in 1890 ranks first all time as the single-season record. His 341 K's in 1890 ranks 22nd. He allowed 200+ walks each of five years, and his 1,704 career walks rank seventh all time. His 1,934 career K's is 55th. He's 25th with 153 wild pitches, and must have been wild with discretion as he doesn't rank among the top 100 in hits batters. He does rank 46th all time in innings pitched.

The whole of his career extends from 1889 to 1901, but only 10 years, as he began in 1889 with Indianapolis (N.L.), was with the Giants 1890 through 1898 less 1896, then was out of the major leagues for two years before coming back for 1901 with N.L. Cincinnati.

The list of best and most by Amos Rusie is worth a scan, with his career data in the second parentheses:

Won: 36 (1894) (245)   E.R.A: 2.54 (1897) (3.07)   P.R: +126 (1894) (+417)
Lost: N/A (174)   Games: 67 (1890) (462)   W.A.T: +8.0 (1893) (+36.2)
Win %: .737 (1897) (.585)   C.G: 58 (1892) (392)   K's: 341 (1890) (1,934)
O.B.%: .322 (1892) (.341)   I.P: 549 (1890) (3,769)   Walks: 289 (1890) (1,704)

He would have been worth the price of an admission ticket when the N.L. Giants were in town in 1890: "Amos Rusie: The One Man Major League Base Ball Game." He lost more than he won in the P.L. year, but then only three N.L. pitchers won more.

STIVETTS, JOHN ELMER "JACK"
P, St. Louis (A.A.) 1889–91, Boston 1892–96

	Career	1890	Best / Most
Won:	202	27	35 (1892)
Lost:	132	21	N/A
Win %:	.605	.563	.686 (1892)
Games:	386	54	64 (1891)
C.G:	278	41	45 (1892)
I.P:	2,887	419	440 (1891)
O.B.%:	.350	.344	.304 (1889)
E.R.A:	3.74	3.52	2.25 (1889)
P.R:	+142	+16	+42 (1891)
W.A.T:	-2.8	-0.6	+1.9 (1896)

Led in: games one year (64 in 1891), O.B.% one year (.304 in 1889), E.R.A. one year (2.25 in 1889), and K's one year (259 in 1891).

Although 1892 was his best year, winning 35 and losing 16 (.686), in 1890 he was in the midst of a transition from quality to quantity; in all during his 11-year career, 1889–99, with St. Louis (A.A.) the first three years he won 72 and lost 50 (.590), he became a .600+ pitcher by virtue of his 1892 season with Boston.

He continued with the Beaneaters through 1898. During the four seasons which followed his best, Jack Stivetts won 84 and lost 57 (.596) with season records of 20–12 (.625), 26–14 (.650), 17–17 (.500), 21–14 (.600).

His telling E.R.A. was consistently well above 4.00 after 1892, and was as high as 4.90 in 1894; when that factor doubles it's time for a major league pitcher to start considering a future beyond baseball, which Stivetts didn't do.

His last three seasons were 11 and 4 with Boston, then 0 and 1, then with the greatest losers in the history of the game, he went out the same at won 0 and lost 4 in the Cleveland Spiders' worst year. His P.L. season, though, was a success in every way, one of the many of Jack Stivetts as a pure National League pitcher.

STRATTON, C. SCOTT "SCOTT"
P, Louisville (A.A.) 1890–93

He was great in 1890, the year of the Players League; he led the American Association in win % and E.R.A., two very vital and informative baseball statistics. His best next to this career season was 1892: won 21, lost 19, .525 Win % with a 2.91 E.R.A.

All three are career best and most for Scott Stratton. In the P.L. year he won 34 and lost 14, .706 win %, with a 2.36 E.R.A., his O.B.% was .260, and his P.R. +72. He pitched in 50 games and completed 44, with 431 innings pitched; his K's were 207, with 61 walks.

His W.A.T. in 1890 counts to +4.4, next best to +4.8 in 1892; the two stats noted above were his only league leaders. In 1890 he was second among A.A. pitchers in wins, fourth in games, third in C.G. and I.P., third in W.A.T., second in shutouts with four, and first in O.B.%.

To summarize the P.L. season for Stratton, for one season this pitcher ranked premier among his peers. Before 1890, with Louisville (A.A.), he began his major league career in 1888, won 10 and lost 17 (.370), and in 1889 he won 3 and lost 13 (.188).

Neither these nor his further data give any indication of what Stratton could achieve. His E.R.A. had been 3.63 and 3.22, and he'd pitched 270 and 134 innings; as peculiar, he reverted back to these levels in 1891, 0 and 0 with Pittsburgh, then 6 and 13 (.316) when he was returned to Louisville.

Actually excepting the brief Pittsburgh interruption, he was a Louisville pitcher from 1888 through early 1894, with marks of 12 and 24 (.333) in 1893, then 1 and 5 (.167) before switching to Chicago, also of course having switched leagues after 1891.

He won 8 and lost 5 (.615) for Chicago in 1894, won 2 and lost 3 (.400) in 1895, and put an end to a quite inferior major league eight-year career. The sum of his benchmarks is brief: 30+ wins one year, 20+ two years, .700+ win % one year, 50+ games one year, 400+ I.P. one year, 300+ three years, and 2.50- E.R.A. two years.

His career line in the record books includes 97 wins and 115 losses, a .458 win %; 231 games, 199 complete, 1,893 I.P., 570 K's and 436 walks, a .344 O.B.% and 3.88 E.R.A.; with SABR-stats of +5 P.R. and +3.2 W.A.T. Scott Stratton was great one season, and had a superlative P.L. season, as an all-star pitcher of the American Association.

SWARTWOOD, CYRUS EDWARD "ED"
OF, Pittsburgh (A.A.) 1882–83, Toledo (A.A.) 1890

An actual "Cy" from Rockford, Illinois, he began with one game for Buffalo (N.L.) in 1881; he got a hit in three at bats, and a walk. He left the major leagues after the 1887 season returning to play in the little Midwest town of Toledo in the P.L. year. He quit again but came back again with Pittsburgh in 1892 for 13 games. Although it was rather brief and disordered, Ed Swartwood had an excellent major league career.

With only 42 at bats counted in 1892, for a .238 B.Avg., the P.L. year was really his last. He led the A.A. in O.B.%, was fifth in B.Avg., and third in walks; among stats less than familiar, he ranks third in total average and third in total player rating.

He's been relegated to obscurity, playing only nine years, but seldom was there a year his performance didn't merit attention. During his career he led his league in hits one year, B.Avg. one year, in O.B.A. two years, doubles one year, and walks one year.

He produced a .300+ B.Avg. each of three years, .400+ O.B.A. one year and 100+ runs one year. 1890 was overall probably the best year for Swartwood. The following shows his career data, 1890, his best and most; let an asterisk (*) indicate league leader.

	Career	1890	Best / Most	Also
At Bats:	2,877	462	471 (1886)	
Hits:	861	151	151 (1890)	177 (*) (1883)
Runs:	607	106	106 (1890)	86 (*) (1882)
R.B.I:	N/A	N/A	N/A	
Walks:	324	80	80 (1890)	
B.Avg:	.299	.327	.356 (1883) (*)	
O.B.A.	.378	.442	.442 (1890) (*)	.391 (*) (1883)
SL.%:	.400	.444	.498 (1882)	
B.R:	+157	+42	+42 (1890)	+35 (1883)
S.B:	120+	53	53 (1890)	
F.R:	-7	+5	+5 (1886 & 1890)	

During his career, Swartwood hit totals of 120 doubles, 63 triples, 15 HRs, and 23 percent of his hits for extra bases; his 1890 sum of S.B. make it clear he could run the bases although his total is far from complete with only four years in the records.

Nonsensical as they appear, the records show him with a total of 4 R.B.I. and 11 K's, both in his last year, with the rest of those columns blank. He made a fair share of benchmarks, including plenty in 1890, and one merits a bit of discussion.

In the year the P.L. played, Swartwood had 151 A.A. hits in 462 at bats, supplemented by 80 walks, with 23 of his 120 career doubles (his 18 led the A.A. in 1882), 11 of his 63 career triples, and three of his career 15 home runs.

This was a very good batter, in many ways, who had a very good year at the bat, and every which way baseball calculates for 1890; perhaps not so for every fan and scholar who studies the stats, but here his .442 O.B.A. and .444 SL.% rate peculiar.

Whether it was with Pittsburgh (A.A.) 1882–1884, Brooklyn (A.A.) 1885–1887, and including Toledo of the American Association in 1890, and perhaps foremost Toledo in the year the P.L. played, each of his teams had in Ed "Cy" Swartwood a fine 1800s baseball player.

THOMPSON, SAMUEL LUTHER "SAM"
OF, Detroit (N.L.) 1885–88, Philadelphia (N.L.) 1889–98

For the record, his career began in 1885. He was outstanding, with a .303 B.Avg., .500 SL.%, +19 B.R., and +6 F.R. He maintained these standards or got better till the day he left the major leagues after the 1898 season, with closing data of .349 B.Avg., .571 SL.%, +6 B.R., and 0 F.R.

Fairly said, his career ended after the 1896 season. He recorded only 13 at bats in 1897 and 63 in 1898. There was a cameo appearance by Sam Thompson with Detroit in 1906, 31 at bats with the Detroit A.L. club, but he didn't nearly do justice to his record.

With Detroit (N.L.) in 1887, he led the league with 203 hits, a .372 B.Avg., .571 SL.%, and 166 R.B.I.; he also scored 118 runs, hit 29 doubles and 23 triples, 11 HRs, and made 24 assists from the outfield. His stats of the P.L. year blend well with these, as typically terrific for Thompson.

In 1893, still with Philadelphia, where he'd switched for the 1889 season, he led the N.L. with 222 hits and 37 doubles, and put a .370 B.Avg. in the record book, along with a .424 O.B.A. and .530 SL.%; this year he hit 11 HRs, scored 130 runs, and had 126 R.B.I.

What have been cited throughout as benchmarks were the norms for Thompson, often well beyond. 1893 was as great as any of his seasons. It was also prelude to the consensus greatest outfield performances in all of baseball history.

Still with the Phillies, sharing the outfields of Huntington Grounds and the University of Pennsylvania Athletic Field with Billy Hamilton and Ed Delahanty, he batted .407, as all three batted .400+. Thompson also hit 27 triples and 13 HRs; his SL.% was calculated at .686.

Thompson was the first player to hit 20+ HRs in a season (1889), the first with 200+ hits and 300+ total bases in one season (1887); he's the best run producer in history.

During his career, Thompson accumulated an average of .923 runs batted in per game; by another, lesser, view he ranks 10th in history with an R.B.I. for each 4.66 at bats.

If defensive luster were necessary, his assists adjusted to a 162-game season equal 32.63, which ranks fourth in history among outfielders. His 283 OF assists ranks 12th, and being part of 65 double plays ranks 15th.

Back to Thompson at the bat. His 128 career HRs stand second among all 1800s players. A bit aside, the world record for career HRs is held by Sadaharu Oh, of the Yomiuri/Tokyo Giants; he hit 868 round trippers during his 1959–1975 career.

For Thompson of the National Baseball Hall of Fame in 1974, and the reasons are plenty, 1890 was one of more than a dozen superb seasons, but he did not play in the 1890 Players League. These are among his N.L. numbers for that year.

He led in hits with a modest total of 172, and in doubles with 41; he was third in R.B.I. and total bases, and fourth in B.Avg. He was not a one- or two-dimension player. Between 1890 and 1896 he averaged 25 outfield assists per year (Willie Mays' season best was 23, Joe DiMaggio 22, Roberto Clemente 27); only Tris Speaker was consistently better than Thompson.

His batting benchmarks include 200+ hits three years, a .400+ B.Avg. one year, .300+ seven years, .400+ O.B.A. four years, .600+ SL.% two years, .500+ four years, 100+ runs 10 years, 100+ R.B.I. eight years, 40+ doubles two years, 30+ four years, 20+ triples three years, 20+ HRs one year, 10+ six years, and he counted 600+ at bats two years.

His B.R. total is a massive +376, including +53 for 1887, +34 for 1892, +45 for 1893, +51 for 1894, and +59 for 1895 when he had 211 hits in 538 at bats, including 45 doubles, 21 triples, 18 HRs (40 percent of hits for extra bases), 11 K's (2.0 percent of at bats), and 31 walks to first base.

His career and season stolen base counts are modest, 229 total, with a high of 29 in 1891. His F.R. marks are excellent, +32 career with +19 in 1891 and +18 in 1892. His career K's known are 226 in 12 years. His career extra base numbers are phenomenal, with 340 doubles, 160 triples, and 127 home runs.

As evidenced by the summary of Thompson's work below, his career K's among at bats would be about 4 percent, and his extra base hits among total hits is 32 percent; by the theorem that equal runs scored and runs batted in over a long career indicate a great player, his related data make the theorem a perfect fit, or vice versa.

Further and fairly said of Thompson, if he'd played seven, maybe 10 more seasons while maintaining his standards, Babe Ruth might be the second name that novice baseball readers would look for in the record books; he is one of perhaps a dozen legitimate candidates for the title of the greatest player in major league history. He played in the N.L. the year the P.L. played.

	Career	*1890*	*Best / Most*
At Bats:	5,984	549	609 (1892)
Hits:	1,979	172	222 (1893)
Runs:	1,256	116	131 (1895)
R.B.I:	1,299	102	166 (1887)
Walks:	450	42	59 (1892)
B.Avg:	.331	.313	.407 (1894)
O.B.A.	.384	.371	.458 (1894)
SL.%:	.505	.443	.686 (1894)
B.R:	+376	+26	+59 (1895)
F.R:	+32	−1	+19 (1891)
S.B:	229	25	29 (1891)

These are the period stats of Thompson, 1876–1889 and 1890–1899. Both lists are exceptionally long:

1876–1889:	1890–1899:
Fifth in Hits	Eighth in Doubles
Third in Triples	Fourth in HRs
Fifth in HRs	Sixth in Extra base hits
Eighth in Extra base hits	Sixth in R.B.I.
Second in Total bases	Eighth in B.Avg.
First in R.B.I.	Second in SL.%
Sixth in SL.%	Seventh in Combo O.B.A. & SL.%
Ninth in Combo O.B.A. & SL.%	

Sam Thompson played for the Philadelphia Phillies of the National League in 1890. He was not quite at the spectacular level of most other years, but was still beyond the imaginings of most major league players.

TIERNAN, MICHAEL JOSEPH "MIKE"
OF, New York (N.L.) 1887–99

He was the premier batter of the National League in 1890, and outstanding for more than a decade. It's beyond explanation that Mike Tiernan hasn't yet been elected a member of the National Baseball Hall of Fame, and in fact through 1989 hadn't been nominated.

1890 might well serve as exemplary measure of Tiernan: first in SL.%, total bases, and batting runs, second in home runs and total average, third in hits and triples, and fourth in runs scored; few if any could measure up to his achievements in the P.L. year.

The New York Giants of owner John Day and field manager Jim Mutrie had in Tiernan the best player in their league, yet the team finished sixth of eight, won 63 and lost 68 (.481 Win %), and 24 games out of first place.

This was excused by one apologist source because the Giants were decimated and doomed by the pursuits and success of their P.L. neighbors, as Tiernan was one of rare few they were able to retain from their 1889 roster despite the reserve clause.

He was exceptional in this regard, and in the fact that he played for only one team and club during his major league career of 13 years. He did play well indeed, except in the field where his F.R. total is -99, and there's not one (+) among his marks.

Otherwise, Tiernan led his league in SL.%, runs, and walks all one year. As is to be seen he excelled at gaining free bases. His K's are rather high for a master at the bat with 318 known and three of 13 years' data missing, and a high of 53 K's in 1890.

	Career	*1890*	*Best / Most*	*Period Stats 1890–1899*
At Bats:	5,906	553	553 (1890)	10th in Runs
Hits:	1,834	168	192 (1896)	Third in Triples
Runs:	1,313	132	147 (1889)	Third in HRs
R.B.I:	851	59	102 (1893)	10th in SL.%
Walks:	747	68	96 (1889)	Seventh in Extra base hits
B.Avg:	.311	.304	.369 (1896)	
O.B.A.	.392	.385	.452 (1896)	
SL.%:	.462	.495	.527 (1895)	
S.B:	428	56	56 (1890)	
B.R:	+309	+40	+48 (1889)	

With the B.R. stat being an after the fact assessment device, those of Tiernan reveal much about him that other data don't. His total is among the highest, as shown his high is +48 for 1889, for the P.L. year +40; also of benchmark class he has a count of +46 for 1896, and two more +30 or better marks.

Further among Tiernan benchmarks are a .300+ B.Avg. seven years, .400+ O.B.A. four years, .500+ SL.% two years, 100+ runs seven years, 100+ R.B.I. one year, 30+ doubles one year, 15+ triples three years, and 10+ HRs five years.

He's not lacking anywhere, except the aforementioned. In fact his record by parts and as a whole rates outstanding; the reason for the Cooperstown error might be in oversight, otherwise it's unknown. What is known of Mike Tiernan is that he was a star in the P.L. year, was 100 percent of the National League, and 100 percent for the New York (N.L.) Giants.

TUCKER, THOMAS JOSEPH "TOMMY"
1B, Baltimore (A.A.) 1887–89, Boston (N.L.) 1890–97

After a career year in the A.A., Tommy Tucker chose the N.L. for 1890, a vital loss and gain for the leagues respectively, but for his chosen team and club he could not nearly compensate for the Beaneaters' loss of Dan Brouthers to the Players League.

The P.L. year of Tucker was a bit above the level he'd established the two years prior to his phenomenal 1889 season; he then leaped and bounded 100 points beyond his prior calculated data. The same holds true for his raw numbers except one; let an asterisk (*) depict league leader:

	1887	1888	1899
Hits:	144	149	196 (*)
Runs:	114	74	103
R.B.I:	N/A	61	99
B.Avg:	.275	.287	.372 (*)
O.B.A:	.347	.330	.450 (*)
SL.%:	.372	.400	.484
B.R:	+3	+20	+50 (*)

He was a better than average batter throughout his 13-year career, 1887–99. "Foghorn," as he was called for reasons now obscure but easily guessed, did well enough though not great on the base paths and at first base.

He stole a total of 352 bases, 85 in 1887 and 63 in 1889; his F.R. total is -11, with -14 in 1892 and -11 in 1893, a best of +6 in 1888. He now ranks seventh all time among 1B with 393 errors, with moderate range.

He set a record at home plate as a batter, involving hitting not batting. He ranks second all time among all players for being hit by pitches 272 times, including 33 times during his stellar 1889 season.

With all his league leader stats shown above, his benchmarks include a .300+ B.Avg. four years and .400+ O.B.A. two years. He never reached the .500+ SL.% level. Each of five years he scored 100+ runs, and one year had 100+ R.B.I.

His 1890 stats and career data are all first class, though none are near his dazzling data of 1889; with his career numbers in parentheses, his P.L. year included a .295 B.Avg. (.290), .387 O.B.A. (.364), .362 SL.% (.373), 104 runs scored (1,084), and 62 R.B.I. (848+).

His strike zone judgment and batting discretion enabled almost a 2:1 ratio in walks and K's; his career sums are 479 and 223 known in eight years. He totaled highs of 61 walks in 1895 and 35 K's in 1892 and 56 walks and 22 K's in the year the P.L. played.

During his career, Tucker collected 6,479 at bats and 1,882 hits, among which are less than expected extra base data:

	Career	1890	Most
2B:	240	17	27 (1896)
3B:	85	8	12 (1888)
HRs:	43	Never had a double digit year.	

His contributions to the three consecutive Boston championship teams of 1891, 1892, and 1893, were journeyman rather than yeoman, and he faded fast after 1897; that year after four games for Boston he switched to Washington, and batted .333 for the year.

His 1898 season consisted of 73 games with Brooklyn and 72 games with St. Louis, a composite .260 as average as it gets for batting averages; his destiny had been set when he joined the Robison brothers' combine. He was relegated to Cleveland for 1899 and played in 127 of the team's 154 games.

Tucker batted .241 in 1899, below average and far below his. He could not have known the feeling of winning more than 20 times, as that poor team was beaten a record 134 times, and finished last of 12 in the N.L. by an unbelievable 84 games.

Sufficiently inspired to quit the major leagues as a player, Tommy Tucker had made for himself a credible above the norm career, including a very solid P.L. season with his new N.L. team, while his former of the A.A. were out of their league.

WELCH, MICHAEL FRANCIS "MICKEY"
P, New York (N.L.) 1883–92

His recently revised 309 career wins ranks 17th all time, 549 starts ranks 24th, 525 complete games ranks sixth, 4,802 innings pitched ranks 14th, 1,850 K's are 59th, and 2.71 E.R.A. 56th. His 274 wild pitches are the second most in history, and Mickey Welch was elected to the National Baseball Hall of Fame in 1973.

Welch, on August 2, 1884, struck out the first nine batters he faced, a record that has remained untouched. His 44 wins and 11 losses (.800 win %) season in 1885 sustains as one of the greatest seasons in history; in 1885 he won 17 consecutive decisions.

He began his major league career with the Troy (N.L.) Trojans in 1880; his won 34 and lost 30 (.531) record and 2.54 E.R.A. left no doubt that he was up to the challenge. Continuing at Troy with a 21 and 18 (.538) record and 2.67 E.R.A. in 1881, he then won 14 but lost 16 (.467) with a 3.46 E.R.A. in 1882.

While Welch produced, Troy didn't, not in terms of the amounts of dollars which they sent the way of the owners of the franchise, or the others who as visitors took portions of the gate receipts with them when they left town.

Some really major league shenanigans put the Troy franchise in dissolution, which reappeared healthy and well in New York City as the Gothams soon to be Giants; at the same time the same sort of tactics moved the Worcester club to Philadelphia.

There's more to the Troy to New York maneuver. The same Metropolitan Exhibition Company which owned the Gothams/Giants also owned the New York City franchise in the American Association, which the company president, John Day, illegally by National Agreement rules, used to build an apparently better 50¢ team at prevailing prices pay per view than their 25¢ team.

The whole of the schemes didn't work out quite as expected; the New York monied men were threatened with revocation of their A.A. franchise, and all the while Welch went with the flow to begin pitching for the New York N.L. club in 1883.

He had another good and productive season, won 25 and lost 23 (.521), with a 2.73 E.R.A.; he was back in original form. The next three seasons of pitching by Welch were spectacular. Among his totals are 116 wins and 54 losses, a .682 win %.

	1884	1885	1886
Won:	39	44	33
Lost:	21	11	22
Win %:	.650	.800	.600
O.B.%:	.308	.276	.337
E.R.A:	2.50	1.66	2.99
P.R:	+23	+63	+18
W.A.T:	+11.2	+7.9	-2.3

There were a couple of subtle hints that he was slipping, but he had three more very good seasons before the P.L. year. In 1887 he won 22, lost 15 (.595) with a 3.36 E.R.A. In 1888 he won 26, lost 19 (.578) with a great 1.93 E.R.A. With a 3.02 E.R.A. mark in 1889, he won 27 and lost 12 (.692).

Came 1890 and the Players League on the field, Welch continued amidst the chaos with the New York (N.L.) Giants, though not up to the levels of his previous 10 years; he won 17 and lost 13 (.567), with a 2.99 E.R.A. for a decimated team.

The balance of his P.L. year record includes 37 games with 33 complete, 268 I.P., 97 K's and 122 walks, .337 O.B.%, +19 P.R. and +3.1 W.A.T. The next year he won 5 and lost 9 (.357), and in 1892 didn't have a record for the game he pitched five innings in, with a 14.40 E.R.A. The great Mickey Welch was finished.

During his career he led the N.L. in win % and shutouts one year, won 40+ games one year, 30+ four years and 20+ nine years, had an .800+ win % one year, pitched in 60+ games two years, 50+ five years, had 60+ C.G. two years, 50+ four years, 500+ I.P. three years, 300+ 10 years, 2.00- E.R.A. two years, 2.50- three years, and 300+ K's one year.

He was busiest in his rookie year, pitching in 65 games, with 64 complete, 575 innings; when he marked up 345 K's in 1884 he allowed 146 walks. His P.R. SABR-stat total is +213 with +63 for 1885, +43 for 1888, and +42 for 1889; his W.A.T. high is +11.2 in 1884, next best +7.9 in 1885 which led the N.L.

He'd come a long way from 34 and 30 in 1880, 44 and 11 midway through his fine career, and was still successful and productive in the year the P.L. played. This is the basic record of Mickey Welch, National League pitcher, New York Giants all the way:

Won: 307	Win %: .585	E.R.A: 2.71	C.G: 525	P.R: +213
Lost: 209	O.B.%: .314	Games: 564	I.P: 4,801	W.A.T: +37.7

Mickey Welch almost joins the very exclusive ranks of pitchers with 100+ more career wins than losses; after Pud Galvin and longtime teammate Tim Keefe, he was the third major league pitcher to join the class of 300+ career wins.

WERDEN, PERCIVAL WHERITT "PERRY"
1B, Toledo (A.A.) 1890 & Many Teams and Leagues

He led his league in triples two years with 20 in 1890 and 29 in 1893, and made 18 in 1891. Between 1884 and 1897 he played in major leagues seven years. His data, teams, and leagues are for a fact and literally all over the 1800s baseball map.

1884: St. Louis, U.A., 18 games, 76 at bats, .237 B.Avg.
1888: Washington, N.L., three games, 10 at bats, .300 B.Avg.
1890: Toledo, A.A., 78 walks, 59 S.B., 113 runs, +37 B.R.
1891: Baltimore, A.A., 102 runs, 104 R.B.I., 52 walks, 59 K's
1892: St. Louis, N.L., 59 walks, 52 K's, +10 F.R.
1893: St. Louis, N.L., 29 triples as noted above
1897: Louisville, N.L., .302 B.Avg., +17 F.R.

During his seven major league years, Perry Werden played in 693 games and collected 2,740 at bats; he made 773 hits for a .282 B.Avg., among which were 109 doubles, 87 triples, and 26 home runs, for a count of 29 percent extra base hits, building a .414 SL.%.

He was walked to first base 281 times, significant in his .358 O.B.A.; he stole 150 bases, the most were 59 in the P.L. year. His batting was good for a +74 B.R., his fielding a +31 F.R. Both R.B.I. and K's are lacking much data, thus unknown. It is known that Werden scored 444 major league runs.

Playing for the Toledo (A.A.) Maumees, aka Black Stockings, nee Blue Stockings, with home games at Speranza Park, Werden had a very good year for a pretty good team; they won 68 and lost 64, a .515 win %, finishing fourth, 20 games out of first place.

Werden played in 128 of their games, had 498 at bats, with 147 hits, for a .295 B.Avg., with 22 doubles, 20 triples, and 6 HRs; a terrific 33 percent of his hits were for extra bases and a .456 SL.%. His 78 walks grew a benchmark .403 O.B.A., and another such mark of 59 S.B. helped along the way to 113 runs scored, with a +1 F.R.

He didn't play many years, or for long in the same place, but when he did Perry Werden was a very good baseball player. In fact had no faults to be found; he recorded a good number of benchmarks, had a couple of very good years, and could have been more perhaps. The year of the Players League was his best, in the A.A.

WHITNEY, JAMES EVANS "JIM"
P, Boston (N.L.) 1881–84, Philadelphia (A.A.) 1890

His first year was 1881, for N.L. Boston, which was spectacular, with a league-leading 31 wins, and 33 losses (.484 Win%). He led the N.L. as a rookie with 66 games, 57 complete, and a 552 I.P.; his 2.48 E.R.A. did not lead, nor his +18 P.R., nor his +5.9 W.A.T.

Jim Whitney got better, and worse. Comparing his career wins and losses with E.R.A. and W.A.T. suggest one of these sets of stats should be quite different; which becomes obvious when his record after the first four years is perused, and he became a losing pitcher.

To recite his early record in a manner other than ordinary would be logical; 24 wins in 1882, 37 wins in 1883, and 23 wins in 1884 are enough to form a perception. Twenty-one then another 21 and 14 losses form the statistical image of the pitcher. A .533 win % then .638 and then .622 say this was a very good major league pitcher.

He was in fact; Whitney was that and more. He's ranked 20th in history with 377 complete games, and 15th with a career .276 O.B.%; in terms of one-on-one confrontations with batters, his career record includes 1,571 K's and only 411 walks, a superb 3.8:1.0 ratio. His 411 walks measured against his 3,496 I.P. results in a very meritorious rate of one walk every 8.5 innings pitched.

To embellish on his excellence, Whitney during his 10-year career won 30+ games two years, 20+ five years, pitched in 60+ games two years, 50+ three years, had 50+ complete games three years, 500+ I.P. two years, 300+ eight years, 2.50- E.R.A. three years, and 300+ K's one year.

That one year of 300+ K's is astounding. In 1883, at his best, Whitney pitched 514 innings. He recorded a league-leading 345 K's, and by the book 35 walks; that's a 9.86:1.00 ratio. There's no such stat, but if there were, it is doubtful any major league pitcher of any era has ever exceeded that bit of datum.

Imaginings aside, to continue the above, Whitney won 18 games in 1885, half his sum of two years before, then he won 12 games in 1886, a third of 1883. Both these latter years he lost 32 games; his win % are .360 and .273, 30 won and 64 lost = loser.

Not a dichotomy, not an anomaly, Whitney just has a very unusual pitching record; he improved to 24 wins and 21 lost (.533) in 1887, then fell again to won 18, lost 21 (.462) in 1888; in 1889 he won 2 and lost 7 (.222), with a 6.81 E.R.A.

He left the Boston N.L. club after the 1885 season and became the all-too-common itinerant: 1886 Kansas City (N.L.), 1887 and 1888 Washington (N.L.), 1889 Indianapolis (N.L.). For the P.L. year he switched team and leagues, was with A.A. Philadelphia.

Measured against his record of nine years, this was almost a non-event. He won 2 and lost 2, was in six games with three complete, pitched 40 innings, early on a week of work, his O.B.% was .407, his 5.17 E.R.A. doubled his best of 2.09 in 1884, and 0.99 more.

Whitney is an uncommon 200+ game major league loser, with 204; he won 191 games, for a .484 win %. SABR-stats assign a +10.2 W.A.T. mark to his career, and a +57 P.R., with totally contrary yearly marks of +51 for 1883, and −52 for 1886.

Whitney didn't pitch in the P.L. of 1890, nor much at all in the major leagues that year, excepting a bit in the A.A. During the whole of the decade he pitched, Jim Whitney was in nearly every baseball way well beyond the ordinary.

WOLF, WILLIAM VAN WINKLE "CHICKEN"
OF, Louisville (A.A.) 1882–91

Born of Kentucky, baseball career exclusive to Louisville, with the very unusual middle and nicknames, William Wolf was an A.A. star in 1890; all his stats are or near benchmark class, and this was by far his best season.

Chicken Wolf of the 1890 Louisville Colonels led his league in hits, batting average, and total bases; he ranks second in doubles and SL.%, third in batting runs, fifth in O.B.A. and in total average. As example his 1890 B.Avg. was .363 and his next best was .300 in 1884.

He didn't lead his league in any stat any other year. His only other benchmarks were his .300 B.Avg., 103 runs scored in 1887, and 17 triples in 1885.

He scored 100 runs in the P.L. year, had 11 triples along with 29 doubles and 4 HRs among his 197 hits, 22 percent for extra bases; in 1885 he hit 17 triples, and also had 23 doubles and 1 HR among 141 hits, for a 29 percent total of hits for extra bases.

His career numbers in this regard, which seem to be the trump suit of Chicken Wolf, are 1,440 hits with 214 doubles, 109 triples, and 17 HRs, 340 of 1,440 hits for extra bases = 24 percent.

His career totals also include 779 runs scored and 207 known R.B.I. in three years, excepting 1892 when he played two games for St. Louis; his total of walks is 229, with highs only in the 30's. He was K's 71 times in the two years known.

He stole 186 bases, with all 11 of his playing years reported, with a high of 46 in 1890. Pardon the oversight, his walks high were 43 in 1890. His B.R. tally is +99 with a high of +45 in 1890, next +18 in 1884. His F.R. count to +39, with a high of +15 in 1883, +10 in 1886, and -3 in 1890.

His calculated stats include: .290 career B.Avg. high .363 in 1890, next .300 in 1884; .326 career O.B.A., high .419 in 1890, next .331 in 1887; .387 career SL.%, high .479 in 1890, next .416 in 1885.

He played in 1,198 games in all with 4,968 at bats, well above the average 1800s major league baseball player on the whole. He had his best year the P.L. year, when William Van Winkle "Chicken" Wolf was an A.A. all-star player.

YOUNG, DENTON TRUE "CY"
P, Cleveland (N.L.) 1890–98, Boston (A.L.) 1901–08

He was an N.L. rookie in the year the P.L. played. If the collection of records achieved by Cy Young were in one century, not nearly split in two, he surely would have been chosen for the National Baseball Hall of Fame with the first wave of inductees in 1936, not being delayed till corrections of 1937 were made.

Among these records, which run the length of a monthly shopping list, he led his league in wins five years, in win % two years, games two years, C.G. three years, I.P. two years, K's two years, E.R.A. two years, P.R. four years, and W.A.T. five years.

Among his benchmarks are 30+ wins five years, 20+ 15 years, .700+ win % five years, 50+ games five years, 400+ I.P. five years, 300+ 16 years, 2.00- E.R.A. six years, and 2.50- E.R.A. nine years.

Among current career ranks are first in wins, first in losses, first in starts, first in complete games, first in innings pitched, 14th in K's, sixth in hit batters, and 21st in wild pitches. In the field he's first in assists by a pitcher, and his assists adjusted to a 162-game season would total 44 for that season.

Young won 20+ games 15 consecutive years. His span which separates career wins from losses is 198 games. He won 2 games and lost 1 in the first modern World's Series in 1903, recording a 1.85 E.R.A. in 34 innings of work in that premier event.

These are some of the reasons the annual major leagues' most valuable pitcher awards have his name. In 1890 Young did well, but who could have imagined what his future would be?

	Career	1890	Best / Most
Won:	511	9	36 (1892)
Lost:	315	6	N/A
Win %:	.619	.600	.778 (1895)
Games:	906	17	55 (1891)
C.G:	749	16	48 (1892)
I.P:	7,357	148	453 (1892)
K's:	2,803	39	210 (1905)
Walks:	1,217	30	N/A
O.B.%:	.304	.311	.240 (1908)
E.R.A:	2.63	3.47	1.26 (1908)
P.R:	+754	+2	84 (1901)
W.A.T:	+100.3	+3.2	+11.6 (1901)

There've been great major league pitchers, and outstanding ones, and better and beyond that, but neither in the 1800s or 1900s has there ever been another quite like this one, who chose the Spiders of Cleveland and the National League as point of origin.

To mention just a few points about his SABR-stats, his span of excellence extended from 1892 through 1908, 17 years. There's hardly many if any other W.A.T. career totals of +100. His +754 total P.R. include a +68 for 1892, +84 in 1901, and six more years of +50 and above, and 11 years of +30 and more.

He led his league in O.B.% five years; his walks include four of 22 counts of 100+ but his career ratio to K's is 2.3 to 1.0. In 1890 Young was just a novice taking his first steps toward one of the greatest major league pitching careers in all of history.

He returned to Cleveland (A.L.) to close out his career in 1909, 1910, and 1911, during which term he won 29 and lost 29 games, then late in 1911 pitched his finale for Boston (N.L.), winning 4 and losing 5 decisions. He'd turned age 44 on March 29.

When the moment came in 1936 to choose the first immortals for perpetual residence at Cooperstown, Cy Young wasn't among the first wave, not because of lack of merits, but rather because he'd been so great in two centuries electors couldn't decide which century would be the most appropriate for his inclusion.

ZIMMER, CHARLES LOUIS "CHIEF"
C, Cleveland (N.L.) 1889–99

Catcher Chief Zimmer made 188 N.L. assists in 1890, which ranks 17th in history for a season by a two position player. He ranks fifth all time in career assists among catchers with 1,580. He's also 20th with 135 double plays, and prorated to a 162-game season his 207 calculated assists ranks 11th best among C's, and he's ranked 11th with 328 career errors.

1895 was the best year at the bat for Chief Zimmer, who would be a leader in organizing the next version of the Brotherhood of Players. A quick glance at his calculated batting stats puts his status well in order, or to the contrary given the span and gaps:

	Career	1890	Best / Most
B.Avg:	.269	.214	.340 (1895)
O.B.A:	.336	.303	.417 (1895)
SL.%:	.369	.291	.467 (1895)

He never led his league in any stat. He was almost exclusively an N.L. player during his 19 years and 1,280 games, excepting 1885 when he wasn't in the major leagues, and 1886 through 1888 in a total of 85 A.A. games for New York and Cleveland.

He began with Detroit of the N.L. in 1884 for eight games, 29 at bats, batting .069. He returned to the league in 1889 with Cleveland, through early 1899 with the worst team in history by no fault of their own, then spent N.L. time between Louisville, Pittsburgh, and Philadelphia through 1903.

Excepting his brief and awful introduction to major league baseball, 1890 was his worst year, until 1901 when he neared his nadir by batting .220, far below his next low of .255 in 1891.

The entirety of benchmarks reached during his long career are included in the brief set of data above; his high in hits was 112 (1891), 63 runs (1892), 69 R.B.I. (1891). His career and P.L. year matches are 1,224 and 95 hits, 617 and 54 runs, and 620+ and 57 R.B.I.

Beyond which the record of Zimmer includes 390 walks (46 in 1890 his high), 323 K's in nine years known (54 in 1890 his high), 151 stolen bases (15 in 1890), and his peak on the base paths was achieved with 18 S.B. in 1892.

His well after the fact but always so informative SABR-stats show a career total of -9 in B.R., with +15 his best in 1895, -13 B.R. in 1890, nearly all -'s. His F.R. career mark very much to the contrary stands at +68, with a high of +19 in 1890, next +18 in 1891, keeping in mind that Zimmer over that very long term played the position of catcher 90 percent of the time.

With defense clearly his best asset on the fields of play, his strength in the greater realm of baseball was in leadership; his establishment of a Players Protective Association has often been cited and alleged as a factor in the founding of the American League.

In the spring of 1900, Clark Griffith, Charles "Chief" Zimmer and Hugh Jennings formed the Protective Association of Professional Baseball Players. It was given high praise by Samuel Gompers, labor rights pioneer, president of the American Federation of Labor, and a baseball fan.

Gompers inadvertently communicated his prospects for a ballplayers union by comparing the Protective Association with the failure of the Brotherhood in 1890.

None of the above baseball persona were factors in the Players League or the Brotherhood. Griffith was elected to the National Baseball Hall of Fame as an executive in 1968. Jennings was elected as a shortstop and standout manager in 1945. Charles "Chief" Zimmer made his greatest contribution to the game and players cause a decade after the Players League played.

Player's League Aside: The Competition Aside

As a closing note on the players who were the competition for the Players League of 1890, one witty and established veteran devised a unique strategy for how to deal with the dilemma of choosing between the leagues: he chose none.

Warren William "Hick" Carpenter was a major league third baseman who began play in 1879. His first three years were with three different N.L. teams. He switched to the A.A. and Cincinnati in 1882, stayed with them through 1889; in 1882 he led the A.A. in hits and batted .342, his only stat above benchmark level.

His career B.Avg. is a very average .259, in 4,638 at bats; his career -81 F.R. is awful even for a hot corner player, which he was almost absolutely throughout his career, which ended back in the N.L. with one game and three at bats for St. Louis in 1892.

He got a hit in that last year and game. He'd missed the 1891 season entirely, and in the year the P.L. played Carpenter didn't; for that matter neither did his team of eight years, not in the A.A. at any rate, for 1890 the Cincinnati club jumped to the N.L. lock, stock, and turnstile.

By his discretion, Hick Carpenter made no new enemies, lost no old friends, only some dollars; perhaps in 1890 he was the wisest persona of all in major league baseball.

6

The Demise of the League

The Players League existed a few more weeks than organized baseball previously had years. When surveyed in terms of dollars and facts, the men of the Players League won in every way except the conclusion; their civil war failed to achieve their quest to win the right to work freely as men, to exist in union as a league.

The causes and reasons for the Players League's demise are many by name; most have the names of backers who betrayed or backed out and ran when the going got tough. The causes and reasons as facts are few; as a formula of cause and effect there were just three: the reserve clause (1879), the National Agreement (1885), and the Classification Plan (1888) = Brotherhood and the Players League.

There was one among the 100 + 40 who dared to defy establishment baseball who may have been the most treacherous of all. His reward was accorded by the title "The Greatest Catcher of the 1800s." Either or both historic claims to fame might be deserved.

As to the hard facts of baseball, as they were after the P.L. had played, when the P.L. was dying that cold November of 1890 some parts of the body suffered extremely; the original entity envisioned and established required external organisms to be implanted for it to exist and function. Then one more was put in a place of power and authority.

With the parts joined as the Players League of 1890, bound by clauses and agreements and plans of their own, the assembly assimilated proved itself to be deficient, less than efficient in function and implementation. Gradual dysfunction of the foreign elements enhanced by faults of the one other which did not belong assured failure and the resultant demise.

Cause of death: a discordant variety of conflicting interests introduced from the external environment, compounded by hostile forces within that environment, one of which was predatory.

John Monte Ward sat in the back room of a common saloon; he was not alone. Albert G. Spalding paid him high compliment, then said Ward, "Pass the wine around, the league is dead, long live the league," words of a proud commander who had suffered a defeat. He could not win no matter the victories within. This was not the pomp and ceremony at the Appomattox Court House in 1865.

Francis Richter wrote, with a certain prescience, "Now that one rival has been knocked out of the ring, the League was not about to let the other get off the ropes."

The specter of the Players League came to an official end shortly before noon on January 16, 1891. By no means were they a nest of gnats; the players of the P.L. played the best season on the fields of the 1800s. They won the attendance game handily over both established opponents, over the N.L. by a score of 981,000 to 814,000. In the end the Players League beat itself.

They won consistently in the courts of law; always the cause was restructured to be the reserve clause. They had the support of the mass of the public despite the efforts of Spalding and his advocates. When all the beans had been counted and divided, the jar of the players was empty. Such was the condition then.

The players were the best of their times, and many are still ranked among the best of all time. They were an anachronism, from a time when free men diametrically opposed to indenture took their cause to the incendiary level, for which they were labeled rebels and renegades.

The inhabitants of Japan were making pottery 11,000 years ago; a thousand wars have since been fought over symbolic artifacts and abstract concepts. Never before had any war been fought over a rule which was not law. The cause of the Players League war was just, despite the precipitant object and subject sustained as baseball law until 1976.

Seasons have come and gone, some better than others in accord with perspective of owner, player, fan, or scribe as spectator. The ashes of the Players League manifesto were stirred a mere decade after its demise; a third Brotherhood was created, the Protective Association of Base Ball Players. The cause was protection in union from the owners' reserve clause.

This socioeconomic phenomenon did not result in the founding of a baseball league, although the American League of Baseball Clubs was indirectly an effect of it. Though players since the first game have been the first feature of it, this was not a players' league; there could never be another like that of 1890.

The hall of fame plaque of William "Buck" Ewing at Cooperstown, U.S.A., makes no mention of the Players League; he was not welcome at the P.L. post-season meeting of the Committee on Negotiations of McAlpin, Goodwin, and Johnson. Nor was any P.L. player welcome at the backer's conference of October 22.

The P.L. backers sat down with the N.L. to work out a peace in November, 11 months before Chris Von der Ahe and John Monte Ward discussed a merger of the A.A. with the P.L. After the fact when the backers abandoned him, Ward had been very tactfully and very thoroughly downsized by Spalding; a man should know his place and abide by it.

For the common Players League player there was not to come any Joan of Arc or Ameterasu with special gifts and blessings which assure perpetual domain to the downtrodden; the P.L. player was left in the condition of the eternal corpse of Japan, a man long dead, half buried and half exposed, never to be looked at or spoken of for fear of the powers of the unknown.

Like the medieval serfs of Western Europe, or the equally decimate and servile gokenin of the Edo Period of Japan, the lords and barons invited into the Players League as loyal backers and contributors in alliance conducted themselves as did the Tozama Daimyo under the realm of Edo, in disgrace cloaked in wealth and dignity.

The P.L. backers were not alone then. In July of 1890 John Day of the N.L. Giants was having serious money troubles. Spalding and Arthur Soden each bought $25,000 of N.L. Giants stock. John Brush tore up the notes he had from Day for prior loans and from sales of players. Al Reach and Ferdinand Abel each put up $6,000. Monied men put at risk by lessers tend to take care of their own.

Frank Brunell reported on the P.L. business season; only Boston made a profit, about $17,000 after paying $60,000 in costs and expenses. New York lost $10,000, Chicago less; Brunell was vague about the other clubs.

On October 21, 1890, the Brotherhood's Eight-Man Central Committee was John Ward, James O'Rourke, James L. White, Arthur Irwin, Fred Pfeffer, George Wood, Ned Hanlon, and Tim Keefe. Manifest and eminent, they had no knowledge of the ledgers.

The *New York Times* included a premature epitaph in their edition of November 13, 1890: "It required but one season to end the existence of the Players' Baseball League ... the organization died a natural death." More than their timing was in error.

And continued: "That malady known in the baseball world as mismanagement caused the death of the Players' League. Blunder after blunder has been made, however to say the sudden collapse must not be attributed to John Ward, if his ideas had been carried out, but the financial men stepped in, their ignorance of baseball, coupled with their desire for notoriety has caused the ruin." But they saw the greater whole of the picture perfectly.

The P.L. Executive Committee held a meeting in Pittsburgh on the 12th of November, wherein an opinion rendered by Judge Bacon of New York was read: "An agreement by the New York P.L. and N.L. clubs was based on an understanding that the two leagues would consolidate, and if not the agreement was void."

Of the ensuing the media knew, the courts knew, obvious and to the point: John McAlpin then resigned his club from the league; Pittsburgh also resigned, but the resignation was tabled. It was not exactly well done if the rules of Parliament were in effect, nor if the game was being played according to Hoyle. "A consolidation meeting would be planned," it was said and written, but not done.

There was more than one P.L. eulogy written, to wit: "Charlie Comiskey, right hand man to Von der Ahe, his strategic and tactical base ball brain; Comiskey would pick up the National Agreement gauntlet where Albert Spalding left it, rule the Chicago White Sox with an iron hand for three decades."

Rarely was it mentioned by men of the media at the time, or in the literature since. Comiskey, who played for the P.L. Chicago Pirates and led them on the field most of the season, was the hub of the infamous Black Sox scandal of 1919–20. Like John D. Rockefeller, Albert G. Spalding, and so many others, he fell in love with every dollar he ever saw, lusting to have and to hold every one to perpetuity. The greed of Comiskey was the unwritten cause of historic wrong. If not for the coming of Kenesaw Mountain Landis and Babe Ruth, major league baseball as commercial business and spectator sport would have died in disgrace, as the American public was disgusted by the whole of that event.

Cite Mr. Comiskey: "The Players League officials, after winning the best fight in the history of the game, threw up the sponge and cried quit; they had the [National] League in the same position you have a drowning man when he has gone down for the third and last time. But when they had him down they let him get up and kick the life out of them." In other words, in his view, the P.L. didn't possess the necessary killer instinct to be successful in its endeavors.

Mr. Comiskey, aside from his history as a player and field manager, was a catalyst and founder of the American League in 1901; one might wonder when and why did his transformation occur. It isn't known if he was a P.L. player-owner, if that was where and when he began to develop his executive concept.

They were a shrewd and determined bunch: Spalding, Robison, Brush, Soden, and the National League company; if there was to be any drowning done, it would not be them that drowned. They were clever and had business acumen. When John Ward picked up their gauntlet, they surmised correctly, it would be a fight to the death. The American Association chose their side, but were of an uncertain mind throughout the fight, the N.L. was aware.

One set of estimates for two of the three leagues of 1890 shows:

	Attendance	Finances
Players League	978,000	-$340,000.00
National League	813,678	-$300,000.00

Further, the A.A. losses were almost as much as the others combined. In other words, the least anxious to fight was twice as great a loser as the willing combatants, but the calculations for 1890 from the *Ohio State Journal* cite the total A.A. loss was somewhere in between $82,000 and $93,000.

A meeting at the Collonnade Hotel in Philadelphia on the 2nd of September may have included discussion of a merger between the A.A. and P.L. There for the A.A. were Von der Ahe, Phelps, and Whittaker; present for the P.L. were Brunell, Johnson, and Ward. The P.L. backed away from the plan of amalgamation soon after. Not at all a wise move by one estimation; the P.L. men had to realize their situation and dilemma by this time. Any such bonding would have been beneficial, if not to turn the tide when all three leagues were daily sinking deeper in debt, then at least to disrupt any strategy the N.L. had to make the kill in which the A.A. was to play any part.

The A.A. men had their own difficulties and dilemma. Their champions-to-be Louisville "Cyclones" (sic, Colonels) would claim 206,000 attendance, but also that they lost money with one of the lowest payrolls in baseball. Contrary to Brunell's, another accounting reported that every Players League club lost money, and that in October the New York club couldn't meet the payroll. The facts to end 1890 facts were: players played great baseball, arguably greater than they would have if not for the Players League; the leagues all lost money, much more so than if not for the Players League.

By the next spring, before the start of the 1891 season, the survivors were at each other's throats. The A.A. officially withdrew from the National Agreement on February 18, 1891; its condition at the moment was mayhem.

Spalding now had been witness to the demise of three other major leagues. Perhaps just doing business, perhaps it was part of him, by the end of 1891 he would add another to his collection as the greatest in his business in history; baseball continued to be played on the fields and business to be done in the only league office.

The 1892 Bostons were the first team to win 100+ games in one season. The league president refused the urgings of Arthur Soden and Julian B. Hart to allow an intraleague post-season series; he recanted in favor of the good old days of the 1880s, and when the point was clarified that there was money to be made.

There was no such spectacle in 1893. The former had given the fans a classic first game, a 0–0 tie in 11 innings, after which Boston won five consecutive over Cleveland, the final three at home; Boston scored 31 runs to the Clevelands' 15.

The 1894 Philadelphias batted .349 as a team, the highest for one season by any team in history. The three Phillies outfielders, and their reserve, all batted above .400; Thompson and Delahanty both .407, Hamilton .404, and Tuck Turner .416, in 339 at bats.

The P.L. men of business were fairly well taken care of for the most part. To the victors belonged the spoils, to pick and choose as they will. The N.L. men took in four A.A. clubs as their own; the plan of the league to expand to 12 teams required four to fill the bottom four spots in their final league standings.

The true founders and men of the Players League were permitted neither accommodation nor mercy. The best were allowed to return to their owners, and some of the better were granted the courtesy. Some among them went to the A.A. for its final season then some with the clubs permitted to continue became National Leaguers.

Untidy and cumbersome, the League of Twelve had been given the name of National League and American Association of Base Ball Clubs, which was soon amended to League Association by men of the media; the first name chosen had been American League, and was rejected as fast as that, only National Association faster.

The date was the 15th of December of 1891; the owners of Boston, Columbus, Milwaukee, and Philadelphia A.A. were all bought out, and a new Chicago franchise which never put a team on the field. Left standing were A.A. Baltimore, Louisville, St. Louis, and the Washington with its tradition of finishing last, no matter what.

The competition was fierce among three of the ex–A.A. teams till near the end of the century. The Browns changed their name to the Cardinals though both continued to be used for a while; they even took the pseudonym Perfectos in 1899 when they finally broke out of the losing trio to finish fifth.

The best show for Louisville was ninth, three times, and 12th at season's end three straight years. The Orioles broke ranks in '93 when they finished eighth, then won three National League championships in succession, a rare feat in major league history indeed after the century turned, but not in the 1800s.

Three (+) consecutive major league championships: Boston Red Stockings (N.A.) 1872–1875 (4); Chicago White Stockings (N.L.) 1880–1882 (3); St. Louis Browns (A.A.) 1885–1888 (4); Boston Beaneaters (N.L.) 1891–1893 (3); Baltimore Orioles (N.L.) 1894–1896 (3).

The A.A. Four in the N.L. League of 12

Year	Baltimore	Louisville	St. Louis	Washington
1892	12th	Ninth	11th	10th
1893	Eighth	11th	10th	12th
1894	First	12th	Ninth	11th
1895	First	12th	11th	10th
1896	First	12th	11th	Ninth (tie)
1897	Second	11th	12th	Sixth (tie)
1898	Second	Ninth	12th	11th
1899	Fourth	Ninth	Fifth	11th

The Orioles were falling, and would fall out of the N.L. in 1900, along with Louisville and Washington; courtesy has its limits. St. Louis would have made it a perfect A.A. foursome, had not the Robison brothers, who owned both St. Louis and Cleveland, switched their better and best to the Cardinals, ex–Browns.

Their lessers had been relocated to Cleveland, which team played one of the worst seasons in history. The N.L. men decided to downsize to eight clubs for 1900, and Cleveland was disenfranchised instead of St. Louis; Louisville had also been joined by process with Pittsburgh at the franchise level, then was cut accordingly.

The number of major league players required to fill the positions on the playing fields was reduced by 67 percent between 1890 and 1900. The N.L. agenda reverted from war profile to business as usual, and after dabbling with the notion that bigger is better reverted to the reliable eight-team format, which was sustained for half a century.

They corrected the fault in structure of expanding to excess, and resumed and continued the historic system of strategy and tactics to control the players and assure the turnstile gate would keep on turning. The men of the N.L. then made a historic error.

A standard admission fee to a game of 25¢ was advised, but could be 50¢; each club was permitted to decide at its own discretion. When options are allowed in such fundamental matters of judgment, problems are almost sure to quickly follow.

Playing rules were modified, and again and again; where there are no standards there cannot be order. Brawls by the players and riots at the ballparks became the featured fare of the N.L. game of the 1890s; contempt became the prevailing attitude with the masses of public.

It didn't matter that alcoholic drinks could be sold at ballparks or not, except to the Christian temperance unions which were established in every domain where such were permitted. It didn't matter that games could be scheduled for Sundays or not, except to the Christian Sabbatarians which long had been established and prominent in every American baseball domain.

The men who were the National League—then the only league—did not or could not realize the mass of external forces, would not consider their own judgment could be in error, and did not bother to be concerned about the public opinion or the force of law.

They became akin to John D. and Morgan and Carnegie, missing the fact that their weighted authority was lesser than the greatest of U.S.A. men then; clearly by virtue of arrogance they were beyond the capacity to comprehend the reality that whether oligarchy, democracy, or republic, all such devices of men have limitations.

Then to their threat albeit salvation from themselves came the American League, with much the same structure, alleging a greatly different code of standards and rules, which some of were facts, and which quickly enough as compromise and courtesy for reasons of dollars would be reduced to the lowest possible condition.

There were no more World's Series, nor were there any World's Series in 1901 and 1902; the old tradition was renewed with the new name in 1930; the owners of the National and American Leagues had by then reconciled their differences, and established the greatest of all sports traditions.

There has been a World Series each fall since, with the exception of 1945 and 1994; 1945 was the year U.S. military logistics had absolute priority, the culminating year of the war to save the world from National Socialism and Imperial Japan.

The Industrial Revolution and the free will determination of the American people proved themselves durable and resilient; there was also fear in the government at Washington, D.C., concerning a gathering of many people in one place, as would be the case in a World Series spectacle venue.

The reason there was no October Classic in 1994 involves the lowest possible baseball condition; it was one of a dozen such conflicts during the latter part of the 20th century between owners and players. In this case push went beyond the limits of tolerance of the public, and again baseball almost killed itself.

"The *Sporting News* confirmed the consolidation of the A.A. and N.L. on December 18 (1891)." Four clubs were "formally accepted into the League, the others were called to submit their buyout prices." On the greater scale, John D. was making the same call of every viable oil company from Pennsylvania to Indiana to California that was not already under the Standard Oil banner.

Von der Ahe had been given a strict lesson in playing hardball U.S.A. business, brutal and ruthless; life went on. Spalding and the N.L. company resumed their singular pursuits. There have been some manifest changes in the interim, but they never did respect the hands that fed them, and as history might ask, "Why should they?"

The games beneath the game went on. Andrew Freedman owned the only New York Giants in 1894; he'd bought 1,200 shares from Richard Croker, the Tammany Hall chief who migrated to England to escape American law. Edward B. Talcott had been an owner of the N.L. Giants, ex–of the Brooklyn P.L. franchise. The Tammany Hall company was a syndicate which did business in governance, in New York City and vicinity with its own standards of ethics and business. Ferdinand Abel, the notorious gambler, was well connected with it.

The N.L. Baltimore and Brooklyn clubs merged between the 1898 and 1899 seasons, and Charlie Ebbets became the surviving Brooklyn club president. Ned Hanlon, with Baltimore when the two clubs were joined, was made the Baltimore president, and a 10 percent owner of both franchises; he was also made the Brooklyn field manager and took most of the great Orioles players with him. They won the National League and by default the world championship in 1899 and 1900.

Such phenomena were typical of baseball near the end of the 19th century. "Syndicate" became synonymous with the game, which was given the label by media men of syndicate baseball.

Frank DeHaas and Stanley Robison raided one of their clubs to make the other competitive. Louisville became entangled in yet another scandal, as Barney Dreyfuss, owner of the N.L. franchise in Pittsburgh, took control of the Louisville club; he then made a trade with himself of four future hall of fame players for $25,000 and several nondescript players.

W.W. Kerr had a large interest in the Pittsburgh franchise then. Henry (Harry) Clay Pulliam became the party vanquished of the Louisville club; he was a lawyer, and the club president. He would become the National League president in 1903, and would commit suicide by gunshot in 1909.

The Players League backers didn't file any petition to discharge bankruptcy when the time came, nor did they sign any documents to declare surrender. One brief citation entitled "The Brotherhood Settlement" summarizes the demise.

"The only real losers in the deal were — Surprise!— the players; in the new National Agreement all players who jumped to the Players' League would revert to the teams [sic, owners] they had played for in 1889." It was as if the P.L. didn't happen.

The return to status quo ante was a natural result. It meant the players would not be free to sell their services on the open market. What had been would be again, baseball law.

One begs to differ, on a point of error in need of correction; after the Players League's demise there was no open market. A year beyond that there would be only the monopoly by the name of the National League of Base Ball Clubs.

7

Closure

An 1890 question: Which established league lost more in player performance? This is given the presumption that all players would have delivered the same in any league as they actually did in the Players League of 1890.

The answer shall be left for the reader to decide. Herein the opinion is cited in terms of P.L. Most Valuable Players, that is M.V.P. with one such symbolic acronym of acclaim for the P.L. pitchers and one for the position players of the P.L.

It should be fairly noted that the P.L. roster of the whole was constructed of approximately 64 percent players who were with N.L. teams in 1889, 21 percent were with A.A. teams in 1889, and the balance with other teams in minor leagues, or did not play in 1889, enabling a much numerically greater selection pool from the N.L.

The teams linked with the players in parentheses are first the team(s) of 1890, then the ex-team(s) of 1889. The position of field manager merits inclusion as an element of the clubs on the playing fields, and these selections are made by ex-league.

The ex–N.L. manager given highest regard for his achievements in the Players League is Mike "King" Kelly (Boston Reds, Boston Beaneaters) who won the only P.L. championship, which in turn required winning a far greater proportion of games on the road than his counterparts, a difficult task then; he also played a fine season in the field the 89 games he was in the Reds' lineup.

His ex–A.A. counterpart in this regard must be Charlie Comiskey (Chicago Pirates, St. Louis Browns), who was the only bench boss from that league to hold the position in the P.L., and his selection thus is by default. While in 88 P.L. games his performance was not at the level of King Kelly, in part due to injury, nor was Comiskey, nor any P.L. persona the fan magnet which Kelly was. Still further it must be noted that Kelly was the object of much temptation to renege his honor, but did not fail the cause.

As a statistical note, while these honors were being assigned the most valuable pitcher and player of the P.L., it came to light that a source used much herein throughout the research for this text, foremost for information involving the A.A., minimally for gathering of data, includes these variations from the accepted numbers.

That source shows Addison Gumbert with 22 wins, not 23; much more significantly he shows Silver King with 32 wins, not 30, and Mark Baldwin with 32 wins, not 34, which were the league high mark; all these second data have been confirmed in various and reliable other sources.

The only variation among batters found shows Buck Ewing as P.L. leader in SL.%, despite having only 352 at bats during 1890. This source as a matter of discretion set 325 at bats as the criterion for this statistical category, contrary to the norm; by the standard of 3.2 at bats or plate appearances per game scheduled for his team, the sum of 400 would be more viable.

By this assessment the best who came to the P.L. of 1890 from other leagues and earned status as M.V.P. or a high rate of consideration include the following.

Ex–National League:
- Charley Radbourn earns the title of Most Valuable Pitcher (Boston Reds, Boston Beaneaters).
- Phil Knell earns second rank as most valuable P.L. pitcher (Pittsburgh Burghers, did not pitch in 1889).
- Addison Gumbert earns third rank as most valuable P.L. pitcher (Boston Reds, Chicago White Stockings).
- Roger Connor earns the title of Most Valuable Player (New York Giants, New York Giants).
- Jake Beckley earns second rank as most valuable P.L. player (Pittsburgh Burghers, Pittsburgh Alleghenys).
- Competition for the third rank as most valuable P.L. player was too close to call, among Hugh Duffy (Chicago Pirates, Chicago White Stockings), Hardy Richardson (Boston Reds, Boston Beaneaters), Jim O'Rourke (New York Giants, New York Giants), and George Gore (New York Giants, New York Giants).

Ex–American Association:
- Silver King earns the title of Most Valuable Pitcher (Chicago Pirates, St. Louis Browns).
- Mark Baldwin earns a tie for second rank as most valuable P.L. pitcher (Chicago Pirates, Columbus Solons).
- Guy Wyehing earns a tie for second rank as most valuable P.L. pitcher (Brooklyn Wonders, Philadelphia Athletics).
- Pete Browning earns the title of Most Valuable Player (Cleveland Infants, Louisville Colonels).
- Dave Orr earns second rank as most valuable P.L. player; his injury precluded a possibility of his finest season (Brooklyn Wonders, Columbus Solons).
- Harry Stovey earns third rank as most valuable P.L. player (Boston Reds, Philadelphia Athletics).

Of the lesser league offender, the American Association, this measure of assessment shows the Philadelphia Athletics and the Columbus Solons suffered worst, with apparently lesser harm to the St. Louis Browns and the Louisville Colonels.

In 1890, in a condition of league decimation, the Athletics finished seventh of the nine teams which played, including the Brooklyn then Baltimore franchise. The Columbus team finished second on the field, with Louisville winning the A.A. pennant, becoming the first major league team to make the great leap forward from last place to first place in a single season.

Of the greater National League offender, Pittsburgh achieved a season among the worst in history; also all doubly damaged, Boston, New Chicago, and New York suffered the loss of star players and great gate attractions.

There is irony, perhaps justice to be found in the facts of 1890, as the owners of these three N.L. clubs were the most egregious offenders to the premise of rights players arguably were entitled to; in the N.L. of 1890 Boston ended its game schedule in fifth place, and New York sixth, while Chicago finished second, somewhat salvaging the status of its owner.

The greatest of U.S.A. men then might not always have won, but they never lost, affirmed by the facts of 1890 P.L. evidence; as for the players who were the P.L. of 1890, they lost, but they were not losers, as evidenced by the better and best adding a great season to their careers filled with successes. In sum, for the Players League players, 1890 was a superb baseball season.

There was no open market in baseball after 1890; after 1891 there was only the National League monopoly. Survival of the fittest for other earthly species is a fairly simple concept; for humans, Americans, men of baseball, the scenario is very complicated.

The natural law as it applies to societies and cultures of all sorts does prevail, but is compounded by unique phenomena called business and politics.

Exemplary among the latter in the U.S.A. were the War(s) of Revolution, then a war to establish national supremacy, then that awful Civil War with all its ramifications and further consequences.

Whichever war one chooses as model, the rebellion by baseball players in 1890 may serve as a microcosmic example of the greater condition; war is a human condition, made by men, of which some stand out prominently. The following stood out in the 1890 war.

ALBERT GOODWILL SPALDING

He was not of this Players League, and to say nemesis would not begin to suffice. He did not want this Players League to exist, and it was because of him foremost that it did not. Cite Albert Goodwill Spalding as star, scion, scourge; as Lucifer is to the devout Christian, he was antithesis, adversary, the enemy. He was all these things, and more.

His motives were mercenary, his means methodical. His name had been spelled differently in the distant past, Spaulding, not Spalding. He represented the National League, as an owner, an executive, as their ambassador with portfolio, granted to him by the other N.L. owners and executives for his skill and his will.

He was certainly not a player in 1890, not in the common sense of the word, no more so than a modern commanding general would be on the front line in a battle. But he had been a player, a pitcher; there was none better during his prime at taking care of pitching business, a standard he continued throughout his business life.

His major league statistics as a pitcher cannot be considered all-telling. He excelled before there was any major league. His baseball career began in 1866, with the Rockford (Illinois) Forest City club. That is the sum of his record known for 1866 and the next year.

Continuing at Rockford in 1868, a rare record shows he pitched in 15 games, won 11 and lost 4, posted no shutouts, had 107 at bats, scored 67 runs, hit 4 home runs, made 9 errors. He remained with this Forest City club (another prominent one existed in Cleveland) through 1869 as an amateur, then he declared as a professional in 1870.

Albert Goodwill Spalding was born on the 2nd of September in 1850, at Byron, Illinois. He died 65 years and a week later on the 9th of September, 1915, at Point Loma, California. Tall for his time at 6'1" his weight is given as 170 pounds, which may have been in his playing days; later in life he was described as portly, which in his time was indicative of prosperity.

Still a very young man in 1870, his records reveal a possibility that he was greatly affected by being paid money to play baseball, as it was then. Data and information are scarce, but SABR has organized a quite comprehensive record for Spalding.

1869 (Amateur)	Pitching	1870 (Pro)
20	Won	7
4	Lost	14
.833	Win %	.333
24	Games	22
Unknown	Innings	Unknown
Unknown	Runs	322

Elementary observation shows a number of significant differences, but it's not likely there were many changes among members of the teams around him in these two years who could have caused them.

1869 (Amateur)	Batting	1870 (Pro)
212	At Bats	110
107	Hits	47
.505	B.Avg.	.427
120	Runs	30
162	Total Bases	66

As a pitcher, the decline in winning percentage stands out most, and as a batter his overall decline in productivity; his batting averages might seem extraordinary, but they were typical for stars.

1869 (Amateur)	Fielding	1870 (Pro)
36	Putouts	Unknown
39	Assists	Unknown
Unknown	Errors	Unknown

Spalding reached his pitching prime at the time of origin of the National Association (of Professional Base Ball Players) in 1871; each of the five years the N.A. (the first major league) existed, he was the first pitcher for the Boston Red Stockings, who finished second in 1871 and won the league championship in every N.A. season thereafter. His numbers explain; he set the standards for what might be achieved, and then exceeded them.

Year	Won	Lost	Win %	Games
1871	20	10	.667	31
1872	37	8	.822	48
1873	41	15	.732	57
1874	52	18	.743	71
1875	57	5	.919	66
Totals	207	56	.787	273

His single season and composite numbers are truly extraordinary, his annualized data are genuinely awesome. There are none better.

Avgs: Won 41   Lost 11   Win % .787   Games 55

Credit fairly given, to the owners who purloined power and took baseball from the players, the National League (of Professional Base Ball Clubs) beginning in 1876 demonstrated greater wisdom in administration, evidenced by their maintaining more systematic and comprehensive records of their teams' and players' performance. The excellence of Al Spalding continued in the first N.L. season, with the Chicago White Stockings, who won the first N.L. pennant.

Year	Won	Lost	Win %	Games	Innings	K's	Walks	E.R.A.
1876	47	12	.797	61	529	39	26	1.75

If not sufficiently impressive, Spalding in 1876 allowed 542 hits and pitched eight shutouts. By modern SABR-stats his pitching runs calculate to a +33, his clutch pitching index +102; his 47 wins led the league, as did his .797 winning percentage.

He pitched in only one more major league game of record, in 1877, then he got down to the business which would be his future, as the owner of a premier sporting goods company which still exists and continues to prosper. Nothing with the name A.G. Spalding has ever known less than success; that would be almost unnatural.

Spalding knew how to take care of business in the pitcher's box, he set the benchmarks, and he dominated like the symbolic eagle; with his pitching credentials thus in order, there is more to be known of this anti-Players League persona.

Spalding learned how to dominate no less in the business office. He would hover over baseball like the eagle over prospective prey; if 1800s baseball men had been garbed in togas, with sashes and tiaras to infer status among egality, his would have been commensurate with the highest in the realm.

Others have put pen to paper in telling the A.G. Spalding story:

Helyar: "Albert Goodwill Spalding tried to export baseball to other countries. The owner of a team and of a sporting-goods empire, he even sponsored a globe-trotting tour of exhibition games, America's top players were watched with indifference, the game took root only in America."

Okrent and Wulf: "The tour lasted nearly six months, and even after touching home, Spalding kept the players going another two weeks in a series of welcome-home exhibitions. They were greeted as heroes—Henry Chadwick called the tour 'The greatest event in the modern history of athletic sports.'"

Zimbalist: "The owner of the Chicago White Stockings, William Hulbert, perceived the organization deficiencies of the NAPBP and in 1876 launched a plan for a new baseball league. Hulbert depended on Albert Spalding, induced him to jump his [Boston] contract and help persuade three other stars to jump with him. Within the Chicago organization, Spalding rose from captain to manager to principal owner. He succeeded in building the White Stockings into baseball's most successful franchise in the 1880's.... In 1905 he established a commission, the commission without a shred of credible evidence concluded the game was invented in Cooperstown, New York, in 1839."

Baseball encyclopedists Turkin and Thompson, with origins in the 1940s, credit Spalding with an assist to Hulbert in devising and organizing the National League, and provide a bit of arcane minutia which impacted the very fiber of baseball for a century afterward.

With another assist to Spalding, he did the persuading. "Hulbert had Judge Orrick C. Bishop of St. Louis draw up a constitution. The Jurist also framed a standard form of player's contract."

This baseball man from the Chicago region, who removed in body for a period of time, but in soul never truly left, came a very long way in a very short time; so much power did he develop that he became able to dictate to every man in baseball, and via the Mills Commission, he was able to dictate history.

Maybe, just maybe, he had a slight bit of a lighter side, a sense of humor that is, though it could have been just another of his economic measures.

Every team needs an official scorer; his is the task of maintaining a detailed coded record of each and every thing that happens during baseball games. One report reveals that Spalding's mother, Elisa Green Williams, was his official scorer. She attended every game, sitting between the wives of the team's biggest stars, Cap Anson and Abner Dalrymple. She scored every play without ever tipping them off that hers was the official version.

This sleight of hand and mind supposedly went on the entirety of each baseball season from 1882 to 1891, on the team that is now the Cubs. Then they were the Chicago White Stockings, of course.

Albert Goodwill Spalding was their owner, and president, and anything else he wanted to be, including awfully tight with a dollar and averse to parting with any not absolutely necessary.

It could be, just maybe, that he made his mother work for her living, or maybe this was just a folklore tale conjectured by a baseball writer at the time.

FRANK BRUNELL

The life and death of the Players League of 1890 could be, and has been by some, reduced to a contest of Ward versus Spalding. The players played, some excelled, some resigned after one game. In the public mind they were the Players League, but there was much more to it.

There were the owner-backers, some dedicated, some disinterested except for fast gains and easy money. When the going got tough, with rare exception they quit and ran, to make the best deals they could with rival league owners, every man for himself.

One of the greater players, Buck Ewing, has been assigned a dual role, as would be in Classic Greek drama or the ancient Japanese Kabuki: he was both scoundrel and scapegoat. Some said that his allegiance to the cause wavered and he went astray; others said he was unjustly accused of betraying his league brethren. Cause for suspicion exists both ways.

In assigning credit or blame for the demise of the Players League an assortment of reasons has been brought forth, but the magnitude and scope and relevance of facts distorted by time cannot now be fairly measured, nor could they then, as the scribes of the time wrote them.

The biography of the Players League involves hundreds of men directly, and the entirety of the baseball public otherwise. The name of Frank Brunell has been mentioned herein some number of times, but his name is seldom to be found among the various P.L. renditions which have been written.

Brunell was chosen to be the secretary and treasurer of the Players League. He kept the records of the players' data, and he kept the records of the owners' dollars as they pertained to the league, and he was keeper of all the league dollars, all of which positions involved trust and responsibility.

It's been written that he was a good friend of John Monte Ward; if so, the details are unknown, as there is nothing to be found as evidence to support such an allegation.

He did work within the sports media of Chicago and Cleveland, locale of the greatest and next to it enemies of the Players League; to say friends would be excessive, but rather than Ward, it's highly probable that Albert Goodwill Spalding and Frank DeHaas Robison were among those he often dealt with on business.

While Ward and Spalding issued statements and diatribe, and the players and owner-backers an occasional quote or opinion, and while Buck Ewing might have repeated some hearsay, nobody was in a position (actually two) to be privy to and filter through any sorts of information about what was happening on the playing fields, and in the offices and back rooms other than Brunell.

His relationship with the Players League may be compared to the bakufu of ancient Japan; the U.S.A. culture and government have had nothing comparable or similar. He was not emperor nor a shogun, neither ruler nor owner, but Brunell was the P.L. central administration. The issue could be raised, was he Marc Antony to the P.L.— et tu Brutus?— as these men were who betrayed Julius Caesar, and by his assassination coupled with their power were able to commit legal murder?

In 1888, after the playing season, Brunell was a Cleveland writer, reporting "The Forest City [A.A. Cleveland] franchise was well run." Upon his leave-taking, Brunell said, "There is no use for honesty, business sagacity or integrity among the [American] Association clubs. The ball is a different kind of ball from that played in the [National] League, nearly as good but one club can not trust another ... that's the way it goes."

Brunell used his job at the *Cleveland Plain Dealer* not only to tout the local Blues, but also as a platform for his trenchant comments on the game. Going into the 1887 season he'd written a second to the opinion "The Cleveland club has brains" then put in comments about the club secretary doing a miserable job and the field manager griping the other clubs were bent on keeping the Blues from improving.

He wrote for and was written about in *Sporting Life*: "Larry Twitchell gave the details of the Brotherhood revolt to Brunell, sporting editor of the *Chicago Tribune*, the first among those interested in the scheme to leak." Brunell in retort wrote: "Your statement that Twitchell gave the scheme away to me is without the slightest foundation in fact."

Sporting Life continued: "Brunell denies that Twitchell was his informant. Twitchell admits he told Brunell about the Brotherhood plan, strange there should be such a contradiction.

"Twitchell was approached by Brunell on the subject of the Brotherhood and its plans for the ensuing season. Brunell apparently was already a confidant of the leaders of the movement . . . satisfied Twitchell that he was on the 'inside' then Twitchell proceeded to tell the whole story to Brunell, giving details, dates, and names.

"Brunell the day after published a full expose of the Brotherhood plot in the columns of the *Chicago Tribune*. After this statement had gone the rounds of the press Brunell came to the front with a denial."

"It is indeed strange that the statements of two parties, Brunell and Twitchell, should be so widely at variance. Further commentary is unnecessary." With this *Sporting Life* ended the debate.

John T. Pickett was under contract for 1890 with Kansas City of the American Association till the owner switched his club to the Western (minor) League, and with the club he took the contracts of his players.

Brunell signed Pickett for the P.L. Philadelphia club, based on the player's statements, further guided in his actions by the legal construction of Pickett's contract with Kansas City; this was the first instance in which a P.L. club departed from the straight and narrow in the matter of approaching players under contract. Recall that Caylor had legal training; Brunell is uncertain.

The matter was investigated, and it was assured that Pickett would be returned to the Kansas City club. He was exceptionally well treated by the Kansas City club; he was paid his full salary in 1889 despite missing half the games because of illnesses.

Pickett admitted that he consented to the transfer of himself from the major league Kansas City to the minor league K.C. club. *Sporting Life* reported "he wasn't worth the row kicked up over him."

Francis Richter was *Sporting Life*, and an associate and rival of Brunell. He'd been a baseball journalist since prior to 1883 when his periodical was established.

The P.L. Philadelphia club lost the Pickett case in its home court. Pennsylvania Judge Arnold ruled decidedly adversely citing Philadelphia (N.L.) v. Hallman (Bill) entered into a contract: "The Court cannot force him [to play] but can rule on him giving service to a third party in violation of a contract.

"To do this is breach of contract and makes him legally liable." The court cited actors versus producers in many similar cases, emphasizing the exclusive rights of employers "requires servants to obey their masters."

Pickett had signed to serve the Kansas City club from April 1, 1890, to October 31, 1890, for $2,200; he was paid a $100 advance in January 1890 by Kansas City, and had been paid a prior $100 advance in December 1889.

Pickett notified Kansas City he was breaking his contract on February 19, 1890, then signed with Philadelphia of the Players League, subsequent to which he was served a subpoena and had to pay $1,000 security.

The case appears to have been dead in the water before any of the pleadings or motions were written; the Wagner brothers, who owned the P.L. Philadelphia club, said they would employ Pickett in easy tasks in their meat stores and allow him time off for practice if he could not play for them in 1890.

Pickett did play for P.L. Philadelphia in 1890, at second base in 100 games; it was written that he was a prime third baseman in his day. He'd played that position in 14 of 53 games in 1889 and never again during his major league career of 189 games.

His career consisted of 189 games and 749 at bats; he batted a composite .252, really not worth the row kicked up over him. As a player he made his own bats and became a craftsman; later he was employed at the Spalding Company factory and designed more bats than any other man in the world. At some point most major league players visited Pickett.

LEAGUE MINUTIAE

None of the P.L. players, nor any 1800s player now ranks among the career top 100 in home runs.

The Players League players hit 311 home runs in 1890, the N.L. 257, and the A.A. 188, for a season total by all players in all three 1890 leagues of 756 home runs, which by coincidence is one more than the U.S.A. champion, Henry "Hank" Aaron in his career.

Teams in all three leagues set records in 1890. The following are some by the Players League including their all-time rank now, also by teams of the National League and American Association.

Players League Team Records of 1890

Team	Stat	#####	Ranks
Boston Reds	Stolen bases	412	15th
New York Giants	Runs scored	1,018	14th
Philadelphia Quakers	Triples (tie)	113	16th
Pittsburgh Burghers	Triples (tie)	113	16th
Buffalo Bisons	Runs allowed	1,199	Third
Buffalo Bisons	Hit by pitches	96	10th

Besides being beaten in every other which way, the Buffalo Bisons were bruised and beaned by a record number of pitches; their most battered was Jay Faatz who was hit 21 times.

The individual single-season records, however, are much greater, as Hugh Jennings (SS, Orioles) was hit 51 times in 1896 and 46 times in 1898; when the Orioles set the season record, they were hit by National League pitches 159 times.

National League Team Records of 1890

Team	Stat	#####	Ranks
Cincinnati Reds	Triples	120	11th
Pittsburgh Alleghenys	Losses	113	Fifth
Pittsburgh Alleghenys	Runs allowed	1,235	Second
Pittsburgh Alleghenys	Roster	46	N/A

There are no known ranks of teams that had the most players on their rosters during a season, however the Pittsburgh Alleghenys (also known as Innocents) tried combinations of at least 46 when on their way into history in the year of the Players League.

American Association Team Records of 1890

Team	Stat	#####	Ranks
Columbus Solons	Opponents B.Avg.	.214	12th
St. Louis Browns	Hit by pitches	95	11th
Philadelphia Athletics	Hit by pitches	87	17th
Toledo Maumees	Stolen bases	421	13th

The Maumees of Toledo were also called the Black Pirates. The only other year Toledo fielded a major league team was in 1884, also in the American Association. In 1890 five of their players each stole 50+ bases and another stole 46 on their way to a record total; Bill Van Dyke (UT) was their leader with 73 stolen bases.

The Star Players of the Players League

Pos.	Name (Alpha)	Team
P	Mark Baldwin	Chicago Pirates
P	Silver King	Chicago Pirates
P	Hoss Radbourn	Boston Reds
P	Gus Weyhing	Brooklyn Wonders
C	Buck Ewing	New York Giants
1B	Jake Beckley	Pittsburgh Burghers
1B	Dan Brouthers	Boston Reds
1B	Roger Connor	New York Giants
1B	Henry Larkin	Cleveland Infants
1B	Dave Orr	Brooklyn Wonders
2B	Lou Bierbauer	Brooklyn Wonders
2B	Joe Quinn	Boston Reds
2B	Sam Wise	Buffalo Bisons
SS	Billy Shindle	Philadelphia Quakers

Pos.	Name (Alpha)	Team
SS	John Monte Ward	Brooklyn Wonders
3B	Bill Joyce	Brooklyn Wonders
OF	Pete Browning	Cleveland Infants
OF	Hugh Duffy	Chicago Pirates
OF	George Gore	New York Giants
OF	Mike Griffin	Philadelphia Quakers
OF	Dummy Hoy	Buffalo Bisons
OF	Jim O'Rourke	New York Giants
OF	Hardy Richardson	Boston Reds
OF	Jimmy Ryan	Chicago Pirates
OF	Harry Stovey	Boston Reds
OF	George Wood	Philadelphia Quakers
P/OF	George VanHaltren	Brooklyn Wonders
MGR	King Kelly	Boston Reds

A summary of the 28 chosen as Star Players by teams includes:

Boston Reds: 6
Brooklyn Wonders: 6
New York Giants: 4
Chicago Pirates: 4
Philadelphia Quakers: 3
Pittsburgh Burghers: 1
Cleveland Infants: 2
Buffalo Bisons: 2

The Feature Players of the Players League

Pos.	Name (Alpha)	Team
1B	Dan Brouthers	Boston Reds
OF	Pete Browning	Cleveland Infants
1B	Roger Connor	New York Giants
C	Buck Ewing	New York Giants
OF	George Gore	New York Giants
P	Tim Keefe	New York Giants
UT	King Kelly	Boston Reds
OF	Jim O'Rourke	New York Giants
P	Hoss Radbourn	Boston Reds
OF	Harry Stovey	Boston Reds
SS	John Monte Ward	Brooklyn Wonders
UT	Deacon White	Buffalo Bisons

A summary of the 12 chosen as Feature Players by teams includes:

Boston Reds: 4
Brooklyn Wonders: 1
New York Giants: 5
Chicago Pirates: 0
Philadelphia Quakers: 0
Pittsburgh Burghers: 0
Cleveland Infants: 1
Buffalo Bisons: 1

The Major League All-Star Teams of 1890

Hardly arbitrary, based on data and facts, and grounded in history, the 33 chosen didn't include many easy decisions; far after the fact, by one source of judgment, these were the All-Star teams of the three major leagues of 1890:

Pos:	Players League	National League	American Association
P	Mark Baldwin	Bill Hutchinson	Scott Stratton
P	Silver King	Tom Lovett	Sadie McMahon
P	Gus Weyhing	Kid Gleason	Hank Gastright
C	Buck Ewing	Jack Clements	Jack O'Connor
1B	Roger Connor	Cap Anson	Perry Werden
2B	Lou Bierbauer	Hub Collins	Cupid Childs
SS	John Monte Ward	Jack Glasscock	Irv Ray
3B	Patsy Tebeau	George Pinkney	Denny Lyons
OF	Pete Browning	Mike Tiernan	Tommy McCarthy
OF	Hugh Duffy	Billy Hamilton	Chicken Wolf
OF	Jim O'Rourke	Sam Thompson	Ed Swartwood

The common rule was set aside that every team must be included. The prime criteria used to make these decisions were individual performance measured against peers at the positions and players' contributions to the relative success of their teams in pursuit of the pennants.

If there were designated hitters then, the N.L. choice would be Oyster Burns; among P.L. players perhaps no less entitled would be Dan Brouthers, King Kelly if a manager was part of the team, Dave Orr, Hoss Radbourn, Hardy Richardson, Harry Stovey.

Those familiar with the hall of fame roster will readily see in the P.L. All Star team five members now, while the N.L. has three, and the A.A. has one; clearly in 1890 the Players League was on the fast track to Cooperstown.

1890 Players in the Baseball Hall of Fame

Players League	National League	American Association
Connie Mack 1937	Cy Young 1937	Wilbert Robinson 1945
Charlie Comiskey 1939	Cap Anson 1939	Tommy McCarthy 1946
Buck Ewing 1939	Jesse Burkett 1946	
Hoss Radbourn 1939	Kid Nichols 1949	
Dan Brouthers 1945	Billy Hamilton 1961	
Ed Delahanty 1945	John Clarkson 1963	
Hugh Duffy 1945	Mickey Welch 1973	
King Kelly 1945	Sam Thompson 1974	
Jim O'Rourke 1945	Amos Rusie 1977	
Tim Keefe 1964	George Davis 1998	
John Monte Ward 1964		
Pud Galvin 1965		

Players League	National League	American Association
Jake Beckley 1971		
Roger Connor 1976		
Ned Hanlon 1996		

The years noted are the years of election; from among these of the Players League three were elected as managers or executives: Mack, Comiskey, and Hanlon. Albert Spalding didn't play in 1890, but certainly was significant. He was elected as an executive in 1939; his affiliation is National League. Wilbert Robinson of the American Association in 1890 was elected as a manager.

Bibliography

Books

Beasley, W.G. *The Japanese Experience: A Short History of Japan.* London, UK: Weidenfeld and Nicolson, 1999. pp. 3, 82, 269–271.

Dewey, Donald, and Nicholas Acocella. *The Ball Clubs.* New York: Harper Collins, 1996. pp. 48, 76–78, 106–107, 125, 146–148, 202–203, 208–209, 303–304, 344–345, 365–366, 417–421, 440, 454, 475, 572–573, 576, 585.

DiSalvatore, Bryan. *A Clever Base-Ballist: The Life and Times of John Montgomery Ward.* New York: Pantheon Books, 1999. pp. 85, 146, 148, 155, 158–159, 164–166, 179, 193, 245, 261, 267, 269–270, 275–276, 280, 284.

Grey, Zane. "The Redheaded Outfield." In *The Fireside Book of Baseball*, Einstein, Charles, ed. New York: Simon and Schuster, 1956. pp. 156–162.

Grossman, Ned. *How to Succeed in Life: Ideas and Principles They Don't Teach in School.* Shaker Heights, OH: Diamond, 1999. p. 47.

Helyar, John. *Lords of the Realm.* New York: Ballantine Books, 1994. pp. 2–3.

Ivor-Campbell, Frederick, Robert L. Tiemann, Mark Rucker, ed. *Baseball's First Stars.* Cleveland: Society For American Baseball Research, 1996. pp. 5–7, 11–13, 22, 36–40, 42, 45, 50, 54, 56, 60, 63–64, 72–74, 83–84, 89–90, 105, 113, 116, 123–125, 130–133, 138, 145, 152–155, 167, 173–174.

James, Bill. *The Bill James Historical Baseball Abstract.* New York: Villard Books, 1986. pp. 13–14, 17, 25–28, 31, 33–35, 42, 44, 51, 60, 64, 68, 77, 94, 315.

James, Bill, John Dewan, Neil Munro and Don Zminda, eds. *Stats All-Time Baseball Sourcebook.* Skokie, IL:, 1998. pp. 478, 969–1001, 1006–1013, 1138–1155, 1157, 1520, 2446, 2451, 2510, 2647.

Koszarek, Ed. "A Simple Little Study: What Wins Major League Baseball Championships." Unpublished. 2000.

_____. "Baseball Story: Von Der Ahe." Unpublished. 2000.

_____. "The 1884 St. Louis Maroons and Other Great Teams." Unpublished. 2000.

Lamar, Steve. *The Book of Baseball Lists.* Jefferson, NC: McFarland, 1993. p. 467.

Lee, Bill. *The Baseball Necrology.* Jefferson, NC: McFarland, 2003. pp. 12, 17–18, 23, 26–27, 32, 45, 48, 50–52, 62–63, 71, 78, 80–81, 83, 86, 90, 92–94, 99, 102, 105, 112–114, 123, 125, 127–128, 133, 142, 149, 151, 154, 157, 159, 161–163, 166, 168, 173–174, 177, 191, 194, 196, 201–202, 205–206, 210, 212, 216–217, 219, 223–224, 228–229, 235, 244–245, 255–256, 262–263, 277, 284, 288–289, 292, 298, 300, 302, 305, 316, 318, 327–328, 334–335, 339, 343, 346, 349, 357, 359, 363, 365, 368, 374–375, 378, 383–384, 386, 388, 390, 393, 403, 406–407, 422, 424–425, 429, 433–434.

Mack, Connie [Cornelius McGillicuddy]. *My 66 Years in the Big Leagues.* Philadelphia: Winston, 1950. p. 78.

Madden, W.C. *The Women of the All-American Girls Professional Baseball League: A Biographical Dictionary.* Jefferson, NC: McFarland, 1997.

Neft, David S., Richard M. Cohen, and Michael L. Neft. *The Sports Encyclopedia: Baseball 2000.* New York: St. Martin's Press, 2000. pp. 741–746.

Nemec, David. *The Beer and Whisky League.* New York: Lyons and Burford, 1994. pp. 49, 118, 139, 167, 185, 207, 214–216, 233–235.

_____. *The Great Encyclopedia of 19th Century Major League Baseball.* New York: Donald I. Fine, 1997. pp. 26, 171.

National Baseball Hall of Fame and Museum. *2002 Yearbook.* Cooperstown, NY: National Baseball Hall of Fame and Museum, 2002. pp. 73, 75, 77–78, 84, 88, 91, 93, 97–98, 100–101, 114, 119–121, 124, 147–148, 151–152, 161–162, 171, 176, 179.

Newspaper Enterprise Association. *The 1972 World Almanac and Book of Facts.* New York: Newspaper Enterprise Association, 1971. pp. 444–445.

Okrent, Daniel, and Steve Wulf. *Baseball Anecdotes.* New York: Harper and Row, 1989. pp. 3, 7, 14, 17, 24–25, 84, 123.

Oppenheimer, Stephen. *Eden in the East: The Drowned Continent of Southeast Asia.* London, UK: Weidenfeld and Nicolson, 1998. pp. 37, 96.

Overfield, Joseph M. "Buffalo and the Baseball Revolt." *Niagara Frontier Magazine* 3, no. 3 (Autumn 1956). pp. 74–80.

_____. "When Baseball Came to Richmond Avenue." *Niagara Frontier Magazine* 2, no. 2 (Summer 1955). pp.30–35.

_____. "Professional Baseball In Buffalo–How It Began." *Niagara Frontier Magazine* 1, no. 2 (Spring 1954). pp. 32–33.

Primedia Reference, Inc. *1999 World Almanac and Book of Facts.* Mahway, NJ: Primedia Reference, 1998. pp. 537, 548, 558.

Reid, John Phillip. *The Authority of Law: The Constitutional History of the American Revolution.* Madison, WI: University of Wisconsin Press, 1993. pp. 27–28.

Ryczek, William J. *Blackguards and Red Stockings: A History of Baseball's National Association, 1871–1875.* Jefferson, NC: McFarland, 1997.

Skipper, John C. *A Biographical Dictionary of the Baseball Hall of Fame.* Jefferson, NC: McFarland, 2000. pp. 69–71, 81, 90–91, 111, 129, 162, 165, 216, 224, 234, 256–257, 289–290, 305–306, 308–309, 323–324.

Society for American Baseball Research. *Baseball Research Journal 28.* Cleveland: Society for American Baseball Research, 1999. pp. 64–65, 120.

_____. *Baseball Research Journal 27.* Cleveland: Society for American Baseball Research, 1998. pp. 4–5, 27.

_____. *The National Pastime: A Review of Baseball History Number 19.* Cleveland: Society for American Baseball Research, 1999. pp. 16–17, 34–35.

Sports in Buffalo Scrapbook (compilation of primary texts, housed at the Public Library of Buffalo and Erie County).

Sullivan, Dean A., ed. *Early Innings: A Documentary History of Baseball, 1825–1908.* Lincoln, NE: University of Nebraska Press, 1995. pp. 96–97, 119, 179, 194–199, 206–208.

Thorn, John, and Pete Palmer, ed. *Total Baseball,* with David Reuther. New York: Warner Books, 1989. pp. 9, 526, 698, 708, 724–725, 728–730, 935–936, 949, 952, 956–957, 965, 980, 984, 988–989, 991–992, 994–995, 1010–1011, 1023, 1033, 1035–1037, 1039, 1044, 1048, 1054, 1056, 1064, 1080–1081, 1095–1096, 1098, 1101–1102, 1108, 1132, 1139, 1143, 1146–1147, 1156, 1159, 1167–1168, 1195, 1198, 1200, 1211, 1217, 1224, 1231–1232, 1241, 1248–1249, 1271, 1287, 1291, 1299, 1318, 1329, 1335, 1337, 1341–1342, 1358, 1360, 1376, 1379, 1390–1392, 1404–1405, 1413, 1420, 1425, 1440–1441, 1444, 1448, 1450, 1456, 1464, 1480–1481, 1483, 1486–1487, 1489, 1494, 1511, 1516, 1519, 1528, 1539, 1542, 1547, 1551, 1553, 1584–1586, 1590, 1593, 1619, 1639, 1645, 1650, 1653, 1656, 1658, 1666, 1669, 1678, 1686, 1690, 1705, 1713, 1722–1725, 1758, 1773, 1775, 1778–1779, 1782, 1788, 1801–1802, 1812, 1821, 1828, 1849, 1853, 1856, 1864, 1893, 1916, 1941, 1943–1944, 1960, 1970, 1973–1974, 1986–1987, 2131–2163, 2289.

Tiemann, Robert L., and Mark Rucker, ed. *Nineteenth Century Stars.* Kansas City, MO: Society for American Baseball Research, 1989. pp. 8, 14, 19–20, 40, 55, 576, 60, 64, 67, 71–72, 75–76, 82, 84, 91, 95–96, 99–100, 102–103, 107, 109, 111–112, 119, 124, 129, 134–135, 141, 149.

Turkin, Hy, and S.C. Thompson. *The Official Encyclopedia of Baseball,* 7th rev. ed., by Pete Palmer. New York: A.S. Barnes, 1974. pp. 8, 12, 650–656, 737.

Wright, Marshall D. *Nineteenth Century Baseball.* Jefferson, NC: McFarland, 1996. pp. 82, 94, 106, 196–200.

Yergin, Daniel. *The Prize: The Epic Quest for Oil, Money & Power.* New York: Simon and Schuster, 1991. pp. 80, 98.

Zimbalist, Andrew. *Baseball and Billions.* New York: Basic Books, 1992. pp. 2–3, 8.

Periodicals

Buffalo Courier
Buffalo Express
London Times
New York Clipper
Players' National League Base Ball Guide 1890
Spalding Guide
Sporting Life
The Sporting News

Index

Aaron, Henry "Hank" 366
Abel, Ferdinand 352, 356
Abel, Gus 41
Adams, Dr. Daniel L. 11, 12
Addison, John 48, 51, 52, 57
Alexander, Grover Cleveland "Pete" 121
All-America World 270
Allen Pasture 158
Altoona Mountain Cities 30
American Association of Base Ball Clubs 3, 10, 13, 23, 24, 25, 26, 27, 28, 31, 32, 34, 36, 37, 38, 39, 41, 42, 45, 46, 48, 50, 54, 56, 80, 93, 107, 114, 156, 178, 179, 181, 185, 198, 202, 206, 210, 214, 215, 221, 223, 230, 234, 235, 240, 243, 250, 265, 284, 292, 295, 299, 301, 302, 306, 307, 309, 314, 318, 322, 324, 335, 336, 337, 342, 344, 353, 354, 359, 364, 365, 366, 367, 369, 370
American Federation of Labor 348
American League 3, 95, 184, 186, 187, 191, 202, 203, 221, 222, 237, 247, 253, 257, 262, 265, 301, 304–305, 307, 348, 351, 353, 356
Andrews, George Edward 69–70
Anson, Adrian Constantine "Cap" 17, 19, 27, 33, 34, 121, 167, 184, 237, 238, 282, 296, 297, 299, 363, 369
Arnold, Judge 365

Bacon, Judge 352
Bakeley (Bakley), Edward Enoch 70–71
Baker Bowl 60, 299, 311
Baldwin, Charles Busted 71
Baldwin, Lady 57

Baldwin, Marcus Elmore 72–74
Baldwin, Mark 33, 62, 63, 359, 367, 369
Ball Park of America 29
Ball Players Protective Association 222
Baltimore Monumentals 30, 234, 241
Baltimore Orioles 37, 89, 95, 125, 126, 142, 144, 145, 148, 149, 170, 189, 223, 245, 269, 276, 301, 305, 306, 307, 323, 333, 354, 355, 356, 367
Bank Street Ground 27
Banks, Ernie 111
Barnes, Ross 18, 19, 45
Barnie, William Harrison "Billie" 28, 32, 37, 41, 137, 148, 305–306
Bartson, Charles Franklin 74
Base Ball Code of Law 10
Bastian, Charles J. 74–75
Beckley, Jacob Peter 62, 75–77, 144, 278, 359, 367, 370
Beecher, Edward H. 77–78
Beemer, John M. 56
Beer and Whiskey League, The 31
Bennett, Charles Wesley 35, 36, 306
Bierbauer, Louis W. 78–79, 367, 369
Billings, James B. 31, 166, 235
Bishop, Orrick C. 21, 363
Black, Ella 278
Blyleven, Bert 299
Bonny (Bonney), Billy 298
Boston Beaneaters/Braves 31, 48, 125, 188, 225, 255, 266, 306, 318, 335, 341, 354, 358, 359
Boston Globe 51
Boston Herald 299
Boston Red Stockings 16, 18, 19, 30, 33, 166, 196, 361

Boston Reds 48–49, 59, 60, 62, 63, 81, 83, 100, 106, 152, 158, 165, 170, 188, 196, 202, 203, 204, 206, 212, 220, 221, 225, 232, 248, 249, 255, 258, 265, 302, 306, 358, 359, 366, 367, 368
Boston Tea Party 6
Boundary Field 162
Boyle, John Anthony 79
Brennan (Dorn), John Gottlieb (Jack) 64, 80
Bresnahan, Roger 186
Brooklyn Atlantics 12, 13, 14, 17, 19, 255, 312, 329
Brooklyn Bridegrooms/Dodgers/Robin/Superbas/Trolley Dodgers 12, 37, 49, 54, 148, 173, 245, 307, 308, 312, 320, 323, 333
Brooklyn Eckfords 12, 15, 16, 255, 312
Brooklyn Excelsiors 12
Brooklyn Gladiators 50, 323
Brooklyn Grays 37
Brooklyn Wonders 49–50, 59, 62, 78, 148, 149, 159, 173, 193, 201, 215, 242, 252, 262, 273, 274, 275, 276, 280, 284, 285, 288, 359, 367, 368
Brotherhood Manifesto 44
Brotherhood of Professional Base Ball Players 3, 4, 7, 32, 34, 35, 41, 42, 43, 48, 49, 57, 115, 119, 120, 144, 163, 166, 167, 176, 196, 197, 217, 229, 233, 239, 252, 265, 273, 278, 282, 283, 284, 285, 286, 293, 296, 306, 348, 349, 350, 351, 352, 365
Brotherhood Park 52, 54, 55, 59, 158, 244
Brotherhood Rebellion 281

Brouthers, Dennis Joseph (Dan) 31, 43, 62, 81–82, 83, 214, 258, 341, 367, 368, 369
Brown, Thomas Tarlton 33, 63, 83–84, 171
Brown, Willard 33, 64, 84
Browning, Louis Rogers (Pete) 62, 85–86, 359, 368, 369
Brunell, Frank 43, 45, 48, 120, 230, 273, 352, 353, 363
Brush, John 9, 11, 32, 41, 53, 260, 352, 353
Buckley, John Edward 87
Buffalo Baseball Hall of Fame 294
Buffalo Bisons 40, 41, 45, 50–51, 57, 59, 71, 78, 87, 90, 92, 100, 112, 116, 117, 123, 126, 130, 131, 140, 141, 142, 151, 157, 161, 162, 176, 183, 188, 213, 228, 235, 253, 272, 273, 290, 293, 301, 366, 367, 368
Buffalo Express 41
Buffington, Charles G. 88–89
Buiner, C.F. 56
Bulkeley, Morgan S. 21, 25, 34, 121
Burkett, Jesse Cail "The Crab" 220, 267, 306–307, 369
Burn, Conrad 32
Burns, Thomas P. "Oyster" 33, 307–308, 369
Byrne, Charles 32, 37, 41, 54

California Angels 169
Candee, Cassius 51
Capitoline Grounds 14
Carnegie, Andrew 5, 20, 35, 42, 73, 95
Carney, John Joseph 89–90
Carpenter, Warren William "Hick" 349
Carroll, Cliff 33, 34
Carroll, Frederick Herbert 33, 34, 91–92, 178
Cartwright, Alexander Joy 11, 121
Caruthers, Robert Lee 172, 308–309
"Casey at the Bat" 34, 303
Caylor, Oliver Perry (O.P.) 23, 27, 28, 29, 31, 37, 43, 165, 282, 365
Chadwick, Henry 12, 14, 15, 24, 25, 43, 103, 121, 282, 290, 363
Champion, Aaron 13
Chapman, John 6
Chauncey, George W. 49, 50
Chicago Colts/White Stockings (Cubs) 16, 17, 19, 23, 27, 51, 117, 139, 184, 208, 217, 237, 239, 270, 274, 297, 299, 300, 354, 359, 362, 363
Chicago Pirates 45, 51–52, 59, 62, 63, 73, 74, 75, 93, 94, 107, 113, 118, 125, 171, 211, 238, 239, 246, 247, 299, 300, 352, 358, 359, 367, 368

Chicago Tribune 43, 365
Chicago White Sox 95, 222, 247, 314, 352
Childs, Clarence Algernon "Cupid" 267, 309–310, 369
Cincinnati Enquirer 23, 29
Cincinnati Outlaw Reds 30
Cincinnati Porkers/Kellys 175
Cincinnati Reds 12, 13, 14, 15, 27, 37, 38, 95, 118, 165, 181, 225, 250, 251, 367
Clanton, Eucal "Uke" 262
Clark, Owen F. "Spider" 64, 92–93
Clarkson, John Gibson 306, 310–311, 369
Classification Plan (1888) 350
Clemente, Roberto 338
Clements, John J. "Jack" 311–312, 369
Cleveland Blues 37, 191, 192, 206, 250, 288, 365
Cleveland Forest Cities 16, 290
Cleveland Indians 78, 262
Cleveland Infants 52–54, 59, 62, 70, 80, 85, 87, 88, 110, 111, 138, 149, 150, 178, 194, 207, 227, 260, 262, 263, 267, 268, 269, 272, 273, 359, 367, 368
Cleveland Leader 53
Cleveland Plain Dealer 43, 51, 365
Cleveland Spiders 52, 95, 103, 206, 221, 250, 266, 268, 269, 309, 313, 327, 335, 347
Clever Base-Ballist, A 22
Clutch Hitting Index 94, 193, 195, 204, 206
Cobb, Ty 121, 211, 257
Collins, Eddie 121
Collins, Hubert B. "Hub" 312, 369
Collins, Phil 60
Collonnade Hotel 353
Columbia Park 186
Columbus Buckeyes/Solons 174, 175, 327, 359, 367
Comiskey, Charles Albert 39, 93–96, 98, 113, 121, 171, 172, 186, 187, 211, 215, 221, 222, 238, 296, 297, 352, 353, 358, 369, 370
Committee on Negotiations of McAlpin, Goodwin, and Johnson 351
Conant, W.H. 41, 166
Confederate States of America 204
Congress Street Grounds 48, 59, 158
Connecticut Mansfields 17, 212, 213
Connor, Roger 42, 62, 96–98, 359, 367, 368, 369, 370
Cook, Paul 97–98
"Cooperstown Baseball Centennial" 233

Corcoran, Thomas William 64, 98–99
Cott, Cornelius Van 54
Cotter, Daniel Joseph 99–100
Crane, Edward Nicholas 64, 100–101, 278, 297, 298
Crane, Sam 298
Craver, Bill 22
Crawford, Sam 257
Croker, Richard 356
Cronin, Jack 186
Cross, Lafayette Napoleon 102–103
Cummings, William Arthur "Candy" 6, 121
Cunningham, Elsworth Elmer 103
Cuppy, Nig 267
Cushman, Charles W. 51

Daily, Cornelius F. 104–105
Daley, William 62, 105–106
Dalrymple, Abner 363
Darling, Conrad 106–108
Davidson, Mordecai 31
Davis, George Stacey 313–314, 369
Day, John B. 11, 28, 37, 41, 49, 54, 167, 340, 352
DeBost, Charles S. 11
Deer, Rob 143
DeHaas, Frank 357
Delahanty, Edward James 108–110, 338, 354, 369
Detroit Tigers 143
Detroit Wolverines 31, 72, 145, 235, 272, 273, 292
DeWald, Charles H. 110–111
DiMaggio, Joe 329, 338
DiSalvatore, Bryan 3, 22
Doe, Alfred George 111
Dorgan, Michael C. 42
Doubleday, Abner 14, 21, 25
Doyle, "Dirty Jack" 79, 267
Doyle, Joseph 37
Dreyfuss, Barney 357
Duffy, Hugh 62, 112–114, 115, 321, 359, 368, 369
Dunlap, Frederick C. 114–116, 299
Duzen, William George 116–117
Dwyer, John Francis 117–118

Earle, Billy 33
Eastern Park 49
Ebbets, Charlie 356
Ebbets Field 216, 299
Emslie, Bob 208
Espenscheid, Frederick 29
Evans, Billy 191
Evans, J.S. 15
Ewing, John 64, 121–122, 276, 278
Ewing, William "Buck" 42, 54, 84, 118–121, 351, 359, 364, 367, 368, 369
Exposition Park 56, 59

Index

Faatz, Jayson S. 64, 122–123, 236, 366
Face, Elroy 111
fantasy players 88
Farrar, Sidney Douglas 64, 123–124, 124
Farrell, Charles Andrew 124–126
Federal League 3, 77, 144, 216
Fenway Park 113
Ferguson, Bob 6, 17, 45
Ferson, Alexander 64, 126–127
Fields, John Joseph "Jocko" 63, 127
Fitzgerald, Charles B. 50, 51
Flagler, Henry 70
Fogarty, James G. "Jim" 33, 34, 64, 128–129, 317
Fogarty, Tim 64
Force, Davy 6
Forepaugh Park 55, 59, 244
Fort Wayne Kekiongas 15, 290
Foutz, David Luther 172, 314–315
Frazier, George 31
Freedman, Andrew 186, 204, 334, 356

Gaffney, John 45
Galvin, James Francis "Pud" 89, 129–131, 343, 369
Gastright (Gastreich), Henry Carl "Hank" 315, 369
Gehrig, Lou 83, 121, 211, 329
Gentleman's Driving Park 162
Gerhardt, G.G. 42
Getzein, Pretzels 306
Gibson, Bob 130
Gilbert, Frank T. 50, 51
Gillespie, James 132
Glasscock, John Wesley "Jack" 315–316, 369
Gleason, William J. "Kid" 64, 132–133, 316–317, 369
Gompers, Samuel 348
Goodwin, Wendell 49, 50
Gore, George F. 133–135, 248, 249, 359, 368
Governors Hill 34
Grant, Frank 40
Gray, James D. 135–136
Great Encyclopedia of 19th Century Major League Baseball, The 17
Gregg, Forrest 215
Griffin, Michael Joseph 136–137, 368
Griffith, Clark 222, 348
Griffith Stadium 60
Grove, Lefty 185
Gruber, Henry John 138
Gumbert, Addison Courtney 139–140, 359
Gunning, Tom 45

Haddock, George Silas 140–141
Hall, George 22

Halligan, William E. "Jocko" 64, 141–142
Hallman, William Wilson 55, 142–143, 365
Hamilton, William Robert "Billy" 83, 204, 317–318, 338, 354, 369
Hanlon, Ned 33, 41, 143–146, 159, 171, 246, 267, 269, 352, 356, 370
Hart, James 296
Hart, Julian B. 48, 354
Hartford Dark Blues 19
Harvard Medical School 11
Hastings, Scott 17
Hatfield, Gilbert 146–147, 278
Hauck, John 37
Hawley, Davis 37, 41
Hayes, John J. "Jackie" 64, 147–148
Healy, Egyptian 33, 34
Hecker, Guy Jackson 319
Heilmann, Harry 214
Helyar, John 4, 362
Hemming, George Earl 63, 64, 148–150
Herancourt, George 37
Higgins, Robert 40
Higham, Richard 96
Hillerich, J. Frederick 86
Hillerich, John A. "Bud" 86
Holbert, Bill 45
Hopper, DeWolf 34
Hornsby, Rogers 121, 298
Hough, O.R. 15
Howe, George 41
Hoy, William Ellsworth "Dummy" 50, 64, 150–152, 188, 368
Hulbert, William 19, 20, 21, 22, 23, 35, 95, 96, 165, 166, 167, 291, 363
Hunter, Catfish 166
Huntington Grounds 311, 338
Hurley, Jeremiah Joseph 152
Husted, William J. 153
Hutchinson, William Forrest 319–320, 369

Ilion (N.Y.) Sunset League Young Stars 294
Indianapolis Hoosiers 241
International League 40, 51, 160
Irwin, Arthur Albert 63, 153–156, 352
Irwin, John 63, 156
Ivor-Campbell, Frederick 2

Jackson, James 30
Jefferson Street Grounds 196
Jennings, Hugh 145, 348, 349, 367
Johnson, Albert L. 52, 53, 54, 56, 230, 259, 260, 266, 268, 353
Johnson, Byron Bancroft "Ban" 95, 121, 186, 187, 222
Johnson, Tom J. 52

Johnson, Walter 121, 329
Johnston, Richard Frederick 157–159
Jones, Charley 45
Joyce, William Michael 62, 64, 159–161, 230, 368

Kachline, Clifford S. 88
Kansas City Athletics 187, 256, 287, 291
Kansas City Cowboys/Unions 80, 241, 252
Keefe, George W. 161–162
Keefe, Timothy John 42, 43, 162–164, 169, 343, 352, 368, 369
Keeler, Wee Willie 121
Kelly, Michael Joseph "King" 3, 42, 48, 49, 64, 120, 164–169, 171, 172, 221, 230, 358, 368, 369
Kennett, W.H. 165
Keokuk Westerns 19
Kerns, James N. 14
Kerr, W.W. 357
Ketcham, Valentino H. 32
Kilroy, Matthew Aloysius 169–171
Kiner, Ralph 257
King (Koenig), Charles Frederick "Silver" 62, 63, 171–173, 359, 367, 369
King George III 11
Kinslow, Thomas F. 173–174
Klein, Chuck 60
Klem, Bill 208, 209
Knell, Philip Louis 63, 174–175
Knight, Lon 45
Koszarek, Edward Joseph 2
Koszarek, Jane Genevieve 2
Kramer, Jerry 215
Krauthoff, Louis 32
Krock, August H. 64, 176–177
Kuehne (Knelme), William J. 63, 177–178
Kuhel, Joe 60

Ladies Day 36
Lajoie, Napoleon 121, 186
Lake Park 299, 300
Lakeland Insane Asylum 86
Landis, Judge Kenesaw Mountain 20, 121, 352
Larkin, Henry E. "Ted" 178–180, 267, 367
Latham, Walter Arlington "Arlie" 43, 64, 180–182
Lennon, M.B. 56
Lewis 182–183
Linton, E.F. 49, 56
Lombardi, Vince 215
London Times 33
Lord Baltimores 17, 328
Louisville Colonels/Cyclones/Eclipse 31, 37, 85, 104, 243, 346, 353, 359
Love, H.M. 55, 56

Lovett, Thomas Joseph 320, 369
Lucas, Henry Van Noye 28, 29
Lyons, Dennis Patrick Aloysius 320–321, 369

Mack (McGillicuddy), Cornelius Alexander "Connie" 40, 50, 64, 95, 121, 170, 183–188, 208, 369, 370
MacMillan Encyclopedia 236
Madden, Michael Joseph "Kid" 64, 188–189
Maddux, Greg 130
Manfield, Joseph 17
Manning, Jack 33, 299, 300
Manning, Jim 33, 34, 222
Mason, Charlie 37
Masonic Home 135
Mather, Elias 28
Mathews, Bobby 45, 290
Mathewson, Christy 121, 233, 294, 329
Maul, Albert Joseph 64, 189–191
Mayo Research Clinic 73
Mays, Willie 338
McAleer, James Robert 191–192, 267
McAlpin, Edwin A. 54, 55
McAlpin, John 352
McCarthy, Thomas Francis Michael "Tommy" 114, 321–322, 369
McGarr, Chippy 267
McGeachey, John Charles 193
McGill, William Vaness 64, 194–195
McGinnity, Joe 186
McGraw, John 82, 95, 109, 118, 121, 145, 182, 186, 187, 212, 267, 333
McKean, Ed 267
McKnight, Denny 24, 27, 37, 235
McLean, John 29
McMahon, John Joseph "Sadie" 322–324, 369
McPhee, John Alexander "Bid" 324–325
McRoy, Robert 192
McVey, Cal 19, 291, 292
Merkle, Fred 208
Merkle Game of 1908 208
Milligan, John "Jocko" 57, 195–196
Mills, Abraham (A.G.) 12, 24, 28, 30, 34
Mills Commission 24, 25, 363
Milwaukee Brewers 175
Milwaukee Cream Cities 30
Minor League Board of Arbitration 212
Mix, Tom 248
Moeller, Danny 301
Molitor, Paul 211
Morgan, John Pierpont 5, 35
Morrill, John Francis 64, 166, 196–197

Morris, Edward "Cannonball" 64, 197–199
Morse, R.C. 31
Morton, Charlie 256
Morton, Sam 256
Moses, Felix 158
Mullane, Anthony John "Tony" 325
Mulvey, Joseph H. 199–200
Murphy, Cornelius B. "Con" 64, 200–202
Murphy, Morgan E. 64, 202–203
Musial, Stan 81
Mutrie, Jim 215, 340

Nash, William Mitchell 203–205
National Agreement 27, 34, 36, 46, 50, 54, 260, 261, 300, 342, 350, 352, 354, 357
National Association of Base Ball Players 3, 12, 15, 16, 19, 29, 131, 166, 212, 213, 250, 290, 291, 304, 328
National Baseball Hall of Fame and Museum 1, 63, 82, 96, 97, 113, 114, 119, 120, 131, 145, 164, 168, 182, 184, 191, 208, 211, 212, 226, 248, 258, 304, 311, 313, 322, 326, 333, 334, 338, 340, 342, 346, 349, 369
National Commission 278
National League 3, 4, 10, 11, 13, 21, 22, 23, 25, 26, 27, 28, 29, 30, 31, 34, 35, 36, 37, 39, 41, 42, 43, 45, 46, 50, 54, 70, 72, 73, 80, 95, 97, 105, 107, 139, 156, 167, 178, 179, 185, 186, 196, 197, 202, 204, 205, 208, 210, 212, 213, 214, 215, 221, 225, 228, 229, 232, 235, 237, 240, 250, 257, 261, 264, 266, 268, 269, 270, 271, 286, 291, 295, 300, 302, 303, 306, 311, 313, 318, 319, 320, 330, 335, 339, 340, 342, 343, 347, 353, 354, 355, 356, 357, 359, 360, 362, 363, 364, 366, 367, 369, 370
Nemec, David 2, 3, 17, 27, 31
New Haven Elm Citys 19
New York Base Ball Club 11
New York Clipper 3, 14, 21, 34, 231, 236, 265, 270
New York Giants/Gothams 11, 42, 49, 52, 53, 54–55, 59, 62, 63, 82, 84, 95, 101, 115, 119, 122, 127, 134, 146, 158, 159, 160, 172, 181, 182, 204, 208, 210, 212, 213, 215, 217, 228, 229, 230, 244, 248, 249, 253, 269, 275, 276, 281, 284, 285, 295, 300, 317, 334, 342, 343, 352, 356, 359, 366, 367, 368
New York Journal 297
New York Knickerbockers 11, 12, 16, 30, 75, 255

New York Metropolitans 30, 37, 173, 185, 206, 214, 215, 216, 271
New York Mutuals 14, 15, 16, 17, 19, 95, 250, 329
New York Times 352
New York Yankees 78, 111, 155, 182, 210, 300
Nichols, Charles Augustus "Kid" 306, 325–327, 369
Nimick, William "Bill" 37, 41, 51, 56, 135, 136, 235
Normandy 29

Oakland A's 187
O'Brien, John F. "Darby" 64, 205–207
O'Brien, Judge Morgan Joseph 36, 49
O'Connor, John Joseph "Jack" 267, 327–328, 369
October Classic 356
O'Day, Henry Francis "Hank" 63, 64, 207–209
Oh, Sadaharu 338
Ohio State Journal 353
Okrent, Daniel 362
Olympic Base Ball Park 51, 59, 162
O'Neill, J. Palmer 41, 53, 56, 135
O'Neill, James Edward "Tip" 63, 209–211
O'Rourke, James Henry "Orator Jim" 18, 42, 84, 211–214, 248, 249, 352, 359, 368, 369
Orr, Dave 62, 64, 214–216, 359, 367, 369
Overfield, Joe 2

Pacific Coast League 151
Palmer, Pete 2
Palmer's Theatre 34
Peace Committee 259, 260
Pearce, Dickey 13
Pendleton Park 158
Pennsylvania State Police 5
Pennypacker, H.C. 55
Pettit, Bob 33
Pfeffer, Nathaniel Frederick "Dandelion" 33, 34, 62, 216–218, 352
phantom ballplayers 88
Phelps, J.H. 37
Phelps, Zach 32, 37
Philadelphia Athletics 13, 14, 16, 19, 33, 37, 55, 80, 179, 185, 187, 191, 203, 230, 240, 302, 322, 329, 333, 359, 367
Philadelphia Blue Jays 311
Philadelphia Centennials 19
Philadelphia Conference 56
Philadelphia Cuban Giants 39, 40
Philadelphia Keystones 30
Philadelphia Live Wires/Phillies 57, 60, 79, 114, 124, 127, 143, 154, 175, 186, 191, 200, 203,

204, 240, 245, 247, 300, 302, 303, 306, 311, 317, 318, 338, 339
Philadelphia Quakers 55–56, 59, 63, 88, 89, 99, 102, 128, 137, 143, 153, 174–175, 195, 196, 200, 240, 243, 244, 245, 302, 311, 366, 367, 368
Phillips, Horace 27, 37
Pickett, John Thomas 57, 218–219, 365, 366
Pierce, Dickey 6
Pietrusza, David 2
Pike, Lipman Emanuel "Lip" 328–329
Pinkney (Pinckney), George Burton 329–330, 369
Pittsburgh Alleghenys/Innocents/Pirates 37, 56, 111, 115, 129, 136, 144, 148, 175, 184, 185, 199, 223, 235, 246, 255, 295, 319, 359, 367
Pittsburgh Burghers 56–57, 59, 62, 63, 76, 91, 112, 127, 130, 135, 140, 144, 145, 152, 177, 190, 199, 223, 255, 270, 278, 359, 366, 367
Pittsburgh Stogies 30
Players' National League Base Ball Guide 1890, The 41
Players Protective Association 348
Playing Rules Committee 41
Poe, Edgar Allan 179
Polo Grounds 59
Postal, Fred 222
Powell, Boog 215
Pratt, Thomas 29
Prince, Charles A. 48, 52
Protective Association of Base Ball Players 351
Providence Grays 224, 225, 281
Pulliam Henry (Harry) Clay 357
Pulliam, William 286

Quinn, Joseph J. 63, 219–222, 367
Quinn, Thomas Oscar 64, 222–223

Radbourn, Charles Gardner "Hoss" 64, 89, 97, 121, 223–226, 326, 359, 367, 368, 369
Radford, Paul Revere 226–227
Rainey, John Paul 64, 227–228
Ramsey, Thomas A. "Toad" 330–331
Ray, Irving Burton "Irv" 331, 369
Ray, W.H. 15
Reach, Al 6, 13, 25, 41, 186, 200, 352
Reach Guide 129
Recreation Park 311
Reid, John Phillip 35
Reilly, John Good "Long John" 43, 331–332

Reserve clause 34, 51, 55, 350
Rhines, William Pearl "Billy" 332–333
Rhoner, Frank 37
Richardson, Abram Harding "Ol' True Blue" 31, 62, 231–233, 359, 368, 369
Richardson, Daniel 42, 228–231
Richmond Virginias 158
Richter, Francis 351, 365
Roberts, Robin 299
Robinson, F.B. 53, 54
Robinson, Wilbert 145, 333, 369, 370
Robinson, William H. "Yank" 64, 233–234
Robison, Frank DeHaas 11, 37, 41, 43, 52, 53, 56, 221, 222, 260, 266, 327, 353, 355, 364
Robison, Stanley 37, 221, 222, 266, 353, 355, 357
Rockefeller, John D. 5, 6, 7, 35, 70, 95, 352
Rockford (Illinois) Forest Cities 16, 304, 361
Rogers, John I. 41, 55, 200
Rose Bowl 176
Rowe, Jack 64
Rowe, John Charles 31, 50, 51, 64, 235–236
Rules Committee for Organized Baseball 209
Rusie, Amos Wilson 206, 334, 369
Ruth, George Herman "Babe" 81, 83, 97, 109, 111, 121, 166, 167, 214, 229, 231, 257, 298, 339, 352
Ryan, James Edward 33, 34, 237–239, 368
Ryan, Nolan 164, 169, 170
Ryczek, David 2

St. Louis Brown Stockings 19
St. Louis Browns/Cardinals/Perfectos) 37, 158, 161, 172, 181, 182, 191, 210, 211, 215, 221, 234, 247, 278, 292, 295, 308, 314, 354, 355, 358, 359, 367
St. Louis Maroons 29, 30, 80, 115, 221
St. Louis Red Stockings 19, 210, 328, 329
St. Paul White Caps 30, 187
Salary cap 9
Sanders, Alexander Bennett 239–240
Scanlon, Mike 29, 37
Schofield, J.W. 14, 15
Seery, John Emmett 241–243
Selee, Frank 221
Sewell, Joe 78
Shannon, Daniel Webster 243–244
Sharsig, Bill 37
Shibe, Ben 170, 186, 187
Shibe Park 187, 191

Shindle, William 57, 244–246, 367
Shire, Moses 40, 51
Shotton, Burt 187
Shugart (Shugarts), Frank Harry 64, 246–248
Simmons, Lew 28, 37
Sisler, George 121
Slattery, Michael J. 248–249
Smith, Charles "Pop" 27
Snyder, Charles Nicholas "Pop" 27, 249–251
Society for American Baseball Research (SABR) 2, 59, 66, 76, 91, 93, 94, 95, 104, 105, 109, 113, 115, 129, 131, 145, 160, 168, 172, 178, 190, 203, 204, 206, 214, 216, 226, 227, 231, 232, 236, 237, 250, 251, 252, 254, 257, 274, 293, 297, 301, 303, 307, 308, 318, 320, 325, 330, 332, 333, 336, 345, 347, 348, 361, 362
Soden, Arthur 11, 22, 28, 41, 48, 166, 352, 353, 354
Somers, Charles 186, 187
South End Grounds 48
South Side Park 51, 59
Southern League 265
Sowders, John 64, 251–252
Spalding, Albert Goodwill 10–11, 17, 18, 19, 20, 21, 23, 24, 25, 32, 33, 34, 39, 41, 43, 48, 49, 51, 52, 53, 57, 72, 84, 89, 93, 95, 121, 128, 139, 165, 166, 167, 171, 219, 239, 270, 280, 281, 282, 283, 284, 286, 291, 295, 296, 297, 326, 329, 350, 351, 352, 353, 354, 356, 360, 364, 366, 370
Spalding Baseball Guide 12, 42, 282
Speaker, Tris 121, 159, 211, 338
Speranza Park 344
Spink, Al 30, 116
Spink, Charley 30
Sporting Life 30, 40, 55, 325, 365
Sporting News, The 30, 39, 129, 220, 356
Sports in Buffalo Scrapbook 39
Sportsman's Park 182
Stafford, James Joseph 252–253
Staley, Harry E. 63, 254–255
Stearns, Frederick Kimball 51, 145, 232, 235, 292
Stengel, Casey 223
Stern, Aaron 32, 37, 54
Sterne, Harry 32
Stivetts, John Elmer "Jack" 266, 335
Stoneham, Horace 175
Stovey (Stowe), Harry Duffield 62, 255–259, 359, 368, 369
Stovey, George 40, 171
Stratton, C. Scott 335–336, 369
Stricker (Streaker), John A. "Cub" 259–261

Stynes, Cornelius William "Neil" 261–262
Sullivan, Marty 33, 34
Sullivan, Ted 93
Sunday (Wacher/Wachter), Arthur (August) 262–263
Sutcliffe, Elmer Ellsworth "Sy" 64, 263–264
Swampoodle Grounds 60, 148, 162
Swartwood, Cyrus Edward "Ed" 336–337, 369
Swett, William E. 264–265
Syracuse Stars 31, 309

Talcott, Edward 54, 55, 56, 356
Tammany Hall 356
Tattersall, John 299, 300
Tebeau, Oliver Wendell "Patsy" 269, 369
Temple, William C. 269
Temple Cup 269
Tener, John Kinley 33, 34, 63, 64, 269–271
Terry, Bill 81, 211
Texas Western 160
Thatcher, J.M. 14, 15
Thayer, Ernest Lawrence 303
Thayer, Judge M. Russell 55
Thompson, S.C. 363
Thompson, Samuel Luther 337–339, 354, 369
Thorn, John 4
Thorner, Justus 29, 165
Tiernan, Michael Joseph 339–340, 369
Tokyo Giants 338
Toledo Maumees (Black Pirates; Black Stockings; Blue Stockings) 31, 344, 367
Tripartite Agreement 27
Troy Haymakers 13, 16, 22
Troy Trojans 328, 342
Tucker, Thomas Joseph 341–342
Turkin, Hy 4, 363
Turner, Tuck 354
Twain, Mark 34
Twitchell, Lawrence Grant "Larry" 271–273, 365

Union Association 3, 28, 29, 75, 80, 100, 105, 116, 156, 157, 221, 222, 234, 241, 248, 249, 299, 307, 321

United States Congress 6
University of Pennsylvania Athletic Field 311, 338

Vanderslice, J.M. 55, 56
Van Dyke, Bill 367
VanHaltren, George Edward Martin 273–276, 368
Vaughn, Harry Francis "Farmer" 276–278
Veterans Committee 298
Virtue, Jake 267
Visner (Vezina), Joseph Paul 62, 278–280
Voight, David Q. 4
Von der Ahe, Christian Frederick Wilhelm "Chris" 13, 26, 32, 37, 38, 73, 93, 94, 158, 172, 181, 215, 259, 260, 351, 352, 353, 356
Von der Horst, Henry 37

Wadsworth, Jack 306
Wadsworth, Louis F. 11
Wagner, George 55, 56, 230, 366
Wagner, J. Earle 55, 56, 200, 230, 366
Wagner, John Peter "Honus" 121, 304
Waldo, H.H. 15
Wallace, Bobby 267
Wallace, John 49, 50, 54
Ward, John Montgomery "Monte" 3, 4, 11, 32, 33, 34, 42, 43, 48, 49, 50, 54, 56, 163, 202, 280–286, 269, 350, 351, 352, 353, 363, 364, 368, 369
Washington Nationals 17, 19, 30
Washington Olympics 14, 16
Washington Senators/Statesmen 60, 92, 109, 111, 115, 148, 159, 175, 184, 185, 192, 208, 221, 222, 227, 229, 230, 232, 237, 243, 250, 264, 271, 301
Watrous, Walter 37
Weaver, Earl 215
Welch, Michael Francis "Mickey" 42, 342–343, 369
Werden, Percival Wheritt "Perry" 344, 369
Western League 32, 95, 187, 365
Westside Park 51
Weyhing, August 287–289, 367, 369

White, James Laurie "Deacon" 18, 19, 31, 50, 51, 64, 188, 235, 289–294, 352, 368
White, Warren 29
White, Will 292
Whitney, Arthur Wilson 294–295
Whitney, James Evans "Jim" 344–345
Whittaker, William 32, 55, 353
Williams, Elisa Green 363
Williams, Jimmy 37
Williams, Ted 81, 215
Williamson, Edward Nagle "Ned" 64, 295–300
Wilmington (Delaware) Quicksteps 30, 307
Wilson, Willie 257
Wiman, Erastus 30, 37
Wise, Samuel Washington 300–302, 367
Wolf, William Van Winkle "Chicken" 345–346, 369
Wood, George A. "Dandy" 33, 34, 302–303, 352
Wood, Jimmy 296
Woodling, Gene 271
Worcester Spy 165
Worchester Ruby Legs 154
World's Series 25, 32, 187, 208, 225, 229, 268, 292, 347, 356
Wright, George 15, 18, 25, 29, 121, 197
Wright, William H. "Harry" 15, 17, 28, 30, 197
Wulf, Steve 362
Wyckoff, Wheeler 32, 37
Wyehing, Guy 359
Wyne, Mike 1

Yale College 11
Yomiuri Giants *see* Tokyo Giants
Young, Denton True "Cy" 266, 346–347, 369
Young, Nicholas (N.E.) 12, 14, 15, 30, 31, 41, 50, 121

Zachary, Tom 111
Zajc, John 2
Zimbalist, Andrew 3, 363
Zimmer, Charles Louis "Chief" 347–349

www.ingramcontent.com/pod-product-compliance
Lightning Source LLC
Chambersburg PA
CBHW081535300426
44116CB00015B/2633